Prehistory of Oklahoma

NEW WORLD ARCHAEOLOGICAL RECORD

Under the Editorship of

James Bennett Griffin

Museum of Anthropology
University of Michigan
Ann Arbor, Michigan

In preparation:

Michael J. Moratto, with contributions by David A. Frederickson, Christopher Raven, and Claude N. Warren, California Archaeology

Published:

Robert E. Bell (Ed.), Prehistory of Oklahoma
James L. Phillips and James A. Brown (Eds.), Archaic Hunters
and Gatherers in the American Midwest
Dan F. Morse and Phyllis A. Morse, Archaeology of the Central
Mississippi Valley
Lawrence E. Aten, Indians of the Upper Texas Coast
Ronald J. Mason, Great Lakes Archaeology
Dean R. Snow, The Archaeology of New England
Jerald T. Milanich and Charles H. Fairbanks, Florida Archaeology
George C. Frison, Prehistoric Hunters of the High Plains

Prehistory of Oklahoma

Edited by

ROBERT E. BELL

Department of Anthropology
University of Oklahoma
Norman, Oklahoma

1984

ACADEMIC PRESS, INC.
(Harcourt Brace Jovanovich, Publishers)
Orlando   San Diego   San Francisco   New York   London
Toronto   Montreal   Sydney   Tokyo   São Paulo

ACADEMIC PRESS, INC.
Orlando, Florida 32887

United Kingdom Edition published by
ACADEMIC PRESS, INC. (LONDON) LTD.
24/28 Oval Road, London NW1 7DX

Library of Congress Cataloging in Publication Data

Main entry under title:

Prehistory of Oklahoma.

    (New world archaeological record)
    Includes index.
    1. Indians of North America--Oklahoma--History--
Addresses, essays, lectures. 2. Indians of North
America--Oklahoma--Antiquities--Addresses, essays,
lectures. 3. Excavations (Archaeology)--Oklahoma--
Addresses, essays, lectures. 4. Oklahoma--Antiquities
--Addresses, essays, lectures. I. Bell, Robert
Eugene, Date   . II. Series.
E78.O45P67 1984   976.6'01   83-12321
ISBN 0-12-085180-6

PRINTED IN THE UNITED STATES OF AMERICA

84 85 86 87   9 8 7 6 5 4 3 2 1

Contents

7. *The Kenton Caves of Western Oklahoma*
Christopher Lintz and Leon George Zabawa

8. *The Woodland Occupations*
Susan C. Vehik

9. *Arkansas Valley Caddoan Formative: The Wister and Fourche Maline Phases*
Jerry R. Galm

10. *Arkansas Valley Caddoan: The Harlan Phase*
Robert E. Bell

11. *Arkansas Valley Caddoan: The Spiro Phase*
James A. Brown

15. *The Plains Villagers: Antelope Creek*

Christopher Lintz

16. *The Western Protohistoric: A Summary of the Edwards and Wheeler Complexes*

Jack L. Hofman

17. *Protohistoric Wichita*

Robert E. Bell

List of Figures

List of Tables

Contributors

Numbers in parentheses indicate the pages on which the authors' contributions begin.

LOIS E. ALBERT (1, 45), Oklahoma Archaeological Survey, University of Oklahoma, Norman, Oklahoma 73019

LARRY D. BANKS (65), Department of the Army, U.S. Army Engineer Division, Southwestern Corps of Engineers, Dallas, Texas 75242

ROBERT E. BELL (221, 307, 363), Department of Anthropology, University of Oklahoma, Norman, Oklahoma 73069

JAMES A. BROWN (241), Department of Anthropology, Northwestern University, Evanston, Illinois 60201

JERRY R. GALM (199), Archaelogical and Historical Services, Eastern Washington University, Cheney, Washington 99004

MARSHALL GETTYS (97), Oklahoma Historical Society, Oklahoma City, Oklahoma 73105

JACK L. HOFMAN (287, 347), Department of Anthropology, University of Tennessee, Knoxville, Tennessee 37916

DAVID T. HUGHES (109), Department of Anthropology, University of Oklahoma, Norman, Oklahoma 73019

CHRISTOPHER LINTZ (161, 325), Department of Anthropology, University of Oklahoma, Norman, Oklahoma 73019

CHARLES L. ROHRBAUGH (265), 303 South Mercedes Drive, Norman, Oklahoma 73069

SUSAN C. VEHIK (175), Department of Anthropology, University of Oklahoma, Norman, Oklahoma 73019

DON G. WYCKOFF (1, 119), Oklahoma Archaeological Survey, University of Oklahoma, Norman, Oklahoma 73019

LEON GEORGE ZABAWA (161), Department of Anthropology, University of Oklahoma, Norman, Oklahoma 73019

Preface

More than 30 years ago David A. Baerreis and I published a Survey of Oklahoma Archaeology, which attempted to bring together the available information on Oklahoma prehistory. I had intended originally to compile a similar summary at the end of 10 years, but somehow the pressure of numerous activities made this impossible. Nonetheless, I strongly believe that one should attempt to summarize available knowledge in specific areas from time to time, not only for colleagues, but because such a summary quickly illuminates deficiencies in the data and suggests new directions for research. Finally, in 1977, I decided to enlist the help of various other Oklahoma specialists to issue a joint summary report on our current knowledge of the region. This volume is the result of this undertaking.

The various authors were selected because of their interest and knowledge of specific areas or topics. I provided them with some general guidelines, a limitation in space and illustrations, and a broad framework. Basically I wanted an up-to-date summary of the topic, with extensive references so readers could go to the original sources if they desired. I believe this goal has been well realized by all the authors.

The amount of published information has grown enormously since the 1951 survey, and it has not been easy to choose what is essential. This contrast between today and 1951 can be seen clearly by comparing the bibliographies of this volume and the 1951 survey. The 1951 survey contained a total of 15 references; this volume contains approximately 940 references.

As editor I have been primarily concerned with matters of style and clarification. I have not directed the authors' conclusions or expressions of individual ideas; in fact, I sometimes disagree with positions that are taken but believe that alternative views or models are essential to continued growth and understanding in the field.

Radiocarbon dates are frequently difficult to locate, or remain unknown for some reason, but charts of available radiocarbon dates have been included with the pertinent chapters. These have been corrected (MASCA) as indicated on the respective charts.

The specimens that are illustrated are in the Stovall Museum collections at the University of Oklahoma unless otherwise noted. So many individuals have been involved in the preparation of photographs and figures that I will mention no one specifically. I do, however, greatly appreciate the efforts made to complete this often troublesome task.

There may be an occasional reader who is surprised to find that there is no mention of runes or the Vikings of Oklahoma. All reputable scholars of runes or Viking history acknowledge that the Oklahoma ''runes'' are modern and are in no way connected with the Vikings. Consequently, this topic is not a part of Oklahoma's prehistory but is rather a topic of modern Oklahoma folklore or fiction.

Finally, I acknowledge the numerous contributors to the book for their interest, cooperation, and personal efforts in making this summary possible. I trust that they will be proud of their contribution. I also express thanks to Mary Goodman and Patricia Kawecki of the Oklahoma Archaeological Survey staff for their work in preparing final copy of the many figures. My wife, Virginia, contributed much to the editing and provided moral support, and for this I am very grateful.

Prehistory of Oklahoma

CHAPTER 1

Oklahoma Environments: Past and Present

Lois E. Albert and Don G. Wyckoff

Introduction

Oklahoma is an environmentally diverse state (Table 1.1). Its annual precipitation varies from about 142 cm (56 inches) in southern LeFlore County to 43 cm (17 inches) at Kenton in the western panhandle. A period of maximum rainfall occurs in the spring—April to June—with a second, lesser maximum about September. The driest part of the year for most areas is winter—December through February. Although mean annual temperatures display a difference of only 2.5–3° C (4–5° F) across the state, the growing season ranges from 222 days in the southeast to 168 days at Kenton. This decrease in length of growing season is partly due to differences in elevation. These range from 110 m (350 feet) at the southeastern corner along Red River to almost 1515 m (5000 feet) on Black Mesa in the panhandle's northwestern corner. Droughts have been recorded for the late 1890s, 1910–1919, the 1930s, and 1951–1957. It appears likely that there were earlier historic droughts (Lawson 1974).

In 1938, Blair and Hubbell published a study of the state's biotic districts. For the present discussion, these have been modified to seven major districts and four minor ones treated as special areas (Figure 1.1). Duck and Fletcher's (1943) habitat types, first published as a map, further define major plant communities within the state. The biotic districts and habitat types have been correlated (Table 1.2) with the physiographic or geomorphic provinces of Curtis and Ham (Figure 1.2). Three excellent bibliographies covering Oklahoma vegetation studies through 1974 are Kelting and Penfound (1953), Milby and Penfound (1964), and Milby (1977). Tables 1.3–1.6 supplement the text of this chapter by listing

1

Table 1.1

Climatic Data for Selected Reporting Stations

Reporting station	County	Biotic district	Latitude Longitude	Elevation, in meters (feet)	Mean annual temperature (°C; °F) (length of record)	Mean annual precipitation (cm; inches) (length of record)	Mean number of frost-free days
Tahlequah	Cherokee	Ozark	35° 59' 94° 56'	86 (846)	16; 60.2 (38 yrs)	109.3; 43.02 (61 yrs)	199
Idabel	McCurtain	Mississippi	33° 53' 94° 49'	50 (460)	17.5; 63.3 (44 yrs)	119.7; 47.11 (53 yrs)	222
Clayton–Tuskahoma	Pushmataha	Ouachita	34° 37' 95° 17'	62 (600)	17; 62.2 (22 yrs)	123.3; 48.56 (54 yrs)	—
Claremore	Rogers	Cherokee Prairie	36° 19' 95° 35'	60 (588)	15; 59.6 (53 yrs)	97.16; 38.25 (60 yrs)	209
Pawhuska	Osage	Osage Savanna	36° 40' 96° 21'	85 (835)	15; 59.4 (51 yrs)	91.82; 36.15 (77 yrs)	200
Enid	Garfield	Mixed-grass Plains	36° 25' 97° 52'	128 (1245)	16; 60.2 (61 yrs)	76.17; 29.99 (67 yrs)	214
Buffalo	Harper	Short-grass Plains	36° 50' 99° 37'	182 (1795)	15; 59.3 (49 yrs)	61.54; 24.23 (57 yrs)	190

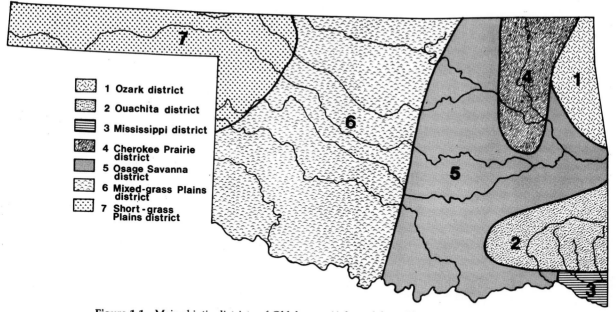

Figure 1.1 Major biotic districts of Oklahoma. (Adapted from Blair and Hubbell 1938.)

1 Ozark district
2 Ouachita district
3 Mississippi district
4 Cherokee Prairie district
5 Osage Savanna district
6 Mixed-grass Plains district
7 Short-grass Plains district

the most abundant plants and animals found in Oklahoma's major biotic districts. By referring to these figures, a more complete picture for each district may be obtained. Statistical data used to construct charts for selected recording stations (United States Environmental Data Service 1966–1979; United States Weather Bureau 1892–1965) in each biotic district were computed on an Apple II microcomputer using Programma software.

Oklahoma's Natural Settings

Ozark District

The Ozark region extends into northeastern Oklahoma from Arkansas and Missouri. The northern portion, the Ozark Plateau, consists of dissected limestones, cherts, and dolomites formed during the Cambrian, Ordovician, and Mississippian periods. To the south, the higher and more rugged Boston Mountains, with a relief up to 245 m (800 feet) from stream bottom to hilltop, are mainly composed of Pennsylvanian sandstones and shales. The streams originating in this region flow southwest or south into the Illinois and Arkansas rivers.

Table 1.2

Correlation of Major Oklahoma Biota with Major Physiographic Provinces

Biotic district[a]	Habitat types[b]	Physiographic or geomorphic provinces[c]

Ozark	Major
	  Oak–hickory forest
	  Oak–pine forest
	Minor
	  Bottomland forest
	  Post oak–blackjack forest
		Ozark Plateau
		Boston Mountains

Ouachita	Major
	  Oak–pine forest
	Minor
	  Oak–hickory forest
	  Post oak–blackjack forest
	  Bottomland forest
		Ridge and Valley Belt
		Hogback Frontal Belt
		McAlester Marginal Hills Belt
		Beavers Bend Hills

Mississippi	Major
	  Bottomland forest
	  Loblolly pine forest
	  Oak–hickory forest
	Minor
	  Cypress bottoms forest
		Dissected Coastal Plain

Cherokee Prairie	Major
	  Tall-grass prairie
	  Post oak–blackjack forest
	Minor
	  Bottomland forest
		Neosho Lowland

Osage Savanna	Major
	  Post oak–blackjack forest
	  Tall-grass prairie
	Minor
	  Oak–hickory forest
	  Bottomland forest
	  Oak–pine forest
		Eastern Sandstone Cuesta plains
		Claremore Cuesta Plains
		Arkansas Hill and Valley Belt
		Northern Limestone Cuesta Plains
		Central Redbed Plains
		Arbuckle Plains
		Arbuckle Hills
		McAlester Marginal Hills Belt
		Dissected Coastal Plains

Mixed-grass Plains	Major
	  Tall-grass prairie
	  Mixed-grass eroded
	    plains
	Minor
	  Sand-sage grasslands
	  Mesquite grasslands
	  Shinnery-oak grasslands
	  Bottomland forest
		Central Redbed Plains
		Western Sandstone Hills
		Western Redbed Plains
		Weatherford Gypsum Hills
		Cimarron Gypsum Hills
		Mangum Gypsum Hills
		Sand areas

Short-grass Plains	Major
	  Short-grass highplains
	Minor
	  Mixed-grass eroded
	    plains
	  Bottomland forest
	  Sand-sage grasslands
	  Piñon–juniper–mesa
		High Plains
		Western Sandstone Hills
		Cimarron Gypsum Hills
		Black Mesa

[a]Blair and Hubbell (1938).
[b]Duck and Fletcher (1943).
[c]Curtis and Ham (1957, 1972).

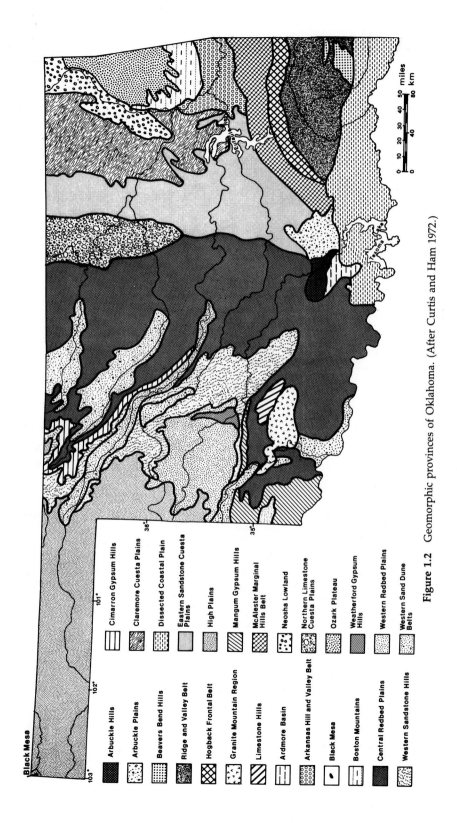

Figure 1.2 Geomorphic provinces of Oklahoma. (After Curtis and Ham 1972.)

Black Mesa

Arbuckle Hills
Arbuckle Plains
Beavers Bend Hills
Ridge and Valley Belt
Hogback Frontal Belt
Granite Mountain Region
Limestone Hills
Ardmore Basin
Arkansas Hill and Valley Belt
Black Mesa
Boston Mountains
Central Redbed Plains
Western Sandstone Hills

Cimarron Gypsum Hills
Claremore Cuesta Plains
Dissected Coastal Plain
Eastern Sandstone Cuesta Plains
High Plains
Mangum Gypsum Hills
McAlester Marginal Hills Belt
Neosha Lowland
Northern Limestone Cuesta Plains
Ozark Plateau
Weatherford Gypsum Hills
Western Redbed Plains
Western Sand Dune Belts

miles
km

Table 1.3

Distributions of Most Important Native Oklahoma Trees and Shrubs[a]

Common name	Scientific name	District						
		Ozark	Ouachita	Mississippi	Cherokee Prairie	Osage Savanna	Mixed-grass Prairie	Short-grass Plains
Box elder	Acer negundo L.	x	x	x	x	x	x	
Red maple	Acer rubrum L.	x	x	x				
Silver maple	Acer saccharinum L.	x	x		x			
Sugar maple	Acer saccharum March.	x	x		x		x[b]	
Ohio buckeye	Aesculus glabra Willd.	x	x		x		x	
Seaside alder	Alnus maritima (Marsh.) Muhl.					x		
Smooth alder	Alnus serrulata (Ait.) Willd.					x		
Serviceberry	Amelanchier arborea (Michx. f.) Fern.	x	x		x	x		
Prairie acacia	Acacia angustissima (Mill.) Kuntze, var. hirta (T. & G.) Robins.						x	
Sand sage	Artemisia filifolia Torr.						x	x
Pawpaw	Asimina triloba (L.) Dun.	x	x		x	x	x	
Saltbush	Atriplex canescens (Pursh.) Nutt.						x	x
River birch	Betula nigra L.	x	x		x	x	x	
Chittamwood	Bumelia lanuginosa (Michx.) Pers.	x	x		x	x	x	
American hornbeam	Carpinus caroliniana Walt.		x					
Water hickory	Carya aquatica (Michx. f.) Ell.			x				
Bitternut hickory	Carya cordiformis (Wang.) K. Koch	x	x	x	x	x	x[c]	
Pecan	Carya illinoinensis (Wang.) K. Koch	x	x		x	x	x	
Shellbark hickory	Carya laciniosa (Michx. f.) Loud.	x		x	x	x		
Nutmeg hickory	Carya myristicaeformis (Michx. f.) Ell.			x				
Pignut hickory	Carya ovalis (Wang.) Sarg.	x			x	x		
Shagbark hickory	Carya ovata (Mill.) K. Koch	x	x			x		
Black hickory	Carya texana Buckl.	?	x		?	x		
Mockernut hickory	Carya tomentosa Nutt.	x	x		x	x		
American chestnut	Castanea dentata (Marsh.) Borkh.	?						
Ozark chinquapin	Castanea ozarkensis Ashe	x	x		x			
Allegheny chinquapin	Castanea pumila (L.) Mill.			x				
Southern catalpa	Catalpa bignonioides Walt[d]					x	x	
Northern catalpa	Catalpa speciosa Ward.					x	x	

6

Common name	Scientific name						
New Jersey tea	*Ceanothus americanus* L.	x		x	x	x	
Inland ceanothus	*Ceanothus herbaceus* Raf.	x		x	x	x	x
Sugarberry	*Celtis laevigata* Willd.	x		x	x	x	
Common hackberry	*Celtis occidentalis* L.	x	x	?	x	?	x
Western hackberry	*Celtis reticulata* Torr.	?		x	x	?	x
Dwarf hackberry	*Celtis tenuifolia* Nutt.	x	x				
Buttonbush	*Cephalanthus occidentalis* L.	x	x	x	x	x	
Redbud	*Cercis canadensis* L.	x	x	x	x	x	
Mountain mahogany	*Cercocarpus montanus* Raf.			x	x	x	x^e
Roughleaf dogwood	*Cornus drummondii* Mey.	x	x	x	x	x	
Flowering dogwood	*Cornus florida* L.	x	x	x	x	x	
Stiffcornel dogwood	*Cornus foemina* Mill.	x			x		
Pale dogwood	*Cornus obliqua* Raf.	x			x		
Hawthorn	*Crataegus* (15 spp.)	x	x	x	x	x	
Hazelnut	*Corylus americana* Walt.	x				x	
American smoketree	*Cotinus obovatus* Raf.			x		x	
Persimmon	*Diospyros virginiana* L.	x	x	x	x	x	
Strawberrybush	*Euonymus americanus* L.	x	x	x^f	x	x	
Wahoo	*Euonymus atropurpureus* Jacq.	x	x	x	x	x	
American beech	*Fagus grandiflora* Ehrh	x	x		x		
White ash	*Fraxinus americana* L.	x	?	x	x	x	
Red ash	*Fraxinus pennsylvanica* Marsh	x	x	x	x	x	
Blue ash	*Fraxinus quadrangulata* Michx.	x		?	?	x	
Honey locust	*Gleditsia triacanthos* L.	x	?	x	x	x	
Plains greasebush	*Glossopetalon planitierum* (Ensing) St. John						x^e
Kentucky coffeetree	*Gymnocladus dioica* (L.) Koch	x		x	x	x	
Carolina silverbell	*Halesia carolina* L.	x	x				
Spring witch hazel	*Hamamelis vernalis* Sarg.	x	x			x	
Southern witch hazel	*Hamamelis virginiana* L.	x	x				
Wild hydrangea	*Hydrangea aborescens* L.	x	x	x	x		
Winterberry	*Ilex decidua* Walt.	x	x	x	x	x	
American holly	*Ilex opaca* Ait.	x	x		x		
Yaupon	*Ilex vomitoria* Ait.		x		x		
Little walnut	*Juglans microcarpa* Berl.				x	x	
Black walnut	*Juglans nigra* L.	x	x	x	x	x	
Ashe juniper	*Juniperus ashei* Buchh.			x			
One-seeded juniper	*Juniperus monosperma* (Engelm.) Sarg.						x^e
Redberry juniper	*Juniperus pinchotii* Sudw.					x	
Western red cedar	*Juniperus scopulorum* Sarg.						x^e

(continued)

Table 1.3 (Continued)

Common name	Scientific name	District						
		Ozark	Ouachita	Mississippi	Cherokee Prairie	Osage Savanna	Mixed-grass Prairie	Short-grass Plains
Eastern red cedar	Juniperus virginiana L.	x	x	x	?	x	x	
Spicebush	Lindera benzoin (L.) Blume	x	x		x	x		
Sweetgum	Liquidambar styraciflua L.		x	x				
Osage orange	Maclura pomifera (Raf.) Schneid.	x	x	x	?	x	x	
Cucumber tree	Magnolia acuminata L.			x				
Umbrella tree	Magnolia tripetala L.			x				
Texas mulberry	Morus microphylla Buckl.					x[f]	x[c]	x[e]
Red mulberry	Morus rubra L.	x	?	x	x	x	x	x[e]
Southern bayberry	Myrica cerifera L.			x		x		
Black gum	Nyssa sylvatica Marsh.	x	x					
Ironwood	Ostrya virginiana (Mill.) K. Koch	x	x					
Hoary mockorange	Philadelphus pubescens Lois.	x	x					
Shortleaf pine	Pinus echinata Mill.	x	x					
Pinon pine	Pinus edulis Engelm.							x[e]
Ponderosa pine	Pinus ponderosa Laws.							x[e]
Loblolly pine	Pinus taeda L.			x				
Water elm	Planera aquatica (Walt.) Gmel.	x	x	x				
Sycamore	Platanus occidentalis L.	x	x	x	x	x		
Cottonwood	Populus deltoides Marsh	x	x	x	x	x	x	x
Honey mesquite	Prosopis juliflora (Swartz) DC.		x			x	x	
Wild plum	Prunus americana Marsh.	x	x			x	x	
Chickasaw plum	Prunus angustifolia Marsh.				x	x	x	x
Oklahoma plum	Prunus gracilis Engelm. & Gray				?	x	x	x
Mexican plum	Prunus mexicana S. Wats.	?	x	?	?	x	x	
Wild goose plum	Prunus munsoniana Wight & Hedr.	?	x			x		
Wild black cherry	Prunus serotina Ehrh.	x	x		x	x	x	
Choke cherry	Prunus virginiana L.						x	
Hoptree	Ptelea trifoliata L.	x	x		x	x	x	x
Prairie crabapple	Pyrus ioensis (Wood.) Bail.					x		
White oak	Quercus alba L.	x	x		x	x		
Southern red oak	Quercus falcata Michx.	x	x	x		x		
Gambel oak	Quercus gambellii Nutt.							
Shinnery oak	Quercus havardii Rydb.						x	x[e]

Common name	Scientific name	1	2	3	4	5	6	7	8	9	10	11	12	13
Bluejack oak	Quercus incana Bartr.				x									
Overcup oak	Quercus lyrata Walt.			x										
Burr oak	Quercus macrocarpa Michx.	x		x					x	x	x			
Blackjack oak	Quercus marilandica Muenchh.	x		x	x				x	x	x			x
Shin oak	Quercus mohriana Rydb.			?					x	?				
Chinquapin oak	Quercus muehlenbergii Engelm.	x		x	x				x	x	x			
Water oak	Quercus nigra L.	x		x	x				x					
Pin oak	Quercus palustris Muenchh.	x		x	x				x					
Willow oak	Quercus phellos L.	x		x	x				?	?				
Dwarf chinquapin oak	Quercus prinoides Willd.	x		x	x				x	x				x
Northern red oak	Quercus rubra L.	x		x					x	x				
Shumard's oak	Quercus shumardii Buckl.	x		x	x				x	x	x			x
Post oak	Quercus stellata Wang.	x		x	x				x	x	x			
Wavyleaf oak	Quercus undulata Torr.													x[e]
Black oak	Quercus velutina Lam.	x		x	x				x	x				
Live oak	Quercus virginiana Mill.				x				x	x				
Piedmont azalea	Rhododendron canescens Sweet	x	x											
Texas azalea	Rhododendron oblongifolium (Small) Millais	x	x											
Fragrant sumac	Rhus aromatica Ait.	x		x	x				x	x	x			x
Winged sumac	Rhus copallina L.	x		x	x				?	x	x			
Smooth sumac	Rhus glabra L.	x		x	x				x	x	x			
Wax current	Ribes cereum Dougl.				x									
Wild gooseberry	Ribes cynosbati L.	x												x[e]
Missouri gooseberry	Ribes missouriense Nutt.	x[g]												
Buffalo currant	Ribes odoratum Wendl. f.													
Black locust	Robinia pseudo-acacia L.	x	x	x					x	x	x			x
Carolina rose	Rosa carolina L.	x	x	x					x	x				x
Leafy rose	Rosa foliolosa Nutt.				x				x	x	x			
Prairie rose	Rosa setigera Michx.	x		x	x				x	x	x			x
Wood's rose	Rosa woodsii Lindl.													
Dwarf palmetto	Sabal minor (Jacp.) Pers.				x[h]									
Peach-leaved willow	Salix amygdaloides Anderss.	x							x	x				x
Carolina willow	Salix caroliniana Michx.	x		x	x				x	x				?
Prairie willow	Salix humilis Marsh.			x					x	x				
Sandbar willow	Salix interior Rowl.	x		x					x	x				x
Black willow	Salix nigra Marsh	x		x	x				x	x				
Western soapberry	Sapindus drummondii H. & A.	x		x	x				x	x				x

(continued)

9

Table 1.3 (Continued)

Common name	Scientific name	District						
		Ozark	Ouachita	Mississippi	Cherokee Prairie	Osage Savanna	Mixed-grass Prairie	Short-grass Plains
Elderberry	Sambucus canadensis L.	x	x		x	x	x	x
Western snowberry	Symphoricarpos occidentalis Hook.							x
Coralberry	Symphoricarpos orbiculatus Moench	x	x	?	x	x	x	
Palmer's snowberry	Symphoricarpos palmeri G. N. Jones							x
Sassafras	Sassafras albidum (Nutt.) Nees	x	x	x	x	?		
Bald cypress	Taxodium distichum (L.) Rich.			x[h]				
American basswood	Tilia americana L.	x	x	x	x	x		
Winged elm	Ulmus alata Michx.	x	x	x	x	x	x	
American elm	Ulmus americana L.	x	x	x	x	x		
Cedar elm	Ulmus crassifolia Nutt.			x		x		
Slippery elm	Ulmus rubra Muhl.	x	x	x	x	x	x	
September elm	Ulmus serotina Sarg.	x	x					
Black haw	Viburnum prunifolium L.	x	x	x	x	x	x	
Southern black haw	Viburnum rafinesquianum Schult.	x	x					

[a] Adapted from Williams (1974).
[b] Caddo Canyons only.
[c] Wichita Mountains area.
[d] Some doubt if species is native to this area.
[e] Black Mesa area only.
[f] Arbuckle Mountains only.
[g] Ottawa County only.
[h] Southeastern McCurtain County only.

10

Table 1.4

Abundant Oklahoma Mammals Native to Oklahoma Biotic Districts[a]

Common name	Scientific name	Ozark	Ouachita	Mississippi	Cherokee Prairie	Osage Savanna	Mixed-grass Prairie	Short-grass Plains
Louisiana white-tailed deer	Odocoileus virginianus louisianae	x	x	x	x	x		
Plains white-tailed deer	Odocoileus virginianus macrourus					x	x	x[b]
Rocky Mountain mule deer	Odocoileus hemionus hemionus						x	x
Pronghorn antelope	Antilocapra americana Americana				x	x	x	x
Elk	Cervus Merriami	x	x		x	x	x	x
American bison	Bison bison bison	x	x	x	x	x	x	x
Black bear	Euarctos americanus americanus	x	x	x	x	x	x	x
Cougar	Felis concolor	x	x	x	x	x	x	x
Bailey bobcat	Lynx rufus baileyi						x	x
Bobcat	Lynx rufus rufus	x	x	x	x	x	x	
Timber (gray) wolf	Canis lupus rubiles	x	x	x	x	x	x	x
Texas red wolf	Canis rufus rufus	x	x	x	x	x	x	x
Coyote	Canis latrans nevrascensis	x	x		x	x	x	x
Coyote	Canis latrans texensis			x			x[c]	
Red fox	Vulpes fulva	x	x	x	x	x	x	x
Kit fox	Vulpes velox velox							x
Gray fox	Urocyon cinereoargenteus ocythous	x	x	x	x	x	x	
Gray squirrel	Sciurus carolinensis	x	x	x	x	x		
Fox squirrel	Sciurus niger rufiventer	x	x	x	x	x	x	
Blacktailed jackrabbit	Lepus californicus melanotis				x	x	x	x
Eastern cottontail	Sylvilagus floridanus alacer	x	x	x	x	x	x	x
New Mexico cottontail	Sylvilagus audubonii neomexicanus							x
Desert cottontail	Sylvilagus audubonii baileyi						x	x[d]
Swamp rabbit	Sylvilagus aquaticus aquaticus	x	x	x	x	x		
Opossum	Didelphus virginiana virginiana	x	x	x	x	x	x	x
Raccoon	Procyon lotor	x	x	x	x	x	x	x
Mississippi valley mink	Mustela vison letifera	x	x	x	x	x	x	x
Common mink	Mustela vison mink	x	x	x	x	x		
Weasel	Mustela frenata primula	x	x	x	x	x	x	
Black-footed ferret	Mustela nigripes				x	x	x	x
Badger	Taxidea taxus berlandieri				x	x	x	x

(continued)

Table 1.4 (Continued)

Common name	Scientific name	Ozark	Ouachita	Mississippi	Cherokee Prairie	Osage Savanna	Mixed-grass Prairie	Short-grass Plains
Muskrat	Ondatra zibethicus	x	x	x	x	x	x	x
Hognose skunk	Conepatus leuconotus							x[d]
Louisiana (striped) skunk	Mephitis mephitis mesomelas	x	x	x	x	x	x	x
Long-tailed Texas skunk	Mephitis mephitis vartans						x	x
Spotted skunk	Spilogale putoris	x	x	x	x	x	x	x
Beaver	Castor canadensis	x	x	x	x	x	x	x
Otter	Lutra canadensis laxaxina	x	x	x	x	x	x	
Blacktail prairie dog	Cynomys ludovicianus						x	x
Rock squirrel	Citellus variegatus							x
Thirteen-lined ground squirrel	Citellus tridecemlineatus	x	x		x	x	x	x
Spotted ground squirrel	Citellus spilosoma							x
Eastern chipmunk	Tiamias striatus	x		x				
Southern flying squirrel	Glaucomys volans	x	x	x	x	x		
Plains pocket gopher	Geomys bursarius	x	x	x	x	x	x	x
Mexican pocket gopher	Cratogeomys castanops					x		x
Fulvous harvest mouse	Reithrodontomys fulvescens	x	x	x	x	x	x	
White-footed mouse	Peromyscus leucopus	x	x	x	x	x	x	x
Deer mouse	Peromyscus maniculatus	x	x		x	x	x	x
Brush mouse	Peromyscus boylei	x	x	x	x	x	x	
Eastern woodrat	Neotoma floridana	x	x	x	x	x		
Southern plains woodrat	Neotoma micropus						x	x
Hispid cotton rat	Sigmodon hispidus	x	x	x	x	x	x	x
Prairie vole	Microtus ochrogaster				x	x	x	x
Pine vole	Pitymys pinetorum	x	x	x	x	x		
Porcupine	Erethizon dorsatum						x	x
Peccary	Pecari angulatus				x	x		
Armadillo	Dasypus novemcinus	x	x	x	x	x	x	

[a]Compiled from Burt and Grossenheider (1964), Duck and Fletcher (1944) and Wildlife Conservation Department (1960).
[b]Present in sand dune and bottomland habitats only.
[c]Wichita Mountains only.
[d]Black Mesa area only.

Table 1.5

Abundant Oklahoma Birds Native to Oklahoma Biotic Districts[a]

Common name	Scientific name	Ozark	Ouachita	Mississippi	Cherokee Prairie	Osage Savanna	Mixed-grass Prairie	Short-grass Plains
Bobwhite quail	Colinus Virginianus	x	x	x	x	x	x	x
Greater prairie chicken	Tympanuchus cupido americanus	x	x	x	x	x		x
Lesser prairie chicken	Tympanuchus pallidicinctus[b]							x
Prairie sharp-tailed grouse	Pedioectes phasianellus campetris							x
Sage hen	Centracercus urophasianus	x			x		x	x
Scaled quail	Callipepla squamata pallida	x			x		x	x
Mourning dove	Zenaidura macroura	x			x	x	x	x
Wild turkey	Meleagris gallapavo silvestrous	x	x		x	x	x	x(?)
American woodcock	Philohela minor	x	x	x	x			
Passenger pigeon	Ectopistes migratorius[b]	x			x	x		
Carolina parakeet	Conuropsis carolinensis[b]	x		x	x	x	x	
Mallard duck	Anas Platyrhynchos	——— common migrant ———						
Pintail duck	Anas acuta	——— common migrant ———						
Pied-bill grebe	Podilymbus podiceps	x	x	x	x	x	x	x
Great blue heron	Ardea Herodias	x	x	x	x	x	x	x
Green heron	Butorides virescens	x	x	x	x	x	x	x
Little blue heron	Florida caerulea	x	x	x	x	x	x	
Common egret	Casmerodius albus	x	x	x	x	x	x	
Snowy egret	Leucophoyx thula	x	x	x	x	x		
American bittern	Botaurus lentiginous		x	x	x	x	x	
Canada goose	Branta canadensis	——— common migrant ———			x	x	x	
Snow goose	Chen hyperborea	——— common migrant ———						
Wood duck	Aix sponsa	x	x	x	x	x		
Turkey vulture	Cathartes aura	x	x	x	x	x	x	x
Black vulture	Coragyps atratus	x	x	x	x	x		
Swallow-tailed kite	Elanoides forticatus	x	x	x	x			
Mississippi kite	Ictinia mississippiensis	x	x	x	x	x	x	x
Sharp-shinned hawk	Accipiter striatus	x	x	x	x	x	x	x
Cooper's hawk	Accipiter cooperii	x	x	x	x	x	x	
Red-tailed hawk	Buteo jamaicensis	x	x	x	x	x	x	x
Red-shouldered hawk	Buteo lineatus	x	x	x	x	x	x	
Golden eagle	Aquila chrysaetos							x
Marsh hawk	Circus hudsonius				x	x	x	x
Prairie falcon	Falco mexicanus		x			x		x

(continued)

13

Table 1.5 (*Continued*)

Common name	Scientific name	Ozark	Ouachita	Mississippi	Cherokee Prairie	Osage Savanna	Mixed-grass Prairie	Short-grass Plains
Sparrow hawk	*Falco sparvorius*	x		x	x	x	x	x
Whooping crane	*Grus americana*	—formerly common migrant————————						
Sandhill crane	*Grus Canadensis*	—migrant————————						
American coot	*Fulica americana*	x			x	x	x	x
Killdeer	*Charadrius vociferus*	x	x	x	x	x	x	x
Common snipe	*Capella gallinago*			x	x	x	x	x
Eskimo curlew	*Numenius borealis*[b]	—migrant————————						
Franklin's gull	*Larus pipixcan*	x			x	x	x	x
Yellow-billed cockoo	*Coccyzus americanus*	x	x	x	x	x	x	x
Roadrunner	*Geococcyx californianus*				x	x	x	x
Screech owl	*Otus asio*	x	x	x	x	x	x	x
Burrowing owl	*Speotyto cunicularia*					x		
Barred owl	*Strix varia*	x	x	x	x	x		
Red-bellied wood-pecker	*Centurus carolinus*	x	x	x	x	x	x	
Red-headed wood-pecker	*Melanerpes erythrocephalus*	x	x	x	x	x	x	x
Hairy woodpecker	*Dendrocopos villosus*	x	x	x	x	x	x	x
Downy woodpecker	*Dendrocopos pubescens*	x	x	x	x	x	x	x
Scissor-tailed fly-catcher	*Muscivora forficata*	x	x	x	x	x	x	x
Horned lark	*Eremophila alpestris*	x	x	x	x	x	x	x
Bank swallow	*Riparia riparia*	—common migrant————————						
Purple martin	*Progne subis*	x	x	x	x	x	x	x
Blue jay	*Cyanocitta cristata*	x	x	x	x	x	x	
Common raven	*Corvus corvax*	x		(early distribution unclear)				
White-necked raven	*Corvus cryptoleucus*					x	x	x
Common crow	*Corvus brachyrhynchos*	x	x	x	x	x	x	
Mockingbird	*Mimus polyglottos*	x	x	x	x	x	x	x
Brown thrasher	*Toxostoma rufum*	x	x	x	x	x	x	
Cedar waxwing	*Bombycilla cedrorum*	—common migrant————————						
Western meadowlark	*Sturnella neglecta*	x			x	x	x	x

[a] Compiled from Duck and Fletcher (1944), Wildlife Conservation Department (1960) and Sutton (1967).
[b] Extinct or nearly so.

14

Table 1.6

Abundant Oklahoma Reptiles and Fishes Native to Oklahoma Biotic Districts[a]

Common name	Scientific name	Ozark	Ouachita	Mississippi	Cherokee Prairie	Osage Savanna	Mixed-grass Prairie	Short-grass Plains
Reptiles								
Common snapping turtle	*Chelydra serpentina*	×	×	×	×	×	×	×
Mississippi mud turtle	*Kinosternon subrubrum hippocrepis*	×	×	×	×	×		
Alligator snapping turtle	*Macroclemys temmincki*	×	×	×	×	×		
Missouri slider	*Pseudemys flordana hoyi*	×	×	×	×	×		
Red-eared turtle	*Pseudemys scripta elegans*	×	×	×	×	×	×	×
Stinkpot	*Sternotherus odoratus*	×	×	×	×	×		
Three-toed box turtle	*Terrapene carolina triunguis*	×	×	×	×	×		
Ornate box turtle	*Terrapene ornata ornata*	×	×	×	×	×	×	×
Prairie lined racerunner	*Cnemidophorus sex-lineatus viridis*	×	×	×	×	×	×	×
Eastern collared lizard	*Crotaphytus collaris collaris*	×	×	×	×	×	×	×
Southern coal skink	*Eumeces anthracinus pluvialis*	×	×	×	×	×		
Great plains skink	*Eumeces obsoletus*				×	×	×	×
Ground skink	*Lygosoma laterale*	×	×	×	×	×	×	
Texas horned lizard	*Phrynosoma corutum*				×	×	×	×
Copperhead	*Agkistrodon contortrix*	×	×	×	×	×	×	
Western cottonmouth	*Agkistrodon piscivoorus leucostoma*	×	×	×	×	×	×	
Eastern yellow-bellied racer	*Coluber constrictor flaviventris*	×	×	×	×	×	×	×
Western diamondback rattlesnake	*Crotalus atrox*	×	×	×		×	×	
Timber rattlesnake	*Crotalus horridus horridus*	×	×	×	×	×		
Prairie rattlesnake	*Crotalus viridis viridis*							
Great plains rat snake	*Elaphe guttata emoryi*	×	×	×	×	×	×	×
Eastern hognose snake	*Heterodon platyrhinos*	×	×	×	×	×	×	×

(continued)

15

Table 1.6 (*Continued*)

Common name	Scientific name	Ozark	Ouachita	Mississippi	Cherokee Prairie	Osage Savanna	Mixed-grass Prairie	Short-grass Plains
Prairie kingsnake	*Lampropeltis calligaster calligaster*	x	x	x	x	x	x	x
Speckled rattlesnake	*Lampropeltis getulus holbrooki*	x	x	x	x	x	x	x
Coachwhip	*Masticophis flagellum*	x	x	x	x	x	x	x
Bullsnake	*Pituophis melanoleucus sayi*				x	x	x	x
Flat-headed snake	*Tantilla gracilis*	x	x	x	x	x	x	
Fishes								
Spotted gar	*Lepisosteus oculatus*	x	x	x	x	x		
Shortnose gar	*Lepisosteus platostomus*	x	x	x	x	x		
Gizzard shad	*Dorosoma cepedianum*	x	x	x	x	x	x	x
Smallmouth buffalo	*Ictiobus bubalus*	x	x	x	x	x		
Bigmouth buffalo	*Ictiobus niger*	x	x	x	x	x		
Blue catfish	*Ictalurus furcatus*			x				
Black bullhead	*Ictalurus melas*	x	x	x	x	x	x	x
Yellow bullhead	*Ictalurus natalis*	x	x	x	x	x	x	
Channel catfish	*Ictalurus punctatus*	x	x	x	x	x	x	x
Flathead catfish	*Pylodictis olivaris*	x	x	x	x	x	x	
White bass	*Morone chrysops*	x		x	x	x	x	
Warmouth	*Chaenobryttus gulosus*	x	x	x	x	x	x	
Green sunfish	*Lepomis cyanellus*	x	x	x	x	x	x	x
Orangespotted sunfish	*Lepomis humilis*	x	x	x	x	x	x	x
Bluegill	*Lepomis macrochirus*	x	x	x	x	x		
Longear sunfish	*Lepomis megalotis*	x	x	x	x	x	x	x
Smallmouth bass	*Micropterus dolomieui*	x	x	x				
Spotted bass	*Micropterus punctulatus*	x	x	x	x	x		
White crappie	*Pomoxis annularis*	x	x	x	x	x	x	
Logperch	*Percina Caprodes*	x	x	x	x	x		
Freshwater drum	*Aplodinotus grunniens*	x	x	x	x	x	x	

[a] Compiled from Miller and Robison (1973) and R. G. Webb (1970).

The Ozark soils developed from the sedimentary bedrocks are Ultisols. These clayey soils form in warm, humid climates with a seasonal deficiency in rainfall. During some portion of the year, precipitation exceeds evaporation so that leaching occurs. The low fertility of these forest soils and the steep mountain slopes are a hindrance to agriculture. Today, crops are grown mainly in the deeper alluvial soils of the valleys.

Hot, humid summers and cool, dry winters characterize the Ozarks' climate. The annual precipitation, though quite variable, has been sufficient to sustain the forest cover. The monthly rainfall pattern, with a growing season of about 199 days, would favor maize horticulture (Figure 1.3).

Dense oak–hickory forest dominates the Ozark Plateau, whereas oak–hickory–pine forest occurs in the Boston Mountains. In addition, some prairie areas are found on flat hilltops and along the forest–prairie border near the western edge of the mountains. The most abundant trees on uplands and dry slopes are blackjack oak, post oak, black hickory, and winged elm. In protected areas, sugar maple, hop hornbeam, redbud, flowering dogwood, linden, white oak, and chinquapin oak flourish. Along the stream banks grow open forests of silver maple, red birch, American elm, cottonwood, sycamore, linden, and several species of oaks. The vegetation for the Ozark area has been described by Wallis (1959), and Gould (1903) listed trees and shrubs for the Boston Mountains. Native animals common to this district include deer, beaver, mink, fox, woodchuck, rabbits, skunk, muskrat, passenger pigeon, hawks, owls, sunfish, catfish, lizards, and snakes.

Ouachita District

Southeastern Oklahoma's Ouachita Mountains form the westernmost exposed portion of a highly faulted and folded uplift extending eastward into Arkansas. The central portion of this uplift is underlain by Devonian novaculite overlain by shales, sandstones, and occasional thin layers of limestone. Along the Arkansas–Oklahoma border, these mountains rise 415 m (1400 feet) above broad valleys whose floors average 300 m (1000 feet) in elevation. Valley floors are covered with Quaternary alluvium. Elevations decrease toward a frontal and ridge system along the western edge of the mountains. The bedrock of the frontal Ouachitas consists mainly of shales interspersed with some limestones and sandstones. This bedrock is of Mississippian and Pennsylvanian age (Sutherland and Manger 1979:6–10). The northern portion of the Ouachitas drains to the Arkansas River by the Poteau River, whereas the southern part drains to the Red River by the Kiamichi, Little, Glover, and Mountain Fork rivers.

Soils formed from Ouachita bedrocks are Ultisols, the same order found in the Ozarks. These thin soils of mountain slopes and uplands are not well suited to agriculture. The deeper alluvial soils in the river valleys are currently used primarily for pasture and crops.

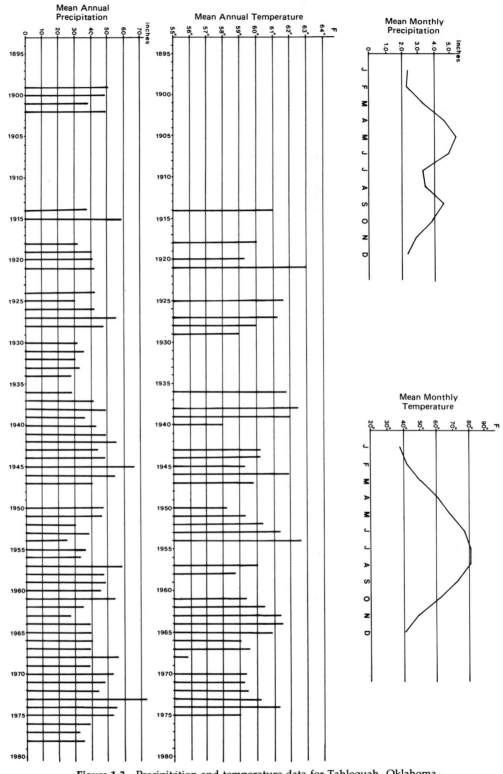

Figure 1.3 Precipitation and temperature data for Tahlequah, Oklahoma.

Many plant and animal species from the Ozarks are also found in the Ouachita Mountains, although some northeastern species are replaced here by southern ones. Oak–pine or oak–pine–hickory forest dominates the habitat types, interspersed with minor amounts of oak–hickory forest, post oak–blackjack forest of the savanna type, and small prairie openings. The major plant association of these mountains consists of shortleaf pine, hickories, black locust, and several species of oaks. In more protected moist areas, linden, sugar maple, and red maple join the assemblage (Figure 1.4). Rich Mountain in LeFlore County, and probably other mountain tops, supports isolated southeasterly species such as southern witchhazel, cucumber tree, and mulberry. On the floodplains of larger streams are found oaks, sweetgum, tupelo, linden, hickories, sugar maple, and shortleaf pine. The oak–hickory forests are similar to those of the Ozarks; in prairie openings the bluestems, dropseed, and Indiangrass are joined by such herbaceous species as aster, goldenrod, and legumes. The native animals included deer, bears, cougars, wolves, foxes, opossums, mink, muskrats, quail, turkeys, herons, hawks, turtles, gar, catfish, and sunfish. Important studies of this area were done by Carter (1967), Little and Olmstead (1936), and Means (1969).

Mississippi District

The Dissected Coastal Plain's northernmost extension lies just north of the Red River in southeastern Oklahoma. The flat to rolling land is cut by the lower drainages of major streams such as the Mountain Fork, Glover, and Little rivers that flow south from the mountains. The elevation ranges from 107 m (350 feet) along the Red River to 215 m (650 feet) in the uplands. Loosely cemented conglomerates of shale, cherts, and sandstone, as well as fine sands mixed with clay underlie the coastal plain. These collectively are termed *Antlers Sandstone*, and were laid down during the lower Cretaceous period (G. D. Ray 1960).

Ultisols dominate the uplands north of the Red River bottoms. The river and stream floodplains consist of Quaternary alluvial deposits. These fertile soils are more favorable for agriculture than the thinner, leached Ultisols.

This district has the state's highest annual average temperature (19° C; 63° F) and rarely experiences extreme cold during the winter. Unlike the rest of the state, the minimum monthly precipitation occurs in August (Figure 1.5). However, because of a high water table, maturing crops usually have sufficient moisture.

Although the dominant habitat type for the district is oak–pine forest, southeastern loblolly pine forest and cypress bottoms forest occur in the southern and eastern portions of the area. The oak–pine forest is similar to that of the Ouachitas, but along the river terraces red maple and holly become important species. Spanish moss hangs from the branches and palmettos have been recorded from wet wooded areas. Native animals include skunks, rabbits, deer,

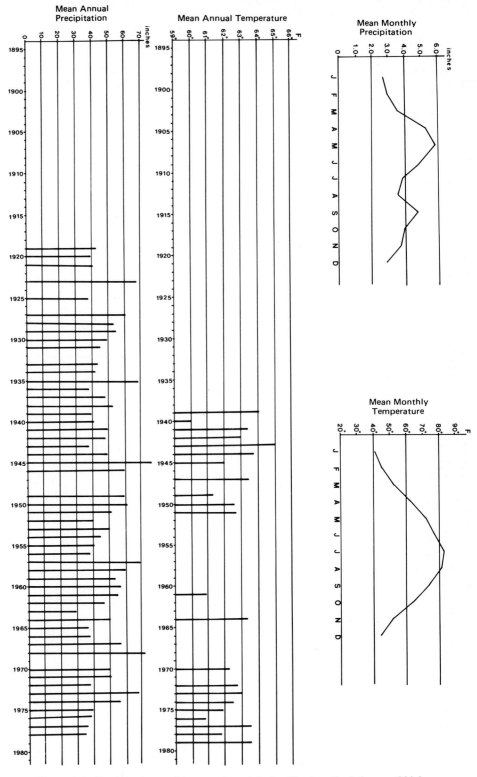

Figure 1.4 Precipitation and temperature data for Clayton–Tuskahoma, Oklahoma.

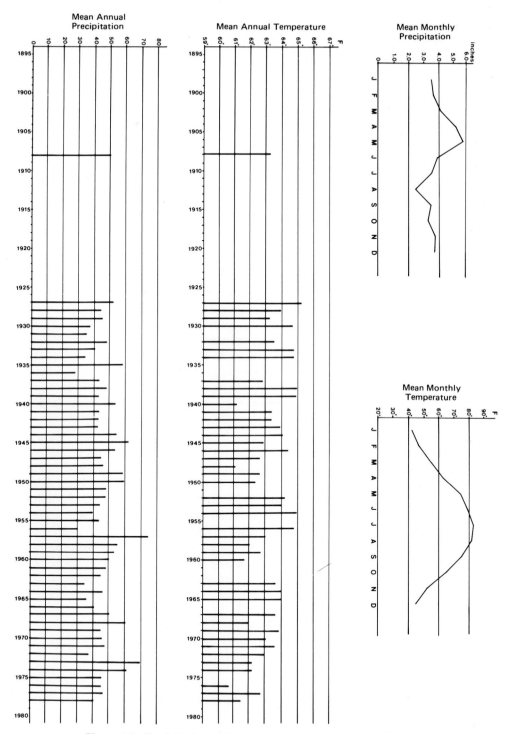

Figure 1.5 Precipitation and temperature data for Idabel, Oklahoma.

squirrels, bears, cougars, foxes, raccoons, quail, turkeys, woodcocks, turtles, snakes, gar, catfish, and occasional alligators.

Cherokee Prairie District

Northeastern Oklahoma's Cherokee Prairie is a southwestern arm of the Tall-grass Prairie of Kansas, Iowa and Illinois. Here, Pennsylvanian shales, lime-stones, and sandstones are strongly dissected, forming breaks and escarpments in the rolling to hilly country. Streams flow through these breaks into the Illinois, Verdigris, Caney and Arkansas rivers. Elevations vary from 260 m (850 feet) in the southeastern tip to 475 m (1550 feet) in the central portion of the Flint Hills (Anderson and Fly 1955). Pimple mounds, commonly found on the prairies, are of natural origin (Murray, 1974), although they are often mistaken for prehistoric Indian mounds or villages.

The most common soils of Oklahoma's prairie are Mollisols. These deep mineral soils contain abundant humus. Most have developed under grasslands with a climate intermediate between arid and humid. The Mollisols found in the Cherokee Prairie contain clayey horizons of varying thicknesses.

Rainfall diminishes noticeably over that of the forested areas to the east. Summers are hot and fairly dry, whereas winters occasionally have extremely cold intervals. Although the annual precipitation and temperature are quite variable (Figure 1.6), crops can be successfully grown on the fertile soils in most years.

Grasses such as little bluestem, sideoats grama, Kentucky bluegrass, big bluestem, Indiangrass, and switchgrass dominate the tallgrass prairie (Anderson and Fly 1955). Other herbaceous plants commonly found include blazing star, sunflowers, asters and yucca. This tallgrass prairie vegetation has been extensively studied (Murray 1974; R. J. Ray 1959; Buck and Kelting 1962; Schaffner 1926; and M. B. Clark 1959). Fingers of post oak–blackjack forest project into the grasslands (Long 1970). The bottomland and ravine forests extend eastern forest species of plants and animals from the Ozarks into the prairie. Augmenting these are species more common to western grasslands, including badgers, jackrabbits, prairie voles, mourning doves, meadowlarks, horned lizards, and bullsnakes.

Osage Savanna District

Diversity in plants, animals, and terrain characterize this area. The savanna is an ecotone, or transition zone, between eastern forests and western grasslands. The flat to rolling terrain with scattered areas of hills ranges from 215 m (650 feet) in the south to about 365 m (1200 feet) in central Oklahoma. The western portion

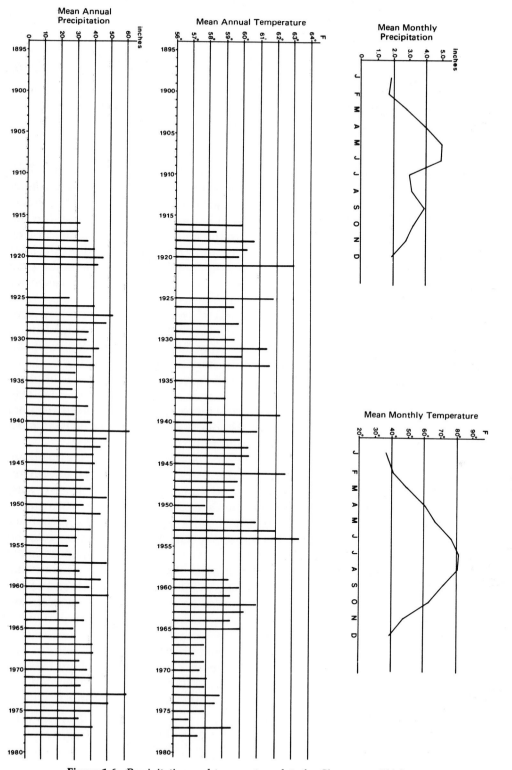

Figure 1.6 Precipitation and temperature data for Claremore, Oklahoma.

of the area is located on the Central Redbed Plains, which are underlain by Permian shales and sandstones. In the southcentral portion, the Arbuckle Mountains, an old system containing Cambrian to Mississippian limestones, Precambrian granites, Ordovician limestones and Mississippian–Pennsylvanian shales and sandstones, rises to 395 m (1300 feet). This complex system is composed of the Arbuckle Hills and Arbuckle Plains. An eastward extension of savanna along the Arkansas River is characterized by scattered hills capped with Pennsylvanian sandstones, whereas mixed limestones and sandstones of the same age form the Northern Limestone Cuesta Plains. The major drainage systems in the northern and central portions, including the Salt Fork of the Arkansas, the Cimarron and the North and South Canadian rivers, flow into the Arkansas River. In the south, drainage is to the Red River; major streams are the Washita, Blue, and lower Kiamichi rivers and the Clear and Muddy Boggy creeks. The southeastern section is an extension of the Dissected Coastal Plain of the Mississippi District.

Soils of the Osage Savanna vary with differences in topography and bedrock. The most widely distributed soil orders are Alfisols, Mollisols, and Vertisols. Alfisols develop where evaporation exceeds precipitation at some time during the year; they are highly weathered soils on stable landforms. Alfisols of this area frequently have a calcium-containing horizon below or within a clayey horizon. In the southeastern extension of the savanna along the coastal plain, the dominant soils are Vertisols. These are clayey soils that develop wide, deep cracks during dry periods. Surface materials fall or are washed into the cracks; water running into the cracks moistens the soils from both above and below and causes further mixing. The result is a uniform texture.

Annual average precipitation is considerably less for the Osage Savanna than for the forested areas to the east. Because the district stretches from the southern to northern borders of the state, there is some variation in the length of growing season. The northern portion more frequently experiences extreme cold during winters than does the area along Red River. Although the annual precipitation and temperature show considerable variation, sufficient moisture for crops is available most years (Figure 1.7).

The savanna is composed mainly of Tall-grass Prairie interspersed with post oak–blackjack forests of varying densities. Westward, short grasses become more abundant. Oak–hickory forest is found on some of the more protected hillsides, whereas areas of oak–pine forest grow in the southeastern part of the district. The most important bottomland trees of the northern portion are elm, pecan, chinaberry, green ash, hackberry, sugarberry, and black walnut. The total number of tree species decreases from about 22 in the east to about 15 in the west (Rice 1965). Central Oklahoma bottomland forests contain persimmon and cottonwood as well as those species found farther north (Penfound 1947; Rice and Penfound 1956). The dominant plants on the Canadian River floodplain include sedges, willow, cottonwood, grasses, cattails, tamarix (not native), American elm, oak, hackberry, boxelder, pecan, grapes, and herbaceous plants

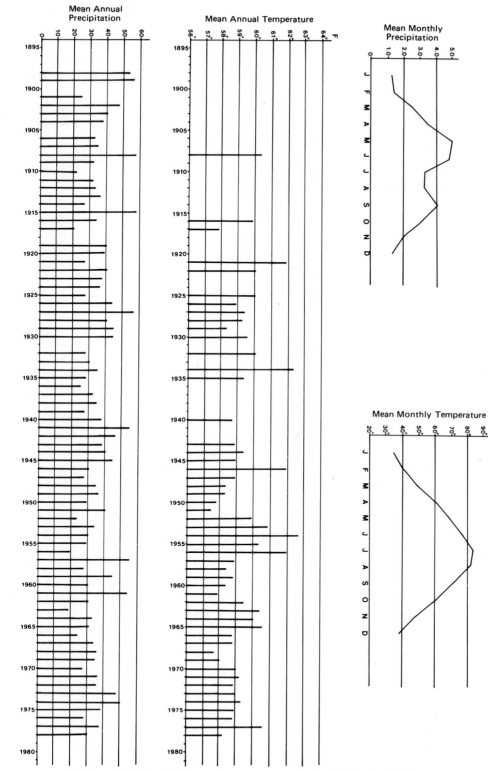

Figure 1.7 Precipitation and temperature data for Pawhuska, Oklahoma.

(Hefley 1937). Dogwood, redbud, hickory, and mulberry are present as small trees in some areas of the central Oklahoma post oak–blackjack forest (Johnson and Risser 1975). Other plant studies in the central portion of the district include Carpenter (1934), Fishman (1936), McCoy (1958), and Carpenter (1937). In the southern part, the post oak–blackjack forests include black hickory and winged elm as well as the oaks (Penfound 1963). Shortleaf pine extends westward into eastern Bryan County (J. Taylor 1965). Buffalo grass is the dominant native grass with smaller amounts of the bluestems and gramas found to the north (Dyksterhuis 1948). Bottomland forests include mainly oaks, elms, pecan, walnut, hackberry, and willow.

The native large animals are no longer present throughout most of the district. Large buffalo herds once thrived on the grasses, whereas deer roamed the bottomlands and areas of upland forest. Many of the small species, such as rabbits, squirrels, birds, and reptiles, still survive.

Mixed-Grass Plains District

The terrain, plants and animals of this district are also quite diverse. The Mixed-grass Plain is an ecotone between the Tall-grass Prairie and the Short-grass Plains. Many of the species found in the eastern part of the state are not represented here, whereas others appear only occasionally.

The flat to rolling eastern portion of the area is underlain by Permian sandstones common to the Central Redbed Plains. The dominant soils are Mollisols and Alfisols. Elevations in the east range from about 300 m (1000 feet) to 365 m (1200 feet); to the west the land rises, reaching elevations of 275 m (1500 feet). Permian sandstones and shales are the principal bedrocks. Along the major rivers (the Salt Fork, Cimarron, North Canadian, South Canadian, Washita, and North Fork of the Red River) are large areas of aeolian sand derived from Quaternary alluvium. Gypsum hills are found in three areas; these are of Permian origin. The dominant soils of the west are Alfisols, Mollisols, and Inceptisols. Inceptisols are young soils that can be formed from many parent bedrocks and under diverse vegetation. The major factor in their formation is a climate in which some leaching occurs, although they still retain weatherable minerals.

Annual precipitation continues to decrease as one approaches the High Plains. The further west one goes in Oklahoma, the more frequent the crop failures become because of variations in annual precipitation and temperature (Figure 1.8). Summers are hot and dry, whereas winters are dry and periodically extremely cold.

Plants include both the bluestem–grama–Indiangrass group common to the prairie and the shorter buffalograss–needlegrass–grama group common to the plains. On the floodplains, cottonwoods, willows, and tamarix grow in thin to dense stands. Some isolated areas of post oak–blackjack forest cover uplands. In

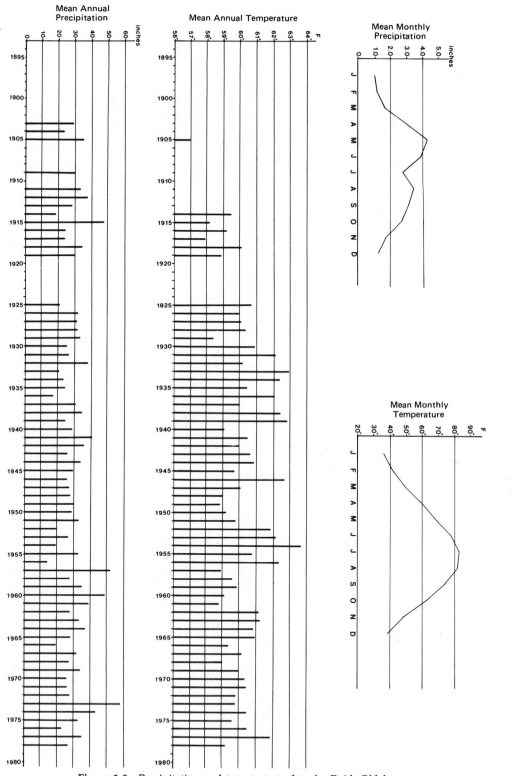

Figure 1.8 Precipitation and temperature data for Enid, Oklahoma.

the sand areas, sand sage, beardgrass, plum thickets, and sumac form the principal ground cover. In the south, shinnery-oak is also found in sandy areas. Abundant native animals in the past were buffalo, coyotes, prairie dogs, prairie chickens, jackrabbits, quail, and snakes.

Some areas of distinctive topography and biota are found in this district. The mesquite grasslands of the Mangum Gypsum Hills in the southwestern corner are an eastward extension of the Texas biotic type. The principal plant association includes mesquite, buffalograss, grama grass, wire grass, and Mormon tea. Prickly pear cactus thickets cover small areas.

The Caddo Canyons are found in the eastcentral part of the area. Isolated eastern forest species, including sugar maple, black walnut, American elm, hackberry, and oaks, form the dominant vegetation. Oak woodland and grasses border the canyons (Little 1939).

The Wichita Mountains are a very old (Cambrian), eroded uplift of granite and other igneous rocks that interrupt the plains. Stony soils derived from these igneous materials support a biota somewhat different from the surrounding plains. Most of the grasses of the valley floors are those of the Tall-grass Prairie; on the hillsides are shorter grasses. Enclosed valleys contain oaks, hackberry, black walnut, American elm, white ash, and woody buckthorn; these forests are more extensive than on the adjacent plain. Post oak–blackjack forests grow on the more exposed slopes.

The extensive grasslands of the Mixed-grass Plains originally supported vast herds of buffalo, whereas deer lived in the wooded areas along streams. Coyotes, wolves, cougars, and bears, as well as jackrabbits, prairie dogs, lizards, birds, and snakes, were also native to the area.

Short-Grass Plains District

Northwestern Oklahoma rises from about 550 m (1800 feet) in Harper County to 1260 m (4100 feet) in central Cimarron County in the panhandle. Mesas in the western part of Cimarron County, however, rise to almost 1515 m (5000 feet). The relatively flat, high plains are underlain by Tertiary and Pleistocene alluvial sands dissected by the North Canadian and Cimarron rivers and their major tributaries. Areas of sand, gypsum hills and sandstone hills extend westward into Harper County from the Mixed-grass Plains. The dominant soils of the district are Mollisols and Alfisols, whereas the mesa area contains Entisols, soils of floodplains or steep slopes that show little weathering, development, or organic matter accumulation.

The High Plains District is the driest area of the state and most frequently experiences crop failures due to drought (Figure 1.9). Summers are typically hot and dry. Because of the increasing altitude, the state's coldest winters and greatest snowfall occur on the plains.

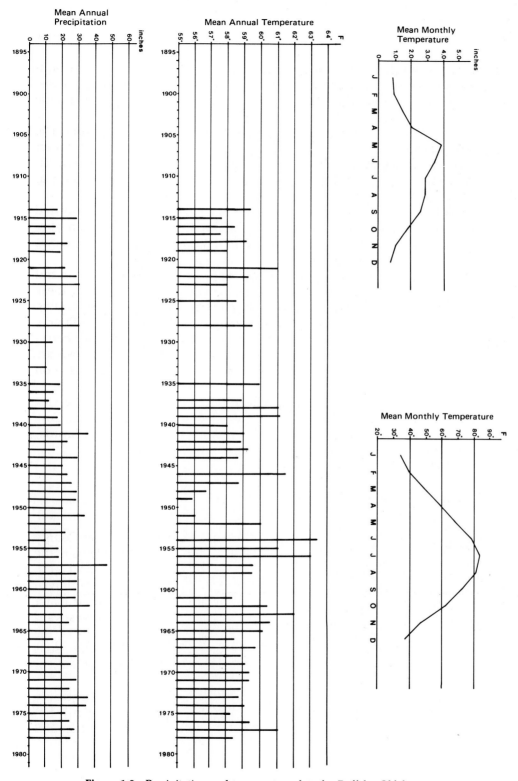

Figure 1.9 Precipitation and temperature data for Buffalo, Oklahoma.

Buffalograss, needlegrass, and the grama grasses dominate the Short-grass Plains. Sagebrush and yucca grow on valley slopes, whereas the sand-sage plant community is found in sandy, streamside areas. These bottomlands also support scattered cottonwoods along the stream margins, with plum thickets and willows on the terraces. Buffalo, antelope, quail, prairie chickens, rabbits, prairie dogs, and rattlesnakes were native to the district.

An eastward extension of the southwestern piñon–juniper–mesa habitat type occurs in western Cimarron County. The mesa areas are formed by canyons cutting through a Cretaceous sandstone. A small area of Tertiary basaltic lava forms Black Mesa (Mesa de Maya) in the extreme northwestern corner of the area. Here, the annual rainfall averages only about 41.5 cm (17 inches) with a growing season of 168 days. Thin soils support a foothills and mountain biota characterized by juniper, ponderosa pine, piñon pine, scrub hackberry, several oaks, yucca, plums, grapes, and prickly pear cactus, as well as some tall grasses, including bluestem. On the stream banks are cottonwoods, willows, cattails, sumac, grapes, and grasses (C. M. Rogers 1953, 1954). Some animals associated with this unique area of Oklahoma include mule deer, eagles, and western chipmunks.

Historical Changes

Narratives written in the early 1800s by visitors to what is now Oklahoma (Table 1.7), then part of Arkansas, tell of large, mature trees that formed open woods. Where there were ravines or stream openings, understory and herbaceous plants abounded. The first botanist known to have collected in the state was Thomas Nuttall, who, in 1819, visited the Ozark, Ouachita, Osage Savanna, and Cherokee Prairie (Tall-grass Prairie) districts when only a few unauthorized white settlers lived west of Fort Smith (Palmer 1927). At that time, the forests were more open and parklike than today. Game, including deer and bear, was plentiful. The travellers who ventured farther west have described unbroken rich grasslands or savannas that supported a variety of animals, including herds of buffalo as well as smaller game.

During the 1830s the government began removing eastern Indian tribes from their homelands to the new Indian Territory. The immigrants cleared timber to build homes, plant crops, and establish trails. They also introduced domesticated crops and animals, as well as a number of European weeds. However, the number of people was not great and most of the land clearance was limited to the eastern third of Oklahoma. At the time of Marcy's expedition of 1849, there were still few settlers along the South Canadian River and much of the land was still in virgin condition (Foreman 1937). None of the eastern Indians settled in the western part of the state, which at that time was still included in their lands.

Table 1.7

Some Exploration of Oklahoma during the Nineteenth Century

Traveller or expedition	Year	Area of Oklahoma visited	Source
Nuttall	1819	Fort Smith, west along Arkansas River; south to Kiamichi River, to Red River; west along Arkansas and along Cimarron and Canadian rivers	Palmer (1927); Bruner (1931)
Long	1820	Across state west to east along South Canadian River	C. M. Rogers (1953); Bruner (1931)
Latrobe–Irving	1832	Northeast	Spaulding (1968); Shirk (1967)
Gregg	1836–1840	Eight trips along Arkansas River and South Canadian River into Texas	Gregg (1926)
Nathan Boone	1843	Fort Gibson, north into Kansas; west, then south to Woods County and North Canadian River; back to Fort Gibson	Fessler (1928)
Sitgreaves-Woodruff	1849–1850	Surveyed northern boundary of Creek Indian country—36°8′42″ north; return to Fort Gibson	Bruner (1931)
Marcy	1849	Fort Smith, west along Arkansas and South Canadian rivers; return to Fort Smith via Texas and southeastern Oklahoma	Foreman (1939)
	1851	Fort Smith to Red River to Wichita Mountains; up North Fork of Red River, return to Fort Smith down Red River and through southeastern Oklahoma	Foreman (1937)
Whipple	1853	Fort Smith to Antelope Hills	Wright and Shirk (1950)
Bigelow	1856	Crossed state east to west	Bruner (1931)
Beale	1858	Along Arkansas and South Canadian rivers	Engle (1934)

Marcy's 1851 expedition to southwestern Oklahoma encountered only Wichitas and some Southern Plains tribes. The records from these expeditions, as well as others of the same period, provide a description of western Oklahoma still in its native condition.

Legal white settlement (other than missionaries, Indian agents and traders, and cattlemen) began in 1889 with the opening of the Unassigned Lands in central Oklahoma. By this time, the buffalo were almost extinct because of government-encouraged slaughter. After 1889, the number of people living in Oklahoma increased rapidly. These settlers came for the purpose of farming the land and building towns, roads, and railroads. The native vegetation began to disappear rapidly as land was broken for farming and as commercial lumbering increased. The 1920s and 1930s were periods of intense lumbering activity.

The 1930s were also a time of drought, one that was especially severe in western Oklahoma. Although all the state experienced clouds of dust, the wind erosion was principally in the High Plains Region. Here, the cultivation of marginal lands, combined with poor farming practices and overgrazing, was responsible for the severe erosion. Studies of grasslands during the period between 1933 and 1940 showed that the margin between Tall-grass Prairie and Mixed-grass Plains had moved eastward 167–242 km (100–150 miles). Four years (1941–1944), including one very wet one (1941) were required for the recovery of the land to its original grass cover (Weaver 1968). Although the drought of the 1950s was almost as severe, improved farming techniques lessened the impact on the land.

Today, few undisturbed tracts of native vegetation still exist. Because of habitat destruction and the introduction of domestic or exotic species—such as starlings, pheasants, house sparrows, European rodents, and carp, which compete for the available resources—native animal populations are lessened and some species are even extinct. Eastern Oklahoma's forests are now in a subclimax condition. Very few mature trees survive because of lumbering and land clearance. Moreover, understory plants are probably more dense, producing a less-open landscape. A few tracts of Tall-grass Prairie can be found in the Flint Hills of north-central Oklahoma, and some Short-grass Plains grassland remains in the panhandle. However, the Oklahoma of today little resembles the lush, sparsely inhabited land described by the travellers of the 1820s.

Prehistoric Environmental Changes

Just as climatic fluctuations have altered Oklahoma's natural settings since A.D. 1800, they also affected the state's prehistoric people, plants, and animals. In fact, stratified deposits of fossil pollen, animal remains, and soils studied in nearby states have yielded clues that the grasslands and forests of the 1800s were but one stage in a development that began some 7000 years ago (Bryant 1977; Delcourt 1979; Delcourt and Delcourt 1979; Gruger 1973; J. E. King 1980; J. E. King and Allen 1977; Wood and McMillan 1976). Moreover, even earlier climatic changes were responsible for plant and animal distributions that would astonish present-day Oklahomans.

Because prehistoric people depended on native plants and animals for food, tools, and shelter, understanding the extent and character of Oklahoma's past environments is important to archaeologists. To date, however, the evidence needed for such understanding is scattered, incomplete, and variable in character. For the following review, information was compiled on Oklahoma's environments during the past 20,000 years, the period that prehistoric people are

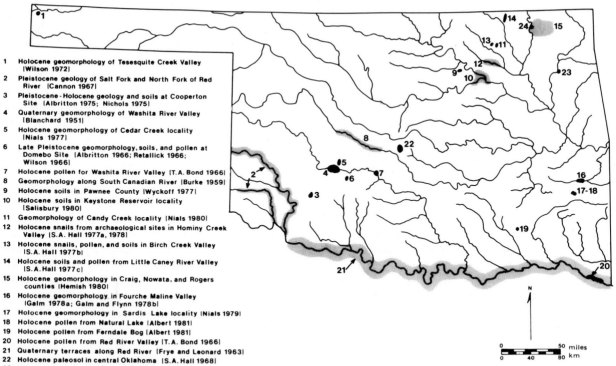

1 Holocene geomorphology of Tesesquite Creek Valley (Wilson 1972)
2 Pleistocene geology of Salt Fork and North Fork of Red River (Cannon 1967)
3 Pleistocene-Holocene geology and soils at Cooperton Site (Albritton 1975; Nichols 1975)
4 Quaternary geomorphology of Washita River Valley (Blanchard 1951)
5 Holocene geomorphology of Cedar Creek locality (Nials 1977)
6 Late Pleistocene geomorphology, soils, and pollen at Domebo Site (Albritton 1966; Retallick 1966; Wilson 1966)
7 Holocene pollen for Washita River Valley (T.A. Bond 1966)
8 Geomorphology along South Canadian River (Burke 1959)
9 Holocene soils in Pawnee County (Wyckoff 1977)
10 Holocene soils in Keystone Reservoir locality (Salisbury 1980)
11 Geomorphology of Candy Creek locality (Nials 1980)
12 Holocene snails from archaeological sites in Hominy Creek Valley (S.A. Hall 1977a, 1978)
13 Holocene snails, pollen, and soils in Birch Creek Valley (S.A. Hall 1977b)
14 Holocene soils and pollen from Little Caney River Valley (S.A. Hall 1977c)
15 Holocene geomorphology in Craig, Nowata, and Rogers counties (Hemish 1980)
16 Holocene geomorphology in Fourche Maline Valley (Galm 1978a; Galm and Flynn 1978b)
17 Holocene geomorphology in Sardis Lake locality (Nials 1979)
18 Holocene pollen from Natural Lake (Albert 1981)
19 Holocene pollen from Ferndale Bog (Albert 1981)
20 Holocene pollen from Red River Valley (T.A. Bond 1966)
21 Quaternary terraces along Red River (Frye and Leonard 1963)
22 Holocene paleosol in central Oklahoma (S.A. Hall 1968)
23 Holocene terrace at Packard Site (Wyckoff 1964a)
24 Holocene floodplain at Lawrence Site (Baldwin 1969; Wyckoff 1981)

Figure 1.10 Sites and localities that have yielded information on Oklahoma's past environments. Black, numbered areas indicate specific sites; stippled areas indicate studied localities.

known to have inhabited the state. This information comes from 24 Oklahoma sites or localities (Figure 1.10); the findings from these sites have been synthesized and arranged according to several climatic episodes attributed to the late Pleistocene and Holocene epochs. These terms refer to the latest part of geological time known as the Cenozoic era. Together, they form the Quaternary period. The Pleistocene epoch was a time of glaciations that created extensive geological deposits, whereas the Holocene is the most recent warm age, one that began about 14,500 years ago and persists to the present (Mercer 1972; Wright and Frey 1965:vii).

Late Pleistocene (Glacial) Environments

Although world-wide cooling apparently began some 70,000 years ago, the last continental ice sheets began accumulating and spreading when an important temperature decline occurred approximately 25,000 years ago (Lamb and Woodroffe 1970). By 17,000 years ago, an ice sheet measuring almost a mile in thickness stretched from northeast Pennsylvania across much of Ohio, the northern two-thirds of Indiana, the northeastern half of Illinois, southern Wisconsin, northern Iowa, and much of South and North Dakota (Flint 1957:313–323). South of this ice mass, a narrow band of tundra covered loess and glacial outwash, whereas spruce forest prevailed over Kentucky, West Virginia, northern Tennessee, and much of Appalachia (Delcourt 1979; Maxwell and Davis 1972). Farther south, pine, fir, and deciduous forests occupied diverse Southeastern settings.

Securely dated, full-glacial pollen records are as yet unknown for Oklahoma. However, springs in southwestern Missouri have yielded 16,000-year-old remains of spruce, mastodon, ground sloth, giant beaver, tapir, horse, and deer (J. E. King 1973; J. E. King and Lindsay 1976; Mehringer *et al.* 1970). More than likely, spruce forest containing these animals also covered much of northeastern Oklahoma. In contrast, a predominance of pine pollen at the base of continuous, but undated, cores from Caddo and McCurtain counties may be evidence that pine forests and/or parklands existed over southeastern and west-central Oklahoma. Although pollen clues to full-glacial settings are not reported for western Oklahoma, 16,000-year-old playa deposits in western Texas and eastern New Mexico yielded high proportions of pine, spruce, grass, and Compositae pollen (Schoenwetter 1975; Oldfield 1975). This pollen assemblage is believed indicative of parklands and boreal forests that existed during a predominantly cool, moist interval called the *Tahoka Pluvial* (Wendorf 1975:261–264). Bison, camel, horse, and mammoth lived in the region during this interval. At the Cooperton site in Kiowa County, southwestern Oklahoma, the 17,000+-year-old remains of a Columbian mammoth occurred in sandy, gravelly sediments that became stabilized, weathered, and eventually eroded (Albritton 1975).

Between 16,000 and 11,500 years ago, the cold, moist conditions ameliorated, causing the glacial advance to slow, to start and stop fitfully, and eventually to retreat. This climatic amelioration appears closely linked to a world-wide warming trend that began some 14,500 years ago (Mercer 1972; H. E. Wright 1972). By 10,000 years ago, the glacial retreat was well underway and significant changes were occurring in plant and animal distributions (Bernabo and Webb 1977:72–73; J. E. King 1980; Webb and Bryson 1972). For example, deciduous forest replaced spruce by 11,300 years ago in northeastern Kansas and, by 10,000 years ago, grasslands were prevalent there (Gruger 1973:248, Figure 3). In contrast, spruce dominated Minnesota settings until some 11,000 years ago when pine began invading from the east; then around 7000 years ago, grasslands expanded into some of Minnesota's pine forests (H. E. Wright 1968). By this time, such animals as mastodons, mammoths, horses, camels, ground sloths, and saber-toothed cats were extinct in North America (Martin 1967; Martin and Guilday 1967).

Although marked climatic and ecological changes occurred between 15,000 and 10,000 years ago, little direct evidence is known for the nature, extent, or rate of change in Oklahoma. In fact, the only dated evidence for this period comes from the Domebo Site in Caddo County (Figure 1.17). Here, 11,000-year-old marsh deposits yielded a grass-dominated pollen profile, elm stumps, many gastropods, and remains of mammoth, extinct bison, extinct tortoise, bog lemming, muskrat, vole, cotton rat, and other rodents and reptiles (Slaughter 1966; Wilson 1966). The Domebo sediments, animals, and plant remains collectively attest to a marshy setting with cottonwood and elm near open grasslands, a situation similar to that of today. However, the presence of spruce pollen, certain snail species, extinct tortoise, bog lemming, and cotton rat are clues that the climate was more moist, with milder winters, than at present. Shortly after 10,000 years ago, this marshy stream setting began to be covered with fine-grained sandy alluvium. This deposit eventually attained a thickness of 12 m (40 feet). This notable alluvial accumulation probably correlates with cycles of stream competency and terrace formation described for the Washita River, the South Canadian, and the Salt and North Forks of the Red River (Blanchard 1951; Burke 1959; Cannon 1967). Such correlations remain to be firmly established through studies of the upland and terrace deposits, their sequences and thickness, and their ages.

In the Red River valley, moderately bedded sands and silts are believed to attest to a late Wisconsin deposition (Frye and Leonard 1963:12–13). Known as the Cooke Alluvial Terrace, this deposit is characterized by the minimal development of soil-weathering profiles and by snail species predominantly like those present today. However, whether the Cooke Terrace or one of three floodplain deposits actually dates within the 15,000 to 10,000 B.P. era of climatic change is still to be determined.

Holocene Environments

The Holocene is characterized by the development of climates and consequent distribution of plants and animals as we now know them, but these developments were neither homogeneous nor continuous. Instead, approximately 14,000 years, and especially the last 10,000 years, of the Holocene are distinguished by intervals of marked environmental change.

After studying numerous southwestern alluvial and soil sequences and after correlating these with European-derived models of temperature change, Antevs (1955) proposed recognizing three periods within the Holocene:

1. *Medithermal,* from 4000 B.P. to present, when moderate temperatures and drought cycles predominated;
2. *Altithermal,* from 7000 to circa 4000 B.P., when a warm, arid climate was prevalent; and
3. *Anathermal,* from 10,500 to 7000 B.P., when an increasingly warm, decreasingly moist climate predominated.

However, recent geological, zoological, botanical, palynological, and dendrochronological findings support the conclusion that the Holocene climatic record is more complex than assumed by Antevs (Ferguson 1969, 1970; C. V. Haynes 1968; Mehringer 1977; C. C. Reeves 1976:222–223). In particular, the climatic changes were not contemporaneous everywhere, and they did not cause similar geomorphic processes or plant and animal responses. Despite such complexities, archaeologists persist in citing Antev's Holocene climatic model to explain changes observed in the archaeological record (Dillehay 1974; Frison 1978b:15–22, 191–211; B. Reeves 1973).

Oklahoma's Holocene records have only recently begun to attract the attention they deserve. Thus, although well studied, dated records are still rare, a growing list of alluviated valleys and marshes or bogs are beginning to yield information about landform, plant, and animal responses to climatic changes during the past 10,000 years. With such information, archaeologists may be able to explain better nearly two-thirds of the human prehistory documented for the state.

Presently, the largest set of Holocene records come from the Washita River Basin in Grady, Caddo, and Washita counties of west-central Oklahoma (Figure 1.10). In Grady County, a Washita River oxbow containing 7.5 m (24 feet) of sediment yielded a continuous, but undated, pollen record consisting of

1. 0–2.4 m (0–8 feet), where oak, hickory, cedar, grass, and disturbance plant pollen is dominant and representative of nearby plant communities that probably were established some 4000 years ago;
2. 2.4–4.5 m (8–16 feet), where grass, ragweed, pigweed, and other disturbance-plant pollen predominates, probably bearing witness to vegetation common during the warm, dry interval of 7000 to 4000 years ago; and
3. 4.5–7.4 m (16–24 feet), where oak and hickory pollen peak and decrease, whereas pine pollen increases, probably attesting to Holocene beginnings and to the waning Wisconsin glacial climate.

The three deposition periods evinced in this pollen record seem to correlate with alluvial and eolian deposits, buried soils, and their contents observed along nearby upland streams. At Domebo Canyon, some 48 km (30 miles) west (Figure 1.10), 12 m (40 feet) of alluvium and four terraces comprise evidence for a long period of aggradation that was interrupted by several erosional episodes during the past 11,000 years. Although Domebo Canyon's Holocene geological units are undated, their characteristics and sequences resemble those recorded and partially dated at Cedar Creek, some 48 km (30 miles) to the west (Figure 1.10). Here, marshy deposits believed contemporaneous with the 11,000-year-old ones at Domebo Canyon are covered by colluvial deposits, as well as by buried soils within terraces. These terraces have been named (from youngest to oldest): Little, Sheppard, Shinn, and Cedar Creek. Some of their characteristics are presented in Table 1.8.

The Domebo Canyon and Cedar Creek geological sequences bear witness to soil horizon development and marshes between 9000 and 11,000 years ago. Such situations are believed the result of stable, more effective, moisture regimes than

Table 1.8

Terrace Sequence and Chronology at Cedar Creek, Caddo–Washita Counties, Oklahoma

Terrace	Height above stream (m; feet)	Comments
Little	0.6–1.2; 2–4	Contains redeposited remains of modern and fossil mammals.
Sheppard	1.8–3.4; 6–12	Contains redeposited remains of modern and fossil animals. Modern alluvial sands are still being deposited on its surface.
Shinn	4.9–6.4; 16–22	Poorly exposed, but contains redeposited fossil animal bones, including many slightly eroded bison remains. Base of terrace yielded a date of 2475 ± 70 B.P. (UGa-1733).
Cedar Creek	6.1–8.9; 20–29	Seems to correlate with Domebo Formation at Domebo Canyon
Upper member[a]		Contains several erosional boundaries; this member lies unconformably over lower. Has a radiocarbon date of 8530 ± 155 B.P. (UGa-1727).
Lower member		Contains many reworked gravels overlain by marshy deposits that often contain molluscs and large-animal bones. Charcoal from near base yielded a date of 9645 ± 110 B.P. (UGa-1728).

Note: Compiled from Nials (1977).

[a]Samples UGa-1730 (8195 ± 185 B.P.) and UGa-172 (9335 ± 125 B.P.) may be relevant but come from redeposited contexts.

exist today. After 9000 years ago, however, began a prolonged period marked by several erosional episodes that were, in turn, interrupted by several brief intervals of stability and slight soil development. Eventually, erosion at both Domebo Canyon and Cedar Creek cut channels that equal those exposed today. Around 2500 years ago, the Cedar Creek locality began to stabilize; marshes then developed and the Shinn terrace began to form. During the 1900s erosion has again been prevalent and has resulted in the formation of the Sheppard and Little terraces.

More than 2 m (8 feet) of sediment dominated by disturbance-plant pollen and 9–14 m (30–40 feet) of alluvium broken by refilled gullies and occasional faint soil horizons are subtle but salient clues to a dry, harsh climate that persisted for perhaps 7000 years in western Oklahoma. The effects and duration of this climate is gradually being documented elsewhere in the state. Along Tesesquite Creek, in the northwestern corner of Oklahoma's panhandle (Figure 1.10), some 12 m (36 feet) of finely laminated sand, silt, and clay apparently accumulated during this period (Wilson 1972). In Cleveland and Pottawatomie counties of central Oklahoma, sand dunes are believed to have formed on a once-stable soil surface (S. A. Hall 1968:151–153). Meanwhile, in Craig, Nowata, and Rogers counties of northeastern Oklahoma (Figure 1.10), recent coal mining and coal test-drilling have exposed at least 6 m (20 feet) of fill that covers outwash fan sediments and coarse-debris slopes with steep angles. These fans and slopes are erosional features that geomorphologists consider typical of semiarid environments. Although these features are undated, they are interpreted as having formed during a long, warm, dry period that persisted between 7000 and 4000 years ago (Hemish 1980:92).

This warm, dry climate's effects and duration in eastern Oklahoma are best documented by long pollen records from Atoka and McCurtain counties. Despite being undated and interrupted by one sterile sand deposit, a 3 m (10-foot) core from Jenkins Reilly Slough (southern McCurtain County; Figure 1.10) yielded a pollen sequence thought to span the postglacial period (T. A. Bond 1966:63–66). This sequence consisted of three zones: 0–137 cm (0–54 inches), where pine, oak, hickory, and some disturbance-plant pollen dominated; 137–151 cm (54–60) and 168–230 cm (66–90 inches), where grass and disturbance-plant pollen was most frequent; and 230–270 cm (90–114 inches), where oak and hickory pollen was prevalent. This latter pollen zone was interpreted to be representative of the early Holocene forest, whereas the 102 cm (40 inches) dominated by grass and disturbance-plant pollen was believed deposited during the succeeding warm, dry period.

Much of the Jenkins Reilly Slough pollen sequence appears to be corroborated by nearly 1.8 m (6 feet) of peat and silt recovered from Ferndale Bog, Atoka County (Figure 1.10). By virtue of its upland setting and its location on the increasingly xeric western margins of the Ouachita Mountains, Ferndale Bog has accumulated a climatically sensitive pollen record (Figure 1.11). Moreover, 10 radiocarbon dates help determine when noteworthy changes occurred in the local vegetation. In particular, the oak, hickory, and pine forest that characterizes the region today was certainly established by 1600 years ago (see the 70-cm zone in Figure 1.11). Between 1600 and 4000 years ago, a forest composed largely of oak and hickory grew here (see pollen record and radiocarbon dates between 70 and 136 cm, Figure 1.11). Significantly, the bog deposit below 136 cm yielded pollen predominantly of grass, Compositae, and disturbance plants, along with notable proportions of oak. All in all, the pollen record from this lowest segment attests to the former presence of grasslands and oak savanna in these now-forested margins of the Ouachita Mountains. Modern analogs to such vegetation may be found in the Osage Savanna, the mixed grasslands and oak forests that now occur some 48 km (30 miles) west of Ferndale Bog.

Although its pollen record does not extend through the Holocene epoch, Ferndale Bog yields noteworthy evidence of the severity and duration of the warm, dry climate that dominated this period. The existence of grasslands and scattered oaks on the Ouachita's margins is undoubtedly a result of decreased effective moisture. Today, these forested uplands average 108 cm (42 inches) of precipitation a year; their evapotranspiration rate is 87 cm (36 inches) (Gray and Galloway 1959:Figure 4). In contrast, the prairie and oak-dominated forests found to the west have evapotranspiration rates that essentially equal or exceed precipitation. Similar conditions must have persisted over the western Ouachitas until 5000 to 4000 years ago. Then, effective moisture gradually increased, eventually enabling the growth of a closed hardwood (oak–hickory) forest. Around 1600 years ago, pine became a notable member of this forest (Figure 1.11). This spread of pine is most probably linked to the development of favorable climatic conditions, particularly an annual average precipitation of 102 cm (40 inches) and an average annual temperature of 10° C (50° F; Fowells 1965:451). Such conditions, however, have apparently not persisted throughout the past 1600 years. Based on the Ferndale Bog record (Figure 1.11), at least three intervals occur when the pine-pollen influx was 20% or less since 550 years ago. These intervals most likely are periods when moisture and/or temperature were not conducive to local pine growth.

Given the record for 4000-year-old, climatic-induced vegetation changes near Ferndale Bog, other Oklahoma locations are perceived to contain clues to the marked effects of changing Holocene climates. For example, at the Packard Site, in Mayes County (Figure 1.10), a firehearth dating 9416 ± 193 years ago (NZ-478) was overlain by 3 m (10 feet) of massive silty clay. This accumulation was interrupted by a thin lens of gravel and is believed to bear witness to the continuous aggradation of sediments eroded from upstream settings. Although horizons marking soil development and stability (and thus the end of an erosion period) were not evident at Packard, a midden-capped horizon at the Lawrence site in nearby Nowata County attests to a Verdigris River floodplain surface that became stable enough for human habitation around 3400 years ago. Here, hunting–foraging people continued to camp until at least 2700 years ago; at some time subsequently, the site was covered with nearly 1.5 m (5 feet) of culturally sterile, floodplain deposits. Other valley settings that apparently stabilized enough for intensive human use around 4000 years ago are along Greasy Creek in Pawnee County and the Fourche Maline–Poteau streams in the Wister Valley (Figure 1.10). Some clues to similar changes in stream regimen seem present among geomorphic and archaeological findings in the Sardis Lake locality (Figure 1.10) of Latimer, Pushmataha, and Pittsburg counties.

Based on the geological, paleontological, and palynological findings at Domebo Canyon, Cedar Creek, Tesesquite Creek, Jenkins Reilly Slough, and Ferndale Bog, Oklahoma settings looked much different between 9000 and 4000 years ago than they do today. In particular, a warm, dry climate that dominated the mid-Holocene had wide-ranging effects. Persisting for some 3000 years, this xeric climate was conducive to erosion that created more sharp relief than is visible today. Plant communities like today's were present but were distributed differently and occasionally were of different composition. Moreover, animals common to such habitats undoubtedly had distributions different from those of today. It is not difficult to envision a predominance of grasslands that supported bison and other prairie animals occurring in eastern Oklahoma settings that now are entirely forested or covered with a mosaic of woodlands and prairies. Clearly, these ancient settings and habitats were important to prehistoric hunting–gathering peoples. How such groups used these lands and their plants, animals, and minerals undoubtedly differs greatly from practices known for late prehistoric and historic natives.

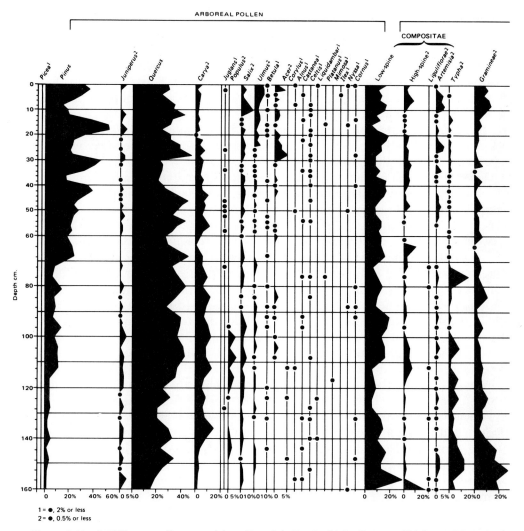

Figure 1.11   A 5000-year pollen record from Ferndale Bog in Atoka County, Oklahoma (top sample and Core IV). Grass, disturbance plants, and oaks dominate the lowest zone and attest to grasslands and scattered woods on this now-forested margin of the Ouachita Mountains. The historically recorded vegetation became established some 1600 years ago. (Adapted from Albert 1981:Figure 26).

Between 5000 and 4000 years ago, Oklahoma's climate began to ameliorate to conditions supporting the historically known habitats and plant communities. The stages entailed in this amelioration are not well documented, nor are the important climatic fluctuations that appear to have occurred during these past 40 centuries. Because some of these short-term climatic changes seem to correlate with, and thus may be causes of, significant cultural changes, the nature, extent, and timing of these climatic fluctuations merit thorough study and documentation. Presently, less than a bare outline is available.

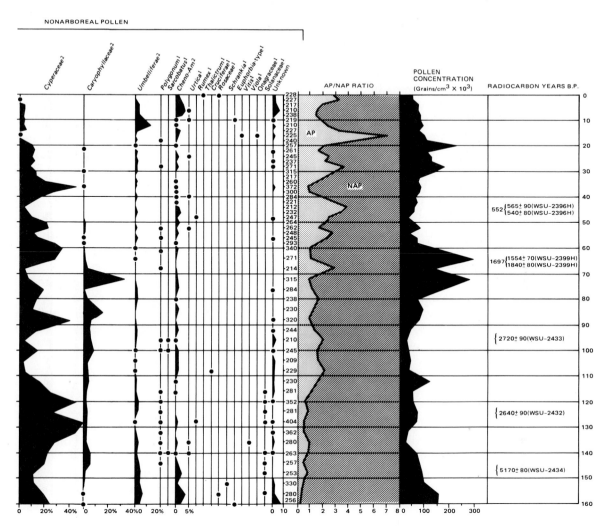

Figure 1.11 (*continued*)

At Ferndale Bog, notable changes in the ratio of tree pollen to non–tree pollen occur at several points in deposits more recent than 5000 years ago (Figure 1.11). Decreasing proportions of tree pollen, especially that of pine (*Pinus* sp.) and oak (*Quercus* sp.), and increasing proportions of disturbance-plant pollen (Compositae and cheno-am) at depths where more total pollen (measured as pollen concentration in Figure 1.11) was deposited probably attests to droughts and/or fire that adversely affected the surrounding forests. Historically, droughts need not have been too long to begin to affect severely Oklahoma woodlands. For example, the 1956–1957 dry years were principally responsible for a loss of 10% of northeastern Oklahoma's forests (Rice and Penfound 1959:604). Thus, declining tree–non–tree pollen ratios at Ferndale Bog depths of 22, 36–38, 48–52, and 86 cm may be clues to important droughts about 250, 400, 800, and 2000 years ago (Figure 1.11).

Some 64 km (40 miles) east-northeast of Ferndale Bog, small Natural Lake on the Jackfork Creek floodplain (Figure 1.10) yielded a short but continuous pollen record believed deposited between 600 and 2400 years ago. Because of its low-land setting and its central location within the Ouachita Mountains, Natural Lake seems to have a record that is less sensitive to climate-induced vegetation changes. However, it does contain evidence for a marked increase of tree pollen around 1000 years ago (Albert 1981:Figure 28). This arboreal pollen increase may represent the result of locally greater effective moisture that began around A.D. 600 or 700.

About this time, a distinctive soil began forming on alluvium in the flood-plains and nearby uplands of the Caney River and its immediate tributaries in north-central Oklahoma (Figure 1.10). Called the *Copan paleosol,* this soil was the floodplain surface from around A.D. 600 to 1300; it is believed (Farley and Keyser 1979:59–60; S. A. Hall 1977b, 1977c; T. J. Prewitt 1980) to have developed under fairly open, grassy settings. Its development, however, was interrupted by ero-sion that began around A.D. 900 and that covered the floodplains with alluvium by A.D. 1300. Environmental conditions then apparently stabilized briefly around A.D. 1400 and allowed another soil to begin developing on the floodplain alluvium (Farley and Keyser 1979:Figure 34).

The A.D. 900–1300 erosional episode in the Caney Basin is most likely the result of increasing dryness. This period corresponds to one zone in the Fern-dale Bog deposit where tree pollen is noticeably less. Moreover, archaeological sites in the Caney and neighboring basins (Figure 1.10) have yielded clues to changes in pollen and mollusc assemblages that attest to drier conditions than before.

Notably, around A.D. 1300, when erosion was becoming most effective in north-central Oklahoma, significant erosion episodes also began in the Teses-quite Creek Basin of the Oklahoma panhandle (Figure 1.10). Here, groves of willow, cottonwood, hackberry, and juniper were flattened and buried by flood-generated deposits of gravel and cobbles. Radiocarbon dates on samples from these trees support the conclusion that destructive floods occurred several times between A.D. 1300 and 1600 (Wilson 1972:207).

Summary

Today's visitors to Oklahoma are frequently struck by the Sooner state's contras-tive scenery, plants, animals, and weather. Due largely to its continental posi-tion relative to warm, moist Gulf air masses, to east-flowing jet streams, and to powerful surges of winter polar fronts, Oklahoma is justifiably famous for its remarkably changing weather. Because these weather variables play on such diverse settings as the stark granite of the Wichita Mountains, the contorted folds of the Ouachitas, the deeply incised Ozark Plateau, and the relatively flat Permian Redbeds, it becomes easier to understand why Oklahoma has habitats with plants, animals, and minerals like those of the fertile Great Plains, the arid Southwest, and the lush southeastern woodlands.

Clearly, Oklahoma as we know it is a land rich in the resources favorable to our society. Moreover, as the following chapters attest, this land's plants, animals, soils, and minerals have long supported the presence, growth, and maturation of many interesting prehistoric societies. Villages, camps, and workshops left by these societies typically yield clues to a range of settings, plants, animals, and minerals favored by the people. Frequently, archaeologists studying such sites have sought to interpret the recovered remains in terms of settings and resource distributions observable today. However, this research practice should be continued with much caution. Although small, a noteworthy body of evidence bears witness to Oklahoma's having undergone significant climatic changes in the past. Oklahoma may now be buffeted by a rather consistent set of air masses and storm tracks, but these have not always been constant in the past. Slight fluctuations in such weather factors have had marked systemic effects on plant and animal distributions as well as on landscape appearances, soil characteristics, and mineral availability. Thus, to begin to appreciate and understand further how Oklahoma's prehistoric peoples maintained themselves through at least 600 generations, archaeologists must continue, and increase, working with specialists trained to document the environmental conditions of the past. Such efforts are now underway, and we can soon expect interesting, sometimes even exciting, results from studying the soils and snails along Delaware Creek in Caddo County, the buried juniper trees of Carnegie Creek canyon (also Caddo County), and buried soils in Washington and Nowata counties. Only with these kinds of multidisciplinary studies will we be able to begin seeing how Oklahoma's prehistoric natives interacted with the environment.

Reference Note

General References: (climate) England 1975; Lawson 1974; Curry 1974; (plants) Duck and Fletcher 1943; Blair and Hubbell 1938; Braun 1950; Bruner 1931; (animals) R. G. Webb 1970; Miller and Robison 1973; Sutton 1967; Duck and Fletcher 1944; Blair 1939; State of Oklahoma, Wildlife Conservation Department 1960; Burt and Grossenheider 1964; (soils) Gray and Roozitalab 1976; Steila 1976; (physiographic or geomorphic provinces) Curtis and Ham 1957.

CHAPTER 2

Survey of Archaeological Activity in Oklahoma

Lois E. Albert

Introduction

Oklahoma archaeology has benefited from the substantial contributions of interested and concerned amateurs. Long before there were professional archaeologists in the state, amateurs began studies that led to recognition of different prehistoric cultures in Oklahoma. Even after professional archaeologists became established, relations between amateur and professional archaeologists remained both cordial and productive, unlike those in some other states. Amateurs have contributed thousands of hours to projects ranging from survey through excavation to processing and analysis.

Recognition of Oklahoma's prehistoric remains resulted in short descriptive articles even before the major incursions of white settlers (Buckner 1878; Robertson 1878). An interest in mounds and other Indian sites continued into the 1880s and early 1900s when the first "scientific" recording and collecting began (W. H. Holmes 1894, 1903) under the auspices of the Bureau of American Ethnology and the United States National Museum. William H. Holmes was the first professional archaeologist to work in Oklahoma. Other collections made for eastern museums at this period went unrecorded or virtually so. Undoubtedly many sites were destroyed when much of the state became farmland at the time of the late-nineteenth-century land runs. The building of towns and a transportation network increased site destruction. One early instance of mound destruction by railroad construction in McCurtain County was documented (Byington 1912).

Joseph B. Thoburn, a historian with an amateur interest in archaeology, was involved in exploring prehistoric remains during the early part of the twentieth century. Thoburn was first associated with the University of Oklahoma and later with the Oklahoma Historical Society in Oklahoma City. He took the earliest known photograph of the Craig Mound at Spiro in 1913 or 1914, and excavated the Ward Mound #1 (also at the Spiro site) in 1916–1917. Thoburn's work continued into the 1920s with excavations at the Bryson site in Kay County, and at mounds and rock shelters in Delaware County (for a listing of Thoburn's work, see M. H. Wright 1946–1947a). In addition to sponsored research during the 1920s by the Oklahoma Historical Society, the Colorado Museum in Denver undertook investigations at the Kenton Caves in Cimarron County (Renaud 1929a).

During the 1930s and early 1940s, amateur investigations were continued in east-central Oklahoma by H. R. Antle, a mathematics teacher at Sulphur. Antle reported one of the few known pictographs in Oklahoma (for a listing of his reports, see Bell 1978). Antle was informally affiliated with the Oklahoma Historical Society and later became the director of the Woolaroc Museum in Bartlesville.

One of the attempts to alleviate the effects of the severe economic depression of the 1930s was the federal Works Progress Administration (WPA) job program. Jobs were provided for the unemployed on public projects, including the excavations of archaeological sites and the cataloging of recovered materials. Money, however, was not provided for analysis and reporting of results because the program was only to provide jobs, not to fund research. Oklahoma's WPA archaeological program was supervised by Forrest E. Clements, a physical anthropologist with the Department of Anthropology, University of Oklahoma. Students from the department supervised the field operations. Records from these digs were frequently sketchy because each supervisor was responsible for several big crews scattered over a large area. Some of the excavated sites were in areas of proposed reservoir construction (also WPA projects), but little systematic survey work was done and many of the sites were previously known.

The Depression was partially responsible for Oklahoma's dramatic crisis in archaeology. In 1933, the Pocola Mining Company, a group bent on selling artifacts for profit, secured a 2-year lease on land containing part of Craig Mound at the Spiro site. Spectacular artifacts looted from burials within the mound were sold to widely scattered museums and private collectors. Less-salable items, such as textiles, wooden articles, or broken pottery, were tossed aside or allowed to disintegrate. The unique artifacts, as well as the large amount of material recovered, captured public interest and resulted in a number of speculative articles about their origin and manner of deposition. Because of the publicity and interest generated by Craig Mound's destruction, Oklahoma's first antiquities law was passed by the state legislature in 1935. As soon as the Pocola Mining Company's lease expired, rights to the site were acquired by Dr. Clements through Oklahoma Historical Society funds and other contributions. WPA-funded excavations at Spiro began in 1936 under the sponsorship of the University of Oklahoma, the University of Tulsa, and the Oklahoma Historical Society. These excavations continued until 1941 (Brown 1966a:33,37).

Archaeological work in the state was abruptly terminated when the United States entered World War II at the end of 1941. Not until after the war was work resumed. The construction of numerous reservoir projects necessitated archaeological surveys and salvage work if anything was to be saved, and Robert E. Bell of the Department of Anthropology directed these activities for several years. Meager funding was provided by the Department of the Interior through the River Basin Survey of the Smithsonian Institution or the National Park Service. Supplemental funding was provided by the University of Oklahoma and volunteer labor was supplied by many students in the Department of Anthropology. Numerous surveys and limited salvage excavations were conducted in several reservoirs. Dr. Sherman P. Lawton, of the University's Department of Communications, undertook numerous surveys and frequently assisted in excavations. By 1962, the volume of contract work with the National Park Service was great enough to employ a full-time staff, and Robert E. Bell was appointed as Director of the Oklahoma River Basin Survey. A summary of archaeological work in Oklahoma reservoirs is presented in Table 2.1.

The ecology movement of the 1960s focused concern on the preservation of cultural as well as natural resources. In 1966, Congress passed legislation, known as the Moss–Bennett bill, authorizing expenditure of up to 1% of the cost of federal projects for cultural resource mitigation. Numerous archaeological sites, both prehistoric and historic, have been located and preserved or salvaged throughout Oklahoma under this bill.

In 1968, Governor Dewey Bartlett requested the State Regents to establish an archaeological survey at the University of Oklahoma. The purpose of this organization was to find and evaluate the state's archaeological resources so that prehistoric Indian sites could be included in a series of interpretive state parks. The archaeological survey was established and the state legislature subsequently created the Oklahoma Archaeological Survey as an official state agency in 1970. The Survey was placed under the supervision of the University of Oklahoma Regents and was quartered at the University of Oklahoma in Norman. In addition to maintaining records for the state's prehistoric sites, the Survey has responsibilities in the areas of public service, education, and basic archaeological research.

Although Governor Bartlett appointed a State Historic Preservation Officer (SHPO) in 1967, an official Office of Historic Preservation (OHP) with full-time staff was not established until 1975. The OHP shares with the Oklahoma Archaeological Survey the responsibility of reviewing the federally funded or licensed projects passing through the State Clearing House. The OHP clears projects dealing with historic properties, whereas the Survey is concerned with prehistoric resources and historic sites with no standing structures.

Table 2.1

Oklahoma Reservoir Studies

Reservoir	Dates	Type of work	Participating organization	Major sites	Funding sources	References
Grand Lake of the Cherokees	1925–1926	Excavation	OHS[a]	Reed	OHS	Thoburn (1926)
	1938	Survey	OU (Anth.)[b]	—	WPA[c]	Grimes (1938)
	1937, 1954	Excavation	OU (Anth.)	Huffaker	WPA	Baerreis (1954)
	1938, 1951–1952	Excavation	OU (Anth.)	Smith	WPA	R. L. Hall (1951); Wittry (1952)
	1938, 1959–1963	Excavation	OU (Anth.)	D1-29, D1-30, D1-47, D1-57	WPA	Freeman (1959b; 1960); Baerreis and Freeman (1961); McHugh (1963)
Lake Wister	1970	Area syntheses	—	Several sites	—	Purrington (1970)
	1939–1940, 1957, 1970–1971	Survey and excavation	OU (Anth.)	Williams Mound, Mackey, Bennett-Monroe, Sam, Wann, Troy Adams	WPA	Newkumet (1940a); Proctor (1957); Sharrock (1960)
	1939–1940, 1971	Excavation	OU (Anth.)	Copeland	WPA	Guilinger (1971)
	1947	Survey	OU (Anth.)	—	NPS[d]	Bell (1947a)
	1974–1975	Resurvey and testing	ORBS[e]	—	C of E[f]	Neal and Mayo (1974); Mayo (1975)
	1976–1977	Testing	ARMC[g]	17 sites	C of E	Galm (1978a)
	1977–1978	Excavation	ARMC	Scott, Wann	C of E	Galm and Flynn (1978b)
Tenkiller Ferry Reservoir	1977–1978	Excavation	ARMC	Curtis Lake	C of E	Galm (1978b)
	1939–1940, 1955	Excavation	OU (Anth.)	Brackett	WPA	Bareis (1955)
	1939–1940, 1954	Excavation	OU (Anth.)	Smullins I	WPA	R. S. Hall (1954)
	1939–1940, 1953	Excavation	OU (Anth.)	Morris	WPA	Bell and Dale (1953)
	1948	Survey	Smithsonian	—	NPS	Wenner (1948b)
	1951, 1969	Excavation	Smithsonian; OU (Anth.)	Cookson	NPS	Israel (1979)
Lake Texoma	1951, 1974	Excavation	Smithsonian; OU (Anth.)	Vanderpool	NPS	Harden and Robinson (1975)
	1973–1974	Resurvey and testing	ORBS	—	C of E	Neal (1974b)
	1940–1941	Survey, testing, and excavation	OU (Anth.)	—	WPA	

Location	Years	Type	Institution	Site	Sponsor	Reference
	1954–1958	Excavation	OU (Anth.)	boat Dock	NPS	Bell (1958c)
	1941, 1960	Excavation	OU (Anth.)	James	WPA	M. A. Ray (1960a)
	1954, 1964	Excavation	OU (Anth.)	Buncombe Creek	OU	Wyckoff (1964c)
	1972	Resurvey	U Texas	—	C of E	Prewitt and Lawson (1972)
Lake Eufaula	1940–1942	Excavation	OU (Anth.)	Groseclose (Eufaula Mound)	Creek Indian Memorial Assn.	Orr (1942)
	1948–1950	Survey	OU (Anth.)	—	NPS	Wenner (1948a); L. Johnson (1950b)
	1948–1950, 1953	Excavation	OU (Anth.)	Kinnear, Huggard, Longtown Creek, Oden, Moody, Stephenson, Bacon	NPS	Proctor (1953)
Fort Gibson Reservoir	1947	Survey	OU (Anth.)	—	NPS	Wenner (1947)
	1949–1950, 1958	Excavation	OU (Anth.)	Harlan	NPS	Bell (1972)
	1968–1970	Resurvey	U Tulsa	—	NPS	W. F. Weakly (1972a)
	1968–1970	Excavation	U Tulsa	Martin-Vincent	NPS	W. F. Weakly (1972b)
	1977	Resurvey	ARA[h]	—	C of E	C. Cheek (1977)
Canton Reservoir	1949	Survey and testing	OU (Anth.)	—	NPS	Bell (1949)
Hulah Reservoir	1949	Survey and testing	OU (Anth.)	—	NPS	Bell (1949)
Heyburn Reservoir	1949	Survey and testing	OU (Anth.)	—	NPS	Bell (1949)
Lake Keystone	1951	Survey	OU (Anth.)	—	NPS	Brighton (1952)
Fort Cobb Reservoir	1955	Survey	OU (Anth.)	—	NPS	B. Williams (1955)
Foss Reservoir	1955	Survey	OU (Anth.)	—	NPS	B. Williams (1955)
	1941, 1951	Excavation	OU (Anth.)	Goodman I	WPA	Gallaher (1951)
	1957–1959	Excavation	OU (Anth.)	Phillips, Mouse	NPS, Bureau of Reclamation	Buck (1959)
Lake Thunderbird (Norman Reservoir)	1955	Survey	OU (Anth.)	—	NPS	B. Williams (1955)
Robert S. Kerr Lock and Dam (Short Mountain Reservoir)	1958	Survey	OU (Anth.)	Sheffield	NPS	Buck (1958)
	1966–1968	Excavation	ORBS	—	NPS	Prewitt and Wood (1969)
	1966–1968	Excavation	ORBS	Harkey–Bennett	NPS	R. Burton & Stahl (1969)
	1967–1968	Excavation	ORBS	Fine	NPS	Eighmy (1969)
	1966–1968	Excavation	ORBS	Tyler	NPS	R. Burton, Bastian & Prewitt (1969)
	1968–1969	Excavation	ORBS	Robinson–Solesbee	NPS	Bell et al. (1969)
	1969–1970	Excavation	ORBS	Tyler-Rose	NPS	Cartledge (1970)

(continued)

Table 2.1 (*Continued*)

Reservoir	Dates	Type of work	Participating organization	Major sites	Funding sources	References
	1969–1970	Excavation	ORBS	Dickson–Haraway	NPS	S. Burton and Neal (1970)
	1967–1971	Excavation	ORBS	Harvey	NPS	R. Burton (1971)
	1967–1970	Excavation	OU (Arch. Surv.) and ORBS	Horton	NPS	Wyckoff (1970c)
Waurika Reservoir	1958	Survey	OU (Anth.)	—	NPS	Lawton (1958b)
	1967	Resurvey	ORBS	—	NPS	Bastian (1967a)
	1972	Testing	ORBS	7 sites	NPS	Rohrbaugh (1972a)
	1972–1974	Excavation	ORBS	4 sites	NPS	Hartley (1974b)
	1976–1977	Excavation	N Tx St[i]	Several sites	C of E	Stevens and Hays (1977a; 1977b)
Hugo Reservoir	1960	Survey	OU (Anth.)	—	NPS	Lawton (1960)
	1969–1970	Excavation	ORBS	Hugo Dam	NPS	S. Burton (1970)
	1970–1971	Excavation	ORBS	6 minor sites	NPS	Rohrbaugh, Burton, Burton and Rosewitz (1971)
	1970–1972	Excavation	ORBS	3 minor sites	NPS	Rohrbaugh (1972b)
	1971–1973	Excavation	ORBS	2 minor sites	NPS	Rohrbaugh (1973b)
	1977–1978	Excavation	MRR[j]	Mahaffey	C of E	Perino and Bennett (1978)
Broken Bow Reservoir	1961	Survey	ORBS	—	NPS	Wyckoff (1961b)
	1964–1965	Excavation	ORBS	Biggham Creek	NPS	Wyckoff (1965a)
	1964–1965	Excavation	ORBS	Bill Hughes, Lamas Branch and Callaham	NPS	Wyckoff (1966)
	1964–1967	Excavation	ORBS	E. Johnson	NPS	Wyckoff (1967a)
	1964–1967	Excavation	ORBS	Woods Mound Group	NPS	Wyckoff (1967b)
Lake Hudson (Markham Ferry Reservoir)	1965–1967	Excavation	ORBS	Beaver	NPS	Wyckoff (1968a)
	1962–1964	Survey and testing	ORBS	—	NPS	Wyckoff et al. (1963)
	1962–1963	Excavation	ORBS	Kerr Dam	NPS	Wyckoff (1963a)
	1962–1964	Excavation	ORBS	Packard	NPS	Wyckoff (1964a)
	1962–1964	Excavation	ORBS	Jug Hill	NPS	Wyckoff (1964b)
	1962–1964	Testing and excavation	ORBS	Other minor sites	NPS	Wyckoff and Barr (1964); Kerr and Wyckoff (1964)

Location	Dates	Type of work	Institution	Site(s)	Agency	Reference
Pine Creek Reservoir	1963	Survey	ORBS	—	NPS	Wyckoff (1963b)
	1964–1966	Excavation	ORBS	Bell, Baldwin, Belk	NPS	Barr (1966b)
	1964–1967	Excavation	ORBS	Bell, Gregory	NPS	Wyckoff (1968b)
	1964–1967	Excavation	ORBS	W. H. Baldwin	NPS	Rohrbaugh (1968)
Mangum Reservour	1963	Survey	ORBS	—	NPS	Wyckoff (1963c)
	1966	Testing	MGP[k]		NPS	Leonhardy (1966a)
Lake of the Arbuckles	1964–1965	Survey and testing	ORBS	—	NPS	Barr (1965a)
Birch Creek Reservoir	1965–1966	Excavation	ORBS	Pruitt	NPS	Barr (1966c)
	1964	Survey	ORBS	—	NPS	Barr (1964)
	1972	Resurvey	Gilcrease	—	C of E	Perino (1972a)
	1974–1975	Testing	ORBS	—	NPS	Gettys, Layhe and Bobalik (1976)
Kaw Reservoir	1976–1977	Testing	U Tulsa	Bryson-Paddock (Buffalo Cliff Village)	C of E	Henry (1977a)
	1926	Excavation	OHS	—	OHS	Thoburn (unpublished)
	1963–1964	Survey	ORBS	Freeman, Hudsonpillar	NPS	Wyckoff (1964d)
	1968–1969	Excavation	ORBS		NPS	Bastian (1969)
	1972–1973	Testing and excavation	ORBS	6 sites	NPS	Rohrbaugh (1973a)
	1973–1974	Survey, testing and excavation	ORBS	Spencer, Vickery	NPS	Rohrbaugh (1974)
	1973–1974	Excavation	ORBS	Von Elm	NPS	Hartley (1974a)
	1974–1975	Excavation	ORBS	3 minor sites	NPS	Hartley (1975b)
	1975–1977	Excavation	ORBS	Bryson-Paddock	NPS	Hartley and Miller (1977)
Webber's Falls Lock and Dam	1975–1977	Excavation	ORBS	21 minor sites	NPS	Young (1978)
	1964–1965	Survey	ORBS	—	NPS	Barr (1965b)
	1965–1966	Excavation	ORBS	McCulley	NPS	Wyckoff and Barr (1967a)
Lake Oolagah	1965–1966	Excavation	ORBS	Other minor sites	NPS	Schneider (1967)
	1966–1970	Excavation	ORBS	Vandever-Haworth	NPS	T. G. Baugh (1970)
	1967–1968	Survey	ORBS	—	NPS	T. J. Prewitt (1968)
	1968–1970	Excavation	ORBS	Lightning Creek	NPS	Baldwin (1970)
	1968–1969	Excavation	ORBS	Lawrence	NPS	Baldwin (1969)
Skiatook Reservoir	1967–1969	Survey	ORBS	—	NPS	Rohrbaugh and Wyckoff (1969)
	1972	Resurvey	Gilcrease	—	C of E	Perino (1972b)
	1974–1975	Testing	ORBS	—	NPS	Gettys, Layhe, Bobalik (1976)

(continued)

51

Table 2.1 (Continued)

Reservoir	Dates	Type of work	Participating organization	Major sites	Funding sources	References
	1976–1977	Testing and excavation	U Tulsa	—	NPS	Henry (1977b)
Copan Reservoir	1969–1970	Excavation	OSU[l]	Weston, Hogshooter	OSU	J. A. Howard (1970)
	1971–1972	Survey	WSU[m]	—	C of E	Rohn and Smith (1972)
	1973–1975	Survey, testing and excavation	ORBS	13 sites	NPS	Vaughan (1975)
	1976–1977	Testing and excavation	U Tulsa	5 sites	NPS	Henry (1977c)
	1974–1979	Excavation	ORBS	3 sites	NPS	Vehik and Pailes (1979)
Albany Reservoir	1972	Survey	ORBS	—	C of E	Neal (1972a)
Parker Reservoir	1972	Survey	ORBS	—	C of E	Neal (1972a)
Clayton Reservoir	1972	Survey	ORBS	—	C of E	Neal (1972b)
	1976–1977	Testing	OU (Arch. Surv.)	33 sites	C of E	Bobalik (1977a)
	1977–1978	Excavation	OU (Arch. Surv.)	Sallee G.	C of E	Bobalik (1978)
Shidler Reservoir	1973	Survey	ORBS	—	C of E	Neal (1973a)
Lukfata Reservoir	1973–1975	Survey and testing	ORBS	—	C of E	Gettys (1975)
Arcadia Reservoir	1973	Survey	ORBS	—	C of E	Neal (1973b)
	1976	Survey and testing	ORBS	—	C of E	Hartley (1976)
Optima Reservoir	1975–1977	Testing and excavation	ARA	Old Hardesty	NPS	Lees (1977)
McGee Creek Reservoir	1976	Survey	ARA	—	C of E	A. Cheek (1976a)
voir	1977–1978	Testing	EA, Inc.[n]	—	C of E	(unpublished)
Candy Lake	1977	Survey	ARA	—	C of E	Leehan (1977)

[a] OHS = Oklahoma Historical Society.
[b] OU (Anth.) = University of Oklahoma, Department of Anthropology.
[c] WPA = Works Progress Administration.
[d] NPS = National Park Service.
[e] ORBS = Oklahoma River Basin Survey (OU).
[f] C of E = Corps of Engineers.
[g] ARMC = Archeological Research and Management Center.

[h] ARA = Archeological Research Associates, Tulsa.
[i] N Tx St = North Texas State University.
[j] MRR = Museum of the Red River, Idabel.
[k] MGP = Museum of the Great Plains, Lawton.
[l] OSU = Oklahoma State University.
[m] WSU = Wichita State University.
[n] EA, Inc. = Environmental Assessments, Inc.

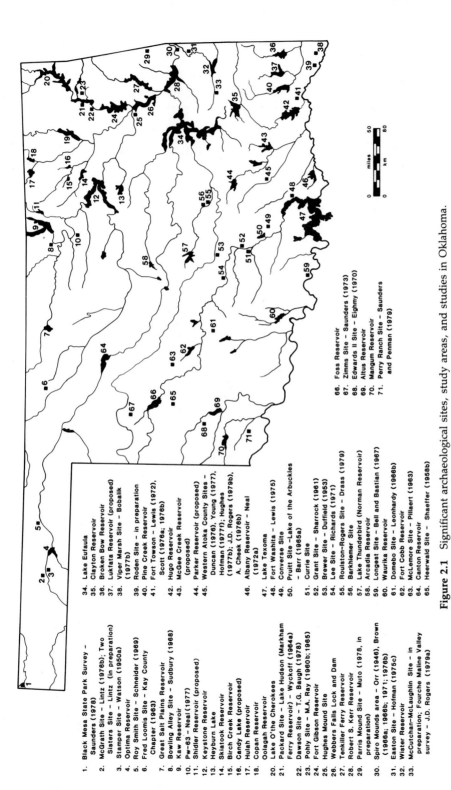

1. Black Mesa State Park Survey – Saunders (1978)
2. McGrath Site – Lintz (1976b); Two Sisters Site – Lintz (in preparation)
3. Stamper Site – Watson (1950a)
4. Optima Reservoir
5. Roy Smith Site – Schneider (1969)
6. Fred Loomis Site – Kay County Chapter (1963)
7. Great Salt Plains Reservoir
8. Bowling Alley Site – Sudbury (1968)
9. Kaw Reservoir
10. Pw–63 – Neal (1977)
11. Shidler Reservoir (proposed)
12. Keystone Reservoir
13. Heyburn Lake
14. Skiatook Reservoir
15. Birch Creek Reservoir
16. Candy Lake (proposed)
17. Hulah Reservoir
18. Copan Reservoir
19.
20. Oologah Reservoir
21. Lake O'the Cherokees
22. Packard Site – Lake Hudson (Markham Ferry Reservoir) – Wyckoff (1964a)
23. Dawson Site – T.G. Baugh (1978)
24. Pohly Site – M.A. Ray (1960; 1965)
25. Fort Gibson Reservoir
26. Hughes Mound Site
27. Webbers Falls Lock and Dam
28. Tenkiller Ferry Reservoir
29. Robert S. Kerr Reservoir
30. Parris Mound Site – Muto (1978, in preparation)
31. Spiro Mounds area – Orr (1946), Brown (1966a; 1966b; 1971; 1976b)
32. Easton Site – Hofman (1975c)
33. McCutchan–McLaughlin Site – in preparation; Fourche Maline Valley survey – J.D. Rogers (1979a)

34. Lake Eufaula
35. Clayton Reservoir
36. Broken Bow Reservoir
37. Lukfata Reservoir (proposed)
38. Viper Marsh Site – Bobalik (1977b)
39. Roden Site – in preparation
40. Pine Creek Reservoir
41. Fort Towson – Lewis (1972), Scott (1978a; 1976b)
42. Hugo Reservoir
43. McGee Creek Reservoir (proposed)
44. Parker Reservoir (proposed)
45. Western Atoka County Sites – Duncan (1976), Young (1977), Hofman (1977f); J.D. Rogers (1979b), A. Cheek (1976b)
46. Albany Reservoir – Neal (1972a)
47. Lake Texoma
48. Fort Washita – Lewis (1975)
49. Converse Site
50. Pruitt Site –Lake of the Arbuckles – Barr (1965a)
51. Currie Site
52. Grant Site – Sharrock (1961)
53. Brewer Site – Duffield (1953)
54. Lee Site – Richards (1971)
55. Roulston–Rogers Site – Drass (1979)
56. Barkhiemer Site
57. Lake Thunderbird (Norman Reservoir)
58. Arcadia Reservoir
59. Longest Site – Bell and Bastian (1967)
60. Waurika Reservoir
61. Domebo Site – Leonhardy (1966b)
62. Fort Cobb Reservoir
63. McLemore Site – Pillaert (1963)
64. Canton Reservoir
65. Heerwald Site – Shaeffer (1958b)

66. Foss Reservoir
67. Zimms Site – Saunders (1973)
68. Edwards II Site – Eighmy (1970)
69. Altus Reservoir
70. Mangum Reservoir
71. Perry Ranch Site – Saunders and Penman (1979)

Figure 2.1 Significant archaeological sites, study areas, and studies in Oklahoma.

Because of both the enhanced availability of funding and stricter mitigation requirements, a rapid growth in American archaeology occurred during the 1970s. The increase in the number of archaeologists working in Oklahoma mirrored this growth. The following short historical sketches of Oklahoma groups' involvement with archaeology illustrate the numerical increase. Significant Oklahoma sites and studies that have contributed to the understanding of Oklahoma archaeology are shown in Figure 2.1.

University of Oklahoma, Department of Anthropology

The university included anthropology in its curriculum quite early in its existence. During the academic year 1905–1906, a Mr. Bucklin taught a course in social ethnology. In 1907–1908, a Department of Sociology and Anthropology was formed, separate from Economics in social studies. This was one of the early American anthropology departments and had as its first chairman the well-known anthropologist, Leslie Spier. These departments have recombined and separated several times, but have been separate departments since 1946.

The Department of Anthropology was depleted during World War II with the departure of its staff. The first faculty member to reinitiate the department in 1945–1946 was Kenneth G. Orr, an archaeologist, who had previously worked with Dr. Clements during WPA times. Orr resigned in 1946 and was replaced by James B. Watson for the academic year 1946–1947. Dr. Watson was an ethnologist but his wife, Virginia, a professional archaeologist, maintained the department's interest in this area. Watson resigned in 1947 and was replaced by Robert E. Bell, an archaeologist, in the summer of 1947. A second position in archaeology was added in 1969–1970 (Richard Pailes) and a third in 1977–1978 (Susan Vehik). In addition, several adjunct faculty have taught specialized courses. At irregular intervals since 1948, the department has offered field schools in archaeology at sites across the state (Table 2.2). A doctoral degree program was initiated in 1967, with the first anthropology Ph.D. degree granted in 1973.

During the 1930s, the Department was involved in federally funded WPA excavations in Oklahoma. A faculty member, Dr. Forrest E. Clements, supervised the program and students acted as field supervisors. Only one person in the program, Joe (Finkelstein) Bauxar, had formal training in archaeology.

In 1946 the department, at the request of the U.S. Army Corps of Engineers, became involved with the renewed reservoir construction activities that followed World War II. Funding provided by the Department of the Interior enabled limited surveys and minor excavations in areas affected by dams and their flood-pool areas (Figure 2.1). The contract unit, Oklahoma River Basin Survey, under the direction of Robert E. Bell, was formed in 1962. The Oklahoma River

Table 2.2

University of Oklahoma Department of Anthropology Field Schools

Year	Site	County	Director
1948	Lake Wister and Ft. Gibson Reservoir	LeFlore Cherokee	Robert E. Bell
1949	Harlan site (Ft. Gibson Reservoir)	Cherokee	Robert E. Bell
1950	Harlan site	Cherokee	Robert E. Bell
1951	Vanderpool site (Tenkiller Reservoir, Morris site)	Cherokee	Robert E. Bell
1952	Morris site	Cherokee	Robert E. Bell
1954	Buncombe Creek site	Marshall	Robert E. Bell
1955	Davis site	McCurtain	Robert E. Bell
1957	Foss Reservoir	Custer	Robert E. Bell
1958	Harlan site	Cherokee	Robert E. Bell
1960	McLemore site	Washita	Robert E. Bell
1963	Shetley Shelter (Markham Ferry Reservoir)	Mayes	Robert E. Bell
1965	Roy Smith site	Beaver	Robert E. Bell
1968	Edwards II site	Beckham	Dewey Buck
1970	Goodman–Baker site	Roger Mills	Don G. Wyckoff
1972	McGrath and Two Sisters sites	Texas	Richard A. Pailes
1973	Two Sisters site	Texas	Richard A. Pailes
1974	Copan Reservoir	Washington	Richard A. Pailes
1975	Copan Reservoir	Washington	Richard A. Pailes
1976	McCutchan–McLaughlin site	Latimer	Don G. Wyckoff
1977	McCutchan–McLaughlin site	Latimer	Don G. Wyckoff
1978	Parris Mound site	Sequoyah	Guy R. Muto
	Salt Creek survey	Osage	Susan Vehik
1979	Salt Creek area	Osage	Susan Vehik

Basin Survey functioned until 1978, when the name was changed to the Archaeological Research and Management Center (ARMC). Since 1962, most of the archaeological research undertaken by the department has been funded by grants obtained by the faculty.

Oklahoma Historical Society

The original concept of an agency to preserve the history of the land was conceived in 1893 by the Oklahoma Territorial Press Association. This concept came to fruition in 1895 when an act signed by Territorial Governor William Renfrew provided funds and designated headquarters at the University of Oklahoma. The Oklahoma Historical Society moved to Oklahoma City in 1904 (Slater 1975:202).

Some of the earliest archaeological work of the Society was carried out by Joseph B. Thoburn. During the 1930s, the Society acted as a cosponsor with other state institutions for the massive WPA excavations. The passage of the National Historic Preservation Act of 1966 led to the appointment of amateur historian George Shirk as the first Oklahoma SHPO in February, 1967. The OHP was established in 1975 and was housed in the Historical Society Building (L. H. Fischer 1979:19). The Society and the OHP work with other state agencies and universities in identifying, listing, and preserving Oklahoma's prehistoric and historic sites.

In the early 1970s the Historical Society was directly involved in archaeological work at historic sites. During 1973–1974 the Society employed a historical archaeologist, Douglas D. Scott. Since that time, testing and excavation programs have been carried out under contract with other state agencies or universities. The Society's *Series in Anthropology* reports the results of the research it supports.

Oklahoma Anthropological Society

The Oklahoma Anthropological Society (OAS) was founded in March, 1952, through the efforts of Robert E. Bell and Karl Schmitt of Oklahoma University's Department of Anthropology. Approximately 40 amateur and professional anthropologists met at Oklahoma University for an organizational meeting, and the Reverend R. C. Swanson of Oklahoma City was elected as its first president. By the end of the first year there were about 120 members and two local chapters at Oklahoma City and Tulsa. The maximum number of local chapters (13) occurred in 1968. At the end of 1979 the OAS numbered about 500 individual and institutional members with local chapters in Ponca City, Tulsa, Muskogee, Oklahoma City, Lawton, and Tishomingo. The Society publishes a newsletter, an annual bulletin, and memoirs or other special publications.

The state society holds two 1-day meetings each year, usually in April and in October. Local chapters usually meet monthly. In addition to these meetings, a number of digs (supervised by professional archaeologists) have been sponsored by the OAS (Table 2.3). Local chapters and individuals have volunteered their time to a number of projects. Members have also designed, constructed, and repaired equipment for both OAS and professional projects. An Oklahoma Anthropological Society Emergency Squad (OASES) file is coordinated with the Oklahoma Archaeological Survey. This file lists OAS members willing to volunteer their free time in various areas of the state when professional archeaologists require assistance on an emergency basis. Society members have also been quite active in reporting site locations and undertaking local research that adds to the state's available data base.

Table 2.3

Oklahoma Anthropological Society Sponsored Fieldwork

Season	Site	County
Spring, 1952	Lacy site, Gv-5	Garvin
Spring, 1953	Brown site, Gd-1	Grady
Fall, 1957	Lee II, Gv-4	Garvin
Fall, 1958	Willingham site, M1-5	McClain
Fall, 1959	Lee II site, Gv-4	Garvin
Spring, 1962	Spring Creek site, My-7	Mayes
Spring, 1963	Duncan–Wilson shelter, Cd-11	Caddo
Spring, 1964	Duncan–Wilson shelter, Cd-11	Caddo
Spring, 1965		
March	Duncan–Wilson shelter, CD-11	Caddo
May	Pruitt site, Mr-12, Lake of the Arbuckles	Murray
July	Duncan–Wilson shelter, Cd-11	Caddo
Spring, 1966	Lee site, Gv-3	Garvin
Fall, 1966	Lee site, Gv-3	Garvin
Spring, 1967	Lee site, Gv-3	Garvin
Fall, 1967	Evans site, Lf-200, Lake Wister	LeFlore
Spring, 1968	Holson Creek site, Lf-9, Lake Wister	LeFlore
Spring, 1969	Lowrence site, Mr-10	Murray
Fall, 1969	Lowrence site, Mr-10	Murray
Spring, 1970	Paul site, Gv-34	Garvin
Fall, 1970	Lake Altus area	Greer
Spring, 1971	Otter Creek #1 site, Hs-25	Haskell
Spring, 1972	Roulston–Rogers site, Sm-20	Seminole
Fall, 1972	Black Mesa State Park survey	Cimarron
Spring, 1973	Tucker's Knob site, Lt-35	Latimer
Fall, 1973	Fort Sill dump	Comanche
Spring, 1974	Mills site, Wn-5, Copan Reservoir	Washington
Spring, 1975	Tucker #3 site, Lt-37	Latimer
Fall, 1975	Ka-11; Hammons site, Ka-20, Kaw Reservoir	Kay
Summer, 1976	McCutchan–McLaughlin site, Lt-11	Latimer
Spring, 1977	McCutchan–McLaughlin site, Lt-11	Latimer
Fall, 1977	Scott site, Lf-11, Lake Wister	LeFlore
Spring, 1978	Converse site, Jn-28	Johnston
Fall, 1978	Converse site, Jn-28	Johnston
Spring, 1979	Converse site, Jn-28	Johnston

University of Oklahoma, Archaeological Research and Management Center

The Oklahoma River Basin Survey (ORBS) was established at the university in 1962. Don G. Wyckoff served as the first full-time staff archaeologist of the unit, while Robert E. Bell was director. Part-time student workers formed a fluctuating staff support. The first contract report was published in July, 1963. During the remainder of the 1960s and the early 1970s the work undertaken by ORBS was primarily in proposed reservoir areas.

In the latter half of the 1970s the types of contracts undertaken expanded with the increasing requirements for cultural resource impact mitigation. In response to this changing emphasis and orientation, the name of the organization was changed in 1978 to the Archaeological Research and Management Center (ARMC). Gerald Galm was the first director of the reorganized unit; he was followed in this position by Rain Vehik. The unit publishes a research report series.

University of Oklahoma, Oklahoma Archaeological Survey

In April, 1970, the state legislature established the Oklahoma Archaeological Survey as an official state agency. The Survey was placed under the authority of the Regents of the University of Oklahoma and was given the status of a research unit under the Vice-Provost for Research Administration. Don G. Wyckoff was the first director and State Archaeologist.

In 1972, the State Archaeologist began reviewing State Clearing House proposals for their impact on prehistoric resources. Minimal staff increases occurred through 1978. At this time the increasing volume of Clearing House reviews and a need to respond more fully to legislated responsibilities necessitated a substantial increase in staff and funding. Contracted environmental studies were shifted to ARMC to avoid potential conflicts of interest.

The State Archaeologist reviews reports of archaeological work done within the state. The Survey also maintains the only complete records on Oklahoma's prehistoric archaeological sites. It coordinates with other state agencies such as the Department of Transportation, the Historical Society, the Office of Historic Preservation, the Department of Tourism and Recreation, and the Oklahoma Conservation Commission in planning and development programs. In addition to working with state agencies, the staff of the Survey conducts basic archaeological research and coordinates planning with federal agencies, such as the Corps of Engineers, the Bureau of Land Management, and the National Park Service.

The Archaeological Survey publishes both professional and popular reports. Its professional publications are the *Archaeological Resource Survey Series* and *Studies in Oklahoma's Past. The Prehistoric People of Oklahoma* is an interpretive series written for the general public.

Phillips University

Phillips University of Enid included an archaeologist (the late Glenn Rose) on its faculty for the past several years. Biblical archaeology was emphasized in the courses offered. The archaeologist's research interest was in the Middle East. Some mammoth remains without cultural associations were excavated in Alfalfa County as a teaching tool for students.

Oklahoma State University, Department of Sociology

The Sociology faculty includes anthropologists with some training in archaeology. The first anthropologist to teach in the department was Morris Siegel (summer semester, 1961). After his death in late summer, 1961, he was succeeded by Martha Royce Siegel until 1967. The department made other additions to its staff in 1968, 1971, and 1974. In addition, an archaeologist was hired on a temporary visiting appointment from 1976 to 1978.

University of Tulsa, Department of Anthropology

The first general anthropology courses at Tulsa University were offered through the Department of Sociology. In 1967, the departmental name was changed to Sociology and Anthropology. The first archaeologist to join the faculty, Ward Weakley, was hired at this time. In 1971, Weakley was replaced by Charles Cheek. A separate Department of Anthropology was established in 1979 with Garrick Bailey as chairman. Five faculty members of the new department had archaeological training or experience.

In 1975, the department established the Laboratory of Archaeology to undertake contract work. A report series, *Contributions in Archaeology*, publishes the results of the Laboratory's work.

Museum of the Great Plains

The Museum of the Great Plains was founded by the City of Lawton in 1961, with Marvin Tong as the director. Early archaeologists on the museum staff included Adrian Anderson, Frank Leonhardy, and Tyler Bastian. Staff revisions in 1971 eliminated positions for archaeologists during the period from 1971 to 1974. Since its founding, however, the staff has undertaken several archaeological contracts and research projects. The best known of these is the work on the Domebo mammoth kill, a Clovis site on the prairie–plains. Presently, the Museum employs a contract archaeologist, John Northcutt, and a part-time staff for washing, cataloging, and survey work.

The Museum maintains exhibits including the archaeology of the Domebo site and later Plains peoples. It also publishes the series, *Contributions of the Museum of the Great Plains.*

Museum of the Red River

The Museum of the Red River was opened in Idabel in April, 1975. This is a private museum sponsored by the Herron Research Foundation, Inc. It was planned as a regional archaeological research center for work in the Red River valley. Its small staff, under the direction of Gregory Perino, has thus far undertaken two major excavation projects in Oklahoma—the Roden site (McCurtain County) and the Mahaffey site (Choctaw County). The results of major projects are published in a museum series.

Gilcrease Museum

The Gilcrease Museum, located in Tulsa, is concerned mainly with the history of the western United States. It exhibits materials from Oklahoma archaeological sites, including Craig Mound at Spiro. The museum undertook some survey contract work, under the direction of Gregory Perino, in Skiatook and Birch Creek reservoirs in 1972. Presently, its staff does not include anyone actively involved in Oklahoma archaeology.

Oklahoma Department of Transportation

The first Oklahoma program alleviating the effects of highway construction on archaeological sites began in 1953. James B. Shaeffer was the program's archaeologist. The project was housed at Oklahoma University's Department of Anthropology under an agreement with the Oklahoma Highway Department. Surveys and salvage projects were carried out throughout the state until the project was terminated in 1962. Much of the data recovered was reported in the Oklahoma Anthropological Society's newsletter and bulletin.

The most recent highway salvage program, the Oklahoma Highway Archaeological Survey (OHAS), was implemented in June, 1972, and quartered with the Oklahoma Archaeological Survey. In 1977, the OHAS moved to separate offices on Oklahoma University's north campus. The number of full-time archaeologists and part-time support staff has varied with the workload. The first Highway Archaeologist was David Lopez; he was succeeded by Rogers Saunders in 1979.

In addition to surveys of proposed construction areas, several major excavations have been completed. These have been published in the series *Papers in Highway Archaeology*.

Oklahoma Conservation Commission

The position of Conservation Commission archaeologist was established in 1973 as an aid in identifying impacts on archaeological resources caused by construction of flood-control/watershed programs. This archaeologist was originally housed with the Archaeological Survey under an agreement between the University and the Commission. The full- and part-time staff has varied in size with the work load. Since the inception of the program, the Conservation Commission archaeologist has been Charles Wallis, Jr. The staff has completed survey, testing, excavation, and preservation projects. The results of these projects have been published in the limited distribution *Letter Report*, *Miscellaneous Report*, *General Survey Report*, and *Research Report* series. In addition to the work done by the staff, excess workload has been contracted to other professional archaeological groups within the state.

Environmental Associates, Incorporated

This commercial company was founded in 1975 in response to the increasing amount of survey work, primarily that connected with Soil Conservation Service environmental impact studies. The company headquarters are in Pauls Valley, with archaeological laboratories in Norman. Throughout its existence, it has worked with the University of Oklahoma and Stovall Museum in preserving and curating materials located during its work.

Archaeological Research Associates

Charles and Annetta Cheek founded the Archaeological Research Associates (ARA), a private research company, in Tulsa in 1975. Survey and testing work under contract to various agencies has been carried out across the state. ARA publishes the results of their work in a small-run research report series.

Benham–Blair and Affiliates, Inc.

Benham–Blair is a multistate engineering organization with headquarters in Oklahoma City. Since 1975, they have incorporated cultural resource information into their environmental impact studies. In October, 1978, archaeological staff was added to implement this work internally. Archaeological laboratory facilities are located with Techrad, the environmental division of Benham–Blair.

Out-of-State Groups

The greatest percentage of archaeological work in the state has been carried out by Oklahoma archaeological groups. Early work by outside groups was mentioned at the beginning of this chapter. During the 1970s projects contracted to non-Oklahoma groups increased with the volume of work. Among the groups working in Oklahoma were the Archaeological Laboratory, Wichita State University, Wichita, Kansas; Colorado College, Colorado Springs; Killgore Research Center, West Texas State University, Canyon, Texas; the Forest Service (USDA), Amarillo, Texas; Archaeology Program, North Texas State University, Denton, Texas; University of Texas, Austin, Texas; Denver Museum of Natural History, Denver, Colorado; Archaeological Resources, Tucson, Arizona; and Espey, Huston and Associates, Inc., Houston, Texas.

The establishment of a professional archaeological program in the late 1940s was the beginning of a concentrated effort to define the prehistoric cultures of Oklahoma and their relationships to each other and to cultures in other areas. The major research emphases during the 1950s and 1960s were the establishment of typologies and of a cultural–historical framework. The increasing amount of funding available for archaeology in the late 1960s and the 1970s resulted in a large increase in the available information and in the number of archaeologists working with it. This new information, especially that from radiocarbon dates, has led to revisions of cultural chronologies in eastern Oklahoma. New excavation and analytic techniques increased the types of information available (for example: activity areas, paleobotanical data from flotation, and reduction sequences from lithic analysis techniques).

Unfortunately, the increased funding for archaeological work became available as a consequence of increased construction and population growth. The destruction of cultural resources has approached crisis proportions in Oklahoma and nationwide. Active cooperation and participation by both amateur and professional archaeologists in salvaging and preserving still-existing resources is imperative. The need for an effective program of public education is urgent. Personnel, time, and funds must be committed in the present if we are to save the past for the future.

Acknowledgments

I thank everyone who responded to my request for information. Too many people helped in my search to thank individually, but special thanks go to Dr. Robert E. Bell, Dr. Don G. Wyckoff, and Larry Neal for their assistance. Much data on the history of Oklahoma archaeology was recalled by Dr. Bell. Don Wyckoff was also an important source of information. In addition, Don read the manuscript and offered many helpful suggestions.

CHAPTER 3

Lithic Resources and Quarries

Larry D. Banks

Introduction

In comparison to any other state or region of comparable size, Oklahoma contains lithic resources in quantity and variety to equal, if not exceed, all others. There are over 35 geologic formations that produce chert in varying degrees of quality and quantity within the state. In addition to the chert, several nonchert materials of archaeological significance also occur in the state. When combined, these materials represent the full range of raw material products needed to supply the lithic industry of every prehistoric culture known in Oklahoma and the adjacent states.

The identification of lithic materials in Oklahoma is relatively well known in comparison to those in most other states. Most of this knowledge, however, is known by a relatively few individuals. Although the chert types may be identifiable, the role of the raw materials in affecting socioeconomics and cultural development in general are poorly understood at this time. Many researchers take the need for accurate identification of lithic materials too lightly and thereby continue to delay the more important potential contribution of this all-important natural resource in understanding the economic anthropology of Oklahoma's prehistoric inhabitants.

This chapter is not a technical paper intended for detailed identification of Oklahoma's lithic resources for two reasons. Space limitations preclude this from happening, but the more important reason is that the basic data for achieving such an accomplishment do not currently exist.

Although lithic materials other than chert are briefly mentioned, the principal objective of this chapter is to address the chert resources as identifiable by geological contexts. In geological literature chert may be mentioned as a lithologic material-type ranging from sand-sized granules, to boulders, to thick-bedded deposits; and, for that reason, reliance solely on geological literature for archaeological needs can often be misleading. The only known satisfactory method of determining the presence of a material and whether or not it was suitable for tool manufacture is by actual field examination. This chapter relies on the results of literature research and on field examination. In researching the geological literature and maps, only those formations that contain chert in forms potentially usable for tool manufacture and with which the author is reasonably familiar are selected for inclusion here.

Lithic Resources

Unlike the other natural resources upon which prehistoric Oklahomans depended that have been subject to considerable alteration, change, or extinction within the past 12,000 years, the basic environmental geology and especially the pre-Quaternary formations have not changed significantly since the introduction of human beings in the area. In fact, the last major geological event that had any effect upon the basic structures of the state was the Laramide orogeny, which produced the Rocky Mountains between 60 and 65 million years ago. The uplift that produced the Rockies caused the general surface elevation of Oklahoma to tilt downward in an easterly direction. Subsequent to the end of the Laramide Revolution, a great Pliocene-aged plain developed eastward from the Rocky Mountains to a north–south line extending roughly from Salina, Kansas, and through Oklahoma City to Fort Worth, Texas. The easternmost edge of this land mass was approximately 228 m (750 feet) thick, and the lithology was made up of sands, clays, silts, and gravels derived from the Rocky Mountains. As a result of late Tertiary and Pleistocene erosion, the land mass dwindled in size to today's remnant, known as the High Plains section of the Great Plains province (Fenneman 1938:14). During the construction of this 10-million-year-old plain, chert, silicified wood, quartzite, and other lithic types were deposited as gravels in the area now known as Oklahoma. The subsequent erosion that removed a major portion of the large Pliocene plain left those same gravels and cobbles strewn southeastward across the surface of the state as modern drainages developed. These gravels provided a significant addition to the other chert resources existing in older geologic strata. Today, the highest elevation in the state is on the flat surface of Black Mesa where the Pliocene land surface was veneered with volcanic basalt. From this point eastward the geologic formations of the state progressively become older in age and lower both in elevation and the stratigraphic sequence.

The state of Oklahoma (Figure 3.1) is divided into seven areas for purposes of discussing lithic resources. The divisions are based on: (1) drainage systems (such as those of the Oklahoma Water Resources Board), (2) age and structure of the geologic systems, and (3) physiographic expressions (Curtis and Ham 1972).

Before the chert formations are discussed by individual areas, some general preliminary remarks are necessary.

As mentioned above, the chert resources of Oklahoma are derived not only from formations within the state, but from extinct and present drainage systems that have brought materials in from other areas; some of the materials derived from outside the state present some of the greatest problems in identification, explanation, and interpretation. The main stems and tributaries of the Arkansas and Red river drainages encompass the entire state of Oklahoma and, in order to have a clear understanding of the chert materials in this area, a certain depth of knowledge concerning chert types from the entire drainage systems flowing through the state is necessary.

The portion of the Arkansas system comprising the North (Beaver Creek) and South Canadian, the Cimarron, and the main stem of the Arkansas head in or near the Rocky Mountains, and flow across and dissect the High Plains section of the Great Plains physiographic province (Fenneman 1931:11–25) before entering the state. In dissecting the High Plains, the Arkansas River and the South Canadian pick up chert and quartzites from the Ogallala, Morrison, and Dakota formations; and from the Texas panhandle area north of Amarillo, Tecovas and Alibates cobbles are added to the drainages. The major chert-producing formations in the headwaters along the eastern flanks of the Rocky Mountains are the laterally equivalent facies of New Mexico's Madera and Colorado's Fountain formations and the Morrison and Lykins formations. The Verdigris and Grand (Neosho) tributaries head in or near the Flint Hills Cuesta of the Central Lowlands province (Fenneman 1938:614–615) before entering the state. The Flint Hills not only extend southward into north central Oklahoma, contributing in-

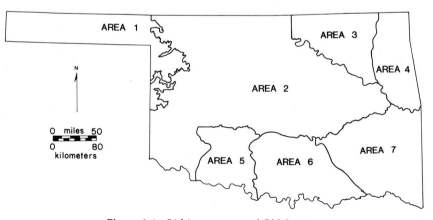

Figure 3.1 Lithic resources of Oklahoma.

place chert deposits of the Foraker, Neva, Cottonwood, Wreford and Florence formations to the state's resources, but the more northerly portion of the Flint Hills provides cherts from an additional seven or eight formations as gravels and cobbles in the Verdigris and Grand River deposits.

An examination of extensive gravel deposits on Arkansas River terraces at John Martin Dam in Colorado by Joe Winters and the author in 1977 produced no chert materials suitable for tool production. In this vicinity, none of the typical Madera–Fountain, Morrison, or Lykins materials was noted. During this same examination (for the Smithsonian Institution), the gravels of the Cimarron were examined south of Springfield, Colorado. The only chert type found here that was suitable for bifacial flaking was a single cobble of Baldy Hill jasper, but it was relatively small. In contrast to these findings, an examination of chert cobbles collected in 1975 by Gregory Perino from the Arkansas River below Keystone Dam indicates a high percentage of cobbles suitable by size and quality for bifacial flaking. The cobbles were primarily, if not totally, derived from Flint Hills and High Plains sources.

The Red River terraces and gravel bars contain cobbles of chert primarily from the Tecovas and from the reworked deposits of the Ogallala formations. Extensive gravel deposits typical of outwash from the High Plains escarpment are concentrated along the Salt Fork of the Red River. The cobbles occur in suitable size and quality for bifacial reduction, but they do become progressively smaller and less concentrated with distance from the High Plains.

Chert-Producing Formations

The stratigraphic column of chert-producing formations (Table 3.1) includes all the formations that have been described in geological literature as containing chert. This does not necessarily mean that the chert in the formations is of a desirable or necessary quality for production of stone tools. For example, some cherts may be brittle or exhibit a splintery rather than conchoidal fracture and therefore would not make suitable tools. Also, chert nodules of high quality may be so tightly embedded in the host-rock matrix that extraction with primitive technology and even modern manual technology is not feasible. Moreover, it should not be assumed that everywhere one of the chert-producing formations appears on a geological map, the area shown is indicative of a source of exploitable chert. One of the reasons chert has not been described in suitable detail for archaeological needs in geological literature is because chert may or may not be a lithologic type common to all outcrops of any given formation. The actual distribution of chert in all but a few of the listed formations is still an unknown, as are detailed descriptions of varieties within each formation. The possibility also exists that isolated facies of the nonchert formations contain sporadic but archae-

Table 3.1

Chert-Producing Formations of Oklahoma

Era	Series	Group	Formation	Member	1	2	3	4	5	6	7	Remarks
Cenozoic	Tertiary Pliocene		Ogallala		X	X						
Mesozoic Cretaceous			Dakota		X	X						
Triassic			Tecovas		X	X						
Paleozoic Permian	Custerian		Cloud Chief	Day Creek		X						
	Gearyan	Chase	Oscar	Herington			X					
			Winfield	Cresswell			X					
				Stovall			X					
			Barneston	Florence			X					
			Wreford	Schroyer			X					
				Three Mile			X					
		Council Grove	Beattie	Cottonwood			X					
			Grenola	Neva			X					
				Americus			X					
			Foraker	Hughes Creek			X					Kay County Flint
				Worland			X					
Pennsylvanian	Desmoinesian		Altamont									
			Oolagah									
	Atokan–Morrowan		Chickachoc							Wapanucka	X	
Mississippian	Chesterian	Jackfork	Markham Hill									
			Wesley									
	Meramecian	Stanley	Ten Mile Creek	Battiest							X	
			Chickasaw Creek								X	
			Moorefield	Bayou Manard				X			X	Equivalent to "J" Beds in Ottawa County "Peoria Flint" and to Warsaw in Missouri
				Tahlequah				X			X	
	Osagean	Boone	Keokuk	Joplin				X				Equivalent to "R" Beds in Ottawa County
				Grand Falls Chert				X				
			Reeds Spring					X				
Devonian			Woodford								X	
			Arkansas Novaculite							X	X	Equivalent to Arkansas Novaculite
			Sallisaw							X	X	Possibly equivalent to Camden chert of Tennessee and Penters chert of Arkansas
		Hunton	Frisco	Cravatt				X		X	Pinetop chert	
			Bois d'Arc					X		X	chert	
Silurian			Chimney Hill	Cochrane				Blackgum		X		
				Keel						X		
				Ideal Quarry						X		
Ordovician		Simpson	Viola							X	Big Fork	
			Corbin Ranch							X		
			Oil Creek									
			Joins									
			Cotter					X				Equivalent to Jefferson City Fm, Missouri

ologically significant localities of chert. Several formations containing chert in conglomerates or in unconsolidated gravels are not listed in Table 3.1 but are mentioned in the text because they may be of localized significance even if they do not exhibit characteristics of having been well known in prehistoric society.

It can be assumed that variable quantities of chert types shown in each of the specific areas also occur as gravels downstream of the outcrop areas shown on the maps (Figures 3.2–3.6). The amount of selectivity required for utilizing those gravel sources, however, can also be assumed to increase significantly with distance from the source of origin.

Area 1

Area 1 contains five relevant lithic types, but only four of them are listed in Figure 3.2; the igneous basalt is excluded. All the formations share physical characteristics of being horizontally bedded and easily accessible because of vertical as well as horizontal exposures that are virtually without ground cover. The eastern boundaries of this area are based on the eastern limits of the High Plains and on boundary lines with surrounding states.

In the westernmost portion of the Oklahoma Panhandle, the Dakota formation produces one of the most extensive quartzite deposits in the state, which were used for stone tool manufacture. This relatively small area of the widespread Dakota formation produces several distinctive quartzite varieties, as do other specific areas, such as the Spanish Diggings in Wyoming and Flint Hill quarries in South Dakota. Throughout the Dakota outcrops from Canada almost to the Mexican border, areas of tightly cemented and well-indurated sandstone (orthoquartzites) often appear, which represent material types atypical of the usual sandstone lithology. Such occurrences exist along the Mora River in New Mexico, in the Springfield, Colorado vicinity, the Wyoming and South Dakota areas mentioned above, and unquestionably in other unfamiliar areas. In the Black Mesa area it is possible that the Tesesquite quartzite reported by Roger Saunders (1978:86) is such a localized phenomena in either the Dakota or the Morrison formation. The Morrison formation produces chert nodules in Wyoming and along the Front Range of the Rockies. Charles Mankin refers to a zone or "agate bed" in northeast New Mexico (Mankin 1972:95–96), but this zone is composed of tiny nodular masses that are unusable for tool manufacture. Chert is unreported in the Morrison formation in the Oklahoma outcrops, but this formation does produce extremely hard silicified sandstone in the Two Buttes area of southeast Colorado (Voegeli and Hershey 1965:57). That possibility also occurs in Black Mesa. *Tesesquite* is likely an appropriate name for a distinctive variety of either the Dakota or the Morrison formation; but in future research it should be appropriately identified by formation. Also, because of the presence of the basalt capstone in the Black Mesa vicinity, partial metamorphism in the

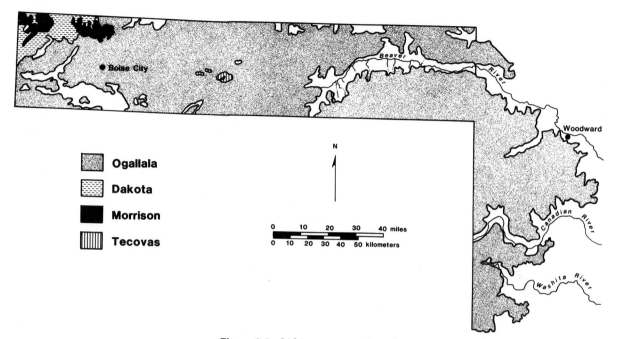

Figure 3.2 Lithic resources, Area 1.

sandstones producing metaquartzite rather than the usual orthoquartzite cannot be arbitrarily ruled out as a cause for the Tesesquite quartzite.

The other principal and potential lithic resources of this area are derived from the Ogallala formation. These resources consist of chert, petrified wood, and quartzites from gravels in the lowermost portion of the formation and possibly from orthoquartzite masses that are known to occur elsewhere in zones of the Ogallala. It is from these masses that the well-recognized Ogallala quartzite cobbles originated. The masses of alternating grey-brown and red colors of the distinctive Ogallala materials have been observed in place in Ogallala outcrops of southeast Colorado, but it is not known whether they actually occur in Area 1. The Ogallala quartzite is probably the single material type most common to the central and southern Great Plains. A northern Plains material that looks identical to the Ogallala "silicified Siltstone" or orthoquartzite (Lopez and Saunders 1973:3) is the "Tongue River silicified sediment" of South Dakota (Porter 1962:268). In the Texas Panhandle, there are eight different localized names for the gravel member of the Ogallala (Byrd 1971:11) in which this same material type occurs and it is referred to by Jack Hughes as "Potter chert" (J. Hughes 1976:2). Another chert type in the Ogallala formation that warrants mention is the brown–tan–white Opaline (Swineford and Franks 1959:111–112) that commonly occurs throughout the Great Plains. Large masses of the material occur east of Guymon and unquestionably elsewhere in the panhandle and further south in Area 2. The material is extremely brittle and badly fractured; in spite of this, flakes and "worked" pieces are frequently found in archaic and later archaeological contexts. The temptation to knap the material seems to have been almost overwhelming, but the results are universally poor. If actual artifacts of the material exist, they are quite rare. This is the material referred to by Hughes as "Ogallala chert" (J. Hughes 1976:2).

In addition to the Ogallala, Dakota, and possibly the Morrison materials, two others of potential significance occur in Area 1. The Pliocene basalt in the Black Mesa area represents the only such material in the state. Unlike finer grained basalt farther west, its usefullness in bifacially flaked tools is limited, but it may occur in other tool forms. Even in the vicinity of the basalt beds, Roger Saunders (1978:89–91) reports only 14 artifacts made of this material from 26 local sites.

The Oklahoma Water Resources report for Region XII (1973:20) indicates small exposures of the Tecovas formation in some of the tributary areas of the North Canadian River in Texas County. Although the typical Tecovas jasper is not mentioned as present, and Robert O. Fay (personal communication, 1982) has not observed any chert in the outcrops, a slight possibility for its presence does exist. In the Tecovas formation in Texas, chert results from secondary replacement but, in those outcrops on the North Canadian, Dr. Fay does not consider the lithologic conditions required for such development to be present. In the headwaters of the Cimarron River in New Mexico, high-quality Tecovas jasper does occur. Christopher Lintz from the Oklahoma Archaeological Survey collected a large piece of the typical yellowish variety from an outcrop referred to locally as *Baker flint*. The Baldy Hill formation (a lateral equivalent of the Tecovas), which produces a distinctive purplish red, mottled jasper also outcrops between the headwaters of the North Canadian and the Cimarron rivers. Cobbles from the Baldy Hill occur in the Cimarron, but it is not known whether this type of material occurs in North Canadian gravels or not. Cobbles from the Tecovas should be expected in the North Canadian from the New Mexico deposits. As the North Canadian flows eastward, the ratio of sand to gravel increases significantly and tends to obscure the gravels anyway.

The lithic materials from this area appear to have been of minimal influence outside the immediate region; but the cobbles and gravels from the Ogallala, the Dakota, and possibly the Morrison quartzites are represented in almost all later formations deposited to the east and southeast.

Area 2

Area 2, which includes nearly a third of the state, is the least productive of lithic resources in terms of geologic occurrence and quality (Figure 3.3). In spite of this, with a foraging type of subsistence, prehistoric inhabitants would not have been without serviceable resources in the form of gravels and cobbles from

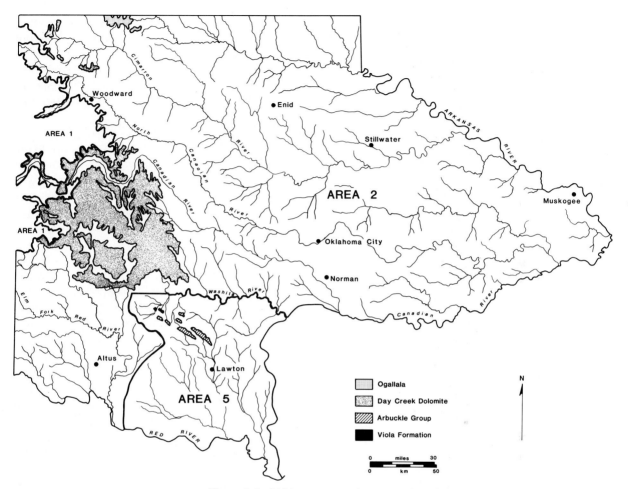

Figure 3.3 Lithic resources, Areas 2 and 5.

most streams and terraces. The cobbles on the interfluves (existing upland terraces from relict drainages) in portions of the area may have played a more important role than the more recent terrace or stream gravels. For example, between the communities of Alva and Enid, terrace deposits that are currently a number of miles away from major streams exhibit significant quantities of high-quality lithic materials in the form of petrified wood (both agate and jasper), as well as nondescript chert types that have been so altered by chemical and mechanical weathering that the original sources cannot be determined without more detailed research. Those terraces have provided rock hounds with major sources of stone used for cutting and polishing for a number of years. The cobbles provided sources of procurement for prehistoric peoples in an area that has no other immediately available sources of in-place chert. Hammerstones and flake debris can be found randomly scattered along the ridges, but there are few specific areas exhibiting concentrated exploitation. These high-level deposits occurring at a considerable distance from the present-day main stem of the Arkansas River can best be attributed to Robert O. Fay's (1965:66–76) suggestion, based on sound geological evidence, that the main stem of the Arkansas once flowed through the valley presently occupied by the Medicine Lodge and Salt Fork tributaries.

The Day Creek dolomite is considered by Roger Bowers (1975:17–19), and a number of geologists to be a lateral equivalent of the Alibates dolomite. The Day Creek produces minor quantities of chertified dolomite similar in color and texture to some of the less vivid and more porous varieties of the Alibates. It was in the Day Creek deposits of southern Kansas immediately north of this area that G. H. Norton (1939:1811) first hypothesized that the silicification (or chertification) in the Day Creek was a result of secondary replacement from silica sources in the Ogallala formation.

David Lopez and Roger Saunders of the Oklahoma Archaeological Survey located some isolated areas in the Day Creek near Woodward, Oklahoma, in 1975 that exhibited evidence of prehistoric exploitation (Larry Neal, personal communication, 1978). In small artifacts and flake debris, this material could be confused with poorer grades of Alibates. However, it is unlikely that its distribution would have anything other than local significance. Individuals conducting archaeological research in the areas of Day Creek exposures, however, should be aware of its possible local significance. The actual distribution of chert in the Day Creek is unknown.

Alibates cobbles and gravels have been found on the Arkansas River terraces derived from the South Canadian as far east as the Spiro site. Three separate Alibates varieties were recovered from natural gravels on the secondary terrace at the north edge of the Spiro site in 1973. The gravels were no larger in diameter than a couple of centimeters, but larger pieces such as one measuring $8.8 \times 5 \times 3.8$ cm found by Gregory Perino below Robert S. Kerr Dam do occur. Also during the Eufaula Lakeshore survey Gregory Perino and Jerry Caffey (1980:135) report that Alibates materials were the third-most-important chert type represented in the project area.

In addition to the gravels and the Day Creek materials, several geologic formations of Area 2, such as the Holdenville, Coffeyville, and Nellie Bly (Oklahoma Water Resources Board Region VIII 1971a:23), contain conglomerates with chert components. The archaeological usefulness of chert conglomerates is questionable, although Lawrence Levick of the Oklahoma Anthropological Society (personal communication, 1976) has located some conglomerate materials resembling brecciated Tecovas fragments west of the Wichita mountains. They were utilized, at least to some extent, by prehistoric knappers. Although significant chert-producing formations do not exist in this area, lithic resources were still available in limited quantity.

Area 3

Area 3 is bordered by the Arkansas River on the south and west and by the drainage divide between the Verdigris and Grand–Neosho rivers on the east (Figure 3.4). The principal chert-producing formations are concentrated in the northwestern portion of the area. This 32-km wide zone is the southernmost extension of the Flint Hills Cuesta of Kansas (Fenneman 1938:614–616), the formations of which extend as far into Oklahoma as the South Canadian River. The characteristic chert in the formations, however, appears to have pinched out in the vicinity or immediately to the north of the town of Fairfax. There are 10 formations that produce chert north of the Kansas line, but not all those formations are known to produce chert in the Oklahoma outcrops. The definite pro-

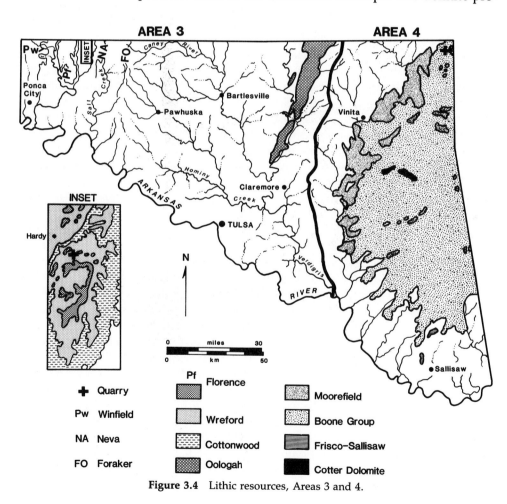

Figure 3.4 Lithic resources, Areas 3 and 4.

ducers of this area are the Florence, Schroyer, Threemile, Cottonwood, Neva, and Hughes Creek members, but two of the formational units (Barneston and Wreford) are the principal producers. In all cases, the chert occurs either as thin nodular lenses subject to pinch and swell structure or as isolated nodules. The chert generally occurs near the crest of the escarpment edges of the rounded hills and mesalike features. Exposures of the chert are generally poor because of the thin, sinuous nature of the outcrops along the edges of the hills.

The cherts in the various formations are distinguishable from each other, but familiarity with the formations and with chert variations in each of them is necessary for differentiation. One of the classic lithic identification problems for Oklahoma archaeologists concerns the proper formational placement of one of the state's best-known chert types from the Kay County quarries. The archaeological problem basically stems from the absence of detailed mapping. Both the Florence member of the Barneston Formation and the Schroyer and Threemile members of the Wreford Formation occur in the same general area, and all three limestone members overlie shale units. The quarries were assigned to the Wreford Formation as early as 1919 by W. H. Twenhofel (1919:907–929), but both the Wreford and the Florence formations share similar lithologies, including chert nodules and lenses. The State Geologic Map of Oklahoma (1955) shows only the Herington and Fort Riley formations of the Chase Group in the immediate vicinity of the quarries, and it indicates the presence of a small outcrop of Fort Riley due east of Newkirk on the east side of the Arkansas river. Chert nodules produced from both locations are identical in all physical characteristics. The detail in this map does not refer to the Wreford formation. The more detailed but smaller-scaled map of the area in the Oklahoma Water Resources Region X (1972:20) indicates that the quarries would more appropriately be assigned to the Wreford. However, neither the Wreford nor the Florence member of the Barneston correlates well with the formations shown on the State Geologic Map of Kansas (Kansas Geological Survey 1964). The detailed Hydrologic Atlas 7 (Oklahoma Geologic Survey 1980) shows both the Wreford and the Florence formations in finer detail. Although both geologic units are shown in the same immediate area, the hilltops producing the Kay County quarries are clearly mapped as the Florence.

The mapping for the Enid Quadrangle (HA-7) is the best existing documentation and should resolve any further controversy of the geologic nomenclature for the quarries. Immediately to the north of the quarries, the Wreford formation contains nodules of blue-gray chert, but they are not lenticular and are so tightly embedded that they cannot be effectively utilized. In terms of archaeological recognition, none of the other cherts in the area approaches that of the Kay County material because of the well-known presence of the Kay County quarries, which extend sporadically along the thin outcrop northward into Cowley County, Kansas. Several quarry areas exist in the general area. The quarries have been referred to in archaeological literature probably as much as any other locality in the Great Plains. They were apparently first cited by C. N. Gould in

1898, and the many references since that time are too many to enumerate. Perhaps the best archaeological discussion of the area is that of Waldo Wedel (1959:476–480) and the best technical description of the chert to date is that of Hubert C. Skinner (1957:41–43).

In archaeological sites, the "Kay County" material usually exhibits colors in varying shades from grayish pink to brick red. However, none of the pink-red coloration has been observed in outcrop materials. Reddish tinges of iron-oxide staining appear in some of the distinctive banding, but the natural colors vary from light gray to blue-gray, and shades of yellow–tan–brown. The reddish coloration and sheen that are typical of archaeological specimens were produced by intentional heat treatment. I have only seen a single Paleoindian artifact (a Clovis point) made of the Florence chert. The point was found on a gravel bar below Keystone Dam. It was yellowish-tan and was highly polished from sand and water abrasion. Archaic artifacts produced from the material are commonly found northward into Kansas as well as in various places in Oklahoma, but they are normally not heat treated. By Plains–Woodland time, artifacts that show evidence of heat treatment began to appear, and by Gibson aspect time practically all artifacts of Kay County material exhibited the effects of heat treatment. It is also during the Gibson aspect that the distinctive material appears to have reached its widest distribution. Artifacts have been found in Caddoan sites along the Red River near Paris, Texas (Mallouf 1976:58–60), and as far south as the George C. Davis site near Alto, Texas. At the Davis site, Dee Ann Story's excavations produced a "Kay County" arrowpoint in a cache of some 125 other points, 6 of which were also made of Keokuk chert from northeast Oklahoma (Shafer 1973:205–208). Robert E. Bell and David A. Baerreis (1951:81–82) document the use of Kay County materials in Washita River focus sites as Waldo Wedel (1959:313–314) does for Great Bend aspect sites near Lyons, Kansas. Several of the largest bifaces from the Spiro site are made from the material. Though Oklahoma lithic materials are of principal concern here, it is also worth noting that direct contacts between Spiro and the Republican River focus are also suggested by the presence of three large bifaces of Smoky Hill jasper excavated by J. B. Thoburn at the Spiro site. The jasper appears to be identical to the type of materials that were produced at the Dooley site excavated by Duncan Strong (1935:69–103) in southcentral Nebraska. Wedel recalls seeing thin, laminated outcrops of the jasper in the banks of Lost Creek to the west of the site (personal communication, 1974). The outcrops are now silted in.

A unique characteristic of the Kay County chert, which is different from other Flint Hills types, is the natural configuration of available nodules. The nodules vary from small, tightly embedded ovate pieces to large, thick globular masses as much as 30 cm in length and 10–12 cm thick. However, in certain areas of the outcrops, such as the Kay County quarries, the chert occurs as lenticular nodules as much as 38 cm in length, 8 cm thick, and 25 cm in width. The wide, flat nodules occur as discontinuous lenses between relatively thin limestone strata that can be peeled back from the cuesta edges with little difficulty. John Reynolds and Martin Stein (personal communication, 1980) from the Kansas State Historical Society have found antler wedges still in place between chert nodules and adjacent limestone strata in quarry excavations of an identical nature to those at the Kay County quarries. The larger chert nodules are not normally as tightly embedded as smaller nodules, and can be removed with relative ease. The quantities and distinctive shapes of high-quality chert nodules, such as the Florence types, which are uniquely conducive to production of large bifaces, are unequaled by any other resource in the state.

By far the largest portion, if not all, of the naturally occurring chert at the most prominent Kay County quarries near Hardy, Oklahoma, was removed prehistorically. The remaining chert at the quarries is primarily debitage from fracturing the limestone and from initial bifacial reduction. Comparisons made between the unaltered Florence outcrops and the quarried areas suggest that the outcrops were exploited from south to north, but the quarrying ended long before the chert sources extending northward into Kansas were depleted.

The other most distinctive, but certainly not one of the best-quality, cherts in this area is the Foraker or Hughes Creek material with its dull, dark blue-gray matrix, in contrast to the white silicified fusilinids. This type of material as well as the Cottonwood and Neva were not widely distributed, at least not in comparison to the Florence. The Foraker material has also been called *Salt Creek* and *Shidler* chert. Although all the other cherts in the southern Flint Hills occur in similar stratigraphic contexts, none of the other Flint Hills types occurs in such convenient forms as does the Kay County material. The term *Kay County* does seem to be an appropriate term for distinction because the Florence outcrops farther north do not seem to exhibit the same form nor the typical banding of this southern facies of the formation.

Along the Verdigris River above the Oologah dam and lake, the Oologah limestone and the Worland member of the Altamont formation, also of the Oologah group, produce distinctive chert types, but both are of very poor quality. The Worland is more uniform in color and texture, and flakes better than the multiveined, fossiliferous, and porous Oologah material. Archaeological sites along the Verdigris River exhibit relatively high percentages of the materials, but they do not appear to have been widely distributed for any appreciable distance.

Two other nonchert lithic materials in this area warrant a brief notation. In exposures of the Seminole formation of Flatrock Creek in the north part of Tulsa, small black phosphatic nodules occur that vary in size up to as much as 3 or 4 cm in diameter. These nodules are almost perfectly round and are identical in appearance to the large, black stone beads that have been found in several Caddoan sites along the Arkansas River but principally at the Spiro site. Nodules like these have also been found infrequently on gravel bars below Tulsa in the Arkansas River. The geologic and geographic distribution of the phosphatic nodules is unknown at this time, but modification required to produce beads from such nodules seems to suggest the probability of their use for such a specialized purpose.

Also, at Webbers Falls on the Verdigris River, the falls were actually caused by a resistant ledge of "siltstone" in the Atoka formation, which crosses the river bed at roughly 90°. This stone, also of unknown distribution, is reputedly the black, dense argillite used for producing large bifacially flaked "hoes" found in the vicinity and farther downstream on the Arkansas River. Fred Schneider (1967:10) refers to the material as "brown to black, micaceous and non-calcareous." Like the phosphatic nodules, the geographic distribution of this distinctive material is unknown. Other Atoka outcrops that are widespread in the area probably contain similar lenses, but the availability of this particular outcrop made possible during low water may have been the primary factor for its use.

Area 4

Area 4 includes the northeast corner of the state from the western edge of the Grand–Neosho river drainage system south to the Arkansas River. It is bordered on the north by the Kansas line and on the east by the Missouri and Arkansas state lines. A mere glance at the chert outcrops shown in Figure 3.4 gives an accurate impression of the significance of the lithic resources of this area. The potential surface outcrop of the Boone group alone covers some 5180 km^2 (Banks 1973:1). The other seven chert-producing formations in the area add another several hundred square miles of potential surface area. It is not only the surface area, however, but the thickness of the formations that make them superlative among the state's resources. The Keokuk is some 76.2 m thick, the Reeds Spring 53.5 m thick, the Tahlequah 9.1 m thick, and the Sallisaw 3 m thick, but only the upper portion is cherty (Huffman 1958:30–44). The chert, of course, does not occur throughout the entire thickness of the formations, but there is no comparison between the sheer mass of the chert in this area with that in all other areas of the state combined.

The four previously mentioned formations constitute the largest and most widely distributed types of the eight chert-producing formations of the area. The Joplin member of the Keokuk contains cherty crinoidal limestone of minimal archaeological significance in quality and quantity. The chert in the Bayou Manard member of the Moorefield is very distinctive with its dense, black, and waxy matrix, occasionally splotched with white fossils, which are mostly crinoidal fragments. The chert is tightly embedded in dense blue-gray limestone; and, although the nodular chert masses may exceed a meter in length, obtaining sizable pieces for bifacial production is difficult at best. Most Bayou Manard artifacts are small and seemingly of a localized distribution along the Grand River. This is the material more popularly known as Red Bird (Wyckoff 1963a:13).

Although the Frisco formation is listed as a potential chert producer of this area because of the well-known materials produced from it in the Arbuckles, actual chert in the Frisco of northeast Oklahoma is not well documented. Thomas Amsden (1961:30) accurately refers to the potential chert in the Frisco here as "rare, but some beds do include small nodules up to 2 or 3 inches long."

The Blackgum formation, which has a total thickness of 10.7 m, is similar to that of the Frisco for potential chert production; and, although accurate descriptions of the chert are unavailable, the formation is described by Robert O. Fay and John Roberts as "a dark gray to black, cherty, glauconitic, fossiliferous limestone and dolomite, with zero to three-foot bed of Pettit Oolite at the base" (Oklahoma Water Resources Board, Region IX 1971b:24). The Pettit Oolite referred to here and the Short Creek Oolite at the base of the Meramecian rocks in Ottawa County (Oklahoma Water Resources Board, Region IX 1971b:26) are of possible archaeological interest. Small artifacts of a light gray silicious oolite occasionally are found in area sites and possibly come from one or both of these two geologic units. The Blackgum formation of northeast Oklahoma is the lateral equivalent of the chert-producing Cochrane of the Arbuckles.

The Cotter dolomite contains what may be the most distinctive chert types of the area. This lateral equivalent of the Jefferson City formation of Missouri produces dense, concentrically banded nodules of a tough and often difficult material to flake. Four different varieties of this material have been previously described (Banks 1973:9–10). The principal outcrops are in the vicinity of Lake Spavinaw, but archaeological specimens of the materials are found in small numbers throughout northeast Oklahoma. More extensive exposures of chert in the Cotter formation occur eastward in northern Arkansas at Norfork Lake than in the small exposures in Oklahoma.

The Grand Falls chert of the Keokuk formation and cherts of the underlying Reeds Spring formation and the overlying Tahlequah member of the Moorefield formation at times occur in the same vicinity and in the same exposure. For this reason there has often been some confusion archaeologically in accurately typing the materials. With comparative analysis, the cherts are easily distinguishable from each other. The pale-blue and more uniformly colored Reeds Spring material is especially distinctive. Some of the weathered Grand Falls varieties are more difficult to distinguish from the Tahlequah materials.

In 1973, 12 varieties of chert from the Grand Falls member of the Keokuk formation were found in one locality (Banks 1973:13–17), but within the past 2 years Don Dickson of the Arkansas Archaeological Survey has found at least an additional 7 distinguishable varieties of the Keokuk types. He has also found a unique red chert in the Joplin member (personal communication, 1981). The Grand Falls chert is widely known as Boone chert in archaeological literature. Because it is the principal chert-producing member in the Boone group and *Boone chert* is widely recognized archaeologically, continuation in use of the term is appropriate. *Grand Falls chert* or *Keokuk chert* are more geologically confined terms. Regardless of which term is used, archaeologists should be aware of the proper geological relationship of the three units' names.

The Sallisaw, often referred to locally as *Barren Fork chert*, is known to have produced relatively large bifaces. Thomas Amsden (1961:45) records blocks of

Sallisaw chert "up to 2 feet in diameter" west of the Tenkiller Dam. It is interesting that a seemingly significant though unquantified portion of late Paleoindian and Early Archaic dart points (Dalton in particular) are made from the Sallisaw chert. Huffman (1958:36) describes the Sallisaw chert as "white to light gray [and] interbedded with calcareous sandstone or sandy limestone." The Sallisaw is distinctive from all other cherts in the area. It is generally more uniform in light gray colors but is frequently stained by iron oxide. Splotches or "eyes" produced by staining are frequent.

The chert formations in this area are all essentially horizontal. Numerous good exposures exist in bluffs and stream cuts, and the clear flowing creeks and rivers of the area contain abundant chert gravels and cobbles. The cherts of the Tahlequah (Peoria quarries) and Grand Falls units are typically fractured but are in large enough pieces to allow production of moderately large bifaces. Easy accessibility to ample chert resources preclude the necessity of actual quarrying in this general area. Many areas exist in the chert exposures where the materials were actively worked, but actual quarries were not developed. Obviously, quarrying represented a considerable expense of energy in comparison to obtaining needed materials from stream gravels and outcrop exposures. Therefore, the reason for the presence of the Peoria quarries is difficult to explain. The Peoria quarries are an exception to the more common method of exploitation in the area. Also, quarrying methods used for the Tahlequah chert in the Peoria area would seem to require different techniques from those used at the Kay County quarries. It is perhaps worth noting that the quarried ridges south of Pierce City, Missouri, are in the Warsaw chert, which is possibly a lateral equivalent of the Tahlequah. Similar to the Kay County quarries discussed previously, a problem with geological nomenclature also accompanies the Peoria quarries. To appreciate the problem, a brief history of the geological state of knowledge for the area is beneficial. In 1915, the Boone cherts of northeastern Oklahoma were discussed in general by L. C. Snider, who stated, in relation to one particular unit, that "the cherts are very dense and almost pure white" (Snider 1915:25). Then, on the next page, he refers to the "pronounced hills of Boone chert [that] rise through the overlying Chester formation and are shown on the accompanying map (PL. 1.). The westernmost of these is the hill about one-half mile east of Pryor" (1915:26).

The only existing publication specifically related to Ottawa County is that by Reed, Schoff, and Branson (1955), but in regard to the area of the Peoria quarries small outliers of only the Hindsville sandstone are shown on the accompanying geological map of the county. They do not refer to the term *Moorefield* in the publication. R. C. Slocum (1955:9–12) introduces use of the term *Moorefield* for the formation overlying the Boone Rocks in parts of Mayes, Delaware, and Adair counties, but does not mention the outliers in the Peoria vicinity. The most detailed geological work in northeast Oklahoma, by G. G. Huffman (1958), does not specifically include Ottawa County, but for the first time the Boone group is divided and the overlying cherts are properly assigned to the Moorefield units, among others, as Post Boone outliers. Like Slocum, however, Huffman did not include the area of the Peoria quarries in his area of study. The state geologic map of Oklahoma (1955) indicates that the quarry vicinity is within the Boone group. The report by Reed *et al.* (1955) was relied upon by Melvin V. Marcher and Roy H. Bingham, (Oklahoma Hydrologic Atlas, No. 2, 1971) in producing the updated geological maps of northeastern Oklahoma (Melvin Marcher, personal communication 1982). Marcher and Bingham do indicate the presence of Moorefield outliers, as do Reed, Schoff, and Branson (1955), in close proximity to Peoria (8 km to the south–southeast and to the north) but not in the immediate area of the quarries.

Based on (1) the discussion with Dr. Marcher, (2) the stratigraphic sequence (i.e., Boone–Moorefield–Hindsville) of other outliers in the general vicinity described by Slocum (1955:16–20), (3) lithologic similarities to outcrops and chert specimens from the Tahlequah member of the Moorefield at Pryor and at Union Mission on the west bank of the Grand River—the same outcrops described as the Boone by Snider but clearly demonstrated by Huffman to be the Moorefield, and finally (4) apparent dissimilarities to specimens collected from other Keokuk (Boone) outcrops, the Peoria quarries have been (Banks 1973:18) and should continue to be considered as outliers of the Tahlequah member of the Moorefield until and if future geological research in the immediate area proves otherwise.

W. H. Holmes reported the quarry pits at Peoria as originally no more "than 10 or 15 feet deep" (Holmes 1919:202); but considering the techniques required to excavate to such depths and as much as 12.2 m in diameter, the quarries represented considerable labor. It is also interesting to point out that the "Peoria" materials respond well to heat treatment, resulting in esthetically pleasing shades of pinkish white with a vitreous luster. Gregory Perino (personal communication, 1973) claims, and probably correctly so, that the influence of Hopewell or later cultures on sites in this area can be recognized by the presence of heat-treated flakes of Tahlequah chert. The material types of the large bifaces reported by Bill Anderson (1968:155–157) from a burial on Gaines Creek near Eufaula and a cache of Florence bifaces are of particular interest here. Of the two artifacts from Gaines Creek, one is heat-treated Tahlequah chert and the other is a variety of chert from the Johns Valley Shale in the Ouachita Mountains. Heat treatment of this blue-black chert from the Johns Valley deposits is detrimental rather than beneficial to its knappability. The material tends to become too brittle at relative low temperatures and to explode at temperatures in excess of 190° C. Also, the unusual 20-piece cache of highly resharpened Kay County bifaces reported by Mike Millsap and Don Dickson (1968:158–159) was heat-treated. Why do the quarried materials appear to be more directly related to heat treatment than do the materials that are not specifically from quarries? Was heat treatment performed solely for functional reasons?

The potential relationships between actual quarrying, heat treatment, and production of artifacts related in some way to ceremonialism need to be examined. The Tahlequah chert is unusually responsive to heat treatment in contrast to other types in the area. Could this characteristic be a factor for the "necessity" of quarrying? It is possible that actual quarrying in this case is more related to ceremonialism of a socioreligious nature than to physical requirements of procurement. W. H. Holmes recognized the presence of two different chert types in the area of Afton Springs and, although the cache of nearly a thousand dart points taken from the springs was probably from the Grand Falls chert and was not heat treated, it is worth noting that Holmes attributed the cache to ceremonialism associated with flint knapping (Holmes 1919:208–209).

This section of the state contains the richest concentration of lithic resources in terms of combined quantity, quality, variety, and size of individually produced pieces. Geologically, the area is complex and the discussion here is oversimplified. The ability to distinguish varieties of the Boone group by specific areas is difficult, if not impossible. Use of trace-element analysis (neutron activation or proton-induced X-ray examination) seems to have little potential for resolving the problem simply because of the magnitude and cost of the task of adequately sampling outcrop areas to obtain the necessary base data.

Chert resources do not occur everywhere as might be implied, but none of the prehistoric inhabitants in the area had any appreciable distance to travel to obtain all the chert necessary for any given stone-reliant society. It is not unreasonable to suggest that the rich lithic resources immediately to the north of the Spiro site and those to the south in the Ouachita Mountains were influencing factors, along with others, in determining Caddoan settlement patterns.

Area 5

The Wichita Mountain region is probably the poorest area in the state in terms of available lithic resources for the production of chipped-stone tools (Figure 3.3). It is also probably the least-known area in the state with regard to such lithic types. Although the Wichita–Arbuckle system bears geologic affinities, the chert-producing formations in the Arbuckles are simply not present or at least are not exposed in the Wichita Mountain area.

The Arbuckle group in the Wichita Mountains is composed of some 1524 m of dolomitic limestone and some soft siliceous lime beds, which contain "occasional cherty limestone, and more rarely thin beds of chert" (Taff 1928:76), but the complete sequence is not exposed completely in any area. The "thin beds of chert" have not been identified with specific formations, but it is likely that they are equivalent to the chert-producing formations of the Simpson group in the Arbuckle Mountains. The best exposure of the Arbuckle group in the Wichita Mountains is "northeast of Blue Creek Canyon where the rocks outcrop in regular succession from the base upward for nearly three miles" (Taff 1928:76), but exposures of chert in any form have not been specifically defined in the area.

The Viola formation, which produces significant quantities of chert in the Arbuckles, crops out immediately to the west and some 4.8 km southeast of

Rainy Mountain Mission north of the Wichita Mountains, but chert resources of the Viola in this area are also poorly known. The Big Fork chert of the Ouachita Mountains is a lateral equivalent of the Viola. The Woodford chert and other pertinent Devonian formations that outcrop in the Arbuckles "so far as known, are concealed by [the] Red Beds" (Taff 1928:78) in the Wichita Mountains.

The Viola and Arbuckle outcrops on the northern flanks of the Wichita Mountains need to be examined for potential chert sources. Judging from the chert types recovered from recent archaeological surveys at Fort Sill (Ferring 1978:386–387), it seems possible that chert sources in the Wichita Mountains, if they exist, were either not known or for some physical reason were considered inadequate to supply needs by prehistoric groups. Most of the archaeological specimens from the Fort Sill investigations were introduced from other areas, such as the Edwards Plateau of Texas and northeast Oklahoma.

Nonchert lithic sources of granite, rhyolite, and other igneous and metamorphic rocks occur in the Wichita Mountains, but none of them warrants specific discussion here.

Area 6

The chert-producing formations in the Arbuckle Mountains and surrounding area equal those in the southern Flint Hills in sheer numbers (12), but the combined total of potential chert produced in the Arbuckle area (Figure 3.5) probably exceeds that of Area 3. With the exception of the Florence chert, the resources of the Arbuckle area certainly exceed those of the Flint Hills in quality. The Woodford and Frisco formations probably produce the most significant amounts of chert in terms of exploitable resources. However, the Cravatt member of the Bois d'Arc formation (a lateral equivalent of the Pinetop chert of the Ouachita Mountains) is thick, and nodules of chert are interspersed throughout the unit. In 1954 W. J. Ford (1954:10) reported a "bed of ten feet of white chert underlying the Simpson group," and R. W. Harris (1957:62) reported a deposit of 3 m (10 feet) of white chert in the Corbin Ranch formation of the Simpson group. It is possible that the two references actually refer to the same type of material. Nevertheless, the chert types from the Hunton and Simpson groups of the Arbuckles have not been defined for archaeological purposes. Consequently, with the possible exception of the Frisco materials, accurate names for the chert types in archaeological literature are nonexistent. For example, the relationship between archaeological specimens reported by Don G. Wyckoff (1973) from the Lowrance site and any specific geological formation is unknown at this time. The most logical source for the weathered Lowrance cobbles would be the Joins or Oil Creek formation, but that is only an assumption. Also, there have been no comparative analyses conducted for the Arbuckle area materials and their lateral equivalents in Areas 4, 5, and 7. Until such a data base is developed, interpretation concerning trade, migration, or even use of specific

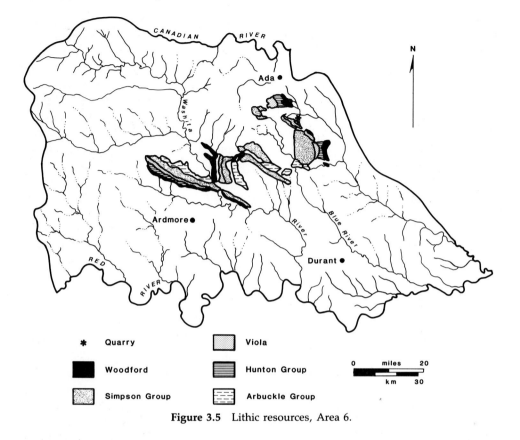

Figure 3.5 Lithic resources, Area 6.

localized outcrops for any given site must be performed on a site-by-site basis, and even then interpretations must be qualified.

The chert in the Frisco formation can be easily confused with specimens of Arkansas novaculite if the site examined is in reasonable proximity to both formations. The Frisco materials near Fittstown may occur in color ranges almost approximating novaculite, but most of the Frisco colors probably result from weathering. In general, the Frisco types are "pale yellow and cream to a light mottled red, gray, and white" (Banks 1973:11). Amsden (1961:25) briefly describes the Frisco chert as "locally present mostly in the form of small light colored vitreous nodules but with some elongate bands up to one-foot thick."

In 1958 Amsden discusses *Hunton Chert* and reports chert materials as "present in parts of the group and locally abundant in some formations" (Amsden 1958:20). Chert is present in varying quantities in the Ideal Quarry, and Keel, Cochrane, Bois d'Arc and Frisco units. Amsden (1958:181) describes the Cravatt member of the Bois d'Arc as 15.24 m thick and containing nodules of chert and beds of chert "2–8 inches thick." The cherts are "brown weathering, partly tripolitic and partly vitreous." He describes the chert in the Cochrane member of the Chimney Hill formation as "irregular nodules and slightly elongated lenses. Light in color but in places almost black. Cochrane chert is common on the Lawrence uplift" (Amsden 1958:45). It is rare in the central Arbuckles but is common in western areas.

The type locality for the Woodford chert is in the vicinity of the town of Woodford. In the Arbuckles, the terms *shale* and *chert* are used interchangeably by geologists in reference to the formation. The Woodford is much more extensive in the Arbuckles than in the Ouachitas, but even here the nature and description of chert in the formation is not well described in geological literature. The southeastern flanks of the Arbuckles that seem to represent the major chert areas are in the headwaters of Boggy Creek and Blue River; consequently, archaeological materials from chert gravels obtained from these streams in the lower parts of their drainages could be easily misinterpreted as derived from the western flanks of the Ouachitas.

Area 7

The Ouachita Mountains of southeastern Oklahoma are the most geologically complex system in Oklahoma in terms of lithic resources (Figure 3.6). Although the same basic formations extend in a roughly linear pattern from west to east, except for that portion east of Atoka that arches to the north before trending eastward, the differences of depositional facies within the formations combined with the complex folding and faulting present difficulties in formational correlation. The two principal geologic groups of the area, the Stanley and Jackfork, are also quite similar lithologically. They both are composed primarily of massive beds of hard quartzitic sandstone with intervening beds of black and often siliceous shale and with chert stringers whose materials are easily confused. It is probably impossible to identify the large numbers of artifacts from sites in the area made from the quartzitic sandstone as being from the Stanley or Jackfork unless the site in question can be specifically related geographically to one group or the other. The cherts in the Stanley and Jackfork, which usually accompany black shale deposits, tend to be quite similar in color, texture, and diaphanousness. Micropaleontology is essentially useless in attempts of identification because of the absence of fossils; trace-element analysis is too costly and time consuming and possibly would not distinguish between the materials any better than would simple comparative analysis; and petrographic analysis on the purer types has little more to offer than does comparative analysis.

With few exceptions, the chert formations of the Ouachita Mountains are poorly exposed under natural conditions. Even where good exposures do occur in bluffs adjacent to stream cuts, the lenticular beds are highly fractured and quite brittle. In the few limestone deposits that contain chert, such as the Wapanucka–Chickachoc and portions of the Pinetop, the chert is not so badly fractured but is so tightly embedded that extraction is difficult. The poor ex-

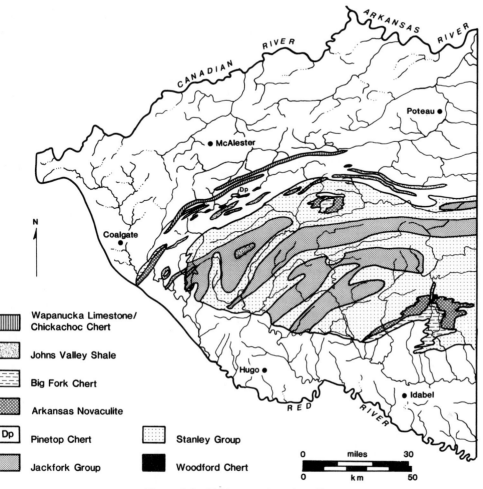

Figure 3.6 Lithic resources, Area 7.

posures result from a combination of the geologic character of the formations, the terrain, and ground cover.

The Ouachita Mountains consist of a series of ranges and individual ridges within the ranges that extend generally in an east–west direction. From Atoka to Hartshorne, however, the ridges and valleys of the western edge of the system are oriented in a more northerly direction at an average of north 45° east. The ridges and valleys are produced by laterally compressed, folded, and warped strata made up predominantly of hard resistant quartzitic sandstone and shale beds of various thickness. Individual beds within the ridges more often than not occur with dips in excess of 50° from horizontal. Because of the near vertical dips, the chert stringers or zones within the formations are also steeply dipping, with very small areas of surface exposure. Even here the ground cover is usually heavy. The thin colluvial soil, detrital rock, and the oak–hickory–pine humus combine to obscure the thin outcrops. Because of the strike and dip of the formations and the brittle and fractured nature of the chert beds, "quarrying" is a generally ineffective method of chert exploitation. The most conducive areas to obtain knappable stone for tool production seems to be in shale formations such as the Caney (Delaware Creek), Johns Valley, and Markham Hill formations, where redeposited boulders occur or in stream and terrace gravels.

The principal chert formations in this area are concentrated in four specific areas: (1) Black Knob Ridge along the western flanks of the Ouachita Mountains. (2) the Winding Stair Range across the northern part of the area, (3) the unique geological feature of the Potato Hills in the northcentral part of the area, and (4) the southeastern portion of the Ouachita Mountains in the central Little River basin of McCurtain County. Within three of the four areas, the Big Fork chert and the Arkansas novaculite formations are the principal chert producers, although the chert beds themselves are highly fractured. The novaculite occurs in larger and more massive beds near the Broken Bow dam site (Rock Pile Mountain) than they do elsewhere in the Ouachitas of Oklahoma. The Woodford and Pinetop cherts occur only in the Winding Stair Range. The Woodford crops out in seven extremely small areas scattered along the crest of the Winding Stair Range from southeast of Pittsburg eastward to Bengal, and the Pinetop is exposed in only two of those areas. The bedded chert is so badly fractured that manufacture of sizable dart points, knives, and other artifacts is prohibitive. When chert fragments can be found weathering out on the surface of the normally steep slopes, the drift can be traced upward to where it began. Even arduous excavation at that point is often fruitless. Perhaps it should not come as a surprise that there are no known "quarries" as such in the area.

As of this writing, the known variability in the chert types is inadequate for the Woodford formation. Thomas Amsden and Robert O. Fay (personal communication, 1982) have expressed informed opinions that the chert is relatively uniform in type. In the Ouachitas it occurs as thin dark gray to black strata interbedded with gray and black fissile shale. Some of the boulders of chert reported by Banks and Winters (1975:35–37) as the Woodford and redeposited in the Caney Shale are now known to have been derived instead from chert beds within the Arkansas novaculite (a lateral equivalent of the Woodford) and redeposited in the Johns Valley Shale.

The late Paleoindian and Early Archaic groups in the southern Ouachita areas and along the Red River seem to have had a preference for the variety of chert types in the Johns Valley Shale. The Pinetop chert that occurs in the Johns Valley is often referred to in geological literature along with the Woodford chert, and the two types occur in the same localities, such as that of Pinetop west of Ti. The Pinetop chert occurs in tightly embedded lenticular masses, from which small solid pieces suitable for bifacial production are difficult to obtain. T. E. Hendricks (1947:Sheet 1) describes the Pinetop chert as "40 feet of chert that is mostly white and light gray [which] weathers brown and very porous." Collections made from the Pinetop in the summer of 1982 include mottled light-blue-gray opaque types that closely resemble some of the "Boone" or Keokuk types from the Ozarks and a high grade of yellowish brown and blue-gray semitranslucent varieties that have been referred to by others (Don Wyckoff, personal communication, 1982) as *Zipper chert*. The Pinetop and Woodford formations are the two chert units of the most limited extent and probably are the most poorly exposed chert units in the Ouachita Mountains.

Because of the absence of quarry areas, obtaining the best-quality materials from the Ouachita formations would seem to have been almost totally fortuitous except for finding concentrations in stream deposits. The possibility does exist that our present-day knowledge is inadequate for understanding the locational procedures used by prehistoric folk in obtaining the larger and better chert resources, which certainly existed in certain areas. Orville D. Hart (1963:25–26) records exotic cobbles of bedded chert in the Markham Hill formation. The chert is defined as "black with a $\frac{1}{4}$ to $\frac{1}{2}$ inch thick rinds [sic] of a white color." He compares boulders of chert and flint of 4×4 feet dimensions with those up to 7 feet in diameter in the top of the Wesley described by Shelburne (1960), and suggests that they came from the same original source. Hart offers no suggestions for the original source of the boulders, but they would most logically have been derived from the older Woodford–Arkansas Novaculite, Pinetop, and Big Fork deposits. It has not been demonstrated that such large boulders occur persistently throughout the formations, but neither have the locations been limited to specific areas.

One of the most distinctive cherts of Area 7 is the Battiest chert, a name suggested by Orville Shelburne (1960:18) for the thin beds in the Ten Mile Creek formation of the Stanley group. This 15.24-cm-thick bed of chert was called the *Smithville lentil* by C. W. Honess (1923:192). In contrast to other types in the area such as the Big Fork, the Battiest exhibits tiny hairline fractures filled with white quartz veins. It has a waxy to vitreous luster on fresh surfaces, and it often contains spicules and radiolaria. Outcrops of the Battiest chert occur about 800 m south of Old Ringgold on the west side of Little River and near the Pine Creek confluence with Glover River, but they do not exhibit evidence of having been quarried. The Battiest is not easily confused with the Chickasaw Creek chert (also from the Stanley group) because of its denseness and color, although weathered pieces may be similar. The Chickasaw Creek type is a dull gray to black chert that occurs in 1–2-foot-thick (30–60 cm) zones with individual beds of 2–3 inches (5–7.6 cm) (Hart:1963:18). This material is infrequently represented in archaeological sites probably because of its generally splintery rather than conchoidal fracture. Orville Shelburne (1960:31) compares the Chickasaw Creek chert to the Wesley cherts in general appearance. Also he (1960:41–43) refers to the presence of "spicular chert" in the lower Atoka formation.

East of Atoka in Black Knob Ridge the Big Fork chert, Arkansas Novaculite, and Woodford chert were mapped in cross section from west to east by T. A. Hendricks (1947). But the Woodford is not recognized in the area by later investigators. Thomas A. Hendricks (1947:Sheet 1) describes the chert of the novaculite formation as "green, brown, and gray novaculite in beds ranging from 1 inch to 1 foot thick." At Black Knob Ridge the novaculite is so badly fractured that sizable pieces of workable stone are almost impossible to obtain from the outcrops. The brown Big Fork chert is the least fractured of the two chert units at Black Knob Ridge, but its brittleness and the near vertical dip of the chert (exposed in the westernmost edge of the Highway 3 and 7 roadcut) would have made aboriginal exploitation of this particular outcrop inaccessible, or at least less than desirable. Northward from Atoka, the Big Fork exhibits a more laminated structure along with increasingly brittle, fracture patterns. The Big Fork formation produces the distinctive chert locally called *Stringtown Flint* from the ridges located at Stringtown. However, the banded shades of gray exhibited on archaeological specimens of the chert are a result of weathering. Unweathered chert occurs in shades of light to chocolate brown. Hendricks (1947) also refers to chert fragments and nodules in the Missouri Mountain shale and Polk Creek shale and boulders in the Johns Valley shale southeast of the Ti Valley and Pine Mountain Faults.

The Wapanucka limestone and Chickachoc chert are lateral equivalents and can more or less be considered as a single unit, although they are differentiated in places by Hendricks (1947:Sheet 1). The cherts in the units are probably the least known or the least recognizable chert types in the Ouachitas. Examination of both units south of Pittsburg reveal that both types are very brittle but, of the two, the Chickachoc is more highly fractured whereas the chert lenses in the Wapanucka are so tightly embedded that removal of selected pieces is nearly impossible. In this locality the Chickachoc is a laminated grayish brown, which weathers to a reddish brown. A small single rock from the unit was a lighter buff color. The rock is brittle and highly fractured. The Wapanucka varies from a light to medium blue-gray to almost black in color. The numerous spicules cause mottling, which makes the Wapanucka chert closely resemble one or more of the varieties of the Keokuk chert from northeast Oklahoma. In small pieces the two different cherts would be easily confused. However, the Wapanucka has a more earthy luster, poorer conchoidal fracture and, in close examination, frequently contains carbonate rhombs, which sparkle in the light. The outcrops of both units are poorly exposed under natural conditions for purposes of chert exploitation.

The Big Fork chert is perhaps best described in the literature by C. W. Honess (1923:74–79), by Charles B. Spradlin (1959:20–26) from outcrops on the Mountain Fork River and by B. W. Miller (1955:11–14) for the Potato Hills area. Spradlin (1959:46) also gives what may be the only description of chert in the Blaylock Sandstone as "chert, red, flinty; in 2-inch beds" at a depth of 3 m below the top of the exposure. The chert from the Blaylock has not been referred to archaeologically, either because of its limited use or nonuse, or because it has not been recognized. In the Big Fork chert outcrop a short distance northeast of the Woods Mound group at Broken Bow Lake, Honess (1923) describes several distinct varieties in the Big Fork chert that are not similarly described elsewhere by himself nor by any other geologist.

Although the actual chert outcrops and stream gravels of the various formations represented in the Ouachita Mountains were unquestionably used in varying degrees by prehistoric inhabitants of the area, the nonchert formations of the Johns Valley shale and the Markham Hill member of the Jackfork appear to be the most likely candidates for production of the highest-quality cherts. In the 1982 investigations by the New World Research Institute at the Bug Hill site at Sardis Lake, a wide range of chert and quartzite types of superior quality and size have been found in the Johns Valley outcrops in close proximity to the Bug Hill site. At least two of the outcrops appear to have been "quarried" along natural exposures. The cherts and quartzites occur in boulder sizes. Past examinations for quarried sources in the chert formations of the Ouachitas appear to have been fruitless because the actual chert beds were much less desirable and accessible than the eroded shales. This geological paradox is logically explained by the fact that exotic boulders of predominantly Arkansas Novaculite, Woodford, Pinetop, and Big Fork chert and quartzites were removed from their parent formations and were redeposited in the younger shale beds prior to the intensive deformation associated with the Ouachita orogeny that left the *in situ* cherts so badly fractured. The shale matrix around the boulders served as a buffer to the fracturing. Based upon preliminary results, production of the larger chert artifacts in the Ouachita Mountains seems to have come from these shale rather than chert formations.

The largest single area of the Johns Valley shale is located in the northcentral and northeast portions of R16E, T1S, and in the adjacent township-range corners to the northeast. Smaller exposures occur east of Atoka in T2S, R12E, and sporadically across the northern Ouachitas from southeast of the Ti community eastward to Stapp. The larger area of the Johns Valley exposures represent the best potential areas of examination for locating places that show evidence of prehistoric quarrying in the Ouachita Mountains.

In addition to cherts in this area, two specific nonchert types, the Hatton Tuff and the Colbert Creek diorite, were principal sources of raw material for manufacture of polished celts. The Hatton Tuff occurs sporadically throughout McCurtain County and an almost unlimited quantity of tuff cobbles are common in Glover Creek, on Little River above the Pine Creek Dam, and in the middle Mountain Fork. The diorite occurs in an extremely limited exposure some 6 m thick and some 800 m in length. The diorite sill, intruded into the Womble schistose sandstone, is described by Honess (1923:210) and Banks and Winters (1975:33). The name *Colbert Creek diorite* was proposed by Banks and Winters for purposes of distinction. An important characteristic of this sill is the fact that the outcrop is so massive that it is difficult to obtain individual pieces small enough to be effectively utilized. Small amounts of drift do occur in Colbert Creek.

Siliceous shales from the Stanley and Jackfork formations were also a source of lithic materials for manufacture of celts, dart points, and ornamental artifacts such as Archaic gorgets and Caddoan earspools (Banks and Winters 1975:26–27). Quartz crystals of unusually large sizes are available throughout the Ouachita Mountains. Flakes from quartz crystals commonly occur in sites of the area, and occasionally complete bifacially flaked dart-points and unifacially flaked arrow-points occur. Quartz crystal was also used as pendants and apparently as fetishes of some sort.

Summary

The lithic materials of Oklahoma had wide influences on cultural developments not only in Oklahoma but in adjoining states. It can be assumed that in the Caddoan periods, and especially in the Gibson aspect, certain lithic materials were used as trade goods or for economic contributions into a larger system outside the Arkansas and Red River drainages. A worthwhile research project would be to document whether or not Oklahoma lithic materials are present at Cahokia, Illinois, or Etowah, Georgia, as they are at the George C. Davis site and other Texas and Louisiana sites.

On March 12, 1981, a 1-day workshop on lithic caches was held at the University of Oklahoma; this produced discussions of some 23 caches from a five-state area. The caches varied from large completed bifaces, preform bifaces, unmodified large flakes, and small dart or arrowpoints to large "tested" blocks of chert. A number of the caches were from nonsite proveniences and were found "accidentally." The James Hemming cache from near Carnegie, Oklahoma, was perhaps the most interesting in terms of anthropological interpretation. The cache contained materials from the: (1) Florence chert, Kay County quarries, (2) Foraker chert, (3) Edwards Plateau of Texas, (4) Grandfalls chert from northeast Oklahoma, (5) Alibates chert (from near Amarillo, Texas), and (6) Obsidian (probably from Jemez, New Mexico).

This cache amplifies the need for additional research into the functional role of economic development in prehistoric cultures. Obviously, the individual(s) represented by the cache was involved in an extensive trade network. Another interesting but not surprising aspect of most of the other caches from Oklahoma is that they also consisted predominantly of Florence, Grandfalls (Keokuk), Tahlequah (Peoria), Arkansas novaculite, and Frisco cherts. It is too much of a coincidence that the major chert types from known quarries in the state are represented by the cached materials.

As other chapters in this volume clearly illustrate, the archaeological resources of Oklahoma are as richly diversified as those of any other state in the United States. They possess the potential physical remnants of evidence necessary for us to reconstruct and understand the dynamic systems through which all prehistoric cultures developed in response to the varied environmental conditions they lived in and exploited. The relationship between cultural development and the natural resources is the essential ingredient in understanding the theory of economic progress in any of the societies involved. Of all natural resources that still possess the potential of providing physical evidence to the intangible aspects in socioeconomics, no others come closer than do the chert resources. Chert is probably the single item of material culture most common to and taken for granted in all the archaeological sites. It is also the single material item that has been associated with people longer than any other. In American archaeology attempts to identify and understand lithic resources stand out as one of the earliest concerns of archaeology. W. H. Holmes (1919), for example, devoted a major publication to this element of material culture, but no other contribution equaling or substantively complementing or altering his work has been attempted since that date. Given this antiquity of association with people and with archaeologists, it is surprising that we do not understand the relationships between this all-important item of material culture and the socioeconomic development of prehistoric societies better than we do. Having available lithic resources sufficient to meet any prehistoric society's needs was tantamount to continuation of the life of the society itself. Yet, there are few, if any, references to chert or any of its varieties in the major texts on economic anthropology.

One could argue that the relationship between the multiple varieties of chert in quality and unlimited quantities and the advanced cultural developments in eastern Oklahoma was no coincidence. Other environmental factors were certainly involved and possibly to a greater extent, but the abundant lithic resources cannot be ignored in the reconstruction of cultural development. This is not the place for a detailed discussion on the subject, but mention is warranted of the status in which chert resources were viewed by various Indian groups as recorded in ethnographic sources. With few exceptions, the availability of chert was usually attributed to being a gift of a divine or mystical nature. Afton Springs in northeast Oklahoma is one of the few known sites in the United States that provides physical evidence suggesting use of the springs as a shrine by a flint knapper or knappers in recognition of the "gift" of chert.

The Hydrologic Atlas produced by the U.S. Geological Survey, Oklahoma Geological Survey, and the Oklahoma Water Resources Board will soon be completed for the entire state. Along with the use of these critical base data, it is also recommended that technical terminology be standardized, Folk's (1965) classification as modified by McBride and Thomson (1970) is perhaps the best basic system to use. The practice of assigning new names totally unrelated to the source of geologic origin should be eliminated for type materials previously "unknown" to those involved in archaeological research. If the types cannot be accurately identified, it is probably more beneficial to other researchers to place such materials in an unidentified category. The role of lithic resources should be reexamined from more anthropological (socioeconomic) rather than from archaeological paradigms. In many cases "selectivity" of certain materials is perhaps better explained by an institutional ceremonialism approach (Ayres

1962:155–176) rather than the traditional archaeological approach based solely on physical properties of the materials and the lithic technology. Valid interpretations of ceremonialism associated with lithic technology from archaeological evidence is indeed a challenge but one that should not be ignored. Lauriston Sharp's presentation (Sharp 1968:341–353) of the role of the stone axe in the Australian Yir Yoront society is a provocative study in attempting to understand the role of a lithic material in any primitive society. Did selected lithic resources in Oklahoma play a role in socioeconomics similar to those in Australia among the Yir Yoront?

The role of the lithic industry (selectivity, procurement, exploitation) in the development of socioeconomics of prehistoric cultures in Oklahoma is one of relatively untapped research potential, but first the raw materials must become as well known to and understood by researchers as they were to the prehistoric folk who used them. There is absolutely no substitute for familiarity with all the chert-producing formations in any given area for accurate lithic identifications and sound anthropological interpretations of their use. There is also no substitute for the use of comparable collections in identifications. Other methods of analysis, such as petrographic, X-ray florescence, and trace-element activation are certainly useful tools in refinement of source areas, but these are only possible after controlled comparative collections have been made.

The past decade or so of achaeological research in Oklahoma has seen a significant increase in the raw materials data base. However, the associated models that have been prepared to explain their use have essentially been concentrated on aspects of lithic technology related to reduction techniques. Until models based on socioeconomics related to the lithic industry are developed and tested, it is likely that the potential for fully understanding cultural developments throughout Oklahoma prehistory will be restricted.

Reference Note

The classification of chert materials developed by Robert L. Folk (1965) and modified by E. F. McBride and A. Thomson (1970) is recommended as a standard for chert studies. Occasional alterations may be required, such as Roger Bowers (1975:24) and Mark A. Sholes (1978:61) point out, but McBride and Thomson provide the best petrographic classification of chert available today. Igneous and metamorphic cherts do occur elsewhere, but the known chert types in Oklahoma are of diagenetic though sedimentary origin. Folk classified all types of sedimentary micro- and cryptocrystalline silicates (flint, agate, chalcedony, jasper, novaculite, etc.) as varieties of chert. Use of this system should serve as the needed unifying element for future lithic studies in Oklahoma. Other references relied upon for preparation of this chapter are Robert O. Fay and John Robert's Oklahoma Geological Survey contributions in the 12-region series by the Oklahoma Water Resources Board; J. A. Taff (1928), Thomas W. Amsden (1958), and R. W. Harris (1957) for the areas of the Arbuckle and Wichita Mountains; Orville B. Shelburne, Jr., (1960), L. M. Cline (1960), Orville D. Hart (1963), C. W. Honess (1923), Mark A. Sholes (1978), whose dissertation is the best technical study of the Arkansas novaculite available, and Thomas A. Hendricks (1947) for the Ouachita Mountains; and George G. Huffman (1958) for the Southwestern Flanks of the Ozarks. For references to actual quarry sites, the sources of C. N. Gould (1898, 1899), W. H. Holmes (1919), and Waldo R. Wedel (1959) are used.

Acknowledgments

I appreciate the many people in Oklahoma and adjacent states who have encouraged and helped develop my personal interests in lithic resources, and I especially thank Joe Winters who has accompanied me on many trips and shared his knowledge of lithic resource locations; Dr. Melvin Marcher, U. S. Geological Survey; Dr. Thomas Amsden, Dr. Robert O. Fay and Dr. Ken Johnson, Oklahoma Geological Survey; Dr. Mark A. Sholes, Montana College of Mineral Science and Technology; Professor Jack Hughes, West Texas State University; Quintus Herron and Gregory Perino, Museum of the Red River; Professor Robert E. Bell, University of Oklahoma; Dr. Don G. Wyckoff and Larry Neal, Oklahoma Archaeological Survey; Lee and Mary Good, Tulsa, Oklahoma; Don Dickson, Arkansas Archaeological Survey; Tom Witty, Martin Stein, and John Reynolds, Kansas Historical Society; Dr. Dennis and Jeanne Stanford, Dr. Waldo and Mildred Wedel, and the late Dr. Clifford Evans, Smithsonian Institution. All these individuals, as well as many others, have contributed to my knowledge in many different ways. I hope in some small way this chapter benefits them.

My family—Billie, Stephanie, Nathan, and Rachel—have all contributed to my ability to pursue a career and my personal interests, often at their expense. My son, Nathan, has often assisted me with field collections and he helped with preparations of the figures for this report. These have been prepared for final printing by Mary Goodman of the Oklahoma Archaeological Survey and I appreciate her special talents. I also appreciate the continued support of my Corps of Engineers supervisors, Dr. Walter Gallaher and Mr. Barry Rought.

This chapter, was typed and initially edited by Suzanne McEntire, Toni Trapp, and Pamela Kirchoff, Word Processing Center of the Southwestern Division Office, Corps of Engineers. I appreciate their hard work and continuing patience.

CHAPTER 4

Early Specialized Hunters

Marshall Gettys

Introduction

Archaeological manifestations of early specialized hunters are largely confined to the western part of the United States, in particular the Greater Southwest and the Plains. In other areas, the economy of early peoples was apparently more eclectic, and in general the archaeological manifestations of these people are termed *Archaic*. In Oklahoma, sites left by the early specialized hunters have been found only in the western portion of the state (Figure 4.1).

Three sites relating to the earliest of the specialized hunters, the elephant hunters, have been reported in the state. The Domebo site (Leonhardy 1966b) and the Cooperton Mammoth site (Anderson 1975b) are single-component sites that have both been excavated relatively recently; they have been well dated and are well understood. However, the finds near Frederick, Oklahoma were reported some years ago, and both the context and the dating of this site have remained controversial (Cook 1927, 1928, 1931; Evans 1930a, 1930b; Gidley 1926; Gould 1926, 1929; Hay 1928, 1929; and Spier 1928). Other finds related to the elephant hunters have been made in relatively isolated contexts, the most significant of which is a cache of choppers and blades found near Anadarko, Oklahoma (Hammatt 1970). Finds of single, isolated Clovis points have been reported by Saunders (1978) and Bell (1948:151).

The later periods of the early specialized hunters, the bison hunters, are represented mostly by surface finds. However, the Nall site, reported by Baker, Campbell, and Evans (1957), has yielded a large concentration of artifacts related to this period.

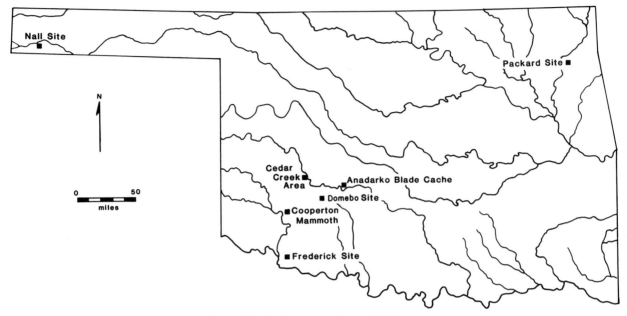

Figure 4.1 Early hunter sites in Oklahoma.

The projectile points of the early bison hunters are generally well made and stylistically unique. Thus they are easily recognized and frequently reported in the literature, often as isolated surface finds. Although such reports do little to add to the specific knowledge concerning the early hunters, numerous reports of "finds" of these distinctive projectile points in combination with a few documented sites does allow for at least a projection of the geographic range of the people involved.

The occurrence of these points has been noted from virtually the entire state. Although most of the finds have been in the western portion of the state (Bell 1948, 1954, 1955; Baker, Campbell, and Evans 1957; D. T. Hughes 1978a), finds have also been reported from the southern portion (Bell 1957a, 1957b), the northern portion (George 1978), and the northeast portion (Bell 1977).

The Elephant Hunters

The Cooperton Mammoth

Although no chipped-stone tools were discovered with the Cooperton Mammoth, there can be little doubt that this site represents the earliest archaeological manifestation in Oklahoma. The association of people and mammoth is based on three aspects of the site: (1) the presence of green-bone fracture, (2) the presence in the immediate vicinity of large stones that do not normally occur in the strata in which the mammoth was found, and (3) the arrangement of the mammoth bones themselves.

Green-bone fracture is a distinctive form of fracture and is easily recognized. Bell (1967:9) noted this fracture in his initial report on the mammoth and Bonfield (1975) elaborated on the process. Although it is impossible to estimate the time required for the bones of the mammoth to lose their green-bone fracturing properties, Bonfield does note that the sediments in which the mammoth was buried were insufficient to produce such fractures regardless of how long the properties might have been retained.

Four lithic artifacts were uncovered in the same unit as the mammoth, a unit that is described as a "sandy reddish-yellow deposit, largely clay or with small inclusions. The pebbles are generally less than two centimeters in diameter" (A. D. Anderson 1975a:145). The largest of the artifacts weighs 8.6 kg (19 pounds) and could hardly be mistaken for one of the natural pebbles. Two of the artifacts have areas that appear to have been battered. One has had two flakes removed (although this may have been by natural causes) and the remaining specimen is an unmodified cobble. All four specimens are granite, a material not particularly amenable to reflecting human workmanship at a simple level.

The stacking of bones is discussed by Mehl (1975:167) as one form of evidence for human association with the Cooperton Mammoth. Although the stacking of the bones may have been the work of scavengers or predators, several combinations of skeletal elements do not seem natural. For example, fragments of scapula were found resting on the skull, some 61 cm (2 feet) above the bone bed.

Relatively little is known of the hunters of this early period. The stones at the Cooperton Mammoth site appear to be associated with the production of bone tools rather than with a non–projectile point kill site. Although the existence of a non–projectile point kill technology would not be unique, the presence of the bone-exploiting tools without any indication of a kill is unique in the literature dealing with these early sites.

The lack of hunting tools at the Cooperton site has led to some interesting speculation about the economic aspects of these early people. If indeed the site is a "chance" bone quarry where these early people happened on a dead or nearly dead mammoth, what was their customary quarry when engaged in hunting? If the economic basis of the people at this period was more diversified than that of the later (12,000 B.P.) mammoth hunters, then the more eclectic economic base of the Archaic culture to the east may have a greater time depth than previously supposed.

The dates associated with the Cooperton Mammoth are not out of keeping with the growing acceptance of the early dates for the entry of man into the New World (Table 4.1). Lorenzo (1978) has reviewed some of the earliest sites in both North and South America with dates that range from 12,600 to 40,000 years ago. More than half the sites reviewed are older than the Cooperton Mammoth dates of approximately 18,000 B.P.

Table 4.1

Radiocarbon Dates for Early Hunter Sites in Oklahoma

Laboratory number	Site and provenience	Date before present (B.P.)	Date (B.C.) based on 5568 half-life	Date (B.C.) based on 5730 half-life	Reference
Gx-1214	Cooperton, tooth plate	19,100 ± 800	17,150	17,723	A. Anderson 1975b
Gx-1215	Cooperton, long bone	17,575 ± 550	15,625	16,152	A. Anderson 1975b
Gx-1216	Cooperton, rib	20,400 ± 450	18,450	19,062	A. Anderson 1975b
TBN-311	Domebo, untreated tusk	4,952 ± 304	3,002	3,151	Leonhardy and Anderson 1966
SM-610	Domebo, lignite wood	10,123 ± 280	8,173	8,477	Leonhardy and Anderson 1966
SM-695	Domebo, wood	11,045 ± 647	9,095	9,426	Leonhardy and Anderson 1966
SI-172	Domebo, bone organics soluble in 2N HCl after initial 2% NaOH	11,220 ± 500	9,270	9,607	Leonhardy and Anderson 1966
SI-175	Domebo, humic acids extracted after decalcification	11,200 ± 600	9,250	9,586	Leonhardy and Anderson 1966
OX-56	Domebo, organic earth	9,400 ± 300	7,450	7,732	Leonhardy and Anderson 1966
R-1070/4	Packard, firepit	9,406 ± 193	7,456	7,738	Wyckoff 1967c
Tx-2190	Perry Ranch, bone	7,030 ± 190	5,080	5,291	Saunders 1976

The Domebo Site

The Domebo site is the oldest site in Oklahoma that can be directly related to other sites of the same tradition, namely the *Llano complex*. This complex is named for the Llano Estacado or Staked Plain, where the type site (Blackwater Draw Locality Number One) is located. Domebo can be considered a typical Llano Complex site in (1) the occurrence of Clovis fluted points and (2) the local topography at the time of the kill that gave the hunters an advantage over the large creatures they hunted. Various other fluted projectile points occur generally in the eastern United States; however, most of these have not been directly related to the Llano complex. The styles of these projectile points are different from the typical Clovis fluted, which is diagnostic of the Llano complex.

The hunters of the Llano complex were apparently very specialized, hunting principally mammoth and taking other game only when mammoth were not available (Wendorf and Hester 1962:166). Apparently the preferred species was Columbian mammoth. At the Domebo site, however, the larger species, Imperial mammoth, was taken. Obviously the taking of such large game required rather sophisticated knowledge of the elephant and its habits. The people of the Llano complex developed mammoth hunting to an art with their pattern of exploitation eventually becoming almost as diagnostic as their distinctive fluted projectile points. The pattern typically utilizes local topographic situations and surface conditions to place the hunters at the advantage.

The utilization of an arroyo provided the hunters with the advantage of height. Another common method was to drive the mammoth into a swampy area where the hunter could maneuver and the mammoth could nct. Wendorf and Hester (1962:166–167) describe the basic pattern as camping near a body of water in a camp site with a good view and then dispatching the animals as they came to water. They noted that mammoths and later bison were killed in this manner.

Retallick (1966:8) postulates that the Domebo kill site may have been swampy at the time of the kill, but Leonhardy and Anderson (1966:25) are undecided as to the nature of the surface at the time of the kill. The exact nature of the kill surface is not as significant as the fact that the mammoth was apparently placed at a disadvantage by the hunter's exploitation of a swampy bottom area to slow the beast down and an arroyo to provide some protection to the hunters.

Artifacts found at the Domebo site include a series of projectile points and tools found in direct association with the mammoth. A second series consisting of a single point and several other tools was found downstream from the skeleton, but these are believed to have been associated with it at the time of the kill. One broken and two complete projectile points were found in direct association with the skeleton. The two complete specimens and a nearly complete specimen found downstream from the mammoth have been classed here as Clovis points, although Leonhardy and Anderson (1966:20) note that one of them is actually more Plainview-like in overall morphology.

Non–projectile point artifacts include only five specimens, three of which are unmodified waste flakes, one of which is a utilized flake, and one of which is a side scraper. The side scraper was found downstream from the mammoth, but because it was made of identical material to the artifacts found in association with the mammoth, it is considered to have come from the kill. The specimen is interesting in that it is made on a blade or bladelike flake typical of the Llano complex. Green (1963) and Hester, Lundelius, and Fryxell (1972:92–97) have discussed the distinctiveness of the blade technology in the Llano complex.

Six radiocarbon dates were obtained for the Domebo Mammoth site. With two relatively predictable exceptions, the dates are virtually identical to those obtained for the Llano complex sites in the Southwest. The average of the four apparently uncontaminated dates is 11,200 B.P. All six dates for the Domebo site are given in Table 4.1.

Anadarko Blade Cache

Hammatt (1970) has reported one of the more interesting finds in Oklahoma, a cache of blades and choppers found near Anadarko, Oklahoma. The find included 26 blades, 4 large cores, and 2 flat discoidal chopping tools. Although the find is isolated and cannot be directly dated, it has been tentatively assigned to the Llano complex based on typological similarity to the tools found in that complex, particularly the use of the blade technique (Hammatt 1970:151). The occurrence of core choppers and discoidal tools is not common in the Llano complex, however.

"Finds at Frederick"

The "finds at Frederick, Oklahoma," reported in the 1920s, present one of the more intriguing problems in Oklahoma archaeology. If these finds are as early as they appear to be, they represent one of the first finds of early man in the New World and one that has for the most part been grossly overlooked by the chroniclers of the history of early man. The circumstances and the prevailing attitude of the day prevented the immediate acceptance of the finds as a legitimate association between people and Pleistocene animals. During the 1924–1926 period, investigations were carried out briefly in the vicinity of Frederick, Oklahoma, by Charles N. Gould and others. They had learned of a gravel deposit that reportedly yielded numerous bones of Pleistocene animals and human artifacts. Although the first find of artifacts is not reported in detail in the first of many articles dealing with the site, the nature of artifacts discovered and the associated animals are listed. The artifacts are seven metates, three arrowheads, and one bead (Gould 1926:92). The associated animals from the bone bed were identified as including ground sloth, camel, peccary, and mastodon, but also three other elephants, some of which may have been mammoth (Gould 1926:92).

The association was questioned by several individuals, including Leslie Spier (1928), who argued for a later deposition of the archaeological material with the earlier faunal material, and O. F. Evans (1930a:476) who also argued in favor of a similar mixing. In September, 1928, a second artifact find was made and the specimen was kept in place by the owner of the gravel pit until it could be viewed by anthropologists and geologists from the University of Oklahoma. As with one of the first Folsom points found in Colorado, this lithic specimen had been removed from the ground and only the original mold of the specimen remained. One of the former skeptics, Leslie Spier, was sufficiently convinced of the association that he considerably softened his stand on the association of people and Pleistocene animals at the site, not without a word of caution, however. Although numerous articles were published concerning the finds, they have been virtually ignored in later summaries of early man studies and appear to have been last noted in a review of early man by Sellards (1940:400–402).

The fauna found with the artifacts (if indeed the association is legitimate) is now known to be commonly associated with the Llano complex. Many of the species noted above occur at Blackwater Draw Locality Number One (Hester *et al.* 1972:226–230). Of course, the primary problem rests on the association of the tools and the fauna. In this light, the statement by Leslie Spier concerning the second find seems most relevant:

> There can be no doubt that the artifacts occur in the pit near the basal portion, on the same level as the fossil remains. An examination of the undisturbed face of the pit, immediately above the position of the finds, showed unbroken, nearly horizontal strata above it. There is no evidence of gullying at this point, whatever may have been the case with respect to the other finds. As the case stands, it looks very much as though the artifacts are of the same antiquity as the fossil animals. At the same time it would be well to reserve final judgement until we are certain that the artifacts are not secondary inclusions. It must be borne in mind that the artifacts are of a distinctly modern type and their occurrence with an early Pleistocene fauna is incongruous when considered in the light of Old World finds. (Hay 1929:94)

Obviously Spier remained conservative in his support. Had the proponents of the finds been pushing for a date in the vicinity of 12,000 years ago instead of a date several times that figure, however, the Frederick finds might have been better received.

Isolated Surface Finds

Isolated surface finds have been reported for several areas in the state, including the Oklahoma panhandle and northeast Oklahoma. Saunders (1978:35) reports a single Clovis point from Cimarron County in possible association with a lithic scatter designated Ci-118. Another Clovis point from the panhandle has been described by Bell (1955:4). A classic Clovis point has been reported by Bell (1977:9) from Tulsa County in the northeast portion of the state.

The Bison Hunters

The hunters of extinct bison can be divided into two groups for the purposes of this discussion: the Folsom hunters and the Plains bison hunters. The Folsom hunters followed the Clovis mammoth hunters and are generally found in the same area except for the far Southwest. The Plains bison hunters are found principally along the eastern edge of the Rockies, extending along the western edges of the Plains. Both groups are characterized archaeologically by very distinctive projectile point forms. The Folsom point is a fluted form, whereas the Plains hunter's types are a series of well-flaked lanceolate or parallel-sided points with several basal forms. The unusually fine workmanship of these points makes them most distinctive as well as very popular with collectors, thus isolated surface finds tend to be reported more often than isolated finds of other artifact types.

Folsom Bison Hunters

No Folsom sites have been excavated in Oklahoma. Such sites have been excavated in the adjacent states of Texas, New Mexico, and Colorado. Surface finds of the distinctive Folsom points have been reported from all areas of the state except the southeast quarter. Baker, Campbell, and Evans (1957:2) have reported a single Folsom specimen from the Nall site in the Oklahoma panhandle. Farther to the south in Caddo County, Folsom specimens have been reported found along Cedar Creek (Bell 1948:151) and in other localities. The Dan Base collection (Bell 1954) contained 10 Folsom points from Caddo County. From the southernmost portions of the state, two Folsom points have been reported, one from Comanche County (D. T. Hughes 1978a:5–6) and one from Marshall County (Bell 1957a:2).

Two recent reports of Folsom specimens are most interesting because they extend the range of such specimens in an unexpected eastward direction. The first of these is a find reported by George (1978:10–12) for north central Oklahoma and the second was reported by Bell (1977:9) for Tulsa County, farther yet to the east. It is interesting to note that the Tulsa find was highly polished and in the same collection as several other highly polished early projectile points. Similar collections of highly polished specimens covering great spans of time in the same spring deposits have been discussed at length by Haynes and Agogino

(1966:817–820). This is not to say that all the specimens reported by Bell (1977:9) came from a single spring, but rather that the polish on specimens of such age is not an unusual occurrence.

Plains Bison Hunters

The Nall site is a blowout area that began to form during the "dust bowl" days of Oklahoma in the 1930s. It is the best-reported site in Oklahoma relating to the Plains bison hunters. It was not until the erosional process had been operating for some time and considerable soil removed that the remains of the early bison hunters began to be noted in the late 1930s and the early 1940s. From 1937 until 1955, a total of 826 artifacts was recovered, only 74 of which were waste flakes (Baker, Campbell, and Evans 1957:2).

Named projectile-point types related to the Plains bison hunters include Midland, Agate Basin, Hell Gap, Scottsbluff, Eden, Frederick (Irwin and Wormington 1970:26–27), Firstview (Wheat 1972:125), Plainview (Bell 1958a:74–75), and Milnesand (Sellards 1955:339) (Figure 4.2). A notched form, Simonson, has also been reported with extinct bison (Frankforter and Agogino 1959) and most recently Willey *et al.* (1978:64–65) have reported a type (Rogers side-hollowed) that has elements of several of these types and the earlier Clovis and Folsom types.

Of the 243 projectile points found at the Nall site that were complete enough for accurate description and assignment to a rough temporal period, only 54 can be reasonably assigned to origins other than the hunters of extinct bison. Thirty-seven of these 54 projectile points are dart points that could not be typed, 15 are small arrow-points of the types generally attributed to the late occupations of the Plains, and 2 are Clovis points, a type discussed above.

Some of the projectile points of the Nall site can be directly related to the named types noted above. With the 54 exceptions also noted above, however, all the projectile points from the site appear to have been in the tradition of the Plains bison hunters. In particular, the Milnesand type is separated from other types; several specimens classed as Plainview with oblique parallel flaking may well be Frederick points; two specimens are noted as suggesting the Eden type (based on a pronounced medial ridge and flaking pattern); and one specimen described and pictured in Baker, Campbell, and Evans (1957:10, Plate 3D) may be Agate Basin. Reexamination of the actual specimens may result in classification of even more specimens from the site in more recently defined types.

A wide variety of non–projectile point lithic artifacts were recovered from the Nall site. Although it is impossible to place them into a well-controlled chronological scheme, as can be done with the projectile points, it seems reasonable to assign the bulk of the artifacts to the hunters of extinct bison. Several classes of artifacts defined by Baker, Campbell, and Evans (1957:11–15) have nearly exact counterparts in the tool types defined by Irwin and Wormington (1970:28–30).

Figure 4.2 Typical early hunter points of Oklahoma. (a,c) Clovis (Terry Nowka collection, Caddo County), (b) Clovis (Skeen collection, Marshall County), (d) Folsom (Hemming collection, Caddo County), (e) Folsom (Skeem collection, Marshall County), (f,g) Agate Basin (Terry Nowka collection, Caddo County), (h) Frederick (University of Oklahoma collection, Kay County), (i) Frederick (Terry Nowka collection, Caddo County), (j) Scottsbluff (University of Oklahoma collection, McCurtain County), (k) Frederick (Hemming collection, Caddo County), (l,m) Meserve (University of Oklahoma collection, McCurtain County), (n) Milnesand (Terry Nowka collection, Caddo County).

This includes two types of gravers, one form of end scraper, and three types of side scrapers. Numerous other tool categories are very similar, but because the respective authors have stressed different criteria in their definition of tool types, the categories do not match as well as those noted above.

Isolated points have been reported from around the state. Bell (1955:4–5) reports six projectile points from western Oklahoma of the types related to the early specialized hunters. Five of these projectile points appear to be types associated with the hunters of extinct bison, although only one can be reasonably linked to a specific type (Specimen 6, which is probably a Frederick point, one of the most recent types associated with the early specialized hunters).

A much more interesting find is a group of early points reported from Tulsa County (Bell 1977:9). Two of the points appear to be typical examples of the Scottsbluff and Eden types, respectively, and are the easternmost examples of these types thus far reported for Oklahoma.

Summary

With the exceptions of the excavations at the Domebo site, the Cooperton Mammoth, and the Anadarko Blade Cache, there have been no excavations in Oklahoma concerned solely with early specialized hunters. Much of this is the result of historical accident; namely, that the great majority of the archaeological work in the state has been done in conjunction with various federal projects that have thus far been concentrated in the eastern portion of the state.

One of the most interesting areas that could be investigated with current Oklahoma data is the variety of problems concerning the relationship of the early specialized hunters (generally a western manifestation) to the early Archaic cultures (generally an eastern manifestation). Although present views of these two groups have been greatly distorted by the historical development of early people research (namely, that kill sites were excavated principally in the west and camp sites were excavated principally in the east), there do seem to be valid differences among the earliest cultures in North America. One of the likeliest places to study the differences between the two cultures would be in locales where the two met, and Oklahoma is such a locale. Several sites from the eastern portion of the state have produced "early specialized hunter-like" projectile points in what are generally considered to be Archaic contexts. At the Packard site, projectile points were recovered that were classed as Agate Basin (Wyckoff 1964a:52), and several other points recovered from the lower levels of the excavations relate to early cultures. At the Bell site, Wyckoff (1968b:45–47) describes several projectile points that fit well into the types described for the early specialized hunters and he even classifies one of the specimens as a Plainview point. More significant than the specific information these sites produced is the fact that the material remains of the earliest cultures can be found in the eastern portions of the state and that the potential is great for research that addresses the problems of early specialized hunter–Archaic relationships.

One of the most pressing problems in the study of early specialized hunters is that of typology. Wheat (1972:152) has noted that several early point types are commonly confused, such as San Jon with Eden–Scottsbluff, Firstview with Milnesand, and Plainview with anything not easily typed as something else. At Hell Gap, the oldest complex was named the *Goshen complex* because the authors did not wish to have their Plainview-like material confused with the abused Plainview taxon (Irwin-Williams *et al.* 1973:46). Closer to home in the Texas panhandle, the Rex Rogers site has produced two projectile points that have features in common with the Clovis, Plainview, and Folsom types, and in the same site, three specimens were found that have been termed *Rogers side-hollowed* but which resemble Simonson, San Patrice, Hardaway, and Dalton (Willey, Harrison, and Hughes 1978:65–66). In Oklahoma, the Nall site is a typical example of the "dumping" of specimens typologically into an artifact taxon, in this case the Plainview type. Detailed analysis of the projectile points from Oklahoma and from the Nall site in particular would do a great deal to alleviate some of the confusion regarding some of these early types.

Generally, the study of the early specialized hunters in Oklahoma suffers from the same problems as the study of early specialized hunters in general: the lack of excavated sites close enough together to develop consistent typologies and chronological controls from site to site and region to region so that other problems can be researched. Oklahoma has manifestations closely related to many of the well-known early complexes of the Plains and the Southwest. However, because the links in Oklahoma are based almost exclusively on surface finds, statements that do more than note the range of these complexes in Oklahoma are tenuous at best. Although the data from the early cultures are sparse in Oklahoma at this time, the potential for research in this time period in Oklahoma is great. Sites have been found from the earliest portion of the period (such as the Cooperton Mammoth) to the latest portion of the period (such as the Nall site), and although surface finds are not abundant, they are sufficient to indicate that the sites do exist.

CHAPTER 5

The Foragers: Western Oklahoma

David T. Hughes

From the very earliest human arrivals to the modern occupants, intensive collection of a wide range of plants and animals (*foraging*) to supplement the regular diet has played a role in the local economy of western Oklahoma. Foraging was the most important activity between the end of the Wisconsin glaciation, when the Pleistocene megafauna became extinct, and the beginnings of agriculture, which brought with it some control over the food supply. This foraging period, often referred to as the *Archaic,* may have begun by about 7000 B.C. and lasted until the start of the Christian Era, or as late as A.D. 500. Within this period, only three sites in western Oklahoma have been extensively excavated: the Boat Dock site (Bell 1958b), the Gore Pit site (Bastian 1964; Hammatt 1976), and the Summers site (Leonhardy 1966a). Three radiocarbon dates have been obtained from the Gore Pit site and one from the Summers site (Table 5.1). Archaic sites that hve been intensively surveyed, collected, and reported but not tested include the Pumpkin Creek site (Wyckoff and Taylor 1971), the Clay and Roberts sites (Saunders 1974b), the Ross site (Hofman 1971), Cd-177 (Hofman 1973b), and the Nall site (Baker *et al.* 1957) (Figure 5.1). The following surveys produced other reportedly Archaic sites: Mangum Reservoir, with 18 sites in Greer County and 14 in Harmon County (Wyckoff 1963c); Arkansas Louisiana Gas Company Pipeline, with 104 sites in 9 counties of central and western Oklahoma (Saunders *et al.* 1972); Crutcho and Soldier Creek Development Project of Oklahoma County, with 5 possible Archaic sites (Lopez 1972); Soil Conservation Service Watershed Protection projects, with 50 possible Archaic sites distributed throughout 19 western Oklahoma counties (D. T. Hughes 1977a).

Two complexes have been identified for the Archaic of western Oklahoma: The Lawton aspect, originally defined in 1960 (Shaeffer 1966:62–86), and the

Table 5.1

Radiocarbon Dates for Western Forager Sites in Oklahoma

Laboratory number	Site and provenience	Date before present (B.P.)	Date (B.C.) based on 5568 half-life	Date (B.C.) on 5730 half-life	MASCA corrected date (B.C.)
GX-2009	Gore Pit (Cm-131) Upper Feature 3	7100 ± 350	5150	5303	—
GX-1558	Gore Pit (Cm-131) Lower Feature 3	6145 ± 130	4195	4379	5080 ± 140
	Gore Pit (Cm-131) Lower Feature 3	6030 ± 130	4080	4261	4990 ± 140
GaK-694	Summers site (Gr-12) Hearth area 2	2770 ± 150	820	903	968 ± 160

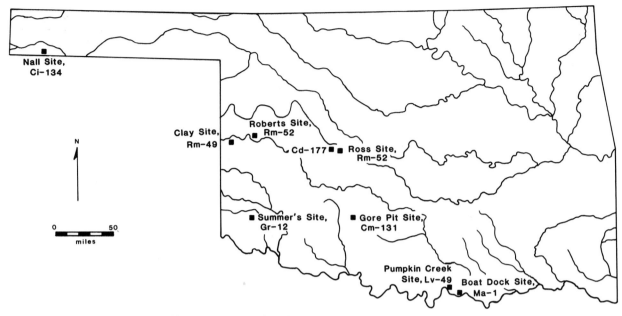

Figure 5.1 Sites of Archaic foragers in western Oklahoma.

Summers complex (Leonhardy 1966a). Gettys (1976), Hofman (1978d), and Hammatt (1976) have commented upon and offered some syntheses of Archaic data for the region.

Forager Complexes

The Lawton Aspect

Extensive surface collections from central and western Oklahoma sites, where local quartzites were the dominant lithic material used in tool manufacture, were the basis for the proposal of the Lawton aspect. Quartzite is considered "a tracer element for the complex" (Shaeffer 1966:63). The sites are normally located on ridge tops or on ridge slopes just below the crests. The Lawton aspect is divided into three temporal phases and two regional foci. The earliest phase, Phase I, characterized by hammerstones, scraper–planes, choppers, curved knives, flint Plainview, and Milnesand points, may be related to the Clear Fork focus of Texas. Quartzite is the dominant material for tool manufacture during the intermediate phase, Phase II, but the tools are smaller and more varied than in Phase I. During late Phase II, a shift to greater use of flint occurs but the scraper–plane and chopper continue as basic artifact forms.

The eastern division of the Lawton aspect, the Little River focus, centers around the Little River in Cleveland County and is marked by a greater use of flint. Characteristic artifacts include a heavy knife, thin, wedge-shaped manos, some Paleoindian-type projectile points, miscellaneous quartzite points, and scraper–planes. The Altus focus, the western division that centers around Lake Altus, is characterized by occasional use of local flint, flint points similar to those of the Eastern Archaic, boatstones, thick manos, and solitary specimens of small adzes, biface oval knives, and scraper-gouges. Clear-Fork-type gouges have been found throughout the Lawton aspect (Shaeffer 1966:65). No radiocarbon dates have been obtained for sites attributable to the Lawton aspect, so precise temporal boundaries cannot be drawn for the phases assigned.

The Summers Complex

Test excavations at Gr-12 in Mangum Reservoir (Leonhardy 1966a) produced a large amount of flint and quartzite artifacts, some bison bone, and hearths. Ogallala quartzite (also called Ogallala chert, Potter chert, and Potter quartzite) was the dominant tool-manufacturing material but there was some use of Edwards chert, Alibates chert, and Tecovas jasper. It is worth noting that the one radiocarbon date obtained from Feature 1 (Table 5.1) was from a very small sample (2.3 grams) and Leonhardy considers the result to be the "maximum age for the site" (Leonhardy 1966:30). The radiocarbon date and the unusual assemblage of artifacts lead Leonhardy to suggest that a new complex be defined. Basic traits for the complex include projectile points similar to the named types Marshall, Lange, Gary, Ensor, Marcos, and Bulverde. Also present are thin oval knives, bifacial Ogallala quartzite implements that may have served as knives, cortical flake and cobble scrapers, Clear Fork gouges, choppers, scraper–planes, gravers, thin grinding slabs, handstones of naturally shaped rock, simple circular fire pits, and small, stone-filled cooking pits. The Summers complex people apparently specialized in hunting bison.

Excavated and Reported Sites

Space limitations prevent more than a brief sketch of other excavated and major reported surface collected sites, eight in all. A check list of artifact styles from each, and the Summers site (Gr-12) is given in Table 5.2.

Excavations were conducted at the Boat Dock site (Ma-1) in 1954 (Bell 1958b). This multicomponent site in the Lake Texoma area may have been used intermittently as a camp site for a long period of time. The Carrollton and Elam foci of Texas may be included among the probable Archaic occupations (Bell 1958b:47).

Table 5.2

Trait Lists for Selected Reported Archaic Sites and Sites with Archaic Components from Western Oklahoma

	Gr-12	Ma-1	Cm-131	Rm-49	Rm-52	Lv-49	Ci-134	Cd-177	Cd-69
Arrowpoints							X		X
Lanceolate points							X		X
Expanding-stem points	X	X	X			X	X		X
Contracting-stem points	X	X	X				X		X
Notched points	X	X	X				X	X	X
Miscellaneous knives	X		X				X		X
Oval knives	X								X
Gravers	X						X	X	
Scrapers	X		X			X	X	X	X
Flake scrapers	X								X
Utilized flakes	X			X	X	X		X	X
Scraper–planes	X		X						
Clear Fork gouge	X	?	X				?	X	
Drills		X				X	X		
Preforms						X			
Prepared manos									X
Prepared metates									X
Grinding stones	X	X	X						X
Grinding slabs	X	X	X						
Celt									X
Hammerstone		X		X	X	X			X
Choppers	X								X
Cores		X		X	X	X			X
Flaked cobbles				X	X	X			X
Nearby lithic source				X	X	X			X

The Gore Pit site (Cm-131) originally contained about 30 charcoal stained concentrations of burned and angular broken rock (Figure 5.2) (Bastian 1964; Hammatt 1976). The area also produced several small concentrations of burned mussell shell. Features 1, 3, and 6, rock middens about 2–3 m (6–8 feet) in diameter, were underlain by at least one concave layer, each of powdery charcoal. A scatter of burned rocks to the north and west of all three features contained small blocks of fibrous charcoal and small quantities of burned mussel shell and bone. These could have been used as earth ovens for food preparation (Hammatt 1976). There are insufficient mussel shells present to indicate that they were associated with all 30 rock middens. No artifacts were found in direct association with the features but surface collections from the area include Trinity, Ensor, Darl, Ellis, Gary, Meserve, Frio, and Abasolo projectile point types. The raw material for all artifacts was predominantly Ogallala quartzite. One slightly flexed, east-oriented burial was found at the Gore Pit site. One radiocarbon date from the apatite fraction of the rib bones (Table 5.1) was obtained. Because this date is about 1000 years earlier than the other dates from the site,

Figure 5.2 Workers from the Museum of the Great Plains excavate one of the burned-rock features at the Gore Pit site. (Photograph courtesy of the Museum of the Great Plains, Lawton, Oklahoma.)

Hammatt (1976:267) proposed that the charcoal dates are more reliable for determining the site's age.

Controlled surface collections were made from the Clay and Roberts sites (Rm-49 and Rm-52) and are reported by Saunders (1974b). Both sites are located at outcrops of gravels rich in quartzite and chert. Detailed analysis of the artifacts and debris indicated that the primary purpose of the occupations at both sites was to obtain and prepare lithic materials. The principle activity was the production of blank flakes from cobbles. There were also some preparation of preforms and possibly some bone and wood working (Saunders 1974:105).

The Pumpkin Creek site, located near outcrops of quartzite and chert gravels, was extensively collected (Wyckoff and Taylor 1971) and yielded projectile points resembling Milnesand, Plainview, Meserve, Dalton variety Greenbriar, Ellis or Darl, and perhaps Scottsbluff, and Eden. Two varieties of drills were identified at the site and one of these may have been made from a Meserve-like artifact. Activities at the site may have included hunting, meat or hide processing, and perhaps bone or wood cutting and scraping (Wyckoff and Taylor 1971:45). The Pumpkin Creek site is probably a single-component site occupied between 7500 B.C. and 5000 B.C.

The Nall site is a multicomponent site in an open deflation area. Surface collections from the site indicate that an Archaic component is present (Baker, Campbell, and Evans 1957). Projectile points include the types Clovis, Folsom, Plainview, Meserve, Milnesand, Angostura, and several triangular stemmed and notched dart points. Several of the reported scrapers resemble Clear Fork gouges (Baker, Campbell, and Evans 1957:Plate 5 A, B, F, and G).

A detailed technological analysis of extensive surface collections from Cd-177, a single-component site, was conducted by Hofman (1973b). Two gravel outcrops on the site produced quartzite and chert, and Ogallala quartzite is the dominant lithic material used on the site. The majority of the Ogallala flakes have prepared striking platforms, which may have been necessary to produce usable flakes from the tough material. Three-fourths of the flakes without prepared platforms were decortication flakes, suggesting that these were not considered important for use to the people working the material. Flaking techniques probably included both hard and soft hammer percussion as well as pressure flaking. Activities at the site probably included hunting (indicated by the presence of one Ellis dart point and one unidentifiable point fragment), preparation of meat, hides, and vegetable matter, and perhaps woodwork for handles and shafts.

The Ross site (Cd-69) is a multicomponent site collected and reported by Hofman (1971). Artifacts include Fresno, Scallorn, Reed, Trinity, Rockwall, Williams, Gary, Hell Gap, Agate Basin, and seven unidentifiable point fragments. The site may have served as a hunting station or camp for Archaic hunters using the Gary, Trinity, and Williams points, with an occupation during the 2000 B.C.–A.D. 500 range (Hofman 1971:114).

Artifacts and Technology

Perhaps the only thing common to all Archaic-related sites reported for western Oklahoma is the predominant use of quartzite, specifically Ogallala quartzite, for tool manufacture. Because the use of quartzite is a characteristic of the Lawton aspect, many sites that produced little other than a few quartzite cores and flakes have been assigned to the Archaic. The use of quartzite alone, however, does not merit this Archaic assignment as quartzite use occurs in later sites. Tool varieties found on over half of the Archaic sites discussed above are expanding and contracting stemmed dart-points, notched dart-points, gravers, utilized flakes, Clear Fork gouges, hammerstones, and cores. Of these, the only ones that would probably not be found on sites of earlier or later foragers would be the varieties of dart points, Clear Fork gouges, and perhaps the gravers. The Clear Fork gouge is one of the few, if not the only, easily recognizable tool type other than a projectile point that is characteristic of the Archaic and appears to have a wide distribution in Western Oklahoma (Hofman 1973b, 1977a).

The projectile-point forms from the Pumpkin Creek site seem to indicate that the earliest foraging cultures in western Oklahoma were derived from the preceding big-game hunting groups. The association of some lanceolate points of the Plano styles with good foraging assemblages could therefore mark the beginning of the Archaic stage in western Oklahoma. The wide range of tools from most of the sites suggests that the Archaic peoples had a highly varied diet. Bison and deer were apparently hunted and freshwater mussels were collected. Although little evidence for the use of small game has been found, this does not preclude its possible contribution to the subsistence base.

On sites that have produced sufficient diagnostic artifacts to indicate their Archaic nature, there is a tendency for local quartzites, specifically Ogallala quartzite, to have been the dominant material used for tool manufacture. Whether such usage was through necessity or preference cannot be determined without more information. Hofman's study of the lithic technology suggests that the techniques used were well adapted to the chipping of this somewhat intractable quartzitic material.

Virtually no work has been done on the settlement technology of the Archaic foragers of western Oklahoma. As Shaeffer noted (1966), most of the sites tend to be on the tops and sides of ridges. The majority of sites studied were short-term multipurpose sites where activities from the initial reduction of lithic resources to the production and use of tools occurred. The only special activity sites for which much information is available are lithic workshop sites (Saunders 1974b).

Summary and Conclusion

It is difficult to conclude much with such sparse data as are available for western Oklahoma. There have been few attempts to utilize the concept of the *Lawton aspect* since its original definition, and there seems to be an unspoken consensus among archaeologists currently working in Oklahoma that it is of little or no use. Therefore, perhaps the Lawton aspect and its related definitions and assumptions should be discarded. It is important to note that the assumptions the concept has made must also be abandoned, especially those related to the quartzite–Archaic interrelationships. If the use of quartzite is indeed a temporal marker, it can only be shown through careful study of sites containing good datable materials.

Although the *Summers complex* has been used no more than the Lawton aspect since its definition, it is potentially more useful because it is based on a campsite that produced a single component and a radiocarbon date. It is important to note that the date for Gr-12 is considered the *earliest possible* date, so that we might be finding components of the Summers complex at later times than at Gr-12.

The area covered in this report represents over half the total land surface of Oklahoma, and the time of the Archaic foragers spans nearly 60% of the time mankind has been known to be present in the state. Despite this, we know less about the time period and area discussed here than we do for almost any other time period and region in the state. There was trade going on with the peoples of the Texas panhandle and the Edwards Plateau, indicated by the presence of flints from these areas, but only more research can give us clues to the nature, importance, and duration of this trade. Only after we understand the character of the exchange networks will we be able to interpret ways and means by which ideas and goods were transported within and across Oklahoma during the time of the Archaic foragers.

CHAPTER 6

The Foragers: Eastern Oklahoma

Don G. Wyckoff

Introduction

From nearly 8000 to 2000 years ago, eastern Oklahoma was inhabited by hunt-ing–gathering people. In contrast to their Paleoindian ancestors, these later hunters usually made side- or corner-notched, unfluted spearpoints with which they killed such modern game as white-tailed deer, elk, turkey, and raccoon. In addition, plants and plant-processing implements were more important to these people than to the earlier Paleoindian bands. Because they practiced hunting and gathering for over 300 generations, these later hunting–foraging people might appear unchanging and dull. But these were dramatic times. Far to the north–northeast, the last vestiges of a continental glacier were melting away. North America was warming, and ice-age distributions of plants and animals were changing markedly. Although unglaciated, Oklahoma also underwent cli-matic and ecological change. During the Holocene, as this postglacial period is known, Oklahoma's plants and animals attained their historic distributions. Given the Holocene changes in economically important plants and animals, eastern Oklahoma's foraging people undoubtedly altered their tool kits and their hunting–gathering practices during their long presence here. For example, some 3000 years ago, neighboring hunting–gathering bands began experimenting with cultivating native plants (Chomko and Crawford 1978; Yarnell 1977). Per-haps prehistoric Oklahomans did likewise? To gain a perspective on the long heritage of these people, information on their sites, remains, assemblages, and ages was compiled and synthesized for what now comprises the eastern half of Oklahoma. This information is presented in chronological order to facilitate comparisons that help discern economic and/or social continuities, cultural change, and gaps in our knowledge.

The Study Area and the Sites

The study area is all of Oklahoma that lies east of Interstate 35, essentially the eastern half of the state's main body (Figure 6.1). Within this area, five major biotic districts are historically recognized (Blair and Hubbell 1938:Figure 1; Duck and Fletcher 1943): (1) Ozark Mountains, 11,330 km² (2.8 million acres), (2) Ouachita Mountains, 12,140 km² (3.0 million acres), (3) Osage Savannah, or Cross Timbers, 34,400 km² (8.5 million acres), (4) Cherokee Prairie, 10,120 km² (2.5 million acres), and (5) Floodplain habitats, 3000 km² (some 0.75 million acres) similar to those along the Mississippi River. The northern two-thirds of this area is drained by tributaries to the Arkansas River, whereas the southern third is part of the Red River Basin. Although thoroughly described elsewhere (see Chapter 1, this volume, by Albert and Wyckoff), this region comprises a major part of the transition between the Eastern Woodlands and the Southern Plains. Consequently, before extensive historic disturbance, the region was a veritable mosaic of prairies and woodlands whose distributions were largely determined by soils, slope, exposure, and climate. It is important to remember, however, that changes in overall temperature and/or precipitation markedly affect the extent and distribution of these grasslands and forests (Borchert 1950; Rice and Penfound 1959:604).

Our information on the Holocene hunting–gathering inhabitants of central and eastern Oklahoma comes predominantly from sites discovered during archaeological salvage programs in proposed reservoir areas. Between 1935 and 1972, 35 major lakes were built, and at least 6 others planned, along the rivers and perennial streams draining this region. Archaeological surveys and testing in these eventually flooded settings resulted in the identification of 15 sites (Figure 6.1) where relatively unmixed deposits yielded tools and trash left by hunting–gathering people. In addition, 26 other sites (Figure 6.1) yielded similar remains, but unfortunately these were commonly mixed with spearpoints, arrowpoints, pottery, and other habitation debris left by later prehistoric people. Thus, although these sites are known to have been frequented by hunting–gathering folk, they are characterized by uncertainties regarding identification of these people's tool kits, how the sites functioned in seasonal activities, and how often these people camped there.

Since 1972, major reservoir planning and construction have slowed appreciably. But due to new federal laws assuring some protection for such cultural resources as archaeological sites, the U.S. Department of Agriculture Soil Conservation Service, the U.S. Army Corps of Engineers, the Oklahoma Conservation Commission, the Oklahoma Department of Transportation, and private industry have increasingly sponsored surveys and tests to locate and preliminarily evaluate archaeological sites affected by their respective projects. This work has resulted in reporting many previously unrecorded sites. Moreover, new information has been generated about the occurrences of ancient camps and workshops along minor tributaries and in uplands. But because the testing conducted at these sites has usually been of small scale, only a few have yielded substantial clues to their functions, ages, or sequence of use by hunting–gathering people. Noteworthy examples are shown in Figure 6.1.

Besides sites affected by various kinds of construction, a few have been studied because they were perceived to contain important information on the region's past inhabitants. The Pohly Shelter, Pumpkin Creek, Roulston–Rogers, and McCutchan–McLaughlin sites (Figure 6.1) have yielded notable clues to tool kits, resource uses, site function, and the chronology of hunting–gathering people. The findings from these sites resulted largely from the interests and efforts of University of Oklahoma students and/or volunteers from the Oklahoma Anthropological Society.

The Sites and Their Ages

Implements and trash left by eastern Oklahoma's hunting–gathering inhabitants are reported for at least 80 archaeological sites (Figure 6.1). This total could be tripled if all locations recorded as containing spearpoints attributable to this period were included. But I choose to limit this synthesis to sites described in published reports and noted for their large collections, their relatively unmixed deposits, or their stratified record of habitation. This latter kind of site, exemplified by locations like 34D1-38, 34My-48, and 34Pu-58 (Figure 6.1), has yielded information needed for recognizing different material culture assemblages, for ascertaining the sequence (i.e., relative age) of these assemblages, and for identifying tool-style changes that help date similar tools from other sites. In contrast, the sites with relatively unmixed deposits (such as 34Sq-23 and 34Ch-75; Figure 6.1) are important for clues to assemblage composition, activity areas within a site, and overall site function. Occasionally, the single deposit and stratified multideposit sites have been radiocarbon dated, thus providing invaluable information about the ages of particular assemblages and the time span for hunter–gatherers in eastern Oklahoma.

One archaeomagnetic and 75 radiocarbon dates are currently reported for middens, hearths, or burials believed left by the hunting–gathering inhabitants of 13 sites in eastern Oklahoma. These dates range from 9416 ± 193 years ago (NZ-498) at the Packard Site to 793 ± 130 years ago at the Wann Site (Table 6.1). The majority (95%) are older than 1800 years ago. In fact, the more recent exceptions come from the Wann Site, a midden reportedly (Galm and Flynn 1978b: 86–89) churned by tree roots, farming, relic digging, and disturbances by late prehistoric people. If these exceptions are excluded because of their likely more recent origin, most dates for hunter–gatherer related contexts fall between 9400 and 2000 years ago.

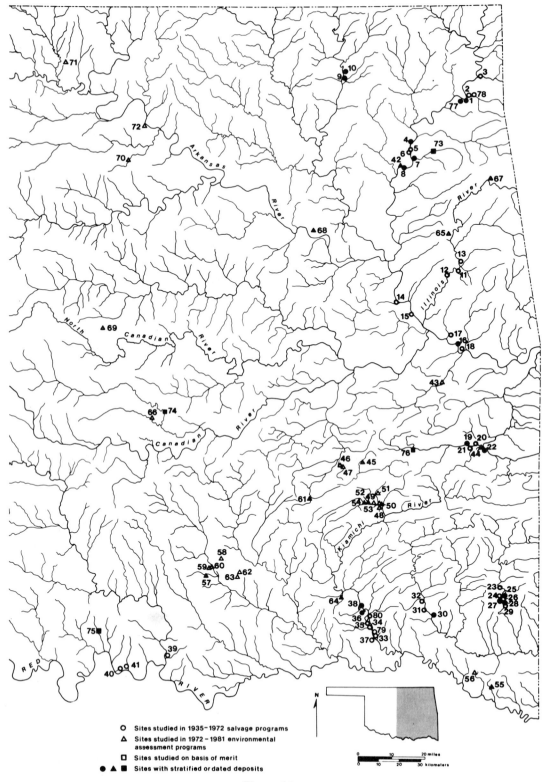

O   Sites studied in 1935–1972 salvage programs

△   Sites studied in 1972–1981 environmental
      assessment programs

□   Sites studied on basis of merit

●▲■ Sites with stratified or dated deposits

Figure 6.1

Figure 6.1 Reported eastern Oklahoma sites with Holocene hunter–gatherer occupations

1. Evans (34D1-38); Baerreis 1951:7-30.

2. Caudill (34D1-59); Baerreis 1951:30-45.

3. McConkey (34D1-21); Baerreis 1951:45-58.

4. Shetley Shelter (34My-77); Wyckoff, Robison, and Barr 1963:37-42; Wyckoff 1967c.

5. Wolf Creek (34My-72); Kerr and Wyckoff 1964:55-80.

6. Jug Hill (34My-18); Wyckoff 1964b.

7. Packard (34My-66); Wyckoff 1964a.

8. Kerr Dam (34My-48); Wyckoff 1963a.

9. Lawrence (34Nw-6); Baldwin 1969; Wyckoff 1981.

10. Craig (34Nw-2); Shaeffer 1966; 41-55.

11. Morris (34Ck-39); Bell and Dale 1953.

12. Cookson (34Ck-12); Israel 1979.

13. Vanderpool (34Ck-32); Harden and Robinson 1975.

14. D. J. Scott (34Ms-48); Schneider 1967:32-57.

15. McCulley (34Ms-50); Wyckoff and Barr 1967a.

16. Harkey-Bennett (34Sq-23); R. Burton and Stahl 1969:111-135.

17. Dickson-Haraway (34Sq-40); S. S. Burton and Neal 1970.

18. Harvey (34Sq-18); R. Burton 1971.

19. Scott (34Lf-11); Bell 1953b; Galm and Flynn 1978b.

20. Sam (34Lf-28); Proctor 1957.

21. Wann (34Lf-27); Sharrock 1960; Galm and Flynn 1978b.

22. Troy Adams (34Lf-33); Newkumet 1940b; Galm 1981:Table 14.

23. Woods Mounds (34Mc-104); Wyckoff 1967b.

24. Hughes (34Mc-21); Wyckoff 1966a:11-47.

25. Callaham (34Mc-68); Wyckoff 1966a:112-152.

26. E. Johnson (34Mc-54); Wyckoff 1967a.

27. Beaver (34Mc-1); Wyckoff 1968a.

28. Lamas Branch (34Mc-42); Wyckoff 1966a:48-111.

29. Biggham Creek (34Mc-105); Wyckoff 1965.

30. Bell (34Mc-76); Wyckoff 1968b:18-94.

31. Gregory (34Mc-98); Wyckoff 1968b:95-153.

32. Belk (34Mc-90); Barr 1966b.:45-79.

33. Mahaffie (34Ch-1); Rohrbaugh et al. 1971; Perino and Bennett 1978.

34. Montgomery (34Ch-70); Rohrbaugh et al. 1971.

35. Houchins (34Ch-75); Rohrbaugh et al. 1971.

36. McKenzie (34Ch-89); Rohrbaugh 1972b.

37. Pat Boyd (34Ch-113A); Rohrbaugh 1972b.

38. Hill (34Pu-58); Rohrbaugh 1972b.

39. James (34Br-11); Ray 1960a.

40. Boatdock (34Ma-1); Bell 1958b.

41. Buncombe Creek (34Ma-2); Wyckoff 1964c:103-140.

42. Dawson (44My-10); T. Baugh 1978.

43. 34Hs-111; Lintz 1978e.

44. Curtis Lake (34Lf-5A); Galm 1978b.

45. Tucker's Knob (34Lt-35); Neal 1974a.

46. McSlarrow (34Ps-62); Penman 1974a:117-139.

47. Blue Creek (34Ps-77); Penman 1974a:140-147.

48. Sallee G (34Pu-99); Bobalik 1978.

49. Natural Lake (34Pu-71); Lintz 1979a.

50. Blessingame (34Pu-74); Lintz 1979b.

51. Lee Kirkes (34Lt-32); Bobalik 1979a.

52. Wheeler Lee (34Pu-102); R. Vehik 1982.

53. Vanderwagon (34Pu-73); Bobalik 1979b.

54. Bug Hill (34Pu-116); R. Vehik 1982.

55. Viper Marsh (34Mc-205); Bobalik 1977b.

56. Bible #1 (34Mc-200); Hughes 1976.

57. Estep Shelter (34At-80); Hofman 1977f.

58. Graham (34At-90); C. D. Cheek et al. 1980.

59. Birch Creek (34At-163); D. T. Hughes 1977b.

60. Mousetrap (34At-175); D. T. Hughes 1977b.

61. Glasscock (34Ps-96); D. T. Hughes 1978b.

62. B. Cook (34At-40); Lopez and Keith 1976:61-63.

63. A. Henry (34At-24); Lopez and Keith 1976:40-42.

64. W. B. Kincade (34Pu-86); Lopez et al. 1979:335-336.

65. J. Woodward (34Ck-92); Lopez et al. 1979:101-103.

66. 34Sm-35; Lopez et al. 1979:451-452.

67. Brazil #1 & 2 (34D1-133-134); Lopez et al. 1979:813-816.

68. 34Wg-108; Hughes 1979.

69. Shingleton #1 (34Ln-42); Wallis 1977b:30-34, 82-111.

70. Camp Creek (34Pw-56); Wallis 1977a:25-29.

71. 34Ka-222; Wallis 1980:54-56.

72. 34Pw-63; Neal and Wheaton 1977.

73. Pohly Shelter (34My-54).; M. A. Ray 1965.

74. Roulston-Rogers (34Sm-20); Drass 1979.

75. Pumpkin Creek (34Lv-49); Wyckoff and Taylor 1971.

76. McCutchan-McLaughlin (34Lt-11); S. Baugh 1982; C. Clark 1980; Powell and Rogers 1980.

77. Smith I Shelter (34D1-55); Purrington 1971:307-353.

78. Cooper Shelter (34D1-48); Purrington 1971:401-432.

79. Burroughs (34Ch-43); Rohrbaugh et al. 1971:91-96.

80. Pate-Roden (34Ch-90); Rohrbaugh et al. 1971:12, 107-108.

Table 6.1

Archaeomagnetic and Radiocarbon Dates Reported for Deposits on Features Left by Eastern Oklahoma's Holocene Hunter–Gatherers

Sample number	Provenience	Uncorrected date before present (T ½ = 5730)	Uncorrected A.D./B.C. Date	References
Wann site (34Lf-27)				
UGa-1961	N3-W8; 55–60 cm	2148 ± 95	198 ± 95 B.C.	Galm 1981:Table 12
UGa-2073	N3-W8; 60–65 cm	1903 ± 65	A.D. 47 ± 65	Galm 1981:Table 12
UGa-2074	N3-W8; 65–70 cm	1633 ± 95	A.D. 317 ± 95	Galm 1981:Table 12
UGa-2075	N3-W8; 75–80 cm	2493 ± 90	543 ± 90 B.C.	Galm 1981:Table 12
UGa-1978	S4-E10; 70–80 cm	1468 ± 135	A.D. 482 ± 135	Galm 1981:Table 12
WSU-2007	S9-E10; 70–80 cm	1967 ± 150	17 ± 150 B.C.	Galm 1981:Table 12
WSU-1784	Test 1; 80–90 cm	793 ± 130	A.D. 1157 ± 130	Galm 1981: Table 12
Williams site (34Lf-24)				
UGa-1515	Midden; 71 cm	2055 ± 55	105 ± 55 B.C.	Galm 1981:Table 15
UGa-1516	Midden; 96 cm	1916 ± 60	A.D. 34 ± 60	Galm 1981:Table 15
UGa-1517	Post; 78 cm	1880 ± 105	A.D. 70 ± 105	Galm 1981:Table 15
McKenzie site (34Ch-89)				
Tx-1483	Level 4; 12–16 in.	1890 ± 70[a]	A.D. 40 ± 70	Valastro et al., 1977:314
Viper Marsh (34Mc-205)				
OU #1153[b]	Hearth #2		A.D. 1–100 ± 40	Bobalik 1977b:5
UGa-1128	Hearth #1	2855 ± 70[c]	905 ± 70 B.C.	Bobalik 1977b:5
Curtis Lake site (34Lf-5A)				
WSU-1723	Stratum IVa; 47 cm	1998 ± 100	48 ± 100 B.C.	Galm 1978b:Table 4; Galm 1981:Table 8
WSU-1724	Stratum IVb; 57 cm	2029 ± 100	79 ± 100 B.C.	Galm 1978b:Table 4; Galm 1981:Table 8
WSU-1725	Stratum IVb; 73–80 cm	2122 ± 120	172 ± 120 B.C.	Galm 1978b:Table 4; Galm 1981:Table 8
McCutchan–McLaughlin site (34Lt-11)				
UGa-1520	N1-W1; 48–53 cm	1915 ± 55	A.D. 35 ± 55	S. Baugh 1982:Table 1
UGa-1521	N1-W1; 93–98 cm	1945 ± 55	A.D. 5 ± 55	S. Baugh 1982:Table 1
UGa-1522	N15-W2; 98–103 cm	2200 ± 55	250 ± 55 B.C.	S. Baugh 1982:Table 1
UGa-2015	S20-E1; 35–40 cm	2250 ± 75	300 ± 75 B.C.	S. Baugh 1982:Table 1
UGa-4043	S6-W4; 35–40 cm	2410 ± 150	460 ± 150 B.C.	S. Baugh 1982:Table 1
UGa-3207	S5-W4; 80–85 cm	2465 ± 60	515 ± 60 B.C.	S. Baugh 1982:Table 1
Tx-3365	S6-W5; 75–80 cm	2480 ± 80	530 ± 80 B.C.	S. Baugh 1982:Table 1
UGa-4044	O-W4; 50–60 cm	2610 ± 145	660 ± 145 B.C.	S. Baugh 1982:Table 1
UGa-2860	O-W5; 90–100 cm	2705 ± 65	755 ± 65 B.C.	S. Baugh 1982:Table 1
Tx-3368	N7-W1; 98–103 cm	2720 ± 50	770 ± 50 B.C.	S. Baugh 1982:Table 1
Tx-3369	O-W1; 100–110 cm	2810 ± 70	860 ± 70 B.C.	S. Baugh 1982:Table 1

Lab no.	Provenience	Radiocarbon age (B.P.)	Calibrated date	Reference
Tx-3366	S6-W5; 95–100 cm	2820 ± 70	870 ± 70 B.C.	S. Baugh 1982:Table 1
Tx-3514	O-W5; 90–100 cm	2900 ± 90	950 ± 90 B.C.	S. Baugh 1982:Table 1
Tx-3812	N1-W1; 93–98 cm	2940 ± 70	990 ± 70 B.C.	S. Baugh 1982:Table 1
Tx-3370	O-W1; 110–120 cm	2950 ± 50	1000 ± 50 B.C.	S. Baugh 1982:Table 1
Tx-3367	N7-W1; 73–78 cm	2990 ± 80	1040 ± 80 B.C.	S. Baugh 1982:Table 1
Troy Adams site (34Lf-33)				
UGa-2079	Test #1; 40–50 cm	2395 ± 480	455 ± 480 B.C.	Mike Mayo, personal communication, 1982
UGa-2078	Test #1; 30–40 cm	2405 ± 80	455 ± 80 B.C.	Mike Mayo, personal communication, 1982
UGa-2081	Test #2; 40–50 cm	3060 ± 215	1110 ± 215 B.C.	Mike Mayo, personal communication, 1982
Lawrence site (34Nw-6)				
Tx-815	Feature 4; 3.3–3.5 ft.	2710 ± 70[a]	760 ± 70 B.C.	Valastro et al. 1972:477–478
Tx-817	Feature 2; 3.5–4.0 ft.	3090 ± 140[a]	1140 ± 140 B.C.	Valastro et al. 1972:477–478
Tx-818	Midden; 4–5 ft.	3150 ± 190[a]	1200 ± 190 B.C.	Valastro et al. 1972:477–478
Tx-816	Feature 10; 4–4.5 ft.	3460 ± 110[a]	1510 ± 110 B.C.	Valastro et al. 1972: 477–478
Bug Hill site (34Pu-116)				
Beta 1413	N24-E10; 50–60 cm	1930 ± 80	36 ± 80 B.C.	R. Vehik 1982:Table 2
Beta 1424	N28-W0; 90–110 cm; (Burial 7)	2175 ± 70	288 ± 70 B.C.	R. Vehik 1982:Table 2
Beta 1412	N28-E2; 40–50 cm	2185 ± 60	298 ± 60 B.C.	R. Vehik 1982:Table 2
Beta 1414	N24-E10; 60–70 cm	2235 ± 55	350 ± 55 B.C.	R. Vehik 1982:Table 2
Beta 1425	N30-W8; 40–50 cm	2340 ± 95	457 ± 95 B.C.	R. Vehik 1982:Table 2
Beta 1415	N28-E2; 70–80 cm	2490 ± 70	612 ± 70 B.C.	R. Vehik 1982:Table 2
Beta 1166	N24-E12; 65 cm; (Burial 9)	2725 ± 85	854 ± 85 B.C.	R. Vehik 1982:Table 2
Beta 1422	N16-W0; 90–100 cm (Burial 4)	2750 ± 70	880 ± 70 B.C.	R. Vehik 1982:Table 2
Beta 1416	N24-E10; 80–90 cm	2860 ± 75	993 ± 75 B.C.	R. Vehik 1982:Table 2
Beta 1421	N41-E2; 110–120 cm	2920 ± 75	1055 ± 75 B.C.	R. Vehik 1982:Table 2
Beta 1423	N28-E14; 70–80 cm; (Burial 3)	3240 ± 105	1384 ± 105 B.C.	R. Vehik 1982:Table 2
Beta 1417	N24-E10; 90–100 cm	3265 ± 70	1410 ± 70 B.C.	R. Vehik 1982:Table 2
Beta 1419	N28-E2; 110–120 cm	3300 ± 90	1446 ± 90 B.C.	R. Vehik 1982:Table 2
Beta 1418	N24-E10; 100–110 cm	3350 ± 70	1497 ± 70 B.C.	R. Vehik 1982:Table 2
Beta 1420	N24-E10; 120–130 cm	3455 ± 125	1605 ± 125 B.C.	R. Vehik 1982:Table 2

(continued)

Table 6.1 (*Continued*)

Sample number	Provenience	Uncorrected date before present (T ½ = 5730)	Uncorrected A.D./B.C. Date	References
Shetley Shelter (34My-77)				
SM-764	Burial #1; 10 ft.	3590 ± 175[a]	1640 ± 175 B.C.	Wyckoff 1967c
Wheeler Lee site (34Pu-102)				
Tx-3712	Stratum II	3234 ± 60	1284 ± 60 B.C.	R. Vehik 1982:Table 1
Tx-3713	Stratum IV	3677 ± 70	1727 ± 70 B.C.	R. Vehik 1982:Table 1
Scott site (34Lf-11)				
WSU-2002	N15-W1; 65–70 cm	2148 ± 100	198 ± 100 B.C.	Galm 1981:Table 10
Tx-2888	N15-W7; 80–90 cm; (Burial 17)	2153 ± 50	203 ± 50 B.C.	Galm 1981:Table 10
UGa-1967	N15-W7; 55–60 cm; (Burial 17)	2215 ± 115	265 ± 115 B.C.	Galm 1981:Table 10
UGa-1971	N15-W1; 50–55 cm	2215 ± 85	265 ± 85 B.C.	Galm 1981:Table 10
UGa-1972	N15-W1; 60–65 cm	2470 ± 75	520 ± 75 B.C.	Galm 1981:Table 10
UGa-1973	N15-W1; 70–75 cm	2505 ± 180	555 ± 180 B.C.	Galm 1981:Table 10
UGa-1968	N15-W7; 90–95 cm	2525 ± 85	575 ± 85 B.C.	Galm 1981:Table 10
UGa-1977	N15-W6; 110–120 cm	2745 ± 135	795 ± 135 B.C.	Galm 1981:Table 10
UGa-1974	N15-W1; 100–105 cm	2850 ± 80	900 ± 80	Galm 1981:Table 10
WSU-2005	N15-W1; 85–90 cm	2925 ± 80	975 ± 80 B.C.	Galm 1981:Table 10
UGa-1975	N15-W1; 130–135 cm	3390 ± 155	1440 ± 155 B.C.	Galm 1981:Table 10
UGa-1976	N15-W1; 145–150 cm	3668 ± 215	1715 ± 215 B.C.	Galm 1981:Table 10
Tx-2890	N15-W7; 150–155 cm	3749 ± 110	1799 ± 110 B.C.	Galm 1981:Table 10
Tx-2893	N15-W1; 150–155 cm	4048 ± 90	2098 ± 90 B.C.	Galm 1981:Table 10
WSU-2006	N15-W1; 115–120 cm	4151 ± 130	2201 ± 130 B.C.	Galm 1981:Table 10
WSU-2003	N15-W7; 165–170 cm	4161 ± 100	2211 ± 100 B.C.	Galm 1981:Table 10
UGa-1970	N15-W7; 170–175 cm	4635 ± 270	2685 ± 270 B.C.	Galm 1981:Table 10
Tx-2889	N15-W7; 120–125 cm	4728 ± 200	2778 ± 200 B.C.	Galm 1981:Table 10
Packard site (34My-66)				
NL-478	Feature 1; 120 cm	9416 ± 193[a]	7466 ± 193 B.C.	Wyckoff 1964a:89

[a]T½ = 5530.
[b]Archaeomagnetic date.
[c]T½ = 5568.

During these nearly 7500 years, most natives living east of the Rocky Mountains were nomads who used unfluted spearpoints, made basketry, increasingly used a ground-stone technology, and developed regionally specialized lifeways based on hunting, gathering, and fishing. Archaeologists traditionally describe these societies as attaining an *Archaic stage* of cultural development (J. B. Griffin 1952a, 1967; Ritchie 1932; Willey 1966:252–266; Willey and Phillips 1958:104–143). J. R. Caldwell (1958:6–18) perceives these people as slowly developing increasingly efficient technologies for exploiting forest plants and animals. However, as recently noted by McMillan and Klippel (1981), these early perceptions of gradual cultural development did not allow for the possibility of pronounced changes in the natural settings. Now that evidence for important ecological changes is accumulating (Delcourt 1979; Gruger 1973; J. E. King 1973; King and Allen 1977), the long record of hunter–gatherer adaptations is even more intriguing.

Although the Archaic cultures of eastern Oklahoma have long interested archaeologists (Baerreis 1951, 1959; Bell and Baerreis 1951:10–14, 19–27; L. Johnson, Jr. 1962; Schambach 1970; Wyckoff 1970b:82–97), cultural sequences and similarities over the area have not been substantially identified. The following pages compile, review, and speculate on what is currently known for three major segments of the approximately 7500 years attributed to this cultural period.

Early Archaic Period

During the 3500 years between 9500 and 6000 years ago, notable environmental and ecological changes occurred in regions that now support the grassland–eastern deciduous forest transition. Although deciduous forest plants and animals apparently expanded westward briefly some 11,000 years ago, grasslands began replacing woodlands in northeast Kansas some 9900 years ago, in Iowa between 9000 and 8000 years ago, in southeast Missouri around 8500 years ago, and in central Illinois some 8300 years ago (Brush 1967; Gruger 1973; J. E. King 1981; King and Allen 1977; Van Zandt 1979). Severe erosion occurred during much of this period that grasslands were expanding, and both are attributed (Anderson, *et al.* 1980:265–266; McMillan and Klippel 1981) to an interval dominated by warm, dry climate.

The Packard Complex

Presently, the only eastern Oklahoma site with isolable deposits actually dated to the early Archaic is the Packard site (34My-66) in Mayes County (Figure 6.1). Here, on a low terrace bordering Saline Creek near its junction with the

Figure 6.2 Examples of tools associated with the early Archaic Pumpkin Creek and Packard complexes.

Pumpkin Creek complex (Pumpkin Creek site, 34Lv-49): (a) Scottsbluff point reworked into end scraper; (b) base of Scottsbluff point; (c,d) Meserve-type points; (e–g) Dalton-Greenbriar variety spearpoints; (h,i) Plainview-type bases; (j) Milnesand-type spearpoint; (k) corner-removed spearpoint; (l,n) chipped bifaces (blanks for tools); (m) section of drill made from Dalton–Greenbriar type point; (o) drill; (p) quartzite chopper.

Grand River, excavations in 1962 and 1963 exposed 3.75 m (12½ feet) of stratified camp deposits (Wyckoff 1964a). Although pottery and arrowpoints were re- covered from the uppermost 60 cm, the remaining 3.3 m of silty clay contained the longest record of Archaic habitations yet found in Oklahoma. Clearly, the location was greatly favored by hunting–gathering people. Its attractiveness was probably due to its proximity to salt springs, to the cool sparkling water of Saline Creek, and to knappable Ozark cherts obtainable from the creek bed and a nearby thick bedrock exposure. The salt springs were only a few hundred yards over a slight ridge and undoubtedly attracted deer and other game sought by prehistoric hunting parties.

At Packard, early Archaic tools and trash predominated between 1.5 and 3.75 m below the surface. Initially, these remains were thought (Wyckoff 1964a:16–21) to correlate broadly with distinct soil horizons, but the observed color changes are now known to result from the silt loam alluvium being gleyed by a fluctuating water table. Although the habitation deposits were not visibly stratified, flakes and implements were concentrated at different depths; these stratified concentra- tions attest to former terrace surfaces that were briefly inhabited while being constantly alluviated.

Of particular interest are the material assemblages clustered at 3.05 and 3.65 m below the surface. The items recovered around 3.65 m (Preceramic Zone IV) include a bifacially flaked drill, 4 bifacially flaked knife sections, 7 flakes used as scrapers or knives, and a chert cobble used as a source (a core) for flake imple- ments. These items were rather scattered, thus inhibiting recognition of a partic- ular activity area; however, most seem relevant for butchering and tool mainte- nance activities. All the chipped-stone tools, plus the 540 recovered flakes, were of local Ozark cherts, principally from cobbles of the microcrystalline Reed Springs variety (Boone Formation). Although undated, these tools, the observ- able knapping practices, and the lithic preferences closely resemble those from a dated zone some 24 inches above.

This dated zone (Preceramic Zone III) was between 2.55 and 3.15 m below the surface and yielded an assemblage that can be called the *Packard complex*. Char- coal from a small, shallow firepit uncovered 3.0 m below the surface yielded a radiocarbon data of 9416 ± 193 years ago (NZ-478), making this the oldest dated assemblage in eastern Oklahoma. Recovered from around this small hearth were 4 cobbles possibly used as hammerstones, a small sandstone abrader, 1243 flakes, 2 flake side scrapers, 2 incidentally used flakes, 4 cobbles used as cores, a bifacially flaked axe, 2 parts of a biface broken while being knapped, 5 sections of bifacially flaked knives, 2 point tips, 1 side-notched spearpoint, 2 lanceolate spearpoints, and a scraper made from a lanceolate spearpoint (Figure 6.2q–y). Most of these objects occurred within 3 m (10 feet) to the west or northeast of the

Packard complex (Packard site, 34My-66): (q) Simonsen-type spearpoint; (r,s) Agate Basin-type spearpoints; (t) end scraper made from Agate Basin-type spearpoint; (u) bifacially chipped double- bitted axe; (v,w) flake knives; (x) end scraper and graver made from flake; (Y) roughly flaked biface blank for tools.

hearth, attesting to the campers' concern with flint knapping, tool manufacture, tool refurbishing, and butchering. Over 90% of the recovered chipped-stone tools and flakes were of the Reed Springs variety of Boone chert, a prevalent Ozark material. The remaining tools and flakes were also of locally available cherts. Thus, the material remains left by these early campers attest to their being regional inhabitants rather than visitors from elsewhere.

To date, lanceolate points like those from around the buried hearth are known for only a few eastern Oklahoma and northwest Arkansas sites. Similar points are reported (Wood 1963) for the lower, but undated, levels of the Breckenridge Shelter in Arkansas. Also, one such lanceolate point (in the collection of Charles Wallis, Sr., of Ft. Gibson, Oklahoma) was found on the surface along Greenleaf Creek in Muskogee County. Because other artifact associations are not well established at these two locations, recognition of a widespread *Packard phase* or *focus* seems premature.

The spearpoints and a few other implements recovered from around the 9400-year-old hearth are stylistically and technologically similar to items used by early Archaic bison hunters elsewhere on the Plains and their eastern margins. In particular, the shallowly side-notched spearpoint (Figure 6.2q) is like those found with 8400-year-old bison skeletons at the Simonsen site and with the deeply buried, 6300 to 7700 year-old camps at the Cherokee Sewer site in western Iowa (Agogino and Frankforter 1960; Anderson and Semken 1980; Anderson and Shutler 1974). In contrast, the two reworked lanceolate spearpoints (Figure 6.2r,s) and one lanceolate point rechipped to a scraperlike form (Figure 6.2t) closely resemble the type known as Agate Basin. This type is reported for 9000- to 10,000-year-old bison kills and camps in eastern Wyoming and adjacent South Dakota (Agogino 1961; Agogino and Frankforter 1960; J. T. Hughes 1949; Irwin, i967; Irwin-Williams *et al.* 1973; Roberts 1943, 1951). Besides similarities with contemporaneously used spearpoints from Iowa, South Dakota, and Wyoming, the Packard complex is characterized by knapping strategies that emphasized the production of chipped bifaces and the use of biface thinning flakes for knives and scrapers. Such practices are commonly discernible among the remains reported for the above-mentioned, distant camps and kill sites. Clearly, the ancient campers at the Packard site were people with strong ties to contemporaneous inhabitants of the Plains.

The Pumpkin Creek Complex and Other Early Archaic Assemblages

Several eastern Oklahoma sites have yielded small collections of tools and habitation debris that attest to early Archaic occupations more recent than the dated one at Packard. Notably, like Packard, these sites are characterized by spearpoints and other distinctive tools that continue to bear witness to a blending of Plains and Eastern Woodlands cultural traits.

One of the largest, most thoroughly studied such collections is reported (Wyckoff and Taylor 1971) for the Pumpkin Creek site (34Lv-49), Love County, in the southwest corner of the study area (Figure 6.1). Here, on severely eroded uplands bordering Pumpkin Creek, were found traces of a small camp and knapping workshop. Indeed, the location was most likely chosen because of exposed Cretaceous gravels (Antlers Formation) that contain many cobbles of easily knappable cherts, quartzites, hematite, and petrified wood. These cobbles were being tested, chipped into biface preforms, or, occasionally, shaped into cores used to produce flakes for cutting and scraping tasks. The recovered collection is dominated by tested cobbles, roughly chipped biface sections (broken during manufacture), cores, and flakes from initial chipping of cobbles and from biface thinning. One area, however, did yield a preponderance of small flakes produced while resharpening scrapers and biface knives or spearpoints (Wyckoff and Taylor 1971:40–43). The actual finished tools recovered here include a hammerstone, a chopper, a well-shaped chipped-stone drill, flake scrapers, flake knives, flakes with prepared graverlike tips, incidentally used flakes, a burin, spearpoints refashioned into scrapers or drills, and several varieties of spearpoints. Examples of these implements are shown in Figure 6.2. Like the Packard site, environmental conditions were not conducive for the preservation of bone, shell, or wooden implements and trash at Pumpkin Creek.

Because the Pumpkin Creek site lacked datable habitation features, our understanding of its age is mainly derived from comparisons of its stylistically distinct tools with similar ones from radiocarbon dated sites. These comparisons support the conclusion that the Pumpkin Creek site occupation is more recent than the 9400-year-old one at the Packard site. For example, two Pumpkin Creek artifacts, a spearpoint stem and a spearpoint reworked into a scraper (Figure 6.2a,b) are directly comparable to the Scottsbluff point type. Scottsbluff points are reported from camps, bison kills, caches, and even cremation burials in Wisconsin, Nebraska, Wyoming, Colorado, and New Mexico (Barbour and Schultz 1932; Frison 1978b:181–191; Hester, et al 1972; Mason and Irwin 1960; Moss 1951; Satterthwaite 1957; Schultz and Eiseley 1935). Geologic and/or radiocarbon dating for these sites rather consistently places them between 6000 and 8500 years old (Mason and Irwin 1960; Moss 1951; Neuman 1967:473; B. Reeves 1973:Table 3). Among the other time-sensitive artifacts from Pumpkin Creek are a Milnesand–Plainview point (Figure 6.2j), 2 Meserve-type points (Figure 6.2c,d), 2 sections of Plainview-type points, and 2 broken and 1 reworked Dalton–Greenbriar variety or Plainview–Golodrina variety spearpoints (Figure 6.2e–g). Also, there is a corner-removed spearpoint (Figure 6.2) that resembles the Ellis type. Although the Ellis type is common to late Archaic and even more recent prehistoric assemblages, corner-removed (expanding stem) spearpoints are known for 7000-year-old deposits at Graham Cave, Missouri, and Modoc Rock Shelter, Illinois (Fowler 1959; Klippel 1971). These same rockshelter deposits also yielded lanceolate spearpoints attributable to the Dalton type and stylistically similar to the Plainview type (Golondrina variety). Plainview, Meserve, and Milnesand points, like those from Pumpkin Creek, tend to be more common to Plains bison kills, camps, and knapping stations, but they are also known from one rockshelter midden in central Texas (Alexander 1963; Crawford 1965; E. M. Davis 1962; Dibble and Lorrain 1968; J. H. Kelley 1974; Sellards 1955; Sellards, *et al* 1947; Wheat 1974). The stratigraphy and radiocarbon dates available for these sites would largely support an age of 7000 to 9000 years ago for the use of lanceolate points like the Milnesand, Plainview, and Meserve examples found at Pumpkin Creek (Alexander 1963:513; E. M. Davis 1962:31, 94; Dibble and Lorrain 1968:29–40; C. Johnson 1974; Krieger 1957:322).

In summary, the Pumpkin Creek site represents a small camp and flint-working station used briefly sometime between 7000 and 9000 years ago. The recovered chipped-stone items consist primarily of tools made from local cherts and quartzite, but two specialized objects (a drill and a graver) are of cryptocrystalline chert that resembles material common to central Texas, some 300 km to the south. These few items may be clues to trade or perhaps even the inhabitants' range of movement. The few, but diverse, spearpoints attest to tool-making ideas shared principally with early Archaic, bison-hunting natives of the Plains. However, the presence of Dalton-like spearpoints also bears witness to ties with early Archaic inhabitants of what is now the prairie border with the Eastern Woodlands. Because this site's assemblage seems unmixed and the result of a blend of traits more common to the east and west, it is herein designated the *Pumpkin Creek complex*. Although detailed comparisons have yet to be made, similar artifacts are reported for nearby sites in Seminole, Atoka, Bryan, and Marshall counties (Lopez *et al.* 1979:451–452; Lopez and Keith 1976:54–56, 60–63; M. A. Ray 1960a; Wyckoff 1964c). Perhaps all these sites result from camping and hunting–gathering activities of the Pumpkin Creek site inhabitants.

East and northeast of the Pumpkin Creek site, several sites are reported where Dalton, Plainview, Meserve, or other early Archaic style spearpoints were found during controlled archaeological excavations. Thus, sites like McConkey, Mahaffey, McKenzie, Sallee G., Blessingame, Biggham Creek, Callaham, Hughes, and Woods Mound Group (Figure 6.1) were undoubtedly inhabited about the same time as Pumpkin Creek. Unfortunately, the shallow and mixed deposits at these sites inhibit isolating and identifying all items left by early Holocene hunters and gatherers. Although particular spearpoints, drills, and spurred end-scrapers might be recognized because of their common association with assemblages at well-stratified sites, few other implements, tool preforms, ornaments, or trash are stylistically unique to early Archaic assemblages. Consequently, early Archaic occupations are evident at several eastern Oklahoma sites, but little is known about their assemblages, activity areas, site function, or frequency of use. Questions about assemblage composition and habitation sequence are especially important for understanding the early Archaic inhabitants of sites like Hughes, Biggham Creek, and Woods Mound Group. These McCurtain County sites (Figure 6.1) yielded Plainview and Meserve points as well as examples of early Archaic point types (i.e., Dalton, San Patrice, Palmer, Kirk, and Big Sandy) that are common to sites in the Southeast (Broyles 1966, 1977; Coe 1964; DeJarnette, 1962; J. W. Griffin 1974; Wyckoff 1965, 1966a, 1967a). The common occurrence of points with Plains and Southeast ties raises the question of whether they are clues to occupations by different groups or by hunting–gathering people familiar with spearpoints typical of areas to the east and west. To date, only three sites provide some evidence bearing on this question.

Along the terrace crest at the Hill site (34Pu-58; Figure 6.1), Archaic materials were found to 1.52 m below the surface (Rohrbaugh 1972b:54–93). Spearpoints from the lowest levels consist of Dalton, Meserve, and several corner-removed forms (Rohrbaugh 1972:Table 2, Plate 12). Occurring with these were utilized flakes, biface preforms, initially knapped cobbles, cores, grinding stones, "nutting" or cupstones, hematite and limonite paint stones, and numerous flakes of quartzite, chert, and jasper. In levels above these earliest remains, occasional parts of Dalton and Kirk points occur and attest to some Southeast-derived styles being adopted by later early Archaic inhabitants. A similar situation is reported (Wyckoff 1968b) at the Bell site (34Mc-76) in McCurtain County (Figure 6.1). Here, on a terrace bordering Little River, habitation remains were found to a depth of 2.25 m. The deepest recovered spearpoint was a section of what is most likely a Plainview-type; some 30 cm above it was found a Kirk point. Unfortunately, these deepest deposits were only tested. Despite the good stratigraphic contexts to help isolate associated tools, the Bell site thus provides little further information on assemblage composition, habitation sequence, or site function within a regional settlement system. Notably, both the Bell and Hill sites have chipped-stone tools and flakes that are predominantly of locally available cherts and quartzites. Thus, they may represent remains of early Archaic groups who were adapting to local settings rather than the remains of temporary camps by wide-ranging nomads.

A similar situation is evinced by finds from Preceramic Zone II (1.5–2.4 m below the surface) at the Packard site (Wyckoff 1964a:100–102). This 90 cm zone is above, and thus later than, the 9400-year-old deposits that yielded the already-described Packard complex. Although it lacked many tools and trash, Packard Preceramic Zone II did yield scattered spearpoints, biface knives, flakes used for cutting and scraping, cores, a polish hematite cobble (tanning stone?), and a chopper (Wyckoff 1964a:90–91). The chipped-stone tools and flakes from Zone II are predominantly of locally available Ozark cherts, but their vertical distributions (Wyckoff 1964a:Tables 1–3) attest to the gradual use of more varieties. The spearpoints are all of indigenous Boone chert and include examples of the Agate Basin type (undoubtedly displaced from Zone III), the Meserve type, Dalton type, and a lanceolate section that resembles the Golondrina variety of the Plainview type (Wyckoff 1964a:Plate 9, Item 4). Spearpoints with affinities to eastern Archaic point styles occur above the specimens from Preceramic Zone II.

Early Archaic Summary

Numerous eastern Oklahoma sites have spearpoints and other distinctive tools like those common to reported sites dating from 9500 to 6000 years ago. But because few studied sites contained stratigraphically isolated deposits, little can be substantiated about local or regional assemblages, habitation sequences, settlement practices, or other adaptive practices. The best-defined and -dated habitation is the 9400-year-old one buried at the Packard site in Mayes County. Here, a small but varied collection of hunting, butchering, bone or wood working, and knapping artifacts attests to a temporary camp used by people familiar with locally available, highly knappable cherts. Designated the *Packard complex*, this assemblage also occurs at an Arkansas rockshelter and comprises the earliest occupations documented for the western Ozarks. The assemblage is especially intriguing because of its ties with very early Holocene, bison-hunting cultures reported from Iowa west into Wyoming.

Although undated, the small Pumpkin Creek site in Love County comprises our second-best source of information on eastern Oklahoma's early Holocene hunters and gatherers. Comparison of its spearpoints with those from dated sites support the conclusion that Pumpkin Creek was inhabited between 7000 and 8000 years ago. The site was a knapping station used by a small hunting party. Locally available chert and quartzite cobbles were tested, preliminarily thinned, and shaped into bifaces. The few nonknapping related artifacts attest to hunting, butchering, and working of bone or wood. The assemblage, designated the *Pumpkin Creek complex*, includes a combination of spearpoints similar to styles prevalent on the Plains and in the Southeast. Other eastern Oklahoma sites contain comparable artifacts. But, because these are made from locally different materials, the sparse collections may represent refuse of regionally different hunting–gathering bands rather than sites frequented by one band. Thus, until more information is available on assemblage compositions, socially distinct manufacturing practices, and settlement patterns, the ties between these sites and the roughly contemporaneous Pumpkin Creek site will remain clouded.

Eastern Oklahoma's early Holocene hunters and gatherers are noteworthy for apparently abundant but scattered small sites, for masterful use of local high-quality cherts in making chipped-stone tools, and for making spearpoints like those common to the Plains and Southeast. Overall, their assemblages seem similar to those of early Holocene bison hunters on the Plains. Perhaps the climatic warming and spread of grasslands during this period stimulated some Plains groups to migrate eastward and to establish hunting–gathering ranges in new settings? Unfortunately, we know nothing about what these people were hunting or gathering. Nor do we know anything about these people's appearances. Skeletal remains of these people or their prey have yet to be found, and the few studied sites have yet to yield clues to their use of plants. Thus, much is still to be learned about these people, their origins, and their lifeways.

Middle Archaic Period

Throughout the two millennia between 6000 and 4000 years ago, warm, dry conditions were prevalent over eastern Oklahoma. Consequently, prairie, or at least savanna-like, habitats existed where oak, oak–hickory, or oak–hickory--pine forests thrive today. For example, pollen findings from the Ouachita Mountains' southwest margins substantiate that grass, disturbance plants, and scattered oaks grew some 5000 years ago where oak and pine occur today (Albert 1981:Figures 26 and 31). Although climatically drier and/or warmer than today, eastern Oklahoma was a land much favored by hunting–gathering people of the Middle Archaic period.

The Grove Focus

Between 1937 and 1940, Works Progress Administration (WPA) archaeological crews working along Grand River exposed partially stratified habitation deposits in many terraces and rockshelters. The lowest, and thus oldest, remains were chipped-stone and ground-stone tools left by hunting–gathering people. After comparing the styles and classes of tools from the Evans, Caudill, and McConkey sites (Figure 6.1), Baerreis (1951) concluded that observed artifact similarities resulted from their being made and used by a western Ozarks' Archaic culture, one he designated the *Grove focus*. Moreover, because the stratified deposits afforded opportunities to study cultural change, Baerreis (1951:58–71) believed he could discern three periods of cultural development: Grove A (the earliest), Grove B, and Grove C. Gradually increasing sedentarism (due to adopting horticulture?) was proposed as the principal factor behind the observed changes. Subsequently, students of these and other Grand River Basin sites have tended to concur with Baerreis's ideas of Grove focus continuity and change (Purrington 1970:522–531; M. A. Ray 1965; Wyckoff 1963a).

Although northeast Oklahoma's Archaic sites are usually attributed to the Grove focus, this construct has become so general in nature that it and its three periods often limit research that might enhance explanations of local diversity and regional ties. For example, were all these sites frequented by hunting–gathering descendents of one society or by unrelated bands who used common implements? How do these sites relate to seasonal and local settlement practices by foraging people? How did these people adapt to the changing environmental conditions documented between 6000 and 4000 years ago? Perhaps the rich, and occasionally deep, sites usually selected for study in salvage situations have, by their nature, biased our perceptions and explanations of eastern Oklahoma's Archaic inhabitants. Given the imperfect stratification manifest at most of these sites, how can we be sure that the stylistic continuities cited as evidence for cultural continuity are not the result of subtle mixing instead? In essence, assumptions basic to the Grove focus concept are suspect. To elaborate further Archaic lifeways and continuities in eastern Oklahoma, more information is needed on specific tool kits, total assemblages, and sites used during discrete intervals of these several millennia. Therefore, I have chosen to review the available site reports in order to recognize different middle Archaic complexes rather than to assign them to broad cultural constructs such as the *Grove focus* as presently defined (Baerreis 1951, 1959; Bell and Baerreis 1951:10–14; Purrington 1970:522–531; M. A. Ray 1961a, 1965; Wyckoff 1963a, 1964a).

The Tom's Brook Complex

One distinctive assemblage is believed to be 5000–6000 years old and to comprise evidence for a continuation of tool making common in early Archaic times. The Tom's Brook complex was first recovered in the lowest levels (11–13) of the Tom's Book Shelter in northwest Arkansas (Bartlett 1963). Presently, the only reported dates are from Stratum 8 of the Paw Paw site in southcentral Arkansas: 1500 B.C. ± 140 (Tx-1549) and 4690 B.C. ± 70 (Valastro, *et al.* 1975:87). In eastern Oklahoma, this complex is identifiable at the Dawson, Pohly, Jug Hill, and Packard (Levels 6–10) sites in Mayes County; at the McConkey (Levels 3–5), Cooper Shelter (Zones 8–9), and Smith I (Zones 5–6) sites in Delaware County; at the Harkey–Bennett and Harvey (prepottery levels) sites in Sequoyah County; the Tucker's Knob Site in Latimer County; the Hughes and E. Johnson sites in McCurtain County; and at the Mahaffey, Burrough, Houchins, and McKenzie sites in Choctaw County (Figure 6.1).

The most diagnostic materials of the Tom's Brook complex are several spearpoint styles (Figure 6.3). Most prevalent are:

1. Those with smoothed expanding stems and concave bases (Johnson type).
2. Those with unsmoothed expanding stems and concave bases (such as Jakie Stemmed and Fairland types).
3. Those with side notches and a straight base (Big Sandy type).
4. Those that have side notches and a concave base (Ensor, Uvalde, Rice Lobed, Frio, Duncan, Hanna, and/or McKean types).
5. Those with broad, slightly expanding stems with straight bases (i.e., Williams, Castroville, and Marcos types).

Occasionally found with Tom's Brook assemblages are such spearpoint types as Calf Creek and Bulverde. Other implements common to these assemblages are large T-shaped drills (Figure 6.3k–l), scrapers and knives fashioned from broken spearpoints (Figure 6.3e–f), large thin flakes with prepared cutting or scraping edges, occasional choppers, roughly flaked blanks (for future spearpoints or knives), and cores for making flakes for tools. As in early Archaic times, the ground-stone tools seem limited to a few grinding stones and "nutting" or

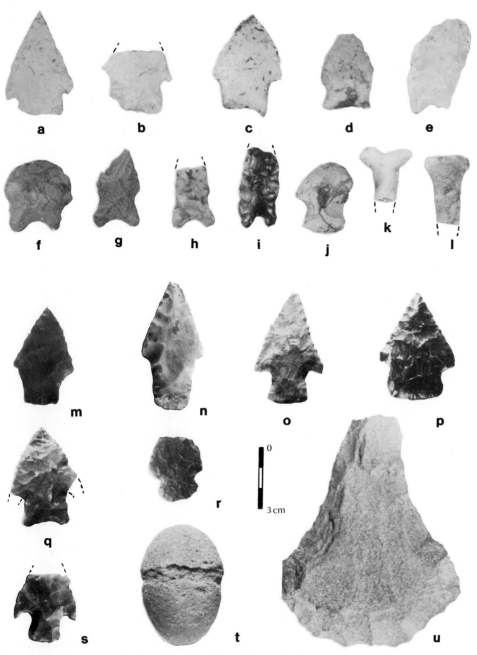

Figure 6.3 Examples of tools associated with middle Archaic assemblages.
Tom's Brook complex (Dawson site, 34My-140): (a,b) Castroville-type spearpoint; (c,d) Johnson-type
spearpoints; (e,f) scrapers made from Johnson-type spearpoints; (g,h) Frio-type spearpoints; (i)
McKean-type spearpoint; (j) scraper fashioned from a corner-notched spearpoint; (k,l) sections of T-
shaped drills.
Trinity aspect (Beaver site, 34Mc-1): (m) Langtry-type spearpoint; (n,o) Bulverde-type spearpoints;
(p) Castroville-type spearpoint; (q) Edgewood-type spearpoint; (r) Palmillas-type spearpoint; (s)
Yarbrough-type spearpoint; (t) grooved cobble (net weight); (u) pear-shaped adze or axe.

cupstones. However, a full-grooved, chipped-and-ground chert axe found in Zone B of the Evans Site is apparently associated with the Tom's Brook assemblage. Also, Zones 5 and 6 of the Smith I Shelter yielded part of a bird leg-bone whistle and a bone awl.

In several ways, Tom's Brook assemblages manifest ties to early Archaic manufacturing ideas. Notably, the overall knapping strategy was predominantly one of working cobbles of quality flint into bifaces that were eventually thinned and shaped into spearpoints. These often have the heavily smoothed stem edges that characterize early Archaic points. Resharpening or reworking spearpoints into scrapers and knives continues, and ground-stone implements are still limited in form and number. Although difficult to evaluate, due to obviously disparate recovery and reporting methods, the knapping of cores for making flake tools seems more common to these assemblages than to earlier ones. A technological feature that does seem important in middle Archaic times is the practice of heating flint to improve its knappability (Mandeville 1973; Mandeville and Flenniken 1974). At the Dawson site, heat-treated Keokuk and Reed Springs cherts are represented by thinned bifaces (preforms) and spearpoints (T. G. Baugh 1978:Table 2). Based on the Dawson site findings, heat treating was practiced after cobbles were partially thinned and shaped.

Some Tom's Brook complex sites have yielded the first clues to actual plants and animals used by eastern Oklahoma's Archaic people. Bone and shell from the Tom's Brook, Cooper, and Smith I shelters attest to hunting deer and other small game as well as collecting shellfish and occasional turtles. Charred nuts from the Paw Paw site, Arkansas (Valastro, *et al* 1975:87) bear witness to fall gathering and, perhaps, seasonal scheduling of activities.

Because few sites were thoroughly tested or excavated, and because Tom's Brook assemblages are rarely found in well-isolated contexts, functional differences are largely undiscernible at this time. The site distributions (Figure 6.1) attest to these people frequenting open camps and rockshelters in the Ozarks and along their western margins. But except for the Dawson site in Mayes County, information is lacking on habitation features, activity areas, and site functions. Testing across the Dawson site revealed the presence of burned limestone (from hearths and/or ovens for heating flint?) as well as clues to different knapping areas (T. G. Baugh 1978). In particular, initial biface knapping was more evident in the southwest part of the site, whereas final biface thinning, biface resharpening, and flake tool use were more apparent in the southeastern part of the site (T. G. Baugh 1978:80–93).

South and west of the Ozarks, only open sites are known to have such assemblages. However, some functional differences seem indicated. Most open sites appear to have been brief camps, but the Tucker's Knob site in Latimer County (Figure 6.1) consists of a large (27 × 12 m), thick (1.05 m) layer of heat-fractured sandstone. A minor camp area is nearby. At least 2 periods of site habitation are evidenced by stratified concentrations of flakes, biface preforms, and spearpoints within the burned-rock deposits (Neal 1974a; Saunders 1974a;

Wallis 1974). However, both periods of site use appear to result from inhabitants related to, and descended from, those responsible for the Tom's Brook complex.

The Tucker's Knob site is distinguished by its many tools relating to hunting and to flint knapping: over 200 spearpoints, 3300 scrapers and knives made from flakes, 194 biface preforms, 18 cores, and 75,000 flakes. Despite knowing the distributions of these abundant items, little is known about the purpose of the heat-fractured rock midden. The many biface preforms and 75,000 flakes show little trace of heat treating; thus the burned rock was not serving as an oven for heating local cherts while making chipped-stone tools. Nor do the many hunting-related tools attest to the heated rocks serving as an oven for roasting game; charred bones were not observed or recovered. In central Texas, similar burned-rock mounds are interpreted (E. R. Prewitt 1981; Weir 1979:63–64) as remains from processing edible plants. But at Tucker's Knob, charred plants (nuts, etc.) were not recovered, and such plant-processing tools as mullers and grinding basins were rare. All in all, Tucker's Knob comprises a major open camp where local chert cobbles were extensively knapped and where some special, repeated activities resulted in a massive accumulation of burned rock. Although this burned-rock midden and the prevalent spearpoint styles (types: Fairland, Frio, Uvalde, and Edgewood) are similar to those left by middle Archaic people in central Texas, all other clues point to the site's use by people native to the western Ouachita Mountains.

Several lines of evidence support the conclusion that the Tom's Brook complex represents traces of scattered hunting–gathering groups. Although these people were undoubtedly adept travelers, their camps are dispersed over several hundred kilometers of rugged eastern Oklahoma–western Arkansas terrain. Thus, I conclude that the sites were not frequented during the seasonal movements of one band. Furthermore, given the plants, animals, and climate that were probably common to this region, it is difficult to imagine what might have attracted one band to traverse it. Finally, the chipped-stone tools reported for these sites are predominantly of locally available stone. Although occasional exotic pieces may occur, they more than likely attest to trade or the movements of small parties from one area to another rather than to the movements of one band.

In summary, at least 16 eastern Oklahoma and 2 Arkansas sites have yielded spearpoints and a few other hunting–gathering tools believed deposited some 5000 to 6000 years ago. Because the sites yielding these artifacts are seldom well stratified, information on assemblages, habitation features, and activity areas is limited. Still, the remains seem similar and are herein interpreted as being attributable to a middle Archaic complex known as *Tom's Brook*. Despite sparse information, the Tom's Brook complex is believed to represent traces of roughly contemporaneous, but locally distinct, hunting–gathering bands that principally inhabited the Ozark and Ouachita uplands. More than likely, during the mid-Holocene these two areas contained markedly different habitats than are found there today. Thus, much paleoecological research will need to be done in conjunction with future archaeological studies of Tom's Brook complex sites if we are to document and explain these people's character and role in the region's past.

The Caudill Complex

Several northeast Oklahoma sites appear to have tools attributable to more recent habitations than those responsible for the Tom's Brook complex. These more recent Archaic camps are believed manifest at the Caudill (Levels 5–6), Guffy 4 (Level 5), Guffy 5 (Levels 4–5), Evans (Zone B), McConkey (Levels 3–4), Smith I (Zones 4–7), Smith II (Zone 2), and Cooper (Zones 6–9) sites in Delaware County. To the south, relevant materials are evidenced at the Wolf Creek (Levels 4–6), Pohly (Levels 5–8 of Upper Unit and Layers A–C of Lower Unit), and the Packard (Levels 5–10) sites in Mayes County. All the Mayes and Delaware county sites are in the Grand River Basin, and most occur along streams draining the western flanks of the Ozark Uplands (Figure 6.1).

Because it was earliest reported at the Caudill site, this second northeast Oklahoma series of middle Archaic assemblages is termed the *Caudill complex*. However, at Caudill, the assemblage is not well separated from debris left by later campers. Only at the Wolf Creek site does the assemblage seem relatively free of mixing. At the other Delaware and Mayes counties sites, Caudill complex assemblages occur in levels that also contain Tom's Brook complex and later assemblages. Such occurrences are interpreted to result from mixing of refuse from at least two intervals of camping, probably by two unrelated groups of campers. It is to be hoped that future research in northeast Oklahoma will focus on finding and studying sites with well-stratified deposits and datable features that will help clarify ages and ties between potentially numerous middle Archaic assemblages.

As yet, sites are unknown that have bone, shell, or vegetal artifacts that are unquestionably attributable to the Caudill complex. Thus, except for some deer-bone awls and deer-antler flakers, the identifiable material culture is composed principally of chipped-stone or ground-stone tools. These latter include occasional pieces of hematite that were scratched or rubbed for red pigment and several grinding stones and cupstones that were preliminarily shaped (by pecking) from sandstone. These implements were most likely used to process seasonally collected nuts, seeds, and berries, but as yet the specific plants that were collected are unknown.

In contrast to the narrow range of ground-stone tools, most Caudill complex assemblages bear witness to a well-developed knapping industry that emphasized use of locally available chert cobbles. Using chert or sandstone hammerstones, these cobbles were occasionally shaped into rough cores from which large flakes could be predictably struck and used as scrapers and knives. A few such cobbles were also made into choppers. More frequently, however, these cobbles were bifacially thinned and roughly shaped into elliptical, ovate, or triangular preforms or blanks. The knapping of these bifacially chipped objects was accomplished with hammerstones and, presumably, antler billets; few of these latter are preserved among the recovered remains. With further thinning and shaping, the rough bifaces were capable of being made into large drills as well as finished knives and spearpoints. Such finish work was undoubtedly accomplished with soft hammers (antler or wood billets) and antler pressure flakers.

Several spearpoint styles are common to the Caudill complex. Especially diagnostic are varieties of large bladed points that have prominent barbs. Most numerous are those which were basally notched so that a parallel-sided stem was created; this style is represented by such named types as Bulverde, Calf Creek, and Smith. Also frequent are basally notched forms with expanding stems: the Marshall and Marcos types are representative. Another prevalent form consists of large bladed points with contracting stems that usually have smoothed-stem edges (i.e., the Hidden Valley and Standlee types). Although not numerous, such point types as Castroville, Williams, Table Rock, and Jakie Stemmed occur in some deposits yielding materials attributable to the Caudill complex. Based on the animal bones recovered from such deposits at the Pohly, Smith, and Cooper sites, the spearpoints described above were used mainly to hunt deer. Turkey, raccoon, and skunk were also killed, and turtle were taken by some means.

Of the recovered projectile point types, the Hidden Valley, Table Rock, and Jakie Stemmed examples have distributions that include much of the Ozarks in Missouri and Arkansas (Adams 1941; Bray 1956; Chapman *et al.* 1960; Wood 1963). This common distribution probably attests to the use of point styles favored by contemporaneous bands of hunters and gatherers. Whether or not these commonly used styles also attest to the bands' being ethnically related remains to be discovered.

The locations yielding Caudill complex materials include both rockshelters and open camps scattered along Grand River and its eastern (Ozark draining) tributaries (Figure 6.1). Although one might conjecture how these two kinds of sites resulted from nomadic, perhaps seasonal, settlement practices, a clear pattern of site use is not evident. Hearths, roasting pits, or traces of dwellings built by the people using the Caudill complex are unknown at these sites. Thus, habitation features cannot be used to delinate functionally different sites. Organic remains are known mainly from the rockshelters, and these remains are overwhelmingly bones of deer. Consequently, little evidence exists for use of the shelters for purposes other than as deer-hunting camps. Moreover, the inhabited shelters and open sites are situated along Grand River and its eastern tributaries, so the distributions of these two kinds of sites seem to offer little insight to seasonally, socially, or economically specialized settlement practices. Such practices may be difficult to discern because the known sites may have been frequented over several centuries when these people were changing their hunting–gathering habits. However, until these sites are radiocarbon dated, little opportunity exists for explaining their use by these middle Archaic people.

The Trinity Aspect

Numerous sites in southeast, southcentral, and northcentral Oklahoma have yielded implements stylistically similar to those of an Archaic culture long recognized in northcentral Texas. Called the *Trinity aspect*, this culture was first identified (Crook and Harris 1952) from findings at 28 sites in the Trinity River's upper drainage, the region centering around Dallas. The materials recovered from these sites bear witness to a common use of similar plants, animals, and minerals, but stratigraphic evidence supports the conclusion that these sites were frequented over a long period. Most are buried in floodplain or first-terrace deposits thought to correlate with 1500- to 4000-year-old alluvial sequences recorded elsewhere in the Southwest. The stratigraphic evidence plus stylistic changes in spearpoints and certain other tools provided a basis for subdividing the Trinity aspect into two sequent assemblages: an earlier Carrollton focus and a later Elam focus (Crook and Harris 1952). Subsequent dating of mussel shells resulted in a nearly 6000-year-old age determination for a site containing a suspected late Carrollton focus assemblage. Thus, the initially determined age for the Trinity aspect is now believed not to be old enough.

At least 30 eastern Oklahoma sites are known to have spearpoints, gouges, and/or stone net-weights that were once considered typical of Trinity aspect assemblages. Few Oklahoma locations, however, have yielded such tools from stratified, isolated contexts, and only one of these contexts (Scott site) has been radiocarbon dated. Locations where Trinity aspect–related material occurred in relatively stratified contexts include the Beaver (50–100 cm below surface), Johnson (Levels 3–5), Bell (Levels 3–5), and Gregory (Levels 5–7) sites in McCurtain County; the McKenzie site (Levels 5–12) of Choctaw County; the Scott site (115–175 cm) of LeFlore County; and the Natural Lake (Levels 3–7), Vanderwagen (Levels 2–5), Blessingame (Stratum III of north terrace and Stratum IV of south terrace), and Hill (0–0 area Levels 4–6 and 0–S10 area Levels 3–7) sites of Pushmataha County (Figure 6.1). Elsewhere, tools like those of the Carrollton and Elam foci appear mixed with earlier and later assemblages at the Boat Dock and Buncombe Creek sites in Marshall County; the James site in Bryan County; site 34Sm-35 in Seminole County; site 34Pw-63 in Pawnee County; the Sallee G. site in Pushmataha County; the Mahaffey, Montgomery, and Pate–Roden sites in Choctaw County; and the Biggham Creek, Hughes, Lamas Branch, and Callaham sites in McCurtain County (Figure 6.1).

The tools attributable to assemblages like those of the Trinity aspect (Carrollton and Elam foci) are mainly of chipped stone. The few pecked-stone objects include grinding stones (typically those used in circular fashion), cupstones (or anvils), net weights (cobbles with a groove pecked around them), and hammerstones. Some sandstone cobbles were occasionally made into net weights by flaking notches into their sides. However, the chipped-stone industry consisted principally of thinning and shaping chert or quartzite cobbles into bifacially flaked spearpoints and knives (Figure 6.3). Although a few chert or quartzite cobbles were made into cores for flakes usable in cutting, scraping, and reaming tasks, most such implements appear to be made from flakes produced while trimming, thinning, and shaping cobbles into bifacially flaked tools. This cobble-to-biface knapping sequence produced many flawed, broken, and unfinished stages of bifacially flaked objects. Some of these broken or unfinished stages were apparently recycled into large scrapers and gouges, the latter being distinguished by concave, steep bit edges. Pear-shaped adzes or axes occur in assemblages of a few sites.

The net weights and gouges comprise noteworthy links to Trinity aspect assemblages, but several spearpoint styles and types are also important clues. In particular, the Oklahoma sites have yielded examples (Figure 6.3) of points with long, smoothed, parallel-sided stems (the Carrollton type); with medium-to-short, parallel-sided stems (Bulverde and Dallas types); with long, contracting stems (Wells type); with broad, contracting stems (Morhiss and possibly the Gary types); and medium-to-short, slightly expanding stems (the Yarbrough, Trinity, and Palmillas types). Along with these may occur occasional examples of the Calf Creek, Langtry, Cassatot River, Smith, Marshall, Edgewood, and Castroville types, forms more common to middle Archaic assemblages to the south, east, and north.

The Oklahoma sites yielding these materials seldom yield traces of the plants or animals used by middle Archaic inhabitants. A few bone scraps attest to the hunting of deer and other small game. Pieces of turtles and mussels also bear witness to species that were foraged. The stone weights or sinkers may be evidence for fish nets or possibly bola weights for ensnaring birds or other game. Occasional charred nut fragments, usually identified as hickory, undoubtedly attest to some of the plants that were seasonally gathered for food or other purposes.

Few Oklahoma sites provide evidence of long or intensive use by middle Archaic people using Trinity aspect–related assemblages. Except for occasional traces of rock-lined hearths and roasting ovens (burned-rock concentrations), habitation features clearly contemporaneous with middle Archaic deposits are rare. Organically rich middens yielding such assemblages are uncommon, although one was perhaps present at the now-inundated James site in Bryan County (M. A. Ray 1960). Some flexed burials found here, and at the nearby Boat Dock and Buncombe Creek sites (Bell 1958b; Wyckoff 1964c), may be middle Archaic interments, but the lack of time-diagnostic grave goods precludes their assignment to this period. In summary, most studied sites are characterized by thin or shallow natural (not midden) deposits where habitation debris appears vertically and horizontally scattered. Although these refuse distributions were undoubtedly affected by postdeposition shifting (due to plant and animal disturbances), the impression is gained that the refuse results from several temporary occupations.

The sparse data on habitation features and the similar assemblages of the Oklahoma sites provide little basis for discerning different site functions or their ties to local and regional settlement practices. The sites themselves are typically on prominent terraces near the confluence of small streams with larger ones. Most studied sites have had less than 10% of their area excavated. Thus, future fieldworkers could contribute much to our knowledge of activity areas, tool kits, and site functions by uncovering larger samples of recognized middle Archaic deposits.

More than likely, the Oklahoma sites were frequented by several different hunting–gathering bands. Regional differences in some tool styles (net weights, for example) and in the material used for knapped tools are potential clues that may help eventual recognition of localities controlled by particular social units. In fact, future research may well ascertain that the Oklahoma sites were inhabited by people unrelated to those responsible for the Trinity aspect sites in north-central Texas. The tools cited above as held in common may represent forms that were popular with many societies for a certain time rather than forms indicative of social ties. Obviously, much remains to be learned about the habitation features, assemblages, use of natural resources, settlement practices, and chronology of these apparently widespread middle Archaic people.

Middle Archaic Summary

Paleoecological findings from the Prairie Peninsula and Ozarks of Missouri bear witness to a warm, dry climate prevailing between 9000 and 4000 years ago (McMillan and Klippel 1981). During this period, hillslope erosion created alluvial fans on terraces; such grassland species as bison and pronghorn became more evident; and people hunted a wider variety of animals, especially forest-edge species, than previously. The drier west flanks of the Ozarks are believed (McMillan and Klippel 1981:238) to have been predominantly prairie, woodlands being largely confined to valley settings.

The above ecological model seems relevant to eastern Oklahoma. Five-thousand-year-old deposits from the base of Ferndale Bog, Atoka County, are dominated by oak and grass pollen (Albert 1981:Figure 31). This pollen spectrum most probably results from the nearby presence of savanna, definitely not from the oak–hickory–pine forest found in this Ouachita Mountains locality today. Thus, as observed in Missouri, grasslands were more than likely prevalent 5000 years ago in eastern Oklahoma settings that support forests today.

Against this ecological backdrop, already accumulated archaeological findings support the conclusion that eastern Oklahoma was extensively inhabited by hunting–gathering people during the Middle Archaic period (6000–4000 years ago). Few Oklahoma sites are well dated to this period, but many have yielded spearpoints and other implements that are stylistically similar to dated assemblages reported for nearby Texas, Arkansas, and Missouri. In lieu of well-dated contexts, archaeologists have previously tended to assign the Oklahoma assemblages to one or two regionally broad, hunting–gathering traditions. But in order to begin to see how these sites might contain clues to different settlement and resource-use practices, similar assemblages have been assumed herein to be roughly contemporaneous and thus assignable to particular complexes. Stratigraphic clues permit recognition of at least three sequent complexes for the Middle Archaic period in eastern Oklahoma. Each is manifest at rather widely dispersed sites and is characterized by locally varying preferences for lithic materials for chipped-stone tools. These characteristics may be indicative of contemporaneous, but different, bands using similar assemblages. More than likely, four or five different hunting–gathering bands were inhabiting eastern Oklahoma during the Middle Archaic period. Whether or not they were linguistically, and thus ethnically, related is uncertain.

In contrast to Early Archaic period sites, many locations inhabited during the Middle Archaic seem to attest to repeated or long-term occupations and to occasional special uses. At least in the Ozarks, both rockshelters and open camps were being frequented. Midden accumulations in both types of sites comprise evidence for repeated, if not continuous, use. Unfortunately, because these middens yield similar assemblages and only rarely preserved organic remains, functionally different habitations are difficult to identify. Sites with only scattered debris undoubtedly attest to camps where hunting and/or gathering parties stayed briefly and refurbished tools or preliminarily processed game, plant resources, or knappable stone. At sites with middens, occasional small hearths and burned-rock concentrations presumably are evidence for comparable activities. A notably exceptional site, however, is Tucker's Knob (34Lt-35), where a large burned-rock midden accumulated from as-yet-undetermined activities. One hopes similar sites will be found and will yield more insight on their layout and function.

Clearly, we are only beginning to understand the complex character of the environment and people existent during the Middle Archaic period. Although long perceived as having a simple hunting–gathering lifeway, these folk were adapting to settings quite different from those known today. We presently know little about their use of plants and animals, little about their range of movements or their settlement patterns, and nothing about their physical characteristics or ethnic ties. Only through sustained research programs in particular regions will these gaps in our knowledge be filled.

Late Archaic Period

Between 8000 and 4000 years ago, atmospheric circulation patterns conducive to warm, dry environmental conditions prevailed in the Midwest. Consequently, prairies and savannas grew in settings far east of their modern distributions, and it is increasingly evident that these open habitats were exploited by people who had adopted noteworthy hunting–gathering strategies (Agogino and Frankforter 1960; Anderson, *et al.* 1980; Fowler 1959; McMillan and Klippel 1981). But around 4000 years ago the previously dominant atmospheric circulation began changing to patterns like those common today. As a result, effective moisture increased. Woodlands became more mesic and they spread into settings that formerly supported grasslands. Between 4000 and 2000 years ago, these notable habitat changes stimulated a variety of social responses, the details of which are only now being discerned. For example, groups living in Missouri, Illinois, and Kentucky had begun raising native sunflowers and sumpweed as well as tropical squash by 1000 B.C. (Chomko and Crawford 1978; Yarnell 1977). Meanwhile, people living in northeast Louisiana were sufficiently numerous and/or organized that they constructed almost 2 km² of parallel ridges and a birdlike mound at Poverty Point (C. H. Webb 1977). Besides attaining an unprecedented level of organization, the Poverty Point inhabitants were engaged in long-distance trade that involved the Gulf Coast, the Ohio and Tennessee valleys, the Middle Mississippi Valley, the Ozarks, and the Ouachita Mountains (C. H. Webb 1977). Clearly, during the Late Archaic period, hunting–gathering people were reaching economic, demographic, political, and/or social thresholds that were important for subsequent cultural developments (J. B. Griffin 1967).

Although details are sparse, eastern Oklahoma's vegetation communities probably achieved their historic predisturbance character and distributions between 5000 and 1700 years ago (Albert 1981:Figures 26, 27, and 31). Undoubtedly, Oklahoma's hunting–gathering people were adapting to gradually changing habitats. Thus, it is important to remember that the studied sites and their contents bear witness to societies living in dynamic relation to a changing land.

During these two millennia, the eastern half of Oklahoma was apparently inhabited by several regionally different societies. In contrast to earlier foraging groups, these latest ones seem increasingly to have preferred to inhabit particular regions, resulting in numerous sites, some of which have thick deposits of trash. The sites with such deposits attest to frequent, if not continuous, occupancy, and they have yielded most of the radiocarbon dates reported (Table 6.1) for the Archaic period in eastern Oklahoma.

The Lawrence Phase

One regional manifestation is represented by similar assemblages reported for open camps and rockshelters along the Grand and Verdigris rivers in northeast Oklahoma. Hereafter called the *Lawrence phase*, this culture is best dated at the Lawrence site, a thick, relatively well-stratified (as well as buried) midden on the bank of the Verdigris River in Nowata County (Figure 6.1). Other related sites are predominantly along the Grand River, some 60 km east, in Mayes and Delaware counties (Figure 6.1): the Kerr Dam site (Occupation Zone II), Shetley Shelter 1.82–2.55 m), Pohly Shelter (mixed in Levels 5 and 6 of Upper Unit ?), the Cooper Shelter (Zone 5), the Smith I (Zone 3) and Smith II (mixed in Zone 2?) shelters, the Caudill site (Levels 3–4), and the McConkey site (Level 2). In southwest Missouri, materials related to the Lawrence phase appear present at a couple of sites, namely the Lewellyn site (34Sn-205) and Jakie Shelter (23By-388; Levels 4 and 5) in the Table Rock Reservoir area (Chapman *et al.* 1960:308–313, 1116–1149).

Of all the above sites, only Lawrence and the Shetley Shelter have yielded radiocarbon dates relevant to Lawrence phase occupations. At the Shetley Shelter, a single flexed-burial resting on bedrock (3.0 m below the surface at the shelter's mouth) was dated at 1650 B.C. ± 175 (SM-764; Wyckoff 1967c). Not long after this burial, people began frequenting the Lawrence site, some 90 km northwest of Shetley (Figure 6.1). The earliest Lawrence dates are between 3400 to 3000 years ago (Table 6.1) and pertain to a developing soil horizon that yielded few artifacts and flakes (Baldwin 1969:Figure 3; Wyckoff 1981). The latest date, 760 B.C. ± 70 (Tx-815), comes from just below the black clay that yielded most of the site's tools, refuse, and habitation features. Thus, the most intense use of the Lawrence site was sometime around 2600 to 2700 years ago. By this time, this Verdigris terrace surface was stabilizing and beginning to develop a sequence of soil horizons.

During the at least 800 years that Lawrence phase groups inhabited northeast Oklahoma, they altered little of their material culture. There is, however, some change evident in their preferred projectile styles. Those common to the earliest Lawrence site assemblages included a Frio-like form and the Table Rock Stemmed type (Figure 6.4). In contrast, the last deposited assemblage still has some of the Frio-like points in addition to such types as Marshall, Williams, Marcos, Afton, Palmillas, Ellis, and Morhiss (Figure 6.4). Most of these same types were also recovered from the sealed off, but undated, Lawrence phase component at the Kerr Dam site (Wyckoff 1963a). A noteworthy addition to the Kerr Dam assemblage were examples of the corner-notched, large spearpoint–knife form classifiable as the Snyders type (Figure 6.4), a type usually thought associated with Woodland period (A.D. 200–500) assemblages in this region. A surprising addition to the latest Lawrence assemblage are corner-notched, small projectiles with narrow hafts; these points (Baldwin 1969:Categories L–O) may well represent evidence for a late Archaic period adoption of the bow and arrow. Baerreis (1951:Tables 3 and 5) reports similar specimens for the Caudill and McConkey sites, but, unfortunately, the suspicion that mixing has occurred inhibits an uncontestable isolation of all items left by Lawrence phase inhabitants.

The common use of such point types as Table Rock, Marcos, Marshall, and Williams comprises evidence that the Lawrence phase people were probably descendents of those responsible for the earlier Caudill complex. As noted for these earlier foragers, the Lawrence phase people had a well-developed knap-

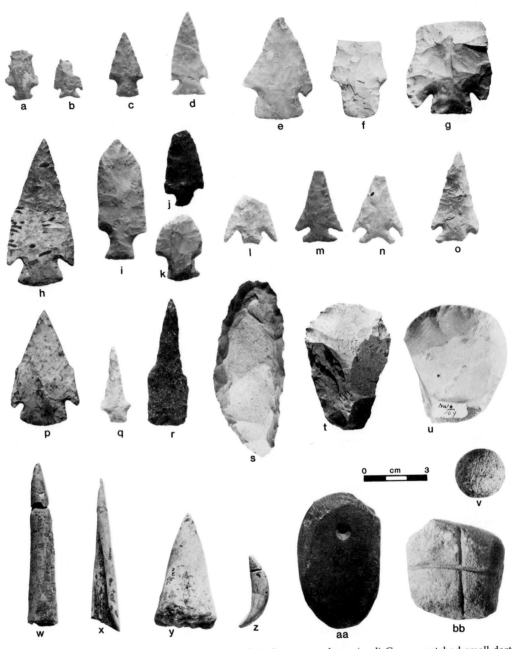

Figure 6.4 Selected artifacts of the Late Archaic Lawrence phase: (a–d) Corner-notched small dart points or arrowpoints; (e) Castroville-type spearpoint and/or knife; (f) broken Morhiss-type spearpoint; (g) incomplete Marshall-type spearpoint; (h,p) Afton-like spearpoints on knives; (i–k) Table Rock-type spearpoints; (l–o) corner-notched (Martindale-like) spearpoints; (q,r) drills; (s) side scraper; (t,u) scrapers; (v) stone ball; (w) antler dart-point tip; (x,y) split-bone awls; (z) canine-tooth pendant; (aa) pendant or unfinished gorget; (bb) grooved stone (weight?). Items j–l come from earliest (3400–3000 years ago) deposits, whereas the remainder are principally from the 2700-year-old deposits of the Lawrence site (34Nw-6), Nowata County, Oklahoma.

ping technology. They apparently obtained high-quality chert from exposed gravel beds as well as from some bedrock exposures. With hammerstones and wood or antler billets, they reduced cobbles or large blanks into bifacially flaked tools (projectile points, point preforms, knives, and choppers) or into cores for producing flakes. These flakes might then be unifacially or bifacially flaked into tools. Heat treating was a technique used to improve the knappability of some chert, but the details about when, how, and how much this technique was practiced remain to be discerned. Among the frequently occurring flake implements are those with steeply retouched (scraping) ends and edges, sharp cutting edges, retouched concave edges, alternately chipped edges, gravers, and steeply retouched pointed ends (Figure 6.4). In addition, some projectile points and flakes were bifacially flaked into long drills with rectangular hafting ends (Figure 6.4). Besides their chipped-stone objects, these people pecked and/or ground sandstone, phosphate, and hematite into grinding basins, mullers, grooved abraders, net weights, balls, ornaments (gorgets), and paint stones (Figure 6.4). From antler, bone, and teeth, they made awls, bone points, flakers, and pendants (Figure 6.4).

Although animal and plant remains were recovered from several sites, there is much to be learned about the character and scheduling of Lawrence phase hunting–gathering practices. For example, such rockshelters as Pohly, Cooper, Smith I, and Smith II yielded mussel shells and bones of diverse animals, but these shelter deposits are too complex to sort, with assurance, the animals and plants brought in by the late Archaic inhabitants. The Shetley Shelter had some stratified deposits and offers some potential for isolating and documenting late Archaic prey. But, to date, the refuse from this site has not been analyzed. Thus, our best source of information is the Lawrence site where some 2700 pieces of animal bone were recovered (Baldwin 1969:83–84), most from the deposit dating around 700 B.C. Much of the bone was burned and broken into small fragments, but of the identifiable pieces, nearly 20% were from deer (Baldwin 1969:83). Over a third of these were from leg bones, bearing witness to deer being killed and quartered away from the camp. Other identified species include raccoon, beaver, squirrel, spotted skunk, coyote, gopher, various turtles, several birds, and some fish. Bison or other animals of upland prairie settings were notably lacking. All in all, the Lawrence phase people were exploiting the surrounding Verdigris bottomland habitats (Baldwin 1969:83).

Because the Lawrence and Kerr Dam sites have the most isolated Lawrence phase deposits, they offer the best clues to site structure and site function. At Kerr Dam, the exposed areas included remains of a rock-lined hearth, surrounding work areas, and nearby knapping areas (Wyckoff 1963a). All these features appear to have resulted from a single encampment, one now buried by 1.2 m of alluvium. In contrast, the Lawrence site contained burned limestone rock ovens, a rock-lined hearth, several refuse-filled pits, and two, clay-lined, possible postholes (Baldwin 1969:76–79). These latter, plus numerous pieces of fired clay, are clues to the former presence of some type of prepared shelter. The burned-rock ovens display some overlapping, providing evidence for the repeated use of this site. All in all, the Lawrence site appears to have been a more substantial and more used camp (a base camp?) than the Kerr Dam site.

The Kerr Dam site is but one of eight Lawrence phase camps in the Grand River Basin (Figure 6.1). These consist of both open sites and rockshelters that, collectively, offer clues to later Archaic settlement and exploitive practices along the Ozark's west border. Some site settings include both open camps (Kerr Dam) and shelters (Smith I and Smith II) adjacent to Grand River. The Smith I shelter was near an abandoned river channel that seasonally might have offered exceptional opportunities to collect fish and mussels (Wittry 1952:2). Other shelters and open camps (Cooper, McConkey, and Caudill) are located along tributaries at short distances above their junctions with the Grand River. Such settings tend to be sheltered by high bluffs and near both bottomland and upland prairie settings. Finally, the Pohly Shelter comprises a small rockshelter situated near a tributary, but in a more upland setting than places like the Cooper Shelter. Because the Lawrence components at most of these sites are difficult to identify with easily isolable deposits, information on their habitation features, assemblages, and refuse is difficult to compile and compare. Thus, functional differences are not distinguishable. However, the Smith I, Smith II, and Cooper shelters did contain numerous flexed burials, some of which are probably of late Archaic age (Purrington 1970; Wittry 1952). These sites also had such apparently contemporaneous features as ash beds (prepared living surfaces?) and midden deposits, all of which are believed to attest to frequent, perhaps seasonal, use. Perhaps the burials, middens, and other features attest to increased shelter use during fall and winter when northeast Oklahoma's weather would have been most adverse for out-of-doors living. Hopefully, future research on comparable sites will allow evaluation of such settlement practices.

Although Lawrence phase foragers principally exploited locally available game, plants, and minerals, they apparently became increasingly involved with regional and long-distance trade. At the undated, but probably early, Kerr Dam site, some chipped-stone tools were identified as made from Peoria and Bolivar flint (Wyckoff 1963a:11–18). If these identifications are still reasonable, the objects are of material that may have been obtained from quarries at least 80 km upriver and, in the case of Bolivar, as much as 160 km to the north–northwest. These same flints are among several exotic materials reported (Baldwin 1969:80–83) for the Lawrence site, an occupation that is probably later than that at Kerr Dam. But in addition to minor amounts of Bolivar and Peoria, the Lawrence inhabitants got at least a fourth of their knappable stone from the Ozarks (Boone chert), some 80 km to the east, whereas 8% was coming from the Kay County locality some 130 km to the west–northwest. At least one flake of obsidian attests to contact with such source areas as the Jemez Mountains in New Mexico or perhaps the Yellowstone region of northwest Wyoming (Baldwin 1969:81). Clearly, the Lawrence phase people were not isolated from the cultural developments that were occurring elsewhere during late Archaic times.

The Wister Phase

For eastern Oklahoma, one of the most intriguing late Archaic developments is evidenced in the northern valleys of the Ouachita Mountains. Here, along tree-shrouded streams that wend through grassy savannas and between oak–pine forested ridges occur numerous open camps, knapping stations, and midden mounds. Because of their numbers, size, and varied contents, these latter became the focus of Oklahoma's WPA archaeological efforts in the 1930s. Twenty midden mounds were extensively dug by large work-relief crews, resulting in the recovery of overwhelming quantities of artifacts and refuse, as well as human and dog burials. The richness of these sites was again demonstrated in the late 1940s when University of Oklahoma archaeologists undertook surveys and excavations to salvage information from sites threatened by the Lake Wister construction and inundation. After analysis of both WPA and the salvage-excavated sites, archaeologists (Bell 1953b; Bell and Baerreis 1951:19–27; Proctor 1957; Sharrock 1960) perceived that the midden mounds represented the long record of a hunting–gathering people who, through time, adopted pottery and the bow and arrow. Their material culture was dubbed the *Fourche Maline focus* (Bell and Baerreis 1951:19), Fourche Maline being the drainage containing most of the studied sites.

Besides representing the remains of a long hunting–gathering tradition, the Fourche Maline focus was interpreted (Bell and Baerreis 1951:27) to result from foraging nomads who continued an Archaic lifestyle long after neighboring groups were becoming sedentary horticulturalists. This interpretation of cultural conservatism has come under scrutiny as more sites were studied and as radiocarbon dates became available. Then, in the 1970s, renewed research around Lake Wister and along Fourche Maline Creek has resulted in refining some previous interpretations of the long hunting–gathering tradition (S. Baugh 1982; Clark 1980; Galm 1978a, 1978b, 1981; Galm and Flynn 1978a, 1978b). In particular, the recent findings support the conclusion that most midden mounds resulted from two major periods of site use: one by hunting–gathering people between 4000 and 2000 years ago and a later one (1700–1200 years ago) by people with pottery, bows and arrows, and probably horticulture (Galm and Flynn 1978b:157–163). Analyses of the human burials provide evidence that the same people are present (McWilliams 1970; Powell and Rogers 1980), but that we are looking at them at different points in time. Bell (1980a) has thus recommended that the term *Fourche Maline phase* be applied to the material culture of the pottery-making folk, whereas that of their hunting–gathering ancestors be called the *Wister phase*.

Most of the reported Wister phase sites are in the Fourche Maline–Poteau Basin, the northernmost valley system in the Ouachita Mountains. Here, Wister phase assemblages are reported and radiocarbon dated for the Curtis Lake (Component 1), Wann (Component 1), Scott (Component 2), and McCutchan–McLaughlin (preceramic zone) sites (Figure 6.1; Table 6.1). In addition, the as-yet-unanalyzed Williams I and Troy Adams sites have pertinent radiocarbon dates (Table 6.1), whereas the undated Sam site has tools (Proctor 1957) like those common to Wister phase assemblages. Recent salvage work at the soon-to-be constructed Sardis Reservoir, in the next valley south of the Fourche Maline drainage, has resulted in the discovery of a major Wister phase occupation at the Bug Hill midden mound, and traces of such assemblages at the Wheeler Lee, Natural Lake, Vanderwagen, and Blessingham sites (Figure 6.1). Although not attributed to the Wister phase by the initial analysts, sites along the Arkansas River and in the southern Ozarks, localities some 90 km north of the Fourche Maline Valley, have projectile points and other tools like those of the Wister phase (Harden and Robinson 1975; A. F. Miller 1977:192–208, 468–472, 475–482, 489–504). It seems quite likely these sites may bear witness to occupations by people related to the late Archaic foragers living in the northern Ouachitas.

Because soils in the Ouachita Mountains are usually leached and acidic, they comprise a poor environment for preserving organic tools and refuse. But because the Wister phase people dumped so much ash, charcoal, and organic refuse on their middens, these sites yielded voluminous amounts of bone, shell, and charred plants. Consequently substantial information is becoming available on the plants and animals that were important to Wister phase foragers (Clark 1980; Galm 1978b; Galm and Flynn 1978b). Their main prey was the white-tailed deer, but turkeys, raccoons, swamp rabbits, cottontails, jack rabbits, opossums, squirrels, beaver, otters, prairie chickens, and both resident and migratory waterfowl were also taken. In addition, these people collected at least eight varieties of mussels, several kinds of turtles (including softshell, snapping, map, slider, and eastern box), and fish (gar, catfish, and drum).

Besides being adept hunters, these people intensively foraged for plants, which they used in diverse ways. Fragmented thousands of charred nut hulls and shells have been recovered from some of these sites. Although difficult to identify and quantify, these fragments attest to much use of the highly nutritious hickory nut and to far less collecting of walnuts and acorns. Hackberries and black haw have been recovered occasionally. Undoubtedly, many other plants were used for food, fiber, and medicine. It is to be hoped that future researchers will continue using techniques that enhance recovery of the minute remains of economically important plants.

Wister phase people may have caught fish with traps and nets, but they are also known to have made hooks (Figure 6.5) carved and smoothed from bone. Besides fishhooks, bones of deer, turkey, and other animals were skillfully cut and ground into awls, spatulates, spearthrower (atlatl) hooks, skewers, handles for chipped-stone tools, knapping billets, pressure flakers, tubes, pendants, hairpins, and beads (Figure 6.5). These items were sometimes decorated with simple (usually geometric) engraved designs. Beads were also made from snails, mussels, hackberry seeds, and even small nodules of phosphate. Larger phosphate nodules were occasionally ground into elliptical spheres, some of which may have been weights for spearthrowers. Such weights were, however, more

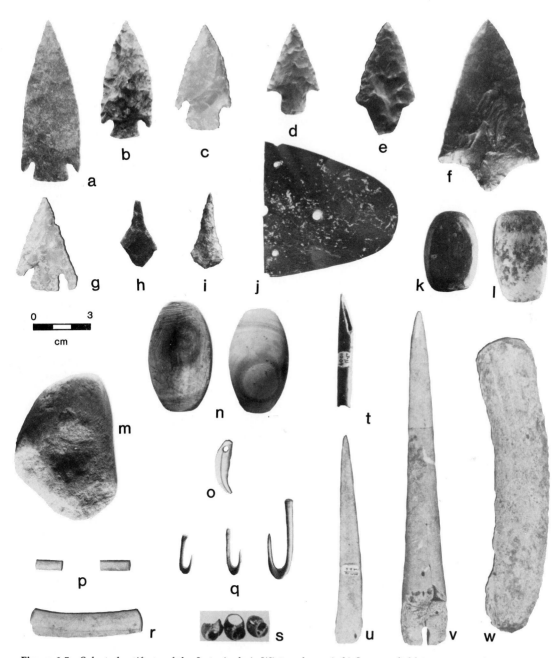

Figure 6.5 Selected artifacts of the Late Archaic Wister phase: (a,b) Summerfield-type spearpoints and/or knives; (c) Bulverde-type spearpoint; (d) parallel-stem spearpoint; (e) Gary-type spearpoint; (f) Gary-type knife; (g) Marcos-type spearpoint; (h,i) drills; (j) elliptical gorget section; (k,l) elliptical spheres of ground-phosphate nodules; (m) cup stone; (n) top and bottom views of a boatstone; (o) canine-tooth pendant; (p,r) bone beads; (q) bone fishhooks; (s) snail beads; (t) bone skewer; (u) split-bone awl; (v) awl made from deer metapodial; (w) antler baton. Items a, c, g, o, p, r, and u–w are from the Bug Hill site (34Pu-116), whereas Items b, d–f, i, k–n, q, s, and t are from the McCutchan–McLaughlin site (34Lt-11). Item j is from the Scott site (34Lf-11).

frequently chipped, pecked, and/or ground from sandstone, hematite, siltstone, or slate into small canoelike forms (boatstones; Figure 6.5). Tabular pieces of slate or shale were cut and ground into elliptical pendants and gorgets (Figure 6.5). These latter frequently display tally marks or geometric designs; they are interpreted to have been ornaments, spearthrower weights, or noise makers (bullroarers).

By far the most common pecked–ground-stone tools in Wister phase assemblages are grinding basins, mullers of several shapes, and the ubiquitous cup or "nutting" stones (Figure 6.5). These latter are either unshaped sandstone cobbles or prepared mullers that have small (32-mm diameter) depressions pecked in their faces. Experimental findings support the contention that these objects were anvils for cracking nuts and, perhaps, for some special knapping procedures.

Although skilled at grinding bone, shell, and stone into ornaments and tools, Wister phase people, like earlier hunting–gathering folks, relied heavily on knapping for many of their implements. The most-utilized materials were local cherts and quartzitic sandstones. In addition, siltstone, novaculite, and a few exotic cherts were used, but never to the extent of locally available chert and quartzitelike sandstone. Actual quarries for these materials are not known, and numerous flakes with waterworn surfaces attest to these people seeking knappable cobbles from nearby gravel beds. A few cobbles were made into cores from which usable flakes could be struck. However, most cobbles were bifacially flaked into blanks that could be further thinned, shaped, and sharpened into axes, ovate-to-triangular knives, and spearpoints (Figure 6.5). The oldest Wister phase deposits typically yield corner-notched spearpoints characterized by expanding stems (such as the Summerfield, Williams, Marshall, Marcos, Lange, and Palmillas types; Figure 6.5), more rarely by parallel-sided stems (i.e., Yarbrough and Bulverde–Carrollton-like types). Through time, however, Wister phase hunters began adopting contracting stem forms (i.e., the Gary and Langtry types; Figure 6.5) of spearpoints. More than likely, all spearpoints were hafted on short foreshafts that were in turn inserted in a longer shaft. Such foreshaft-hafting allowed these objects to be used as knives as well as spears or darts. Many so-called spearpoints show edge resharpening and microscopic edge wear that attest to their serving as more than projectile points (Galm and Flynn 1978b:138–148). Piercing, cutting, and scraping implements were also fashioned from flakes produced while splitting or thinning cobbles into blanks for axes, knives, or spearpoints.

Between 1200 and 800 B.C., while Wister phase people were heavily using base camps in the Ouachita Mountains, other hunting–gathering people developed a complex society that was responsible for several remarkable sites in the Lower Mississippi Valley (C. H. Webb 1970, 1977). One of these people's notable achievements was their acquisition of desired raw materials through trading networks that stretched as far north as Michigan, as far east as Alabama, and as far west as Oklahoma (C. H. Webb 1977:Figure 28). Argillite (a form of siltstone) and several knappable cherts were obtained from eastern Oklahoma and have been recovered at the Poverty Point site in northeast Louisiana (C. H. Webb 1977:37–42). Although Poverty Point's residents more than likely got these materials from Wister phase people, it is unclear what the latter received in return. The most obvious exotic items reported (Galm 1978b:66–70; Galm and Flynn 1978b:148–153, 163) for Wister phase sites are occasional spearpoints of Boone and other Ozark-derived cherts, materials that might have come from 90 to 110 km north of the Fourche Maline Valley. Perhaps some gorgets, atlatl weights, and the rare bannerstones found at a few Wister phase sites comprises clues to trade with Poverty Point people.

While the highly organized, semisedentary Poverty Point people were building complex earthworks in the Lower Mississippi Valley, Wister phase people were leaving a distinctly different archeological record in the Ouachita Mountains. This record is most visibly represented by the numerous sheet middens and midden mounds found along the Poteau River, Fourche Maline Creek, and their several large tributaries. Along Fourche Maline Creek, such midden deposits seem to occur every kilometer or so; similar distributions are believed present along the Poteau. When excavated, these sites are revealed to contain complicated midden deposits, including visibly and texturally similar, but discontinuous and noncontemporaneous, sequences of midden-laden silt and silt loam. Such deposits often contain traces of compacted living surfaces, some with occasional scattered postmolds that presumably result from pole-frame dwellings actually built on the midden. Other discernible habitation features include rock-lined hearths, ash beds (hearths?), burned-rock concentrations (roasting ovens?), numerous human burials, and infrequent dog burials. Although seldom well investigated, areas adjacent to the midden deposits usually bear signs of habitation, too. All in all, these sites are characterized by similar habitation features, deposits, tool kits, and refuse. For this reason, the midden mound locations are thought to represent base camps inhabited by small bands of hunters and gatherers. Some sites, however, were favored apparently for special reasons. For example, the Scott site (34Lf-11; Figure 6.1) has yielded more mussel shells than most analyzed sites, a fact that probably results from the site's being near shoals favored by shellfish.

Whether or not nearby midden mounds were inhabited contemporaneously or during different seasons or years remains to be determined. Given their proximity, it seems unlikely that all were occupied during the same season or year. Such use would have created a situation in which plant and animal resources within easy walking distances would have been susceptible to rapid depletion. More than likely, the Wister phase base camps were frequented in different seasons or years. Scatters of flake debris and occasional tools found in nearby uplands have not been well studied but most likely are traces of secondary camps that were frequented by hunting, plant gathering, knapping, or other special task parties. Notably, rockshelters used by Wister phase people have yet to be identified and studied in the Oklahoma portion of the Ouachitas. Such sites are known, however, and, one hopes, will contribute more insight to our knowledge of Wister phase settlement practices and resource uses.

Despite the lack of some critical information, the Wister phase sites still comprise evidence for a significant late Archaic cultural development in eastern Oklahoma. The available radiocarbon dates span the same 4000–2000-year-ago period when southeast Oklahoma habitats were becoming as mesic as those known today (Albert 1981). The fact that many Wister phase sites are partially buried by unstratified alluvium and are exposed in stream banks is interpreted as evidence that Wister phase people were adapting to changing environmental conditions. The nature and extent of these adaptations and changes remain to be fully explained by future researchers.

Other Late Archaic Occupations and Complexes

Late Archaic occupations have been identified at a number of sites in the southern flanks of the Ouachitas, in the bordering strip of Gulf Coastal Plains, and in Cross Timbers settings west of both the Ouachitas and the Ozarks. Although assemblages representative of such occupations are undoubtedly present, seldom have they been recovered from well-stratified and adequately dated deposits. Consequently, one can seriously question the composition and age of tool kits, assemblages, and habitation features left by the late Archaic inhabitants of these other eastern Oklahoma regions. Moreover, questions can be raised about the usefulness of assigning these artifact collections to particular complexes or cultures.

One example of the above situation is the *Lamas Branch complex*. This term was applied (Wyckoff 1968a:69–87) to artifacts recovered from five sites studied in the Broken Bow Reservoir area of McCurtain County. The sites are: Lamas Branch, Beaver, E. Johnson, Woods, and Biggham Creek (Figure 6.1). Subsequent to the study of these sites, similar tools were perceived (Wyckoff 1968b:187–203) at the Bell and Gregory sites, open camps with deep deposits that are now innundated by the Pine Creek Reservoir in McCurtain County (Figure 6.1). Although identified as the remains of late Archaic occupations, the Lamas Branch complex more than likely is the mixture of assemblages left by middle Archaic and late Archaic hunting–gathering parties. Of the original sites, only Beaver contained an assemblage in a relatively isolated deposit, and the Beaver assemblage has herein been attributed to the middle Archaic Trinity aspect. Moreover, since definition of the Lamas Branch complex, several spearpoint styles thought typical of late Archaic assemblages have been found elsewhere in relatively stratified contexts believed deposited over 4000 years ago. All in all, the composition of the Lamas Branch complex needs reexamination and probably redefinition. Despite this problem, the seven sites mentioned above have yielded presumably late Archaic styles of spearpoints (Gary, Darl, Williams, Marshall, etc.) and most probably were frequented by late Archaic people. Unlike the Wister phase sites some 130 km to the north, none of these open sites is characterized by organically rich middens or distinctive habitation features. They have yielded a variety of chipped- and/or ground-stone tools (including elliptical gorgets like those found at Wister phase sites), and they may represent base camps or often-used secondary camps.

Along the lower Kiamichi River, notable late Archaic occupations have been reported (Perino and Bennett 1978; Rohrbaugh 1972b:133–137; Rohrbaugh et al. 1971:141) at the Mahaffey, Burroughs, Montgomery, Pate–Roden, McKenzie, and Hill sites (Figure 6.1). All are open locations where late Archaic tools and trash were identified among the materials mixed with, or lying directly below, deposits yielding the earliest pottery known for southeast Oklahoma. The purported late Archaic assemblages are characterized by some expanding or parallel stem spearpoints and by many contracting-stem (Gary type) examples. In addition, biface knives, blanks for biface tools, flake scrapers, flake knives, mullers, cupstones, and occasional gorget fragments occur. The chipped-stone industry seems heavily focused on quartzitic sandstone, local cherts and jasper, and some imported material (i.e., novaculite). The few habitation features clearly associated with the late Archaic occupations include remnants of rock-lined hearths and occasional concentrations of fire-cracked rock.

Although not in the Kiamichi River drainage, the recently studied (Bobalik 1977b) Viper Marsh site in southern McCurtain County (Figure 6.1) closely resembles the late Archaic occupations in the Hugo Reservoir area. In particular, Viper Marsh findings bear witness to a dispersed occupation by hunting–gathering people who were predominantly using contracting-stem dart points and who were bringing in knappable stone (usually novaculite) to this chert-poor location. Stylistically, their chipped-stone and ground-stone tools are directly comparable to those noted for the Wister phase, the Lamas Branch complex, and the Hugo Reservoir late Archaic assemblages.

Also similar are late Archaic assemblages identified for the James, Boat Dock, and Buncombe Creek sites. These are but three of the numerous, frequently used camps known along Red River in the area now flooded by Lake Texoma (Figure 6.1). But here, like elsewhere, late Archaic assemblages have largely been separated and identified on the basis of projectile point styles from deposits that contained earlier and later materials as well. Thus, until assemblages are recovered and studied from well-stratified contexts, we really know little about late Archaic occupations along the upper course of Red River.

In 1962, the Archaic assemblages reported for the Lake Texoma area and the Fourche Maline Valley were noted (Leroy Johnson 1962:268–280) to bear many similarities in composition with the massive WPA collections from the Miller and Yarbrough sites of northeast Texas. Moreover, after comparing the evidence for material-culture change from sites with deep deposits, L. Johnson (1962:268) believed the late Archaic inhabitants of northeast Texas and southeast Oklahoma underwent a similar sequence of culture change. Having recognized these similarities, Johnson proposed that all these sites were bearing witness to a single regional culture, one he dubbed (L. Johnson 1962:269) the *La Harpe aspect*. But because many of the referenced sites now seem to be locations with mixed assemblages, because the La Harpe aspect is synomynous with late Archaic, and because the term's use tends to mask poorly understood sequences and adaptations, continued recognition of the La Harpe aspect can be questioned. Until we have more data to better evaluate local assemblages, local chronologies, and regional ties, I would argue that continued use of the La Harpe aspect concept serves little purpose. In fact, it probably detracts from our developing a substantial basis for perceiving late Archaic people and their lifeways.

Finally, we have begun to accumulate some knowledge of late Archaic occupations in the Cross Timbers. Most such findings originate from testing, evaluating, and mitigating sites affected by Soil Conservation Service construction of upstream watershed impoundments. These findings are seldom adequately dated or of sufficient scope (due to amount of testing) to allow recognition of local or regional late Archaic groups. But some of the studied sites have yielded clues to assemblages from fairly well-stratified deposits, for example the Roulston–Rogers, Estep Shelter, Birch Creek, Glasscock, Mousetrap, and 34Wg-108 sites (Figure 6.1). In addition, one notable cluster of tested sites in Atoka County (Estep, Graham, Birch Creek, and Mousetrap; Figure 6.1) seem to bear witness to late Archaic occupations at different kinds of sites. The Estep Shelter comprises a very small overhang (with good preservation of bone and shell) that was used by a few foragers, whereas the Graham, Mousetrap, and Birch Creek sites are sizable open camps with large accumulations of heat-fractured rock. All in all, some site variability is evident and perhaps can eventually be used to develop testable models of late Archaic seasonal foraging practices and band composition in this locality. Presently, however, none of these late Archaic deposits has been radiocarbon dated and established as contemporary.

Late Archaic Summary

To date, the Ferndale Bog, Atoka County pollen record (Albert 1981) provides our best evidence that eastern Oklahoma began undergoing pronounced ecological change some 4000 years ago. Between then and some 2000 years ago, the plant communities found in the Ozarks, Ouachitas, and Cross Timbers are believed to have attained their historic compositions and distributions. Also, there is accumulating evidence that many valleys underwent major aggradation during these 2000 years. Within these changing settings, hunting–gathering bands seem to have increasingly focused their attention on particular localities. At least the available archeological record supports the conclusion that many hunting–gathering folks maintained themselves along the west border of the Ozarks and in the northernmost valleys of the Ouachita Mountains. In these two settings, numerous large sites occur that are often characterized by deep midden deposits. Although similar tools and trash are recovered from sites in both regions, the sites are believed to have been inhabited by at least two unrelated groups. Their material cultures have herein been called the *Lawrence* and *Wister* phases.

For both cultural manifestations, the best-studied sites are probable base camps, places that were frequented often by several families and were used as a base of operations for diverse hunting–gathering activities. Except for these important sites, we have little substantial information on other kinds of places used by the Lawrence phase and Wister phase people. One hopes future researchers will have opportunities to fill in the gaps and explain these people's settlement practices and adaptations during these millennia of significant ecological change.

South and west of the regions inhabited by Lawrence phase and Wister phase folks occur a scatter of studied sites that were probably occupied by similar foraging bands. Because of inadequate information on assemblage compositions, assemblage ages, and site distributions, it is difficult to ascertain the character, settlement practices, or sociocultural ties of these groups to those of the Lawrence and Wister phases. Regardless of these limitations, the accumulating evidence attests to the fact that most of the eastern half of Oklahoma was inhabited by late Archaic people. Their sites and material remains offer many opportunities to learn how hunting–gathering people coped with noteworthy environmental change. More than likely, the successful adaptations of some of these people helped lay the groundwork for the later adoption of farming and the subsequent (A.D. 800–1200) rise of Caddoan societies.

Conclusion

Thirty years ago, the first synthesis of Oklahoma archaeology summarized (Bell and Baerreis 1951:96) the Archaic period by noting that there was evidence for a long, but undated, sequence, one best represented by the Grove focus in the western Ozarks and by the Fourche Maline focus in the northern Ouachita Mountains. Today, we are able to date the duration of this stage of cultural development and to begin perceiving evidence for many local adaptations to previously undocumented environmental changes. People dependent on foraging have clearly inhabited eastern Oklahoma for at least 7500 years, or from 9500 to 2000 years ago. Moreover, they apparently acquainted themselves readily with the locally available plants, animals, minerals, and settings, while developing several regionally different cultures. Whether or not these represent the remains of related people has yet to be determined. Likewise, we still do not know whether or not the sequence observable in one region occurs nearby in largely unstudied watersheds. We are certain, however, that the archaeological record for the sequence and character of hunting–gathering societies is far more complex than was ever realized. The challenge for the future is to improve our recovery and analytical techniques so that we can continue to identify and explain increasingly specific parts of this long human record.

Reference Note

This synthesis relies on reports of archaeological sites where implements, refuse, and habitation features were found in datable, stratified and/or unmixed deposits. Key references for such sites are: Baerreis 1951; Baldwin 1969, 1970; S. Baugh 1982; T. Baugh 1978; Bell 1953b; Burton and Stahl 1969; Clark 1980; C. D. Cheek *et al.* 1980; Drass 1979; Galm 1978a; Galm and Flynn 1978b; Hofman 1977a; D. T. Hughes 1977b; Neal 1974a; Powell and Rogers 1980; M. A. Ray 1965; Rohrbaugh 1972b; Rohrbaugh *et al.* 1971; Shaeffer 1966; Wyckoff 1963a, 1964a, 1966a, 1968a, 1968b, 1981; and Wyckoff and Taylor 1971. Although less securely dated or identified (due to mixing), materials left by prepottery hunting–gathering people also occur at sites reported by Barr 1966b; Bell 1958b; Bell and Dale 1953; Bobalik 1977a, 1977b, 1978, 1979a, 1979b; R. J. Burton 1971; Burton and Neal 1970; George and Wyckoff 1980; Gettys 1975; R. S. Hall 1954; Harden and Robinson 1975; D. T. Hughes 1978b, 1979; Israel 1979; Kerr and Wyckoff 1964; Lintz 1978d, 1979a, 1979b; Lintz *et al.* 1981; Lopez and Keith 1976; Lopez *et al.* 1979; McClung 1980a, 1980b; A. F. Miller 1977; Neal and Wheaton 1977; Penman 1974a; Perino and Bennett 1978; Perino and Caffey 1980; Prewitt and Lawson 1972; Proctor 1957; Purrington 1970; M. A. Ray 1960a; Schneider 1967; Sharrock 1960; Wallis 1976, 1977a, 1977b, 1980, 1981; Wittry 1952; Wyckoff 1964b, 1964c, 1965, 1967a, 1967b; Wyckoff and Barr 1967a; Wyckoff *et al.* 1963.

Acknowledgments

This chapter benefited from the thoughtful comments of Richard Drass and the proofreading of Pat Kawecki. Also, appreciation is expressed to Dr. Rain Vehik (University of Oklahoma Archaeological Research and Management Center) for the loan of artifact negatives for the Lawrence, Bug Hill, Scott, and Beaver sites.

CHAPTER 7

The Kenton Caves of Western Oklahoma

Christopher Lintz and Leon George Zabawa

Introduction

The Kenton Caves are seven of many rockshelters located in the northwestern corner of the Oklahoma Panhandle (Figure 7.1; Table 7.1). Expeditions during the late 1920s through early 1940s recovered a large amount of perishable materials because of the dry conditions within the caves. Thus, the region represents one of the few areas in western Oklahoma from which archaeologists have information about both perishable and nonperishable aspects of material culture.

The caves are located in the Tesesquite Creek Valley, a tributary of the Cimarron River, in the Black Mesa area of Cimarron County. This area is characterized by flat-topped mesas bordering gradually tapering stream valleys 8–10 km in length. The mesas are erosional remnants of sandstone and orthoquartzite deposits formed during the Mesozoic era (Fenneman 1931:40; Stovall 1943:22). The valleys were created prior to the Pleistocene, but soils in the valley bottoms range from Pleistocene to Recent in age (Wilson 1972). The vegetation is an extension of Rocky Mountain vegetation composed primarily of the piñon–juniper type with scattered trees predominantly confined to the upper slopes and rock outcrops. The floodplains and uplands are mixed grassland savannas (Duck and Fletcher 1943; Bruner 1931; Kapustka 1974; Risser, Risser, and Goodnight 1980). The fauna is that typical of the short grass and piñon–juniper ecotonal area.

Past environmental conditions in the Tesesquite Creek Valley and adjacent areas may have been somewhat different than the present. Geomorphic studies

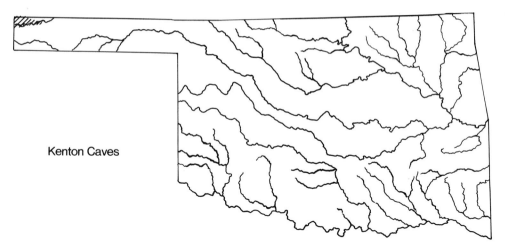

Figure 7.1 Location of Kenton Caves.

in Tesesquite Creek Valley have shown that major changes have occurred in vegetation (Wilson 1972). Buried willow, cottonwood, hackberry, juniper, and possibly pine stumps measuring up to 1 m in diameter are indicative of a valley forest. The bottomland forest extinction has been radiocarbon dated at 327 to 621 years ago (circa A.D. 1329 to 1723). These dates only reflect the termination of the bottomland forest, and not the time for development. If several centuries were necessary for the development of the forest, then woodland conditions may have been present when the caves were occupied (Wilson 1972:206–207).

History of Investigations

Although local ranchers and sheepherders have known about the caves for years, their importance was only recognized through the persistent efforts of William "Uncle Billy" Baker, the panhandle farm agent and respected avocational archaeologist. Baker's son, Ele, is credited with "discovering" Basketmaker Cave No. 1 (34Ci-50) in June 1928. Immediately, Baker contacted Dr. Leslie Spier at the Department of Anthropology, University of Oklahoma (Baker 1929a). Previous commitments, however, prevented the University from initiating fieldwork in the panhandle, so Baker agreed to monitor and preserve the site.

The 1926–1927 excavations at the Folsom early man site in New Mexico, and the development of a Southwest cultural classification at the 1927 Pecos Conference renewed interest in cultural surveys throughout the Southwest. The Colorado Museum of Natural History launched an extensive archaeological sur-

Table 7.1

Correlation of Cave Names and Expeditions to the Kenton Caves

Site number	Cave name	Expedition and year	Reference
34Ci-50	Cave No. 1	Renaud 1929	Renaud 1930a
	O-2 (Site Oklahoma-2)	Renaud 1929	Renaud fieldnotes
	Unnamed	Baker–Thoburn 1929	Baker 1929b
	Basket Maker Cave 1	Thoburn 1930	Thoburn correspondence; U.S.G.S. Topographic Map
	Mummy Cave	I. W. Mathews *et al.* 1933	Anonymous 1968
	Ci-Ke-I	Ele Baker 1934	FERA catalog number
34Ci-39 and Ci-68	Twin Caves	Renaud 1929	Renaud 1930a
	Black Caves	Wm. Baker n.d.	Baker field notes; Ele Baker, personal communication, 1980
	Labrier Site	Ponca OAS-1968?	Archaeological Survey Site forms
	Red Devil District	Lintz 1976	National Register forms
34Ci-68[a]	East Twin Cave	Renaud 1929	Renaud 1930a
	Cave No. 2	Renaud 1929	Renaud 1930a
	O-4 (Site Oklahoma-4)	Renaud 1929	Renaud fieldnotes
	Wet Cave	Wm. Baker	Ele Baker, personal communications, 1980
	Red Devil Cave	Lintz 1976	National Register forms
34Ci-39[a]	West Twin Cave	Renaud 1929	Renaud 1930a
	Cave No. 3	Renaud 1929	Renaud 1930a
	O-5 (Site Oklahoma-5)	Renaud 1929	Renaud fieldnotes
	Dry Cave	Wm. Baker	Ele Baker, personal communications, 1980
	Black Cave	Wm. Baker	Wm. Baker fieldnotes
	Red Sun Cave	Lintz 1976	National Register forms
34Ci-48	Unnamed	Thoburn 1930?	None
	Pigeon Cave	Ponca OAS-1968?	Archaeological Survey Site forms
34Ci-49	Basket Maker Cave II	Thoburn 1930[b]	Thoburn, correspondence
		Henry 1978	Henry, personal communications, 1980
34Ci-69[a]	Bat Cave	Vaughn 1928	Baker 1929a
34Ci-70	Unnamed	Stovall 1940	None—gratiffi dates and sponsor are present on wall of cave.
Unknown	Unnamed	Tate 1938[b]	Fieldnotes, Tate correspondence

[a]Site placed on National Register of Historic Places.
[b]Gratiffi at 34Ci-49 indicates WPA removal of cave paintings; portion of main chamber or smaller chamber to west may have been excavated by Tate in 1938.

vey program starting in northeastern New Mexico and adjacent areas. By November, 1928, Nelson J. Vaughan, the scout for the Colorado Museum party, reached the Kenton area and made inquiries about Bat Cave (34Ci-69). William Baker met Mr. Vaughan and showed him the newly discovered cave, 34Ci-50, after obtaining assurances that the Colorado Museum party would not disturb it (Baker 1929a).

However, on July 14, 1929, the Colorado Museum party under the direction of Dr. Etienne B. Renaud quietly conducted a brief survey and limited testing at three rockshelters in Oklahoma. The survey apparently located four rockshelters and five open sites (Renaud 1929d). Bat Cave (34Ci-69) was not tested because its northern orientation was believed to make it unsuitable for habitation. Renaud's excavations at Basketmaker Cave I (34Ci-50) and the Twin Caves (34Ci-39, 34Ci-68) lasted less than a month (Renaud 1929d; Baker 1929a). A series of excavation summaries were quickly released (Renaud 1929a, 1929b, 1929c, 1930b, 1930c), with more detailed descriptions appearing in both English and French (Renaud 1930a, 1930d, 1932).

Outraged by this breach of agreement, Baker organized a small crew of Boy Scouts in July 1929 and spent 1 day salvaging additional materials from 34Ci-50. Newspaper accounts indicate that Baker was planning to excavate other nearby shelters with deep bedrock grinding basins (Rucker 1929). Although no notes exist, his collection contains materials from the Twin Caves (34Ci-39). At a later date, he was also involved in digging other caves in the Tesesquite Valley as well as several shelters north of Boise City (Baker n.d.; Ele Baker and Bill White, personal communications, 1980).

Baker was instrumental in publishing newspaper articles concerning the removal of important Indian artifacts from state school land by the Colorado Museum party (Anonymous 1929a, 1929b; Baker 1929a; Rucker 1929). To investigate these charges, Governor Holloway directed Dr. Joseph Thoburn, historian from the Oklahoma Historical Society, to visit and report on the status of the Kenton Caves. After a brief visit in July, 1929, Thoburn sought private funding to continue excavations. Following the 1929 Pecos Conference, Thoburn returned to the Kenton area and appointed Baker to direct the official excavations for the State of Oklahoma. The length of the Baker–Thoburn excavations at 34Ci-50 is uncertain; the results, however, were published in detail (Baker 1929b).

During the winter, Thoburn sought funding for additional excavations under the Cooperative Ethnological and Archaeological Investigations Act (Public Law 248, 70th Congress 1928). The Smithsonian Institution matched a $1000 fund established by the Oklahoma Historical Society. With a $2000 budget, Thoburn spent the 3 summer months of 1930 directing excavations at Basketmaker Cave I (34Ci-50), Basketmaker Cave II (34Ci-49), and perhaps Pigeon Cave (34Ci-48). Unfortunately, little has been published about this lengthiest of all organized archaeological expeditions, and nothing is known about the work or the materials recovered.

Professional interest in the Kenton Caves waned after the 1930 excavations. However, the publicity about the cave's contents attracted many local people. A favorite school, church, or community pastime of the 1930s was to picnic at the caves and to search for souvenirs. During the course of such activities, three burials were found in 1933. In May, Mrs. I. W. Mathews discovered a desiccated or naturally mummified child at 34Ci-50 while on a school outing from Keyes; and a short time later, two adults—a mummified man and a partially mummified woman—were unearthed from the same shelter by Merrill McGee, John Tharp, and Pard Collins (Anonymous 1968:10D; Hollis 1979).

The recovery of mummified remains prompted Forrest Clements from the University of Oklahoma to sponsor a Federal Emergency Relief Administration (FERA) supported field party in June, 1934. Ele Baker directed four other workers in the clearing of 34Ci-50. Because much of the cave had been previously excavated by Renaud, William Baker, Thoburn, and various groups on weekend outings, only a small amount of materials were recovered (Bell 1953c).

Excavations near Kenton shifted from archaeology to paleontology during the latter half of the 1930s. Under the direction of Dr. J. Willis Stovall, Works Progress Administration (WPA) crews worked on sites in Ellis, Cimarron, and Texas counties, Oklahoma. The Cimarron County crew was under the supervision of Mr. Crompton Tate. After 35 months, the quantity of dinosaur remains began to diminish. In an effort to continue the WPA project, Tate shifted to the excavation of Indian remains from a cave in April 1938. Only a small quantity of prehistoric materials and almost no perishable items were recovered (Tate n.d.). This departure from paleontology was short lived. With much of the cave deposits left intact, Stovall terminated the Cimarron County field crew after less than a month at the cave (Tate 1938; Stovall 1938). Correspondence indicates that Dr. Forrest Clements from the University of Oklahoma was planning additional work at the cave in June, 1938, but apparently the project was never funded (Stovall 1938).

By late May, 1940, Stovall personally supervised five laborers on a 2-week excavation at 34Ci-70 for the WPA (Stovall 1940). It is not certain if this is the same site excavated by Crompton Tate because there are no records describing the site location. Although the shelter was totally cleared, the results have never been published and all but four items have been misplaced.

With the outbreak of World War II, major excavations in the Kenton area ceased. Several articles were published describing unique artifacts from the shelters (Baker and Kidder 1937; Renaud 1939), and a number of cultural summaries have been written (Clements 1943; Renaud 1947; Bell and Baerreis 1951; M. A. Ray 1961a; Campbell 1969, 1976; Saunders 1982). Within the last 20 years, several surveys have been conducted in adjacent areas (M. A. Holmes 1972; Campbell 1973; Lintz 1976a; Ludrick 1966; Muto and Saunders 1978; Saunders 1978; Saunders and Saunders 1982; Haury 1982). Limited excavations at two rockshelters and two open sites in North Canyon were conducted in the Fall of 1973 (Nowak and Kranzush n.d.). Recently, the University of Tulsa excavated a trench through the talus midden at Thoburn's Basketmaker Cave II (34Ci-49), and tested the terrace in front of 34Ci-115 near Lake Carl Etling (Don Henry, personal communications 1981).

The recovered artifactual remains from the Kenton Caves have been scattered. Materials from Renaud's excavations are in the University of Denver Department of Anthropology. William Baker's materials are in the No Man's Land Museum at Panhandle State University, Goodwell, Oklahoma. Some of Thoburn's materials are on display at the Oklahoma Historical Society in Oklahoma City; but the small quantity of remains suggests that much has been loaned or lost. The three mummies were divided among the principle finders. The mummified child was kept for a time under a bed at J. R. Butler's home, in John Tharp's garage, in Pard Collins' house, and even hung on the back of an upstairs door at the Kenton Hotel before being donated to the No Man's Land Museum (Hollis 1979). For over 15 years the mummified woman was kept in the attic storage area at the Kenton Hotel before being moved to a "museum" in Brownie Collins' house at Kenton. During the 1950s, Willis Stovall allegedly took the adult mummies; however, there is no trace of them at the University of Oklahoma. Materials from Ele Baker's 1934 excavations are at the Woolaroc Museum near Bartlesville and the Stovall Museum at the University of Oklahoma. The location of Crompton Tate's materials is unknown, but they may be with the WPA dinosaur materials at the University of Oklahoma. Only four items from Stovall's 1940 excavations are available at the Stovall Museum, University of Oklahoma. The location of the atlatl reported by Baker and Kidder (1937) is unknown. Finally, the recently excavated materials from 34Ci-49 are at the University of Tulsa.

Stratigraphy

Little is known about the internal structuring of the cave's deposits. This is due to the general lack of records, the excavation techniques (which were primitive by today's standards), and the changes in excavation methods (which varied from one project to another). To test each of the three caves, Renaud dug four vertical trenches; one along the central cave axis, another across the back wall, and diagonal trenches from the center mouth to each back corner. His artifact recovery techniques are not specified. William Baker used shovels and sifted the soil, but the methods of provenience control are not discussed. Thoburn's recovery techniques are largely unknown, except that he "blasted" the rocks blocking the cave. Unpublished maps by Stovall are the only records of horizontal and vertical location of materials from any of the early excavations.

The size of the caverns and depths of cultural deposits vary considerably. The best stratigraphic information is from 34Ci-50 (Baker 1929b:18; Bell 1953c). This shelter had 1.7 m of deposits, but artifacts were only found in the upper 1.2 m.

Although the relationships of the complex strata are unclear, multiple occupations are indicated in the stratigraphic descriptions. Several of the caves have internal structures reflecting different activity areas. In describing the east cave at 34Ci-68, Renaud (1929d, 1930a:130) mentions the presence of two roughly circular, vertical rock enclosures measuring 2.20 m in each corner of the cave. They may represent storage cists or small rooms (Campbell 1976). The west cave at 34Ci-39 and 34Ci-49 have clusters of bedrock grinding basins, indicating mealing areas. Both Baker (1929b:18) and Renaud (1930a) mention a series of charcoal hearths on the north side of 34Ci-50, separate from layers of grass, sage brush, small twigs, and leaves on the cave's south side, which may have been used as flooring or bedding. Although discrete activity areas are suggested, spatial patterning within the shelters are not well understood from these few passing comments.

Material Remains

A wide variety of material has been secured from the caves. Lacking clear artifact provenience, it is impossible to delineate material change through time within any shelter, or even to demonstrate that the six shelters were occupied by the same groups. The following description of materials must reflect a mixture of several cultural assemblages.

Plants provided both food and raw-material resources for a variety of utilitarian items. Foodstuffs include both domesticated products and wild floral resources. Cultivated plants include ears and shelled kernels from several varieties of corn, and stems, seeds, and rinds from either squash or pumpkin gourds (Renaud 1930a; Baker 1929b; Thoburn 1930). Analysis of corn indicates that both small and large ears of 8-, 10-, 12-, and 14-row varieties are present (Cutler 1959; J. C. Winters 1975) (Figure 7.2 a–g). A comparison of the corn varieties indicates that the "temporal provenience could range anywhere from Basketmaker III (A.D. 300) through late Prehistoric Plains, 'Puebloid,' Apache or related cultures" (Winters 1975:3). Several specimens of "early" pod corn have also been recovered (Anonymous n.d.). The pod corn resembles the earliest corn from Bat Cave in New Mexico; but this variety could also be contemporaneous with the other corn varieties (Paul Minnis, personal communications 1982). Thoburn (1930) reports the recovery of beans; if the identification is accurate, however, beans are very rare. These cultigens were supplimented by acorns, hackberry, cactus, sand plum, crocus bulbs, and other wild fruits and berries (Renaud 1930a). Often the cultigens were recovered in paired woven-grass or prairie-dog-skin bags. These bags and their contents may either represent one means of storing garden seed by suspending it away from rodents, or reflect the means of transport. Some idea of food preparation is also indicated. Corn cobs were found encased in baked clay, and three circular cakes made of acorn and wild plum or

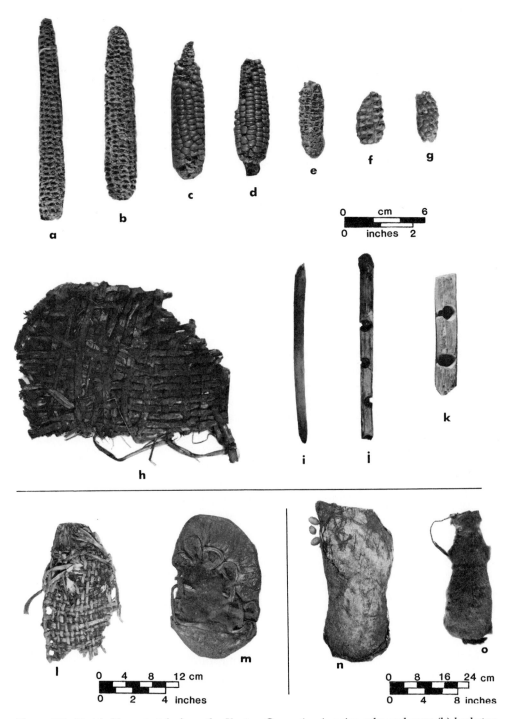

Figure 7.2 Perishable materials from the Kenton Caves: (a–g) maize cobs and ears; (h) basketry fragment; (i) fire drill; (j–k) fire-drill hearths; (l) woven sandal; (m) leather sandal; (n) skin bag stuffed with (squash?) seeds; (o) prairie-dog skin stuffed with maize kernels. Specimens courtesy of the Oklahoma Historical Society, Oklahoma City.

cherry were found at 34Ci-50 (Baker 1929a; Renaud 1930). The cakes measured 10–15 cm in diameter and less than 5 cm thick. A central hole through each cake may represent a suspension hole for cooking or storage. Corncobs impaled on short sticks may have served as bait for snaring small game.

Other plant remains were used to make a variety of items. Clothing and ornaments made from plants include several varieties of square- and round-toe sandals made of yucca leaves and padded with bark; a piece of twined fabric representing either clothing or a bag; and chinaberry-seed beads (Renaud 1930a). Although sandals are most common, mats and baskets are also known. The few examples were made of yucca or bark by four methods: coiling, simple plaiting, twilled plaiting, and single-strand twining. Small bundles of grass within loose netting formed "bags" for storing seeds. Bark and cattail leaves were occasionally used to make string, but yucca-leaf cordage served as the common binding material. The majority of cordage is two ply, but some three-ply and two-strand, two-ply cords are known. The recovery of knotted yucca and grass shows that the half hitch, double half hitch, square wreath, and a number of other knots and loops were known. True textile fabric is rare and is only represented by the previously mentioned clothing article. No nets have been found.

Game was obtained by the curved nonreturnable "boomerang" throwing stick, the atlatl (spear thrower), and the long bow. No snares or traps have been conclusively identified. Slotted and unslotted hardwood foreshafts reflect the use of compound darts, and the nock portion of at least one arrow shaft has been found, in addition to a wooden knobbed bunt.

Wood was also used in friction fire-drill basins and in a wide range of "crochet needles," hairpins, pegs, and other pointed sticks. Sticks with flattened blades may have been used as weaving battons, or in making baskets. Some sticks were used as pine pitch applicators. Several wooden tubes and wooden beads were also found. Many worked and unworked sticks were found with knotted yucca leaves wrapped around them, as well as small wooden shafts wrapped with shredded vegetable fibers.

The uses of tied bundles of grass, twigs, and sagebrush are uncertain. Some may reflect brushes or brooms, whereas others may merely reflect the means of transporting and storing raw materials for subsequent use. Some thick wads of knotted corn leaves, tied with yucca, show extensive wear as if they were used as general cleaning or scouring pads. The use of pine cones is uncertain. Finally, the layers of grass within the caves may have served as beds, or padded activity areas.

As with floral resources, faunal materials were well preserved. Pieces of fresh-water mussel shell and a crayfish claw have been recovered, along with the bones of bison, deer, antelope, elk, jackrabbit, cottontail rabbit, coyote, wildcat, badger, rodents, turtles, eagles, and turkeys (Renaud 1930a). Thus, a wide exploitation pattern involving a number of different settings is indicated.

Besides food, fresh-water mussel shells were perforated and shaped into pendants, or notched along the edge and used as scrapers and fleshers. Other ovate and circular pieces of ground mussel-shell may be bead or pendant blanks, or shell inlays. Large marine-shell disc beads and *Olivella* shell beads indicate that the people were part of an exchange system extending to the ocean.

Land animals were used in a wide variety of ways. Animal skins were fashioned into fur-lined moccasins and bags. The bags were made from prairie-dog skins complete with fur, legs, tail, and head, with cordage for a carrying strap. Leather pouches were made with and without the hair from deer, antelope, buffalo, or prairie-dog hides and used to store corn and gourd seeds. Skins were also cut into strips and braided together into furry thongs, or incorporated with yucca cordage. A small piece of a rabbit-fur blanket was recovered. A deer-hoof pendant tinkler was found on a thong with several bird-bone beads. The function of a feather bundle tied with yucca fiber is unclear. The bone technology is limited. Mammal leg-bones were split and sharpened into several varieties of awls that may have been used to manufacture basketry and leather goods. A perforated bone "shaft wrench" was also recovered. Bird bones were commonly used to make tubes and beads.

Pottery was not found by most of the expeditions. Newspaper accounts, however, mention prehistoric ceramics (Rucker 1929) and nearly 40 sherds were listed by Crompton Tate (n.d.) on the shipping roster. The Tate sherd sample has been lost and no descriptions are available. The William Baker collection from 34Ci-50 contains one cordmarked sherd with angular quartz temper, six corn cob or cordmarked sherds with fiber tempering, and three black plainware sherds with fine black-sand temper. Two fragments of an unusual black-sand-tempered clay pipe are also present. The pipe has a groove with punctations around the outside rim of the bowl, a broad smooth bowl, and at least three encircling grooves with punctates below the bowl. It is uncertain whether the specimen is an elbow or straight pipe form.

Local orthoquartzite was used to make a variety of chipped- and ground-stone tools. Primarily Tesesquite and Dakota quartzites were employed to make chipped-stone tools; small quantities, however, of opalite and jasper were also used (Lopez and Saunders 1973:3; Lintz 1976b). The lithic assemblage is rather crude with flake and bifacial knives, drills, borers, gravers, scrapers, choppers, cores, modified flakes, and manufacturing debris often being represented. A few stone arrowpoints and an occasional dart point were recovered by Tate (n.d.), and William and Ele Baker. The dart points include an unfluted "fishtail" form attributed to Paleoindian occupations, and the Williams type plus other unidentified kinds of large corner-notched forms. In comparison, the small corner-notched Scallorn, and to a lesser extent the small side-notched Washita and Harrell points and unnotched Fresno points are more abundant than the dart points.

Ground-stone items include grooved honing stones for sharpening awls and sticks, grooved shaft-smoothers, and oval grinding basins with one-handed manos. Hammerstones and "polishers" were also found, as were anvil stones with vegetal material still adhering to the working surface. One selenite pendant with a yucca string attached through the perforation and a small fragment of a possible black slate gorget were found at 34Ci-50.

Historic trade-items are very rare. The William Baker collection, however, has a small box of white, green, light blue, dark blue and black glass seed and pony beads from 34Ci-39.

Although occasional isolated human bones and teeth were found during the sponsored excavations, the best articulated burials were unearthed by amateurs. Nothing is known about the adult male burial. Both the woman and the child were buried in semiflexed positions (Anonymous 1968:10D; Hollis 1979). The woman was buried with a mat or coiled basket over her head (Bell 1953c; Hollis 1979). The child was underneath a heavy rock and was buried with a necklace of 16 *Olivella* shell beads and a grass bag of corn ears under his legs. Based on stature, the child may be about $2\frac{1}{2}$ years old (Archie Hood, personal communication 1982). He does not appear to be clothed, although close examination shows what may be part of a G-string. The lack or scarcity of clothing suggests that death may have occurred during the spring or summer. The skeletons do not have deformed heads (Bell 1953c).

Several of the caves have painted or scratched-rock art motifs. A reported polychrome painting at 34Ci-49 was apparently removed by the WPA crews. Most of the identifiable painted figures are anthropomorphic, although the styles vary considerably (Figure 7.3). Some are solid-painted, square-shouldered

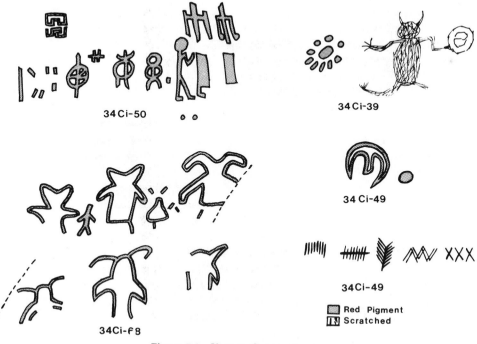

Figure 7.3 Kenton Cave rock art.

adults dressed in kilts or mantas in association with naked children. Others are outlines of long eared or horned figures. Other painted motifs include the sun or flower, Najahe crescent, and phi designs. Most of the grooved petroglyphs include a series of tally marks, zigzags, feathers, and X motifs. One exception is the lightly scratched horned anthropomorphic figure holding a shield at the west shelter of the Twin Caves (34Ci-39). In general, rock-art sites are abundant in the Black Mesa region (Burchardt 1958; Campbell 1973; T. Clark 1969; Lawton 1962; Moorehead 1931:117; Renaud 1937). The variations in the stylistic designs suggests that several different traditions are represented.

Interpretation and Conclusions

Cultural assignment of the Kenton Cave material has been extensively debated. Heavily influenced by the newly constructed Pecos classification and noting some similarities in the perishable assemblage, Renaud (1930a:34) thought the materials represented a stage above the seminomadic hunter and below the sedentary Pueblos. He suggests that the materials were "an early, very primitive phase of the Basketmaker culture, an incipient stage preceding its more complete characterization elsewhere." He suggests a date of circa 1500 B.C. for the Kenton caves based on the presence of basketry, painted figures, and maize, and on the absence of pottery from his 1929 excavations. Similarly, the absence of pottery and small points from the published literature has led M. A. Ray (1961a) to attribute the materials to an Archaic lifestyle. Another summary acknowledges considerable antiquity, but stops short of dating the materials (Bell and Baerreis 1951:17). These earlier summaries were based on materials from one or two expeditions and secondary sources, and have not considered the full range of materials available from the shelters. In general, cultural affiliations are tenuous because there is little stratigraphic information available to segregate the assemblages, and there is a paucity of comparable perishable materials from the Plains region to the east.

Undoubtedly the caves have considerable antiquity. Stovall (1943:119) found late Pliocene-age horse and camel bones beneath the cultural remains at 34Ci-70. The recovery of an unfluted "fishtail" point from 34Ci-50 may indicate some late Paleoindian or early Archaic use of the shelters. The large corner-notched points, wooden atlatl, and pod-corn may be indicative of later Archaic occupations; these items, however, are rare and could well coincide with subsequent use of the caves. Although projectiles and pottery were not abundant, most of the styles are post-Archaic. The many Scallorn and, to a lesser extent, Washita, Harrell, and Fresno points, along with the long bow, suggest occupations by both Woodland and Plains Village stage groups. In addition, numerous Woodland and Plains Village sites have been recorded in the adjacent Black Mesa State Park on South Carrizo Creek (Saunders 1978), and in the environmentally similar Chaquaqua Plateau in Southeastern Colorado (Campbell 1969; 1976). The recovery of thin, black-sand-tempered plainware pottery and glass beads from the shelters, as well as numerous adjacent pictograph sites depicting mounted Indians, suggests both protohistoric and historic use of the caves. Undoubtedly even sheepherders and cowboys used the caves, although nothing in the material assemblage reflects their use.

No radiocarbon dates have yet been reported from the six Kenton Caves. One date of A.D. 560 ± 150 (no lab number reported) was obtained from a rockshelter in North Canyon, some 12.8 km northeast of the Tesesquite Valley (Nowak and Kranzush n.d.). The radiocarbon dates obtained by the University of Tulsa from Thoburn's cave 34Ci-49 have yet to be published.

Research to further our understanding on the Kenton Caves based on firm stratigraphic information may soon be available from the University of Tulsa excavation. The caves, however, are only a small part of a larger settlement system within the Tesesquite Valley. The regional prehistory should also concentrate on studying other site situations within a broader area base. A number of site types in various topographic situations are already known—including stone structures, bison kills, terrace sites, lithic quarries, and tipi rings (Muto and Saunders 1978). These other sites must be studied in conjunction with the caves to correct the distorted exploitative-settlement situation in the mesa and canyon land area. Intensive survey of the Black Mesa State Park has tentatively defined shifts in the settlement pattern between the Woodland and Late Prehistoric periods (Saunders 1978). Between A.D. 200 and 1000, Woodland groups located major habitation camps on stream terraces and caves, whereas specialized activity sites were located on bluff tops, talus slopes, and stream terraces. The Late Prehistoric groups, however, (A.D. 1000–1500) located camps and villages on bluff tops, in addition to the stream terraces and shelters. Perhaps defense became a concern in the selection of campsite locations (Campbell 1969; 1976).

Additional study of the existing Kenton Cave materials would not be without merit. A detailed botanical analysis of the number and variety of floral remains could determine what resources were grown, which areas were exploited, and perhaps the seasons of occupations. Similarly, a study of faunal remains might be helpful in interpreting the exploitation patterns at the caves. A detailed description and analysis of the remaining artifacts would help establish a comparative basis for materials from other sites in the region.

Little definitive information can be provided from a literature review. Scattered artifact collections, inadequate material descriptions, poor provenience information, and a lack of specialized studies severely limits our present knowledge of the cultural resources located in the mesa and canyon lands of the northwestern Oklahoma panhandle.

Acknowledgments

The organization of this chapter is based on a draft report prepared by Roger Saunders, and it is with extreme regret that he declined coauthorship of this version. Many people opened their files and institutions during our studies. We thank Ele Baker, Bill White and Mrs. I. W. Mathews for their personal recollections about the early work at the caves, and Don Henry for information about the recent University of Tulsa fieldwork. Hellen Pushmueller of the Department of Anthropology, Denver University; Lynn Barnes and Martha Blaine of the Oklahoma Historical Society; Harold and Joan Kachel of the No Man's Land Museum; K. D. Meeks of the Woolaroc Museum; and Candace Greene and Robert Bell of the Stovall Museum gave us access to records and allowed us to examine collections on display and in storage. In addition, Waldo Wedel of the Smithsonian Institution; Jack Haley of the Western History Archives, University of Oklahoma; Don Wyckoff of the Oklahoma Archaeological Survey; Jiri Zedik and L. R. Wilson of the Oklahoma Geological Survey; and Rose King, secretary of the Oklahoma Anthropological Society, checked additional records and helped run down leads. Archie Hood and Paul Mennis provided their specialized expertise. Roger Saunders provided the artifact plate. Finally, Charles Wallis, Jr., listened and challenged many ideas during the formative stages of this chapter.

CHAPTER 8

The Woodland Occupations

Susan C. Vehik

Introduction

Woodland occupations of Oklahoma are not well known, principally because of a lack of diagnostic artifacts, clear stratigraphy, and radiocarbon dates. It is necessary to address briefly each of these problems before trying to synthesize what we know about Oklahoma Woodland occupations.

On the Great Plains, Woodland occupations are considered to reflect the extension, direct and indirect, of developments that occurred in the woodland area of the upper Midwest. Plains Woodland sites have, traditionally, been identified by the presence of pottery that was elongated in form, had conoidal bottoms, and was frequently cord marked and grit tempered. Also, at least on the eastern margin of the Plains, there are sherds resembling Hopewellian zone-decorated wares. In addition to pottery, corner-notched dart and arrowpoints, shell disc beads, burial in mounds or ossuaries, an increase in the frequency of grinding stones, and the appearance of tools associated with horticultural activities are also considered diagnostic.

Unfortunately, many items that serve successfully as diagnostics for the Woodland in other areas of the Plains are absent, infrequent, or nondiagnostic in much of Oklahoma. Pottery is infrequent, especially in earlier sites, and in some areas of the state it seems to remain infrequent. As a result, little is known of vessel shape and, from what information is available, it appears that tempering and surface finish were variable (Hartley 1974a:129) and Purrington 1970:531–543.

Projectile points, the other artifact class most commonly used to assign temporal and cultural affiliations, present difficulties similar to those outlined for pottery. Corner-notched points (both dart and arrow forms) seem to reach their highest frequencies during the Woodland time period in Oklahoma. However, they also appear in the Late Archaic and extend into the post-Woodland (Wyckoff *et al.* 1963 [citing Baerreis 1951]; Purrington 1970:10–13). Contracting-stem dart points reflect much the same pattern as corner-notched points. Also, projectile point forms more characteristic of earlier and later groups are present in Woodland occupations. Finally, there is the possibility that arrowpoints appear earlier in the grasslands whereas dart points remain dominant in the woodland areas until post-Woodland times.

It is presently difficult to use the increased frequency of grinding stones as a diagnostic because few Woodland sites have been adequately excavated to permit trust in quantitative values. Also, grinding stones are quite task specific and sites at which grinding activities were not engaged in would be undersampled. In addition, problems would certainly be encountered in distinguishing Woodland sites from post-Woodland sites on this basis.

Tools directly associated with horticultural activities are few. Stone hoes occur in eastern areas of the state during the Woodland time period but they have also been found in sites dating to both earlier and later periods (Wyckoff and Barr 1964:23–27; S. S. Burton 1970:41). For the most part, tools associated with horticultural activities do not become frequent until late, when the transition was being made to post-Woodland occupations.

Shell disc beads are infrequent and may reflect the general paucity of Woodland burials (in which shell disc beads are most frequently found).

Also, it must be noted that the nature of early ceramic occupations in southeastern Oklahoma reflects a different set of diagnostic artifacts and attributes. These occupations are prominently characterized by a thick plainware tempered with grog and, less frequently, grit and other materials (this form continued as a utilitarian ware into the subsequent Gibson aspect). These early ceramic occupations are commonly known as Fourche Maline and bear certain, still mostly undefined, relationships to the southeastern United States. Although not commonly so considered, it has been suggested that the Fourche Maline ceramic components be considered part of the Woodland period or stage (Galm 1978a:26). No doubt these Fourche Maline groups exercised some, as yet mostly undefined, influence on cultures resident in other parts of Oklahoma. This may be one of the reasons why the Southern Plains Woodland deviates from the situation in the more northerly portions of the Plains.

The situation here then is that many artifact types considered to reflect Plains Woodland occupations are either absent, infrequent, or are also found in earlier and/or later occupations. The net effect is that it is difficult to assign a site or site component to the Woodland.

Many of the problems just noted are a result of or compounded by the lack of distinct stratigraphic separation of occupation levels in many sites. Thus, relatively shallow sites may have the products of several occupations intermixed. Also these sites have frequently been further mixed by plowing. Finally, even further compounding this situation, is the use of fairly large arbitrary excavation levels and the lack of research directed toward defining stratigraphic differences.

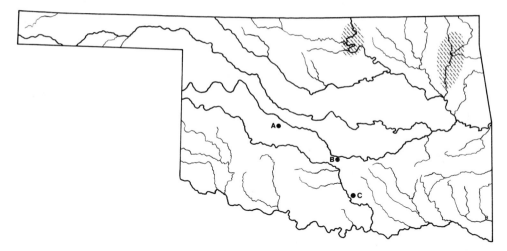

Figure 8.1 Woodland sites in Oklahoma: A, Duncan–Wilson site; B, Brewer site; C, Pruitt site. Hatching indicates northeastern and northcentral (especially Kaw Reservoir) areas.

Although there are quite a few radiocarbon dates for the Woodland they come from only a few sites in widely scattered localities. For the most part, this represents the exigencies of contract archaeology that has been generally underfunded and is concentrated in the eastern portion of the state.

Unfortunately, at the present time there is little that can be done to alleviate the difficulties discussed above. More effort is needed in defining stratigraphic positions, obtaining radiocarbon dates, and refining artifact typologies. It is with these problems in mind that we begin our survey of Oklahoma Woodland occupations.

The distribution of sites presently assigned to the Woodland indicates a tendency to cluster into three groups: (1) Ozark Plateau and Neosho Lowland, or northeastern Oklahoma; (2) the northern Cuesta Plains, or northcentral Oklahoma, and (3) the southern area of the Central Redbed Plains and adjacent areas, or southcentral Oklahoma (Figure 8.1). This distribution reflects the concentration of archaeological activities and probably does not reflect adequately the original distribution of Woodland occupations. However, because the three areas show distinct differences in their Woodland occupations, each is discussed separately.

Northeastern Oklahoma

The Woodland occupations of northeastern Oklahoma are generally organized by a tripartite system: Delaware A focus, Cooper focus, and Delaware B focus. There are few radiocarbon dates available for these foci and most of them are in dispute.

Much of the discussion that follows is based on Purrington (1970) who re-analyzed and reorganized material from Works Progress Administration (WPA) projects. It should be kept in mind, however, that site deposits seem to have been subjected to frequent mixing and that perhaps too much faith was placed on contents of relatively thick arbitrary levels. In addition to Purrington, information was also derived from the following sources: Baerreis 1951, 1953; Baerreis and Freeman 1961; Baerreis *et al.* 1956; Bell and Baerreis 1951; R. S. Hall 1954; Kerr and Wyckoff 1964; McHugh 1963; M. A. Ray 1965; Wyckoff 1964d; Wyckoff and Barr 1964; and Wyckoff *et al.* 1963.

The Delaware A focus is considered to have been a gradual development out of the Late Archaic Grove C focus. The appearance of contracting-stem projectile points such as Gary and Langtry is one criteria used to separate Delaware A from Grove C. This presumably occurred sometime around A.D. 1 or shortly thereafter. Ceramics, including Delaware Plain and Delaware Cord-Marked, are thought to have appeared after contracting-stem points.

Only eight sites or their components have been assigned to the Delaware A focus, and these include Cooper Shelter, Huffaker 2, Evans 2 (Zone 4), Smith I and II (Zones 1 and 2), Guffy 4 (Levels 3–5), Guffy 5 (Levels 2–4), and possibly Area 6 of the Reed Site. With the exception of the first three, most of the others seem to be of mixed or doubtful assignment.

There is an equal number of rockshelter and open sites. Except for the two Smith shelters, which are in the eastern Neosho (Grand) River bluffs, the Delaware A focus sites occur on eastern tributaries of that river.

Direct evidence of Delaware A focus subsistence resources is minimal. Unidentified bone and shell debris has been noted for some of the shelters. In at least one instance, shell represented 80% of the recovered faunal remains.

More general knowledge about subsistence practices may be obtained by organizing artifacts into functional categories in the manner proposed by Fowler (1959) and Winters (1969). Purrington (1970) has already organized his data in this manner and reference should be made to him for details. Rockshelter sites tend to be dominated by items associated with hunting and kill-processing activities. Open sites have a wider range of material and, although hunting and kill processing were the most frequently represented activities, plant processing was relatively more frequently represented than it had been in the shelters. Other activities represented in open sites included lithic processing and woodworking.

Pottery is seldom found in Delaware A but what there is can generally be assigned to the types Delaware Plain and Delaware Cord-Marked. Delaware pottery is tempered with grit (crushed sandstone) and/or shell. Both jar and bowl forms are represented and these have conoidal to flat-disc bases. In general these forms resemble the Woodward Plain forms of the later Neosho Focus. Delaware Cord-Marked occasionally had cord-wrapped stick impressions, incised chevrons, or barrel-shaped punctates on the lip.

The predominant chipped-stone artifacts are projectile points. Gary and Langtry varieties of contracting-stem points are most common. Other point types, such as Marshall, Marcos, Guffy, Williams, Delaware, McConkey, Table Rock Stemmed, and Smith (all either [1] straight-stemmed, [2] large expanding-stemmed, or [3] small barbed or expanding-stemmed points), continue from the Archaic. Also found were Cooper, White River Elliptical, Sequoyah, Scallorn and Reed points (all either corner-notched dart points or triangular, stemmed, or notched arrowpoints), which are characteristic of later Woodland or post-Woodland groups.

The remainder of the chipped-stone inventory includes knives, scrapers, drills, single- and double-bitted axes, and hoes. Knives consist of a variety of forms, mostly unhafted, but some had contracting-stem bases. It is possible that some items now more frequently classified as preforms or blanks may have been included in the knife category. Scrapers include bifacial and unifacial forms, which are sometimes found in combination with side scrapers and knives. Disc scrapers are relatively infrequent.

Ground-stone items include manos (ovoid to subrectangular), which may have one or more pits in one surface, grinding stones (similar to manos but with minimal intentional modification), milling slabs (rare, either flat tabular or deep basin in form), nutting stones, hammerstones, flat and grooved abraders, and ground hematite chunks.

Bone and shell tools were relatively rare. There were a few antler and bone flakers, a possible bone flesher, bone beamers and bone awls (mostly made of splinters). Shell artifacts include turtle-shell bowls, mussel-shell disc beads, and mussel-shell hoes with central perforations.

Data regarding Delaware A focus burial procedures are lacking, although it is possible that Cooper Shelter was a burial area from Grove C through the Neosho focus. So few grave goods were found in association that it is difficult to assign burials confidently to a specific focus.

Data indicating the nature and direction of Delaware A focus external relationships are minimal. Cord-marked pottery with conoidal bases and grit tempering is similar to that of the Central Plains and the Ozark Highland. The appearance of Cooper projectile points and disc scrapers has been taken to indicate minimal Hopewellian influence. Thus, on the basis of present evidence, Delaware A focus seems to reflect cultural developments mainly to the north and east.

The Cooper focus appeared in northeast Oklahoma sometime during the Delaware A focus. Three radiocarbon dates are available from the two Cooper sites (Table 8.1). D1-33, believed to be the earlier of the two sites, has a date of A.D. 991. Although certainly later than the A.D. 1 to 500 range for Kansas City Hopewell (A. E. Johnson 1976:5) this date is not out of line with the circa A.D. 900 date for Hopewellian material in southeastern Kansas (Marshall 1972:232). D1-49, which is supposed to be later on the basis of its ceramic relationships, has a very late date and a date that seems to be too early (Table 8.1). At present it seems safe only to conclude that the temporal range for the Cooper focus is unknown. Whatever its beginning date, Cooper is marked by an increase in Cooper points (which resemble Snyders) and by the appearance of zone-stamped pottery.

Four sites have been assigned to the Cooper focus: two Cooper sites, Cope-

Table 8.1

Radiocarbon Dates: Woodland Occupations

Laboratory number	Site and provenience	Date before present (B.P.)	Date (A.D.) based on 5568 half-life	Date (A.D.) based on 5730 half-life	MASCA corrected date (A.D.)[a]	Reference
Tx-1907	Von Elm (Ka-10) F. 2, pit, charcoal	1750 ± 80	200	148	214 ± 109	Hartley 1974a:77
Tx-1908	Von Elm (Ka-10) F. 2, pit, charcoal	1360 ± 60	590	549	610 ± 72	Hartley 1974a:77
Tx-1909	Von Elm (Ka-10) F. 2, pit, charcoal	1740 ± 60	210	158	219 ± 84	Hartley 1974a:77
Tx-1910	Von Elm (Ka-10) F. 3, pit, charcoal	1470 ± 50	480	436	516 ± 78	Hartley 1974a:80
Tx-1911	Vickery (Ka-41) F. 1, pit, charcoal	1520 ± 80	430	384	472 ± 115	Rohrbaugh 1974:43
Tx-1782	Freeman (Os-59) F. 3, pit, charcoal	530 ± 80	1420	1404	1377 ± 91	Valastro et al. 1977:312
Tx-1780	Daniels (Ka-77) Area A, hearth, charcoal	770 ± 70	1180	1157	1179 ± 98	Valastro et al. 1977:313
Tx-1781	Daniels (Ka-77) Area B, F. 1, pit, charcoal	1060 ± 100	890	858	913 ± 145	Valastro et al. 1977:313
Tx-2352	Hammons (Ka-20) F. 1, pit, charcoal	1600 ± 80	350	302	367 ± 117	Young 1978:86
Tx-2353	Hammons (Ka-20) F. 1, pit, charcoal	1870 ± 70	80	24	47 ± 113	Young 1978:86
Tx-2354	Hammons (Ka-20) F. 2, hearth, charcoal	1810 ± 190	140	86	170 ± 246	Young 1978:86
Tx-2355	Hammons (Ka-20) Level 9 (54"), charcoal	1470 ± 130	480	436	508 ± 176	Young 1978:86
I-9621	Sunny Shelter (Os-135), 40–50 cm, charcoal	920 ± 80	1030	1002	1046 ± 103	Henry 1977b:94
I-9622	Sunny Shelter (Os-135), 90–100 cm, charcoal	1175 ± 80	775	740	795 ± 124	Henry 1977b:94
SMU-372	Big Hawk Shelter (Os-114), 50–60 cm, charcoal	1131 ± 56	819	785	845 ± 87	Henry 1977c:95
SMU-379	Big Hawk Shelter (Os-114), 70–80 cm, charcoal	1322 ± 48	628	588	648 ± 61	Henry 1977c:95
SMU-380	Big Hawk Shelter (Os-114), 80–90 cm, charcoal	1538 ± 83	412	366	452 ± 122	Henry 1977c:95
SMU-381	Big Hawk Shelter (Os-114), 90–100 cm, charcoal	1618 ± 60	332	283	350 ± 90	Henry 1977c:95
WIS-449	Weston (Os-99), Unit I, charcoal	990 ± 60	960	930	985 ± 76	Howard 1971:29
I-9620	Painted Shelter (Os-129) 50–60 cm, charcoal	1450 ± 80	500	456	526 ± 113	Henry 1977b:68

Lab no.	Provenience and material	Date ± SD			MASCA corrected[a]	Reference
WIS-309	Cooper (Dl-49), 8–12″, late component, charcoal	680 ± 55	1270	1250	1273 ± 70	Bender et al. 1969:230
WIS-313	Cooper (Dl-49), 8–12″, late component, charcoal	1840 ± 60	110	55	123 ± 80	Bender et al. 1969:230
WIS-307	Cooper (Dl-33), 8–12″, early component, charcoal	980 ± 55	970	941	991 ± 71	Bender et al. 1969:230
WIS-198	Copeland Shelter (Dl-47), 48–52″, late Woodland, charcoal	590 ± 50	1360	1342	1346 ± 62	Bender et al. 1968:166
WIS-201	Copeland Shelter (Dl-47), 48–52″, late Woodland, charcoal	580 ± 50	1370	1353	1352 ± 63	Bender et al. 1968:166
GaK-899	Pruitt (Mr-12) F. 8, pit, charcoal	1260 ± 90	690	652	712 ± 127	Barr 1966c:125
GaK-900	Pruitt (Mr-12) F. 8, bell-shaped pit, charcoal	1140 ± 90	810	776	833 ± 138	Barr 1966c:125
Sm-692	Duncan–Wilson (Cd-11), Level 8, charcoal	865 ± 195	1085	1059	1097 ± 254	Lawton 1968:10
Sm-693	Duncan–Wilson (Cd-11), Level 10, charcoal	918 ± 195	1032	1005	1045 ± 269	Lawton 1968:10
Sm-772	Duncan–Wilson (Cd-11), Level 15, charcoal	1430 ± 170	520	477	540 ± 227	Lawton 1968:10
Sm-773	Duncan–Wilson (Cd-11), Level 20, charcoal	1520 ± 70	430	384	447 ± 243	Lawton 1968:10
Tx-865	Currie (Gv-22), house, log, charcoal	580 ± 70	1370	1353	1348 ± 83	Lintz 1974:48–49
Tx-861	Currie (Gv-22), house, log, charcoal	800 ± 70	1150	1126	1163 ± 97	Lintz 1974:48–49
Tx-860	Currie (Gv-22), house, log, charcoal	910 ± 70	1040	1013	1057 ± 88	Lintz 1974:48–49
Tx-833	Currie (Gv-22), house, post, charcoal	870 ± 70	1080	1054	1107 ± 104	Lintz 1974:48–49
Tx-831	Currie (Gv-22), house, post, charcoal	780 ± 70	1170	1147	1169 ± 101	Lintz 1974:48–49
Tx-830	Currie (Gv-22), house, charred corn cob	890 ± 70	1060	1033	1087 ± 97	Lintz 1974:48–49[b]
Tx-832	Currie (Gv-22), house, burned thatch	710 ± 70	1240	1219	1259 ± 87	Lintz 1974:48–49
Tx-857	Currie (Gv-22), house, burned thatch	560 ± 80	1390	1373	1360 ± 94	Lintz 1974:48–49
Tx-858	Currie (Gv-22), house, burned thatch and vines	830 ± 50	1120	1095	1143 ± 77	Lintz 1974:48–49
Tx-862	Currie (Gv-22), house, burned vines	560 ± 70	1390	1373	1362 ± 85	Lintz 1974:48–49
Tx-863	Currie (Gv-22), house, burned vines	790 ± 60	1160	1136	1163 ± 90	Lintz 1974:48–49
Tx-864	Currie (Gv-22), house, burned vines	650 ± 70	1300	1281	1296 ± 90	Lintz 1974:48–49

[a] MASCA dates corrected following procedures outlined by Rippeteau (1974).
[b] Corn cob date corrected by subtracting 250 years.

land 2 Zone Three and Evans 2 Zone Three. The Cooper sites are large open sites at the juncture of Honey Creek and the Neosho. The other two sites are shelters on a tributary of the Neosho.

With the exception of brief mention by Bell and Baerreis (1951:30) that decayed bone, along with deer and bison teeth, had been found at the Cooper sites, there are no data relating directly to subsistence practices. Purrington (1970:394–396) studied only a portion of the Cooper sites material, but does not indicate functional categories. At the two shelters, hunting and kill-processing tools are most frequent, whereas plant-processing tools occur infrequently.

Baerreis (1953) originally organized the pottery from Cooper into four types: Cooper Zoned Stamped, Ozark Zoned Stamped, Cowskin Dentate Stamped, and Honey Creek Plain. Purrington (1970) further subdivided Cooper Zoned Stamped on the basis of tempering. Cooper Zoned Stamped now has two varieties, one with quartz grit-temper and the other with grit and shell temper (like the Delaware types). Decoration techniques include incising, stamping, embossing, and punctation. Organization of these techniques into designs is variable but usually is accomplished in a zone format alternating dentate stamping with smooth areas. Base form is rounded to slightly conoidal.

Ozark Zoned Stamped is tempered with clay, or clay and grit. Decoration techniques are similar to those outlined above. There is considerable overlap in designs between Cooper Zoned and Ozark Zoned but the latter seems to have made greater use of crosshatching and lesser use of punctation. There is also an apparent tendency toward the contraction of decoration to the upper rim area. A similar trend is seen in Weaver ware from Illinois (Baerreis 1953).

Cowskin Dentate Stamped has grit and shell temper. Decoration techniques include incising, stamping and punctation, with these limited to the lip or rim–lip area. Designs are relatively simple diagonal or horizontal arrangements and there is little or no zonation. Base form ranges from round to slightly conoidal.

Honey Creek Plain is the plainware for the preceding types. Considering Purrington's redefinition of ceramics from this area, some of these sherds could not now be distinguished from Delaware Plain.

Discussion of the other artifact categories is somewhat hampered by the fact that Purrington analyzed only projectile points from D1-33, drills from D1-49, and superficially considered scrapers from D1-49. The remainder of the material from these two sites has been only briefly described by Bell and Baerreis (1951).

One of the major diagnostic characteristics for Cooper focus is the high frequency of Cooper corner-notched points, which resemble corner-notched specimens from Kansas City and Illinois Hopewell sites. Other types include Gary, Langtry, Marshall, Williams, Scallorn, Alba, Young, Fresno, and Sequoyah. The latter five are small arrowpoint forms and are relatively infrequent.

Knife forms are little different from those in Delaware A. Disc scrapers seem to have been the most frequent scraper form, however, unifacial and bifacial end scrapers also occur. Other chipped-stone artifacts include the combination knife–end scrapers, drills (some of which are reworked Cooper points), and chipped-stone axes.

Information about ground-stone artifacts is principally from Bell and Baerreis (1951) although there is some information from the two shelters. Large numbers of oval manos and a few oval basin milling slabs are found at the Cooper sites. In addition to these there are flat abraders, nutting stones, some fragments of a polished hematite perforated gorget, and a polished hematite boatstone.

Two fragments of a small pottery figurine were recovered from D1-33 (Figure 8.2a). The head fragment is portrayed with a rounded coil of hair on the right rear side of the head and elongated ear lobes. The other fragment includes the area from the waist to the knees, with the figure portrayed wearing a breech-cloth. These two fragments resemble figurines from other Hopewellian areas.

Based on the preceding information it appears that the two Cooper sites may have been permanently occupied villages. The shelters, on the other hand, appear to represent temporary hunting camps.

Little is known about burial practices. No mound burial is known for the area. Bell and Baerreis (1951:33) suggested that Cooper shelter was a burial area for some of the residents of the Cooper sites. There is little evidence for or against this proposition, except for the stratigraphically variable placements.

The Cooper sites and the Cooper focus in general are thought to reflect a Hopewellian intrusion into the northeast Oklahoma area. There are a small number of potsherds resembling material from Kansas City Hopewell. In addition, the trend in Cooper focus ceramics toward a contraction of decoration to the rim–lip area is also represented in the Illinois Hopewell series, southeast Kansas Hopewell, and in Kansas City Hopewell. The use of grit as temper is also shared with Kansas City and Illinois Hopewell (southeast Kansas material is clay tempered). Projectile point types also resemble those of Kansas City and Illinois Hopewell. It is presently impossible to locate more explicitly the source area for the Cooper focus.

The nature of the relationship between the Cooper focus and the indigeneous residents is also presently undefined. Not much is known about the geographical distribution of Cooper focus sites but the available evidence seems to suggest that they stayed relatively close to major drainages. It has been suggested by Purrington (1970:535) that Delaware A continued through and beyond Cooper focus, perhaps assimilating Cooper in the process.

The Cooper focus is suggested to have been in decline by A.D. 700 (Purrington 1970:538). None of the three presently available radiocarbon dates can serve to affirm or revise that date.

The Cooper and Delaware foci are followed by the Delaware B focus. Delaware B is essentially a continuation of Delaware A with the addition of some Caddoan traits. No dates are available to suggest when those traits might have first appeared. Most likely, this was sometime after A.D. 900. As for a termination date there are two dates centering around A.D. 1340 from the Copeland 2 shelter and these apparently date a zone having an intermixture of Woodland

a

b

c

d

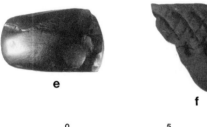

e

f

g

h

i

j

k

l

m

n

o

and Neosho focus material. Considering that the dates for the Neosho focus center on A.D. 1400, a date around A.D. 1300 appears to be an acceptable termination date for Delaware B occupations.

The following sites are included in Delaware B: Guffy 4 (Levels 1 and 2), Guffy 5 (Level 1), possibly Reed 6, Smith 1 Shelter (Zones 1 and 2), Cooper Shelter (Zone 2), and Evans 2 (Zones 1 and 2). The latter three sites have mixed deposits. With the exception of Smith 1, which is in the east Neosho River bluffs, all sites are on tributaries of the Neosho. Cooper and Reed are shelters whereas the rest are open sites. No faunal remains are mentioned for any of these sites. All of them are dominated by tools associated with hunting and kill-processing activities. Guffy 4 seems to have been intensively occupied, has evidence for a wide range of activities, and thus may have been a village site. Guffy 5, although seemingly less intensively occupied, shows a similar range of material.

What limited evidence there is, then, suggests a combination of village sites on river floodplains and hunting camps in similar locations as well as in bluff shelters. There is no unequivocable evidence for the practice of agriculture.

The ceramic inventory is dominated by Delaware Plain and Cord-Marked. In addition, there is a shell-tempered plain and cord-marked series, a limestone-tempered plain and cord-marked series, and varying amounts of Woodward Plain-Neosho Variety, which is a Neosho focus trait. Caddoan sherds are absent to very rare.

The chipped-stone assemblage is marked by increased frequencies of small arrowpoints, including: Fresno, Young, White River Elliptical, Reed, Haskell, Scallorn, and Sequoyah. Gary, Langtry, Cooper, Marshall, Marcos, Williams, Guffy, Delaware and Table Rock Stemmed are not infrequent.

Other chipped-stone material includes knives, scrapers, drills, axes, and hoes. Knife forms include some that are small and ovate in shape, as well as some with contracting-stemmed bases. Scrapers include the bifacial and unifacial end-scrapers noted earlier, a new combination side- and end-scraper with a medial ridge, and disc scrapers. The latter is relatively rare, however. Single- and double-bitted axes seem to have increased in frequency, as did the chipped-stone hoes.

Ground stone includes manos, small and minimally modified grinding stones, milling slabs, nutstones, grooved abraders, ear spools, and chunks of such

---

Figure 8.2 Artifacts from Woodland occupations in Oklahoma: (a) Pottery figurine, Cooper site, northeast Oklahoma; (b) Ozark Zone Stamped rim sherd, Cooper site, northeast Oklahoma; (c) Cooper Zone Stamped rim sherd, Cooper site, northeast Oklahoma; (d) corner-notched dart point, Cooper site, northeast Oklahoma; (e) hematite celt, Hammons site, northcentral Oklahoma; (f) Ozark Zone Stamped rim sherd, Hammons site, northcentral Oklahoma; (g) Williams-type point, Hammons site, northcentral Oklahoma; (h) Gary-type point, Hammons site, northcentral Oklahoma; (i) elliptical scraper, Hammons site, northcentral Oklahoma; (j) bone pinhead, Brewer site, southcentral Oklahoma; (k) Scallorn-type point, Brewer site, southcentral Oklahoma; (l) limestone and crushed sandstone tempered vessel, Brewer site, southcentral Oklahoma; (m) bone needle, Brewer site, southcentral Oklahoma; (n) bone awl, Brewer site, southcentral Oklahoma; (o) stone pipe, Brewer site, southcentral Oklahoma.

minerals as hematite, chalk, and galena. The ear spools are thought to reflect Caddoan influences.

Bone and antler tools include awls, flakers, beamers, fleshers, a fishhook, and a deer-mandible sickle. Shell artifacts include turtle-shell bowls and centrally perforated mussel-shell hoes.

There are presently no data available regarding burial practices.

We have already noted that Caddoan cultures were influencing Delaware B. The Reed site, which is the most northern known Spiro focus ceremonial center, is about 13 km downstream from the Guffy sites at the confluence of the Cowskin with the Neosho. Dates for Reed concentrate between A.D. 1000 and 1250 (uncorrected). Purrington (1970:543) has suggested that the Guffy sites may have continued to be occupied by Delaware B people after the founding of Reed. It is possible that Spiro focus influences on Delaware B may have ultimately transformed the latter into the Neosho focus.

Before proceeding on to the second group of Woodland sites, there is another class of archaeological sites that seems to belong to the Woodland. This class consists of burned-rock mounds positioned on bluff tops overlooking river valleys. What few radiocarbon dates there are center around A.D. 400–500. Unfortunately, because the mounds contain minimal artifactual material, we do not know what their function was and we cannot assign them to any particular archaeological unit. In fact, they may be accretional and utilized for different purposes through time (Vehik and Pailes 1979: 207–210).

Northcentral Oklahoma

West of the Ozark Plateau is the Cross Timbers (postoak–blackjack forest) and tall-grass prairie area of northcentral Oklahoma. This area produces most of the Woodland sites and radiocarbon dates, however, no foci or phases have been identified. As a result the material was organized using the following procedures. Those sites with radiocarbon dates were organized sequentially, their artifact inventories characterized by projectile point and ceramic styles and then those sites with relatively similar dates and artifact styles were grouped together to form broad temporal–stylistic units. The final step was to add to these units other sites in the area based on their shared stylistic features. With few exceptions only excavated sites were used. Major references for this section include: Bastian 1969; Gettys, Layhe and Bobalik 1976; Hartley 1974a, 1975b; Henry 1977a, 1977b, 1977c; J. A. Howard 1970, 1971; Leehan 1977; Neal 1974b; Rohrbaugh 1973a, 1974; Vehik and Pailes 1979; and Young 1978.

The Hammons site in the Arkansas River Valley has the earliest radiocarbon dates for this area (Table 8.1). The most extensive occupation is thought to be Woodland, but a short-term Plains Village occupation may be represented in the upper two levels. Four dates were obtained, with three coming from features in Levels four and five, whereas the fourth came from the ninth 6-inch level. The fourth date of A.D. 508 is thought to be incorrect because it was stratigraphically lower than the other three samples, which yielded earlier dates. Excluding that A.D. 508 date, the three remaining dates overlap in the area from A.D. 100 to 250.

Seven sherds of Cooper Zoned, Ozark Zoned, and Cowskin Dentate were also recovered. The majority of the projectile points belong to the Williams corner-notched dart point category, but contracting-stem forms also occur. In addition, obsidian and disc scrapers were also recovered.

In the Kaw Reservoir area of the Arkansas River Valley, the following sites may also date to the same time period as Hammons: Hudsonpillar (Ka-73), Jim Butterfield (Ka-119), Daniels A (Ka-77), Spencer-2 (Ka-11), Spencer-3 (Ka-121), Greenhagen (Ka-92), Dry Creek (Ka-90), School Land (Ka-75), Sarge Creek (Os-58), and Keith Fruits (Os-100). To the east of Kaw and mostly within the Cross Timbers are the Thomas (Wn-6), Hogshooter (Wn-18), and Williams (Os-160) sites. Artifacts associated with these sites include: Cooper Zoned pottery, Ozark Zoned pottery, Cowskin Dentate pottery, Williams or other large corner-notched points, contracting-stemmed points, disc scrapers, and obsidian. Usually more than two of these categories were present at a site.

These Woodland occupations appear to date from circa A.D. 100 to 300 and are characterized by infrequent pottery tempered with sand and/or grit, bone, and clay. Sherd surfaces are most frequently smoothed, although cord-marking does occur and relative percentages may vary from site to site. Also present but relatively rare are Cooper Zoned, Ozark Zoned, and Cowskin Dentate pottery.

The chipped-stone inventory consists of projectile points, scrapers, drills, notches, gravers, cores, and manufacturing debris. Williams and other corner-notched dart points are the most frequent projectile point types. However, contracting-stem forms, especially Gary, and small projectile points, such as Scallorn also occur. Scraper forms include discs, hafted or stemmed types, large and small end-scrapers similar to those generally called snub-nosed and thumbnail, and elliptical types. Drills include those with straight as well as expanding bases.

Ground-stone consists of manos, flat grinding basins, a few nutting stones, tabular abraders, hammerstones, and hematite chunks. Also a wedge-shaped hematite celt and a boatstone fragment were recovered.

Bone and antler tools are relatively infrequent. One fragment of a bison-scapula hoe has been recovered, as have several deer-antler flakers.

Artifact assemblages from most sites seem to indicate an emphasis on hunting and, in the Kaw Reservoir especially, lithic processing. A much wider range of activities and a greater emphasis on plant processing can be found in the Thomas, Hammons, Hudsonpillar, and Williams sites. Burned daub and/or subsurface features are also frequent in these sites. Thus there seems to be indicated a mixture of semipermanent multipurpose sites and specialized hunting and/or lithic processing sites.

Not much information is available regarding resource exploitation. Floral and faunal remains are not generally well-preserved in this area and retrieval of such information has not been emphasized. At Hammons, land turtle was most frequently represented, followed by bison, deer, and rabbit.

For the most part, all the sites included here are open sites. The sites in the Kaw Reservoir area are primarily on Arkansas River terraces whereas farther east they may be buried under alluvial sediments (Vehik 1982a:69). There are not enough sites from the Cross Timbers area to construct a settlement pattern.

In addition to open and shelter sites, burned-rock mounds are found in the eastern portion of the area. An analysis of those in the Copan Reservoir area of the Caney River suggested that most appear to have been built early in the Woodland sequence and that tools associated with plant processing are most consistently present (Vehik and Pailes 1979:207). There seems to have been some reuse of the mounds by later Woodland or post-Woodland groups. Most of this material is associated with hunting and/or kill-processing activities.

Nothing is known of burial practices.

External relationships can be seen with the Cooper focus in northeastern Oklahoma or with other Hopewellian groups. The Cooper, Ozark, and Cowskin sherds from Kaw are tempered with limestone or clay and either grit, sand, or bone. Young (1978:120) has indicated that these tempering materials are infrequent in northcentral Oklahoma and that, therefore, the vessels producing the sherds may have been manufactured elsewhere and traded in. Although limestone is a frequent source of the grit in the northeastern Oklahoma Hopewellian decorated sherds, there is only one example of it in the Kaw material. Most of the Kaw decorated sherds are tempered with clay and sand. Sand and sand–clay are the dominant temper forms for the rest of the pottery from these sites. Therefore, at least on the basis of temper, the Kaw Hopewellian sherds could just as easily be indigeneous. However, their relative infrequency might still be used in support of Young's proposition.

The Ozark Zoned sherd from the Copan Reservoir area is clay tempered. Clay tempering is common to Ozark Zoned in northeastern Oklahoma (Baerreis 1953). It is also similar to Cuesta Decorated Dentate Stamped in southeastern Kansas.

The presence of obsidian suggests wider relationships and possible, albeit probably marginal, participation in the Hopewellian trade network. The obsidian at the Hudsonpillar site was suggested to be from the Yellowstone area (Bastian 1969:19).

The second group of Woodland sites is typified by the Von Elm site in the Kaw Reservoir area. There are several occupation areas at this site but only one, Area C, has been dated. Three dates of A.D. 214, 219, and 610 were obtained from Feature Two. A fourth date of A.D. 516 pertained to Feature Three. Although it is possible that more than one Woodland occupation is represented there are few data to support such a proposition. Thus it is assumed that one occupation is represented and the area of overlap between the radiocarbon dates indicates that that occupation dates between A.D. 300 and 550.

The predominant pottery at Von Elm Area C is a smoothed, sand-tempered ware, but some cord-marked pottery also occurs infrequently. By far the majority of projectile points in this area are Scallorn, with Gary a distant second.

The Vickery site (Ka-41), also in Kaw Reservoir, yielded a date of A.D. 472. This date specifically pertains to Area A, which seems to have had only one occupation. With the exception of a very limited number of sherds, the ceramics were smooth surfaced and it is suspected that they may have been tempered with crushed limestone, which has since !eached out (Rohrbaugh 1974:35). Scallorn points were dominant, followed by Gary and Fresno. With the exception of the possible limestone temper, this site seems to present a situation similar to that outlined for Von Elm.

Three rockshelter sites (Os-114, Os-129 and Os-135) in the Cross Timbers area have provided dates ranging from A.D. 325 to 795 and thus seem to belong to the time period being considered here. Unfortunately the dated levels contained very little material. Mostly they show a mixture of small arrowpoints and contracting-stemmed dart points.

Other sites that may be included here are Glenn Peel (Ka-100) Areas B and D, Von Elm Area A, and Os-155. The first two are in the Kaw Reservoir area and the last is in the Cross Timbers. These sites possess, to varying degrees, some of the following artifacts or attributes: smooth sand- or limestone-tempered pottery with some cord-marking, clay-tempered pottery that could be smoothed or cord-marked, and an almost equal ratio of large to small projectile points. It is also possible that the Kaw Reservoir sites belong to the preceding Woodland group because there is obsidian present and cord marking is more frequent than in Von Elm and Vickery.

This second set of Woodland sites is characterized by an increased frequency in pottery, most of which is smooth surfaced. Tempering is most frequently sand followed by limestone ("cell") and clay.

The chipped-stone industry includes projectile points, perforators, bifaces and knives, scrapers, drills, gravers, notches, double-bitted axes, and miscellaneous lithic manufacturing debris. Projectile points are most frequently represented by Scallorn, with Gary the major dart form. In general, there is either a one-to-one relationship between small and large points or the former are more frequent. Knives are predominantly ovate in form. Scrapers includes alternately beveled forms as well as large and small end-scrapers (thumbnail and snub-nosed). Major differences with the preceding period are seen in the absence of stemmed scrapers, disc scrapers, and elliptical scrapers. The thumbnail and snub-nosed scrapers seem to have increased in frequency.

Ground stone includes manos, a few of which have a keeled appearance, flat-surfaced grinding basins; tabular, concave, and grooved abraders; and a stone bead. No bone or antler tools were recovered. Also no burials are known.

Almost no information is available from the Kaw Reservoir area on resource utilization. Remains in the Cross Timbers' shelters are dominated by turtle fragments followed by deer, rabbit, and fish. Mussells and nuts may also have been an important food resource. Bison remains are very infrequent, however. Henry

(1977c:130) suggests occupation of at least the Big Hawk Shelter (Os-114) during late summer and autumn.

With the exception of Os-155, all the sites in the Cross Timbers area are shelters. The remaining sites in the Kaw Reservoir are open sites, with the exception of Os-155. However, none of the sites in the Kaw Reservoir area is in the Arkansas River Valley. Some of them are near the juncture of tributary streams with the Arkansas. In general, there appears to be a trend toward the occupation of areas away from the Arkansas River (Vehik 1982a:69).

The shelter sites seem to have been occupied principally for hunting activities, whereas Os-155 seems to have been occupied principally for plant processing. Both areas of the Glenn Peel site seem to have been occupied for hunting and lithic processing activities. This same range of activities was conducted at the Vickery site with the addition of plant processing. Finally, Von Elm site shows a wide range of activities and the presence of subsurface features along with burned daub suggest a more permanent occupation.

There is virtually no evidence indicating the direction or nature of any external or exchange relationships. Studies of lithic resource utilization suggest the possibility that adaptations were isolated, localized, or independent (Ferring 1982:204; Vehik 1982b).

The third group of sites includes Black Hawk Shelter (Level 6), which provided a date of A.D. 845. Artifacts recovered include a burin, a notch, a Scallorn point, a contracting-stemmed point, a small diamond-shaped point, and unutilized flakes. It is also in this level that pottery first appears. This pottery is shell tempered and comparable to Woodward Plain–Reed Variety (Henry 1977c:119). Also, in Level 7, one each of the Washita and Fresno point types were found. This deposit seems to be transitional to post-Woodland occupations.

Area B of the Daniels site (Ka-77) has a date of A.D. 913. The ceramics are all smoothed and bone is the most frequent temper. However, shell, sand, and clay were also utilized. The majority of the projectile points are small in size, with Fresno most frequent. This portion of the Daniels site could represent either late Plains Woodland or early Plains Village occupations.

The Weston site (Os-99) in the Cross Timbers consists of several mounds, of which two were used at least partially for burial. One of these mounds produced a date of A.D. 985. Frequency distributions for each artifact class (i.e., the class *projectile point*) are available for each mound, but more specific breakdowns for types are unavailable. As a result we must assume that the mounds were contemporaneous. Apart from grinding implements, however, the cultural inventory is rather meager. There are no ceramics and the majority of points are of the Scallorn type. What meager evidence there is suggests a Woodland affiliation.

Level 5 of Sunny Shelter produced a date of A.D. 1046 and two retouched flakes along with a Washita point. There is not enough material here to make a cultural assignment.

The last two dates are for sites in the Kaw Reservoir area. Area A of the

Daniels site has provided a date of A.D. 1179. The artifact assemblage shows a mixture of small and large points, with Williams most frequent. Also present were Scallorn, Washita, and Shetley points. Only one sherd, cord-marked with bone temper, was found. Provenience information by level is not available but the site was fairly shallow. It is possible that there were two occupations, one represented by the large points and the cord-marked sherd and the other by the small points and the radiocarbon date. A variety of different interpretations can also be formulated, however.

The Freeman site (Os-59) has a date of A.D. 1377, which is too late for a Woodland occupation. Freeman seems to have had a rather complex occupational history ranging from the Archaic through Woodland and Plains Village. Bastian (1969:113) notes that all the aboriginal features and diagnostic Plains Village artifacts were found south of a late Woodland artifact concentration. Because the date is from a feature it may be that it is more applicable to the Plains Village occupation.

The northern area of Freeman was dominated by Fresno and Washita–Reed points. Other forms included were Huffaker, Scallorn, and Gary. In addition an alternately beveled knife or scraper was found. The majority of the pottery was cord-marked with bone, clay, or "cell" temper.

Other sites that might belong in this third Woodland group include D. E. Spencer (Ka-62), Scott (Ka-52), and Von Elm Area D. All sites are dominated by Scallorn points, with Fresno, Washita, Huffaker, Alba, and Gary points less frequent. Pottery tempering is varied but includes sand, limestone, grit, and clay, or combinations of these. Surfaces may be smoothed or cord-marked.

The third group of Woodland sites is difficult to characterize. In some instances we begin to see a transition to post-Woodland occupations. This transition begins around A.D. 850 or perhaps earlier. Its terminal date is not set and may be variable from area to area.

Pottery from these sites is quite variable in temper and surface treatment.

The chipped-stone inventory includes projectile points, preforms (which can include knives and bifaces), snub-nosed and thumbnail scrapers, notches, gravers, hoes, and lithic manufacturing debris. Most of the projectile points are small and Fresno and Washita are more frequent. The variety of knives includes alternately beveled forms.

Ground stone includes manos, of which a few are keeled. In addition there are grinding basins with flat and concave working surfaces, nutting stones, tabular abraders, grooved abraders, a crinoid-stem disc, and chunks of limonite and hematite.

No bone or antler tools are associated with these occupations.

Burial practices are known from one site. This burial was in a slight pit dug in the center of the mound floor. Above it was an arrangement of rock slabs and metates forming a pavement. Most of the artifacts were part of the mound fill. The burial was of an adult, which was very poorly preserved.

Data on resource exploitation are again meager and most of it comes from the shelters in the Cross Timbers area. Turtle, deer, rabbits, and mussels continued to be major resources, but there is a large increase in fish remains.

Very little can be said about settlement patterns. The shelters and burial mounds are in the Cross Timbers. Also in that area, especially in its more eastern portions, are the burned-rock mounds. Again, sites tend to be farther removed from the Arkansas, but those at the later end indicate a return to the valley, especially at points where tributary streams enter the Arkansas valley (Vehik 1982a:69).

The shelters seem to have been used principally as hunting camps. The burned-rock-mound occupations seem to have been more directed to hunting and kill processing (Vehik and Pailes 1979:207). The open sites seem to have been occupied for hunting and kill processing but at least at some of the sites there is evidence for plant and lithic processing. None of the sites yielded any evidence for relatively permanent occupation.

Data regarding external relationships are limited. It is possible that the Cross Timbers area was influenced by the intrusion of Caddoan groups into northeast Oklahoma. External relationships of groups in the tall-grass prairies are indecipherable at the present time. Similarities in ceramics have been noted with Early Plains Village sites in Central Kansas, to Pomona Ware and Riley Cord Roughened in northern and eastern Kansas, and to Pruitt Cordmarked in southern Oklahoma (Hartley 1974a:59–65). The present sample of ceramics from northcentral Oklahoma is not large enough to confirm or reject any of the postulated affiliations.

Southcentral Oklahoma

To the south of Kaw Reservoir in southcentral Oklahoma we have our third and smallest group of Woodland sites. Only four sites, Duncan–Wilson, Brewer, Pruitt, and Currie belong to the group. References for these sites include Barr 1966c, Duffield 1953, Lawton 1968, and Lintz 1974.

Duncan–Wilson Rockshelter (Cd-11) is potentially a very informative site but unfortunately there are stratigraphic problems, so it is only briefly discussed here. Most of what follows is based on Lawton's (1968) interpretations.

One group of material includes Levels 20–17 and seems to date from about A.D. 450 to 550 (Table 8.1). There was no pottery in these levels and Ellis, Gary, and Marcos were the dominant projectile point types. In addition there were disc scrapers, Clear Fork gouges, nutting stones, grinding stones, and fire hearths, some of which were rock ringed. Floral remains were dominated by hackberry and walnut. Faunal remains include rabbit, turtle, deer, and birds.

Levels 15–13 of Duncan–Wilson formed yet another group with an initial date of A.D. 550 and an unknown terminal date. Ellis and Gary points are still predominant but Scallorn, Huffaker, and Marcos also occur. Clay-tempered cord-marked pottery appears but is infrequent. Other artifacts include hafted knives, disc scrapers, Clear Fork gouges, and grinding stones. Floral remains are dominated by hackberry but a gourd fragment was also recovered. Faunal remains were dominated by rabbit, turtle, and deer.

Levels 12–10 formed another group with a termination date of A.D. 1045. Fresno, Washita, Reed, Bonham, and Scallorn points were dominant. Other artifacts include thumbnail scrapers, a few disc scrapers, an alternately beveled knife, grinding stones, milling basins, shell-disc beads, and obsidian. It is impossible to determine from Lawton's report which pottery types occur in what levels (Lawton 1968:88). The general impression is that cord-marked, clay-tempered pottery continued. Turtle, rabbit, and deer apparently remained dominant, but bison remains are evident for the first time. Walnut and hackberry dominate the floral remains with piñon nuts appearing in small amounts.

Levels 9–7 date from around A.D. 1050 to approximately A.D. 1600. There is a mixture of Woodland and Plains Village materials in these levels. Fresno, Washita, Huffaker, Scallorn, Reed, and Gary are the most frequent point types. The major pottery type is that designated as *Pruitt-like,* which is shell tempered and cord marked (Pruitt has limestone temper). In addition there are scapula hoes, bone digging-stick tips, squash knives, metates, and the first completely worked manos. Bison is still a minor component of the fanual inventory, with deer, turtle, and rabbit prevailing. There are also some corn kernels and cobs present but walnut and hackberry are still dominant.

The Brewer site in McClain County appears to be a Woodland village site as several storage pits as well as wattle and daub were recovered. The majority of the pottery was limestone and/or sand tempered. Surfaces were cord marked and a narrow strip under the lip was sometimes left plain. Large punctates were also occasionally used, although nothing is mentioned about placement. Bases are generally conoidal, although a few may have been flattened. Vessel form does not appear to be as elongated as in many other conoidal-based vessels. The next most frequent pottery type was shell tempered, smooth surfaced, flat based, and had strap handles (this could reflect a second late Plains Village occupation). Duffield (1953:63) also mentioned a sand-and-clay-tempered sherd with surface decoration "crudely like Hopewell sherds from northeastern Oklahoma." Because the sherd was not illustrated it is difficult to tell what was meant by that comment.

Projectile points were infrequent but include mostly Gary with one Scallorn. Other artifacts include flake end- and side-scrapers, a couple of ovoid bifaces (Duffield calls one a hoe), manos, bone fishhooks, bone pins, bone flakers, bone shaft-wrenches, bone awls, bone beamers, bone needles, shell scrapers, centrally perforated shell hoes, and a stone elbow-pipe. A dog burial was also recovered. Floral remains included acorns and walnuts or hickory nuts. Faunal remains were dominated by deer, but also recovered were antelope, bison, rabbits, turtles, birds, and mussel shells.

The Pruitt site (Mr-12) is on a tributary of the Washita River near the boundary that separates the Plains from the Arbuckle Plateau. The two radiocarbon dates for the site average to around A.D. 770. Pruitt was divided into four areas that contained features (mostly pits of various shapes) and scattered postmolds. Barr (1966c:92) suggests that there was both a Plains Village and a Woodland occupation of the site. There is, however, a mixture in the various pits of the materials he considered diagnostic of the two periods. This seems to indicate only one occupation. Barr (1966c:98), however, suggests Plains Village reuse of Woodland pits.

The majority of the projectile points were small and dominated by Scallorn and Young, followed by Morris and Reed–Washita. All identifiable dart points were Gary. Other chipped-stone artifacts included a variety of knife fragments, expanded-base drills, core end- and side-scrapers, a disc scraper, utilized flakes, gouges, bifacial choppers, cores, and hammerstones. Ground stone consists of manos, milling slabs, nut stones, tabular abraders, celts, and chunks of glauconitic mica, hematite, and limonite. Bone artifacts include splinter awls, beamers, and flakers. Shell artifacts consist of a scraper and five centrally perforated hoes.

Pottery can be divided basically into two almost-equally frequent types. Pruitt Cord-Marked has crushed limestone temper and cord-marked surfaces. The cord marking is frequently smoothed over in an area just below the lip (similar to Brewer). Bases are conoidal. The second type is unnamed but it has crushed-bone or limestone temper with some occasional use of sand or clay. Surfaces were cord marked and then smoothed over. Barr (1966c:75) notes a strong similarity of this second type to Lindsay Plain of the Plains Village tradition Washita River focus.

Floral remains include corn and walnuts, with hickory nuts most frequent. Faunal remains include mostly turtles and mammals, with the latter dominated by deer. Apparently no bison were recovered. The remaining faunal remains included fish, molluscs, and turkey, along with other birds.

Little can be said about trade relationships. Some connections to the east are suggested by the presence of Reed Punctated and Williams Incised pottery. Reed Punctated is now recognized as a component of Pennington Punctate–Incised and Crockett Curvilinear (R. E. Bell, personal communication, 1978). Brown (1971b:220) includes these as part of the Harlan phase, which dates to before A.D. 1200.

The last site of this group is Currie in Garvin County. Although the site description has not yet been published, except for a brief description by Lintz (1974), there are 12 radiocarbon dates available. The dates are for a rectangular house with four central support posts, an entryway extended to the southeast, and walls of upright poles. This is essentially the Washita River focus house pattern. The dates range from A.D. 1057 to 1362, with an average of A.D. 1210.

Artifacts found on the house floor include straight-stemmed arrowpoints similar to Alba and Bonham. Pottery was rarely cord marked, it "was not shell tempered" and it had circular bases (Lintz 1974:28).

Evidence for a second occupation is suggested in the upper 10 cm of the fill. Here the pottery was shell tempered and the projectile points were of the Washita type.

Because of the difference between the artifacts in the upper fill and those in association with the house, Lintz (1974:28) suggested that the site was transitional between Plains Woodland and Plains Village. Although the artifact descriptions are quite vague, it appears to this author that Currie is basically a Washita River focus site.

Summary and Conclusions

In general, for northeast Oklahoma it seems that there may have been a cultural continuation from the Late Archaic through the Delaware foci and into the Neosho focus. Although there is a continuation represented in many of the artifact types, the populations did not exist in a vacuum. Ceramics seem to have been introduced from the northeast and these were then followed by an apparent intrusion of Hopewellian peoples who brought a variety of different artifact styles. It appears that these intruders may ultimately have been assimilated by the indigeneous Delaware A focus groups. Subsequently, new influences, this time from the south, were received by the indigeneous groups and the result is recognized archaeologically as the Delaware B focus. Late in Delaware B there was another direct intrusion into the area, this time by Caddoan groups. This may have resulted in changing Delaware B into the Neosho focus.

The earliest Woodland occupations of the northcentral area date to between A.D. 100 and 300. It is presently impossible to determine whether these occupations are a continuation from resident Archaic groups or not. The greater frequency of smoothed as opposed to cord-marked pottery is a situation found commonly on Hopewellian and other Woodland sites during this period. Some sherds do, however, resemble fairly closely Hopewellian stamped pottery. Corner-notched dart points are most frequent and may also reflect northeastern influences. In addition to these there are Gary points and small projectile points, such as Scallorn. Special purpose camps for hunting–kill processing and lithic processing are most frequent but relatively permanent villages are also known. At least in the Kaw area, land turtle, bison, deer, and rabbit were the prominent faunal resources. There is no definitive evidence for agriculture.

A second group of northcentral Woodland sites seem to date from about A.D. 300 to 800. Although there is little evidence pro or con, it seems most likely that these sites represent a continuation from the earlier Woodland groups. Most of the pottery is smooth surfaced and there seems to be less variety in the tempering material. Small projectile points, especially Scallorn, are as frequent as or more frequent than the large dart points. These small points may represent the introduction of the bow and arrow and, if so, it seems that this equipment became dominant earlier in the tall-grass prairie area than in the oak–hickory forest of northeast Oklahoma. Also, although we certainly do not have an adequate sample of sites, it appears that temporary camps associated with hunting–kill processing are more frequent than previously. At least in the Cross Timbers area, turtle, deer, rabbit, fish, and nuts seem to have been the major food resources. There is little evidence for bison and none for agriculture.

Beginning around A.D. 800 in the northcentral area, sites begin to display characteristics more common in post-Woodland occupations. The presence of shell and bone tempering may reflect trends seen in the Caddoan area of southeast Oklahoma. Projectile points are mostly small and, although Scallorns are dominant, Fresno and Washitas, among others, occur more frequently. In the Cross Timbers area, turtle, deer, rabbit, mussels, and fish were the major resources. There is at present no unequivocable evidence for villages. Most sites seem to be temporary hunting–kill processing camps. This is a trend that seems to continue through early post-Woodland occupations (Vehik and Pailes 1979:11). This may be a product of sampling error because it is increasingly apparent that the villages were on high terraces, which did not get sampled in the archaeological surveys.

For the southcentral Oklahoma area it seems likely that the transition from the Archaic to Woodland occupations occurred some time prior to A.D. 450. Brewer may date to about this time period or slightly later. Unlike the Kaw area, most of the pottery is cord marked and this trend is noted for most later Plains Woodland sites. There is insufficient evidence to argue whether or not Woodland groups were intrusive into the area. The Pruitt site seems to represent a slightly later development of the same cultural tradition represented at Brewer. The presence of a ware similar to Lindsay Plain of the Washita River focus suggests the possibility that perhaps, with some differences, Pruitt and the Custer focus may be equivalent culturally and that both reflect transition from Woodland to the Plains Village Washita River focus. Major animal resources were turtle and deer. It does not seem that bison was important until Washita River focus times. By circa A.D. 800, agriculture appears to have been initiated. Although we do not have an adequate sample, we do know that relatively permanent village sites existed.

In the process of attempting to characterize Woodland occupations in Oklahoma several problems, in addition to those outlined in the introduction, were encountered. One of these problems is the dating of Hopewellian occupations. Hopewell in the Lower Illinois Valley dates between 100 B.C. and A.D. 400; in the Kansas City area it is between A.D. 100 and 500; in northcentral Oklahoma, they are seemingly between A.D. 100 and 300 or slightly later; in southeast Kansas, they range between A.D. 700 and 900; and in northeast Oklahoma, they are between A.D. 123 and 1274. Although there is not space to document it fully here, it is suggested that the dates for the latter two areas are in error. The general concurrence of dates from the first three areas provides some support for such an interpretation.

Throughout the preceding pages there have been consistent references to the absence or infrequence of bison in the various faunal assemblages. Instead, the major large mammal resource seems to have been deer. Dillehay (1974:187) has suggested that climatic change was the primary cause for the absence of bison between A.D. 500 and 1200–1300. He also seems to imply that a dry–warm period would probably be responsible for such a situation (Dillehay 1974:185). Unfortunately, there are very few climatic data available for Oklahoma. Some questionable data from the Cross Timbers area suggest an increase in arboreal vegetation circa A.D. 200, and this may have lasted until circa A.D. 900, when it decreased sharply (Vehik and Pailes 1979:206).

The last point to be stressed is that both the northeastern and southcentral areas show continuous, relatively permanent occupation throughout the Woodland and into the post-Woodland. The northcentral area seems to reflect an early establishment of semipermanent Woodland villages but through time they were replaced by more temporary occupations. This situation appears to change with Plains Village occupations, which appear to be more sedentary, especially late in time. Climatic changes and/or cultural developments can be offered as causal factors. Unfortunately, there are few relevant data available.

This completes our review of Woodland occupations in Oklahoma. Although there are a number of definitional, as well as anthropological, problems to be worked on in regard to these occupations, it is certainly not the case, as seems to be the more common belief, that Woodland occupations were sparse or nonexistent outside the northeastern area of Oklahoma.

CHAPTER 9

Arkansas Valley Caddoan Formative: The Wister and Fourche Maline Phases

Jerry R. Galm

Archaeological investigations in the Arkansas Basin began in earnest over 40 years ago with the Works Progress Administration (WPA)-sponsored excavations at the Spiro Mound complex. In 1939 the emphasis of the WPA archaeological program shifted to the numerous "black mound" sites situated along Fourche Maline Creek and the Poteau River southwest of Spiro. Excavations conducted between 1939 and 1942 were centered in the vicinity of the confluence of these drainages in the area to be inundated by the proposed Wister Lake. These excavations and the subsequent investigations of Bell in 1947 to 1948 provided data for the first synthesis of prehistory in the southern portion of the Arkansas Basin (Bell and Baerreis 1951:19–27). The work of Bell and Baerreis provided a description of a manifestation previously designated the *Fourche Maline focus* (Krieger 1947:202). Included within this focus were component assemblages containing an early type of plainware pottery. The recognition of this ceramic type, Williams Plain, as an important member of pre-Caddoan artifact assemblages raised many questions relating to the temporal placement and areal extent of the Fourche Maline focus. Unfortunately, answers to these questions were not forthcoming and only recently have the data necessary to provide further interpretations of the Fourche Maline focus become available.

This chapter provides descriptive summaries of the recently defined Wister and Fourche Maline phases (Bell 1980a; Galm 1978b, 1981; Galm and Flynn 1978b) and a synopsis of Formative development in the Arkansas Basin of eastern Oklahoma. Although the emphasis of this chapter is on Fourche Maline, it is pertinent to review the full cultural sequence in the area defined as the Wister Valley (Galm 1978a:4). This sequence is derived from Galm (1981) and is based primarily on excavations conducted at the Curtis Lake, Scott, and Wann sites during the two-phase Wister Lake Archaeological Project (Galm 1978a, 1978b; Galm and Flynn 1978b). Previous investigations in the valley (Newkumet 1940a, 1940b, 1940c, 1940d, 1940e, 1940f; L. Howard 1941; Watson 1947; Bell and Baerreis 1951:19–27; Bell 1953b; B. Williams 1953; Proctor 1957; Sharrock 1960; Guilinger 1971; Irvine 1980) and recent studies in areas west of the valley (Wyckoff 1976; Wyckoff and Woody 1977; Lintz 1978e; J. D. Rogers 1979a; Powell and Rogers 1980; C. Clark 1980; S. D. Baugh 1982) also have contributed to the current understanding of Fourche Maline in the Arkansas Basin. No attempt has been made to provide an exhaustive review of Fourche Maline investigations or of the artifact data presented in this study. This information is presented in various reports that should be consulted by the interested reader (Bell 1980a; Schambach 1970; L. Johnson 1962; Galm 1978a, 1978b, 1981; Galm and Flynn 1978b).

The Study Area

The study area is confined to the Poteau River and its tributaries, which comprise the watershed for the southern portion of the Arkoma Basin in extreme eastcentral Oklahoma (Figure 9.1). The Poteau River and its largest tributary, Fourche Maline Creek, drain the northern Ouachita Mountains in an area defined as the Poteau Basin. The Poteau River joins the Arkansas near the town of Spiro, Oklahoma, and drains an area of about 4890 km^2 in eastern Oklahoma and western Arkansas (Oklahoma Water Resources Board 1970).

The majority of sites discussed in this chapter are concentrated in an area defined as the Wister Valley (Figure 9.1). Fourche Maline manifestations are known to be present in other parts of eastern Oklahoma, western Arkansas, and eastern Texas, in addition to the Wister Valley and environs. However, in-depth consideration of sites and cultural sequences in these areas is beyond the scope of this study. The Wister Valley encompasses the floodplains of the Poteau River and Fourche Maline Creek within the area defined by the furthermost extension of slackwater impounded by Wister Dam. The dam was completed in 1949 below the confluence of the Poteau and Fourche Maline, forming Wister Lake. The valley is approximately 128 km^2 and is bounded on all sides by formations of the Ouachita Uplift.

Throughout this study reference is made to the Poteau Basin or the area lying between the Arkansas River valley and the Kiamichi Range of the Ouachita Mountains. There is evidence to indicate that the prehistory of this area is significantly different from that portion of the Arkoma Basin north of the Arkansas River valley and from the Red River Basin to the south. Accordingly, no attempt has been made to expand the present consideration of *Fourche Maline* beyond the Poteau Basin. For purposes of this discussion, the Poteau Basin has not been extended into neighboring Arkansas but is restricted to eastcentral Oklahoma.

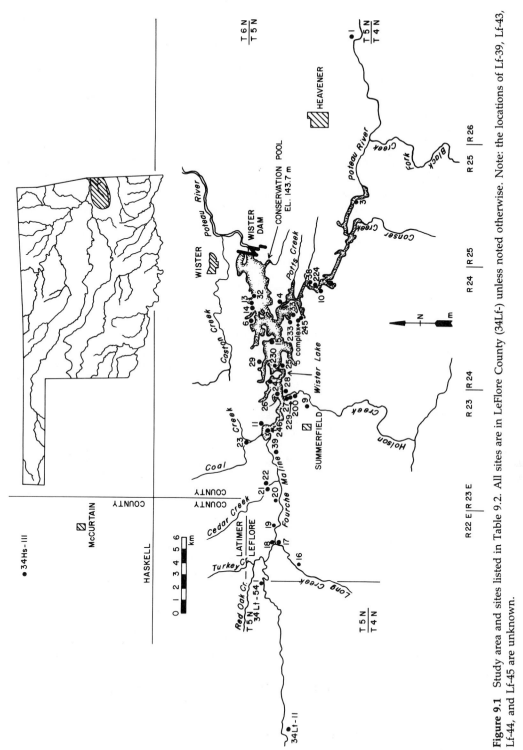

Figure 9.1 Study area and sites listed in Table 9.2. All sites are in LeFlore County (34Lf-) unless noted otherwise. Note: the locations of Lf-39, Lf-43, Lf-44, and Lf-45 are unknown.

History of Investigations

The earliest archaeological investigations conducted in the valley were sponsored by the WPA under the direction of Forrest E. Clements of the University of Oklahoma. Starting in 1939, field crews from the University of Oklahoma initiated a program of complete or partial excavation on at least 24 sites. In 1942, World War II brought an abrupt halt to these investigations. The war also interrupted the analysis of recovered materials and most of the sites excavated during the WPA archaeological program remain unanalyzed. A chronological sequence of archaeological investigations in and around the valley is presented in Table 9.1. A summary of site investigations is presented in Table 9.2. Apart from the brief surveys of Virginia Watson in 1946 (Watson 1947), the next major work in the valley was conducted by Robert E. Bell of the University of Oklahoma in 1947 to 1948. Bell's investigations focused on excavations at the Scott site (34Lf-11) and led to the first published synthesis of archaeology in the Wister Valley (Bell and Baerreis 1951:19–27). The deeply stratified Scott site (Bell 1953) provided valuable new data on the Fourche Maline focus (Krieger 1947) and was to be the last major investigation in the valley for nearly 30 years. In the intervening period, reports were prepared on WPA excavations at the Sam (Proctor 1957), Wann (Sharrock 1960), and Copeland (Guilinger 1971) sites. These reports added information on artifact sequences at each site, but provided few new insights on the growing confusion surrounding the Fourche Maline focus construct. At the center of this controversy were the dual concerns of chronological ordering and geographical distribution of sites assigned to the Fourche Maline focus. Despite early indications that sites in the Wister Valley contained components representing Archaic (preceramic), Woodland, and Gibson aspect occupations (Bell and Baerreis 1951:19–27), additional data were required to provide further interpretations.

Sites recorded in the Wister Valley are dominated by extensive midden deposits, long noted for their organic and artifactual richness. These midden locales occur in large numbers (Galm 1978a) and have been the source of continuing interest since the onset of WPA-sponsored excavations. The WPA program provided the first indications of the complexity of these midden sites and the difficulties encountered in distinguishing well-defined stratigraphic sequences (Newkumet 1940a). Depths of the midden deposits ranged from under 1 m to over 3 m, with the horizontal extent of the midden consistently less than 1 ha. Previous research at midden sites suggested relatively continuous occupations and an attendant accretion of cultural debris resulting in a slightly mounded appearance (Bell and Baerreis 1951:19–27; Bell 1953; Newkumet 1940a). Bell and Baerreis's discussion of "Fourche Maline" sites provides an accurate description of their physical characteristics (1951:19–20).

> The Fourche Maline sites are represented by accumulations of village debris or midden deposits situated on the bank of a river or stream. These middens are characterized by a black colored earth which contains, scattered throughout the deposit, considerable

Table 9.1

Sequence of Archaeological Investigations in the Poteau Basin

Year	Investigation	Publication/report
1936	WPA excavations begin at Spiro.	Orr 1946; Brown 1966a, 1966b, 1971, 1976b.
1939	WPA survey of the Wister Valley (Phil J. Newkumet).	Newkumet 1940a.
1939–1942	WPA excavations begin in the valley (University of Oklahoma) under field supervision of P. J. Newkumet and Lynn E. Howard (U of O).	Newkumet 1940a, 1940b, 1940c, 1940d, 1940e, 1940f, 1940g; Howard 1941; Proctor 1957; Sharrock 1960; Guilinger 1971.
1946	Resurvey and survey of the upper Poteau River by Virginia Watson (U of O).	Watson 1947.
1947	Test excavations at 34Lf-11, 34Lf-10, 34Lf-4, and 34Lf-3, conducted by Robert E. Bell (U of O).	Williams 1953; Bell and Baerreis 1951.
1948	Second season excavations by Bell at 34Lf-11 (Scott site).	Bell 1953b.
1965	Limited testing conducted at 34Lf-1 by Bell.	
1967	Excavations by the Oklahoma Anthropological Society (OAS) at 34Lf-200 (Evans site), field supervisor Terry Prewitt (U of O).	
1968	Test excavations by the OAS at 34Lf-9 (Holson Creek site), Terry Prewitt field supervisor.	
1968–1969	OAS excavations at 34Lt-54 (Runner site), I. C. Gunning field supervisor.	
1974–1975	Resurvey and survey of proposed Wister Reservoir enlargement area by Larry Neal and Michael B. Mayo (U of O).	Mayo 1975.
1976–1977	Excavations at 34Lt-11 on Fourche Maline Creek under direction of Don G. Wyckoff (Oklahoma Archaeological Survey).	Wyckoff and Woody 1977; Wyckoff 1976, 1979.
1976–1978	Wister lake Archaeological Project investigations under direction of Galm (U of O).	Galm 1978a, 1978b, 1981; Galm and Flynn 1978a, 1978b.

amounts of clam shell, animal bones, charcoal, fire cracked rocks, various artifacts, human burials, occupational surfaces and other miscellaneous objects. No house patterns have been found at any of the sites although occasional post holes were encountered within the middens.

Unfortunately, little progress has been made in clarifying culture–historical problems and refining the Fourche Maline focus construct since these early investigations. As a result, the term *Fourche Maline,* depending on the source,

Table 9.2

Summary of Sites Investigated in the Poteau Basin of Eastern Oklahoma

Site number	Site name	Year	Type of investigation	Supervisor	Sponsor
34Lf-1	—	1965	Testing	Bell	OU
34Lf-3	Conser	1947	Testing	Bell	OU
34Lf-4	Cantrell	1947	Testing	Bell	OU
34Lf-5A	Curtis Lake	1976	Excavation	Galm	ARMC-OU
34Lf-5B	Miller Locality	1977	Testing	Galm	ARMC-OU
34Lf-5C	Briar Locality	1976–77	Excavation	Galm	ARMC-OU
34Lf-5C	Kelly Locality	1977	Excavation	Galm	ARMC-OU
34Lf-5C	Locality 2	1977	Testing	Galm	ARMC-OU
34Lf-9	Holson Creek	1968	Testing	Prewitt	OU
34Lf-10	Ward	1947	Testing	Bell	OU
34Lf-11	Scott	1947–1948/1976–1977	Excavation	Bell/Galm	OU/ARMC-OU
34Lf-13	Henry Heflin II	1941/1977	Excavation/Testing	Newkumet/Galm	WPA-OU/ARMC-OU
34Lf-14	Henry Heflin I	1941	Excavation	Newkumet	WPA-OU
34Lf-15	Lee Redwine II	1940	Excavation	Newkumet	WPA-OU
34Lf-16	Sol Thompson	1941	Excavation	Howard	WPA-OU
34Lf-17	S. O. DeHart II	1942	Excavation	Howard	WPA-OU
34Lf-18	S. O. DeHart I	1941	Excavation	Howard	WPA-OU
34Lf-19	Mrs. Hooks	1941	Excavation	Newkumet	WPA-OU
34Lf-20	Copeland	1940–1941	Excavation	Newkumet	WPA-OU
34Lf-21	N. E. Conner	1941	Excavation	Newkumet	WPA-OU
34Lf-22	John Smith	1940	Excavation	Newkumet	WPA-OU
34Lf-23	Henry Peck	1940	Excavation	Newkumet	WPA-OU

34Lf-24	J. W. Williams I	1939–1940	Excavation	Newkumet	WPA-OU
34Lf-25	J. W. Williams II	1940	Excavation	Newkumet	WPA-OU
34Lf-26	Bennett Monroe	1940/1976	Excavation/Testing	Newkumet/Galm	WPA-OU/ARMC-OU
34Lf-27	Omer Wann	1940/1976–1977	Excavation	Newkumet/Galm	WPA-OU/ARMC-OU
34Lf-28	James M. Sam	1940/1977	Excavation/Testing	Newkumet/Galm	WPA-OU/ARMC-OU
34Lf-29	Raymond Mackey	1940/1977	Excavation/Testing	Newkumet Galm	WPA-OU/ARMC-OU
34Lf-32	Dan Akers	1941	Excavation	Newkumet-Howard	WPA-OU
34Lf-33	Troy Adams	1940/1976–1977	Excavation	Newkumet/Galm	WPA-OU/ARMC-OU
34Lf-38	W. O. Brewer	1941	Excavation	Newkumet-Howard	WPA-OU
34Lf-39	Shippey	1941	Excavation	Howard	WPA-OU
34Lf-43	J. J. Phillips	1941–1942	Excavation	Howard	WPA-OU
34Lf-44	Wes Willard	1942	Excavation	Howard	WPA-OU
34Lf-45	Sy Watkins	1942	Excavation	Howard	WPA-OU
34Lf-200	Evans	1967	Testing	Prewitt	OAs
34Lf-224	Meander	1977	Testing	Galm	ARMC-OU
34Lf-229	Rowsey	1977	Testing	Galm	ARMC-OU
34Lf-230	Pot Breaker	1977	Testing	Galm	ARMC-OU
34Lf-233	Ashmore	1977	Testing	Galm	ARMC-OU
34Lf-245	Anderson Branch	1977	Testing	Galm	ARMC-OU
34Lf-246	Roscoe	1976	Testing/Mechanical stripping	Galm	ARMC-OU
34Lt-11	McCutchan–McLaughlin	1976–1977	Excavation	Wyckoff	OASu
34Lt-54	Runner	1968/1977	Testing	Bell/Galm	OAS/ARMC-OU
34Hs-111	—	1978	Profiled	Lintz	ARMC-OU

Note: ARMC-OU = Archaeological Research and Management Center; OAS = Oklahoma Anthropological Society; OASu = Oklahoma Archaeological Survey; OU = University of Oklahoma; WPA = Works Progress Administration; 1940/1976 = separate investigations.

can convey one or more of the following meanings: (1) a focus, as defined by McKern (1939); (2) an archaeological area; (3) a site component; (4) a site complex; or (5) a site type.

In addition to the problems of interpreting the cultural chronology and content of components included in this focus, there has been virtually no systematic examination of subsistence–settlement patterns. Adaptive strategies have been inferred to be based on the hunting–gathering–fishing triad reflective of an "Archaic" lifestyle. There has been tacit recognition of the continuity of this lifestyle through time, and, accordingly, a relatively stable pattern of occupations throughout the cultural sequence. Likewise, settlement patterns were envisioned as relatively stable in view of the obvious multiple componency of the sites excavated (Bell and Baerreis 1951:19–20; Wyckoff 1970b; Bell 1953). The apparent uniformity of adaptations seen in sites within the valley has had the effect of further clouding interpretations of subsistence–settlement patterns and external relationships.

Bell (1980a) presents a synopsis of Fourche Maline that includes a recommendation for the subdivision of this focus into two cultural phases. These phases, Wister and Fourche Maline, were identified by the presence of preceramic (Wister phase) and ceramic-bearing (Fourche Maline phase) components previously combined in the Fourche Maline focus (Bell 1980a:118–120). In documenting the various uses of the term *Fourche Maline*, Bell acknowledges that without further refinement of temporal placement and cultural content this concept lacks interpretive value at either a local or regional level of investigation. He summarizes the current status of Fourche Maline as follows (Bell 1980a:112–113):

> This survey of materials associated with the label Fourche Maline clearly indicates that the term is being used in a variety of ways by different individuals. This is largely a result of the fact that the generalized Fourche Maline as described in the 1950's extends over much too long a time span from the Archaic to periods of ceramic production. It has become a convenient label for archaeological assemblages which appear to represent "Pre-Gibson" times or what we think of as lacking the major characteristics of the Caddoan development. . . . we appear to have a continuum at least from the Late Archaic up to the formation of what can be termed Caddoan. . . . Consequently, we have no general consensus as to when Fourche Maline appeared nor how long it lasted. When this is the case, it should not be surprising that so-called Fourche Maline relationships are indicated almost everywhere. . . . It is necessary to revise or abandon the term Fourche Maline as it is currently employed if we are to communicate with each other in trying to unravel the prehistory of the Caddoan area (Trans-Mississippi South).

Following the recommendations of Bell (1980a), expanded definitions of the Wister and Fourche Maline phases have been developed (Galm 1981). As indicated earlier, the data incorporated in discussions of these phases have been provided by the recent excavations at Wister Lake. Additional data on these phases are derived from the excavations at the McCutchan–McLaughlin site in nearby Latimer County, Oklahoma (Wyckoff 1976, 1979; Wyckoff and Woody 1977; C. Clark 1980; Powell and Rogers 1980; S. D. Baugh 1982). Summaries of the cultural sequence developed from these investigations and the Wister and Fourche Maline phases are presented below.

The Cultural Sequence

A major goal of recent investigations in the valley was to identify archaeological units and place them in a well-dated sequence. As Stoltman (1978:703) has pointed out, "It is impossible to attain a mature understanding of modern prehistoric archaeology without taking explicit cognizance of the dimension of time." To date, over 60 radiocarbon assays have been obtained from sites in the area (Galm 1981; S. D. Baugh 1982; Lintz 1978e). These dates were instrumental in the development of a cultural sequence for the Wister Valley and vicinity (Galm 1981). A summary of radiocarbon dates from the Poteau Basin is provided in Table 9.3. This suite of dates documents an extensive occupation of the area during the Wister phase, circa 1500–1300 B.C. However, the temporal span of the Fourche Maline phase is not as clear from these assays. A suggested range of circa 300–200 B.C. to A.D. 700–800 is proposed for this phase on the basis of these dates, stratigraphic evidence, and artifact content. Surprisingly few acceptable dates fall in the period circa 300 B.C.–A.D. 400 and may indicate either a smaller resident population in the area and/or a change in settlement pattern. Whatever the cause, the available dates for the Fourche Maline phase suggest that changes in settlement patterns occurred at the end of the preceding Wister phase. Further examination of the nature and causes of changes occurring between these phases requires additional study.

With the accumulation of artifactual, radiocarbon, and stratigraphic data it has been possible to establish a culture–historical sequence and thereby resolve many of the problems associated with the term *Fourche Maline*. The revised cultural sequence is presented in Figure 9.2 and follows the taxonomic scheme of Willey and Phillips (1958). Although derived primarily from research in the Wister Valley, this sequence is extended to include the entire Poteau Basin segment of the Arkansas watershed in eastcentral Oklahoma.

As part of the development of this cultural sequence, a review of site components in the Wister Valley and surrounding area was conducted in order to provide a chronological ordering of occupations. Unpublished site records, published reports, and artifact collections provided the data for this assessment (Galm 1981). A preliminary ordering of site components is presented in Table 9.4. Although this evaluation of site components is provisional, it is based on comparison to the cultural content, radiocarbon dates, and stratigraphic evidence from the Curtis Lake, Scott, and Wann sites (Galm 1978a, 1978b; Galm and Flynn 1978b). Most of the sites listed in Table 9.4 were excavated during the WPA program, but were never analyzed. This ordering of cultural components

Table 9.3

Radiocarbon Assays from the Poteau Basin, with Emphasis on the Wister and Fourche Maline Phases

Site	Sample number	Laboratory number	Square	Depth from surface (cm)	T½ = 5568 years B.P.	T½ = 5730 years B.P.	T½ = 5730 uncorrected calendric date
34Lf-5C (Curtis Lake)	CL-3	WSU-1722	N13-E0	40–50	1275 ± 100	1313 ± 100	A.D. 637 ± 100
	CL-4	WSU-1723	N6-E2	47	1940 ± 100	1998 ± 100	48 ± 100 B.C.
	CL-5	WSU-1724	N6-W2	57	1970 ± 100	2029 ± 100	79 ± 100 B.C.
	CL-6	WSU-1725	N15-W4	73–80	2060 ± 120	2122 ± 120	172 ± 120 B.C.
34Lf-11 (Scott)	S-14	Tx-2891	N15-W1	25–30	1500 ± 140	1545 ± 140	A.D. 405 ± 140
	S-3	UGa-1965	N15-W7	40–45	1940 ± 90	1998 ± 90	48 ± 90 B.C.
	S-15	Tx-2892	N15-W1	40–45	2160 ± 70	2225 ± 70	275 ± 70 B.C.
	S-16	UGa-1971	N15-W1	50–55	2215 ± 85	2281 ± 85	331 ± 85 B.C.
	S-4	UGa-1967	N15-W7 (Burial)	55–60	2150 ± 115	2215 ± 115	265 ± 115 B.C.
	S-6	Tx-2888	N15-W7 (Burial)	80–90	2090 ± 50	2153 ± 50	203 ± 50 B.C.
	S-17	UGa-1972	N15-W1	60–65	2470 ± 75	2544 ± 75	594 ± 75 B.C.
	S-5	WSU-2002	N15-W1	65–70	2085 ± 100	2148 ± 100	198 ± 100 B.C.
	S-18	UGa-1973	N15-W1	70–75	2505 ± 180	2580 ± 180	630 ± 180 B.C.
	S-19	WSU-2005	N15-W1	85–90	2840 ± 80	2925 ± 80	975 ± 80 B.C.
	S-7	UGa-1968	N15-W7	90–95	2525 ± 85	2601 ± 85	651 ± 85 B.C.
	S-20	UGa-1974	N15-W1	100–105	2850 ± 80	2936 ± 80	986 ± 80 B.C.
	S-25	UGa-1977	N15-W6	110–120	2745 ± 135	2827 ± 135	877 ± 135 B.C.
	S-21	WSU-2006	N15-W1	115–120	4030 ± 130	4151 ± 130	2201 ± 130 B.C.
	S-8	Tx-2889	N15-W7	120–125	4590 ± 200	4728 ± 200	2778 ± 200 B.C.
	S-22	UGa-1975	N15-W1	130–135	3390 ± 155	3492 ± 155	1542 ± 155 B.C.
	S-9	UGa-1969	N15-W7	135–140	3850 ± 155	3966 ± 155	2016 ± 155 B.C.
	S-23	UGa-1976	N15-W1	145–150	3555 ± 215	3668 ± 215	1712 ± 215 B.C.
	S-10	Tx-2890	N15-W7	150–155	3640 ± 110	3749 ± 110	1799 ± 110 B.C.
	S-24	Tx-2893	N15-W1	150–155	3930 ± 90	4048 ± 90	2098 ± 90 B.C.
	S-11	WSU-2003	N15-W7	165–170	4040 ± 100	4161 ± 100	2211 ± 100 B.C.
	S-12	UGa-1970	N15-W7	170–175	4500 ± 270	4635 ± 270	2685 ± 270 B.C.
34Lf-27 (Wann)	W-5	UGa-1963	N3-W8	15–20	1530 ± 85	1576 ± 85	A.D. 374 ± 85
	W-6	UGa-1964	N3-W8	25–30	1955 ± 80	2014 ± 80	63 ± 80 B.C.
	W-1	WSU-1781	Test Unit 5	20–30	Modern		
	W-10a	UGa-1960	S2-W8	20–30	1170 ± 75	1205 ± 75	A.D. 745 ± 75
	W-10b	UGa-1962	S2-W8	20–30	1190 ± 60	1226 ± 60	A.D. 724 ± 60
	W-2	WSU-1782	Test Unit 2	30–40	1930 ± 170	1988 ± 170	38 ± 170 B.C.
	W-14	UGa-2072	N3-W8	35–40	1365 ± 165	1406 ± 165	A.D. 544 ± 165
	W-11	Tx-2894	N2-W13	40–50	1220 ± 80	1257 ± 80	A.D. 693 ± 80
	W-7	UGa-1957	N3-W8	45–50	1625 ± 90	1674 ± 90	A.D. 276 ± 90

Sample	Lab No.	Provenience	Depth			
W-3	WSU-1783	Test Unit 5	50–60	1620 ± 100	1669 ± 100	A.D. 281 ± 100
W-8	UGa-1961	N3-W8	55–60	2085 ± 95	2148 ± 95	198 ± 95 B.C.
W-15	UGa-2073	N3-W8	60–65	1848 ± 65	1903 ± 65	A.D. 47 ± 65
W-16	UGa-2074	N3-W8	65–70	1585 ± 95	1633 ± 95	A.D. 317 ± 95
W-17	UGa-2075	N3-W8	75–80	2420 ± 90	2493 ± 90	543 ± 90 B.C.
W-12a	UGa-1978	S4-E10	70–80	1425 ± 135	1468 ± 135	A.D. 482 ± 135
W-12b	WSU-2007	S4-E10	70–80	1910 ± 150	1967 ± 150	17 ± 150 B.C.
W-4	WSU-1784	Test Unit 1	80 ± 90	770 ± 130	793 ± 130	A.D. 1157 ± 130
34Lf-33 (Troy Adams)						
Ad1	UGa-2076	Test Unit 1	10–20	1055 ± 110	1087 ± 110	A.D. 863 ± 110
Ad2	UGa-2077	Test Unit 1	20–30	1160 ± 160	1195 ± 160	A.D. 755 ± 160
Ad3	UGa-2078	Test Unit 1	30–40	2405 ± 80	2477 ± 80	527 ± 80 B.C.
Ad4	UGa-2079	Test Unit 1	40–50	2395 ± 480	2467 ± 480	517 ± 480 B.C.
Ad6	UGa-2081	Test Unit 2	40–50	3060 ± 215	3152 ± 215	1202 ± 215 B.C.
34Lf-5C (Kelly Locality)						
5K-1	WSU-1780	S1-E5	19	1220 ± 120	1257 ± 120	A.D. 693 ± 120
34Lf-24 (Williams I)						
A	UGa-1513	6:18	30	850 ± 50	876 ± 50	A.D. 1074 ± 50
B	UGa-1514	6:9	43	720 ± 60	742 ± 60	A.D. 1208 ± 60
C	UGa-1515	14:23	71	1995 ± 55	2055 ± 55	105 ± 55 B.C.
D	UGa-1516	5:11	96	1860 ± 60	1916 ± 60	A.D. 34 ± 60
E	UGa-1517	2:10	78	1825 ± 105	1880 ± 105	A.D. 70 ± 105
34Lt-11 (McCutchan–McLaughlin)						
F	UGa-2017	O-S8	10–15	1315 ± 75	1354 ± 75	A.D. 596 ± 75
E	UGa-2016	O-S8	15–20	1185 ± 75	1220 ± 75	A.D. 730 ± 75
S	UGa-4042	S6-W4	25–30	1515 ± 165	1560 ± 165	A.D. 390 ± 165
T	UGa-4043	S6-W4	35–40	2410 ± 150	2482 ± 150	532 ± 150 B.C.
D	UGa-2015	S20-E1	35–40	2250 ± 75	2317 ± 75	367 ± 75 B.C.
A	UGa-1520	N1-W1	48–53	1915 ± 55	1972 ± 55	22 ± 55 B.C.
U	UGa-4044	O-W4	50–60	2610 ± 145	2688 ± 145	738 ± 145 B.C.
I	Tx-3367	N7-W1	73–78	2990 ± 80	3079 ± 80	1129 ± 80 B.C.
G	Tx-3365	S6-W5	75–80	2480 ± 80	2554 ± 80	604 ± 80 B.C.
R	UGa-3207	S5-W4	80–85	2465 ± 60	2538 ± 60	588 ± 60 B.C.
M/N	Tx-3514	O-W5	90–100	2900 ± 90	2987 ± 90	1037 ± 90 B.C.
O/P	UGa-2860	O-W5	90–100	2705 ± 65	2786 ± 65	836 ± 65 B.C.
B	UGa-1521	N1-W1	93–98	1945 ± 55	2003 ± 55	53 ± 55 B.C.
Q	Tx-3812	NL-W1	93–98	2940 ± 70	3028 ± 70	1078 ± 70 B.C.
H	Tx-3366	S6-W5	95–100	2820 ± 70	2904 ± 70	954 ± 70 B.C.
J	Tx-3368	N7-W1	98–103	2720 ± 50	2801 ± 50	851 ± 50 B.C.
C	UGa-1522	N15-W2	98–103	2200 ± 55	2266 ± 55	316 ± 55 B.C.
K	Tx-3369	O-W1	100–110	2810 ± 70	2894 ± 70	944 ± 70 B.C.
L	Tx-3370	O-W1	110–120	2950 ± 50	3038 ± 50	1088 ± 50 B.C.
34Hs-111						
TC-1	UGa-1979	Strat Profile	137–147	1645 ± 75	1694 ± 75	A.D. 256 ± 75

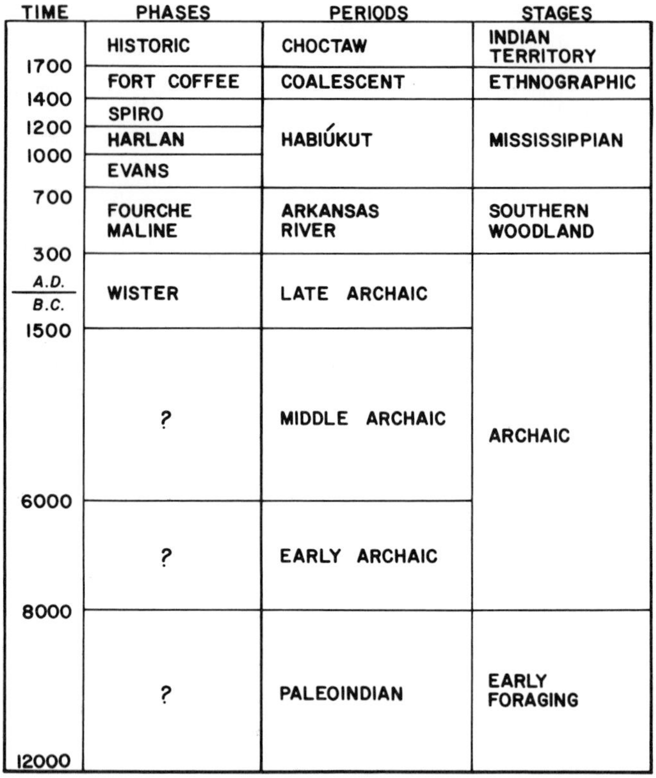

TIME	PHASES	PERIODS	STAGES
1700	HISTORIC	CHOCTAW	INDIAN TERRITORY
1400	FORT COFFEE	COALESCENT	ETHNOGRAPHIC
1200	SPIRO		
1000	HARLAN	HABIÚKUT	MISSISSIPPIAN
700	EVANS		
300	FOURCHE MALINE	ARKANSAS RIVER	SOUTHERN WOODLAND
A.D. / B.C.	WISTER	LATE ARCHAIC	
1500			
	?	MIDDLE ARCHAIC	ARCHAIC
6000			
	?	EARLY ARCHAIC	
8000			
	?	PALEOINDIAN	EARLY FORAGING
12000			

Figure 9.2 A revised cultural sequence for the Poteau Basin.

therefore provides a temporal framework that can be tested during future research.

Late Archaic Period

Wister Phase

The Late Archaic period is marked by extensive occupation of riparian environments. Late Archaic components occur in large numbers, often as the lowermost occupations of midden and mound sites (Galm 1978a:33). There is every indication that a larger population resided in the valley during the Late Archaic than was present in the Middle Archaic period.

Late Archaic components from the valley are grouped under a single phase, the Wister phase, following Bell (1980a:119). The Wister phase spans a consider-

Table 9.4

Preliminary Summary of Cultural Component–Cultural Phase Relationships at Sites in the Poteau Basin

		Phase/period[a]							
		Historic	Fort Coffee	Spiro	Harlan	Evans	Fourche Maline	Wister	Middle Archaic period
34Lf-1	Curtis Lake	0	0	+	+	0	0	0	0
34Lf-5A	Briar Locality	0	×	+	0	+	×	×	0
34Lf-5C	Kelly Locality	0	0	×	+	+	0	0	0
34Lf-5C	Victor	0	0	0	0	0	0	×	0
34Lf-6	Holson Creek	0	0	×	+	0	0	0	0
34Lf-9	Ward	0	0	×	+	0	×	×	0
34Lf-10	Scott	0	0	+	0	×	×	×	+
34Lf-11	Heflin II	0	0	+	×	0	×	×	0
34Lf-13	Heflin I	0	0	+	+	0	+	+	0
34Lf-14	Redwine II	0	0	×	+	0	×	×	0
34Lf-15	Thompson	0	0	0	+	0	+	×	0
34Lf-16	DeHart II	0	0	×	+	+	×	×	0
34Lf-17	DeHart I	×	0	0	0	0	×	+	0
34Lf-18	Copeland	0	0	0	0	0	+	×	0
34Lf-20	Williams I	0	0	×	+	×	+	×	0
34Lf-24	Williams II	0	0	+	0	×	+	×	0
34Lf-25	Bennett Monroe	0	0	0	+	0	+	×	0
34Lf-26	Wann	0	0	0	0	0	×	×	0
34Lf-27	Sam	0	0	×	+	×	+	+	0
34Lf-28	Mackey	0	0	+	+	+	×	×	×
34Lf-29	Akers	0	0	+	0	+	+	+	0
34Lf-32	Troy Adams	0	×	+	+	0	0	×	0
34Lf-33	Pot Breaker	0	0	0	0	×	+	×	0
34Lf-230	Ashmore	0	0	0	0	0	0	×	0
34Lf-233	Anderson Branch	0	0	0	0	0	+	+	0
34Lf-245		0	0	0	0	0	0	0	0
34Lf-246	Roscoe	0	0	+	×	0	0	0	0
34Lt-11	McCutchan–McLaughlin	0	0	+	+	+	×	×	0
34Lt-54	Runner	0	+	+	0	0	+	×	0
34Hs-111		0	0	0	0	+	×	×	0

[a] × = strong indication of component; + = possible presence of component; 0 = absent or not identified.

able period of time (ca. 1500–300 B.C.) and may require further subdivision with the accumulation of additional data. Components assigned to this phase have been identified at Curtis Lake, Scott, Wann, Williams I, and Mc-Cutchan–McLaughlin (Wyckoff 1976; Wyckoff and Woody 1977). An even larger list of components referable to this phase is suggested by the artifact content of sites excavated during the WPA program (Table 9.4).

The later, limiting dates on this phase correspond to the appearance of ceramics in the valley sequence. Late Archaic assemblages from the Poteau Basin resemble collections reported throughout eastern North America at a similar time depth, in terms of the kinds of artifacts and technologies represented. Other similarities can be found in subsistence–settlement patterning and patterns of disposal of the dead (cf. H. D. Winters 1968, 1969; W. S. Webb 1974; Dye 1980; Morse 1967; J. B. Griffin 1967) over wide regions of the eastern United States.

In components of the Wister phase, contracting-stemmed point forms (primarily Gary) co-occur with a variety of expanding-stemmed–corner-notched styles. Ground-stone (e.g., manos, boatstones, pendants), bone (e.g., awls, pins, atlatl hooks), and shell (e.g., beads, discs, pendants) technologies, in addition to chipped-stone technology, appear to be well developed during the Wister phase (Bell 1980a; C. Clark 1980). Perhaps the most significant aspect of Wister phase components is that many of the artifact styles and technologies that first appear during the Late Archaic persist as dominant forms, in some instances for several millenia. This is the case for contracting-stemmed points that dominate chipped-stone samples into the Habiúkut period and may also apply to styles of bone and shell artifacts (e.g., bone whistles and beads, shell pendants and beads). Overall, chipped-stone technology along with patterns of lithic raw material utilization appear to change very little until the Habiúkut period and the appearance of small point forms.

Burials are the most common type of feature recorded during the Wister phase. Other occupational features represented include pits, ashy concentrations, and rock concentrations. Features in general are not well represented nor are they very informative.

Indications of trade in nonlocal raw materials and/or artifacts are present in components of the Wister phase. Copper items, principally in the form of rolled beads, and marine shells, occurring as pendants and beads, are the best examples of trade. The latter artifacts generally occur in burial contexts. A pattern of flexed burials with few material associations is first recognized during the Wister phase and persists throughout the valley chronological sequence. The occurrence of materials of nonlocal origin in burial contexts provide the first indications in the valley of a concern for individual status and the afterlife. In all likelihood, copper recovered from valley sites was obtained from the Lake Superior region or from sources in northcentral Oklahoma (Wyckoff 1980:Table 57). Marine shells were derived from the Gulf Coast (Wyckoff 1980:486). The direction of trade in nonlocal raw materials and/or artifacts more than likely continues with little change into the Habiúkut period (cf. Wyckoff 1980).

Subsistence strategies during the Wister phase are dominated by nut collecting (primarily *Carya*), the hunting of deer and small game, and the harvesting of aquatic resources, including fish, turtles, and freshwater mussels. Late Archaic through Arkansas River period occupations reveal only minor changes in this pattern of exploiting the resource area. The taxa of plants and animals represented at sites in the Wister Valley reveal a consistent use of riparian, forest-edge, and aquatic habitats throughout the Wister and Fourche Maline phases. The economies of peoples residing in the area during these phases of prehistory appear to be relatively stable.

Indications of seasonality of occupations during the Wister phase are restricted to the fall. However, the suggestion of seasonal, fall occupations most likely is overemphasized by the available data. An alternative interpretation based on consideration of a wider range of data, such as depositional sequences, chemical profiles, radiocarbon dates, and artifactual content, is that occupations occurred on a year-round but intermittent basis. This is not to suggest that all occupations at midden mound sites occurred on a year-round basis. Rather, it is proposed that the major occupations at midden mound sites were year-round, or were at least of several season's duration. Moreover, it is apparent that this intermittent pattern of semipermanent residency is best preserved in the artifactual, occupational, and depositional records at multicomponent sites in this area.

Base camps comprise the most frequent and inclusive settlement type identified in the Poteau Basin. Base settlements are suggested by a diversity of implement forms, the quantities of floral and faunal remains represented, and the intensity of occupations reflected in the depositional records of cultural components in midden mound sites. A pattern of base camp settlements, from which exploitation of riparian, forest-edge, and aquatic habitats is directed, is well established by the Wister phase.

Arkansas River Period

Fourche Maline Phase

The concept of a Southern Woodland stage in the prehistory of the Poteau Basin is derived from the Woodland pattern as defined for the eastern United States (J. B. Griffin 1967) and the geographically defined Trans-Mississippi South construct (Schambach 1970). Cultural interaction during this period (ca. 300 B.C.–A.D. 800) focused on eastern Texas and the lower Mississippi Valley. Only minimal interaction with groups residing north and northeast of the study area is posited, at least during the early segment of this period. Indications of trade or interaction with Hopewellian-related peoples located north of the Arkansas River (Baerreis 1939, 1953; J. B. Griffin 1967:Figure 3, 186) are virtually nonexistent. Although relationships to the general pattern of Woodland occupations in the eastern United States are not disputed, the southern orientation of cultural interaction and to a lesser extent, the variability in environments, underscore differences in the development and evolution of specific cultural sequences.

The Trans-Mississippi South construct (Schambach 1970:16–27) lacks the temporal focus reflected in the Southern Woodland concept and thus does not impart the cultural characteristics of this segment of prehistory. Encompassed within this stage are ceramic-bearing cultures occupying woodland environments west of the Mississippi River, including the Ouachita Mountains, portions of the southern Ozark Mountains, and the West Gulf Coastal Plain of northeastern Louisiana, southwestern Arkansas, and eastern Texas. This includes most of the area defined by Schambach (1970:22–24) in his Trans-Mississippi South construct. Temporally, Southern Woodland cultures began with the appearance of ceramic technology and end with the appearance or domination of Mississippian cultures.

The definition of the Arkansas River period derives from the presumed source of dominating cultural influences. The Arkansas River valley most likely provided a major commercial and communication link to southeastern cultures, most notably those of the lower Red River drainage and the lower Mississippi Valley. The Ouachita Mountains are a barrier to trade and travel between the Arkansas and Red River drainages. The presence of this geographical barrier no doubt had a direct bearing on the significance of the Arkansas River valley as a thoroughfare for the exchange of material goods and ideas.

The definition of the Fourche Maline phase (ca. 300 B.C.–A.D. 800) follows the recommendation of Bell (1980a:119–120). Dominant artifact forms found in components of this phase include Williams Plain pottery, contracting-stemmed (Gary) points, and a variety of chipped-stone implements, such as double-bitted axes (Bell 1980a; Schambach 1970:19). However, these forms cannot be restricted in distribution to this phase nor are they by themselves an indication of a specific culture. As noted above, most artifact forms and related technologies first appear during the preceding Wister phase and continue in use into the succeeding Habiúkut period.

Components of this phase predating circa A.D. 400 are poorly documented, possibly indicating a smaller resident population in the valley during this period (Galm 1978b:74–76). In any case, the Wann site currently provides the only example of a component assigned to the early segment of the Fourche Maline phase. A review of this component and the later-dating components at Curtis Lake and Scott (Galm 1978b; Galm and Flynn 1978b) suggest that subsistence–settlement strategies changed very little in the Fourche Maline phase from the preceding Wister phase. The fewer number and decreased thickness of components of this phase suggest changes in settlement patterns that are not entirely clear at present.

Ceramics, dominated by Williams Plain, increase in frequency during later segments of this phase. Ceramic technologies are represented by grog–grit–bone-tempered plainwares, including Williams Plain and LeFlore Plain. LeFlore Plain occurs later in the cultural sequence than Williams Plain, although the exact date of introduction cannot be ascertained. Sherds with a high percentage of bone tempering inclusions occur in the earliest samples of Williams Plain as a minor variety. The frequency of bone tempering increases in late components of the Fourche Maline phase. Decorated ceramics include incised varieties of Williams Plain (Newkumet 1940a; Galm and Flynn 1978b:206–213, 269–276; Irvine 1980) followed in time by incised variants of LeFlore Plain. Decorative motifs include incised parallel diagonal lines, "ladder" designs, and crosshatch patterns. Most attempts at decoration are uneven and relatively crude. Basketry impressions are present on the bases of Williams Plain vessels and sherds, thus indicating the technique of manufacture. The techniques of weaving plant fibers indicated by these impressions, although first documented during the Fourche Maline phase, probably have much greater time depth. Other changes in artifact styles or frequencies from the preceding Wister phase are difficult to distinguish at present.

An early–late or early–middle–late subdivision of the Fourche Maline phase may be warranted but is difficult to document with the available data. The appearance of small points, such as the Scallorn style, may occur as early as circa A.D. 600 and may be a clue to cultural changes warranting further subdivision of the Fourche Maline phase. The upper, limiting dates on the Fourche Maline phase are tentative, but an influx of material traits associated with the westward expansion of Mississippian influences (and possibly peoples) can be placed at circa A.D. 700–800 in this area (Wyckoff 1980:152, 156–171; Bell 1972:259; Story and Valastro 1977). The appearance of Mississippian-related materials (e.g., decorated ceramics, small point varieties) marks the beginning of the Evans phase in the valley sequence.

Overall, the Fourche Maline phase appears to represent a continuation of the cultural adaptation that began in the Wister phase. Sites occupied during the Wister phase were reoccupied, especially during the late segment of the Fourche Maline phase. Artifact assemblages and subsistence strategies reflect only subtle changes in the transition from the Wister phase to the Fourche Maline phase. Besides the introduction of ceramics, the only other notable change in the artifact assemblage is a reduction in the frequency of occurrence of expanding-stemmed–corner-notched projectile points–knives. Occupational features, subsistence evidence, and at least aspects of the settlement pattern, parallel patterns established during the Wister phase.

The appearance of ceramics thus marks the transition from Late Archaic to Arkansas River period occupations. Ceramics remain the key element in distinguishing what otherwise appear to be similar cultural adaptations. To what extent the addition of ceramics affected socioeconomic patterns during the Fourche Maline phase is not apparent in the archaeological record.

Formative Development in the Poteau Basin

Late Archaic Period

The beginning of the Wister phase marks the establishment of a cultural pattern that corresponds to the development of regionally-defined Late Archaic adaptations throughout eastern North America (Caldwell 1958; H. D. Winters 1969, 1974; Cleland 1966). The regional differentiation of adaptations during the Late Archaic may reflect an increased knowledge and exploitation of locally available food resources (Caldwell 1958). Alternatively, the apparent stability of developing lifestyles during the Late Archaic period may be the result of a greater efficiency and adaptability of subsistence pursuits (Cleland 1966, 1976). Testing of these and other hypotheses (H. D. Winters 1974) will require further investigation of adaptive strategies.

The pattern of stable, diversified, and regionally-discrete Late Archaic adaptations may have greater time depth than previously inferred (Caldwell 1958) for eastern North America (e.g., Tennessee, Ohio, and Illinois river valleys). However, the transition from Middle Archaic to Late Archaic occupations appears to be an accurate assessment of the time depth for this pattern in the Poteau Basin.

Similarities in inferred lifestyles and even artifact assemblages underlie Late Archaic manifestations in eastern North America (cf. J. B. Griffin 1967:178–180). The possibility of a gradual diffusion of selected traits and ideas into the Northern Ouachita Province during the Late Archaic is suggested by gross stylistic similarities to artifact forms in regions south and east of the study area. The LaHarpe aspect (L. Johnson 1962:268–280) accommodates many of the Archaic traits found in the Wister phase and subsequent Fourche Maline phase. Both contracting and expanding point "stemming traditions" extend over a broad region of eastern Texas, eastcentral Oklahoma, southwestern Arkansas, and presumably northwestern Louisiana during the Late Archaic (L. Johnson 1962:268–270; Bell 1958b; Bell and Baerreis 1951:19–27; Wyckoff 1966a; Schambach 1970).

Schambach's (1970:20–30) definition of the Trans-Mississippi South as a natural area construct provides a geographic framework for the interpretation of cultural interaction. Although the area encompassed by the Trans-Mississippi South construct is too broad to provide meaningful cultural insights (Schambach 1970:Figure 1), developmental sequences within a smaller core area probably are culturally related. Extensive cultural interaction probably occurred between the Ouachita and Arkansas drainages in western Arkansas and the Poteau Basin throughout the cultural sequence.

Areal affinities are suggested between the Wister phase, the Lamas Branch complex (Wyckoff 1966a, 1970b) in the Southern Ouachita Mountains, and the late White Oak phase (early Dorcheat phase?) in the Mid-Ouachita Region of Arkansas (Schambach 1970:Table 23, 388–394). Similarities in contracting-stemmed and corner-notched–expanding-stemmed point styles and general lithic assemblages provide a strong basis for comparison of sites in these areas. The absence of radiocarbon dates for sites in the Lamas Branch complex (Wyckoff 1966a:85–87) and the Mid-Ouachita sequence (Schambach 1970), however, weakens closer consideration of developmental relationships. Equally important is the absence of even preliminary definitions of subsistence–settlement patterns and systems in adjacent areas of Arkansas, Louisiana, Texas, and southeastern Oklahoma. The development and refinement of local sequences is a necessary first step in the explication of relationships within this area. For the time being, trait correspondences, mainly in the form of stylistic similarities in point assemblages, are suggestive of broad, interregional cultural relationships within the Trans-Mississippi South (Schambach 1970). The nature and extent of these relationships remain to be examined at a future date.

Beyond the area and site complexes included within the Trans-Mississippi South, only very general relationships to the Wister phase can be projected. The Grove focus of northeastern Oklahoma (Baerreis 1951; Bell and Baerreis 1951:10–15) shares few similarities with the Wister phase. Artifacts included in this focus most likely date from the Middle Archaic and Late Archaic periods (Purrington 1970) but are difficult to compare with Wister Valley assemblages. In all likelihood, the Grove focus is more closely linked to Late Archaic manifestations in regions to the north and east. This would suggest that different cultural traditions developed north and south of the Arkansas River during or prior to the Late Archaic period. Whatever the time depth of this proposed development, at least portions of the area north of the Arkansas in northeast Oklahoma manifest culture histories at variance with the Wister sequence in the following period (Arkansas River) of prehistory. The influence of Hopewellian cultures north of the Arkansas (Baerreis 1953, 1939; J. B. Griffin 1967) during the "Woodland" stage has no parallel south of the Arkansas River in eastern Oklahoma.

Indications of interaction between peoples occupying the valley during the Wister phase and more removed areas of the eastern United States are limited. Major Late Archaic manifestations in the central Wabash (Winters 1969), Green (W. S. Webb 1974), Ohio (Janzen 1977), and Tennessee river valleys (Webb and DeJarnette 1942) serve as illustrations of regionally discrete Late Archaic adaptations. Indications of trade or contact with these or other major Late Archaic complexes in the eastern United States during the Wister phase is problematic. However, trade patterns in the Wister phase resemble those described for other Late Archaic Midwestern and Eastern cultures (cf. H. D. Winters 1974). The exchange of copper and marine shell, in particular, is well represented and may be one expression of more extensive links between Late Archaic manifestations throughout eastern North America.

Perhaps most surprising in the definition of the Wister phase is the virtual absence of direct evidence for interaction with the Poverty Point culture (Ford and Webb 1956; C. H. Webb 1977). A trade in lithic raw materials from the Poteau Basin to Poverty Point has been suggested (C. H. Webb 1977:15, 38), although no indication of direct contact between these Late Archaic manifestations is apparent. Baked clay objects, plummets, jasper beads, and steatite vessels, all characteristic of Poverty Point culture (C. H. Webb 1977:28–53), are not represented in components of the Wister phase. Contracting-stemmed points (Gary) dominate hafted biface samples in Wister phase and most Poverty Point collections (C. H. Webb 1977:Table 5, 37), but are a dubious indication of cultural interaction. Potential trade routes connecting the two areas during the chronological span of Poverty Point culture (ca. 1700–500 B.C.) (C. H. Webb 1977:4–5) most likely were centered on the Ouachita River. Peoples of the Wister phase are likely to have had some contact with the Poverty Point culture, but no strong relationship was developed.

Arkansas River Period

The definition of the Fourche Maline phase has helped clarify the temporal position of components formerly included in the Fourche Maline focus. Along with a refined segregation of preceramic (Wister phase) and ceramic-bearing (Fourche Maline phase) components, the available evidence points to restricted occupation of the valley during the early segment of the Fourche Maline phase. Prior considerations of the Fourche Maline focus as an early representative of thick-ware ceramic complexes (Orr 1952:243–244) or formative traditions (J. A. Ford 1969) in the eastern United States are questionable in view of the earliest dates for the Fourche Maline phase (ca. 300 B.C.). Thick-ware types, such as Schultz (Fischer 1972), Marion (J. B. Griffin 1952:98), Fayette (J. B. Griffin 1943:667–672), and Vinette I (Ritchie and McNeish 1949:100), found at sites in the midwestern and northeastern United States form an Early Woodland ceramic tradition apparently predating the appearance of Williams Plain in the Wister Valley. Williams Plain resembles Tchefuncte Plain (Orr 1952:243; Haag 1971:15; P. Phillips 1970:162–163) from the lower Mississippi Valley in terms of paste, temper, and, to some extent, form and surface treatment. However, a wider range of vessel forms occur in Tchefuncte Plain (P. Phillips 1970:162–165) and to date there is no evidence of podal supports in samples of Williams Plain. Williams Plain also resembles the type, Baytown Plain (Greengo 1964:23–35; Phillips et al. 1951:82) from the lower valley, although as P. Phillips (1970:162) points out, "The propriety of separating *Tchefuncte* from *Baytown* may be questioned." The temporal placement of Tchefuncte Plain at about 200 B.C. (P. Phillips 1970:Figure 2; Haag 1971:15) corresponds to the appearance of Williams Plain in the Wister Valley. Both Tchefuncte and Williams ceramics appear to represent regional variations of an "Early Woodland" complex in their respective areas of development (P. Phillips 1970:15–16; Orr 1952:243–244). More detailed comparison of these ceramic types will require additional analysis. However, it is apparent that Formative development in Poteau Basin exhibits strong ties to the Southeast, particularly the lower Mississippi Valley. The appearance of Williams Plain most likely marks a "developmental" transition out of the Late Archaic in this area and may represent a northern variant of lower Mississippi Valley plainwares where this transition has greater time depth.

No examples of early cord-marked (Fischer 1972:147) or fiber-tempered (e.g., Wheeler series; Haag 1942; Sears and Griffin 1953; Jenkins 1974) ceramics have been recovered from the Wister Valley. Temporally, the appearance of Williams Plain in the Poteau Basin at circa 300–200 B.C. overlaps with the Alexander series (late subphase?) in the lower Mississippi Valley and the western middle Tennessee Valley (Dye 1973, 1980).

As noted earlier, interaction with Cooper Hopewellian groups residing north of the Arkansas River (Baerreis 1939, 1953; J. B. Griffin 1967) is minimal. Exchange with Hopewellian-related groups to the north currently is indicated by only several "trade" sherds out of the many ceramic collections examined to date. Examples of Marksville ceramics (Toth 1974) also occur infrequently in valley collections. The possibility of social conflict between Cooper Hopewellian and Fourche Maline peoples cannot be ruled out (Galm 1978a:240–241) and may explain the limited exchange of trade materials.

Comparability of data sets poses a major problem in evaluating regional patterns of cultural interaction during the Arkansas River period. Further refinement of the Mid-Ouachita sequence (Schambach 1970), as well as the development of other well-dated local sequences is an important part of refining regional interpretations. At present, Fourche Maline components in the Poteau Basin appear to be culturally linked to sites along the Arkansas (Bond 1971) and Ouachita (Schambach 1970) rivers. These and surrounding (Lintz 1978e; Vehik and Galm 1979) areas hold the most promise for the refinement of patterns of interaction and exchange during the Arkansas River period. As defined in this study, components of the Fourche Maline phase comprise a pattern of cultural adaptation not fully documented outside the Poteau Basin. Until such documentation is provided, extension of this phase over a wider region of eastern Oklahoma and western Arkansas is not warranted.

Acknowledgments

Thanks are extended to Daniel Landis for typing the final draft, to Pamela K. Rutan for preparation of the graphics, and to the staff of Archaeological and Historical Services, Eastern Washington University, for assisting in the completion of this chapter.

CHAPTER **10**

Arkansas Valley Caddoan: The Harlan Phase

Robert E. Bell

Introduction

The Harlan phase represents an early Caddoan occupation that is found in the Arkansas River valley drainage in eastern Oklahoma. The origins are to be found in older Formative periods represented by Fourche Maline, and it is followed by the Spiro phase, which represents a cultural climax within the Arkansas Valley. The general time period represented by the Harlan phase ranges from A.D. 900 to 1200. These dates, however, are somewhat arbitrary divisions of a cultural continuum and modifications are to be expected, especially at the beginning of this phase (Table 10.1).

The phase is named after the Harlan site in Cherokee County, a mound center that provides the basic characteristics for this period (Bell 1949, 1972). A number of other sites have Harlan phase occupations present, and Wyckoff (1974:57–58), on the basis of artifacts or radiocarbon dates, has assigned a number of additional sites or site components to this time period. These include the following: Spiro (Brown 1966a, 1966b, 1971b, 1976b), McCarter (Shaeffer 1957), Wendtland (Schneider 1967), Fine (Eighmy 1969), Vanderpool (Harden and Robinson 1975), Jensen (Wyckoff and Barr 1964), Reed (Purrington 1970; Thoburn 1931), Lillie Creek (Purrington 1970), School Land I (Duffield 1969), and School Land II (Duffield 1969). In addition to the above sites, the following appear to have Harlan phase occupations present: Norman (Finkelstein 1940), Brackett (Barreis 1955; L. Howard 1940), Hughes (Orr 1946, 1952), Huffaker (Baerreis 1954, 1955), Eufaula (Orr 1941, 1942), Sam (Proctor 1957), Cookson (Israel 1969), Copeland (Guilinger 1971), Plantation (Briscoe 1976, 1977), and Parris (Muto 1977, 1978).

Table 10.1

Harlan Phase Radiocarbon Dates

Laboratory number	Site and provenience	Date before present (B.P.)	Date (A.D.) based on 5570 half-life	Date (A.D.) based on 5730 half-life	MASCA corrected date (A.D.)	Reference
M-856	Harlan site (Ck-6), Unit 4, Layer A, charcoal	610 ± 150	1340	1322	1320 ± 100	Bell 1972:254
M-858	Harlan site (Ck-6), Unit 4, Layer A, charcoal	610 ± 75	1340	1322	1325 ± 65	Bell 1972:254
Tx-471	Harlan site (Ck-6), Unit 4, Layer A, charcoal	770 ± 70	1180	1157	1185 ± 75	Bell 1972:254
Tx-593	Harlan site (Ck-6), Unit 4, Layer A, charcoal	860 ± 70	1090	1064	1110 ± 80	Bell 1972:254
M-64	Harlan site (Ck-6), Unit 4, Layer A, charcoal	1280 ± 300	670	632	700 ± 300	Bell 1972:254
M-859	Harlan site (Ck-6), Unit 4, Layer B, charcoal	820 ± 150	1130	1105	1145 ± 145	Bell 1972:254
Tx-470	Harlan site (Ck-6), Unit 4, Layer B, charcoal	810 ± 70	1140	1116	1155 ± 75	Bell 1972:254
Tx-588	Harlan site (Ck-6), Unit 4, Layer B, charcoal	990 ± 50	960	930	985 ± 45	Bell 1972:254
Tx-589	Harlan site (Ck-6), Unit 4, Layer B, charcoal	1050 ± 50	900	868	930 ± 70	Bell 1972:254
Tx-590	Harlan site (Ck-6), Unit 4, Layer B, charcoal	1220 ± 50	730	693	750 ± 70	Bell 1972:254
Tx-594	Harlan site (Ck-6), Unit 4, Layer B, charcoal	860 ± 50	1090	1064	1110 ± 70	Bell 1972:254
Tx-597	Harlan site (Ck-6), Unit 4, Layer B, charcoal	1100 ± 50	850	817	880 ± 60	Bell 1972:254
Tx-586	Harlan site (Ck-6), Unit 4, House 2, charcoal	880 ± 70	1070	1044	1100 ± 80	Bell 1972:254
Tx-587	Harlan site (Ck-6), Unit 4, House 2, charcoal	960 ± 50	990	961	1010 ± 50	Bell 1972:254
Tx-596	Harlan site (Ck-6), Unit 4, House 2, charcoal	900 ± 70	1050	1023	1090 ± 90	Bell 1972:254
Tx-598	Harlan site (Ck-6), Unit 4, House 2, charcoal	840 ± 60	1110	1085	1130 ± 80	Bell 1972:254

M-860	Harlan site (Ck-6), Unit 4, Layer C, charcoal	775 ± 150	1175	1152	1175 ± 145	Bell 1972:254
Tx-469	Harlan site (Ck-6), Unit 4, Layer C, charcoal	860 ± 70	1090	1064	1110 ± 80	Bell 1972:254
Tx-591	Harlan site (Ck-6), Unit 4, Layer C, charcoal	980 ± 50	970	941	990 ± 50	Bell 1972:254
Tx-592	Harlan site (Ck-6), Unit 4, House 3, charcoal	920 ± 70	1030	1002	1060 ± 80	Bell 1972:254
Tx-595	Harlan site (Ck-6), Unit 4, House 3, Layer C, charcoal	960 ± 40	990	961	1010 ± 40	Bell 1972:254
Tx-599	Harlan site (Ck-6), Unit 4, Layer C over House 3, charcoal	1090 ± 50	860	827	890 ± 60	Bell 1972:254
Tx-603	Harlan site (Ck-6), Unit 6, House log #2	960 ± 60	990	961	1010 ± 60	Bell 1972:254
Tx-605	Harlan site (Ck-6), Unit 6, House, charcoal	860 ± 60	1090	1064	1110 ± 80	Bell 1972:254
Tx-607	Harlan site (Ck-6), Unit 6, House log #1	930 ± 60	1020	992	1040 ± 60	Bell 1972:254
M-1092	Harlan site (Ck-6), Unit 7, Phase A fill, charcoal	1090 ± 100	860	827	885 ± 115	Bell 1972:254
Tx-606	Harlan site (Ck-6), Unit 7, Phase A fill, charcoal	830 ± 60	1120	1095	1140 ± 80	Bell 1972:254
M-1094	Harlan site (Ck-6), Unit 7, Phase B fill, charcoal	820 ± 100	1130	1105	1135 ± 100	Bell 1972:254
Tx-466	Harlan site (Ck-6), Unit 7, Phase B fill, charcoal	720 ± 70	1230	1208	1250 ± 60	Bell 1972:254
Tx-610	Harlan site (Ck-6), Unit 7, Phase B fill	970 ± 70	980	951	1005 ± 65	Bell 1972:254
M-1093	Harlan site (Ck-6), Unit 7, House under Phase D, charcoal	1360 ± 100	590	549	630 ± 90	Bell 1972:254
Tx-467	Harlan site (Ck-6), Unit 7, House under Phase D, charcoal	1020 ± 50	930	899	965 ± 55	Bell 1972:254
Tx-608	Harlan site (Ck-6), Unit 7, House under Phase D, charcoal	1000 ± 50	950	920	980 ± 50	Bell 1972:254

(continued)

Table 10.1 *(Continued)*

Laboratory number	Site and provenience	Date before present (B.P.)	Date (A.D.) based on 5570 half-life	Date (A.D.) based on 5730 half-life	MASCA corrected date (A.D.)	Reference
Tx-609	Harlan site (Ck-6), Unit 7, House under Phase D, charcoal	970 ± 70	980	951	1005 ± 65	Bell 1972:254
Tx-602	Harlan site (Ck-6), Unit 2, village house post, charcoal	930 ± 70	1020	992	1045 ± 75	Bell 1972:254
M-65	Harlan site (Ck-6), Test Area 4, House 3, charcoal	720 ± 200	1230	1208	1215 ± 175	Bell 1972:254
Tx-468	Harlan site (Ck-6), Test Area 4, House 3, charcoal	720 ± 50	1230	1208	1250 ± 40	Bell 1972:254
Tx-600	Harlan site (Ck-6), Test Area 4, House 3, charcoal	960 ± 60	990	961	1010 ± 60	Bell 1972:254
O-398	McCarter site (Ms-15), Area A charcoal	1160 ± 100	790	755	815 ± 125	J. Miller 1963:118
Tx-485	Fine site (Sq-13), Trench C structure, charcoal	840 ± 60	1110	1085	1140 ± 80	Valastro et al. 1968:390
Tx-617	Fine site (Sq-13), Trench C structure, charcoal	920 ± 60	1030	1002	1050 ± 70	Valastro and Davis 1970:261
M-819	Reed site (Dl-1), Near South house, charcoal	1100 ± 150	850	817	865 ± 165	J. Miller 1963:117
Wis-46	Reed site (Dl-1), House under mound, charcoal	1050 ± 60	900	868	940 ± 60	Bender et al. 1965:404
Wis-49	Reed site (Dl-1), House under mound, charcoal	1070 ± 80	880	848	910 ± 90	Bender et al. 1968:167
Wis-243	Reed site (Dl-10), Cache pit #1, charcoal	750 ± 55	1200	1177	1220 ± 40	Bender et al. 1968:167
Wis-246	Reed site (Dl-11), Village unit 11, charcoal	820 ± 60	1130	1105	1150 ± 70	Bender et al. 1968:167

Wis-247	Reed site (Dl-11), Sq. 4:5, 16–20" deep, charcoal	890 ± 55	1060	1033	Bender et al. 1968:167
Wis-249	Reed site (Dl-11), Sq. 1:5, 28–32" deep, charcoal	870 ± 60	1080	1054	Bender et al. 1968:167
Wis-250	Reed site (Dl-11), Sq. 4:7, 40–44" deep, charcoal	840 ± 60	1110	1085	Bender et al. 1968:167
Wis-251	Reed site (Dl-11), Sq. 4:7, 24–28" deep, charcoal	800 ± 60	1150	1126	Bender et al. 1968:167
Wis-252	Reed site (Dl-11), Sq. SE 1:16, 4–8" deep, charcoal	770 ± 60	1180	1157	Bender et al. 1968:167
Wis-253	Reed site (Dl-11), Sq. 3:7, 32–36" deep, charcoal	670 ± 55	1280	1260	Bender et al. 1968:167
Wis-42	Lillie Creek (Dl-41), Structure in mound, charcoal	760 ± 90	1190	1167	Bender et al. 1965:403
Wis-257	School Land I (Dl-64), Sq. NE 14:18, 24–30" deep, charcoal	790 ± 55	1160	1136	Bender et al. 1968:473
Wis-258	School Land I (Dl-64), Sq. NE 10:3, 8–12" deep, charcoal	710 ± 55	1240	1219	Bender et al. 1968:473
Wis-259	School Land I (Dl-64), Sq. NE 9:27, 4–8" deep, charcoal	900 ± 50	1050	1023	Bender et al. 1968:473
Wis-260	School Land I (Dl-64), Sq. NE 9:29, 12–16" deep, charcoal	870 ± 60	1080	1054	Bender et al. 1968:474
Wis-255	School Land II (Dl-65), Sq. NE 34:1, 8–12" deep, charcoal	790 ± 60	1160	1136	Bender et al. 1968:473
M-818	Norman site (Wa-Nr-1), Unit 1A, 2nd substage, charcoal	1050 ± 150	900	868	J. Miller 1963:117
O-595	Norman site (Wa-Nr-1), House #3-1, charcoal	1000 ± 100	950	920	J. Miller 1963:116

(continued)

Table 10.1 (Continued)

Laboratory number	Site and provenience	Date before present (B.P.)	Date (A.D.) based on 5570 half-life	Date (A.D.) based on 5730 half-life	MASCA corrected date (A.D.)	Reference
O-606	Brackett site (Ck-43), Test pit #4, charcoal	700 ± 100	1250	1229	1265 ± 65	J. Miller 1963:117
M-817	Hughes site (Ms-5), House 3, charcoal	1050 ± 150	900	868	920 ± 150	J. Miller 1963:116
O-594	Hughes site (Ms-5), House 8, charcoal	875 ± 100	1075	1049	1110 ± 110	J. Miller 1963:116
Wis-44	Hughes site (Ms-5), House 1, charcoal	730 ± 80	1220	1198	1245 ± 65	Baerreis and Bryson 1965:72
M-816	Spiro site (Lf-40), Craig mound, basal section, charcoal	1170 ± 150	780	745	810 ± 160	J. Miller 1963:116
M-1670	Spiro site (Lf-40), Craig mound, F. A-24, charcoal	1230 ± 110	720	683	750 ± 130	Brown 1967:78
SM-886	Spiro site (Lf-40), Craig mound, F. B-76, charcoal	685 ± 100	1265	1244	1270 ± 80	Brown 1967:79
Tx-4	Spiro site (Lf-40), Craig mound cedar post	1144 ± 165	806	772	835 ± 175	Stipp et al. 1962:45
Wis-130	Spiro site (Lf-40), Craig mound, F. B-189, charcoal	780 ± 70	1170	1147	1170 ± 80	Brown 1967:79
Wis-156	Spiro site (Lf-46), House, fire pit 5, charcoal	1020 ± 70	930	899	960 ± 70	Bender et al. 1967:539
O-2262	Spiro site (Lf-46), House 2, charcoal	725 ± 100	1225	1203	1215 ± 105	Brown 1967:79
M-1667	Spiro site (Lf-51), Brown mound, A-3, charcoal	940 ± 100	1010	982	1055 ± 155	Brown 1967:78
UGS-1401	Plantation site (Mi-63), Area A, F. 1, charcoal	935 ± 115	1015	987	1055 ± 125	Briscoe 1976:12
UGa-1845	Parris mound (Sq-12), Test Trench 3, charcoal	875 ± 110		1075	1120 ± 110	Muto 1978
UGa-1846	Parris mound (Sq-12), Test Trench 1, F. 2, Cut 5, charcoal	1090 ± 230	860	860	925 ± 255	Muto 1978

Wyckoff (1980:174–85) in his study of the Arkansas Basin Caddo, has added Harlan components at several other sites: Bill Ross, Box Car, Mackey, Troy Adams, Littlefield (Lf-60), Choates 2, Hall, Littlefield 4, and Goff Shelter. In addition, 25 sites known only from surface collections are included in Caddo II, the Harlan phase time period. There are undoubtedly many additional Harlan phase sites to be identified, but identification is often difficult because of limited or specialized activities or the presence of additional occupations.

The Harlan phase sites are concentrated along the Arkansas River valley and its major tributaries such as the Poteau, Illinois, and Neosho (Grand). Settlements extend westward along the Arkansas and Canadian rivers into the Claremore Cuesta Plains, but these appear to represent frontier thrusts into the prairie plains, and form a western periphery of Harlan settlements. The sites clearly favor a location with access to the hardwood forested zones of eastern Oklahoma, ranging from the McAlester Marginal Hills Belt on the south to the Ozark Plateau and Neosho Lowland in the north. Many sites occur along the Neosho River valley, which forms a boundary line between the oak–hickory forest of the Ozark uplift and the tall-grass prairie of the plains. Settlements located on the prairie plains, however, are less frequent and the Eastern Sandstone Cuesta Plains appears to mark the western limits of the occupied area. The larger sites tend to be located at strategic locations in floodplain bottomland areas that also had easy access to the resources of both oak–hickory forest lands and the tall-grass prairie (Figure 10.1).

The sites represented include two broad types: sites having mounds and sites lacking mounds. The mound sites may have only a single mound or several of them. The Harlan site contains five mounds arranged around an open area and covers about 8.5 ha. Sites having only one mound may cover 2 ha or less. The

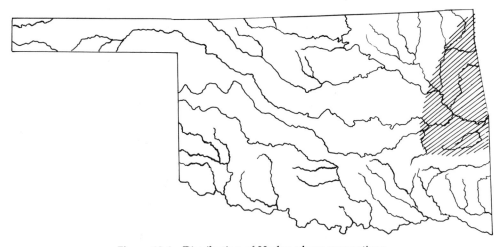

Figure 10.1 Distribution of Harlan phase occupations.

non–mound sites are usually less than 1 ha in area and represent small villages, farmsteads, base camps, secondary camps, or special-activity areas.

The settlement pattern indicates a scattered series of mound sites that served as local or regional community centers, which were surrounded by a series of small satellite communities and farmsteads. These satellite communities supported the mound centers by a trade and exchange network controlled by a religious and political authority centered at the major sites. The Harlan site represents one example of these centers with the presence of substructure mounds, mortuaries, and the final burial place for the tribal elite. It functioned as the administrative and ceremonial center for the region but was probably subject to a higher authority situated elsewhere, probably at Spiro.

The Harlan phase sites are located in a region that offers considerable resources for exploitation of natural resources. The Ozark highlands offered outcrops of limestone, sandstone, shales, and dolomite, commonly interbedded with flints or cherts that were good materials for chipped-stone artifacts. Other natural products include galena, hematite, limonite, phosphate nodules, siltstones, and cannel coal, all of which were utilized. Red cedar and osage orange were probably important woods not only for local products but for items used in trade.

Basic subsistence was based on agriculture, hunting, fishing, and gathering with considerable differences in emphasis from site to site. Bone debris is scarce at the Harlan mound center but smaller non–mound sites often obtain indications of important hunting activities. Faunal materials from the School Land sites indicate utilization of deer, bison, opossum, raccoon, dog, bobcat, beaver, rabbit, elk, turkey, great horned owl, longnosed gar, catfish, and turtles. At School Land I, deer and bison constitute 90% of the bone debris. A nearby site, School Land II, displays a somewhat different faunal assemblage, suggesting variations in hunting emphasis or practices from village to village.

Farming is assumed to have been important although actual plant remains are rare. Gardening equipment such as hoes and seed processing equipment, however, are well represented.

Trade and exchange become of increasing importance during the Harlan phase; in fact, it probably represents a major economic activity. This is reflected in the appearance of exotic goods such as conch shell, copper, trade wares in pottery, such as Coles Creek Incised, and flints from distant sources. Lithic materials are represented from deposits in Kay County, Oklahoma, the Amarillo dolomite quarries in Texas, and Arkansas novaculite. A necklace of small stone beads found at the Harlan burial mound appears to have originated in the Southwest. Indications of this increased trade activity with the presence of valued exotic goods, especially simple conch shell and copper items represents one characteristic of the Harlan phase, and differentiates it from the earlier formative period.

The Harlan site provided the best information about the Harlan phase and represents a major mound center. The site has five mounds arranged around an open area or *plaza* that overlooks the Fourteen Mile Creek river valley. The small number of houses discovered and the general absence of midden debris suggest that the site was not inhabited by many people and was not a village in the usual sense; rather, it was the tribal mortuary and ceremonial center to which a dispersed supporting population gathered in times of crisis or to honor their dead.

One large rectangular flat-topped mound dominates the site area. This mound measures 40 m in width and 49 m in length at the base and rises to a height of 4.3 m. Cross sections indicate that it was built in four construction episodes that increased the size and height of the mound. Prior to mound construction, a structure had been present upon the original ground surface and this structure provided the orientation for the superimposed construction periods representing the mound. The mound platform lacked evidence for structures or indications of special features in the areas excavated. Radiocarbon dates from the mound suggest a span of about 200 years for its utilization (Table 10.1).

The remaining mounds include two mortuary mounds, a composite burial mound composed of three conjoined conical-shaped units, and a specialized mound containing a large rectangular-shaped rock feature. This latter mound is poorly understood because similar features have not been found elsewhere, and the radiocarbon dates appear very early (A.D. 700). Perhaps it is not to be associated with the Harlan phase but rather with an earlier development or formative period.

The mortuary mounds represent mounds that have been constructed over the remains of a mortuary structure that was destroyed upon removal and burial of the contained remains. One mound had buried a single mortuary structure but the other one contained three superimposed mortuaries, one built on top of the other but separated by layers of earth representing mound construction phases. The initial mortuary was built on the original ground surface and, upon destruction, it was buried by a mantle of earth that formed the surface for the construction of the second mortuary. After destruction of the second mortuary it was buried to provide a new surface for the third mortuary. This third mortuary was finally destroyed and then covered over with a final cap that completed the mound.

The mortuary structures are similar in form to the houses in the villages, a square structure having four large, centrally placed posts for supporting the roof (Figure 10.2). Measurements from three mortuaries at Harlan range from 6.7 by 7.3 m to 10 by 10 m. The walls were made with upright wooden posts that served as reinforcing for a wattle-and-daub plastered wall. The roof was covered with thatch supported on a cane and wooden framework. The entranceway is usually marked by shallow parallel trenches or rows of post holes forming a short hall-like entrance passage into the interior. The entranceway is sometimes marked by an elevated clay platform and indications of special preparation. The

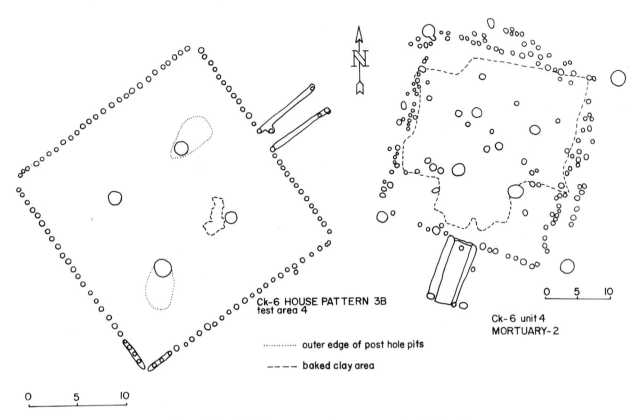

Figure 10.2 Posthole patterns of structures at the Harlan site.

interiors are not marked by special features although numerous extra postholes commonly surround the walls or appear in the interior, suggesting structural reinforcement or special constructions. That these structures functioned as mortuaries is indicated by the general absence of debris or rubbish on the floors, as if the structure had been cleaned out prior to destruction, the absence of interior fire places, and the presence of postholes for closing the entranceway. The finding of human skull fragments in the mortuary area also supports this usage, and indicates that the clearing of the mortuary for interment elsewhere was not always complete.

Excavations at the Harlan site indicate that mortuary structures were used for housing the dead. When the mortuary was filled (or for other cultural reasons), the contained remains were removed and buried in the nearby burial mound. After burial, the mortuary was burned and destroyed, covered over with earth, and a new one was constructed over the same spot. The burial remains found within the burial mound also support this idea. Many burials were apparently deposited at the same time and these occur in layers to indicate different burial episodes in mound construction. The skeletons are commonly disarranged and are often incomplete, suggesting various stages of decomposition of the body prior to burial. Artifacts are often widely scattered but clearly belong together and represent a single interment phase.

The Harlan site burial mound was composed of three small, conjoined conical mounds placed in a north–south line at the eastern side of the site area. The north end formed the largest unit and measured 2.1 m in height and 15.2 m in diameter. The conical units decreased in size toward the southern end, the smallest mound measuring 1.1 m in height and 10.7 m in diameter. A small amount of earth had been placed within the areas between the conical mounds to connect them with a low earthen saddle, thus forming a single linear mound out of the three subunits. The burials, however, were concentrated within each of the three conical units.

The burials contained within the mound were dominated by single flexed individuals, commonly in very poor condition and usually incomplete. Multiple burials, cremations, and bundle burials also occur with isolated bones or single skulls. Burial associations were found with 55.6% of the graves and there is a trend for burial items to increase and become more elaborate in the later burials. Artifacts found with the early burials include flint bifaces, bone pins, copper-coated wooden pins, natural concretions, deer-mandible sickles, stone pipes, black stone beads, chunks of galena, stone celts, and Coles Creek Incised and Williams Plain pottery. Artifacts found with the later burials include pulley-shaped stone earspools, wooden earspools, tubular shell beads, conch shells, ring-type stone earspools, copper beads, an effigy pipe, Woodward Plain pottery (Reed variety), and other pottery wares.

The burial mounds were built up by accretion in depositional phases that were similar in all three of the mound units. Some of the earliest graves had been placed in shallow pits on the original ground surface. Other burials appeared in layers and clearly represented a single interment event, presumably from the deposition of remains removed from a mortuary. Although burials may have been placed in the burial mound at other times, it appears that there were three or four major periods of deposition. At each time, the human remains were taken from the mortuary and deposited in each of the three burial mound units. The burials were then covered over with earth to complete one burial episode. As the new mortuary became filled and its contents removed, another burial interment would follow.

The significance of deposition within three different parts of the mound remains unknown, although it apparently reflects social differences that were incorporated into the funeral activity. There are some differences in the associated artifacts, not only in frequency but their presence or absence. Yet it is clear that the three subunits were used at the same time and that burials were deposited in all subunits. For example, portions of the same pottery vessel (Pennington Punctate Incised) appeared in the same depositional phase in each of the three units. Stone earspools from matching pairs were often found at considerable distance from each other. That this represented the deposition from clearing out a mortuary is indicated by the incompleteness of the skeletons, displacement of the bones, scattering of associated artifacts, and evidence for contemporaneous burials.

The presence of cremation is interesting in view of Swanton's (1942:238) observation that the Caddo cremated the bodies of men who died on war expeditions. Cremations appear in all three subunits and throughout the utilization of the mound. Although sex data are not available, burial goods associated with cremations suggest individuals of high status.

The smaller mound sites, which are more numerous, usually have only a single mound and it may vary from site to site. The Lillie Creek site has a single structure mound (mortuary?), and a burial mound was present at the Eufaula site. The non–mound sites have evidence for structures, scattered middens, and occasionally small cemetery areas. The sites are usually situated close to the river upon a terrace immediately above the flood plain. The size is normally less than 1 ha and the number of structures recovered ranges from a single house to a small village cluster. The School Land I site produced a total of nine houses, not counting overlapping floor plans; some of the houses have clearly been rebuilt or shifted in their orientation.

The typical house structure is almost square in outline, about 7 m across, with a parallel trench-type entranceway at one side, and four large interior posts for supporting the roof. Construction is similar to the mortuaries with a wattle-and-daub wall and a grass-thatched roof. A central fireplace occurs in the interior and occasional postholes suggest reinforcement or special interior features. Wall replacement, wall reinforcement, and the rebuilding of structures over the same general area appear very typical of the sites investigated (Figure 10.3).

Figure 10.3   Two superimposed house patterns found at the Harlan site, Test Area 4.

Industries

The following sketch of industries associated with the Harlan phase is based primarily on the type site itself plus materials from the Harlan phase at the Spiro site. It should be pointed out that other types of sites, such as small villages, farmsteads, base camps, and the like, will not have many of these items that are associated with the major centers. The smaller satellite communities have a less elaborate inventory and more items that appear to continue in use from earlier times.

Chipped-stone materials include various finished artifacts as well as debitage from their manufacture. Debitage is chiefly of local materials, however, and most exotic flints appear to have been brought in as finished products through trade.

Small projectile points or arrowheads are perhaps the most common chipped-stone item. These occur in a variety of named types, including Scallorn, Reed, Huffaker, Alba, Homan, Hayes, Morris, Agee, Sequoyah, Ashley and Pocola. These are commonly of nonlocal materials (Figure 10.4).

Larger projectile points or dart points also occur in small numbers. The more common types include Gary, Langtry, Ellis, and Edgewood, although other types may be represented by one or two examples.

Large bifaces that represent either spearpoints or knives are also present. These are usually leaf-shaped, with or without notches or modification for hafting. Some examples from the Harlan site have stains on the basal section apparently resulting from the original hafting or wrapping. Named types include the Mineral Springs biface and the Kay point. These are commonly made of nonlocal materials.

Other chipped-stone items include flake scrapers with secondary chipping along the end or side, a single flint drill, spatulate shaped celts, chipped hoes or digging tools, and pecking hammers. The spatulate-shaped celts have been shaped by a chipping process, but were then ground and polished to provide the final finish. The chipped-stone digging tools are commonly made of shale, either roughly rectangular or oval in outline with evidence of usage and wear on the bit edges. The pecking hammers were used in the manufacture of pecked- and ground-stone artifacts.

Artifacts of ground stone include both items for everyday utilitarian usage as well as articles of adornment and indications of status. Milling basins and hand stones (mullers) for food processing are represented. Anvil stones marked with cups or pits for cracking nuts or other hard materials were used. Stone celts were a common burial association and occur in two broad classes: a thick ovate form having a rather wide base, and a more slender type with a more pointed poll. There is a single flared celt or spud from the Harlan site of the elongate form (Brown 1976b:177–181), apparently an early form of this artifact.

Stone beads (forelock beads?) are very characteristic of the Harlan phase. They are commonly made of black phosphate nodules but other materials are repre-

Figure 10.4 Cache of projectile points from Burial 4, Harlan site.

sented, such as shale, sandstone, and even hematite. They are typically globular, tubular, or barrel-shaped with drilled perforations. Examples of unfinished specimens also occur, suggesting local manufacture of some examples. One necklace of small stone-disk washerlike beads appears to be a trade item from the Southwest region. Simple flat stone pendants also occur (Figure 10.5).

Stone earspools are well represented. They are most commonly of the pulley-shaped type although examples of the "napkin ring" type also occur. The earspools usually occur in matched pairs and many have been covered with a copper veneer on the exterior or outer face of the spool. None of the Harlan site examples is decorated and there is a trend for an increase in the diameter of the spool through time.

Stone pipes are represented by the T-shaped pipe of the Chandler type (Brown 1976b:230). This form also occurs in clay. A single clay-stone effigy pipe was recovered at the Harlan site. It depicts a human figure standing upright and

Figure 10.5 Artifacts from the Harlan site (Ck-6): (a) T-type stone pipe, Burial 19, Specimen 341; (b) copper long-nosed god mask, Burial 37, Specimen 586; (c) copper plate fragment, Burial 89, Specimen 598; (d) spindle-shaped copper-covered wooden beads, Burial 54; (e) copper-coated stone earspool, Unit 1C, Specimen 270; (f) galena, Unit 1A, Specimen 781; (g) fragment of copper plate, Burial 41, Specimen 315; (h) copper-coated stone ear-spool, Burial 114, Specimen 379; (i) black stone beads, Burial 118, Specimen 890; (j) flat stone pendant, Unit 1A, Specimen 317.

carrying a small pouch in one hand. Other details are obscured by the poor condition, although a second figure and the rattles of a snake are suggested.

Bone artifacts are scarce but this probably reflects preservation because bone was in poor condition in all parts of the site. Artifacts include bone awls, a beamer, bird-bone beads, a fishhook, deer-jaw sickles, and pins. These latter specimens were probably hairpins as they resemble wooden hairpins found at the site.

Both conch shell and mussel shell were utilized. Mussell shells were used as shell hoes and possibly for disk-shaped shell beads. The conch shells are represented chiefly by fragments although three relatively whole shells suggest the presence of plain shell cups. None of the conch shell specimens shows any indication of cutting, perforations, or engraving, although preservation is poor and decorations could have become eliminated. Shell was also used for disk and tubular-shaped beads of various sizes.

Wooden objects are represented by a few specimens that were preserved because of the copper veneer attached to the wood. Wooden earspools, wooden hairpins and wooden spindle-shaped beads are all present and were associated with burials. Wooden bowls are reported from this phase at Spiro.

Copper was used as a veneer for wooden and stone objects as well as for solid copper artifacts (Figure 10.5). Copper items include fragments of flat copper plates, some of which show embossing, a flat hair or head ornament, flattened globular beads, the long-nosed god mask, hairpins, a tubular-shaped fragment, and a rattle. The rattle, although badly preserved was apparently of wood or a small gourd with a copper veneer.

Additional miscellaneous articles include the presence of galena and hematite, presumably for the use as pigments. The galena is represented by irregular or rounded chunks showing abrasions from rubbing or grinding the surface. One galena bead is known. Indications of pigments were present in some burials by a small mass of colored clay in light grey, green, red, and red-brown. Natural concretions, a fossil shell, and chalk stone also appear as grave offerings. Some unidentified small globular seeds were also used as beads.

Indications of cordage (two ply), reed and cane matting, and coiled basketry are present.

Pottery is well represented with a variety of named and unnamed types (Figure 10.6). Vessel forms include small jars, deep jars, various sized bowls, and bottles. Handles and lip tabs are also present. Decorations include incising, engraving, punctates, and the use of a red slip. Some wares appear to be trade items derived from some outside source whereas others were locally made. Named pottery types include the following: Coles Creek Incised, Crockett Curvilinear Incised, Davis Incised, Hickory Fine Engraved, Holly Fine Engraved, Leflore Plain, Pennington Punctate Incised, Sanders Plain, Spiro Engraved, Williams Plain, and Woodward Plain. Fingernail punctates and clay-pinched designs are also present.

Figure 10.6 Pottery vessels from the Harlan site (Ck-6) burial mound: (a) Spiro Engraved bottle, Burial 94, Specimen 585; (b) Leeched shell-tempered bottle, Burial 37, Specimen 1237; (c) Holly Fine Engraved jar, Burial 114a, Specimen 580; (d) Crockett Curvilinear Incised vessel of unusual form, Burial 73, Specimen 878; (e) Pennington Punctate Incised bowl, Burial 114a, Specimen 378; (f) Beaver Pinched (?) jar, Burial 99, Specimen 880.

Harlan Phase Internal Change

The Harlan phase appears to have a duration of approximately 300 years. Throughout this time span many of the cultural characteristics—for example, the house pattern—appear to have been quite stable; on the other hand, there are differences in the cultural inventory from early to late Harlan times. From evidence at the Harlan site, some artifacts are characteristic of early Harlan periods whereas others are typical of late Harlan phase. One has the subjective impression that trade and items to be associated with a social elite become of increasing importance and abundance. It appears reasonable that as more research is done and the time period is better understood, that further subdivisions within the Harlan phase will be necessary.

Considering only the evidence from the Harlan site, it is clear that burial offerings increase from early to late times. In the early burials, 40.9% of the graves have burial goods; in the late burials, 76.5% of the graves have burial goods. There is also a related trend in mortuary size, the later mortuaries being somewhat larger in floor area than the earlier ones. The social significance of this increase in mortuary size, however, is not clear.

Goods associated with early burials include black stone beads, large bifaces, bone hairpins, copper-coated wooden hairpins, galena, stone celts, Coles Creek Incised pottery, Williams Plain pottery, Spiro Engraved, stone pendants, and stone pipes. Some of these are exclusively early items and do not appear in late burials.

Burial goods associated with late burials include stone earspools of the pulley and "napkin ring" type, wooden earspools, conch-shell cups and tubular beads, copper beads, greater amounts of copper, clay pipes, an effigy pipe, Woodward Plain pottery, and a clay-tempered pinched ware. Many of these items do not appear in early graves.

There are a few articles that appear in an intermediate period: the flared celt or spud, spindle-shaped wooden beads with a copper veneer, the long-nosed god mask, Holly Fine Engraved pottery, and Pennington Punctate Incised pottery.

Without radiocarbon dates from the burial mound, the appearance of some items remains uncertain. The following table, however, indicates what appears to be the most diagnostic items for the early and late periods:

Early Harlan phase	Late Harlan phase
Black stone beads	Stone ear-spools, pulley type
Galena	Utilization of conch shell
Bone pins	Copper ornaments including embossing
Copper-coated wooden pins	
Stone celts	Effigy pipes
Coles Creek Incised	Stone spuds
Williams Plain	Woodward Plain

One of the most interesting questions regarding the Harlan site itself is why the site was abandoned, apparently sometime after A.D. 1200. The Norman site, a large mound center, is located only 5 km away on the nearby Grand river and present radiocarbon dates indicate that it was occupied during the Harlan phase and for some time afterward. Burial goods found at the Norman site suggest a Spiro phase occupation, possibly extending into the Fort Coffee phase. In addition, many items present at Harlan are absent at the Norman site, and vice versa. It would appear that, for some social reasons not presently understood, the political–religious control once centered at the Harlan site was shifted to the Norman site, and the Harlan mound center fell into disuse.

External Relationships

The Harlan phase development is concentrated with the Arkansas River drainage and its relationship to Caddoan expressions along the Red River are not understood. The Caddoan developments along the Red River and the Arkansas River, although closely related, are quite different in a number of cultural characteristics and should be investigated independently. Cultural differences between the two regions, such as architecture and mortuary customs, appear to have a lengthy history, and such differences may reflect an early division in the Caddoan linguistic stock.

Within the Arkansas River basin the origins of the Harlan phase remain uncertain. There are indications that it may have developed within the region out of the older Fourche Maline phase. On the other hand, the distribution of Harlan phase sites, importance of trade and exchange, new cultural characteristics, and increased cultural complexity suggest that a new people may have entered the region. If this is the case, they most certainly came from the east or southeast, not from the west or north. As our understanding of Fourche Maline becomes improved, perhaps this matter will be resolved.

One feature of the Harlan phase is its expansion into new territories, especially toward the north along streams flowing out of the Ozarks Uplift. This is especially evident in the Neosho River valley along the western edge of the Ozarks. During the time period around A.D. 900 to 1000, one can note the expansion of the Harlan phase into many new areas. One has the impression of a dynamic society expanding into new territories that were quickly incorporated into a region dominated by the Harlan phase elite.

I have suggested previously (Bell 1980b) that this expansion not only included parts of Oklahoma, but that it extended northward into the eastern Central Plains region. The presence of Harlan phase artifacts in northwestern Arkansas, southwest and western Missouri, and at sites along the Missouri River in Nebraska and Iowa indicate contact with the Arkansas valley area. Such artifacts as pottery types, stone earspools, copper-coated wooden hairpins, and Caddoan type arrowpoints were obtained from Harlan phase peoples in some manner, possibly by means of a trade and exchange system that operated within this region. Chapman (1980) has noted a number of typical Harlan phase (Caddoan) artifacts found in Missouri in the Loftin phase and the Stockton complex. Items are also found in the Nebraska phase (Blakeslee and Caldwell 1979), the St. Helena phase (Cooper and Bell 1936), and Upper Republican sites in both Kansas and Nebraska (W. R. Wedel 1959; Witty 1978). It is obvious that artifacts originating in the Harlan phase area of Oklahoma are also present in regions to the north as far as the Central Plains.

Although the distribution of these artifacts can be understood in terms of a widespread trade network existing beyond the area dominated by Harlan phase people, the presence of typical Harlan phase house patterns (a square structure with four central roof supports and entrance passage) suggests that a movement of peoples was involved. Similarities in the house patterns, along with the Harlan phase type artifacts, at the Loftin site and other sites representing the Nebraska, Upper Republican, and Smoky Hill phases, suggest that more than simple trade is involved. Although artifacts may be obtained by trade or other contacts, parallels in house patterns and constructions imply a more intimate relationship.

Moreover, radiocarbon dates for the sites and house structures concerned appear at approximately the same time as the Harlan phase expansion. Consequently, I have suggested that the Harlan phase population not only expanded into new areas of Oklahoma, but also to the north and northeast as far as the Missouri valley. These people contributed to and represent the ancestors of Caddoan populations represented in the Central Plains region.

CHAPTER 11

Arkansas Valley Caddoan: The Spiro Phase

James A. Brown

Introduction

The Spiro phase represents the Caddoan tradition in the Arkansas valley drainage at the peak of social complexity and cultural elaboration. Dating to between A.D. 1250 and 1450, Spiro phase sites are found throughout eastern Oklahoma north of the Kiamichi range of the Ouachitas (Figure 11.1). The principal and most famous site in the Caddoan area is Spiro, which is located near the eastern edge of the state. Its fame is a result of the widely publicized circumstances surrounding the discovery of the principle mound's contents and the repute its artifacts have as art objects. Consequently, the material culture of Spiro has become one of the best known of any in Oklahoma.

Habitat

Spiro phase sites are located primarily in the floodplain and valleys of the Arkansas River and its principal tributaries in eastern Oklahoma (Poteau, Grand, and Illinois rivers). The most heavily occupied physiographic zone is the butte and valley terrain of the Arkoma Basin (Figure 11.1). To the north, in the Ozark Uplift zone, occupation is sparse; south in the Ouachita Mountain zone little is known about occupation. Throughout the region an oak–hickory forest covered the uplands except for pockets of tall-grass prairie. The river valleys were oc-

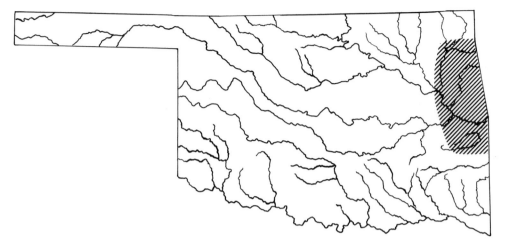

Figure 11.1 Spiro phase in Oklahoma.

cupied by a mesic vegetation. The oak–pine forest zone of southeast Oklahoma does not seem to have been occupied. The prairies were larger and more continuous at the western edge where grassland was interspersed with patches of post oak and blackjack oak savanna. Likewise, the bottomlands changed character from east to west. In the vicinity of Spiro the bottoms held predominately a southeastern bayou vegetation that changed to a floodplain gallery forest in the western part of the drainage above Webbers Falls (Thwaites 1905:233). Climate is warm, humid, and continental.

Settlement Patterns

Three basic site types are the civic–ceremonial center, the village and various categories of impermanent camps (shelters, mines, etc.). The civic–ceremonial centers are distinguished from other sites by the presence of public buildings and a buried structure mound or a platform mound. Habitations are not found around these structures. At Spiro the associated population was distributed in small, isolated sites within a 3-km radius. This site and Norman are the largest centers and contain the greatest number of different mounds. Both contain a complex of conjoined platform mounds and a pyramidal mound. At Spiro, the larger and more important of the two sites, a conjoined platform mound (the Craig mound) consisted of four units in a line about 120 m long and connected by saddles. The largest unit at the north end was constructed last and over the location of a previously dismantled mortuary structure. A sequence of such large structures were constructed and dismantled during the Spiro phase. The last of these, which I call the *Great Mortuary*, enclosed an estimated area between 180 and 280 m², depending upon alternative reconstructions. The same mound type at Norman (Md. A or WgNrI) consisted of only two conjoined units. Excavation in one disclosed a platform structure. Just north of the mound were the remains of at least four superimposed surface structures enclosing 60.5–97.5 m². They were placed in the same location to the mounds as the Great Mortuary was toward the southern three units of the Craig mound. The pyramidal mound at Spiro stood approximately 5.5 m (Brown mound), and the Mound C (WgNr III) at Norman stood about 2.1 m high. The Norman site also contained other earthworks in the form of accretional burial mounds and buried structure mounds.

The Spiro phase centers are arranged in a hierarchy of at least two levels and perhaps a third. Spiro and Norman occupy the top, with Spiro the more important. The lower level centers consist of simple buried structure mounds. An example is the Sol Thompson site (Lf 16). Between these two well-defined levels is a category of platform mound sites that do not constitute a clearly separate level because either they may belong to the preceeding Harlan phase (Reed) or they may not be independent centers (Skidgel and Cavanaugh), but satellites of Spiro instead. These lesser centers consist of a single pyramidal mound and associated ground-level public buildings that were laid out on the same orientation. The Reed site (Dl 1-11) is a peripheral center servicing the northern groups on the Elk river.

Habitation sites are relatively small. Half are 1.5 ha or less in size. The settlement with the largest confirmed site is the 8-ha Horton site. The next in size is Littlefield I (ca. 4 ha) that contains at least 15 regularly arranged structures oriented on the cardinal directions. Next are a group about 2 ha in size. The smallest are hamlets and farmsteads of one to two structures. A thoroughly excavated example of a farmstead is the Cat Smith site, which consists of 2 structures, 1 subsurface feature, and 2 burials within a 15-by-30 m area. Impermanent sites consist mainly of shelters (e.g., Owl Cave, Pohly) that were used for season exploitation of resources or for ritual purposes.

Structures

The common building is square to rectangular in ground plan and usually has two central supports positioned in the center of the floor along the longitudinal axis and arranged in such a way as to suggest a gabled roof (Figure 11.2t). Alternative support frameworks are known. The large structures at Norman have four supports in a square arrangement. Other lack visible interior supports. The doorway was usually centered in the long axis and was often protected by an extended entryway. The walls were set in individual postholes or in trenches and were covered with clay daubed over horizontal cane laths or grass thatch. The roof was apparently thatched with grass (Wyckoff 1970c:18).

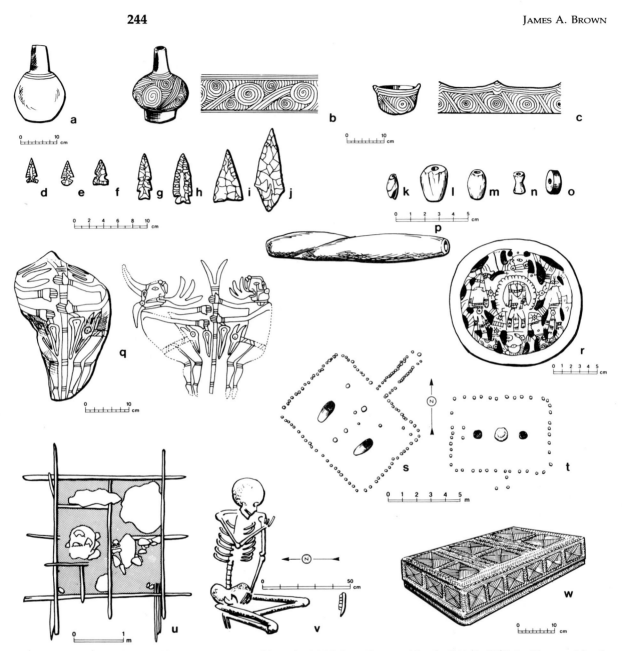

Figure 11.2. Spiro phase artifacts, structures, and burials: (a) Hickory Engraved bottle (B88-1); (b) Spiro Engraved bottle (B100-1); (c) Spiro Engraved bowl (B189-1); (d) Haskell point; (e) Keota point; (f) Washita point; (g) Sallisaw bokoshe point; (h) Sallisaw point; (i) triangular lance point (BrB3/5); (j) Gary knife point; (k) *Olivella*-shell bead; (l) massive barrel-shaped bead; (m) barrel-shaped bead; (n) phalange-shaped bead; (o) disc-shaped bead; (p) columella bead; (q) engraved *Busycon* shell cup with design after Phillips and Brown 1975; (r) engraved shell gorget; (s) ceremonial structure (Skidgel mound site); (t) domestic structure (Littlefield I site); (u) litter burial (B62); (v) semiflexed burial with deer-mandible sickle (EvB1); (w) basket burial. All items from Spiro except structure plans.

The large number of sites of the Spiro phase found in the Spiro vicinity probably indicates a concentration of population around this civic–ceremonial center. The unusual density of this concentration is implied by the bluff-crest location of many settlements around Spiro. This population is probably an aggregate of many communities including those settlements that were formerly located along secondary streams, such as Lee creek, which has a gap in recorded occupation during this time (Mayo and Muto 1979).

Subsistence

A broad spectrum of plants and animals were utilized for food, with cultigens dominating the plant sector and deer, raccoon, turkey, and fish probably dominating the animal. The limited amount of systematically collected data available suggest an animal procurement pattern essentially the same as that documented by Smith (1975) in the Mississippian Lowlands. One potentially significant addition is bison hunting, but so few bones are found in Spiro phase sites that it is difficult to measure the importance of this hunting pattern. Bison appear to have had a nonsubsistence importance because its wool was utilized to fabricate the yarns of twillwork bags found at the Craig mound. As testimony to the interest in this animal are the depictions of bison in shell engraving of the Craig school (Phillips and Brown 1979:IV:176). The list of animals taken shows a strong preference for river bottom and upland forest-edge species. Fishing, musseling, and capturing migatory waterfowl were part of the subsistence practices of this period. Salt was available locally from springs on the Arkansas river.

A cultivated plant complex of corn and other domesticated plants, probably including squash, beans, sunflower, and gourd, testifies to a well-established agricultural system, although the relative importance of this sector of the economy is not known. Corn remains have been found in Spiro phase components at Norman (Wg 2), Horton (Sq 11), Bowman (Lf 66), and Jones (Lf 75). The presence of the other plants is based on the contemporary Ozark Bluff Shelter materials (Gilmore 1931). The deposits from which most of the perishables come dates to the Mississippian period according to radiocarbon dates and artifact associations (Brown n.d.b). Native plants were probably utilized intensely to judge from the Ozark shelter record (Yarnell 1981).

The available information on the distribution of sites indicates that settlement location was influenced strongly by the distribution of prime arable land. Land that is both productive and easily tilled with light hand-tools is not widely distributed in the Caddoan territory. These lands are concentrated in portions of the bottoms of the Arkansas valley and secondary streams. The upland soils south of the Ozark Uplift are inherently poor as agricultural soils because they are derived from sandstones and shales. The small size and scattered distribution of sites point to long fallow cultivation practices (slash-and-burn type), and ultimately to a large degree of local subsistence self-sufficiency.

Food Processing

Corn and nuts were presumably ground with milling stones. The pecked centers on the faces of manos were probably aids in breaking up hardened corn kernels. Further grinding was accomplished through rotary and back-and-forth grinding. Food storage was managed primarily in aboveground facilities because cache pits are rare (cf. Sheffield site, Prewitt and Wood 1969:8). Pits that do occur are probably hearths and food-processing pits (Wyckoff 1970c:22).

Resource Exploitation

The basic rocks and minerals utilized were drawn from local sources. They included sandstone, hematite, silicified ("Webbers Falls") siltstone, galena, clays, and red and yellow ochre. Chert sources were divided between Ozarkan and Ouachitan formations. Both outcrops of rocks and and gravel beds were exploited. Some of the identified sources of chipped-stone artifacts are Boone, Moorefield, Cotter, Peoria, Bolivar, Novaculite, Zipper cherts, and quartzites.

Other materials utilized were bone, antler, animal hair, bird feathers, wood, and grasses. Cane (*Arundinaria gigantea*) and cedar (*Juniperus virginiana*) wood and bark are commonly present at Spiro.

Industries

Chipped-stone working was diverse and refined. Materials ranged greatly in size and quality. A large number of uses were made of flake tools that were often taken from locally available sources, including river cobbles. The bipolar technique was commonly used for small nodules. Several different core types indicate a corresponding number of flaking techniques. Bifacially chipped tools were produced from better materials, although course-grained siltstones were regularly utilized to produce hoe blades (Figure 11.3i). Other tools include choppers, cobble cutting implements, bifacially chipped knives (ovate and beveled "Harahy" form), drills, end-scrapers, Gary knife points, triangular lance points, and arrowpoints in various styles (Figure 11.2d–j).

Ground-stone techniques for grinding and polishing stones were well developed. Quartz crystal artifacts were finished with a high polish. Ground-stone tools include manos, milling slabs, grinding basins, anvils, celts, adzes, polishing discs, sandstone hones, files, and abraders. More specialized artifacts include T-shaped pipes (Figure 11.3l) and ceremonial celts. Pipes of this type were crafted at Spiro where drilling waste is found.

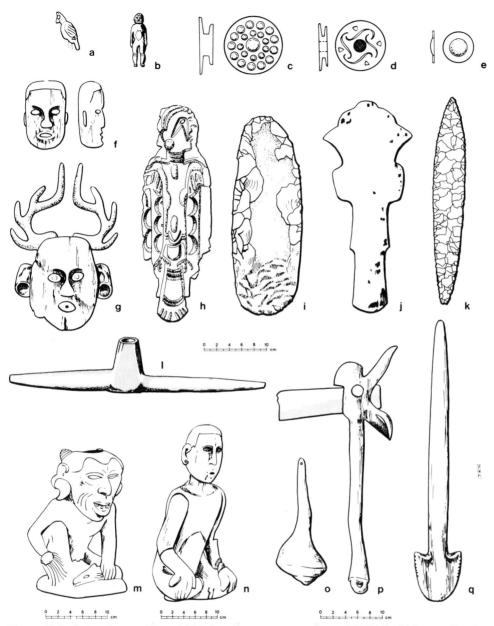

Figure 11.3 Spiro phase artifacts: (a) bird staff, copper-covered wood (BrB6-9); (b) human figurine pendant, shell (B36-2); (c) pulley-shaped earspool, unperforated, stone; (d) pulley-shaped earspool, perforated, copper-faced stone (B51-23); (e) composite ear-disc ornament, stone core, shell ring (B51-43); (f) human head rattle, copper-covered wood (B122-13a); (g) human face mask, copper-covered wood; (h) headdress plate, sheet copper (A6-7); (i) spade head, chipped stone; (j) mace-form club, chipped stone; (k) ceremonial biface, chipped stone (B39-7); (l) T-shaped pipe, stone (B99-6); (m) human effigy pipe, (B99-3); (n) mortuary figure, wood; (o) *Busycon* pendant, shell; (p) "woodpecker" axe, copper axe head, shell eye and wooden handle; (q) elongate axe head, stone (B8-2). All items from the Spiro site.

Bone and antler were used to make implements and components of headgear. Tools include a bison-bone digging tip, deer-jaw sickle, deer-ulna awl, deer-metacarpal awl, and split-bone awls. Specialized artifacts include pins, bird-bone beads, and polished headdress pieces.

Cedar wood was well preserved in the Craig mound mainly through the protection of copper sheathing. Wooden artifacts include carved bowls, mortuary figures, human maskettes, clubs, litters, headdress plaques, beads, earspools, ear ornaments, knives, antlers, hair buns, and hairpins (Figure 11.3a,g,n).

Locally available freshwater shell was utilized for hoes, scrapers, and sometimes disc beads. The large numbers of marine-shell objects such as most of the beads, cups, and other artifacts were imported in finished form. However, some cups were embellished locally with engraved drawings, and sometimes broken cups were fashioned into gorgets, beads, and other small objects (Figures 11.2q,r, and 11.3b).

Baskets were produced almost entirely from cane. A variety of techniques were employed. Large baskets were produced on coiled foundations, the impressions of which are sometimes found on the bases of pots. Plaited matting is common at Spiro, and a well-developed twillwork technology is evident. Both conoidal baskets and rectangular forms are known. Elaborate examples of the latter are the lidded chests that held the remains of elite burials in the Great Mortuary (Figure 11.2w). The tops of these baskets have float weave patterns decorated with blackened splints. The diversity of this technology can be inferred from the study of Scholtz (1975).

The diversity of textiles preserved from the Craig mound attests to a well-developed craft without the benefit of the true loom. Twined sacks and bags were made mainly of lagomorph (*Lepus* or *Sylvilagus* spp.) hair and mixtures of animal hair and vegetal fibers. Both very coarse textiles and fine cloth were made, including open-work designs produced by the bobbin lace technique. Kilts, fringed skirts, headbands, sashes, and three kinds of cloaks or mantles are preserved. The latter consist of feather–fur cloth in which tufts of these materials were tied to wefts, dye-resist decorated cloth, and a polychrome, twined tapestry textile in which a design is outlined by black yarn stitchwork. Feathers used were turkey and some goose down. Colors were produced by the use of madder dyes (red) and other materials.

A diverse ceramic technology was present, making use of both shell and grog tempers. Surfaces were sometimes specially treated by high burnishing and decorated by a red or black slip. Surface modeling, punctating, incising, and engraving were employed as decorative techniques, although decorated surfaces are not common. A diversity of vessel shapes are known, including jars, bottles, miniatures, hooded bottles, "seed jars," bowls, footed vessels, and beakers. Bowls are often carinated and sometimes possess broad strap handles that are otherwise found on a minority of jars. A distinctive feature of jar and bowl shapes is a flat disc base. The bases and lower bodies of these vessels appear to have been manufactured in coil-foundation baskets.

Dress and Ornament

Our knowledge of Spiro dress and ornament derives mainly from engraved-shell depictions and secondarily from grave goods in elite burials. Because the human subject-matter of this art pertains to male warriors, chiefs, and ritual functionaries, we know nothing about adult female and child dress. Burial associations in cemeteries are of little aid because few personal objects are present.

Basic clothing seems to have been quite simple, consisting of belted sash, a woven skirt, and moccasins or boots. A feather- or fur-tufted cape or cloth was also worn, presumably in cold weather, although some of the more elaborate capes seem to have been ceremonial costumery that were chiefly clothing. These capes were rectangular textiles thrown over the shoulders and were secured with ties at the upper corners. Many of these articles of clothing were woven textiles. The skirts are depicted as decorated with geometric designs (Figure 11.4a).

Upon this foundation male dress was further elaborated with ornaments on the head, hair, and body. The head was a prime spot for displaying identity and status through ornamentation. The large number of different combinations of ear, hair, headdress, and facial treatments present were presumably the means for representing identity. Except for the uniformity in which chiefly status was expressed, no two combinations were quite alike. Hair was dressed in roaches of different styles, in double buns on top and in back, and most commonly as a ponytail. In front, a lock of hair was invariably secured with one or more massive shell beads to drape in front of the face. This "beaded forelock" seems to be a mark of warrier status at Spiro and elsewhere in the Mississippian East. Feathers, sometimes pendant from flexible staffs, were secured in back, and raccoon pelts were tied into the hair. Earlobes held various styles of ear ornaments. Copper-faced earspools (both the pan-Mississippian perforated form and the distinctively Caddoan unperforated form) were most common, some of which were carved in elaborate designs (Figure 11.3c.d). Other forms include bossed ear discs and various spool and plug forms, most of which have eastern analogues (Figure 11.3e). Artwork shows beads and feathers pendant from these ear ornaments. Facial painting and tattooing perhaps completed Spiro headdressing. On the head were various bands, caps, and ornaments. A woven headband was perhaps the least symbolically specific. Headgear more specifically belonging to the elite consists of hairpins and caps to which antlers or frontally oriented plaques were attached. The pin ornaments consisted mainly of repoussé copper sheets in the form of falcons, bilobed arrows (in depictions only), and crescent or serpentine feathers (Figure 11.3h). The caps were more complex. White-tailed deer antlers of copper-sheathed wood were attachments. The plaques ranged in size from the large unsupported square or round copper plates to smaller copper-faced wooden plaques. On these plaques are designs in themes similar to the hair ornaments, including war and fertility symbols. The body was further

ornamented by beaded choker necklaces, wristlets and draped necklaces. Raccoon pelts were sometimes tied around the arms. A shell gorget was sometimes worn with the choker.

The symbolically most basic ornaments of the elite were the columella pendant on a draped shell bead necklace and the bellows-shaped apron (Figure 11.3o). These two items constituted essential elements of the chiefly uniform throughout the Mississippian region.

More specialized ceremonial dress complemented customary garb. A falcon costume consisted of a beaked mask and a cape, which probably carried wing feathers embroidered onto a polychrome textile. A snake costume also seems to have existed from artwork depicting long snakeskin marked robes. A basic supplement to these and other possible costumes are the rattles, of which the human and turtle effigies are outstanding. The head rattles, which appear to belong to the falcon costume, symbolize severed human heads—presumably taken in battle (Figure 11.3f).

Burial Practices

A diversity of burial practices are recorded that mirror the large number of statuses supported by the hierarchical social organization of the Spiro phase. Both inhumation and cremation were practiced, either as a final interment or as a temporary stage before selective exhumation of bones. Other practices are suggested by the partly disarticulated burials found in burial pits at the Craig and Brown mounds. Thus at least four distinct programs are present: (1) inhumation without exhumation; (2) storage or exhumation of a partly dismembered skeleton, leading to the preservation of skull, axial skeleton, and some of the limbs; (3) complete dismemberment, leading to the curation of skull elements only; and (4) cremation. From these programs a number of distinct burial types can be derived that signify different social statuses.

Undisturbed inhumations are found in cemeteries and local burial plots. Flexed, semiflexed, and extended positions occur (Figure 11.2v). Uniform orientation rules are absent. Both adults and children are found in cemeteries although the latter are greatly underrepresented. This is the only place that chil-

---

Figure 11.4 Spiro phase artifacts: (a) woven skirt, red with tan design, courtesy Smithsonian Institution, Specimen 423353, Negative 78-1771. Length approximately 1.07 m between ties; (b) Sanders Engraved bowl, 40-cm diameter, Specimen Lf-Cr-1, B. 36–39; (c) Poteau Plain bowl, 40-cm diameter, Specimen Lf-Cr-1, B. 90-5; (d) detail of pottery appliqué on Vessel h, longest strip is 7 cm long; (e) appliqué nodes on pottery, Specimen Lf-Cr-1, B. 120-5, largest node is 3.5 cm across; (f) Poteau Engraved sherd, Owl Cave, longest dimension is 12.3 cm; (g) pottery handle with appliqué node, Specimen Lf-Cr-1, D160, 4.6 cm high; (h) Woodward Appliqué vessel, 32.5-cm diameter at the rim, Specimen Lf-Cr-1, B. 56-2; (i) Woodward Appliqué tripod vessel, 16-cm diameter at the rim, Specimen Lf-Cr-1, B. 162-19; (j) Poteau Plain bottle, 25.2 cm maximum diameter, Specimen Lf-Cr-1, B. 182-25. (Photograph of ceramics by Jim Tribble.)

dren are found outside the elite graves. Most burial plots are small in keeping with the size of the resident population (e.g., Cat Smith). When present, grave goods consist of pottery vessels and utilitarian implements. Larger cemeteries are uncommon and are known mainly from the Horton site and sites in the Fort Coffee locality (Rohrbaugh 1982). A diversity of interment practices are recorded in this cemetery that signify social group affiliation.

Burials subjected to post mortem manipulation are found mainly in the civic–ceremonial centers where they are associated with mortuaries. Partial disarticulation is reserved for adults who evidently achieved high social standing in the community. The scanty evidence available, which does not indicate a bias toward either sex, suggests a broad basis for attaining rights to this burial treatment. These burial types predominate in the centers. More complete disarticuation and cremation were treatments reserved for the elite. Cremation, which is the more traditional of the two treatments, was supplanted at Spiro but retained at Norman. Large basins were constructed to process cremations. At the base of the Craig mound and adjacent to the Great Mortuary was a 4.9-m-diameter crematory basin with a vertical rim 49 cm high and a flight of stairs inside descending to the floor.

At Spiro a simple disarticulation process replaces cremation by Great Mortuary times. The disarticulated remains were placed in two different funerary facilities. The premier of the two was contained within a wooden-pole litter that was the expression of top office (Figure 11.2u). They ranged in enclosed area from .56 to 2.79 (or 3.90) m². On these funerary biers the condensed remains of the deceased were nestled among piles of sumptuary grave goods. The second form was burial with marine shell and copper grave goods in a twillwork basketry chest (Figure 11.2w). The chest burial was open to both adults and children, whereas the litter burial was restricted to adults (of which the only sexed individual was male). The only other high-status burial found in the Great Mortuary was a lavishly accompanied interment of the partly disarticulated form. All are adults, and one identifiable skeleton is female. All three are specialized burial treatments pertaining to the apical social group of the region, of which two are novel to the Great Mortuary. Of these, the one premier burial type is contained on an office-specific litter bier.

Trade

Patterns of both outside trade and exchange internal to the region can be distinguished in the patterning shown by the sources of artifacts found at Spiro and other sites. The internal exchange is presumably the result of trade between local communities, and in the case of Spiro it is manifest as a flow of gifts and offerings to the center. This internal exchange constitutes a fundamental means for regular provisioning at the local level, especially when food is in temporary short supply. Artifacts made from materials available within the Spiro phase area are very common in all sites. Some from highly localized sources within the area indicate considerable movement of goods within the area. The most conspicuous are the black silicified siltstone hoe blades at Spiro that are made of Wapanuka formation material (Figure 11.3i). Numerous chert artifacts made from Ouachita Uplift sources and Peoria chert, for example, are other traceable examples. The less-tangible exchange in foodstuffs, however, would logically constitute the fundamentally important commodity in this flow. Corn, squash, and beans would have been produced in every community, but a mechanism of exchange would have been essential to alleviate temporary local shortages of food in bad harvest years. However, some commodities such as bison meat and salt, which were more available in the west, would have been more evenly distributed through exchange.

The role of chiefs in the flow of goods and foodstuffs is disclosed by the appearance of locally produced goods in the Great Mortuary shrine, along with highly valued copper, marine shell, and other exotic objects. Among the textile garments were fur- and feather-cloth cloaks, examples of which are also found at the local level in burials in dry shelters of Oklahoma and Arkansas (e.g., Bollin Cave [3 NW-31], D. R. Dickson, personal communication, 1980; Harrington 1924, 1960). We can surmise that these robes found their way into the principle mortuary shrine through chiefly appropriation of valuable goods made from locally available materials in communities throughout the Spiro domain. Textiles of spun bison hair may be another example. Although these appropriated items are a manifestation of internal trade, their concentration may have been to facilitate external trade.

Distinct external trade patterns are disclosed by grave goods. In this the chiefs held a principal role that is well documented by the aggregation of exotic objects of all classes—both high-valued copper and low-valued utility pottery—in elite graves at Spiro and to a much lesser extent in those at Norman and Reed. The source of the greatest amount of goods are the phases in the Red River valley contemporary with Haley. The greatest portion of exotic materials (pottery, projectile points, and pigments) comes from this region.

Next in importance is the Memphis area of the Mississippi River valley (400 km east of Spiro). A large number of ceramic types can be traced to this area (e.g., Neeley's Ferry Plain, Bell Plain, effigy ware, Barton Incised, Parkin Incised, Old Town Red, Nashville Negative Painted, Walls Engraved, red-on-white, and polychrome pottery). The Dover chert bifaces from eastern Tennessee and the massive effigy pipes of east Arkansas bauxite may have been acquired through this area (Figure 11.3k,m). Other objects originated even farther away, whether they were acquired from those sources directly or through intermediaries. The maces of Illinois novaculite (Kaolin chert) come from Union County, Illinois (Figure 11.3j). Most galena comes from the Potosi district of eastern Missouri (Walthall 1981). Long distance transport from the southern

Appalachians is indicated by such items as Hiawasse Island Red-on-Buff pottery, "Mound C" style gorgets of the Dallas phase, Bennett style gorgets, mica, carved limestone bowls and ceremonial axe heads of marble and chlorite schist (Figure 11.3q). These objects are from an area dominated by Dallas phase culture, and by the centers of Moundville and Etowah (Figure 11.3p, q). Copper may have been acquired here too (Woolverton 1974). Marine shells, however, must have been taken from Gulf waters, most likely off the coast of Florida (Figure 11.2k). Specific links to Moundville and Etowah are implied by the stylistic cross-ties in artwork found at Spiro.

A small amount of material can be attributed to the West (e.g., Alibates flint), but there existed important long-range trade ties to the Southwest that must have been the source for the rare cotton cloth (King and Gardner 1981). This area also seems to have been an important beneficiary of Spiro trade because the marine molluscan shell beads and the Caddoan and Mississippian pottery occasionally found in Washita River and Antelope Creek sites probably came from the East (Bell 1973).

Society

Spiro phase society was basically organized into communities of residential groups. These groups occupied one or more houses and were probably composed of families related to each other through a core of women. The analysis of the Sheffield site argues in favor of a closer consanguineal relationship of adult women than men. The direction that this evidence points to conforms to the prevalent pattern kinship present in all historic Caddoan speaking groups.

Social Rank

Beyond the local community a strong hierarchy of individuals and families seems to obtain. This hierarchy is attested to by graded differences in size and wealth of civic–ceremonial centers and by distinctions in the treatment of the dead. Cooperative relations among leaders would have been cemented by alliances through gift-giving and intermarriage among high-status families. In the creation and maintenance of alliances the authority of the chiefs was confirmed through custom and ritual. The allegiance of the ordinary individual was assured through the distribution of food and other commodities and through the sharing of war booty.

Evidence for the economic activities of chiefs come to us principally through burial goods. The Great Mortuary, which was the mortuary–treasure house of the paramount lineage contained stockpiles of both locally produced artifacts and exotic items. Great stacks of wealth that were piled on and next to the three types of elite burials were formed of textile garments, marine-shell cups, various copper objects, and shell and pearl beads. This record of primitive wealth accumulation represents the apogee of social display in Spiro society. Mortuary shrines of lesser-ranking centers (e.g., Norman) disclose a much more limited inventory of grave goods. The relative poverty of the lesser centers accords well with their smaller size. Exotic items were probably sumptuary goods that were reserved for the elite and distributed as gifts by the Spiro paramount to subordinates living elsewhere. For instance, copper repoussé plates of the hawk cut-out design are found in number at Spiro but sparingly at lesser centers, for example an elite burial at Norman and what may have been one marked by a plate from Reed. A similar role was played by shell gorgets among lesser-ranking individuals meriting only cemetery burial (e.g., Morris). The thousands of pounds of shell beads of many different sizes and shapes quite possibly performed a similar role, except that the beads could have been more freely exchanged than the copper headdresses, which were important symbols of rank.

Warfare

Recent comparative studies have shown the functional utility of matrilineal organization in suppressing intergroup warfare within a polity. If such a kinship organization existed in the Spiro domain, it would help explain the total lack of archaeological evidence of intergroup warfare. There are no stockades around villages, and the civic–ceremonial centers lie in isolated locations unprotected by any visible physical barriers.

The suppression of internal conflict was counterbalanced by organized external warfare. War expeditions were an important feature of Spiro society. Military themes dominated Spiro iconography, and combat weapons constitute the source for status emblems in the form of axes, clubs, and bow and arrow elaborations. Trophy heads appear to have been collected and ritually displayed.

Smoking

Smoking was an important social activity for which a number of distinct pipe types were in service, perhaps for equally different social functions. Large stemmed pipes of the T-shaped form constituted a basic ritual type, for which there was a special ritual variant with two bowls and two stems (Figure 11.3l). This pipe type is a local development from the ancient stemmed pipe. Other important ceremonial pipes are the massive effigy pipes, in stone or pottery, and representing humans and various animals (e.g., puma, frog). These pipes were generally imported (Figure 11.3m). Pottery examples are local. Complementing these pipes are a number of elbow pipe forms, both with and without stems.

Religion

The popular religion was strongly imbued with beliefs in the power residing in animals, their representations, and in natural objects. Different expressions of animalistic belief are recorded in the numerous depictions of people and animals in Spiro art and in specific articles of dress and ritual. Procreative magic beliefs are implied by the depictions on shell of bison and fish pierced with arrows. The animalistic basis for leadership is conveyed in the deer-antler headdress worn by specific men and by the depiction of one among a group of animals (snakes, cats, etc.) with the same headgear. An antler headdress of copper-covered wood came from the Craig mound, and a well-known human mortuary mask features identical antlers (Figure 11.3g).

A different category of leadership is associated with the falcon or hawk cult. War prowess is communicated by the copper plate and engraved shell representation of warlike falcon impersonators brandishing a club in one hand and grasping a severed head in the other. Falcon depictions were used in a number of different representations in elite headgear, and the bird's-eye markings were carried over into the widely found facial marking known as the *forked* or *weeping eye* (Figure 11.3h). There is evidence that each animal species had specific powers. The falcon had a military one, and other animals (e.g., woodpecker, cat, rattlesnake) probably possessed powers similar to those of categories widely held among southeastern Indians (Hudson 1976). Among these were the messenger service of small birds used by shamans. Small birds mounted on staffs from the Craig and Brown mounds attest to use of a tool of sorcery widely employed in the historic southeast (Figure 11.3a). Other aspects of shamanism, which were likewise controlled by the elite, are attested to by the quartz crystals, fossils (including a mastodon molar), and oddly shaped rocks and deformed antlers found in the Great Mortuary and elsewhere.

Few of these beliefs crystalized into formal cults. None can be directly related to the ancestor cult that dominated Spiro social and religious life. The purpose of this cult was the propitiation of the ancestors of the leading lineages in each community. The mortuary or charnel house of each community functioned as the shrine. Each evidently held the remains of the high-status individuals of that community, together with important ritual objects, wealth, and various objects presented as gifts to the ancestors. These contents have to be largely inferred because our knowledge of Spiro phase shrine contents is restricted to the Great Mortuary deposit in the Craig mound. This deposit, although imperfectly known due to the destruction wreaked on it by the plundering of the so-called hollow chamber for relics, has disclosed a unique record of lavish mortuary behavior from the sections salvaged by professional archaeologists. This record is unique because it represents the buried contents of the dismantled mortuary. Numerous seated human statues in wood, which undoubtedly were ancestor figures, reveal the shrine nature of this deposit (Figure 11.3n). Other artifacts supporting this function are the wooden mortuary masks (Figure 11.3g) and the

30 or more miniature wooden mortuary masks found in a single basket. The other grave goods in the Great Mortuary attest to the storehousing of great wealth with the dead. Material representation of the ancestor cult is also contained in iconographic features such as face masks, skulls, and human long-bones.

The remains of the mortuary shrines are usually found beneath small mounds that were erected over the site of the dismantled structure. The floors of these structures are usually cleaned of any midden, unlike most habitation structures. The contents were probably placed in nearby burial mounds. These mounds contain layers of secondary human remains that testify to episodes of wholesale removal of skeletons and artifacts from a repository such as a mortuary.

The basic architecture of these structures is identical to ordinary habitations, but their specialized function is revealed by the doorways that are blocked by movable posts or clay platforms in the extended entryways (Figure 11.2s). Fireplaces are often absent as well. In short, these structures were carefully constructed at ground level, with the exception of the structures that appear to have been erected on top of the main cone of the Craig mound over the location of the Great Mortuary.

In the major civic–ceremonial centers, platform mounds were used in the performance of fire rites. At Norman and Skidgel the mount summits were given over to the building of fires rather than to supporting an enclosed structure. Massive ash beds are found there and few postholes. The sacred uses of fire appear to be very important and are represented in another guise by the crematory basins found near the mortuaries.

The Southern Cult

Spiro has earned a great reputation as one of the three major centers of the Southern Cult, the other two being Moundville and Etowah. Numerous objects, designs, and symbols are found in common among the three centers. Most of these objects at Spiro are trade goods from the East. This includes the engraved shell executed in the Braden style complex, most of the repoussé copper, and many ritual items such as ceremonial celts, bifaces, maces, monolithic axes, and human effigy pipes (Figure 11.3f,h,j,m,q). This exotic component to the ceremonial equipage and trappings of power does not diminish the fact that the essential emblems of power of the Southern Cult were well integrated into Spiro society, albeit at the apex only. Ceremonial objects included various club forms as status emblems and carved pipes as ritual objects (Figure 11.3m,p,q). A wide variety of ear and hair ornaments bear insignia whose form was inspired by the ceremonial objects and key animal symbolism. Specific items also constituted a uniform of the elite, consisting of a columella pendant and bellows-shaped apron (Figure 11.3o). One of the most important features of the Southern Cult was the widespread recognition of a falcon impersonation cult that emphasized the warlike qualities of this bird (Figure 11.3h). A specific costume went with this status, and a wide variety of motifs take their inspiration from this bird (e.g., the forked eye). The warlike character of the Southern Cult symbolism is manifest in the falcon cult and in the employment of arms of war and spinoff symbols as emblems of high status. A secondary category of symbolism is connected with the ancestor and mortuary cults. Others have more ambiguous meanings ("cross," "sun circle," "open eye," and "barred eye"). Not all ceremonial objects recognized in the East found acceptance in the Spiro Phase. A few examples of the discoidal occur as trade items without the least evidence that the game of chunky common in the East was adopted in the Caddoan area.

Art

Spiro has provided an extradinary record ot its artistic expression in the form of engraved shellwork and works in other media (pottery, wood, copper, and stone). Chance preservation of this shellwork in the Great Mortuary at Spiro has allowed us to know more about Spiro art than other Mississippian societies. A long-standing autochthonous tradition stands behind this artwork (Figure 11.2q,r). Only the latest phase of this tradition (Craig C) is definitely contemporary with the Spiro phase.

The Craig style is characterized by a strong prediliction to bilateral symmetry in the treatment of subjects on both shell gorgets and cups. In the latter, a sculptural effect is achieved through subordination of the design to the longitudinal and transverse axes. One of the specializations of this style is the incorporation of sculpted relief in engravings and the full face frontal representation of figures. A great diversity of themes are represented. Many are standard subjects in Mississippian art (e.g., warriers, death elements, weapons, human heads, falcons, rattlesnake, cat, raccoon, and other animals). Uncommon elsewhere are the genre subjects of this style (warriers in dugouts, human arrow sacrifice, etc.). An even more distinctive theme is the depiction of dancers in pairs that hold serpent staffs (Figure 11.2q). This subject is very common at Spiro and evidently holds great ritual meaning that is without parallel in the Braden style complex.

Human Population

Studies of the human skeletal material from various cemeteries of the Spiro phase (Horton, Morris, and Spiro) indicate a population that was genetically transitional between the peoples of the Great Plains and the Southeast. Stature is average with means of 168 cm for males and 155 cm for females. As befitting a population that was organized into social ranks, major differences in health and nutrition existed among this population. High tooth-wear and tooth-loss in the lower-ranked segments contrasts with the light wear and low tooth-loss among the Spiro elite. In addition, up to one-third of the adult skeletons from Horton and Morris exhibit periostitis that Brues (n.d.) believes is indicative of endemic syphilis or other treponema. The relative proportions of this condition are not available by social rank. Among the local populace the infectious disease load was higher than that in the skeletons from the Red River Caddoan (Mires 1982), but the quantity of corn in their diet was probably less, as indicated by the lower rates of dental caries and less evidence of dietary deficiencies. Uniting this population was the practice of cranial deformation among some of the adults (both male and female). This deformation is the circular type that produces marked flattening of the frontal profile.

Chronology

The Spiro phase represents a taxonomic refinement of the old Spiro focus of Orr (1946, 1952). The latter, which represented a developmental sequence of considerable duration, has been divided into culturally distinct units with temporal limits. The Spiro phase approximates the former Middle and Late Spiro (Orr 1946) or the Brown and Clayton components (Orr 1952). The type provenience at Spiro is the Great Mortuary, to which other grave lots in the Craig mound—both from layers overlying the Great Mortuary and those immediately beneath—have been added to form the Spiro phase component at Craig mound. Artifacts from this set of proveniences are distinct from those from the Harlan site that are dated significantly earlier by radiocarbon (Bell 1972). Although the Craig mound assemblage includes highly specialized ritual objects and exotic items rarely found outside the site, time-sensitive artifacts and craft attributes exist that provide reliable links to habitation and other civic–ceremonial sites that are dated mainly in the thirteenth to fifteenth centuries (Table 11.1). The mean ^{14}C age of the Great Mortuary has been calculated to be A.D. 1389 ± 39 by the averaging methods of Long and Rippeteau (1974). This date (corrected by the MASCA formula) can be regarded as the median age of the Spiro phase time span. Rohrbaugh (1982) has refined further the limits of this phase.

Diagnostic of this phase is a ceramic complex dominated by the Woodward ceramic series and a red- or black-slipped companion ware, Poteau Plain (Figure 11.4c,j). Williams Plain and LeFlore Plain are absent. Distinctive decorative treatments on the shell-tempered wares consist of Woodward Appliqué (Figure 11.4d,e,g,h), Braden Punctate, and Poteau Engraved (Figure 11.4f). Distinctive vessels forms include legged jars (Figure 11.4i), rim-effigy bowls, and wide-mouthed bottles. A general diversity of ceramic forms in all pastes distinguishes this phase from others of this tradition. There are other distinctive attributes of

Table 11.1

Radiocarbon Dates from Spiro Phase Proveniences

Laboratory number[a]	Site and provenience	Material tested[b]	Date before present (B.P.)	Date (A.D.) based on 5568 half-life	Date (A.D.) based on 5730 half-life	MASCA corrected 5730 date (A.D.)[c]	References
M-815	Spiro: Burial 62 (Great Mortuary)	s	580 ± 75	1379	1353	1353 (1260–1410)	Crane and Griffin 1963:238
M-1662	Spiro: Burial 62 (Great Mortuary)	s	550 ± 100	1400	1384	1380 (1294–1424)	Crane and Griffin 1968:87
M-1663	Spiro: Burial 62 (Great Mortuary)	w	680 ± 100	1270	1250	1260–1290 (1190–1360)	Crane and Griffin 1968:87
M-1664	Spiro: Burial 108 (Great Mortuary)	fw	400 ± 100	1550	1538	1440 (1398–1610)	Crane and Griffin 1968:87–88
M-1665	Spiro: Burial 155 (Great Mortuary)	s	490 ± 120	1460	1446	1410 (1326–1500)	Crane and Griffin 1968:88
SM-885[d]	Spiro: Burial 155 (Great Mortuary)	s	1558 ± 157	392	347	420 (290–554)	Brown 1967:79
M-54	Spiro: wood poles (Great Mortuary?)	w	640 ± 250	1310	1291	1310 (1071–1450)	Crane 1956:665
O-596	Spiro: wood poles (Great Mortuary?)	w	500 ± 100	1450	1409	1390 (1310–1430)	Bell 1961
M-309	Spiro: marine shell	s	480 ± 200	1470	1456	1410 (1260–1610)	Crane and Griffin 1959:180
TX-57	Spiro: wood poles (Great Mortuary?)	w	530 ± 105	1420	1405	1390 (1310–1430)	Tammers et al. 1964:155
WIS-135	Spiro: Burial 174	c	710 ± 70	1240	1219	1240 (1190–1310)	Bender et al. 1967:539
M-1661	Spiro: Burial 10	c	550 ± 100	1400	1384	1380 (1294–1424)	Crane and Griffin 1968:87

Lab no.	Provenience	Material	Age estimate	Date	Corrected date	MASCA date	Reference
M-1668	Spiro: Artifact 6	c	1250 ± 110	700	664	700–724 (614–850)	Crane and Griffin 1968:88
M-1671	Spiro: Burial 162	c	1225 ± 110	725	689	730–760 (620–880)	Crane and Griffin 1968:88
WIS-254	Cat Smith: House 1	c	560 ± 60	1390	1374	1374 (1314–1410)	Bender et al. 1968:474
TX-615	Cat Smith: House 1	c	650 ± 60	1300	1281	1301 (1240–1351)	Valastro and Davis 1970:261
TX-616	Cat Smith: House 1	c	630 ± 60	1320	1302	1312 (1252–1372)	Valastro and Davis 1970:261
TX-493	Cat Smith: House 2	c	770 ± 70	1180	1158	1200–1220 (1110–1258)	Valastro et al. 1968:391
TX-614	Cat Smith: House 2	c	800 ± 60	1150	1127	1187 (1097–1230)	Valastro and Davis 1970:261
TX-619	Sheffield: Feat. 2	c	440 ± 70	1510	1497	1429 (1390–1500)	Valastro and Davis 1970:259
TX-489	Sheffield: Feat. 4	c	790 ± 200	1160	1137	1190 (980–1350)	Valastro et al. 1968:391
WIS-256	Sheffield: Feat. 4D	c	500 ± 60	1450	1435	1405 (1365–1430)	Bender et al. 1968:474
TX-618	Horton: Feat. 1C	c	780 ± 70	1170	1147	1204 (1090–1247)	Valastro and Davis 1970:262
TX-627	Horton: Feat. 1C	c	440 ± 90	1510	1497	1427 (1387–1507)	Valastro and Davis 1970:262
TX-819	Horton: Feat. 4	c	1120 ± 100	830	798	860–880 (730–968)	Valastro et al. 1972:475

[a]This list excludes M-14 and TX-4 that are considered faulty age estimates by their respective laboratories (Deevey, Flint, and Rouse 1967).

[b]c: charcoal; f: fabric; s: marine shell; w: cedar wood.

[c]The column of MASCA dates includes the corrected average date (based on the 5730-year half-life) followed by the corrected age-range, calculated according to the instruction of Ralph, Michael, and Han (1973).

[d]Date SM-885 is absurdly old; other early dates (M-1668, M-1671, and TX-819) were probably run on old charcoal accidently included in Spiro phase features.

this phase. Jars lack the expanded or "stilt" form of the flat base that is common earlier, and all bottle types (including Spiro and Hickory Engraved) possess straight or nearly straight necks (Figure 11.2a). A distinctive pedestal bottle base (Figure 11.2b) and bottle neck "step" (Figure 11.2a) occur in this phase.

Projectile points are dominated by triangular outlines, and are modified by different base shapes and notch orientations to yield a number of distinct types (e.g., Fresno, Washita, Reed, Morris, Keota, Haskell) (Figure 11.2d–h).

Within the Spiro phase, trends can be detected that may eventually warrant subdivision of this phase. Up to the period of the Great Mortuary at Spiro, such types as Sanders Engraved (Figure 11.4b) and Paris Plain are found. Afterwards such types as Friendship Engraved, Nash Neck Banded, and a variety of Avery Engraved appear that presage more frequent presence in the later Fort Coffee phase. These changes accompany the initiation of a new constructional cycle at the Craig mound that resulted in the platform mound at the north end of this mound complex. This cycle probably reflected the reorganization of Spiro society into a more consolidated hierarchy.

Connections

Trade items provide clear indications of contemporaneity of the Spiro phase with the Sanders focus in the Southwest; the early McCurtain focus to the south; the Graves Chapel, Mineral Springs, and Haley phases to the southeast; and the Mid-Ouachita focus and Parkin phases to the east. The range of time delimited by these connections spans distinct periods, the earlier of which is represented by Sanders and the later by McCurtain. The Spiro phase falls between the well-known Alto and Belcher phases of the southern Caddo Area. Early artifact cross-ties are composed of Sanders Engraved, Maxey Noded Redware, and the Red River pipes of the Graves Chapel style. Late cross-ties include Friendship Engraved, Hodges Engraved, Glassell Engraved, Nash Neck Banded, Avery Engraved, and Howard points (Bohannon 1973). Other items less specific to time are Haley Engraved, Handy Engraved pottery, and Hayes, Toyah, Massard, Coryell, and Granberry parker points.

The Spiro phase does not seem to be confined to Oklahoma. A pattern of finds of diagnostic artifacts points to an extension of the phase into neighboring districts of the Arkansas and Missouri Ozarks and along the Arkansas River. The McClure complex, 48 km miles downstream from Spiro closely conforms to an assemblage of this phase (Hoffman 1977). In some of the Ozark Bluff shelters there are Spiro phase materials of Woodward Appliqué pottery (House 1978; Dellinger and Dickinson 1942) and distinctive basketry and fabrics (Scholtz 1975). Father north on the White River the Loftin site shows close affiliation (Chapman 1980). In the opposite direction, on the Red River, lie the Sanders and Nelson foci that constitute regional variants of the Spiro phase (Krieger 1946; Wyckoff 1970b).

Reference Note

The description of this phase rests basically on information from five sites: Spiro, Norman, Horton, Cat Smith and Sheffield. These sites have been isolated as representative of this phase by the chronological investigations of Brown 1980c, Bell 1972, Cartledge 1970, and Rohrbaugh 1982. Pertinent descriptions of the Spiro site are contained in Thoburn 1931; Brown 1966a, 1966b, 1971b, 1976b, n.d.a.; Burnett 1945; Clements 1945; Orr 1946, 1952; Hamilton 1952; J. D. Rogers 1980, 1982b; and Wyckoff 1968c. Special studies of various aspects of the site can be found in Brown 1967; Phillips and Brown 1975, 1979; Hamilton *et al*, 1974; Bell 1947b; Duffield 1964a; Watson 1950b; Baerreis 1957; Brown 1971a, 1975, 1976a, 1981a, 1981b, n.d.a; J. B. Griffin 1952a, 1961; King and Gardner 1981; Krieger 1945; J. H. Howard 1968; Waring and Holder 1945; Wyckoff 1970c; T. J. Prewitt 1974; Waring 1968. The most recent bibliography of Spiro is by Hofman (1977e). Descriptive studies of other sites are: Norman (Finklestein 1940), Horton (Shaeffer 1958a, Wyckoff 1970c), Reed (Purrington 1970), Sheffield (Prewitt and Wood 1969), Moore (Rohrbaugh 1982), Morris (Bell and Dale 1953), Cat Smith (Wyckoff and Barr 1967b), Choates (Orr 1946:248–249, Rohrbaugh 1982), Littlefield I (Orr 1946:242–243), Owl Cave (Lawton 1964), and Sol Thompson (Galm 1978a:222–227). Settlement pattern studies can be found in: Wyckoff (1970c); Brown, *et al*. (1978) and subsistence data are contained in Cutler and Blake (1973), Duffield (1969), Galm (1981), and Wyckoff (1970c). Structure plans are reported by Wallace (1962) and J. D. Rogers (1982b), lithic technology is commented on by Galm (1978a), and osteological observations have been made by Brues (1958, 1959, n.d.) and Miries (1982).

CHAPTER 12

Arkansas Valley Caddoan: Fort Coffee and Neosho Foci

Charles L. Rohrbaugh

Introduction

This chapter concerns one cultural–historical unit, the Fort Coffee focus, which, by the time this appears in print, will have been defined out of existence. The Neosho focus, however, should remain considered as a unit of the Midwestern Taxonomic System until such time as firm temporal and geographical control over the material can be established.

Bell and Baerreis (1951) based their definition of the Fort Coffee focus primarily on K. G. Orr's (1946) preliminary work on the Works Progress Administration (WPA) excavations near Spiro, Oklahoma. Orr's definition of the focus was based on material recovered from several sites. The type component, *Fort Coffee component*, was not defined at a single site, but rather by a group of sites—Gertrude Bowman, Granville Bowman I, and the Skidgel cemetery—in the vicinity of the historic military post. Fort Coffee was seen as the latest of a number of components that comprised the focus. The occupation at the Choates—Holt site was seen as the earliest of these. It was followed by components at the Littlefield site (Li-I) and at the Lymon Moore cemetery (Mo-I). Orr was uncertain about the relationship of material recovered from a cemetery near the Braden Schoolhouse.

Additional material recovered since 1951 has been attributed to the Fort Coffee focus (Figure 12.1). Defined as an independent Turkey Bluff focus (Lehmer 1952), material from the Cookson and Morris sites has been considered as a variant of the Fort Coffee focus by most researchers. Most of the additional material recovered since 1951 came from salvage excavations associated with the

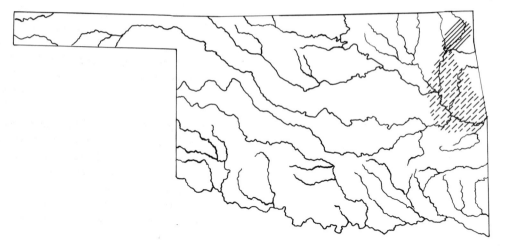

Figure 12.1 Fort Coffee (broken hatching) and Neosho (solid hatching) foci in eastern Oklahoma.

construction of the Arkansas River Navigation System by the United States Army Corps of Engineers. The following list includes all reported sites with recognized Fort Coffee focus components:

WPA sites
    Littlefield I (Orr 1946)
    Choates–Holt (Orr 1946)
    Moore (Orr 1946, Keith 1973)
    Gertrude Bowman I and Granville Bowman (Orr 1946)
    Skidgel Cemetery (Orr 1946)
    Braden Schoolhouse Cemetery (Orr 1946)

Early salvage work
    Morris (Bell and Dale 1953, Brues 1959)
    Cookson (Lehmer 1952, Israel 1979)
    Horton (Shaeffer 1958a, Brues 1958, Wyckoff 1970c)

Late salvage work
    Cat Smith (Wyckoff and Barr 1967b)
    Sheffield (Prewitt and Wood 1969)
    Tyler (Burton, *et al.* 1969)
    Robinson–Solesbee (Bell *et al.* 1969)
    Fine (Eighmy 1969)
    Tyler–Rose (Cartledge 1970)
    Harvey (Burton 1971)
    Wybark (Lopez 1973)

A number of these reports have attempted to summarize the Fort Coffee focus (Wyckoff 1970c; Cartledge 1970; R. J. Burton 1971), but the WPA excavations have only recently been reported in detail (Rohrbaugh 1982).

In speaking of the *Fort Coffee focus* I am considering the material as a focus of the Fulton aspect (Midwestern Taxonomic System) and not the phase called *Fort Coffee* in the system used by Brown (1966a, 1966b, 1967, 1971a, 1971b, 1976b) in his monumental work on the Spiro site. Brown recognizes four phases of Caddoan development in the Arkansas Valley: Evans, Harlan, Spiro, and Fort Coffee. The Harlan phase is present at Spiro but is best known from the type site in Cherokee County, Oklahoma (Bell 1972). This phase is securely dated at the Harlan site and ended an early period of Caddoan development around A.D. 1250. The Spiro phase is seen as lasting from around this time to about A.D. 1450. The following Fort Coffee phase lasts from A.D. 1450 to no later than about A.D. 1600.

Rohrbaugh (1982) has demonstrated that the material assigned to the Fort Coffee focus represents a period of cultural development in the Arkansas Valley that is primarily contemporary with the Spiro phase at the Spiro site. The relationships are complex between the units of the Midwestern Taxonomic System and the units of the newer system developed by Brown from that suggested by Willey and Phillips (1958). The older system has all but passed out of useage and I discuss the Fort Coffee focus here as a backdrop to introduce more current ideas on the culture history of the region. The following table attempts to clarify the relationships between the units of the two systems.

Foci	Absolute dates (A.D.)	Phases
Contact period	ca. 1600	Contact period
		Fort Coffee
	1450--	
Fort Coffee		Spiro
	1200--	
		Harlan
Spiro		Evans
	800	

Dating of the material that has been assigned to the Fort Coffee focus is based on a large series of radiocarbon dates from a great number of sites. Table 12.1 lists these dates with their respective proveniences.

Most of the material that Orr considered as representative of the Fort Coffee

Table 12.1

Radiocarbon Dates: Spiro and Fort Coffee Phases

Laboratory number	Site and provenience	Date before present (B.P.)	Date (A.D.) based on 5568 half-life	Date (A.D.) based on 5730 half-life	Tree-ring corrected date (A.D.)	Reference
Tx-519	Fine (SQ18); charred post, H.1	500 ± 70	1450	1435	1395 ± 35	Valastro et al. 1968:390
Tx-485	Fine; charred posts, Trench C	840 ± 60	1110	1085	1140 ± 80	Valastro 1968:390
Tx-617	Fine; charred post, Trench C	920 ± 60	1030	1002	1050 ± 70	Valastro and Davis 1970:261
Tx-623	Fine; charred log, H. 1	620 ± 80	1330	1311	1315 ± 75	Valastro and Davis 1970:261
Tx-621	Fine; charred log, H. 1	780 ± 60	1170	1147	1175 ± 65	Valastro and Davis 1970:261
WIS-254	Cat Smith (MS52); charred post, H. 1	560 ± 60	1390	1373	1360 ± 50	Bender et al. 1968:474
Tx-616	Cat Smith; charred log, H. 1	630 ± 60	1320	1301	1310 ± 60	Valastro and Davis 1970:261
Tx-615	Cat Smith; charred log, H. 1	650 ± 60	1300	1280	1295 ± 55	Valastro and Davis 1970:261
Tx-493	Cat Smith; charred post, H. 2	770 ± 70	1180	1157	1185 ± 75	Valastro et al. 1968:391
Tx-614	Cat Smith; charred post, H. 2	800 ± 60	1150	1126	1165 ± 65	Valastro and Davis 1970:261
Tx-619	Sheffield (SQ22); charcoal, F. 4D, trash pit	440 ± 70	1510	1497	1445 ± 55	Valastro and Davis 1970:259–260
WIS-256	Sheffield; charcoal, F. 4D, trash pit	500 ± 60	1450	1435	1400 ± 30	Bender et al. 1968:474
Tx-489	Sheffield; charcoal, F.4, circular floor (?) area	790 ± 200	1160	1136	1165 ± 185	Valastro et al. 1968:391
Tx-486	Harvey (SQ11); charcoal, F. 5, bell-shaped pit	390 ± 60	1560	1549	1470 ± 50	Valastro et al. 1968:391
Tx-611	Harvey; charcoal, F. 5	550 ± 60	1400	1383	1365 ± 45	Valastro and Davis 1970:259
Tx-627	Horton (SQ11); charcoal and flotation charcoal, F. 1 trash pit	440 ± 90	1510	1497	1450 ± 60	Valastro and Davis 1970:262
Tx-618	Horton; charcoal and hickory nutshell, F. 2 trash pit	780 ± 70	1170	1147	1170 ± 80	Valastro and Davis 1970:262

Lab number	Sample description				Reference
Tx-819	Horton; charcoal, F. 4 trash pit	1120 ± 100	830	796	850 ± 120	Valastro et al. 1972:475
Tx-625	Tyler (HS11); flotation charcoal, F. 2 trash pit	420 ± 70	1530	1517	1460 ± 50	Valastro and Davis 1970:262
Tx-624	Tyler; flotation charcoal, F. 5 trash pit	450 ± 110	1500	1486	1445 ± 75	Valastro and Davis 1970:262
WIS-43	Bowman III (LF66); charcoal center post, H. 1	560 ± 80	1390	1373	1355 ± 55	Bender et al. 1965:403
WIS-1111	Moore (LF31); charcoal center post, House 3	575 ± 70	1375	1358	1355 ± 55	Bender 1979[a]
WIS-1112	Moore; charcoal center post, H. 3	560 ± 60	1390	1373	1375 ± 35	Bender 1979
WIS-1113	Moore; wood and nut charcoal, F. 8, trash pit	370 ± 65	1580	1569	1515 ± 95	Bender 1979
WIS-1109	Jones (LF69); charcoal center post, H. 4	400 ± 65	1550	1538	1465 ± 55	Bender 1979
WIS-1116	Jones; charcoal center post, H. 1	630 ± 70	1320	1301	1310 ± 70	Bender 1979
Tx-3793	Same as WIS-1116	680 ± 50	1270	1250	1275 ± 45	Rohrbaugh 1982:138
WIS-1114	Littlefield IV (LF82); charcoal center post, H. 1	565 ± 65	1385	1368	1360 ± 50	Bender 1979[a]
Tx-3796	Same as WIS-1114	620 ± 60	1330	1311	1320 ± 60	Rohrbaugh 1982:138
WIS-1118	Littlefield I (LF60); charcoal center post, H. 1	490 ± 70	1460	1445	1405 ± 35	Bender 1979
Tx-3794	Same as WIS-1118	490 ± 70	1460	1445	1405 ± 35	Rohrbaugh 1982:138
WIS-1117	Ainsworth (LF80); charcoal center post, H. 1	485 ± 65	1465	1450	1400 ± 30	Bender 1979[a]
Tx-3791	Same as WIS-1117	450 ± 50	1500	1487	1425 ± 25	Rohrbaugh 1982:138
WIS-1132	Humic acids from WIS-1117 dated to check reliability of date	480 ± 90	1470	1456	1405 ± 45	Bender et al. 1981:148
WIS-1115	Ainsworth; charcoal center post, H. 2	470 ± 55	1480	1466	1415 ± 25	Bender 1979
Tx-3792	Same as WIS-1115	450 ± 70	1500	1487	1420 ± 30	Rohrbaugh 1982:138

(continued)

Table 12.1 (Continued)

Laboratory number	Site and provenience	Date before present (B.P.)	Date (A.D.) based on 5568 half-life	Date (A.D.) based on 5730 half-life	MASCA corrected date (A.D.)	Reference
WIS-1119	Littlefield III; charcoal center post, H. 2	650 ± 70	1300	1281	1295 ± 65	Bender 1979
Tx-3795	Same as WIS-1119	680 ± 50	1270	1250	1275 ± 45	Rohrbaugh 1982:138
Tx-3916	Edgar Moore B1	540 ± 160	1410	1396	1345 ± 105	Rohrbaugh 1982:139
Tx-3917	Edgar Moore B17	440 ± 190	1510	1497	1470 ± 160	Rohrbaugh 1982:139
Tx-3918	Edgar Moore B44	510 ± 160	1440	1425	1385 ± 125	Rohrbaugh 1982:139
Tx-3919	Edgar Moore B52	490 ± 170	1460	1445	1425 ± 165	Rohrbaugh 1982:139
Tx-3920	Edgar Moore B62	470 ± 170	1480	1466	1460 ± 150	Rohrbaugh 1982:139
Tx-3921	Edgar Moore B65	470 ± 150	1480	1466	1455 ± 135	Rohrbaugh 1982:139
Tx-3922	Edgar Moore B67	500 ± 160	1450	1435	1390 ± 130	Rohrbaugh 1982:139
Tx-3923	Edgar Moore B69	450 ± 190	1500	1487	1470 ± 160	Rohrbaugh 1982:139
Tx-3924	Edgar Moore B82	480 ± 180	1470	1456	1435 ± 175	Rohrbaugh 1982:139
Tx-3925	Lymon Moore B1	330 ± 120	1620	1610	1525 ± 115	Rohrbaugh 1982:140
Tx-326	Lymon Moore B3	500 ± 200	1450	1435	1430 ± 180	Rohrbaugh 1982:140
Tx-3927	Lymon Moore B11	300 ± 130	1650	1641	1595 ± 165	Rohrbaugh 1982:140
Tx-3929	Lymon Moore B23	430 ± 80	1520	1507	1450 ± 60	Rohrbaugh 1982:140
Tx-3930	Lymon Moore B27	290 ± 160	1660	1651	1610 ± 190	Rohrbaugh 1982:140
Tx-3931	Lymon Moore B35	560 ± 200	1390	1373	1350 ± 150	Rohrbaugh 1982:140
Tx-3915	Lymon Moore B46	410 ± 160	1540	1528	1495 ± 135	Rohrbaugh 1982:140
Tx-3913	Moore, 1969 excavations B1	460 ± 90	1490	1476	1440 ± 60	Rohrbaugh 1982:140
Tx-3914	Moore, 1969 excavations B3	450 ± 190	1500	1487	1470 ± 160	Rohrbaugh 1982:140
Tx-3915	Moore, 1969 excavations B4	320 ± 110	1620	1620	1540 ± 110	Rohrbaugh 1982:140
Neosho Focus Dates						
O-2126.	Jug Hill (MY18); charred post, rectangular house	325 ± 100	1625	1615	1535 ± 110	Wyckoff 1964b:5
O-2162	Jug Hill; charcoal, F. 6,	550 ± 100	1400	1383	1340 ± 80	Wyckoff 1964b:5

[a] These dates are shown as they were reported by Bender (1979) to the author. They were rounded to the closest decade when reported by Bender, Baerreis, Bryson, and Steventon (1981:147–148): WIS-1111 (580 ± 70), WIS-1114 (570 ± 70), WIS-1117 (480 ± 70).

focus in the Spiro locality represents occupation of the area during the Spiro phase. Fifteen sites were located in this area of about 95 km² in the northern bend of the Arkansas River just upstream of the confluence of the Poteau River. These 15 sites are:

Site	Name	WPA designation
34LF31	Moore	LfMoI, Lymon Moore LfMrIII, Edgar Moore 1969 excavations
34LF60	Spencer Littlefield I	LfLiI
34LF63	Spencer Littlefield II	LfLiII
34LF64	Spencer Littlefield III	LfLiIII
34LF82	Spencer Littlefield IV	LfLiIV
34LF62	Choates–Holt	LfCtII/HoI
34LF42	Gertrude Bowman I	LfBoI
34LF65	Gertrude Bowman II	LfBoII
34LF66	Gertrude Bowman III	LfBoIII
34LF67	Granville Bowman	LfBmI
34LF68	Squire Hall	LfHaI
34LF78	Hamilton	LfHnI
34LF75	Louis Jones	LfJoI
34LF69	Skidgel I	LfSkI
34LF80	Garrett Ainsworth	LfAhI

There are only two sites in this list that are dominated by material representing occupations during the Fort Coffee phase. All the others are Spiro phase components, contemporary with the Spiro phase at the Spiro ceremonial center and representing hamlets where the people responsible for the construction of the ceremonial center lived.

The two Fort Coffee phase sites are the Lymon Moore cemetery at the Moore site and the Skidgel cemetery. There is a single house at the Jones site with a radiocarbon date indicating its construction during this phase. There is a Fort Coffee phase component at the Choates–Holt site, but the major occupation of this site is during the Spiro phase. Absent from the list is the component at the Geren site (LfGeI) located just south of the Skidgel cemetery. The presence of circular house patterns there suggests it may have been a Fort Coffee phase component. Orr believed these houses an early form but, although there is no evidence firmly establishing their temporal provenience, most researchers feel they represent a very late form. Additional examples of the circular house occur at the Choates–Holt site.

Conspicuously absent from the list is the Skidgel Mound (LfSkII, 34LF70). It is omitted only because there is virtually nothing from it to describe. The mound was a low, two-stage pyramidal structure with two associated houses, built on a high point to the south of the Skidgel cemetery and the Jones houses. The two houses were located to the northeast of the mound and the mound overlaps one of them. This situation indicates that the houses were public structures associated one with each of the mound construction stages. Both houses are two-center-post, rectangular structures with extended trench entranceways. Both are oriented away from the cardinal directions, characteristic of late houses. It is suspected that the Skidgel Mound was built during the Spiro phase. The only indications of a pre-Spiro phase occupation in the area of historic Fort Coffee are two four-center-post square houses at the Gertrude Bowman I site (34LF42, LfBoI).

It is my feeling that the concept of a *Spiro phase* should be limited to the components of the Spiro locality. Control of time at other sites in the Arkansas River region is not nearly so refined and there is considerable change in material culture as one moves to the west along the river and up its tributaries. The use of the concept to denote an area-wide complex also prejudices thought toward the idea that there was political unity over a wide area during this period, with the social group at Spiro in control of the entire area. This may or may not be the case, but prejudicing thought along these lines will not lead to a critical evaluation of the complex relationships between such centers as Norman on Grand River, Brackett on the Illinois River, and Eufaula on the Canadian River, all of which show evidence of occupation during the period.

Control of material culture through time and space during the period of the Spiro phase has become sophisticated to the extent that it is perhaps now better to think of the period as characterized by a Spiroan *culture,* as that term is used by Willey and Phillips (1958). The use of the concept of Spiroan culture allows us to establish phase sequences outside the Spiro locality. The establishment of a Norman phase of Spiroan culture, or a Eufaula phase, forces us to consider developments in these remote areas and to compare these developments with those of the Spiro locality.

Material culture complexes during the period of the Fort Coffee phase are considerably less diverse than those during the period of the Spiro phase. This is in part due to the greater complexity of the Spiro phase social system: less variation in the structure of the system responsible for the Fort Coffee phase led to less variation in the material culture through which it is recognized. Changing social organization from the Spiro to the Fort Coffee phase, seen in changing complexity of cemetery organization in the area, indicates that the late system was more egalitarian and, likely, composed of fewer and more mobile people. It is reasonable to think of the entire Arkansas River region as participating in a single Fort Coffee phase social system, albeit a much simpler one than that of the preceding phase.

The Spiro Phase Village

The WPA sponsored crews of the late 1930s and early 1940s uncovered more than 50 two-center-post rectangular houses in the Spiro locality (Figure 12.2). There are indications that this was a relatively small portion of the entire sample,

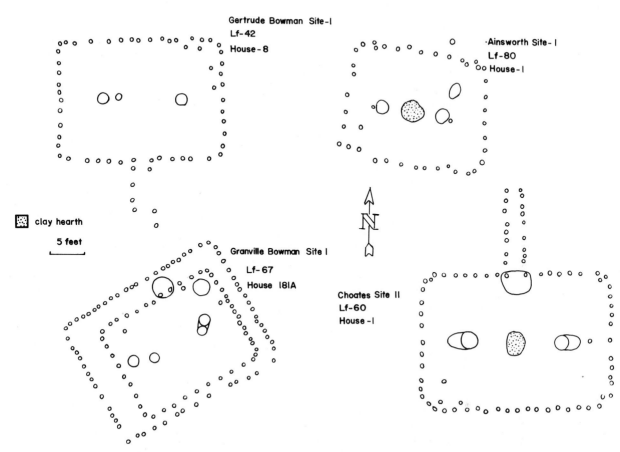

Figure 12.2 Examples of Fort Coffee and Neosho focus house patterns.

however. This house form apparently remained in use into the Fort Coffee phase, but by far the majority represent occupation during the Spiro phase.

There are radiocarbon dates from the center posts of 9 of these houses in the locality (see Table 12.1). These dates indicate that 8 of the houses were constructed during the Spiro phase. Six were apparently constructed during the last century of the phase, however. These figures tempt me to speculate that there were perhaps 50 of 60 houses standing on the uplands overlooking the Arkansas River bottoms, and in the bottoms themselves, during the last century of the phase. It is reasonable to visualize this community as a single village. The leaders of this village undoubtedly controlled events at the Spiro Mound ceremonial center.

The presence of a number of Spiro phase cemeteries suggests this picture may be somewhat simplistic. The Edgar Moore cemetery, with more than 80 individuals, is organized in such a way as to suggest that it may be a village cemetery. The very similar Gertrude Bowman I and Granville Bowman site cemeteries contain an array of artifacts that probably represents the interment of a group of people that is of roughly the same size as in the Edgar Moore cemetery. It is tempting to infer that these, and perhaps as yet undiscovered cemeteries, represent the cemeteries of a number of distinct villages in the locality during late Spiro phase.

It is clear that there were social distinctions between the people buried in the Edgar Moore cemetery. There are several paired burials in this field that are accompanied by greater quantities of artifacts and seemingly by artifacts of greater quality than is usual among burials that are not paired. These paired burials indicate that there were individuals among those who were buried in flat cemeteries who were afforded greater attention at burial than was the case with the majority of the population. Of course, it is presumed that there were a number of classes in the population the members of which were buried in Craig Mound at Spiro and not in these cemeteries at all (see Brown 1971a).

The Bowman site cemeteries are in the vicinity of historic Fort Coffee. It appears there was a distinct community in this area during the Spiro phase, composed of a number of houses, the local cemeteries, and a ceremonial center with public houses at the Skidgel Mound. There were apparently other houses at the Louis Jones site as well. This situation is not duplicated at the Moore site; the Spiro phase occupation there is limited to the Edgar Moore cemetery and to a few houses uncovered during the 1969 excavations. WPA records indicate a few houses at the site were left unexcavated and some of these were probably Spiro phase structures. There is no evidence there was ever any public facility in the area, however.

The nature of storage facilities during Spiro phase is poorly understood. Many of the sites attributed to the later Fort Coffee phase have been excavated at least in part by stripping off topsoil with heavy machinery. This has led to the identification of many refuse-filled pits scattered between houses. Few Spiro phase sites have been excavated in this manner and there are few areas at Spiro phase sites that have had large areas exposed in conventional excavation techniques. The Choates–Holt site is an exception. There, in the process of exposing two large circular structures, a two-center-post rectangular house and a number of refuse-filled pits were uncovered. These pits can be viewed as interior features of the circular structures, but their contents indicate that they are Spiro phase pits. One contained a piece of a copper-covered earspool such as those recovered from burials at Spiro. Without its artifacts, the Spiro phase community may not differ radically from the later Fort Coffee phase community.

The house type of the Spiro phase does change through time, but the changes are subtle and ill-suited for relative dating purposes. Spiro phase houses are two-center-post rectangular structures usually containing a central hearth. They are usually 6–8 m long and 4.5–6 m wide. The length-to-width ratio is generally about 1.33/1.0. There is a decrease in size from early to late in the phase. Houses shrink by about half from about 54 to about 27 m² from the thirteenth and fourteenth centuries to the early fifteenth century A.D.

There is a change in orientation of the houses also. Those that have their center posts aligned from east to west, or very close to it, produce an earlier assemblage of artifacts than those oriented considerably away from the cardinal directions. It is probable that houses oriented directly north to south are generally early also. Not all cardinally oriented houses are early and not all noncardinally oriented houses are late, however. Rather, there appear to have been more cardinally oriented houses early in Spiro phase than there were later in the period.

These houses often have prepared baked clay floors and occasionally have extended entranceways with posts set into excavated trenches. Considerable amounts of wattle and daub are usually recovered with them, indicating the closely spaced wall-supports were plastered. Similar structures are shown in a photograph presented by Swanton (1942:Plate 15) with pitched thatched roofs. Evidence of interior partitions and baked clay features occurs. Where building material has been identified it has generally been identified as cedar.

The material attributed to house mixtures of the WPA-sponsored excavations represents both a great deal of sheet trash that has accumulated over and around the houses as well as material from the houses themselves. Further, there are few data from temporally secure contexts such as refuse-filled pits. No distinctive Spiro phase midden contexts have been excavated in the Spiro locality. Middens from other areas show mixtures of material from before and after the Spiro phase. Thus, our knowledge of the material culture of this phase is not only limited to burial contexts at the Spiro site itself, but is limited to material from similar contexts in the Spiro locality: flat cemeteries. This material is considerably different from that recovered from Craig Mound, however, and clearly represents material culture on a more mundane level than does that impressive collection.

Spiro phase burials at the Edgar Moore cemetery are usually semiflexed, supine, primary, single interments. Fully flexed individuals occur but appear to be restricted to youths and females. Burial on the side is frequent, but prone burials are not common. Extended burials are quite rare, if they are properly considered part of the burial program at all. There is one burial that may be a secondary interment, but it may also have been disturbed by vandals. There is one Spiro phase burial in the Lymon Moore field that rests on a burned surface, but evidence of the use of fire in this burial program is otherwise absent. There is ample evidence that some individuals were buried either in pairs in the same grave, or were buried with precise knowledge of the position of other burials in the field. These pairs of individuals, usually oriented in opposite directions, sometimes appear to have satellite burials associated with them. They are additionally distinguished by the presence of greater numbers of artifacts and the presence of distinctive types of artifacts, such as bottles, large chipped-stone bifaces, elbow pipes, and so forth.

There are few absolutely diagnostic items associated with Spiro phase cemeteries. One of these is the complicated engraved bottle, and other bottles with

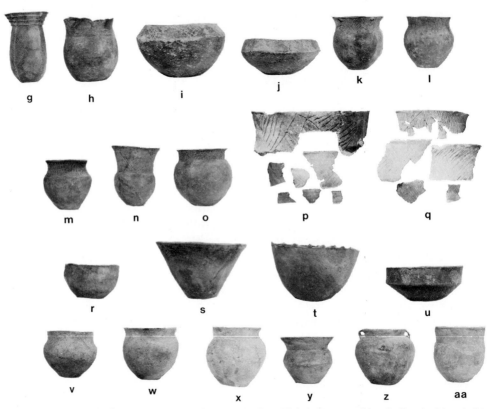

Figure 12.3 Fort Coffee ceramics: (a) Edgar Moore Site, Blakely Engraved bottle (height 20 cm); (b) Lymon Moore Site, Hudson Engraved bottle (height 24 cm); (c) Edgar Moore Site, Complicated Engraved bottle (height 20 cm); (d) Edgar Moore Site, Complicated Engraved bottle (height 21 cm); (e) Edgar Moore Site, Complicated Engraved bottle (height 20 cm); (f) Edgar Moore Site, Complicated Engraved bottle (height 23 cm); (g) Lymon Moore Site, Emory Punctate Unique form jar (height 19 cm); (h) Lymon Moore Site, Emory Punctate C3 form jar (height 18 cm); (i) Lymon Moore Site, Womack Engraved C form bowl (maximum diameter 23 cm); (j) Lymon Moore Site, Womack Engraved C form bowl (maximum diameter 21 cm); (k) Lymon Moore Site, Braden Incised C1 jar (height 15 cm); (l) Lymon Moore Site, Woodward Appliqué C1 jar (height 14 cm); (m) Lymon Moore Site, Braden Punctate C1 jar (height 14 cm); (n) Edgar Moore Site, Braden Punctate A form jar (height 16 cm); (o) Lymon Moore Site, Braden Punctate C3 jar (height 16 cm); (p) Braden Incised variations (scale ca. 1:6); (q) Braden Incised variations (scale ca. 1:4.25); (r) Edgar Moore Site, Poteau Plain A

similar forms (Figure 12.3). This group includes specimens that compare to such named types of bottles as Avery Engraved, Ripley Engraved, Spiro Engraved, Hatchell Engraved, Blakely Engraved, and plain bottles. These forms are not found in later Fort Coffee phase cemeteries although pieces of them occur in Fort Coffee phase trash contexts.

Another diagnostic of the Spiro phase cemetery is the Woodward Appliqué jar. These jars, otherwise indistinguishable from Woodward Plain jars, are decorated with appliques strips, nodes, lugs, and strap handles. Sometimes these are additionally embellished by fingernail punctations. The decoration of the bodies of such forms distinguishes another type characteristic, but not diagnostic, of Spiro phase: Braden Punctate. Braden Punctate and Braden Incised jars occur in Fort Coffee phase cemetery contexts, but the punctated variant is characteristic only of the Spiro phase (Figure 12.3).

Poteau Plain, predominantly a bowl type, is extremely characteristic of Spiro phase cemetery contexts, but is not diagnostic. The type occurs in Fort Coffee phase cemeteries and is a persistent, if relatively minor, part of the assemblage found in Fort Coffee phase trash contexts. The shape of these bowls is distinctive in Spiro phase cemeteries. Their sides are usually quite straight. The same bowls in Fort Coffee phase cemeteries more commonly have slightly rounded sides. However, Poteau Plain bowl sherds recovered from Fort Coffee phase trash contexts usually have severely straight sides. It appears that during the Spiro phase there was a selection for severe bowl profiles as grave furniture. In the later Fort Coffee phase this shape is apparently not so closely related to cemetery contexts, but is the general shape of most Poteau Plain bowls (Figure 12.3).

One series of vessels apparently disappears from material assemblages at the end of the Spiro phase. These are the vessels that came from, or were influenced by ideas from, the Mississippi Valley to the east. Such types as Mounds Place Incised and Bell Plain occur in Spiro phase contexts but not in later Fort Coffee phase. Similarly, there are a few unique items, such as a rattle bowl and a simple unrestricted bowl with opposite bird-head effigies from the Gertrude Bowman I site. Artifacts indicating interaction with peoples of the Ouachita River region of southwestern Arkansas and with the Red River region of southeastern Oklahoma occur in both Spiro and Fort Coffee phases, but artifacts indicating interaction with the Mississippi Valley are characteristic only of the Spiro phase.

---

form bowl with two tabs (maximum diameter 15 cm); (s) Edgar Moore Site, Poteau Plain B1 bowl (maximum diameter 28 cm); (t) Edgar Moore Site, Poteau Plain B2 bowl with scalloped rim (maximum diameter 24 cm); (u) Edgar Moore Site, Poteau Plain C form bowl (maximum diameter 22 cm); (v) Edgar Moore Site, Woodward Plain A form jar (maximum diameter 15 cm); (x) Edgar Moore Site, Woodward Plain B form jar (maximum diameter 15 cm); (y) Edgar Moore Site, Woodward Plain C1 jar (maximum diameter 15 cm); (z) Edgar Moore Site, Woodward Plain Compound jar (maximum diameter 13 cm); (z) Edgar Moore Site, Woodward Appliqué C2 jar with lug handles (maximum diameter 16 cm); (aa) Edgar Moore Site, Woodward Plain C3 jar (maximum diameter 15 cm). (All measurements approximate.)

Spiro Phase Subsistence

There is no doubt that the production of a crop of corn was one of the more important annual events in the round of Spiro phase subsistence activities. Remains of corn have been recovered from a number of Spiro phase contexts in the Spiro locality. However, this is the extent of our knowledge of Spiro phase agriculture. No other cultigens have been identified. Our knowledge of plants these people collected is little better.

It is reasonable to assume from what is known about the subsistence of peoples of eastern North America that Spiro phase agriculture depended on a variety of crops, principal among which were corn, beans, and squash. It is reasonable to infer that these people were slash-and-burn agriculturists, using the sandy soils of the Arkansas River bottom and its natural levees as farm plots. The only agricultural implements found in this assemblage in the Spiro locality are a few perforated mussel shells, presumably hafted for use as hoes, and a bison-scapula digging-stick tip from the Ainsworth site (LfAhI, 34LF80). This is presumably because these tools were made from impermanent materials such as bone, shell, and wood. The later Fort Coffee phase assemblage contains a much greater number of these items as well as a greater array of other tools of perishable materials. The loss of the Spiro phase assemblage is undoubtedly the result of poor preservation.

Spiro phase exploitation of animals is poorly understood for the same reasons. Our lack of data on the faunal assemblage has also been compounded by the lack of excavation in midden contexts in the area. The white-tailed deer was apparently a dietary mainstay. Such bone as is found in Spiro phase contexts is usually deer bone. There is controversy over the importance of bison at this time, but there is no doubt that bison bone does appear in this context. The use of this animal may have increased from the Spiro to the Fort Coffee phase, although there are few data on which to base such an assertion; but the use of the buffalo was certainly not an invention of Fort Coffee phase society.

The nonagricultural subsistence activities of the period of the Spiro phase in the Arkansas River region probably did not take place in the Spiro locality. Our best evidence suggests that a great deal of this activity took place in the hilly areas of the Ozark Mountains to the north and in the Ouachita Mountains to the south. One example of this is a small rockshelter high in the drainage pattern of Petit Jean Creek in west central Arkansas, no more than 2 km south of the drainage of the Arkansas and no more than 80 km by air from the Spiro locality. This small site, Sliding Slab Shelter (3SB29) (Harden *et al.* 1981), produced a large faunal assemblage that apparently represents occupation of the shelter during the Caddoan period, from about A.D. 800 to after 1450 (Rohrbaugh 1981).

The faunal assemblage from the shelter (Marrinan 1981) is dominated by white-tailed deer bone. Almost 25% of the biomass represented in the complete assemblage was deer. One fragment of elk bone represented the only other large mammal recovered.

According to one interpretation, the bulk of the faunal material from the shelter represents debris deposited during the period of the Caddoan tradition. If the shelter were occupied primarily during the late fall and winter, some fires would have been necessary. These would have been used for smoking meat (see Swanton 1946:372–381). The large quantities of ash produced in this process would have been useful in aiding in the removal of hair from the hides. The large accumulation of mussel shell found in the shelter would have been a source for scraping tools, and many modified shells were recovered from the deposits. Nut hulls, brought to the shelter with the hickory and walnuts that were thick through the deposits, would have been a ready source of tannic acid for tanning.

The processing of nut meats was important also. Natives of this region are reported to have collected large quantities of nuts, and the production of a "nut milk" was common. Crushed nuts were boiled, allowing the shells to sink and a thick, rich broth to rise. This nut milk was an important ingredient in many southeastern dishes (Swanton 1942:122, 1946:364–367).

It is easily imagined that Sliding Slab Shelter was used as a kind of intensive exploitation center during the Caddoan period. A relatively small group of men and women may have come to the shelter in the late fall. They would have returned to a valley bottom village in the spring, quite possibly bringing quantities of hides, nut milk and perhaps other products as well (Rohrbaugh 1981:189–190).

The Fort Coffee Phase Community

The two-center-post rectangular house that characterizes the Spiro phase village continues in use into the period of the Fort Coffee phase. Dates on these houses from the Spiro locality, and from other areas, indicate this. Yet, it is also believed that the circular houses at the Choates site, and others, are features of this late phase. Houses associated with Fort Coffee phase debris are often less regular in floor plan than their earlier counterparts, although the degree to which this is influenced by excavation techniques is uncertain.

The 1969 excavations at the Moore site uncovered three houses, at least one of which belongs to the Spiro phase occupation, and a large series of refuse-filled pits. This is a common community plan for the Arkansas River region during this period.

Fort Coffee phase burials at the Lymon Moore cemetery differ from Spiro phase burials at the Moore site. Whereas Spiro phase burials appear randomly oriented, the burials of the Lymon Moore field are consistently oriented with their heads to the west. There are characteristics of the early burials that relate to the age and sex of the individual, but the sexes are segregated in the Lymon Moore field and are characterized by distinctive tool kits.

Virtually all the burials are semiflexed. Most are supine and all are primary, single interments. Females are buried with a distinctive tool kit. All the deer-mandible sickles and deer-ulna awls occur in female burials. Males are characterized by a more lavish and varied set of associations, although there are no items diagnostic of male burials. The sexes are segregated with the females on the east and the males on the west, with an area of admixture in between.

The Spiro phase, Edgar Moore cemetery is organized in such a way as to suggest there were distinct social classes within the population buried there. The positions of the individuals in the field, and the affinities of certain artifact categories to these positions, suggest there were social distinctions among the population that transcended age and sex. This is not true of the Fort Coffee phase, Lymon Moore cemetery. Here virtually all the variation can be explained in terms of age and sex. The burials of the oldest males are the most elaborate and the burials of the youngest females are the least elaborate. The Spiro phase cemetery organization implies a society in which social position was inherited at birth. The Fort Coffee phase cemetery organization implies a society in which social position could only be acquired in life.

In contrast to the material assemblage of the Spiro phase, that of the Fort Coffee phase is relatively distinctive. A particular constellation of ceramic and stone artifact types, which occurs in burial and refuse contexts, makes it relatively easy to distinguish. The most distinctive ceramic types include Hudson Engraved, Womack Engraved, Emory Punctate and Nash Neck Banded (Figure 12.3). The small triangular unnotched Fresno point is not unique to the Fort Coffee phase but is common in this context. Similar shapes of small projectile points, such as the Talco and Shetley types, are unique to the phase, however.

Fort Coffee phase assemblages are characterized by the relative scarcity of Poteau Plain vessels and the corresponding abundance of Woodward Plain wares. Over 90% of the ceramics were Woodward Plain sherds. This is the result of a drastic increase in the use of the jar form during the Fort Coffee phase. This form represents about 23% of all jars and bowls in Spiro phase contexts, but almost 50% of jars and bowls in the Lymon Moore cemetery and 65% of jars and bowls in the Fort Coffee phase refuse-filled pits at the Moore site. The size of jars increases also. Although very large Woodward Plain and Woodward Appliqué jars occur at Spiro (Brown 1971b; 138, Figure 20), they have not been found in other Spiro phase contexts in the area. Vessels of capacities of greater than 8 liters are relatively common in Fort Coffee phase refuse contexts. Braden Incised, another jar form, is also characteristic of the phase. Braden Punctate occurs, but is not as common as in Spiro phase contexts (Figure 12.3).

Indications of influence from the Mississippi Valley disappear from the Fort Coffee phase ceramic assemblage. In such types as Hudson Engraved, Emory Punctate and Nash Neck Banded, however, there is indicated an increased influence from peoples of the Red River variant of the Caddoan tradition. A single sherd of a Simms Engraved vessel suggests influence from the same direction (Figure 12.3).

Fort Coffee Phase Subsistence

The most distinctive context of the period of Fort Coffee phase in which corn kernels have been found is Feature 5 at the Harvey site (R. J. Burton 1971). This pit contained a Talco-type small projectile point, diagnostic of the Fort Coffee phase in the Spiro locality, and other artifacts characteristic of the phase. Charcoal from the pit was dated at A.D. 1560 ± 60 (Tx-486), a characteristic date for the phase. Two burned seeds, appearing to be sunflower or squash, were also found.

Indirect evidence of agriculture during this period is available in a number of tools from the Moore site. Such tools as polished deer mandibles, polished bison scapulae, and perforated mussel shells are inferred to have been used as sickles, hoes or digging tools, and shell hoes, respectively.

The exploitation of animals did not apparently diminish with the end of Spiro phase. A study by Pillaert (n.d.) of the faunal debris from the refuse-filled pits at the Moore site suggests that around 30% of the diet of mammalian species was white-tailed deer. The meat represented by bison bone, however, represented around 60% of the meat from mammals. Less-important species included bear, beaver, woodchuck, rabbits, raccoon, opossum, and squirrels. There were duck, turkey, quail, and passenger pigeon bones in the sample. A great many reptile bones, primarily turtle, were recovered. Various fish species were also represented in the sample. In total, bones of mammals represented over 90% of the useable meat available, followed by bones of fish, birds, and reptiles (see Rohrbaugh 1982:562).

Neosho Focus

Certain broad similarities have been noted between the material Orr assigned to the Fort Coffee focus and material from the Neosho focus of Delaware and Mayes Counties in northeastern Oklahoma (Figure 12.1). Much has been written about the Neosho focus since it was summarized by Bell and Baerreis in 1951. With the exception of a single site, however, these have been reports of WPA excavations carried out under the supervision of D. A. Baerreis. The best general survey of the material is Freeman's (1962) summary of her dissertation (1959a). This was an analysis of six rockshelters and three open sites on the Grand (Neosho) River in Delaware County. It criticized a number of hypotheses on the origin of the assemblage made by Baerreis in a number of papers (1939b, 1940, 1941, 1953, 1960) and summarized data from a number of technical reports (Baerreis and Freeman 1959, 1961; Freeman 1959a, 1960). The Jug Hill site (34MY18) (Wyckoff 1964a, 1964b; Wyckoff et al. 1963), was an open site salvaged as a result of the construction of Markham Ferry Reservoir on Grand River. It is in Mayes County about 80 km by air south of the Delaware County sites. Both Wyckoff (1970c) and Purrington (1971) have subsequently commented on the material.

Baerreis (1941) suggested a date of around A.D. 1650 for the assemblage. Freeman contested this late date and suggested it was contemporary with the late Caddoan manifestations, and Baerreis (1960) later agreed on a date around A.D. 1350 to 1400. Two radiocarbon dates from the Jug Hill site indicate a late occupation (Table 12.1).

Little is known about Neosho focus settlement pattern save that it integrated the use of rockshelters with open sites. Freeman believed the shelters were occupied year-round by one or two small family groups.

> The wide variety of artifacts present in the Neosho focus components in the rockshelters; hunting tools, tools for preparing hides, sewing, pottery for cooking, indicate that many activities were carried on in the rockshelters. These sites are most probably year round dwelling places for one or two families. The open sites were not large enough to have been summer dwelling places for the entire Neosho focus population in Delaware County, but could have been gathering spots for a few families engaged in gathering or agricultural activities. (Freeman 1962:6)

Most of the Delaware County rockshelters were located in the bluffs along steam valleys tributary to Grand River. Two were peripheral to terraces and floodplains of the river. Only one open site contained a large sample of Neosho focus material. A number of refuse-filled pits and postholes were found here. Such features were also found at the Jug Hill site. Other open sites in Delaware County had small samples of this material above Archaic assemblages.

The irregular series of post holes found at the Jug Hill site was interpreted (Wyckoff 1964b) as the remains of a roughly rectangular house oriented with the long axis from northwest to southeast and measuring 3.7 by 5.8 m. Contained within the pattern were a baked-clay basin and two refuse-filled pits. Other pits were found in the area of the house. No interior supports were located.

No burials were recovered from the Jug Hill site. Freeman briefly describes rock shelter burials. "Grave goods were sparse, consisting of a bowl, a grooved shaft abrader, and shell beads with a child and a section of twilled matting with an adult. All burials were primary. Positions varied from extended to partially flexed. Both single and multiple burials were found" (Freeman 1962:5).

A number of tool types—half-socketed bison-scapula hoes, perforated mussel-shell hoes, handstones, and grinding basins—suggested agriculture was important although no cultigens were found. Bone and shell were not preserved at the Jug Hill site. Freeman believed that the bottomlands below the rockshelters could have supported agricultural plots. No such sites were found, perhaps because of WPA sampling procedures.

Acorns, nutting stones and mussel shells in the deposits imply the importance of gathering and collecting. Large numbers of small unnotched triangular projectile points of the Fresno and Shetley type were recovered, but the small notched triangular form was rare. A variety of large projectile point forms were recovered.

The variety of artifacts made from bone suggests a faunal assemblage similar to the Fort Coffee phase assemblage at Moore.

> Tools made of antler included flakers and drills. Flakers were also made of deer ulnas. Turtle carapaces made into bowls and a plaque made of a turtle plastron were found. Awls were made from deer ulnas, deer cannon bone, bird bone, longitudinally split bone, and splinters of bone worked only at the tip or else completely worked into a rod shape. A single rib edge or neural spine awl was found. Deer bones were also made into beamers (cannon bone) and shaft straighteners or wrenches (radii and ulnas). A bone flesher and a bone fishook were found at one rockshelter. (Freeman 1962:4)

Within a few years of the publication of the definition of Woodward Plain (R. L. Hall 1951), the type was being used as a category for all shell-tempered plainware in eastern Oklahoma. Freeman and Buck (1960) attempted to isolate two varieties: Woodward Plain Reed variety from the assemblage at the Reed site, and Woodward Plain Neosho variety from one of the open sites and four rockshelters in Woodward Hollow of the Delaware County locale. The Reed site is an early Caddoan tradition site in the vicinity. Thus, the two samples were temporally isolated; one before the end of the thirteenth century and the other after the beginning of the fourteenth century A.D.

Some researchers contend there are quantitative differences by which one can distinguish body sherds of the two varieties, but no usable explication of such differences has yet appeared. Bell (1972:247) has implied that one distinctive difference is that the Reed variety is heavily leached. This distinction has been picked up by various other researchers in recent years (Briscoe 1977:131–134; Galm 1978:128; Galm and Flynn 1978b:204; and Muto 1978:102). Unfortunately leaching has nothing to do with the definition of these varieties and the only mention of it in the Freeman and Buck paper is in reference to the Neosho and not the Reed variety (1960:8). Furthermore, the leaching of temper from the paste of shell-tempered ceramics has been shown not to be temporally significant in at least two extensive studies (Brown 1971b:145; Israel 1979:153).

Freeman and Buck (1960) demonstrated that there were distinctive variations in vessel forms in the two samples. Perhaps most significant, the Neosho variety sample of 237 rim sherds showed much more variety than did the 225 rim sherds from the Reed site. Furthermore, the sample from Reed was dominated by jar forms whereas the Neosho sample contained a great number of bowl sherds. Viewed strictly from a temporal perspective, this sequence is both similar to and distinct from the situation in the Spiro locality.

Another clear difference in these areas is the lack of slipped bowls in the northern area. None of the material in either sample was even polished. This lack of slipping and polishing is also seen at the Jug Hill site. Poteau Plain does not exist in the area.

Decorated ceramics of the Delaware County area have received much attention. Neosho Punctate is a form associated with both bowls and jars, but primarily with jars. With the possible exception of a slightly finer surface texture, the type is otherwise indistinguishable from Woodward Plain. Punctation, with elliptical, round, or wedge-shaped tools; incising; and the fixing of appliqué nodes are the decorative techniques. Lip puncation or incision is a common mode, particularly on bowls. Bowl bodies are rarely decorated. Punctation and incision commonly occur together.

Braden Incised, Braden Punctate, and Woodward Appliqué, the decorated jar types of the Spiro locality, are considerably different from these jars of the Neosho type. Most of the modes of Neosho Punctate occur on jars of the Spiro locality, but in significantly different combinations and motifs. The combination of punctation and incision is less common. The execution of the motifs is better. Lip notching or punctating is not a feature of jars in the area, nor does lip punctation occur on bowls. The most characteristic motif of the Braden Incised type does not occur on Neosho Punctate vessels: opposed triangular zones of oblique incisions extending from the lip to the upper shoulder. Whereas punctation is used as an integral part of the complex angular and curvilinear motifs on Neosho Punctate vessels, its most common appearance on Braden Puncate vessels is in horizontal bands around the neck. Fingernail punctations or similar marks made with tools are common on Braden Punctate jars but are rare or absent on Neosho Punctate vessels.

The Neosho Punctate type has never been associated with ceramics of the Caddoan area. It has formed a significant part of a continuing argument, introduced by Baerreis (1939), on the origin of the complex. Baerreis believed that the modes of decoration were similar to Oneota ceramics from Wisconsin, Iowa, Nebraska, and Missouri, and that other artifacts were similar to this complex as well. Because Oneota had been linked with the Chiwere Sioux occupations of these states, he suggested that the Neosho focus represented the debris of Dhegiha Siouan groups; that is, either the Osage or Kansa. He suggested a late intrusion of these peoples into northeastern Oklahoma in the seventeenth century A.D.

Freeman attacked this hypothesis (1959a, 1962), attempting to demonstrate that the complex developed out of existing Archaic and Woodland assemblages.

> The Neosho focus then, may have been in existence prior to the time of developed Oneota sites in Missouri and the Plains. The design of Neosho Punctate pottery is reminiscent of Oneota designs but cannot be said to be Oneota. It is suggested that the design is a result of contact with a proto-Oneota group and not because the Neosho focus peoples were part of the migration of Oneota peoples to the west. (Freeman 1962:10)

A pre-Oneota date is suggested by the dates from Jug Hill, but the presence of historic trade items on this site is intriguing. Such artifacts were not bound by the WPA crews and were not found in context at Jug Hill, but their presence must be noted. A red, grainy "clay-stone" (Wyckoff 1964b:49) pipe fragment similar to catlinite in color but not texture, a rolled-copper tinkler, a rolled-copper bead and a triangular copper piece were found. An elbow pipe of similar material was found on the surface of an untested Neosho focus component not far away (1964b: 49–50).

The Spiro Locality and Delaware County

It is apparent that no direct relationship can be established between the Neosho focus material and the Spiro and Fort Coffee phases in the Spiro locality, or in the drainage of the Arkansas River below its confluence with the Canadian, for that matter. Still, it is also apparent that the Neosho focus material is contemporary with at least part of the sequence in the Spiro locality. It is a reasonable working hypothesis that the Neosho focus material, and the material from the Reed site, represent a distinct but essentially similar sequence to that in the Spiro locality. It is reasonable to conceive of the peoples of these two areas interacting closely during the period of the Spiro phase, perhaps to the extent that leaders of the Delaware County area were interred in Craig Mound at Spiro. It is reasonable to see the subsistence pattern of the Delaware County area in essentially the same terms as we see it in the Spiro locality: agricultural villages, perhaps not as compact as those of the Spiro locality, dissolving in nonagricultural seasons to collect the resources of the eastern flanks of the Ozark Uplift. A closer examination of sites in the Delaware County area will be needed before these hypotheses can be accepted or rejected, however.

CHAPTER 13

The Plains Villagers: The Custer Phase

Jack L. Hofman

Introduction

The Custer phase is interpreted as an early Plains Village complex that developed out of southern Plains Woodland manifestations and is antecedent to the Washita River phase. This is an over simplification of a dynamic process of cultural change and interaction involving numerous small groups of prehistoric hunting–foraging–gardening people who inhabited a diversified environment from central to western Oklahoma. Interpretation of the archaeological unit originally designated *the Custer focus* has in some ways changed very little since 1951 when the complex was first defined. What has changed is not our reconstruction of the economy or life-style of these people, but our understanding of the age and distribution of the complex. That is, the way in which this archaeological unit, Custer, articulates with other archaeologically constructed complexes in time and space. The following is one possible interpretation of the way the Custer phase fits within the archaeological picture of western Oklahoma. This interpretation is intended to form both a target that can be attacked with hypotheses testing of hypotheses and a base that can be built upon with further research. Even the word *phase*, which I choose to use here, may prove to be inappropriate as a better understanding of the Custer complex emerges. This study elaborates and refines the definition of the Custer phase presented in Hofman (1978c).

287

The Setting

Between A.D. 800 and 1100 western Oklahoma was somewhat different than it is today. There were expanses of open tall-grass and mixed-grass prairie intermingled with stands of post oak, blackjack oak, and shinnery oak. Herds of bison and antelope roamed the region and there was probably a plentiful supply of turkey, deer, and elk. Topographically, the region was probably similar to that of today. Deep canyons in Permian sandstone and gypsum dissect some locales. Others are typified by rolling hills, flat eroded spaces, sand dunes, or the granite peaks of the Wichita Mountains.

Figure 13.1 indicates the known distribution of Custer phase components and this distribution includes a number of physiographic and vegetative regions. The area between 98 and 100° west longitude and 34 and 36° north latitude, which contains the documented Custer components, has a subhumid climate. The region, as a whole, slopes gently to the southeast and elevation ranges from over 600 m to about 300 m (2000 to about 1000 feet) above mean sea level. Major drainages flow to the southeast and include (from north to south) the Canadian, Washita, and Red Rivers. Each major river is fed by numerous tributaries of various sizes, many of which have perennial springs where water is available during even the driest years. These tributaries were much used by the prehistoric people. The rivers and many tributaries provide niches of riparian forest and a variety of plant and animal species not common to the open plains (Hofman 1978b). A number of relict species are found in some canyon bottoms where vegetation is protected from the drying winds (Little 1939).

The modern vegetative pattern places this region at the western edge of the tall-grass prairie and the eastern fringe of the short-grass high plains. Because

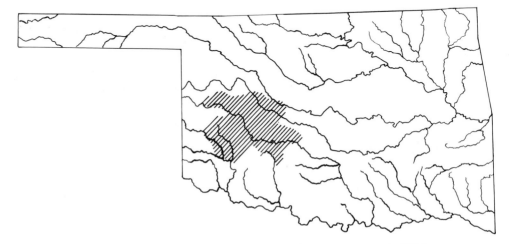

Figure 13.1 Established distribution of Custer phase components in Oklahoma.

this border is known to move as much as 160 km (100 miles) due to variations in precipitation and grazing (Shelford 1963), it is a zone known for extreme fluctuations in productivity and fairly rapid shifts in species densities. Records from the past 75 years indicate the average annual precipitation for the region varies from 55 to 80 cm (22 to 32 inches). The area is very dry due to strong prevailing winds that cause an evapotranspiration potential exceeding the amount of precipitation. The modern growing season varies from 200 to 210 days and extends from about the first of April to near the first of November.

With a variable water supply and even greater extremes in temperature, prehistoric gardening activities were probably precarious at times. We do not know many details of the environment in western Oklahoma between A.D. 800 and 1100, but we have documentation of recent extreme conditions for this region and of significant climatic changes in similar plains localities during prehistoric times (Reher 1977). We can predict that the 250-to-300-year period during the Custer phase was not one of stable ecological conditions. There were times of varying moisture (Kraenzel 1955; Weakly 1943). Varying vegetative productivity correlated with changes in major plant species frequencies, and changes in the size of resident herd animal populations (Dillehay 1974) indicate a cyclical or oscillating situation in which a few years of reliable rainfall may result in more productive vegetation and, in turn, larger herds and better garden production. Dry years could result in crop failure and severe damage to grazing areas. In such a situation, using the diversified riparian and plains plant and animal communities may have been expedient, even critical, to supplementing the assumed bottomland gardening economy.

Settlement and Economy

Because the settlement of these prehistoric peoples is closely tied to their economic basis, the settlement and economy of Custer peoples are discussed together in this section. For the purpose of the present discussion, Custer sites are assigned to one of three types: hamlets, camps, and shelters. *Hamlets,* such as Goodman I, Mouse, Phillips, Edwards II, and Hodge are identified by evidence of house structures, storage pits, a relative abundance of pottery, and/or the presence of horticultural implements. A variety of sites from isolated farmsteads to small villages are probably represented in this category.

Camps, such as represented by the Ross site and Bk-23, are indicated by a limited variety and quantity of Custer phase characteristics. These include projectile points, cutting and scraping tools, small quantities of ceramics, and the absence of evidence for houses or storage. Ceramics would not necessarily be found at a hunting or specialized resource collecting camp, but without them assignment of these small sites to a particular Late Prehistoric manifestation becomes very tenuous. These camps were probably repeatedly occupied and are generally located in upland areas near tributary streams. *Shelter sites*, of which Duncan–Wilson is an excellent example, are located in canyons and near bluffs. These sites may have evidence of either long-term habitation or short-term camping activities. Their protected settings make them particularly suitable for occupation during specific seasons.

The activities of Custer people are believed to have differed significantly during various parts of the year. The annual cycle of their activities as it is vaguely understood, at present, can be broken down into two primary components. These are the growing season and the winter season.

The Growing Season

The livelihood of Custer peoples included riverbottom gardening activities. For this part of the year, extending from March or April through October, they may have lived in small villages or hamlets and directed their economic activities from these permanent sites. The entire group may not have remained in the settlement for the entire growing season. The hamlets apparently consisted of a few houses scattered along a high terrace or ridge, often near the juncture of two primary water sources. The houses were of post, wattle-and-daub construction and probably had thatched roofs. Cache pits used for storing vegetal products, dried meat, and valuables occur in and adjacent to these structures. When no longer suitable for storage, these pits were filled with trash.

Locating permanent hamlets on high ground ensured against flooding after torrential summer storms and the winds or breezes on these more prominent positions helped clear the living area of flying insect pests. By locating permanent habitation sites near two water sources, Custer peoples were often provided with naturally irrigated alluvial bottomland for their crops, as well as with more potable spring water from a smaller tributary. The rivers of the area generally carry a high sediment load, often with high saline content, and their waters are not ideal for drinking.

Wood supply is another reason they may have favored stream confluence situations for their permanent settlements (W. W. Caldwell 1977; D. E. Griffin 1976, 1977). By settling near the mouth of a tributary, prehistoric people could have exploited the wood resources typical of the river's entire length plus the bonus of wood from along a secondary stream. Wood was critical for fuel, construction, and artifacts.

Horticultural related activities required at least semipermanent occupation of sites situated near suitable garden plots, but settlement was not always along primary rivers. If riverbottom situations were preferred for gardens, then the presence of permanent settlements in upland situations along secondary streams, such as at the Heerwald site and Duncan–Wilson shelter may indicate a sizable population for the region, competition for land, and the need to cultivate plots in less-desirable niches. Upland site locations were also used, however, in response to various needs, such as wild resource procurement and protection from harsh weather during winter months. Hunting and limited purpose gathering and/or processing sites were probably reutilized. When limited activity sites were located some distance from the primary habitation sites, overnight stays may have been necessary and accumulation of limited Custer phase remains would result.

Hunting was a routine activity and a wide range of species were utilized. Table 13.1 provides only a minimal estimation of the variety of animal resources hunted or used. Deer, elk, bison, turkey, and small game were probably hunted year-round. Some species, such as land terrapins, were available primarily during frost-free periods. These small reptiles were apparently important as they are present on all sites where faunal material was recovered and studied in detail. Bison-hunting expeditions may have occurred during the summer between planting and harvest times. The importance of fishing is unknown and this problem requires further research. Fish remains were present at the Duncan–Wilson shelter in levels dominated by Custer phase ceramics and evidence of fish was also found at the Keith site.

March and April would have been a time for preparing garden plots and planting. We have no direct evidence of the species grown in Custer phase gardens (with the possible exception of remains from Duncan–Wilson shelter where maize was found in possible Custer phase contexts) but we can assume that maize, beans, squash, and sunflowers were probably cultivated. Wild plant resources were important for fuel, food, construction materials (thatch, wattle, posts), domestic equipment (matting and basketry), and artifacts (bows, arrow shafts, handles). Plant remains from lower ceramic levels at Duncan–Wilson shelter (Levels 7–15), which are here interpreted as Custer phase in age, include hackberry, plum, persimmon, gourd, walnut, oak, and hickory.

The Winter Season

By the end of October remaining vegetal produce was probably prepared for future use and storage in underground cache pits. In the late fall of most years, village groups might embark on a major bison hunt to provide meat, grease, robes, and other necessities for the winter months. After a successful hunt the group could split up into smaller units and live in winter camps situated in riverbottoms, canyons, or other protected settings.

Winter hunting expeditions could have resulted in numerous short-term camps (Gilmore 1932) and scattered kill sites. Such camp sites used during bison-hunting operations probably contain minimal diagnostic evidence. It is possible that some small sites in southwestern Oklahoma with a limited quantity and variety of Custer phase characteristics, such as Bk-23 and Bk-28 (Barr 1966a) along Elk Creek in Beckham County, actually represent temporary camps used during hunting and/or gathering excursions.

Table 13.1

Fauna Represented at Excavated Custer Phase Components

Taxa	Goodman I (Cu-1)	McLaughlin I (Cu-4)	Shahan II (Cu-7)	Phillips (Cu-11)	Mouse (Cu-25)	Hodge (Cu-40)	Edwards II (Bk-44)	Duncan–Wilson (Cd-11; Levels 7–15)
					Sites			
Bison	x	x	x	x	x	x	x	x
Elk	—	—	—	—	—	—	—	x
Deer	x	x	x	x	x	x	x	x
Antelope	—	—	—	—	—	—	x	x
Bobcat	—	—	—	—	—	—	—	x
Dog	—	—	—	—	—	—	—	x
Beaver	—	—	—	—	—	—	x	—
Badger	—	—	—	—	—	—	x	x
Raccoon	—	—	—	—	—	—	—	x
Opossum	—	—	—	—	—	—	—	x
Skunk	—	—	—	—	—	—	—	x
Squirrel	—	—	—	—	—	—	—	x
Prairie dog	—	—	—	x	x	—	x	—
Jackrabbit	—	—	—	—	—	x	—	—
Cottontail	—	—	—	x	x	x	x	x
Rodents (various: gopher, mole, rat)	x	x	x	x	x	x	—	x
Turkey	—	—	—	—	—	—	—	x
Birds (various)	x	—	—	x	x	x	—	x
Fish (various)	—	—	—	—	—	—	x	x
Turtles (various)	—	—	—	x	—	x	x	x
Mussels (various)	x	x	x	x	x	x	x	x
Snails (various)	—	—	—	—	—	x	x	x

Kill sites of bison are little known in southwest Oklahoma. Two Late Prehistoric kills of single bison are documented from Caddo County. One is from
Domebo Canyon and produced a triangular unnotched arrowpoint in association with a bison (Anderson and Chappabitty 1968). The second is from White
Canyon and had a side-notched triangular point in association (Hofman 1980a;
Hofman and Morey 1981). These two kills represent hunting activities of Custer
or later times. Such kills may have been common throughout the late Prehistoric
period. Larger kills of definite Late Prehistoric age are not reported from the
Custer area, but late sites such as reported by Speth and Parry (1978) and Lintz
(1976a) may eventually be documented. Bison hunting by plains Indians during
the late fall and early winter is apparently a very old pattern (Ewers 1955; Frison
1978b; Reher 1977). It is probable, however, that bison hunting was carried out
intermittantly throughout the year depending on opportunity and need.

Available evidence does not allow determination of the importance of various
species to Custer economy, but all excavated Custer components have produced
faunal remains of bison as well as deer (Table 13.1). Faunal data are reported in
detail from only three Custer components and only one study provides such
essential information as elements and minimum number of individuals per species (Penman 1974b). I believe the Pate site (GV-49) represents, or at least includes, a Custer phase assemblage. But, the relevence if its fauna to the Custer
phase (Penman 1979) must await analysis of the artifacts. Nevertheless, we
know that both bison and deer were important resources during Custer times.
Lintz (1974:51) argued that deer was the favored and primary meat source for
Custer people, but I argue against acceptance of this interpretation based on the
evidence at hand. Future detailed studies of faunal resources from Custer sites
will be essential to learning more about the economy of these people, but some
comments about bison and deer exploitation are in order because these species
played an important part in the livelihood of Custer people.

Hunting Patterns

Deer have a restricted home range or foraging area, generally less than 1.6
km² (600 square acres) in extent and their predictable movements within this
territory make them very susceptible to hunters. Deer are usually found solitary
or in groups of a few individuals, although during the winter they may bunch in
larger groups of as many as 25 individuals. When killed, a deer could be dressed
in the field and carried back to the hamlet. This might be done by leaving the
dressed deer essentially intact or the animal might be quartered and carried back
in sections to the site. In either instance the vast majority of deer bone from each
deer might be brought back to the hamlet, and could eventually turn up in the
archaeological record (M. Brown 1975:77).

Bison, on the other hand, being much larger and more gregarious than deer,
were generally hunted and processed differently. The bulk of bison resources

utilized by Plains Villagers were derived from annual summer and fall hunts. But, utilization of single bison kills may have followed much the same pattern as for communal kill situations. When a bison kill was made it was common practice to strip the meat from the bones, dry it, mix it with melted fat or grease, and pack it for transport back to the camp or hamlet (Gilmore 1932). This resulted in distinctive assemblages of bison bone at kill and camp sites (Brown 1975; Todd 1978; Wood 1968). Perishable bison elements such as the hide were also heavily relied upon but leave little evidence in the archaeological record. Select bones, such as the scapulae, tibiae, and rib sections might be salvaged for use as tools. Long bones might be processed for their grease and marrow (Leechman 1951; S. C. Vehik 1977). But, in many situations the bulk of bone material at a bison kill would not be redeposited back at a village site (Wood 1968; Todd 1978). Therefore, bison utilization by Plains Villagers such as the Custer phase people may be underrepresented if only bone frequencies from hamlets are depended upon for our interpretations. We must remain conscious of such potential inherent biases in the archaeological record if our interpretations are to be realistic. Also, the importance of species as contributors to prehistoric diet depends on the amount of meat or number of calories an individual of the species provides as well as on the number of individuals that are utilized. Many rabbits and turtles are required to provide the same amount of meat as one deer. Likewise, it requires the meat of 3 or 4 deer to equal that produced by a single bison (Smith 1975; White 1953).

Material Culture and Industries

Industries of the Custer phase are represented in the archaeological record by characteristics common to students of Late Prehistoric Plains Village complexes. Custer phase assemblages are distinctive not by their peculiarity but by the relative frequencies of specific artifact types. The discussion that follows emphasizes, by necessity, nonperishable artifacts of ceramic and stone and resistant organic artifacts of bone and shell. Artifacts of skin, hide, hair, sinew, wood, fiber, and similar materials are known only indirectly, if at all. There is little doubt that Custer peoples used many such perishable items but they are not preserved in the open camp sites. Baskets, bags, nets, matting, twine, rope, hafts, or handles, wooden utensils, and garments can be assumed, and one hopes future research will shed light on these aspects of the Custer phase lifeway.

Information on the architecture of the Custer phase is limited to evidence from three house patterns (Figure 13.2). Two of these are from the Goodman I site and the third was recorded at the Mouse site. These structures share several general characteristics. Each was apparently of wattle-and-daub construction with posts for wall supports. A hearth was present near the center of each structure, but interior roof supports exhibit no consistent pattern. The largest house at the

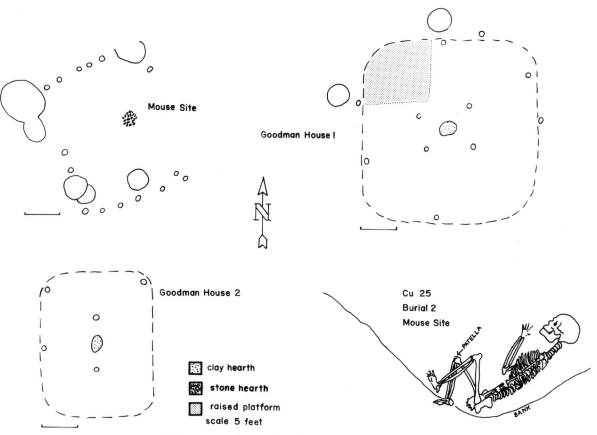

Figure 13.2 Custer phase house patterns and burial.

Goodman I site had four interior posts placed around the central hearth, the second Goodman I house had two interior supports, whereas the Mouse site house had no discernible interior support posts. The roof covering was presumably of thatch, bundles of swamp grass placed in a shinglelike fashion on a light roof-frame. In outline the houses were rectangular with rounded corners and all lack visible evidence of entryways. Cache pits occur near the walls of two structures and these could be on the interior or exterior. House 1 at the Goodman I site had a raised platform approximately 2.4 m (8 feet) square in the northwest corner. The significance of this feature is unknown, but raised platforms or altars are sometimes found in rectangular houses of the later Panhandle aspect. In size, the structures measure from 4.5 to 7.2 m (15 to 24 feet) on a side, with the 7.2 m (24 foot) square structure at the Goodman I site the largest, having a floor area of about 172.5 m² (575 square feet). The smallest structure was at the Mouse site and had a floor area of 85.5 m² (285 square feet). The mean floor size of the three documented Custer phase structures is 117.9 m² (393 square feet).

The predominant artifacts from most Custer sites are pottery sherds. The pottery was a coarse utilitarian ware typified by globular cooking and storage vessels. No systematic study of vessel sizes has been conducted but most of the jars apparently had a capacity of 3.8 to 7.6 liters (one or two gallons) or less. Surface treatment varies from smooth to cordmarked or smoothed-over cordmarked, the latter most common. This pottery has been termed *Stafford Cordmarked* and *Stafford Plain*, but systematic study is needed to determine the actual relationship of these types to the Lindsey Plain and Lindsey Cordmarked of Washita River sites in central Oklahoma. Of all the reported pottery from Custer phase sites, about two-thirds is cordmarked or smoothed-over cordmarked and only one-third is smooth. The frequency of cordmarking from site to site varies from about 25 to 100%. Vessel forms vary from direct-rimmed vessels with round or pointed bases to shouldered vessels with everted rims and round or flat bases. Shouldered vessels with flat bases are always smooth surfaced and these vessels may have lip tabs or strap handles. Decorations are not common but applied nodes or punctates and notched rims are occasionally found on smooth sherds or vessels, and diagonally cordmarked lips sometimes occur on cordmarked vessels. Smooth vessels rarely exhibit burnished surfaces.

A variety of materials were used as temper, but the paste can generally be described as coarse. Grit and grog (crushed rock and sherds) were important tempering agents with caliche, sandstone, limestone, gypsum, or sand often forming a large percentage of the paste. Bone was also used in varying amounts and was generally mixed with grog or grit. The importance of grog as a temper may well be underestimated due to the relative difficulty in identifying this substance. Shell was a less-common temper but is found in the smooth-surfaced sherds at some sites. Some of the limestone used as temper is full of fossil shell which also occurs in some sherd assemblages. The significance of temper as a temporal indicator for the area is unknown. Variations in tempering material may relate to availability of various materials throughout the region. Sherds and vessels of Custer phase pottery are illustrated in Figure 13.3.

Other ceramic and clay artifacts include figurines, usually human forms, and occasional discs made from potsherds. Figurines are reported from Goodman I and Mouse, both of which were permanent sites indicated by house structures and both of which produced burials. The figurines were not recovered from burial contexts, however. Figurine function remains questionable, but the occurrence of figurines with a burial at the McLemore Site (Pillaert 1963) of the later Washita River complex is suggestive.

Stone artifacts (Figure 13.3) include a variety of arrowpoint styles. Corner-notched arrowpoints in the range of the Scallorn type are found at all Custer sites that have more than 50% cordmarked pottery. Triangular side-notched and unnotched types such as Washita and Fresno are almost always represented. Scrapers include the typical Plains style end-scraper, side-scrapers, spokeshaves, and pointed scrapers or reamers. Flake knives and beveled-edge knives are found, but the diamond-beveled or Harahay knife is not common. Both expanding-base and plain-shafted drills occur, as do large dart points. The latter

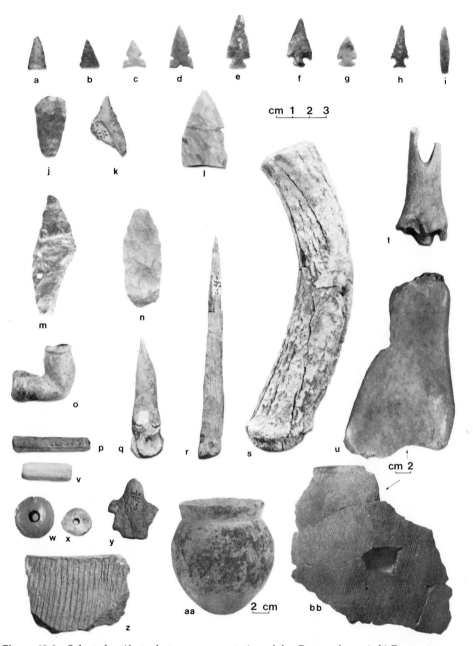

Figure 13.3 Selected artifacts that are representative of the Custer phase: (a,b) Fresno-type arrow-points; (c) Washita-type arrowpoint; (d) Harrell-type arrowpoint; (e–h) varieties of corner-notched (Scallorn-type) arrowpoints; (i) drill; (j) end-scraper; (k) pointed scraper; (l) beveled-knife section; (m) beveled knife; (n) elliptical knife; (o) stone pipe; (p,v) bone beads; (q,r) bone awls; (s) antler handle; (t) section of bone-shaft wrench; (u) bison-scapula hoe; (w,x) shell-disc beads; (y) clay figurine fragment; (z) cordmarked rim sherd; (aa) undecorated pottery vessel; (bb) large rim section from a cordmarked vessel. Specimens a,b, m, o, p, v, u, and aa are from the Goodman I site (Cu-1); Specimens c–h, l, n, x, and bb are from the Phillips site (Cu-11); Specimens i–k, q–t, w, y, and z are from the Mouse site (Cu-25).

may represent the reutilization of older items that had been found. The most common chipped-stone tools are flake knives and scrapers that show minimal or no intentional modification.

Ground-stone artifacts include unifacial and bifacial grinding stones, often without pecked or shaped edges, grinding basins, abraders, and arrow-shaft smoothers. Celts occur infrequently, but one specimen is known from the Keith Site and a second is reported from the lower ceramic levels at Duncan–Wilson shelter. Celts from Heerwald may be of post–Custer phase age. Ground-stone elbow pipes made of fine-grained red sandstone and other unidentified stone are recurrent on Custer sites but are never plentiful. Like the figurines, they usually occur on the major habitation sites. Cobbles representing hammerstones and pecking stones are common. Some of the quartzite cobbles were apparently sharpened and used for pecking or shaping grinding stones and similar items.

Bone artifacts form a distinctive and important part of Custer assemblages but are generally found in small numbers. Bison-scapula hoes and bison-tibia digging stick tips have a frequency of about one per component and bone awls made from various elements are only about twice as common. Limited numbers of arrow-shaft wrenches and scored ribs are found. Antler sections were used as handles and probably as knapping tools, but are again infrequently recovered. Bird-bone beads appear at several sites in limited numbers.

Shell artifacts include occasional scrapers or spoons and disc-shaped beads made from freshwater mussels. An unreported burial from Foss Reservoir in Custer County, which may represent a Custer phase interment, produced over a hundred shell disc beads (John Flick, personal communication, 1976). The beads are very similar to those reported from Woodland ossuaries in the Central Plains (Kivett 1953). *Olivella*-shell beads were recovered from one burial at the Goodman I site.

Trade and Interaction

There is minimal evidence of trade between people of the Custer phase and those outside the region. Much of the evidence that indicates interaction or potential contact with other areas is of a general nature and could have resulted by diffusion of ideas. Characteristics such as cordmarked globular jars and corner-notched arrowpoints did not originate in southwestern Oklahoma, but their presence does not imply continued contact with outsiders. Even the limited number of items that definitely originated from outside the known Custer phase area do not necessarily demonstrate close trading relationships with other groups. Exotic flints and shells could possibly represent the sojourns of a few individuals. Although there are a number of possible models that could explain the dispersal of cultural materials throughout the area (Blakeslee 1975; Wood 1974), I suspect that much of the trade occurred in the form of village-to-village exchanges all along the Canadian, Washita, and Red River drainages.

Exotic lithic materials that found their way into Custer assemblages include obsidian, Kay County flint, and Alibates flint, in increasing order of importance. Only a few flakes of obsidian are presented in Custer components and finds of Kay County flint are also limited. These materials indicate interaction to the west (obsidian from the New Mexico area) and north (Kay County flint from north-central Oklahoma). Much of the Alibates flint recovered from Custer sites could represent the utilization of gravels that have washed down the Canadian and, to a lesser extent, the Washita Rivers. But not all the Alibates in western Oklahoma is derived from exploitation of these relatively small river-deposited cobbles. A cache of large Alibates biface reduction flakes from the Heerwald site probably indicates the transport of blanks from the Alibates quarry area in the central Texas Panhandle (Lintz 1978f). A large Alibates knife from Burial 2 at the Goodman I site also suggests that not all Alibates used in Custer times was derived from river gravels.

Several sites in the western Oklahoma area have produced marine shell in burial contexts (Hofman 1977b), but only one such find can definitely be assigned to the Custer phase. Burial 2 at the Goodman I site produced 29 *Olivella*-shell beads that originated from the Pacific coast and indicate contact between people of the Custer phase and those to the west. *Olivella*-shell beads were also found at the Duncan–Wilson shelter.

Interaction within the Custer area is also indicated. Fragments of granite grinding stones have been found as much as 80 km (50 miles) from a source in the Wichita Mountains area.

Burial Customs

Only five burials are documented that can be assigned to the Custer phase with certainty. Two of these are from the Goodman I site and three are from Mouse. All these cases indicate the placement of individuals in a flexed position with the head oriented in an easterly direction (where orientation could be determined). Associations occur with three of the five individuals and include pottery vessels, an elbow pipe, two large flint knifes, *Olivella*-shell beads, bird-bone beads, and possibly projectile points. The pottery vessels were smooth surfaced, and the present lack of evidence for cordmarked vessels in burial contexts could argue for the strictly utilitarian nature of Stafford Cordmarked jars. Burial associations are not restricted to adults and in general the funerary pattern of the Custer phase appears very similar to that for the Washita River complex (Lopez 1970). It is not known whether a large cemetery area exists on Custer sites or if individuals were randomly placed within or near the habitation areas. The Foss Reservoir burial containing many perforated shell disc beads is a very interesting case and, if similar burials are found in definite Custer contexts, strong similarities with the Central Plains Woodland (Keith focus) materials will be indicated. A burial example is shown in Figure 13.2.

Internal Chronology and Change

Table 13.2 summarizes the available radiocarbon dates from Custer phase components. Although few in number, these dates fill an important gap between those available for the Woodland materials from the Pruitt site (Barr 1966c; Wyckoff 1966b) and those from Washita River sites. These dates are the basis for my interpretation that Custer was a transitional phase between Southern Plains Woodland and Washita River. The four dates bracket a time frame starting at circa A.D. 800 and ending about A.D. 1100. At least until additional Custer dates are forthcoming, I accept this time estimate as realistic for the Custer phase.

If, Custer phase represents a time of growth and change in the lives of Southern Plains villagers, then we can expect temporal and spatial diversity within this archaeological unit. Based on knowledge of the preceeding Woodland and later Washita River complexes in the region, an outline of Custer phase changes can be suggested. Perhaps more fundamental than changes in artifact styles, however, is the suggestion of a general increase in population and settlement density during Custer times. Information from Washita River habitation sites indicates that they are larger on the average than Custer sites and generally produce a greater quantity of cultural materials. This may indicate more intensive exploitation of limited areas. Also the number of sites potentially assignable to the Custer phase (based on frequencies of pottery types) appears, from non-systematic investigation, to be less than the number that represent Washita River habitation. If Washita River sites are more common, this implies closer spacing of habitation sites and perhaps a larger population. Another line of evidence that merits further investigation is the potential change in house size. Custer phase houses have an average floor area of about 117 m² (390 square feet) whereas the two reported Washita River houses have an average floor area of 192 m² (640 square feet). Although the available samples are inadequate to be conclusive, the possibility of increasing structure size is interesting. Taken together, increases in the number and size of sites, the size of houses, and the intensity of agricultural activities (perhaps reflected by more numerous and diversified bone gardening tools) from Custer to Washita River times, may all reflect increasing population pressure in the region.

Artifactual changes within the Custer phase are believed represented by ceramic and stone artifacts. The ratio of cordmarked to smooth pottery decreases through time. Thus, early Custer assemblages have a higher frequency of cordmarked sherds and vessels whereas in late components smooth-surfaced ceramics are common. The frequency of decorations such as appliqué nodes and fillet strips increases in proportion to the quantity of smooth-surfaced pottery. The occurrence of lip tabs and strap handles is also limited to smooth vessels with only rare occurrences of lip tabs on cordmarked specimens. The range in vessel shapes and perhaps in the size range also appears to increase through time so that the ceramic industry by Washita River times is much more diversi-

Table 13.2

Radiocarbon Dates for the Custer Phase

Laboratory number	Site and provenience	Date before present (B.P.)	Date (A.D.) based on 5568 half-life	Date (A.D.) based on 5730 half-life	MASCA corrected date (A.D.)	Reference
M-1091	Mouse (Cu-25): F. 19	1000 ± 100	950	920	980 ± 110	Crane and Griffin 1965:132
Tx-807	Edwards II: F. 8	1141 ± 70	810	775	830–850 ± 100	Valastro et al. 1972:475
Tx-808	Edwards II: F. 7	980 ± 70	970	940	1000 ± 80	Valastro et al. 1972:475
Tx-809	Edwards II: F. 3	1100 ± 80	850	820	890 ± 90	Valastro et al. 1972:475

fied than in the earlier Custer period when ceramic vessels were close mimics of preceeding Woodland styles. Initially vessel forms were large jars with direct or inverted rims, slight shoulders, and conoidal or rounded bases. As a result of influence, probably from the east, the manufacture of vessels with prominent shoulders, everted rims, rounded or flat bases, and smooth surfaces increased.

A seriation of Custer phase sites based on the frequency of cordmarked and smooth-surfaced pottery was prepared (Hofman 1978c) and compared to the frequency of three broad groupings of arrowpoint styles: triangular unnotched, triangular side-notched, and corner notched. The results indicated that sites with less than 50% cordmarked pottery had predominantly triangular un-notched arrowpoints and few or no corner-notched arrowpoints. This probably indicates a general trend in which Fresno-type points become more common through time at the expense of Scallorn varieties. The frequency of Washita points remained fairly constant in the samples studied. The common usage of diamond-beveled knives apparently develops during late Custer or post-Custer times.

The addition of several bone-tool types to the material culture inventory apparently also occurs during late or post-Custer times. Bison-frontal hoes, bison-ulna picks, and deer-mandible sickles are as yet unreported from Custer sites. These artifacts, and probably ceramic pipes as well, can be considered as markers of terminal or post-Custer occupations in the region for the present. Overall then, Custer phase represents the transition from a Plains Woodland complex to a well-developed Plains Village complex known as Washita River. Due to differential acculturation rates, the artifacts that constitute Custer assemblages represent an interesting and diversified blend of Woodland and Late Prehistoric attributes. The changes in popularity of particular artifact styles was probably not consistent throughout the area. There may have been lag in the spread and acceptance of certain traits.

Speculations

The origin of the Custer people may be a local development from existing Woodland groups, and the Custer complex is believed by most researchers to represent prehistoric Caddoan speakers possibly ancestral to one or more of the tribes later to form the Wichita Confederacy (Newcomb and Field 1967). I accept these two interpretations as the most reasonable ones presented to date. There are, however, a number of questions that are raised by their acceptance.

If we work under the assumption that the Custer phase represents a group of the prehistoric Caddoan linguistic stock, then we need to determine their time of arrival on the Southern Plains from the Caddoan heartland to the east (Wyckoff 1974). If we also accept that the Custer phase represents an indigenous development, then we must conclude that at least some of the Plains Woodland groups in western Oklahoma who formed the base for Custer development were also of Caddoan background. The acceptance of Central Plains Woodland traits by these people indicates that they were probably no longer in close contact with the Caddoans to the east, or that they also had interaction with groups to the north. We might conclude, then, that at least some of the Caddoan stock who were later to coalesce and be recognized as the Wichita and other Southern Plains Caddoan tribes, were present on the Southern Plains before Woodland times (prior to A.D. 500) and perhaps during the Archaic period. The contracting-stemmed dart point (Gary type) is only one of several possible indications of similarities between the material culture of the Southern Plains Archaic groups and those in the Caddoan area proper during late Archaic times.

The interpretation originally presented by Buck (1959) that Custer represents the results of a migration of Central Plains Woodland peoples south into the western Oklahoma area is not favored here, but should not be discounted altogether. It is conceivable that late Archaic peoples in western Oklahoma were first heavily influenced by the Central Plains Woodland groups and later by Caddoans spreading westward during Washita River times. (Bell 1961, 1973).

The end of the Custer phase as a distinctive complex is also explainable in several ways. One interpretation is as follows. During the 100-year period, A.D. 1050–1150 and thereafter, there was a strong influx of ideas and possibly people up the Canadian and Washita River valleys that brought rapid change to the material culture of the Custer phase. This change is reflected especially in the ceramic complex. This may also be a time of population increase in the area and a period of intensified horticultural endeavors. Sites such as Currie (Gv-22) may represent this Custer–Washita River phase transition. The spread of a smooth-surfaced ceramic complex eventually reached extreme western Oklahoma where by A.D. 1200–1300 the vast majority of ceramics from all sites were smooth surfaced, with the exception of possible Panhandle aspect components (Hofman 1977c, 1980b; Leonhardy 1966a; Pillaert 1963).

Although it is easy to argue for the contribution of Custer to the development of the Washita River complex, we can argue that Custer may also have contributed at least in part to the Panhandle aspect. The distribution of Custer and Panhandle sites are essentially contiguous and will probably be shown to overlap considerably when the actual distributions are better known. Rectangular houses, cordmarked globular pottery, and a general Plains Village artifactual complex are present during Custer and appear later in the Panhandle aspect. One architectural trait of the Panhandle aspect, the rear platform or altar found in some rectangular structures, may have a Custer phase antecedent in the platform in House 1 at the Goodman I site.

The Cave Creek site (Leonhardy 1966) suggests possible contemporaneous occupation of western Oklahoma by Panhandle aspect and Washita River peoples. Evidence from some sites (Saunders 1973; Hofman 1977c) indicates a possible eastern spread of the Panhandle aspect after A.D. 1450 and perhaps a partial coalescence of Panhandle and Washita River culture in the old Custer phase territory.

Research Needs

Some basic research needs for a better understanding of the Custer phase are listed here.

1. Systematic recovery and analysis of subsistence data is a critical area of need if we hope to develop an understanding of Custer phase economy and settlement. To date no Custer site has been systematically excavated with the recovery of micro and macro plant and faunal remains as a significant part of the recovery goals.

2. Dating of the Custer phase is inadequate at present. If dates were available from a large number of Custer sites as well as earlier and later sites throughout the region then systematic studies using such techniques as trend surface analyses (Roper 1976) could provide valuable data on the movements and historical connections of the various groups involved.

3. A program of extensive survey and testing will be required before significant statements can be made about the distribution, spacing, and settlement of Custer groups and before we can assess the population of Custer times relative to that of earlier and later complexes in the region.

4. There are a number of collections from sites in central and western Oklahoma (e.g., Paul Site [Gv-34]; Pate Site [Gv-49]; Goodwin-Baker Site [Rm-14]; Currie [Gv-22]) that when reported will help solve some of the existing problems of the Custer phase and its relationship to Washita River. As badly as data are needed on small-scale vegetal remains and on faunal assemblages, our first step in continuing the study of Late Prehistoric complexes in western Oklahoma must be the analysis of extant collections. By doing so, we may better understand the kind of questions that need asking.

Reference Note

This chapter draws on information from a series of site reports, specialized studies, and summary papers. The Goodman I site (Cu-1) was reported by Gallaher (1951); McLaughlin I (Cu-4)[1], Williams (Cu-6), and Shahan II (Cu-7) were reported by Brighton (1951); the Phillips (Cu-11) and Mouse

---

[1]Unfortunately, due to an error in calculation, the McLaughlin I Site (Cu-4) was previously included in the Washita River phase (Hofman 1978c). This site should be considered as part of the Custer phase as indicated by the high frequency (52%) of cordmarked Stafford pottery. Three sites, Goodman II (Cu-2), Shahan I (Cu-3), and McLaughlin II (Cu-5), which were originally included in the Custer focus (Brighton 1951; Bell and Baerreis 1951; Lintz 1974; Hofman 1975a), are not included in the Custer phase here (see Hofman 1978c). These sites have only 7%, 2%, and 1% cordmarked Stafford pottery, respectively. These frequencies are within the range of cordmarked pottery frequencies of Washita River sites and are, therefore, not distinguishable from Washita River sites based on the limited samples.

(Cu-25) sites were reported by Buck (1959); Edwards II (Bk-44) by Eighmy (1970); Hodge (Cu-40) by Hofman (1974); and Keith (Cd-8) by Hofman (1978a). In addition to these sites, Custer phase components are believed to be represented at the Heerwald site, Cu-27 (Shaeffer 1965; Hofman 1976b); Little Deer, Cu-10 (Hofman 1978b); Duncan–Wilson Bluff Shelter, Cd-11 (Lawton 1968); Barrow Pit site, Cm-127 (Shaeffer 1961); Ross, Cd-69 (Hofman 1971); Bk-23 and Bk-28 (Barr 1966a); Gr-3, Gr-6, and Ki-3 (Burton and Burton 1969); and the Pate site, Gv-49 (Penman 1979).

Other sources include Penman's (1974b) study of the Hodge site fauna and discussions of the Custer "focus" in Bell and Baerreis (1951), G. N. Keller (1961), Buck (1959), J. T. Hughes (1974), Lintz (1974), Hofman (1975a, 1978c), and Bell's (1973) summary of the Washita River focus. General information on the life of Plains Villagers, particularly of Caddoan speakers, is derived from Newcomb and Field (1967) and Holder (1970). Data on the area's ecology is derived from Bruner (1931), Burt and Grossenheider (1976), Curtis and Ham (1972), Gray and Galloway (1959), Kraenzel (1955) and Shelford (1963).

Acknowledgments

My sincere appreciation is extended to Don G. Wyckoff, Christopher Lintz, and Robert E. Bell, and Pat Hofman for their efforts in helping me with this chapter. Especially, I am indebted to Timothy G. Baugh and Don Wyckoff for considerable help in the final stages of preparation.

CHAPTER 14

The Plains Villagers: The Washita River

Robert E. Bell

Introduction

Identified sites of the Washita River people are located in the central section of Oklahoma, chiefly along the Washita River valley and its tributaries (Figure 14.1). A few sites of this period are known along the South Canadian River valley, but the watershed separating the North and South Canadian rivers appears to mark the northern boundary of the settlement area. This area falls into two physiographic regions, the Western Sandstone Hills and the Central Redbed Plains. The southern margins are roughly marked by the Arbuckle and Wichita mountains, and the eastern edge abuts the Eastern Sandstone Cuesta Plains, an area dominated by the Post oak–Blackjack Cross Timbers. The western margins are less well known but appear to be marked by the Western Redbed Plains. It should be noted that surface finds from sites outside this area suggest related materials, but these are poorly known and are not included herein.

The altitude of the area ranges from 600 m in the west to 300 m in the east. The rock outcrops are generally red shales or red sandstones of Permian age. The rocks are not hard, and they erode to produce a slightly rolling plain with few escarpments. The surface slopes from west to east, and the streams follow this slope, cutting shallow narrow channels and ridges into the broad flat-topped plain. Local relief is low and would rarely exceed 30 m from the stream bed to the crest of adjacent hills.

The Washita River valley shows evidence of several stages of alluviation. Terrace remnants of at least two old floodplains occur at about 1.5 and 7.6 m

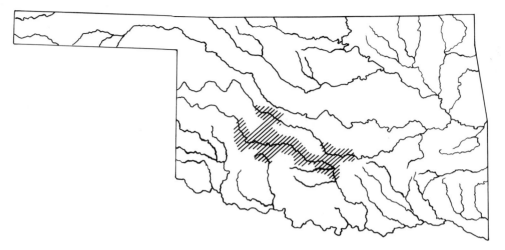

Figure 14.1   Washita River focus

above the present floodplain. The present floodplain varies from 0.8 to 3.2 km in width, with a total valley width ranging from 3.2 to 9.6 km. There are numerous meander scars and oxbow lakes which mark channel changes over the years.

The soils of the area are predominantly sandy and occur in considerable depth. The soils are of medium to great fertility, and they support a varied agricultural economy today. The climate is temperate with an average rainfall of about 76 cm per year. This average, however, is misleading as the range is considerable. Chickasha, for example, which has an average annual precipitation of 78.25 cm, has a recorded minimum of 41.47 and a maximum of 120.52 cm (McKay 1953:83). The rainfall is erratic, with drought or violent storms very typical, especially during the growing season. The rainfall, moreover, is likely to be localized, with heavy rains in some areas and drought conditions in others.

The mean annual temperature ranges from 14.5 to 17.8° C within the area, but it varies a great deal during the seasons. August is the hottest month, and temperatures may reach 49.9° C, with an average of 28.4° C. Winter temperatures may go as low as −26.1° C, but this is unusual as the January average is 4.17° C. The growing season average is 120 days per year. The last killing frost in the spring usually occurs in mid-April, whereas the earliest killing frost of the fall occurs in the early half of October. These will vary considerably, however, from year to year.

The natural resources in terms of rocks and minerals are not especially favorable, particularly from the aboriginal point of view, because flints or cherts for tools are limited to small pebbles or gravels. These can be found in alluvial deposits throughout the area but they tend not to be of good knapping quality. The majority of stone outcrops are sandstones or shales, although limestone and granite are available along the southern fringes of the area. Other items available include asphalt, clays, gypsum, various copper minerals (such as malachite and chalcocite), magnetite, hematite, and limonite (McKay 1953).

The plant and animal resources today are considerably modified, as a consequence of white settlement. Early settlers have stated that the region was formerly typical tall-grass prairie with timber limited essentially to the bottom lands and along stream courses. Vegetational zones include the Mixedgrass Eroded Plains, Tallgrass Prairie, and Post oak–Blackjack Forest types (Duck and Fletcher 1943). The various ecological zones represented offered a variety of plant and associated animal resources for the aboriginal populations. Faunal resources were diverse and debris from site excavations suggest the extent to which these were utilized by the Washita River people.

Radiocarbon Dates and Physical Anthropology

There are six radiocarbon dates available for Washita River sites, and these are presented in Table 14.1. The date from Lee II, however, is modern and of no value. It is not known if this date resulted from an error in the radiocarbon laboratory or if it was incorrectly identified in the field. The remaining five dates are from three different sites, but the large margin of error on two of the dates renders them less helpful than is desirable. There is clearly the need for additional radiocarbon dates from Washita River sites. The dates do overlap, however, and suggest an occupation ranging from around A.D. 1000 to 1400. It is suggested elsewhere (Bell 1968:8) that the major occupation falls between A.D. 1150 and 1375. One date from McLemore (C-1245) suggests an earlier occupation, however, and this should be reevaluated with reference to site data and possibly additional assays. The date of A.D. 1035 suggests that the McLemore site may shed light upon the transition from Custer to Washita River in western Oklahoma.

The physical type represented by the Washita River people is best known from burials recovered at the McLemore site (Brues 1962). The skeletons exhibit considerable variation, and Brues recognizes three basic types: (1) a Basket Maker-like skull, which is relatively small, narrow, parallel-sided, and fairly high; (2) a more characteristic Plains-type skull having rugged features, a rather low vault, a sloping forehead, strong brow ridges, and a heavy face; (3) a type resembling the round-headed modern Pueblo population of the Southwest. In general, the population tends to be mesocephalic or brachycephalic; it exhibits a long face, the parietal bosses are developed, and the saggital ridge or keel is prominent. There is no suggestion of any skull deformation. The stature for males averages around 169 cm and for females around 155 cm. The group differs from populations studied from eastern Oklahoma, although individual skulls can be duplicated among populations found in the southeastern and south-

Table 14.1

Washita River Radiocarbon Dates

Laboratory number	Site and provenience	Date before present (B.P.)	Date (A.D.) based on 5568 half-life	Date (A.D.) based on 5730 half-life	MASCA corrected date (A.D.)	Reference
WIS-123	Brown site (Gd-1), Test Pit 1, charcoal	700 ± 70	1250	1229	1265 ± 55	Bender et al. 1967:539
M-820	Lacy site (Gv-5), House post, charcoal	800 ± 150	1150	1126	1160 ± 140	J. Miller 1963:117
O-1322	Lee II (Gv-4), Pit 3, Sq. N1-L4, 55-inch depth, charcoal	100 ± 100	1850	Modern	Modern	J. Miller 1963:117
C-1245	McLemore (Wa-5), Feature 4, pit, 10–36 inches, charcoal	950 ± 150	1000	972	1035 ± 155	J. Miller 1963:117
R-829/1	McLemore (Wa-5), Feature 17, pit, 10–24 inches, charcoal	575 ± 50	1375	1358	1350 ± 40	J. Miller 1963:117
R-829/2	McLemore (Wa-5), Grid B, Square S3-R12, 18–24 inches, charcoal	630 ± 55	1320	1301	1315 ± 55	J. Miller 1963:117

western parts of the United States. Obviously, the population representing the Washita River people is not homogeneous in its characteristics, and additional data are needed.

Burial statistics from the McLemore site indicate that survival was difficult and there was a short life expectancy. Approximately 38 individuals out of 100 live births survived to the age of puberty. No skeletons were recovered that represented individuals who had lived beyond age 55, and only 17% of the total population lived beyond age 35. Infant mortality was very high, as 36.5% of the babies died at less than 1 year of age. Two young adult female skeletons have been recovered that were accompanied by the remains of newborn infants, suggesting that death occurred at the time of childbirth. There is the suggestion, however, that females lived longer than the males.

The reasons for this low survival rate are not clear, as the bones do not reflect an especially disease-ridden population. There are no indications of diet deficiency, such as scurvy, which is sometimes indicated among groups farther to the east. There is some evidence of conflict and violent death, but the rugged way of life probably contributed greatly to a short life span.

One skeleton, that of a young girl, shows a deformity of the vertebrae, possibly a result of injury. Mild arthritis is present on some individuals. Tooth wear, tooth decay, and tooth abcesses are common; toothache was apparently a common ailment.

Settlements

The Washita River settlements are all small in size and could be accommodated in an area of from 0.8 to 2.0 hectares. A house count is not possible as only two houses have been excavated, each from a different site, but the occupational areas suggest a small number of structures. The number of burials recovered from two sites, 15 at Grant and 52 at McLemore, also suggests a small number of inhabitants. The distribution of sites indicates a dispersed, almost rural population, living in small-sized villages or hamlets containing from two or three up to a dozen houses and numbering fewer than 100 individuals. The hamlets or farmsteads are dispersed along the Washita River drainage, sometimes separated by several kilometers and at other times clustered together within sight of each other. Although the settlements are small in size, they are numerous and, if contemporary, suggest a relatively dense population as compared with adjacent regions.

These small communities appear to represent permanent base camps or villages located adjacent to a reliable water supply and sandy-loam soils that were easy to cultivate with simple tools. There are indications of occupations at rock-shelters and other localities, suggesting specialized activity sites or resource exploitation areas, but these are not well understood with reference to the presumed base localities. The village locations are characterized by the presence of permanent houses; numerous cache pits or refuse pits; occasional scattered postholes, which suggest arbors, food drying racks, or specialized structures; scattered midden debris; and an associated cemetery. There appears to be no particular village planning other than to comply with the local topography. Although individual burials are sometimes found within the village area, the cemetery is usually located outside the occupational area, but relatively close by.

The known Washita River houses are square or rectangular in shape and are constructed of wood and daub. The interior floor area ranges from 40.87 to 78.0 m^2, indicating a considerable range in house size. Interior features include support posts for the roof, cache or storage pits, a hearth or cooking area, and occasional post holes suggesting internal divisions or special features. Wall construction was formed by upright wooden posts placed about 45 to 75 cm apart, with the intervening areas filled in with sticks, grass, cane, and daub, and the final wall plastered over with clay. The roof was a grass thatch placed on a network of small poles supported by centrally placed interior roof supports. Examples of two house plans are illustrated in Figure 14.2.

Cache pits or storage pits are another common village feature. These are sometimes found within the houses but are more commonly scattered throughout the village area. These are circular, cylindrical pits, ranging from 90 to 150 cm in diameter and from 90 to 150 cm in depth. They were initially used for storage but were eventually abandoned to become a convenient place to dispose of refuse. Although cached materials have been found in such pits, most of them that have been excavated were filled with refuse and midden debris.

Burials placed in small cemetery areas are usually found close to the village area. There appears to be no special planning of the cemetery area because graves sometimes overlap or intrude one upon the other. The dead were placed into a pit-type grave in a flexed or semiflexed position, the body lying in an east–west direction with the head to the east. Single burials are most common although multiple burials are reported. Grave offerings may occur with the burial and usually were placed around the head or around the main body area. Common grave items include pottery vessels, tools or implements, or articles of adornment, such as shell beads. There are some indications that certain objects occur only with males or females, and there are some hints of minor status differences as reflected in burial goods. For example, Burial 34 at the McLemore site was associated with the following items: 1 pottery vessel, 2 long-bone awls or pins, 4 flint knives, 2 mussel shells, a lump of raw clay, and 1 piece of selenite. Another nearby burial of similar age and sex had no associations at all.

Three adult burials found at the McLemore site show evidence of the individuals having been killed by violent action. One young male had been shot by an arrow, the head of which was still imbedded between the vertebrae; and two skeletons, a young adult female and a middle-aged man, had serious skull damage from blows to the head. All three were killed by violent action and were subsequently buried within the local cemetery area.

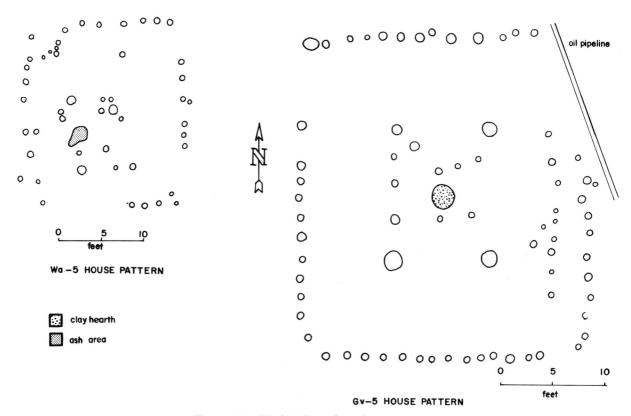

Figure 14.2   Washita River focus house patterns.

Subsistence

Subsistence of the Washita River people is best indicated by refuse and debris recovered from the village middens and refuse pits. From this it is evident that hunting, fishing, gathering, and gardening activities all contributed to the food resources. The proportional role of each, however, has not been evaluated, and it undoubtedly varied from site to site and from year to year. Hunting and horticulture were of primary importance, with fishing and gathering serving to vary the diet or supplement needs in times of emergency.

The identification of animal bones from the sites gives some idea of the game and meat animals. It is not clear, however, when a bone represents the remains of a food animal or that of an animal killed for some other reason, possibly for the skin, the teeth, or for yet some other purpose. Also, small-animal bones, such as those of gophers or moles, may be later intrusions into the site. The bones of food animals were commonly split and broken in order to extract the marrow, but this applied chiefly to the larger animals. Small-animal bones, such as those of the rabbit, are usually not broken; yet many of these smaller animals were certainly killed for food.

Animal bones recovered from the sites include the bison, deer, elk, antelope, wolf, dog, badger, coyote, raccoon, beaver, lynx, opossum, cottontail rabbit, jackrabbit, cotton rat, ground squirrel, gopher, turtles, wild turkey, duck, prairie chicken, and crow. There are, in addition, other bird and small-mammal bones that have not been identified. From the quantity of bones present, it is clear that deer and bison provided the basic meat supply. Elk, antelope, rabbit, turtles, and birds were utilized, but combined they represent less than 10% of the total bone refuse.

Fishing and the gathering of mussels are indicated by the fish bones and shells found at the sites. Several varieties of mussels were collected, and the shells were sometimes used for various utensils or ornaments. The recovery of fish bones varies considerably from site to site, apparently reflecting the local availability, but several kinds of fish bones have been recovered. These include flathead catfish, blue catfish, drum, sucker, and gar. Some of the fish were quite large in size, as vertebrae up to 2.5 cm in diameter are common. Bone fishhooks and the fish gorge indicate hand-line fishing was practiced. No data are available to suggest that these people used fish traps or weirs, nor is there any indication for the use of the harpoon.

The exploitation of the local flora is indicated by recovered plant remains, although this evidence is limited because no extensive flotation samples have been collected. Occasional nutshells such as pecan, hickory, walnut, and piñon have been found, and other plant remains include hackberry, wild cherry, plum, persimmon, Kentucky coffee bean, and *Chenopodium* seeds.

Cultivated plants are known from carbonized samples of corn, beans, and gourds that have been recovered from middens or refuse pits. The location and extent of cultivated areas, however, remain unknown. The sites are situated on terrace deposits characterized by sandy loam soils that could be cultivated easily with primitive agricultural implements. At all known sites, farm land suitable for small-scale cultivation is available close to the village area. Crop production was probably more analogous to gardening than to farming, with each family planting and harvesting according to its own requirements. One has the impression that a subsistence level was maintained, perhaps with great difficulty at many times, but that surplus resources were rare and occurred temporarily only after a rich harvest or successful hunt. The general lack of luxury goods and the absence of specialists suggest a subsistence economy only.

Artifacts

The production of consumer goods such as tools, utensils, and household equipment was more of a handicraft activity than a formal industry. Although some skilled craftsmen undoubtedly existed and may have bartered some surplus, most individuals probably produced their own necessities for daily living.

Stone artifacts are the most common cultural item on Washita River sites. These are made from sedimentary, metamorphic, and igneous rocks, or various siliceous materials such as chert or flint. Articles made from stones lacking a conchoidal fracture, such as sandstone, shale, diorite, or granite, were made by a pecking, grinding, and polishing process with the use of a hard pecking hammer and rubbing stones or abraders. The chipped-stone materials were shaped by percussion flaking done with a hammerstone or by pressure flaking done with a section of bone or antler.

Pecked- and ground-stone items include the milling basin (metate) and mano, the mortar and hammerstone, the cupstone or nut stone, celts, grooved abraders for smoothing arrowshafts or bone tools, perforated sandstone disks, whetstones, and elbow pipes.

Chipped-stone artifacts include a variety of arrowpoints, chiefly Washita and Harrell, small drills or perforators, knives (especially beveled forms), and several kinds of scrapers (typical artifacts are shown in Figure 14.3). Chip debris or specimens represent various stages in manufacture and indicate that all the above artifacts were made at the sites.

Articles made from animal bone or antler are also plentiful and represent a wide variety of tools and implements (Figure 14.4). Numbers of unfinished objects that illustrate the method of manufacture have been found. Large pieces of bone were roughly shaped or trimmed by removing flakes or irregular pieces with a hammerstone. The smoothing of rough areas and the shaping were done with abraders or whetstones. Cutting was done by a sawing technique in which deep grooves were cut or scraped into the bone with a stone or piece of flint. When the cut was deep enough, the bone was broken or snapped along the groove, and the rough edges were ground off. Bones of the bison and deer were preferred, but other animal bones were also used. Certain bones were commonly selected for specific tools, and these were conserved in anticipation of future needs.

Objects made of bone or antler include scapula hoes, bison-skull scoops or hoes, digging-stick tips, deer-jaw sickles, beamers, several types of awls, knives, spatulas, chisels, picks, flakers, drifts, shaft wrenches, notched-bone rasps, scrapers, fishhooks, balls or game pieces, arrow nocks, handles, and ornaments. Of the latter, bird-bone beads, tubes, deer-toe tinklers, and pendants are most common, although antler pieces that suggest headgear decorations are present. Bone was obviously an important resource that was easily available and met many needs of the community. Individual specimens often show indications of resharpening, modification after damage, or a high polish from extensive use.

Clay was utilized chiefly for daub and ceramics although other uses are indicated. Clay daub was used as a plaster or as a caulking in house construction, and some storage pits appear to have been lined with a thin clay layer or plastered wall. Some fire hearths have baked clay areas, but it is not clear if they were specially prepared by adding clay or if the burning simply baked the

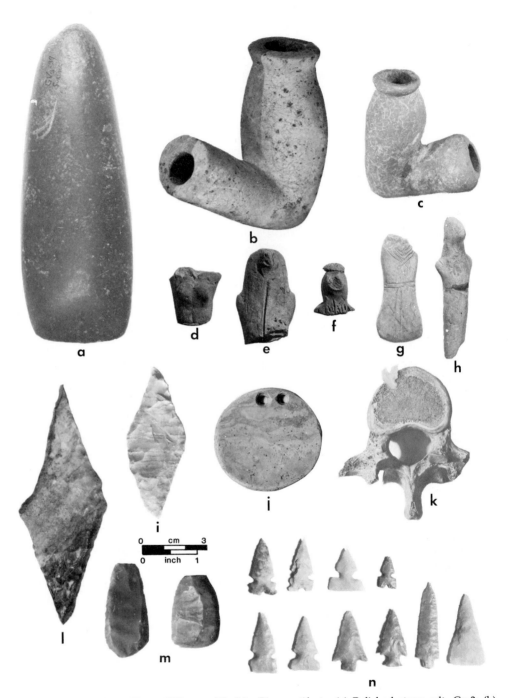

Figure 14.3 Southern Plains Villagers: Washita River artifacts. (a) Polished stone celt, Gv-3; (b) stone pipe, Wa-5; (c) stone pipe, Wa-5; (d) clay figurine, torso section, Wa-5; (e) clay figurine, head and shoulder section, Wa-5; (f) clay figurine, head with topknot, Wa-5; (g) clay figurine with ornamentation, Gv-2; (h) clay figurine, Gv-2; (i) alternate beveled flint knife, Wa-5; (j) conch-shell ornament, Wa-5; (k) projectile point imbedded in first lumbar vertebrae of a young female adult, aged around 24 years, Cu-27. This burial also included an 8-month-old fetus. (l) Alternate beveled flint knife, Gv-2; (m) two flint end-scrapers, Gv-2; (n) assorted projectile points, Gv-3.

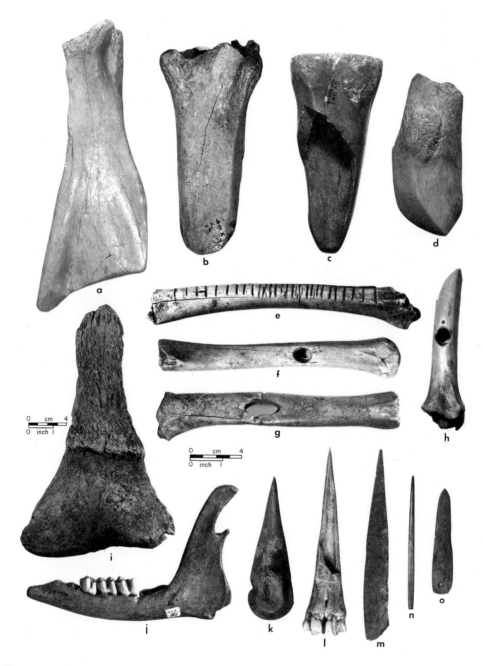

Figure 14.4 Southern Plains Villagers: Washita River bone artifacts. (a) Bison-scapula hoe, Gv-2; (b) bison-tibia digging-stick tip, Wa-5; (c) bison-tibia digging-stick tip, Gv-1; (d) bone knife or fleshing tool, Wa-5; (e) grooved deer-bone shaft, Gv-2; (f) bone arrow-shaft wrench, Gv-2; (g) bone arrow-shaft wrench, Gv-3; (h) broken arrow-shaft wrench, Gv-4; (i) bison-horn core hoe, Gv-2; (j) deer-jaw sickle (note string groove), Gv-4; (k) bone awl or perforator, Wa-5; (l) bone awl or perforator, Gv-2; (m) flat bone awl or perforator, Gv-2; (n) bone awl or pin, Gv-2; (o) perforated flat bone perforator, Wa-5.

317

surrounding soil. Pottery, however, represents the most abundant clay product found on the sites.

Ceramics

Suitable clays for making pots can be found along the stream banks close to most of the sites. No evidence of digging or exploitation of clay deposits is now known. Certain exposed clays were surely preferred, however, for either their quality or convenience of access, because rolls or loaves of raw clay are sometimes found at the sites. The raw clay is generally of rather poor quality and requires the addition of a tempering material before it can be shaped and baked to produce a satisfactory container. Various materials were added to the clay as tempering; these materials include crushed mussel shell, sand, crumbled sandstone or limestone, caliche, crushed bone, or other angular particles. Individual sherds or vessels may have only one or may have several of these items added to the clay. The assortment of materials used for tempering the clay suggests that the craftsmen utilized whatever was handy or readily available rather than that they were influenced by any particular cultural preference.

The pottery was made by a hand-shaping process using the technique of adding a ring of clay around the circumference of the vessel to build up the walls. Broken sherds showing poor welds suggest that this was sometimes done by the use of short strips that formed segments of the ring section. Each ring section was added one at a time around the pot; there was no overlapping of a continuous ropelike coil of clay. The vessels often show rather rough interiors as well as finger impressions left by the potter in binding the clay rings together. The exterior was smoothed by rubbing, and the tool marks commonly are evident. The vessels and sherds show considerable variation in the quality of the pottery. Some examples are made of well-kneaded clay and have been carefully shaped and smoothed whereas others appear to have been poorly mixed and show more careless execution. The paddle-and-anvil technique was also used in binding the clay pieces together, and the specimens exhibiting this usually show the cord impressions from a cord-wrapped paddle on their exterior.

The actual firing or baking process is not known, but an open fire must have been used because the vessels are unevenly baked and show irregularities in color from uneven heat. The thicker pieces are frequently badly fired and, when the tempering is especially abundant, they crumble and break very easily.

The Washita River people produced a variety of vessel forms: globular and vase-shaped jars, deep bowls, bottles, and miniature vessels. Other forms such as a human-effigy bowl, bowls with animal heads attached to the rim, and seed jars have been found, but these are rare and probably represent trade wares. The most popular vessel is a globular or vase-shaped jar with a rounded or flattened

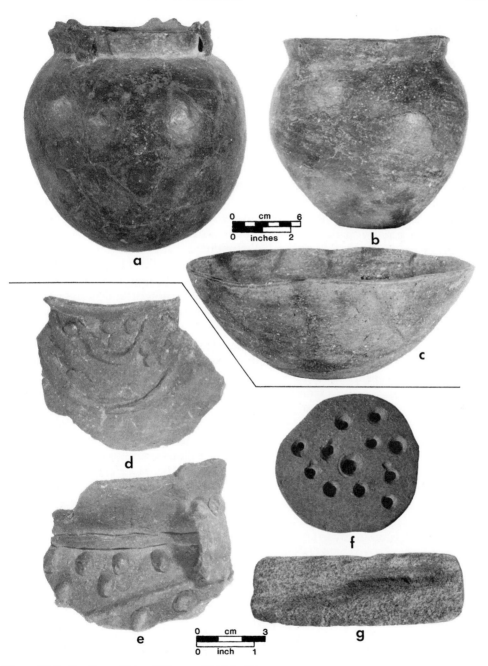

Figure 14.5 Southern Plains Villagers: Washita River ceramic artifacts. (a) Pottery jar with four handles, Gv-2; (b) pottery jar, Gv-2; (c) pottery bowl, Gv-2; (d,e) pottery rim-sherds with appliqué strips and pellets, Gv-3. (f) pottery perforated disk, Wa-5. (g) sandstone grooved abrader, Gv-3.

base. The typical base is a small, flat disk-type base, although some conical bases occur; vessels with this latter type of base will not, of course, sit upright without supports (Figure 14.5).

Pottery decoration is minimal. Usually the vessels are a plain-surfaced ware, or, less commonly, cord marked, and of a varying brown or gray color. Handles are present, and they commonly occur in groups of four spaced equally around the neck or rim. The handles were riveted to the vessel wall in the rim or neck area. Two lip tabs were frequently placed immediately above the handle, projecting vertically above the rim. Decoration, when present, is usually limited to small conical pellets of clay that were stuck upon the surface to form a row or ring of nodes around the neck of the vessel. Additional fillets or strips of clay were sometimes also added beneath the nodes in simple garland or V-shaped patterns. Painting, incising, or engraving appears only on occasional trade sherds. The pottery appears to have been primarily a utility ware, produced simply for service and without embellishment.

Other clay products include perforated disks (shaped from sherds), clay elbow pipes, figurines, and some unidentified objects. Among the latter are small barrel-shaped cups or containers, about 7.5 cm in height and with a corncob-roughened exterior. In these cup-shaped objects, the clay is poorly prepared, often without tempering, so that it breaks easily. The walls are very thick, and the interior sometimes shows a red or reddish-yellow stain. These objects have a small capacity and their use remains unknown, although a paint cup appears to be a reasonable assumption.

Crude human figurines were also made from clay. The bright red clay usually lacks tempering particles and is poorly baked; consequently, whole specimens are scarce. The figures are simply done with the shoulders and head areas emerging from a cylindrical body. Details of arms and legs are usually not indicated, but the head and torso are sometimes more carefully defined. Female breasts, head ornaments or hair dressing, and incisions or punctates to mark body decoration are sometimes present. Both males and females are represented in these figurines, which range in size from 5 to 15 cm in length. The purpose of the figurines is not known although Schmitt and Toldan (1953) suggested that they were children's toys.

Other irregular or broken fragments of baked clay have sometimes been found, but these remain unidentified.

Other Material Remains

Information on textiles, matting, or basketry is essentially lacking except for cord impressions on sherds. Such impressions indicate cordage of varying diameter and simple plaiting of loosely woven fabric.

Direct evidence for the use of wood, leather, and hides is also very meager although the presence of scrapers, bone beamers, awls, and similar tools suggests their presence.

Shell was utilized in a minor way for a number of purposes. Mussel shells were plentiful in the streams; not only was the meat undoubtedly eaten but the shell was used for various tools or ornaments. Mussel shells frequently show wear along the edges indicating use as a scoop, spoon, or scraper; some notched examples could have served as shredders for obtaining fibers. Crushed shell was used as tempering for pottery, and small fragments were cut and shaped into beads or small ornaments. Flat disk beads and short tubular beads were made of shell; also small ornaments and carefully shaped pieces appear to have been inlays for decorating wood or other perishable artifacts. Small snail shells and *Olivella* shells were cut and prepared for beads. Burial associations indicated that beads were used not only for necklaces but that they were also attached to garments for decoration.

Other natural materials besides stones used for tools or implements include hematite, limonite, selenite, steatite, and asphaltum. Pieces of hematite and limonite clearly provided raw materials for pigments, and asphaltum was certainly used as an adhesive. The use for selenite and steatite remains uncertain at this time.

Exotic Goods

Trade or contact with surrounding areas is indicated by the presence of items that were not locally available. These include raw materials such as flint, and consumer goods such as pottery or piñon nuts. With the exception of flint, items obtained from surrounding areas are not plentiful and are usually limited to one or two examples at each of the sites. Items that may have been traded to individuals from other areas include hides or skins, bone tools or implements, wood (osage orange) or wooden objects, hematite, pottery, asphaltum, and food stuffs. Articles received by the Washita River people include various flints, steatite, selenite, seashell ornaments, earspools, and piñon nuts. The sources for various materials suggest that exchange or contacts were chiefly east and west, probably reflecting the natural routes furnished by the stream valleys.

Flint for the manufacture of arrowheads, knives, or scrapers is the most abundant import. The local sources were chiefly small pebbles; consequently, flint of good quality and suitable for large artifacts, such as beveled knives, was in demand. Debitage and finished artifacts are present from three identified quarry sources: the Frisco outcrops in Pontotoc County, the Kay County quarries near Hardy in northern Oklahoma, and the Alibates quarries near Amarillo, Texas. Some finished flint artifacts may also have been acquired through trade, but the chip debris suggests that most of them were made locally from raw materials.

Pottery was also acquired from surrounding areas and is represented by whole vessels and sherds, although these trade items are not common. That the items are actually trade items and not locally made copies is indicated by differences in the paste and tempering and by the quality of the objects themselves. One of the most interesting vessels is a human effigy bowl (Pillaert 1963:Plate 16), which was found with an infant burial at the McLemore site. This vessel form is most similar to examples from the Tennessee–Cumberland area of Tennessee, and it is unique for Oklahoma. The right leg of the effigy had been broken and was lost prior to placement in the grave; this is indicated by the broken surface, which was worn and partially smoothed. The vessel was apparently highly valued even though damaged.

Occasional sherds having a red slip and incised or engraved designs were derived from peoples living in eastern Oklahoma. Some cord-marked sherds appear to have come from the west, although some wares thus decorated were made locally.

Other items of foreign origin include a conch-shell ornament and a fragment from a decorated stone earspool. These objects were apparently obtained from the Caddoan neighbors to the east. Selenite, *Olivella* shells for beads, and piñon nuts were brought in from the west, possibly from the Custer focus or Antelope Creek peoples of the High Plains region. Trade and exchange, although represented by a few miscellaneous artifacts, do not appear to have played a very important role other than in the case of flint.

Speculations

The origins of the Washita River population remain uncertain at this time. Furthermore, it is not entirely clear when they departed from the Washita River valley, where they went, or what actual historic population is represented. It appears most likely that they are ancestors of the Wichita and related tribes that occupied the southern Plains region in historic times, but this supposition requires more supporting evidence than is now available if it is to be considered a conclusion. More dates are needed to control better the time factors, and additional excavations should be done to answer specific questions relating to the problems involved.

According to our best evidence for dating, the Washita River people occupied the region between A.D. 1150 and 1375. Earlier and later dates may be forthcoming, but the five radiocarbon assays now available suggest this time bracket. By A.D. 1100 or 1150 the Washita River people were already settled along the Washita River valley. Their way of life reflects a cultural adaptation to a prairie–plains environment that was already established. This implies adaptation to the plains environment prior to the above dates. This may have taken place in the Washita River valley area or elsewhere, but at present it is not clear where this might have occurred.

The question of origins for the Washita River people needs to be considered. One older complex found in central Oklahoma, known as the *Pruitt complex* (Barr 1966c), appears to date around the period from A.D. 700 to 800. This complex has been considered, largely upon the basis of ceramics, as a late Plains Woodland manifestation derived from the east. The Pruitt complex does share some features with Washita River, however, and might well represent the ancestor of the Washita River population, but the Pruitt complex is too poorly known at this time to evaluate this potential relationship.

The Custer focus, which lies to the west of the Washita River area, offers another possibility. Radiocarbon dates for the Custer focus are available from two locations, the Mouse and Edwards II sites, and suggest an occupation ranging from A.D. 800 to 1000. These dates suggest that at least a portion of the Custer focus precedes the Washita River focus in time, and that it may be ancestral to the Washita River assemblages. There are many similarities between the Custer focus materials and Washita River, and Lintz (1974) and Hofman (1975a) have suggested that the Custer material represents an early phase of the Washita River development. Although this may be the case, it overlooks potential ancestral relationships with the Pruitt complex that was present to the east of the Washita River area. Because both the Custer focus to the west, and the Pruitt complex to the east, share characteristics with Washita River villages, perhaps both contribute to its development.

The abandonment of central Oklahoma by the Washita River peoples around A.D. 1400 is not understood at the present time. Climatic changes or the intrusion of other populations derived from the west may have been important factors. We do find archaeological sites in western Oklahoma that appear to have been occupied during the period from A.D. 1400 to 1600, and that appear to represent unidentified peoples. Such sites as Edwards (Bk-2), Taylor (Bk-8), and Little Deer (Cu-10) are distinctly different from Washita River, and the suggestion has been previously made that some of these may represent Kiowa or Apache groups that were moving onto the Plains from the Southwest. Because these groups appear in the archaeological record at about the same time that the Washita River people abandoned their area, this suggestion merits consideration and further research.

It is also during this time period (A.D. 1400 to 1600) that one finds indications of increased Plains influences among the Caddoan occupations in the Arkansas River valley of eastern Oklahoma. Whether this represents an increased cultural interaction or an eastward retreat of the Washita River peoples into the Arkansas valley area remains unknown.

Identification of the Washita River people with known historic tribes remains uncertain, although I favor identification with the Wichita and related tribes. The Wichita were in the Great Bend area of the Arkansas River around A.D. 1540, and Wedel (1959) reports other archaeological sites in Kansas that could well represent a transitional period from Washita River to Wichita. This continuum in development, however, also requires further research and evaluation.

Reference Note

One group of Southern Plains Villagers that occupied central Oklahoma around 600 to 800 years ago is identified as the Washita River focus. A summary paper on these people was published by Bell in 1973 and no major fieldwork has been done in the region since that time, although some comparative studies have appeared. Our overall knowledge about the Washita River people remains quite limited as it has not received adequate attention. The most extensively excavated sites are McLemore and Grant, but the other known sites have been limited to small tests or surface collections.

Current published information about individual sites includes the following: Brown site (Bell 1953a; Schmitt and Toldan 1953; M. Phillips 1975); Clements (Cd-57) (Saunders 1974a); Duncan–Wilson rockshelter (Lawton 1968); Grant (Sharrock 1961; Ahshapanek and Burns 1960); Lacy (Oakes 1953; Hofman 1976a); Lee I (Schmitt 1950; Richards 1971); Lee II (Pillaert 1962); Max Thomas (Lawton 1958a); McLemore (Pillaert 1963; Brues 1962; Lopez 1970); Ross (Hofman 1971); Van Schuyver (Sharrock 1959a); Wa-4 (Carley 1974); and Willingham (Sharrock 1959b, Kerr 1964). Other articles that deal with Washita River materials or their relationships to surrounding areas include those by Bell (1971), M. K. Davis (1965), Evans (1951, 1952, 1958), R. S. Hall (1952, 1953), Hofman (1975a, 1976b), Jordan (1960), Lintz (1974), Troike (1955), S. Vehik (1976), and Wyckoff (1961a).

CHAPTER 15

The Plains Villagers: Antelope Creek

Christopher Lintz

Introduction

Along major drainage systems of the Southern Plains in Texas and Oklahoma panhandles are distinctive late prehistoric sites that are designated the *Antelope Creek focus*. Although the greatest density and the largest known sites are located near the Alibates "flint" quarries on the Canadian River in Texas, other closely affiliated sites have been found in Roger Mills and Beckham counties in western Oklahoma, and Beaver and Texas counties in the Oklahoma Panhandle. The culture's boundaries roughly coincide with the High Plains physiographic province within an area drained by the Canadian and North Canadian rivers (Figure 15.1).

Antelope Creek Taxonomy

Despite early excavations and surveys along Wolf Creek and the Canadian River between 1907 and 1921, the first attempt to organize numerous sites into a cultural unit was by Moorehead (1931). Most cultural designations applied throughout the 1930s and 1940s were merely terms of convenience that lacked both an explicit classificatory system and a rigorous and precise definition of the culture unit. Many had descriptive, geographics, or implied generic relations in their names. Thus a term such as *Stone Slab House Culture* (Holden 1931:43)

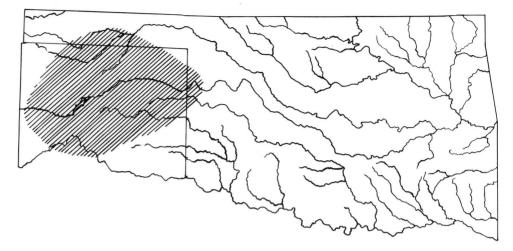

Figure 15.1 The Antelope Creek area.

describes one of the distinctive features of the manifestation; *Texas Panhandle Culture* (Moorehead 1931:122), *Canadian Culture* (Holden 1933:39), *Panhandle–Canadian Culture* (Holden 1932:504), and *Panhandle Culture* (Moorehead 1931:128; Holden 1932:39; Lowrey 1932; G. H. Haynes 1932; C. S. Johnson 1939) all geographically place the culture unit; whereas *Post Basketmaker Culture* (Studer 1931a), and *Texas Panhandle Pueblo Culture* (Studer 1952, 1955) imply cultural affiliations with groups to the west.

Sayles was the first to employ an explicit taxonomic system. Following the Southwestern Gladwin–Gladwin Taxonomic system, he proposed the term *Panhandle phase* and defined the distinctive traits (Sayles 1935). Despite major excavations at Antelope Creek and Alibates, few reports were published during the late 1930s and early 1940s and Sayles's term was never widely adopted.

In 1946, Krieger synthesized the manifestation and employed the Midwest Taxonomic system used in defining other Plains culture units. Noting widespread differences, he postulated that several regional variants would eventually be recognized. Krieger proposed the terms *Panhandle aspect* for the cultural manifestation throughout the Texas and Oklahoma panhandles, and explicitly defined one subdivision, the *Antelope Creek focus* for the Texas Panhandle. The type site was Antelope Creek 22, which had a large contiguous multiroom structure. Krieger's terminology replaced all previous culture constructs.

In Oklahoma, a large site on the Stamper ranch was excavated in 1933 to 1934, and although unpublished was well known in professional circles. It was reported to be different from Antelope Creek focus sites but its cultural affiliation remained unclear for many years (Clements 1945:68). The *Cimarron focus* was proposed as the Oklahoma counterpart to Antelope Creek (J. B. Griffin 1946:85). However, lacking description of distinguishing characteristics, this term was never accepted.

Description of Stamper site architecture and artifacts appeared 16 years after excavation. Watson (1950a) used Stamper as the type site for defining the *Optima focus* of the Panhandle aspect. Stamper differed from Antelope Creek 22 in architecture and minor artifactual details. The majority of rooms at Stamper were individual unit structures scattered across a broad terrace. Watson postulated that the Optima focus was geographically separate and perhaps somewhat earlier than the Antelope Creek focus.

Salvage excavations in the Sanford Reservoir, Texas, during the 1960s cast doubt on the validity of a geographical distinction between Antelope Creek and Optima foci. Excavations at three sites with single-unit structures led Duffield (1964b) to question the architectural differences of the manifestations. Subsequent excavations at 41-Pt-8, 41-Pt-25, and 41-Mo-7 forced Green (1967:187) to expand the Antelope Creek definition to include single-room dwelling sites.

At the same time, excavations at the Roy Smith site in Oklahoma disclosed a large contiguous room structure that dated earlier than the Stamper site (Schneider 1969). Clearly the temporal and geographical distinctions in architecture between Antelope Creek and Optima were invalid. Instead of abolishing the Optima focus and utilizing the expanded Antelope Creek focus designation, Schneider (1969:176) suggested that both foci terms be dropped and Krieger's broader Panhandle aspect be retained for sites in both areas. In essence, the Panhandle aspect would have no defined focus subdivisions.

Recently the Panhandle aspect has been revived and modified to include the Apishapa focus in contrast with the Antelope Creek focus (Campbell 1969, 1976). The Apishapa of southeastern Colorado and northeastern New Mexico shares the use of stone-slab house construction and other generalized Plains Village traits. However, many architectural and artifactual differences exist on the specific level (Campbell 1976; Lintz 1974, 1976b, 1978b, 1978c).

In this chapter, the Panhandle aspect is considered to have two geographically and culturally distinct foci subdivisions: Apishapa and Antelope Creek. The Antelope Creek focus concept used herein follows Green's (1967) expanded definition and includes sites in Oklahoma that were formerly considered part of the Optima focus.

Community and Settlement Patterns

Architecture within the Antelope Creek focus is distinctly different from any other Plains Village complex. The use of stone-slab wall foundations frequently permits observations on community patterns even before sites are excavated. Unfortunately the community pattern is quite complex and shows a wide variation in house styles. Sites can range from single-room dwellings to villages containing more than 35 rooms. Stamper, Handley, Alibates 28 Unit II, and Cottonwood Ruins are large villages consisting mainly of freestanding one-room buildings; whereas Roy Smith, Tarbox, Saddleback, Alibates 28 Unit I, and Antelope Creek 22 have contiguous multiroom structures. Saddleback and Alibates 22 respectively contain 33 and 25 rooms in a single structure.

Antelope Creek structures also display a wide range of variation and size. Five basic room patterns have been recognized on the basis of shape, size, and co-association of interior features (Figure 15.2).

Room Pattern 1 is characterized by a large (12.6–60.3-m^2 area), semisubterranian rectangular room with an eastward extended vestibule averaging 2.6 m long by 0.7 m wide. At Antelope Creek 22, Alibates 28, and Coetas Ruin, intact roofs over the vestibules indicate that the entry clearance was only 0.7 m high. The central portion of the floor extending from the east to west walls is depressed 22 cm below the adjacent floor benches. However, the width of the benches is more consistent (1.71 ± 0.18 m) than the width of the central floor channel (1.83 ± 0.72 m). Interior features are associated with the different floor surfaces. The floor channel contains a central hearth and associated ash pits, an altar or raised platform along or recessed into the west wall, and an entry step and entry columns along the east wall. The floor bench may contain corner bins

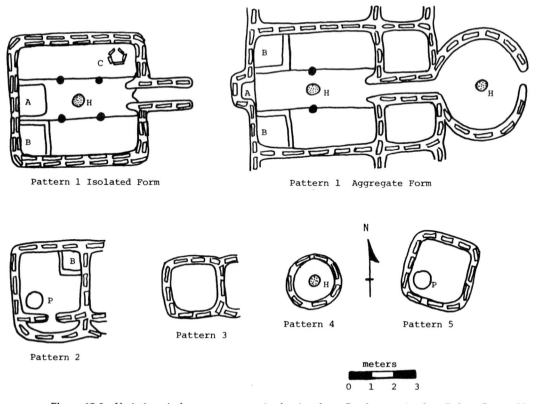

Figure 15.2 Variations in house structures in the Antelope Creek area. A, altar; B, bin; C, cist; H, hearth; P, pit.

and storage cists or pits. Collars around hearths, raised rims along floor bench edges, raised altar platforms, bin walls, depressed channels, elevated vestibule openings, entry sills, and steps all serve to segregate materials from discrete activity areas. Many rooms have four interior support posts along the edges of the channel, but in general a pair of interior posts are added for every 14 m^2 of floor space. The walls are estimated to be about 1.9 m tall. The roof form is uncertain, but flat or hipped are the most-common postulated forms.

Room Pattern 1 occasionally forms the dominant unit in a larger aggregation of rooms and is thought to be the core of a household cluster. The complex configuration of large contiguous structures at Tarbox Ruin, Antelope Creek 22, and Alibates 28 (Unit I), predominantly represent the repetitous placement of multiple household clusters in a north–south line. In addition to the dominant room, the most-common aggregate form includes smaller (2.4–7.2-m^2 area) storage rooms flanking the vestibule entrance, and a large (6.7–18.7 m^2) circular or rectangular anteroom at the east end of the vestibule. Access to these smaller rooms can be gained from the vestibule, other small rooms, or from outside the structure. Passage between small rooms is gained through ground-level doorways or upper wall openings. At Alibates 28 Unit I, midden debris was added to the small storage rooms in order to raise the floor levels above the top of the extended vestibule.

Room Pattern 2 consists of large (7–10-m^2 area) rectangular room with a single small (1–4.5-m^2 area) narrow room placed to the south. Interior features are limited to occasional storage pits and perhaps storage bins. Wall gaps between rooms indicate interior ground-level doorways, but exterior access may have involved upper wall openings. Several rooms may occur together as a contiguous aggregate separate from Room Pattern 1 structures. However, both patterns may occur at the same site.

Room Pattern 3 is a small (2–12-m^2 area) circular or rectangular structure with stone-slab walls and earthen floors. Interior features and ground-level entryways are absent. This pattern often occurs as an isolated unit or rarely in pairs at sites with isolated Pattern 1 rooms. The size is similar to the storage rooms flanking the vestibules in the aggregate form at Room Pattern 1. Most may have served similar functions.

Room Pattern 4 consists of a small (2.6–4.8-m^2 area) circular structure with stone-slab walls and a hearth either centrally located or against the east wall. These isolated units occur at small sites that often lack Pattern 1 rooms. The size range of these rooms is considerably smaller than the circular-shaped antechambers associated with Room Pattern 1.

Room Pattern 5 is a small (5.5–8.5-m^2 area) rectangular isolated structure with an interior bell- or basin-shaped storage pit near one corner. This pattern occurs at sites with isolated Pattern 1 rooms. The storage pit makes this room pattern distinct from the storage rooms flanking the vestibules in the Pattern 1 aggregate form.

A further departure from traditional Plains Village architecture is the frequent use of vertically oriented stone slabs that act as adobe wall footings. Stone-slab foundations were predominantly used regardless of structure size or form. The aggregate form of Pattern 1 may have a single or double row of stone slabs as a foundation upon which alternating layers of adobe and horizontal masonry was added. The stones are generally not dressed or carefully placed along and within the walls. Some walls with double slab rows have rubble-filled cores. Other minor variations in wall construction include the use of puddled adobe walls, adobe "blocks," post-reinforced walls, and a combination of posts between the foundation stones.

Storage pits occur within large rectangular rooms or as exterior units. Three types of pits include a flat-bottomed variety with stone-slab walls and floors; a flat or basin variety with stone-slab walls; and a basin-shaped pit that lacks stone. All three types range from 0.6 to 1.8 m in diameter; the basin-shaped pits are usually 0.9–1.2 m deep. Bell-shaped storage pits are present inside Pattern 5 rooms at Alibates Ruin 28.

The village layout can also be variable. In a few instances, architectural layout is confined by spatial limitations imposed by topography. The contiguous-room buildings at Saddleback and Arrowhead Peak ruins nearly fill all available mesa-top ground. However, space was not a limiting factor for contiguous-room structures at Antelope Creek 22, Alibates 28 Unit I, Tarbox, Coetas, and Roy Smith sites. Room placement at most sites seem largely unplanned and rambling. Even at large contiguous-room sites, planning is limited to individual household aggregate units that seem to be strung together in an accretionary fashion. None of the large contiguous-room sites shows consideration of the entire building configuration. At other sites, isolated-room buildings may occur at irregular intervals along terrace edges. The houses are not placed around a common plaza or communal area.

The possibility of warfare in Antelope Creek sites, as indicated by numerous burned structures, a few inaccessible mesa-top sites, a pile of 11 skulls inside a burned house at the Footprint site, and an occasional arrowpoint embedded in human bone (Eyerly 1907) adds dimension to the settlement and community pattern picture. However, no site has reported ditchworks and palisade fortifications. Except for burned structures, most sites do not show evidence of hostilities; the burning may merely reflect local mortuary customs. Certainly the numerous small and large sites with dispersed structures suggests peaceful conditions during a portion of the Antelope Creek florescence.

No intensive survey of the Panhandle region has specifically examined Antelope Creek settlement patterns. Most architectural sites occur on first and second terraces above floodplains along major river drainages. Little is known about sites along small tributaries or on the upland Plains; late prehistoric campsites are occasionally reported. The relationship between large and small sites remains to be explored; they seem to be contemporary with each other. Seasonality studies based on Antelope Creek faunal collections suggest that some small sites with isolated circular rooms, such as Roper and Pickett, were occupied during the summer and possibly represent specialized field huts. Other differences in site size may reflect hamlet–farmstead relationships.

Economy

The economy is based directly on a hunting–gathering–horticultural subsistence strategy which may have been augmented indirectly by trade with adjacent peoples. Hunting activities focus on bison, antelope, and deer that primarily inhabit the grassy High Plains uplands. Most bones from large herbivores have been intentionally broken to extract marrow and bone grease for consumption and cosmetics. Smaller mammals consumed include rabbits, prairie dogs, ground squirrels, pocket gophers, badgers, coyotes, raccoons, bobcats, and wood rats. Most inhabit the edge breaks and grassy upland environs. The upland playas and bottomland sloughs and creeks provided waterfowl (ducks, geese, swans), turtles, frogs, fish, and mussels. These aquatic animals contributed little to the total dietary intake but certainly provided culinary variety.

Evidence for domesticated animals includes occasional dog bones, but it is not certain whether they were consumed. The absence of dog burials suggests that they were not highly revered pets. Turkey remains have not been identified in osteological samples. The mention of turkeys in some early reports may reflect modern faunal resources rather than identification of archaeological remains. There is no evidence that turkeys were raised or eaten by Antelope Creek peoples.

Floral products collected and consumed have been more difficult to recover and identify. Noncultigen remains include acorn, hackberry, mesquite, grasses, wild buckwheat, cattail stems, plums, persimmons, prickly pear cactus, and Indian mallow. Most were obtained along the river drainages and breaks regions.

The contribution of horticultural products to the diet is also difficult to assess. Domesticated plants include 8-, 10-, and 12-row cobs of pop or small flint corn and "Southern Plains–Pima–Papago–Basketmaker" corn, squash, or pumpkin, and beans. The abundance of tibia digging-sticks and scapula hoe-blades at most sites suggests that cultigens were locally grown rather than obtained through trade. No prehistoric fields or water control systems have been recognized in the Panhandle region, but their use is strongly suspected.

Industries and Arts

The Antelope Creek artifact assemblage is a main indicator that the peoples are culturally related to Plains groups rather than to Puebloan peoples (Figure 15.3). Many artifact types have counterparts in Apishapa, Washita River, and Upper Republican assemblages, yet there are subtle differences that significantly separate Antelope Creek from these other complexes.

Chipped-stone artifacts are abundant. Most are made of local Alibates "flint."

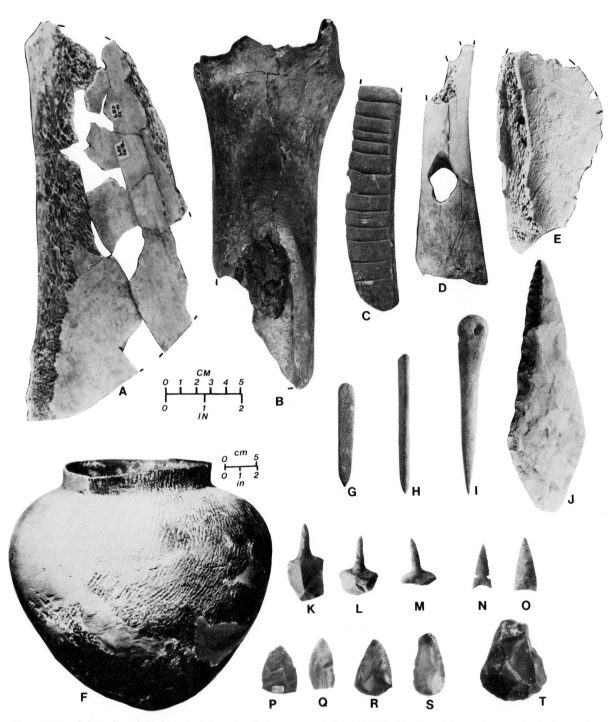

Figure 15.3 Selected artifacts from Antelope Creek focus sites. A, hoe; B, tibia digging-stick tip; C, rasp; D, shaft straightener; E, squash knife; F, cordmarked jar; G–I, awls; J, diamond-beveled knife; K–M, drills; N,O, points; P–T, scrapers.

The predominant projectile points are small unnotched and side-notched forms, although larger corner-notch "dart" points occur at most sites in small numbers. Bifacially flaked knives include ovate-to-diamond-shaped alternately beveled knives and, more rarely, corner-notched or stem-hafted knives. Side- and end-scrapers are plentiful; two distinctive forms are thick "keeled" end-scrapers, and thin triangular "guitar pick" scrapers. Drills and reamers include flake base, expanding base and T-base forms. Chipped axes and picks are scarce. Many sites contain large bifacially shaped core blanks of Alibates and caches of flake blanks and tools.

Pecked- and ground-stone artifacts are more limited. Small oval, one-handed manos and grinding basin fragments are common at most sites. Many specimens show heavy battering and may have been systematically broken. Bedrock mortars occur at some sites, but pestles have yet to be reported. Hammerstones are common and were used to manufacture and maintain chipped-stone and bone tools and to extract marrow and grease from food bones. Awl sharpeners are usually amorphous nodules of abrasive stone with one or more irregular grooves. They contrast with the finely made rectangular shaft smoothers that sometimes occur in paired sets. Siltstone and red argillite elbow pipes occur in small numbers at most sites. The bowls are usually barrel-shaped with a thin, slightly flaring lip that occasionally is incised. Green-stone celts are extremely rare and may represent trade items.

Bone artifacts produce the greatest range of artifact types. Bison scapula were manufactured into hoes and squash knives. The hoes have been roughly shaped by percussion and have the entire glenoid area and spine removed. Bison-tibia digging-sticks are twice as common as hoes. Most specimens have a socketed hole burned in the end. A wide assortment of awls are present, including rib-edge awls, split-rib awls, splinter awls, and split deer-metapodial awls with and without the head intact. On rare occasions, awls are decorated with dots and straight line incisions. Unique to the complex is a short, bluntly pointed awl or pin with a square cross section. Eyed needles are rare. Another long slender tool has a thin spatulate tip with a rounded end. Grooved and notched bison-rib "rasps" are common, but shaft straighteners are rare. Deer and antelope antlers served as billets and pressure flaking tools. Bone discs and short tubular beads also occur.

Local mussel shells were used as scrapers or spoons. Most wear occurs on the lip, which may be serrated. A major use of shell was for jewelry. Occasionally local mussels were fashioned into pendants, but most shell jewelry was imported; disc beads, *Olivella* beads, columella beads, conch pendants and gorgets, and conus shell tinklers were probably traded into the area from the west.

Ceramic artifacts include a limited range of items. Perforated sherd discs, straight "cloud blower" pipes, and globular clay beads are rarely found, but cordmarked sherds occur at most sites in abundant quantities. The pottery consists of heart-shaped jars with wide mouths. Straight rims are placed vertically or slightly flaring on the broad shoulders of the jars. Most of the vessels are large; a reconstructed vessel from the Two Sisters site has a volume in excess of 17 liters. The vessels are made by loosely coiling sand, mica, or crushed-quartz-tempered clay fillets into rough form and welding them together with a cord-wrapped paddle. The cordmarking is vertically oriented on the rim and upper shoulders, but increasingly overlaps and approaches a checkered pattern near the base. Sometimes the impressions are smoothed over and obliterated.

Decorations occur on less than 3% of sherd samples. When present they are confined primarily to the rim and lip areas. The most common motifs include punctating and diagonal tool impressions on the lip; pinching of the lip–rim juncture; and punctating or finger gouging a single row of dots around the rim. More rarely the upper rim may have a single band of incised chevrons, or the upper body vessel may be incised. Modeling of the vessel is rare, but includes appliqué fillets on the body, undulating and cambered rims, loop handles, or a single horizontally oriented lip tab.

Little is known of wooden artifacts because they are poorly preserved and rarely recovered. Coiled basketry has been found at several sites, and twined and plaited baskets and "woven mats" have been found only at Alibates 28 (Studer 1934:90). Most specimens have been found within houses, but basketry with burials at the Footprint site documents their use as mortuary containers.

The artistic range of expression is also poorly documented. Embellishments of bone tools and ceramic vessels have been briefly mentioned. A red-stone tubular pipe has been recovered with an incised bird design, but it may represent a trade item. Worn and faceted pieces of hematite, limonite, and other paint stones occur at many sites, but the use of paint is poorly understood. One triangular beveled knife from Antelope Creek 22 and several other otherwise unmodified large slabs from storage pits at the Two Sisters site have been coated with red paint. Occasional petroglyphs have been found in direct association with Antelope Creek sites. Human Footprint motifs were found on recessed altar slabs at the Footprint site, and stylized turtle and bison pecked in relief occur on bluffs near Alibates Ruin 28.

Trade, Exchange, and Influence

Examination of trade relationships between Antelope Creek peoples and adjacent groups is hindered by an inability to recognize trade materials equally from all directions. Puebloan trade materials are easily identifiable by their use of exotic materials and distinctive motifs, but similarities in material culture between Antelope Creek and other contemporaneous Plains groups—Washita River, Apishapa, and Upper Republican—make it difficult to recognize trade items from the east and north. Consequently, interactions among various Plains groups has not been as thoroughly examined as that with Southwestern groups.

The single most important resource that Antelope Creek peoples controlled was Alibates agatized dolomite. This choice silaceous material outcrops intermittently as two stratigraphically separate zones within the Permian exposures in the middle of the Texas Panhandle. Some 550 prehistoric quarry pits are visible around an outcrop on Alibates Creek. Although Alibates chert has been used for almost 12,000 years, the presence of large bifacially shaped quarry blanks at distant late prehistoric sites suggests that intensive mining and rough shaping of Alibates trade nodules did not occur on a large-scale basis prior to the Antelope Creek focus. Both finished tools and quarry blank bifaces and flakes were traded with adjacent groups during the late prehistoric. The presence and proportions of Alibates tools and debris in adjacent areas to the west, north, and south may serve as a rough indicator of exchange. However, knappable-size nodules of Alibates occur in Canadian River gravels as far as Arkansas, and caution must be exercised when using Alibates as a trade indicator to the east.

Southwestern trade items have been found in small quantities at most Antelope Creek sites. The classes of trade materials from the Southwest include marine shell artifacts (*Olivella* shell beads, conus tinklers, columella shell beads, conch-shell pendants and gorgets), exotic silaceous materials and minerals (obsidian, mica, and turquoise), and Southwestern pottery vessels and pipes. Fifteen Southwestern pottery types have been reported from Antelope Creek sites (Crabb 1968; Baerreis and Bryson 1966). Most types originate in the Rio Grande and upper Pecos river valleys within an area roughly bounded by Albuquerque, Jemez, Espanola and Pecos, New Mexico.

Trade items from Plains groups are harder to recognize because of similarities in material culture. Nevertheless, red-stone (catlinite?) pipes, flint tools made from Niobrara jasper, and occasional sherds with collared rims and incised or punctated bodies attest to trade ties with Central Plains groups. Possible trade or influence with adjacent Washita River peoples may be reflected in a small amount of ceramics with strap handles and sherds with horizontal and vertical lip tabs.

Trade with Caddoans beyond the Cross Timbers appears to be negligible. Single Caddoan sherds have been reported from Antelope Creek 24 and 41 Pt-8. The few green-stone celts from the Panhandle may be trade items from either the Caddoan area or the Southwest.

Burial Customs

Antelope Creek people were buried in hilltop cemeteries adjacent to villages, or less commonly in the village middens and within houses. Graves may be left unmarked, covered with rocks, or, rarely, slab lined. The type of grave markings in general does not seem to correlate with burial location, except that slab-lined graves have not been found within houses. If burials occur within houses, almost invariably they are located in the largest room at a site. The "burial rooms" found at Stamper, Footprint, Antelope Creek 22A, and Alibates 28 Unit I are all extensively burned and show long-term reuse. Some burial pits were noted above floor level, indicating that the burials postdate the room's occupation. The grave offerings that accompany these later burials clearly indicate that they are Antelope Creek peoples.

Most burials are single interments; however, multiple interments have been reported from inside rooms at the Footprint and Tarbox sites as well as the Fred Loomis hilltop ossuary. Body positions are primarily flexed to semiflexed, but individuals may be on their sides, backs, or may even be sitting within the grave. Extended burials have been reported but are extremely rare. The head orientation of burials shows considerable range. The orientations listed in descending order of preference are toward the east, west, south, southeast, north, and southwest. No data are available to determine whether the orientations correspond to celestial alignments.

Mortuary offerings are not common. Less than 30% of the graves have produced grave goods. Most offerings are personal adornments—disc and *Olivella* shell beads and pendants, turquoise beads, and conch-shell gorgets have been found near the head, neck, and wrist areas. More rarely, utilitarian items such as projectile points, laurel leaf and diamond-shaped beveled knives, bone awls, mussel shells, basketry, pottery, and stone elbow pipes have accompanied the burials. Although population profiles are not well understood, there seems to be no age or sexual discrimination against inclusion of grave offerings.

Cultural Origins

Antelope Creek origins have long been a matter of speculation. Numerous theories have been advanced, but as additional investigations refined cultural assemblages within Antelope Creek and adjacent manifestations, inconsistencies with most theories became apparent. The five cultures most often cited for Antelope Creek origins are Puebloan, Upper Republican, Caddoan, local Woodland, and Apishapa.

Many early investigators were impressed by the contiguous-room architecture employing stone masonry and postulated a Puebloan origin for Antelope Creek. However, the architectural resemblance is only superficial. Analogous room patterns and details of altar and central channel feature in Room Pattern 1 are not present in the Southwest. Material culture traits between the two areas are quite different and common items are so scarce in one area or the other that they suggest trade goods. Antelope Creek artifacts suggest a Plains origin with an overlay of Southwestern influences. Perhaps the most damaging evidence comes from skeletal materials. Osteometric and dentition analyses of burials from Antelope Creek 22, Alibates 28, and Footprint sites indicate that Antelope Creek focus populations are phenotypically closer to central Plains (Upper Republican) populations than to Pecos Pueblo populations (D. K. Patterson 1974; D. E. Patterson 1974). More recent discrete trait analyses of crania from Antelope Creek, Upper Republican and Washita River indicate that the Footprint peoples most closely resemble the Washita River peoples at the McLemore Site (Johnson and McWilliams 1978). Although the samples are small, these studies support the notion for Plains rather than Southwestern origins for Antelope Creek.

Similarities in subsistence strategies, numerous ceramic, bone, and stone tools, and generalized architectural patterning have led some to suggest an Upper Republican origin for Antelope Creek (Watson 1950; Bryson, et al. 1970). Both areas have such distinctive artifacts as globular cordmarked pottery, diamond-shaped beveled knives, side-notched points, drills, scapula hoes, bone awls, beads, and stone elbow pipes. Upper Republican house forms are reminiscent of Antelope Creek's Pattern 1: both contain single, square rooms with eastward "entrances."

Dates for Upper Republican are slightly earlier and overlap Antelope Creek dates. An onset of drought conditions at A.D. 1200 in the Central Plains is cited as a cause for the rapid southward migration. Presumably a drought would have collapsed the subsistence base in the Central Plains by reducing horticultural productivity and by altering bison migratory routes around the desiccated areas.

Upper Republican and Antelope Creek differ in a number of unique items and decorative styles. Antelope Creek frequently reports tibia digging-sticks, manos and metates, and bone rasps, whereas Upper Republican has bone beamers, bone gorgets, bow guard bracelets, fishhooks, and pottery elbow pipes. The distinctive Upper Republican collared rim on jars is reported less often than Southwestern trade sherds at Antelope Creek sites. A few sites in Texas reportedly have a "high proportion of collared sherds" (Crabb 1968:84; see also J. T. Hughes 1968:189). One such site also yielded Sante-Fe Black-on-white (B/W), Wiyo B/W, Galisteo B/W and Rowe B/W trade sherds (Crabb 1968). Recent tree-ring correlations indicate that all four types were made between A.D. 1300 and 1375 (Breternitz 1966; Baerreis and Bryson 1966; Honea 1973; Smiley et al. 1953). These dates are considerably later than one would expect if Upper Republican peoples were responsible for the rise of Antelope Creek.

In architecture, the Upper Republican square house pattern and interior features are mirrored in numerous other Plains Village and Caddoan culture complexes. Such widespread architectural similarities may reflect underlying commonality between Caddoan woodland and Caddoan prairie groups. Antelope Creek is unique in floor channels and altar feature traits.

Although both Upper Republican and Antelope Creek peoples were in contact and exchanged ideas, if not peoples, the proposed rapid southward migration in A.D. 1200 seems unlikely for the origins of Antelope Creek.

Several investigators posited Antelope Creek origins in the Caddoan area of eastern Oklahoma (Hobbs 1941; Bell 1961). Prior to adequately dated complexes in Oklahoma, Bell suggested Southern Plains Village complexes reflect late Gibson aspect Caddoan peoples who were drawn up major river systems to the Plains area by population pressures in the Southeast. This model accounted for a decline in Caddoan ceremonial complexity during the later Fulton aspect and a similarity in bone and stone tools between the Ft. Coffee focus Caddo and the Plains Village Washita River focus. The three Plains Village complexes in western Oklahoma formed a single continuum, with Washita River earliest and Antelope Creek latest. Differences between the Plains Village complexes reflect local specializations and borrowing of ideas as the Caddoans pushed farther onto the Plains.

As dates for these manifestations accumulated, it became apparent that the model did not work. Evaluation of dates suggests that most Plains Village complexes are earlier than Fulton aspect Caddo. The total Caddoan area becomes smaller, rather than larger (Bell 1968:48). Actual Caddoan influences in western Oklahoma and Texas are relatively scarce (Hofman 1978c). Although Caddoan origins for Antelope Creek seem unlikely, it continues to be cited in recent literature (J. E. Keller 1975).

Recognition of earlier Woodland peoples residing on the southern High Plains has led some to postulate a local origin for Antelope Creek (J. T. Hughes 1968; Lintz 1978a). The demonstration of Woodland peoples in the area has been well substantiated (J. T. Hughes 1962, 1979; W. R. Wedel 1975; Green 1967; Mitchell 1975; Lintz 1978d; Etchieson 1979). However, little is known about specific assemblage details. Local origins for Antelope Creek is an appealing idea because it requires no population displacement. Woodland manifestation shares with Antelope Creek such traits as cordmarked pottery, keeled end-scrapers, slab metates, and manos. Presumably the same general cultural transitions that are occurring for the Woodland–Custer–Washita River foci east of the High Plains are also occurring in the Texas Panhandle. Antelope Creek, however, receives additional influences from either Apishapa or the Southwest.

A major problem with accepting this model is the lack of reported transitional- and intermediate-stage sites. Presently available radiocarbon dates are limited to one site for the High Plains Woodland occupation: 1650 B.C. to A.D. 850 (W. R. Wedel 1975). Dates for Antelope Creek abruptly begin at A.D. 1200 (Bryson, *et al.* 1970). If Antelope Creek's development occurred simultaneously with Washita River's, then some sites in the Panhandle area should date to the ninth to twelfth centuries. None has been reported to date. The absence of Woodland house sites gives the impression that local Woodland peoples may have been nomadic groups from adjacent areas who were temporarily exploiting the High Plains. Many of these problems may simply reflect the small sample of excavated Woodland sites and an archaeological preoccupation to dig sites with masonry architecture.

General architectural and material culture similarities between Apishapa and

Antelope Creek foci have led some to suggest a phylogenic relationship (Campbell 1969, 1976). Both cultures share a horticultural–hunting subsistence base, projectile points, snub-nose scrapers, globular cordmarked pottery, slab metates, oval manos, and flexed burials. Architecturally, both have circular structures made with vertical and horizontal slab masonry. Campbell (1976:89) has suggested that the progressive Antelope Creek developed out of Apishapa by adopting new traits from groups living to the north and east. The borrowed traits include square house patterns, beveled knives, scapula hoes, tibia digging-sticks, and bone rasps. In order to derive Antelope Creek houses from Apishapa architecture, Campbell postulates a developmental sequence involving circular to square isolated houses, to large contiguous-room structures. However, available radiocarbon dates do not support such a sequence (Lintz 1978b). Such architectural traits as the central floor channel and altar–bench feature are unique to Antelope Creek and cannot be derived from Apishapa, Southwest, or Plains cultures. One has to wonder why major readjustments in house forms and subsistence-related tools were necessary by Antelope Creek peoples when both groups had similar basic economies. Undoubtedly there are strong relationships between the two cultures, but the phylogenic relationship has yet to be conclusively demonstrated.

Cultural Dynamics

Culture change within Antelope Creek is poorly understood. The problem stems not from a scarcity of dated sites but from a lack of quantified descriptive reports. Virtually nothing is known about changes in the artifact assemblage, and little is known about community-pattern development.

Aside from the postulated functional differences between hamlet and field-houses, most community-pattern variations have been viewed as architectural dynamics. Previous developmental sequences postulated changes from isolated-room structures to multiroom structures (Crabb 1968; J. T Hughes 1968), or from isolated circular to isolated rectangular to multiunit structures (Campbell 1976). Contrary to these models, available radiocarbon dates indicate that multiunit structures tend to be earlier than isolated rooms (Lintz 1978b). There is also a tendency for later rooms in isolated structures to be larger than rooms in early contiguous-unit structures. Perhaps the breakdown in contiguous-room patterns reflects dispersal of peoples into smaller units in response to deteriorating local resources with an onset of drier conditions in the Texas Panhandle after A.D. 1300 (Duffield 1970:265). However, temporal, spatial, seasonal, functional, ecological and sociopolitical differences could also have contributed to architectural diversity.

Historical Affiliations

A problem equally as puzzling as cultural origins is the subsequent development of Antelope Creek into historically identifiable tribes. Between A.D. 1450 and 1500 Antelope Creek is caught in the radical changes and migrations that swept cultures throughout the Plains and Southwest. Additional droughts and possible Apache intrusions into the southern Plains have frequently been cited as contributing factors for the abandonment of the region.

By 1541 Coronado records only nomadic bison-hunting groups in the Texas panhandle. The permanent villages are gone and the ruins are not worthy of comment. Furthermore, none of the archaeologically or historically documented cultures on the Plains area after the sixteenth century lived in stone-slab houses, used many forms of stone and bone tools, or decorated their pottery as did the Antelope Creek peoples. Although the culture pattern cannot be traced with certainty after A.D. 1500, there is no evidence that the people suffered genocide. The cultural continuity has been difficult to trace and several historical connections have been suggested.

Grinnell's 1893 Pawnee origin myth alluding to a former occupation in stone houses somewhere to the southwest has led Hughes (1968) to postulate a combined Antelope Creek–Lower Loup origin for the Pawnee. Furthermore, the antecedents of Pawnee earthlodge altar feature may lie in Antelope Creek architectural patterns. However, Grinnell's is unique among many myths in suggesting a southwestern origin for the Pawnee, and the altar similarity offers a meager thread of continuity. Other architectural and artifactual traits are dissimilar.

Other investigators have speculated that Coronado's nomadic Teyas Indians were Antelope Creek peoples who changed their subsistence base, settlement pattern, and other aspects of culture to meet deteriorating climatic conditions (Schroeder 1962). This suggestion does not require a rapid replacement of different cultural groups in the Panhandle between A.D. 1500 and 1541. Rather, the culture shed an extensive sedentary-oriented artifactual inventory during a transition to nomadic lifestyles. Unfortunately it is virtually impossible to test because no Teyas sites have been archaeologically identified in the Panhandle, and the cultural traits remain poorly known.

Another possibility suggests that Antelope Creek peoples coalesced with other western Oklahoma Plains Village groups and moved toward the east. The association of Antelope Creek architecture with a Washita River artifact assemblage at a sixteenth-century village site in western Oklahoma is cited as support for the merging of cultures (Saunders 1973; Lintz 1978a). Cultural similarities in bone and stone tools between the Washita River focus and the Ft. Coffee focus suggests an eastward drift of peoples (Hofman 1978c). Campbell (1976) suggests that the Great Bend aspect of southcentral Kansas received a direct influx of Antelope Creek peoples; however, cultural similarities are not particularly strong.

These suggestions are not mutually exclusive; more than one could be correct. It is apparent that the Antelope Creek focus did not remain intact. A variety of family or other social unit responses to cultural pressure of the early 1500s may have occurred. Certainly a number of historically recorded cultures are in northern Texas and western Oklahoma for which we have no archaeological information. The historical identification(s) of Antelope Creek may never be resolved to everyone's satisfaction.

Reference Note

Our knowledge of the Antelope Creek focus is based on information accumulated from numerous excavations and surveys conducted since the pioneering efforts in 1907 by professor T. L. Eyerly at the "Buried City" (Handley Ruins). Most archaeological work has been conducted on sites along the Canadian River and information obtained from these Texas sites is used to supplement knowledge of the culture extending into Oklahoma.

The best-known excavated sites in Texas include the Antelope Creek 22 site (Baker and Baker 1968a, 1968b; Hobbs 1941; Holden 1930; C. S. Johnson 1939; Lowrey 1932; Moorehead 1931; Patterson 1974; Studer 1955), Antelope Creek 22A site (Baker and Baker 1968a), Antelope Creek 23 (Baker fieldnotes), Antelope Creek 24 site (Baker and Baker 1968b; Duffield 1970), Alibates 28 site (Baker and Baker 1968a, 1968b; Bousman 1974a; Duffield 1970; Mason 1929; D. K. Patterson 1974; D. E. Patterson 1974; Studer 1939, 1955), Alibates 28A site (Baker and Baker 1968b), Alibates 30 site (Baker and Baker 1968b), Arrowhead Peak site (Green 1967), Coetas site or Ruin 55 (Studer 1934), Conner site (Duffield 1964b, 1970), Cottonwood Ruin (Holden 1929; Moorehead 1921, 1931), CR-1 site (Glasscock and Glasscock 1955), Footprint site (Green 1967; D. K. Patterson 1974; D. E. Patterson 1974), Handley's Ruins (Eyerly 1907, 1910; Moorehead 1921, 1931; Holden 1929; Ellzey 1966), Landergin Mesa site (Moorehead 1921, 1931), Medford Ranch site (Duffield 1964b, 1970), 41-Mo-7 site (Green 1967), Pickett Ruin (Carter and Carter 1958; Duffield 1970), Turkey Creek site (Bandy 1976; Green 1967), Roper Ruin (Duffield 1970), Saddleback Ruin (G. H. Haynes 1932; Holden 1932, 1933), Sanford Ruin (Duffield 1970), Spring Canyon site (Duffield 1964b, 1970), Tarbox Ruin (Holden 1929; Moorehead 1931), Black Dog Village (J. E. Keller 1975), South Ridge site (Etchieson 1979), and Lookout Pueblo (Lowrey 1932). Published village and mortuary sites in western Oklahoma include Hedding site (Shaeffer 1965), Zimms site (Flynn 1983; Saunders 1973), and the Fred Loomis site (Kay County Chapter 1963), whereas excavated Oklahoma Panhandle sites include Roy Smith site (Schneider 1969), Stamper site (Watson 1950a; C. S. Johnson 1934), McGrath site (Lintz 1976b), and Two Sisters site (Lintz 1973b, 1979c). Other unpublished village sites in the Oklahoma Panhandle include Mayer site, Nash I site, Clawson–Fast site, and the Hamby site. Smaller nonarchitectural sites have been found east of the High Plains, which contain ceramics reminiscent of Antelope Creek wares. The Shawver site (Hofman 1977c), Cave Creek site (Leonhardy 1966a), and Hodge site (Hofman 1974) are three such localities that appear to represent camps occupied by Antelope Creek peoples while they were gathering resources or trading with groups in the Redbed Plains region of central and western Oklahoma. Information from excavations at these sites, as well as a number of surveys (Bousman 1974a, 1974b; W. Davis 1962; L. G. Johnson 1950a; Studer 1931a, 1931b; Mason 1929; Etchieson 1981) and previous regional syntheses (Sayles 1935; Krieger 1946; Bell and Baerreis 1951; Studer 1955; Wedel 1961; J. T. Hughes 1968, 1979; Campbell 1976; Lintz 1978a, 1979b) form the corpus of data from which this chapter is derived.

The culture has been well dated using radiocarbon dates (Baerreis and Bryson 1966; Pearson, et al 1966; Valastro, et al. 1977; Bender, et al. 1966, 1967, 1971; Schneider 1969; J. E. Keller 1975; Lintz 1978b), archaeomagnetism (Flynn 1983; Lintz 1973b; Saunders 1973), and crossdating of Southwestern ceramic types (Krieger 1946; Baerreis and Bryson 1966; Crabb 1968). Table 15.1 summarizes the radiocarbon dates, using both uncorrected and MASCA corrected dates. These data, supported by the other techniques (Table 15.2), indicate that Antelope Creek flourished between A.D. 1200 and 1500.

Table 15.1 Radiocarbon Dates for Antelope Creek Sites

Laboratory number	Site and provenience	Date before present (B.P.)	Date (A.D.) based on 5568 half-life	Date (A.D.) based on 5730 half-life	MASCA corrected date (A.D.)	Reference
WIS-117	A-439—housefill	440 ± 75	1510	1500	1430 ± 85	Bender et al. 1967:531
WIS-120	A-439—floor	600 ± 85	1350	1330	1340 ± 95	Bender et al. 1967:531
WIS-128	A-439—S.E. corner post (F. 1)	620 ± 70	1330	1310	1320 ± 80	Bender et al. 1967:531
WIS-114	Alibates 28, Unit 1, Room 1	600 ± 75	1350	1330	1340 ± 85	Bender et al. 1967:531
WIS-116	Alibates 28, Unit 1, Room 19?	630 ± 70	1320	1300	1310 ± 80	Bender et al. 1967:531
WIS-129	Alibates 28, Unit 1, Room 19	770 ± 75	1180	1160	1220–1200 ± 85	Bender et al. 1967:531
WIS-101	Alibates 28, Unit 2, Room 24	600 ± 70	1350	1330	1340 ± 80	Bender et al. 1966:529
Tx-259	Alibates 28, Unit 2, Room 24	480 ± 80	1470	1455	1410 ± 90	Pearson et al. 1966:464
WIS-118	Arrowhead Peak—composite	620 ± 70	1330	1310	1320 ± 80	Bender et al. 1967:532
Tx-1493	Black Dog Village—F. 13 (Structure 2)	280 ± 150	1670	1660	1610–1520 ± 160	Valastro et al. 1977:305
Tx-1513	Black Dog Village—F. 17 pit; south of Structure 3	420 ± 70	1530	1515	1430 ± 80	Valastro et al. 1977:305
Tx-1499	Black Dog Village—F. 17 pit; south of Structure 3	350 ± 90	1600	1590	1500–1470 ± 100	Valastro et al. 1977:305
Tx-1498A	Black Dog Village—F. 17 pit; south of Structure 3 (bone apatite)	500 ± 70	1450	1435	1405 ± 80	Valastro et al. 1977:305
Tx-1498B	Black Dog Village—F. 17 pit; south of Structure 3 (bone collagen)	1110 ± 200	840	805	880–860 ± 210	Valastro et al. 1977:305
Tx-1489	Black Dog Village—F. 6, Structure 4	510 ± 60	1440	1430	1400 ± 70	Valastro et al. 1977:305
Tx-1490	Black Dog Village—F. 6, Structure 4	470 ± 60	1480	1470	1420 ± 70	Valastro et al. 1977:305
Tx-1491	Black Dog Village—F. 6, Structure 4	460 ± 60	1490	1475	1420 ± 70	Valastro et al. 1977:305

Tx-1488	Black Dog Village—F. 6, Structure 4	390 ± 50	1560	1550	1450 ± 60	Valastro et al. 1977:305
Tx-1512	Black Dog Village north central post, Structure 5	980 ± 170	970	940	1000 ± 180	Valastro et al. 1977:305
Tx-1497	Black Dog Village—altar area, Structure 5	610 ± 50	1340	1320	1330 ± 60	Valastro et al. 1977:305
Tx-1496	Black Dog Village—floor fill, Structure 5	590 ± 60	1360	1340	1350 ± 70	Valastro et al. 1977:305
Tx-1495	Black Dog Village—S.E. corner floor fill, Structure 5	300 ± 50	1650	1640	1600–1510 ± 60	Valastro et al. 1977:305
WIS-410	Canyon Country Club Cave N2/N-S, Level 1	400 ± 60	1550	1540	1440 ± 70	Bender et al. 1971:478
WIS-411	Canyon Country Club Cave N1/W1, Level 1	300 ± 50	1650	1640	1600–1510 ± 60	Bender et al. 1971:478
WIS-403	Canyon Country Club Cave N1/W1, Level 2	670 ± 50	1280	1260	1290–1260 ± 60	Bender et al. 1971:478
WIS-421	Canyon Country Club Cave N1/W1, Level 2	700 ± 60	1250	1230	1250 ± 70	Bender et al. 1971:478
WIS-402	Canyon Country Club Cave N-S/N1, Level 2	1260 ± 55	690	650	690 ± 65	Bender et al. 1971:478
WIS-408	Canyon Country Club Cave E-W/W1, Level 3	620 ± 45	1330	1310	1320 ± 55	Bender et all. 1971:478
WIS-95	Canyon Country Club Cave N1/W1, Level 3	800 ± 75	1150	1130	1190 ± 85	Bender et al. 1966:529
WIS-89	Coetas (Ruin 55) (A-611) Room 1	520 ± 70	1430	1415	1390 ± 80	Bender et al. 1966:529
Tx-258	Coetas (Ruin 55) (A-611) Room 1	430 ± 80	1520	1505	1430 ± 90	Pearson et al. 1966:463
WIS-92	Coetas (Ruin 55) (A-611) Room 1	690 ± 60	1260	1240	1260 ± 70	Bender et al. 1966:528
WIS-94A	Coetas (Ruin 55) (A-611) midden	490 ± 70	1460	1445	1410 ± 80	Bender et al. 1966:528
WIS-94B	Coetas (Ruin 55) (A-611) Room 2 Fill	520 ± 85	1430	1415	1390 ± 95	Bender et al. 1966:528

(continued)

Table 15.1 *(Continued)*

Laboratory number	Site and provenience	Date before present (B.P.)	Date (A.D.) based on 5568 half-life	Date (A.D.) based on 5730 half-life	MASCA corrected date (A.D.)	Reference
Tx-257	Currie Ruin—House Fill	830 ± 100	1120	1095	1180–1110 ± 110	Pearson et al. 1966:463
WIS-100	Currie Ruin—House Fill	670 ± 75	1280	1260	1290–1260 ± 85	Bender et al. 1966:530
WIS-176	Currie Ruin—House Fill	480 ± 90	1470	1455	1410 ± 100	Bender et al. 1967:531
WIS-99A	Footprint (41Pt-25) Room 1, Floor	420 ± 80	1530	1515	1430 ± 90	Bender et al. 1966:529
WIS-99B	Footprint (41Pt-25) Room 1, Floor	520 ± 80	1430	1415	1390 ± 90	Bender et al. 1966:529
WIS-102	Footprint (41Pt-25) Room 2, post hole 2	520 ± 70	1430	1415	1390 ± 80	Bender et al. 1966:529
WIS-122	Footprint (41Pt-25) Room 3	660 ± 70	1290	1270	1290–1260 ± 80	Bender et al. 1967:531
WIS-90A	Handley (A-609)—midden	640 ± 70	1310	1290	1310 ± 80	Bender et al. 1966:530
WIS-90B	Handley (A-609)—midden	740 ± 80	1210	1190	1230 ± 90	Bender et al. 1966:530
WIS-97	Handley (A-609)—midden	360 ± 75	1590	1580	1500–1460 ± 85	Bender et al. 1966:529
Tx-260	Palisades Shelter Test Pit 5 (30–36")	465 ± 85	1485	1470	1420 ± 95	Pearson et al. 1966:464
WIS-108A	Palisades Shelter Test Pit 5 (30–36")	630 ± 75	1320	1300	1310 ± 85	Bender et al. 1966:530
WIS-108B	Palisades Shelter Test Pit 5 (30–36")	600 ± 75	1350	1330	1340 ± 85	Bender et al. 1966:530
WIS-98	Palisades Shelter Test Pit 5 (36" hearth)	330 ± 75	1620	1610	1520–1470 ± 85	Bender et al. 1966:530
WIS-132	Palisades Shelter House 1, NW hearth	870 ± 70	1080	1055	1095 ± 80	Bender et al. 1967:531
WIS-126	Pickett Ruin (A-116) Exterior or Midden	710 ± 70	1240	1220	1240 ± 80	Bender et al. 1967:531
WIS-134	Roper (A-62)—composite	650 ± 70	1300	1280	1300 ± 80	Bender et al. 1967:531
WIS-141	Roper (A-62)—composite	580 ± 70	1370	1355	1355 ± 80	Bender et al. 1967:531
WIS-137	Roy Smith—Test Pit B (Feature 3)	750 ± 70	1200	1180	1220 ± 80	Bender et al. 1967:533

Lab number	Provenience	Date			Date	Reference
WIS-124	Roy Smith—N3-R13 (Feature 2)	730 ± 70	1220	1200	1230 ± 80	Bender et al. 1967:533
WIS-121	Roy Smith—Room A (between floors)	730 ± 75	1220	1200	1230 ± 85	Bender et al. 1967:533
WIS-142	Roy Smith—Room G N36-R1 (disturbed)	570 ± 60	1380	1360	1360 ± 70	Bender et al. 1967:533
WIS-145	Roy Smith—Room I N36-R5, Ash	700 ± 50	1250	1230	1250 ± 60	Bender et al. 1967:533
WIS-147	Roy Smith—Room I N37-R4, Ash	700 ± 70	1250	1230	1250 ± 80	Bender et al. 1967:533
WIS-148	Roy Smith—Room I N37-R5, Ash	730 ± 65	1220	1200	1230 ± 75	Bender et al. 1967:533
Tx-255	Sanford Ruins—Midden North of Room 4	700 ± 90	1250	1230	1250 ± 100	Pearson et al. 1966:463
Tx-256	Spring Canyon—Midden NE of Main Structure	550 ± 90	1400	1385	1380 ± 100	Pearson et al. 1966:463
WIS-83	Stamper—Exterior Refuse, Trench NE of House 3	650 ± 70	1300	1280	1300 ± 80	Bender et al. 1966:528
WIS-84	Stamper—Interior House 3, SE corner	650 ± 80	1300	1280	1300 ± 90	Bender et al. 1966:528
Tx-3260	Two Sisters—Feature 9, pit beneath west wall of Room 5, Structure A	890 ± 50	1060	1033	1073 ± 60	Lintz 1979c
Tx-3261	Two Sisters—Feature 6, pit inside Room 5, Structure A	510 ± 50	1440	1425	1395 ± 60	Lintz 1979c
UGa-2508	Two Sisters—Floor, Room 1, Structure B	545 ± 55	1405	1388	1380 ± 65	Lintz 1979c
UGa-2509	Two Sisters—Feature 13, pit; lowest level, Room 1, Structure A	600 ± 50	1350	1332	1342 ± 60	Lintz 1979c
UGa-2217	Zimms site, Interior Post 2	1065 ± 60	885	853	923 ± 70	Flynn 1983
Tx-3303	Zimms site, Wall Post 7	900 ± 50	1050	1023	1063 ± 60	Flynn 1983

Table 15.2

Archaeomagnetic Dates for Antelope Creek Sites

Laboratory number	Site and provenience	Date (A.D.)	Comment
O.U. 927	Alibates 28, Unit II, Room 7, Central hearth	Modern	Polar position reflects weathered feature sediments left exposed since 1938 excavations.
O.U. 788	Two Sisters, Room 1A, Central hearth	1385 ± 34	—
O.U. 887	Two Sisters—Room 1B, Burned south wall	1420 ± 25	Collected as oriented blocks; recollected at archaeomagnetic laboratory.
O.U. 888	Two Sisters—Room 1B, Central hearth	1320 ± 10	Collected as oriented blocks; recollected at archaeomagnetic laboratory.
O.U. 830	Zimms—Floor, south edge of central channel	950 or 1450 ± 19	Polar position near cross over in master curve.

CHAPTER **16**

The Western Protohistoric: A Summary of the Edwards and Wheeler Complexes

Jack L. Hofman

Introduction

The period between A.D. 1500 and 1750 in western Oklahoma is poorly documented archaeologically, but represents a time of dynamic social interaction and cultural change. This chapter organizes available data from this period into a useful framework and reviews present problems and research needs. This discussion of protohistoric archaeological remains is only an approximation, one to be revised and corrected after additional fieldwork and analytical studies are completed.

The Cultural Setting

Coronado's chroniclers provided the first historical documents on the Indians who lived in the Southern Plains area between the Pueblos of eastern New Mexico and the Wichita of Quivira. Unfortunately, the information recorded about Plains occupants is brief. Later, Spaniards, including Oñate in 1601 and Ulibarri in 1706, led excursions onto the Plains after 1600 but they too provide precious little information on the nomadic hunters of the region. In the 1700s, however, the French were in contact with the settled Wichita and Caddo along the Arkansas and Red Rivers (Hartley and Miller 1977; Sudbury 1976a; Jelks 1967; Harris *et al.* 1965). With Spanish on the west and French on the east, the cultural stage in the Southern Plains was set for diverse social contacts that created an adaptive niche exploited by nomadic bison hunters and traders. These wide-ranging people developed symbiotic and interdependent relationships with the more settled groups to the east and west. These Southern Plains hunters are generally believed to have been Apacheans and related peoples, although the Jumano and others were active in the area for part of this period. The Jumano were apparently absorbed into the Apache groups during the first quarter of the eighteenth century (John 1975:194). The Comanche apparently did not become prevalent in this region until sometime well after 1700.

Spanish and French contact with and influence on groups bordering the Southern Plains began and rapidly accelerated after 1550. The native technologies of the Southern Plains tribes were gradually replaced by European goods. Between 1750 and 1800 the technological transition from native to European goods was nearly complete but cultural materials were not all that changed. Introduction of the horse and increased demand for European goods resulted in intensified exploitation of, and increased dependence on, such tradable resources as bison robes, meat, salt, and slaves. The impact of this economic reorientation had social and political ramifications as well. Access to European materials may have been primarily indirect. Plains residents were middlemen in trading materials of Caddo or Wichita origin to Pueblos, and in trading Pueblo items to the Wichita and Caddo. In a similar fashion some French and Spanish goods were distributed whereas others were retained by Southern Plains residents. Evidence for long-distance trading helps to demark this period of aboriginal occupation in the Southern Plains. Trade between Plains hunting tribes, Puebloans, and settled Plains villagers undoubtedly had ancient roots, but the intensity of this trade apparently increased tremendously after European contact. By 1700, Southern Plains Indians were relying partially on metal tools and were dependent on horses obtained from the Spanish Southwest. They were also trading with eastern Prairie Villagers for guns and a wide variety of European, primarily French, materials. Previously established trade networks along which seminomadic plainsmen redistributed various products throughout adjacent areas were basic to these interactions.

Edwards Complex: 1500–1650

The Edwards Complex is defined on the basis of information from four sites in Greer, Beckham, Roger Mills, and Washita counties of southwest Oklahoma. (Figure 16.1). These sites have produced archaeological materials distinctive enough to warrant separate recognition as the *Edwards complex*, after the most thoroughly investigated site. The four best known Edwards complex sites are Edwards I (34Bk-2), Taylor Area B (34Gr-8), one component at Goodwin–Baker (34Rm-14), and Duncan (34Wa-2). Several sites in southwestern Oklahoma, such as Bell (34Bk-9), are probably related but are presently unreported.

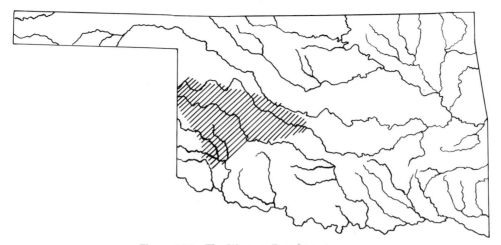

Figure 16.1 The Western Protohistoric area.

The Edwards I site was partially excavated by A. Dewey Buck, Jr. and students of the 1968 University of Oklahoma Archeological Field School. Their excavations revealed part of a circular ditch enclosure that has been interpreted as a defensive earthwork (Weymouth 1981; Figure 16.2a). A similar ditch, also interpreted as part of a fortification, was exposed during 1981 test excavations at the Duncan site (Figure 16.2b). A third ditch, encountered at the Taylor site, has been interpreted as a fortified earthwork (Burton and Burton 1971) but may represent a natural feature (Weymouth 1981). Materials at the Goodwin–Baker site, considered typical of the Edwards complex, were found in one area of this repeatedly occupied site. A series of post molds in this area may represent an arbor or similar structure. Evidence for more permanent or substantial Edwards complex habitation structures was lacking. Description of the overall settlement pattern and annual life cycle of the Edwards complex people will remain impractical until further surveys and specific site studies have been completed.

Artifacts (Figure 16.3) presently form our most reliable basis for identifying Edwards components. Ceramics are predominately plain-surfaced, sand-tempered sherds that are usually gray in color. A very small percentage of the ceramics are tempered with combinations of sand and bone, clay, or shell. Because of the small, friable sherds, vessel forms are poorly understood. In general, however, the vessels appear to have been round based and shouldered. Rims are everted or straight and usually have rounded lips. A bowl form may also be represented. Appendages are rare or absent, but decorations consisting of notched rims and fingernail punctates occasionally occur. Sherds with incised or appliqué decorations also apparently belong with this complex, and some sherd surfaces may be either brushed or burnished. Approximately 70% of the sherds from the surface of the Edwards I site (1900 sherds) and a similar percentage of sherds from the test excavations and surface of the Taylor site (2929

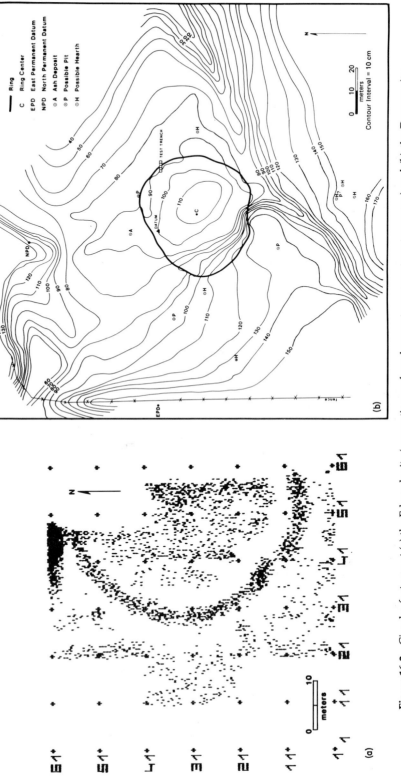

Figure 16.2 Circular features at (a) the Edwards site (magnetic map based on proton magnetometer survey) and (b) the Duncan site.

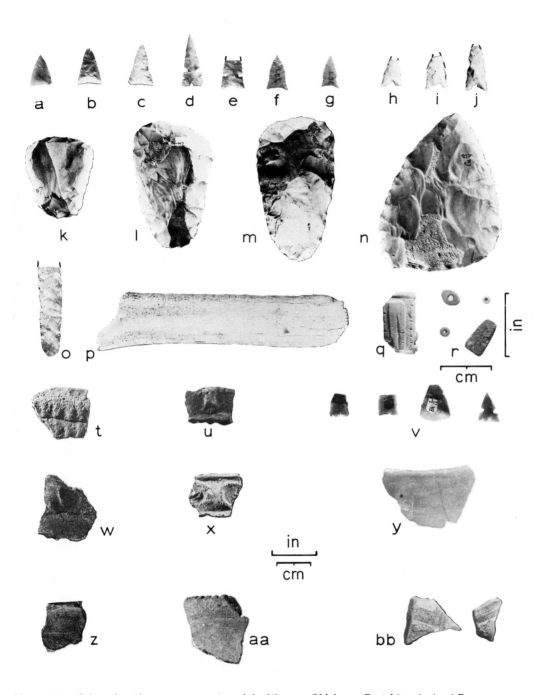

Figure 16.3 Selected artifacts representative of the Western Oklahoma Protohistoric: (a–c) Fresno-type arrowpoints; (d) Huffaker-type arrowpoint; (e) Washita-type arrowpoint section; (f,g) examples of "fishtail" arrowpoints; (h–j) sections of Garza type arrowpoints (k–m) end-scrapers of Kay County flint; (n) ovate knife of Kay County flint; (o) section of ensiform "pipe" drill; (p) section of metapodial bone flesher; (q) section of "elaborate form" (Pecos) claystone pipe; (r) turquoise beads; (s) pendant of malachite; (t) neck banded rim-sherd of clay-tempered pottery; (u, w, x) rim sherds of Emory or Nash Neck Banded types; (v) arrowpoints of obsidian; (y) rim sherd of Pecos glaze-paint pottery; (z) rim sherd of Little Deer ware (plain variety); (aa) rim sherd of sandy ware; (bb) sherds of Picuris glaze-paint wares. Specimens a–u, w, and x are from the Little Deer site (Cu-10); Specimens v, y–bb are from the Edwards site (Bk-2).

sherds) fall within this description. Sherd frequencies are not available for the Goodwin–Baker component. An important though usually small percentage (2–5%) of the pottery from Edwards complex components is Puebloan, most of which was derived from Pecos and Picuris. A number of sherds, representing up to 2% of each site's sample, have been identified as Pecos Glaze V or Plain Red Ware. Micaceous, thin gray pottery comparable to upper Rio Grande Pueblo utilitarian wares frequently accompanies the imported glaze and red wares. Most of the remaining sherds from these sites probably result from earlier occupations by people using pottery similar to that found on Custer and Washita River sites. Tubular plain or decorated ceramic pipes of the type reported from Pecos are represented by a specimen found by Lawrence and Gene LeVick from the Taylor site and the Edwards I site.

Lithic assemblages from Edwards complex sites yield distinctive tool types and chipped-stone materials. Arrowpoints are predominantly triangular unnotched Fresno forms (about 70% or more) but side- and/or base-notched (Harrell, Washita, and Garza types) as well as other triangular and corner-notched forms are represented. Flake-base drills, ensiform pipe drills, biface and uniface tools, beveled knives, as well as end- and side-scrapers are common. Flake tools with a wide variety of edge form attributes are very frequent and often exhibit retouching. Such ground-stone artifacts as grooved abraders, grinding stones, and metates are also common. Small turquoise and malachite ornaments occur, some of which are perforated for suspension. Over 70% of the chipped-stone tools are of Alibates and similar agatized dolomites (such as Tecovas) found in the Texas Panhandle. Kay County flint from northcentral Oklahoma constitutes about 10% of the stone tools. Obsidian that is almost certainly from the Jemez region of New Mexico (Baugh and Terrell 1982; Sappington 1980) and Edwards chert from central Texas are both represented by about 4% of the artifacts. A few pieces of obsidian probably from the Government Mountain area of Arizona are also included. Obsidian comprises a consistent, but small percentage (usually less than 10%) of the chipped-stone debris. The remaining chipped-stone tools are made of miscellaneous local or unidentified cherts and quartzites. These percentages are based on approximately 700 chipped-stone tools and over 900 pieces of debris from the surface of the Edwards I Site (T. Baugh 1982). The relative frequencies of these lithic types are believed to be comparable to those for the Taylor and Goodwin–Baker and Duncan components, but no absolute counts are available for these sites.

Distinctive bone tools include bison-metatarsal fleshers, usually with toothed edges, that are documented from the Edwards and Taylor sites (T. Baugh 1982; Hofman 1978b:66). Bison-scapula hoes apparently belong with this complex but occur in limited numbers. Because most of our present knowledge of Edwards complex tools is derived from surface finds, there is at present no other information on bone, plant, or shell artifacts.

No European trade items are reported from the Edwards site but a single glass trade bead was purportedly found on the Taylor site (Burton and Burton 1969:17). This surface find is in a private collection and has not been compared with dated bead samples of European origin. Because no other trade items are known for Edwards complex sites, we assume European trade articles were few, if represented at all. The paucity of such trade objects may result from the sites having been occupied before European trade was well established on the Southern Plains.

The Edwards complex is interpreted to date between A.D. 1500 and 1650. This estimate is based on a series of artifact types and several radiocarbon dates from the Edwards site. The Southwestern Glaze sherds from Edwards and Taylor are comparable to Glaze V (A.D. 1600–1700) ceramics at Pecos (Kidder and Shepard 1936; T. Baugh 1982). The serrated metapodial fleshers are believed (Hofman 1975b) to date after A.D. 1500 in Oklahoma. The paucity (or possibly the absence) of European items may indicate that the complex should date prior to intensive trade in European items in the region. Wyckoff (1970a) suggests a date during the 1600s for the Goodwin–Baker component and the Taylor site Area B is believed (Burton and Burton 1969) to be of similar age. Five radiocarbon dates from the Edwards site are listed in Table 16.1. Sample Tx-812 is believed to date Late Prehistoric (pre-Edwards Complex) occupation at the site. The remaining dates, however, relate to the time of the Edwards Complex component at Edwards I. These samples (Tx-810, Tx-811, Tx-813, and Tx-814) range from about A.D. 1500 to about A.D. 1650.

The economy of Edwards complex peoples was apparently based primarily on bison and trading. Bison bones were the dominant animal remains in the refuse of the Edwards complex sites (Monk 1982). It is likely that gardens were also maintained, judging from the few bison-scapula hoes and ethnohistorical reports for the area. Horses were not evidenced by archeological findings, but they were reportedly in use in the area, at least in limited numbers, by 1650. Many protohistoric Southern Plains groups, such as the Edwards complex people, supplemented their own resource gains by trading meats, hides, leather products, and salt for horticultural produce from the Pueblos and Prairie Villages. The primary evidence for trade is in the form of pottery and stone artifacts from the Southwest and Southeast. These artifacts probably represent only a small part of the trade between eastern New Mexico Pueblos, Caddoan Villagers and Edwards complex people. Such perishables as horticultural produce, dried vegetables, blankets, meats, salt, robes, leather items, and woods (bois d'arc) were also traded. During the latter part (ca. 1625–1650) of the Edwards complex, horses, slaves, and European items such as metal tools were probably traded as well. Emphasis on cultural interaction to the west during the Edwards complex may reflect a historical connection between the Edwards complex people and those of the eastern New Mexico area (Bell 1973:185; Jelinek 1967; Opler 1975), and may not represent an increasing trade by native occupants of western Oklahoma.

Table 16.1

A Summary of Radiocarbon Dates from the Edwards Site, 34Bk2, Beckham County, Oklahoma

Laboratory number	Provenience	Date B.P. (1950)	Date (A.D.) based on 5568 half-life	Date (A.D.) based on 5730 half-life	MASCA corrected date (A.D.)	References
Tx-810	Post Hole 3	310 ± 70	1640 ± 70	1631	1590–1510 ± 80	Valastro et al. 1972:475–476
Tx-811	Circular ditch enclosure	200 ± 70	1750 ± 70	1744	1650 ± 80	—
Tx-812	Post Hole in Square S12-R5	550 ± 70	1400 ± 70	1384	1380 ± 80	—
Tx-813	Post Hole 1	290 ± 70	1660 ± 70	1651	1610–1520 ± 80	—
Tx-814	Post Hole 2	450 ± 70	1500 ± 70	1487	1420 ± 80	—

Wheeler Complex: 1650–1725

The Wheeler complex was originally defined in 1967 (Bell and Bastian 1967:124–127) from materials recovered at the Wilson Springs (34Cd-5), Scott (34Cn-2), and Little Deer (34Cu-10) sites in Caddo, Canadian, and Custer counties of west central Oklahoma (Figure 16.1). The following discussion is based primarily on the Little Deer site in Custer County, the only extensively analyzed Wheeler assemblage (Hofman 1978b). Because none of the Wheeler sites has been excavated, there is little information on houses, burials, fortifications, site structure, or settlement patterns for this cultural complex. A small site (34Cd-218) on a creek in northern Caddo County may represent a Wheeler complex limited activity camp (Hofman 1973a). The limited artifact collection from this very small camp included a serrated bison-metatarsal flesher exhibiting cut marks made by a metal tool. This site is interpreted as a hunting or processing camp used by people of the Wheeler complex.

Artifacts attributed to the Wheeler complex (Figure 16.3) are, in most respects, very similar to those of the Edwards complex. There are, however, some important differences. The predominant pottery continues to be thin, dark gray and is tempered with sand or combinations of sand and other materials. This ceramic grouping comprises nearly 90% of the Wheeler complex sherds from the Little Deer site. Fewer than 2% of the Little Deer ceramics are Southwestern in origin. These include Pecos Glaze V and micaceous sherds. Therefore, it appears that the relative frequency of Puebloan sherds is less for the Wheeler complex than for the Edwards complex. The two Pecos Glaze V sherds from Little Deer are believed to represent the latter part of the Glaze V period (approximately A.D. 1650–1700), and the micaceous sherds apparently date after 1680 (Warren 1979:242). Three tubular decorated Pecos pipe fragments (Kidder's 1932 "Elaborate Form") have been found at Little Deer. The ceramics provide evidence for the greatest material cultural similarities between the Edwards and Wheeler complexes. The only potentially significant difference in ceramics now apparent is that Wheeler components have fewer and less-varied Southwestern sherds and a lack of Southeastern Caddoan pottery.

There are several important differences between the stone-tool assemblages but primary among these is the different use of lithic materials (Table 16.2). Kay County flint is the dominant material represented in the chipped-stone artifacts and debris from the Wheeler complex occupation at Little Deer; this material is most frequent at other Wheeler complex sites as well. Alibates and Edwards chert are important minor types for chipped-stone tools at the Little Deer site (Table 16.2). In contrast, the Edwards complex assemblage at the Edwards I site contains much more Alibates and obsidian and considerably less Edwards chert. Obsidian is scarce at Little Deer and other Wheeler complex assemblages such as Scott and smaller nearby sites.

The different chert types used by Edwards versus Wheeler complex people

Table 16.2

Comparison of Chipped-Stone Material Types from the Edwards and Wheeler Complxes

	Edwards complex		Wheeler complex	
Lithic type and source	Edwards site surface artifacts (n = 691) (%)	Edwards site surface debris[a] (n = 924) (%)	Little Deer site surface artifacts (n = 402) (%)	Little Deer site surface debris (n = 558) (%)
Alibates and Tecovas (Texas Panhandle)	73	62.2	19.9	17.7
Kay County (north-central Oklahoma)	11	6.4	50	51
Edwards (central Texas)	4.6	3.0	13.9	14.3
Obsidian (New Mexico)	4.2	11.2	<1	—
Quartzites	3.9	3.0	8.6	9.7
Miscellaneous cherts (local)	3.5	11.9	7.5	7.2

[a]The Edwards site surface collection was not controlled and exotic types such as obsidian may be overrepresented.

may reflect changing networks of exchange, resource procurement, and cultural interaction. For the Edwards complex, about 80% of the lithic material was derived from the Texas Panhandle, New Mexico, or local sources. In contrast, 65% of the Wheeler complex lithics are derived from northcentral Oklahoma and central Texas. Only 15% are local and 20% from western sources. This shift in the derivation of lithic resources could reflect an important change in interregional group relationships. People of the Wheeler complex were obviously emphasizing trade with the Wichita (Taovayos and related groups) who lived along the Arkansas River near the Oklahoma–Kansas border. Perhaps, by this route, the Wheeler complex people were also indirectly in contact with French traders. Communication and trade between Wheeler people and the eastern New Mexico Pueblos (and indirectly with the Spaniards) was apparently of less intensity than such interaction during Edwards complex. For a further discussion of Wheeler complex cultural contact see Hofman (1978b:82–86). Interaction of the Edwards complex people appears to have been very distinctive in emphasis (T. Baugh 1982). During the Edwards complex, trading with the Pueblos and Caddo hamlets along the Red River was perhaps most important and trade or contact with the Arkansas River area villagers was secondary.

In addition to differences in lithic materials, some tool types characterize the Wheeler complex. Large end- and/or side-scrapers are one tool type that helps distinguish the Wheeler from the Edwards complex. These large scrapers are usually made of Kay County flint and appear to be similar in all respects to specimens from protohistoric Wichita sites on the Arkansas River (Sudbury 1976a; Hartley 1975a; Hartley and Miller 1977). These large scrapers are very common in the Wheeler complex assemblages at the Little Deer and Scott sites but occur only occasionally in Edwards complex assemblages. Projectile point frequencies appear to differ as well. Unnotched triangular arrowpoints constitute 85% of the Little Deer sample, whereas they comprise about 70% at the Edwards Site. Harrell and Washita types are represented in small numbers in both complexes. Garza points (triangular with a single basal notch) are seldom represented at Wheeler complex sites. The remaining stone tool assemblages reported for the Wheeler complex are comparable to those of the Edwards complex. Plain-shafted pipe drills, flake-base drills, flake tools, grooved abraders, grinding stones, and turquoise are represented. Bone artifacts include scapula tools (ppossibly scapula hoes), toothed bison-metapodial fleshers, and awls.

European trade items are also recorded from Wheeler sites. Although they are few in number, a varied assortment of trade goods are present. Glass beads are known from the Little Deer and Scott sites, and lead sprues, balls, and gun flints have been found at Little Deer. In addition, metal tools are indirectly evidenced by distinctive cut marks on bone artifacts (Hofman 1978b:66). The chronological position of the Wheeler complex has been discussed by Bell and Bastian (1967:124–127) and Hofman (1978b:71–74). No radiocarbon dates are available but A.D. 1650–1725 or 1750 is believed a realistic estimate for this culture. This estimate is based on sherds of late Pecos Glaze V, micaceous sherds, tubular decorated Pecos pipes, large end-scrapers like those used by protohistoric Wichita along the Arkansas River, bison-bone fleshers, and evidence of a variety of European trade materials believed to be of French origin.

Primary differences between the Edwards and Wheeler complexes can be summarized as follows:

1. Lithic material of the Edwards complex is primarily Alibates dolomite and secondarily Kay County chert, obsidian, and Edwards chert, whereas the predominant Wheeler complex lithic material is Kay County chert with lesser amounts of Alibates and Edwards chert and very little obsidian (Table 16.2).
2. Greater quantities and more varied Southwestern ceramics are associated with the Edwards complex than the Wheeler complex. In addition, the Edwards complex includes a variety of Southeastern Caddoan pottery.
3. The Wheeler complex includes more materials of European origin than the Edwards complex. Some Edwards assemblages apparently lack European items.
4. The Wheeler complex appears to be later than the Edwards complex.

Related Sites, Finds, and Complexes

In Oklahoma, Plains assemblages of protohistoric or very late prehistoric age are known from several sites. Most of these cannot be discussed here as detailed information about them is not available. A detailed report is available, however, for the Lowrance site (34Mr-10) in the Washita River drainage of southcentral Oklahoma (Wyckoff 1973; L. Taylor 1973). Assemblage B at Lowrance has been compared to the Wheeler complex (Wyckoff 1973:143; Hofman 1978b:76). Characteristic materials of Assemblage B include thin, gray sandy-paste pottery, triangular unnotched arrowpoints, flake-base drills, and large end-scrapers. These sherds are very similar to those of the Wheeler and Edwards complexes. Lowrance chipped-stone tools are distinctive in that they are predominantly local materials, with a few Alibates, obsidian and Kay County pieces present. No European trade goods were found at Lowrance. Wyckoff (1973:144) suggests a date from the late 1500s to the late 1600s for this Lowrance component.

It is difficult to assess fully relationships between Assemblage B at Lowrance and the Wheeler and Edwards complexes, partially due to the lack of information on protohistoric sites in the intervening area. The assemblage from Lowrance is comparable in several respects to both the Edwards and Wheeler assemblages, but until additional data are available we are unable to determine which affinity is strongest or if the Lowrance component relates to a third distinctive complex.

A complete vessel of thin, black sandy-paste pottery was reported by Vincent Dale (1973) from Texas County in the Oklahoma Panhandle. This vessel is similar to the sandy-paste pottery from the Edwards and Wheeler sites, and it is the only complete vessel of this ceramic type from Oklahoma. No materials were found with the vessel, but it probably results from protohistoric activity in the Panhandle region by people related to those in southwestern Oklahoma.

In west Texas, the Floydada Country Club site (Word 1963), Montgomery site (Word 1965), Pete Creek site (Parsons 1967), and the Garza components at the Lubbock Lake site (Holliday 1977; E. Johnson et al. 1977) have protohistoric occupations. These Texas sites all contain sandy-paste, dark thin-walled ceramics, and usually Puebloan derived pottery. At the Montgomery site, for example, 85% of the pottery is believed to be Puebloan utilitarian wares. Triangular notched and unnotched arrowpoints, flake-base drills, end-scrapers, and sometimes serrated metapodial fleshers are found. Most of the Texas sites contain an abundance of bison bone. European trade items are rare. Lithic materials are typically Edwards chert and Alibates (or Tecovas), but obsidian occurs in notable quantities. Two dates from the Garza levels at Lubbock Lake (A.D. 1635 ± 50 and 1665 ± 60; E. Johnson et al. 1977:104) apparently indicate occupations during the sixteenth and seventeenth centuries. These west Texas protohistoric occupations have not been summarized in a comprehensive fashion and no archaeological complexes have been defined that can be used to organize these assemblages into a systematic framework. It may eventually be feasible to incorporate them into the Edwards complex. Evaluation of interrelationships between these sites and those in western Oklahoma will be possible only after detailed comparative research.

Probably the best-known protohistoric complex in the western Plains region is the Dismal River aspect, documented primarily through study of sites in western Nebraska and Kansas and eastern Colorado (Hill and Metcalf 1942; Champe 1949; W. R. Wedel 1959; J. H. Gunnerson 1960, 1968; Wood 1971; Schlesier 1972). Dismal River is believed to represent Apachean occupations of the Central Plains between A.D. 1675 and 1725. These assemblages share a number of common characteristics in ceramic and lithic artifacts with the Edwards and Wheeler complexes (Hofman 1978b:79–82; T. G. Baugh 1982) and other Southern Plains protohistoric assemblages. A limited amount of Rio Grande Pueblo material is reported from the Dismal River sites, as are some European trade items. There can be little doubt that most of the Southern Plains sites discussed above are part of the same archaeological tradition as Dismal River. This is not to imply that all the groups represented were genetically related. To assume that all the Southern Plains protohistoric assemblages with black sandy pottery represent activities of Apachean groups would be premature. Dismal River sites apparently postdate some of the Southern Plains components and we can appropriately look to the Southern Plains for Dismal River antecedents.

Speculations

The actual relationship between the Edwards and Wheeler complexes is unknown, but the sites attributed to these complexes represent the activities of related societies. Changes in the trade patterns of these groups through time could have resulted in the differences observed between assemblages of the Edwards and Wheeler complexes. It is also possible that both represent a number of distinct bands or subtribes who were competing for specific resources and for European trade goods. These groups may have been historically related and were almost certainly in continued contact. Edwards and Wheeler may represent a continuum of culture change. The presence of fortification ditches at the Edwards and Duncan sites in southwest Oklahoma is of special interest. Do these features represent efforts to protect people from raiding by hostile groups living in the region, or conflict with people from other areas?

The presence of Puebloan artifacts on the sites could result from movement of small groups as well as trade. Some Pueblo people are known to have fled the Spanish-dominated Southwest during the seventeenth century. For example, members of Picuris Pueblo lived for a time with Plains Apache groups. It is likely that the Pueblo people carried valued articles with them to the east and they probably continued to make pottery following traditional Pueblo designs and techniques. Although trade may be primarily responsible for occurrences of Puebloan artifacts in western Oklahoma, the possibility that a few Pueblo Indians lived in this region during part of the seventeenth and into the eighteenth century cannot be discounted.

The Edwards I site and apparently several other Southern Plains protohistoric sites predate sites of the Dismal River aspect. As presently understood, Dismal River occupations date between A.D. 1675 and 1725. If Dismal River has its roots, at least partially, in the spread of Athapaskans out of the Southwest, then there should be Athapaskan sites on the Southern Plains that predate some Dismal River occupations. In looking for possible Southern Plains complexes from which Dismal River may be derived, the Edwards complex, and to some extent the Wheeler complex, are candidates. It is also evident that some of these people remained in the Southern Plains area and were contemporary with the groups composing the Dismal River aspect. Apachean occupation of the Southern Plains is believed to have began before and to have continued after occupation of the Dismal River sites.

However, Apachean people were not the only ones active in the Southern Plains during the sixteenth and seventeenth centuries. Therefore, we should not assume that all assemblages that are in some way comparable to Dismal River are necessarily Apachean. Activities of groups such as the Jumano, Caddo, and others could be represented by archaeological remains in the region.

The impact that bison-hunting tribes moving into the area from the Southwest had on the native villagers is not well understood. It has been suggested, and is quite plausible, that nomadic newcomers harassed settled Southern Plains villagers of the Washita River complex and Panhandle aspect. The apparent abandonment of Washita River and Panhandle aspect village sites during the last half of the fifteenth century may have resulted in part from the eastern spread of Athapaskans and/or other groups. By the mid-sixteenth century this transition seems to have been complete for some of the Panhandle aspect and Washita River villagers may have left the area and moved to the north and east. By the seventeenth century this portion of the Southern Plains was dominated by hunting, trading, and possibly horticultural groups. These are probably the people encountered by Coronado, Oñate, and others.

It is possible that some descendants of the Washita River phase and Panhandle aspect peoples were incorporated into the western protohistoric societies. I am not, however, in agreement with T. Baugh's (1982) hypothesis that the Edwards complex represents a cultural continuum with the Washita River phase, or that the Edwards complex represents an ethnic group ancestral to the Wichita. My basic reason for disagreement is that the ceramic technology of the Edwards complex is distinct from that of the Washita River phase (Hofman 1978c), the Great Bend aspect (W. Wedel 1959), and the protohistoric Wichita on the Arkansas River in northern Oklahoma (Hartley and Miller 1977; Sudbury 1976a). It is presently widely accepted that the Washita River phase represents groups ancestral to the Wichita and related tribes. The ceramics of the Washita River phase are more similar to those of the protohistoric Wichita in terms of form, paste, and color than are the ceramics of either of these manifestations to the Edwards complex pottery (Hofman 1978b:83–84). Pottery from Edwards and Wheeler complex sites does not fit easily within the apparent Wichita ceramic tradition as represented from Washita River phase through the protohistoric

Arkansas River villages. Rather, ceramics from the western protohistoric assemblages compare most favorably with that of the Dismal River aspect and to some extent with protohistoric Athabaskan (Navajo and Jicarilla) ceramics and Eastern Pueblo utilitarian wares. Neither does the presence of horticulture and its associated technology constitute a valid argument for assignment of the Edwards complex to the Wichita or other Caddoan group. T. Baugh's hypothesis is an important alternative to consider, but it is premature to assign the Edwards and Wheeler complexes to a specific ethnic group(s).

Research Needs

Many of the present problems facing the study of protohistoric occupations in western Oklahoma are of a cultural–historical nature. When we have a better understanding of chronology, sites, and assemblages the archaeological complexes can be refined and questions addressed regarding economies, European contact and its effects, settlement, and interrelationships of the groups represented by these archaeological remains. Some specific problems include the need for

1. More radiocarbon and archaeomagnetic dates in order to make comparisons between sites and complexes more meaningful; at present there are no absolute dates for the Wheeler complex.

2. Information on community organization and architecture, which is now extremely limited for the period; no Wheeler complex sites have been excavated.

3. Detailed reporting of available surface collections, private collections, and available excavated materials. This reporting is essential and will enable a more comprehensive evaluation of the protohistoric complexes and facilitate their comparison.

4. Additional work in unstudied or poorly known regions. Until this is accomplished, there can be little hope of filling the gaps in our knowledge of settlement or intersite and intercomplex relationships in the Southern Plains area.

Reference Note

This presentation is based on both archaeological and ethnohistorical references. Information on the Wheeler complex is derived from Bell and Bastian (1967b) and Hofman (1978b), whereas information on the Edwards complex comes primarily from the Edwards I site (Baugh and Swenson 1980; Baugh and Terrell 1982; T. Baugh 1982; Bell 1973:185; Hofman 1978b:75), Area B of the Taylor site (Burton and Burton 1969:14–19, Tables 2 and 4), one area of the Goodwin–Baker site (Wyckoff 1970a), and the Duncan site (Neal 1982; T. Baugh 1981). Additional protohistoric materials that cannot be assigned with confidence to either the Wheeler or Edwards complex include a vessel from Texas County (Dale 1973) and Assemblage B at the Lowrance site in Murray County (Wyckoff 1973; L. Taylor 1973).

Archaeological data on the Dismal River aspect are from Champe (1949), J. H. Gunnerson (1960, 1968), Hill and Metcalf (1942), Schlesier (1972), and W. R. Wedel (1959). Comments on protohistoric components in western Texas are based on reports by Holliday (1977), Johnson *et al.* (1977), Parsons (1967), and Word (1963, 1965). Upper Rio Grande Pueblo site data are primarily from Pecos Pueblo (Kidder 1932, 1958). Ethnohistorical information is derived from Bolton (1908), Forbes (1960), R. I. Ford (1972), D. A. Gunnerson (1956, 1974), John (1975), J. C. Kelley (1955), Kessell (1979), Lange (1953, 1957, 1979), Opler (1971, 1975), Riley (1978), Schroeder (1962, 1979), Thomas (1935), M. M. Wedel (1981), Wedel and Wedel (1976), and Winship (1896).

Acknowledgments

I extend special thanks to Timothy G. Baugh, Don G. Wyckoff, Christopher Lintz, and Pat Kawecki for their efforts toward completion of this chapter.

CHAPTER 17

Protohistoric Wichita

Robert E. Bell

Introduction

Archaeological sites in Oklahoma that have produced evidence of trade and contact with Europeans during the period from A.D. 1600 to 1800 are rare. Of the sites known, only two have been subjected to partial excavation and the rest are known chiefly from surface collections. Our best information comes from the Bryson–Paddock (Ka-5) and Deer Creek (Ka-3) sites in northern Oklahoma on the Arkansas River, and the Longest (Jf-1) site in southern Oklahoma on the Red River (Figure 17.1). These sites have been identified as representing the Wichita Indians, who inhabited the southern Plains in historic times. The designation *Wichita* is used here in a broad sense to include not only the Wichita proper but the affiliated tribes that were a part of the Wichita confederacy. These include the Wichita, Iscani, Taovayas, Tawakoni, Waco, and Kichai. The three sites mentioned above are usually attributed to the Taovayas although it is known that the various groups frequently occupied the same village area. Our present knowledge does not permit clear distinctions between the various groups as far as the archaeological record is concerned.

There are several other sites that may represent early Wichita occupations: Adkins (M1-17), Baum (Ka-70), Beard #1 (Ka-46), Butterfield (Ka-119), Cn-22, Cn-23, Gordy (Ka-141), Hartshorne (Ka-42), Hinz (Wa-4), Keith (Cd-8), Leche #2 (Os-54), Little Deer (Cu-10), Olson (Ka-117), Scott (Cn-2), Scott (Ka-52), Shotts (Jk-27), Van Rollins (Cn-21), and Wilson Springs (Cd-5). These sites have produced trade materials or Wichita-style flint scrapers but excavation and additional research may modify the idea that these represent Wichita occupations.

363

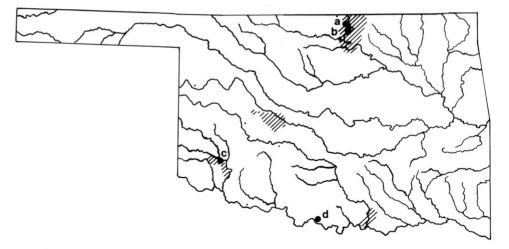

Figure 17.1 Protohistoric Wichita area: (a) Bryson–Paddock, (b) Deer Creek, (c) Devil's Canyon, (d) Longest; hatching indicates other, isolated sites.

The three major sites—Deer Creek, Bryson–Paddock, and Longest—are generally attributed to the Taovayas who were actively engaged in trade with the French during the eighteenth century. The early maps and documents, however, are often not as precise as one would like and the identifications are subject to considerable controversy. The historical discussions regarding identification of these sites can be found in Bell, *et al.* (1967), Harper (1953), Hartley and Miller (1977), McRill (1963), Sudbury (1976a), and M. Wedel (1981).

It seems possible that the Deer Creek and Bryson–Paddock sites represent the two Paniouassa (Wichita) villages visited by Claude Du Tisne in 1719. The location of the Paniafsas Indian town and fort on the John Mitchell map (M. Wedel 1981: Figure 18, p. 64) coincides well with the location of the Deer Creek site. The name *Fernandina* also refers to the Deer Creek site, but the origin of this name remains uncertain and it does not appear on early maps until around 1830.

The Longest site situation on Red River has been identified as San Bernardo, a fortified Wichita village (Taovayas) that was an important trade center by 1760.

The historical records suggest that the Deer Creek and Bryson–Paddock sites were most intensively occupied during the period from 1700 to 1750, and that the Longest site flourished after 1750. Apparently pressures from the Osage in disrupting French trade flowing up the Arkansas River valley could be avoided by shifting the villages to the Red River in southern Oklahoma. The present archaeological evidence does not refute this suggestion, but excavations at the Deer Creek site may necessitate modifications of this view.

There are four radiocarbon dates available from the Bryson–Paddock site (Table 17.1). Two of these are from a modern charred log and can be discounted. The other two dates suggest an occupation earlier than 1700, but this might be

Table 17.1

Protohistoric Wichita Radiocarbon Dates

Laboratory number	Site and provenience	Date before present (B.P.)	Date (A.D.) based on 5568 half-life	Date (A.D.) based on 5730 half-life	MASCA corrected date (A.D.)	Reference
Tx-2356	Bryson–Paddock Feature 5, pit, burned log	35 ± 70	1915	1914	Modern	Hartley and Miller 1977:194
Tx-2357	Bryson–Paddock Feature 5, pit; same sample as Tx-2356	Modern	Modern	Modern	Modern	Hartley and Miller 1977:194
Tx-2359	Bryson–Paddock Feature 4, pit, charcoal	190 ± 60	1760	1755	1695 ± 45	Hartley and Miller 1977:189
Tx-2360	Bryson–Paddock Feature 7, pit, charcoal	290 ± 70	1660	1652	1560 ± 80	Hartley and Miller 1977:204

expected. This particular time period is troublesome because of fluctuations in the radiocarbon–dendrochronology curves that make precise dating difficult. The trade materials suggest an occupation from around 1720 to 1750 for the Bryson–Paddock site, and until additional radiocarbon dates or other evidence become available the trade goods are likely to be most accurate for dating purposes.

The major sites as well as others that may represent Wichita occupations are concentrated in a wide band from north to south in central Oklahoma rather closely following the Central Redbed Plains physiographic region. This is an area dominated by Tall-grass Prairie vegetation with its associated flora and fauna. The Cross Timbers belt or Post oak–Blackjack forest region lies to the east and does not appear to have been heavily exploited, as the potential Wichita sites lie chiefly to the west. This region is characterized by low relief dominated by shales and sandstone outcrops. The Deer Creek and Bryson–Paddock sites fall in the western margins of the Northern Limestone Cuesta Plains and have good resources of flint locally available. The Kay County flint quarries are only 16 km to the northeast and other outcrops of limestone containing flint nodules occur in the immediate site areas.

Settlement Patterns

A comprehensive view of the Wichita settlement pattern cannot be formulated at this time because research has been limited to the three major sites and only two of these have been partly excavated. It is clear, however, that these are large concentrated villages situated on large rivers that provided access to the French trade centered at New Orleans. Other sites producing trade items or Wichita-related materials appear to be specialized localities or limited occupational sites related to these major villages.

The major village sites are all large in total extent. The Deer Creek site covers an area of approximately 13 ha and the Longest site occupies about 14 to 16 ha. The Bryson–Paddock site, covering about 4 to 5 ha, appears to be the smallest of the three. All three sites are situated on higher lands near the river on terraces above the flood plain.

A distinguishing feature of the villages is the presence of a large circular or oval-shaped earthwork or fortification. Other obvious surface features include numerous low mounds and shallow depressions. Excavations have also revealed the presence of houses, numerous storage or refuse pits, burials, occasional postholes, and scattered midden areas.

The earthwork located at the Deer Creek site forms a large circular area that is open at one end, is rather horseshoe shaped, and measures approximately 134 m across the diameter. It appears as a ditch but is not continuous; one area opposite the open end appears to represent an entryway to the interior of the enclosed area. The ditch today is from 0.6 to 0.9 m deep in places and the surface on each side suggests that some of the ditch fill was piled along the edges. This feature suggests a circular fortification having a ditch and embankment but, until excavation, no conclusions can be finalized.

A large, oval-shaped ditch has been discovered at the Longest site also. It forms a large oval approximately 80 m wide and 118 m long. This feature, however, has been cultivated for many years and is not evident upon the surface other than by the presence of bone fragments that have been plowed up from the ditch fill. A cross section was cut across this feature in 1967 to reveal the presence of a wide ditch measuring 3.6 m across at the top, with sloping side walls forming a ditch about 1.2 m in depth. No indications of postholes or a fortification wall were found at that time.

Thoburn mentions the existence of a similar earthwork at the Bryson–Paddock site; this is apparently circular or horseshoe shaped with the opening facing the river. Fieldwork at the Bryson–Paddock site did not investigate this feature.

The villages clearly are not contained within these circular earthworks because evidence of structures, midden mounds, and scattered debris are to be found in many areas surrounding these enclosures. They appear to represent fortifications at which the villagers could assemble for protection in times of attack.

Excavations have revealed the presence of house structures of varying size and form at these sites (Figure 17.2). Random postholes also suggest the existence of possible food-drying racks, arbors, fences, enclosures, or other similar features. There are indications of three different forms of structures: (1) a round or circular structure similar to the historic Wichita grass house; (2) an oval-shaped structure also used as a living area or covered arbor similar to the historic Wichita; and (3) a larger circular structure believed to be a community or specialized village feature.

The round or circular structures are best known from the Longest site and the Upper Tucker site immediately across the Red River in Texas. These houses range in size from 6 to 10 m in diameter. The construction was located in a shallow saucer-shaped depression with an outer ring of postholes providing evidence of the exterior wall. A second ring of larger postholes appears in the interior. These indicate roof supports for the outer ring of posts that were leaned against the inner ring to form a beehive-shaped structure. The floor plan is similar, if not identical, to Wichita grass houses of historic and present times. There is a fireplace at the center, and extra postholes sometimes suggest additional interior supports, special features, or replacement of initial constructions.

Another type of residence is represented by an oval-shaped house constructed in a saucer-shaped depression. These range in size from 4 by 6 m to larger houses measuring as much as 6.7 by 11 m. The oval-shaped depression over which the structure was erected varies in depth, but it may be from 30 to 45 cm in depth at the center. The posthole arrangement varies somewhat from example to example, but generally posts are arranged around the edges of the depres-

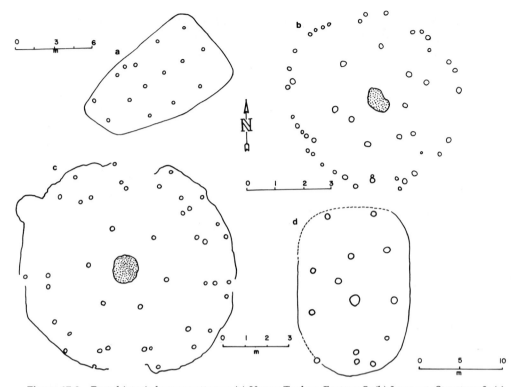

Figure 17.2 Protohistoric house patterns: (a) Upper Tucker, Feature 5; (b) Longest, Structure 3; (c) Longest, Structure 1; and (d) Bryson–Paddock, Structure B. Shaded areas indicate clay hearths.

sion with a series of roof support posts placed in a line along the center, following the long axis of the structure. A central fireplace is usually present. Like the circular houses, the oval-shaped houses commonly contain evidence of household debris scattered over the floor areas.

The Bryson–Paddock site also produced evidence of a larger circular structure that is believed to represent a community or specialized structure. The posthole pattern is not as clear as one would like, but it appears to represent a large circular house measuring approximately 12 m in diameter. The central area is marked by a fireplace and it is surrounded by an inner ring of posts, apparently used for roof supports. Although the ring patterns are incomplete and some extra posts occur, the outer areas appear to be represented by two rings of postholes. The structure resembles the circular houses but it is larger in size; it is not placed in a depression but is constructed on level ground and is marked by the general absence of cultural debris. It appears unlike any other structures reported and apparently served some different village function.

It is believed that all these structures were grass-covered houses similar to the historic Wichita. The general absence of daub and the presence of burned grass "silica clinkers" indicate that this was the case.

Another characteristic of the Wichita village sites is the presence of numerous small circular or oval-shaped mounds. These vary in size from small mounds, easily overlooked, no more than 20 cm in height, up to larger mounds measuring 0.6–0.9 m in height. The diameter varies according to height but ranges from 6 to 12 m. These mounds are quite numerous and appear scattered throughout the village area. There are around 60 to 65 mounds indicated for the Deer Creek site, and an equally large number were formerly present at the Bryson–Paddock site. Cultivation, however, has leveled off most of the mounds at the Bryson–Paddock site as well as at large areas of the Longest site, but their former existence is suggested by concentrations of village debris.

These mounds were first thought to represent the remains of former house locations, but excavations at the Longest site indicated that they were composed entirely of village refuse—broken animal bones, ash, charcoal, various artifacts, soil, and debitage. They represent concentrated middens, trash mounds, or midden mounds and appear to contain no special features. Without more extensive village site excavation they cannot be associated with specific house structures.

Another common feature associated with the village sites is cache or storage pits. These may occur close to the houses or almost anywhere in the village area and are usually filled with trash or midden deposit when excavated. The pits vary in form and are represented by cylindrical, bowl-shaped, and bell-shaped pits. The latter are smaller at the top and flare outward, with the largest diameter at the floor of the pits. The size varies considerably from the smaller examples, measuring 45–60 cm in diameter and 50–60 cm in depth, to large pits measuring 150 cm in diameter and 150 cm in depth. Most of them, however, are around 90 cm in diameter and 90–120 cm in depth. They contain village debris or midden material—animal bones, artifacts, flint debris, broken rocks, charcoal, and so forth. Some examples have sterile soil lenses present that divide the pit interior into an upper and lower section. Whether this represents a temporary abandonment with the resulting wash-fill or a purposeful seal remains unknown. Pits found at the Longest site suggest that grass liners were sometimes used and that covers may have been supported by ledges or cut-out areas made in the wall of the pit. The pits were used for temporary storage and when abandoned became a convenient place to dispose of refuse.

Burials

Burials have been found only at the Longest site, so our information regarding burial customs is quite limited. A total of seven burials have been found and these were in two different areas of the site, both appearing to be at the peripheries of the occupational areas. Mr. Longest reports plowing up burials in various locations, which also suggests that no special cemetery area was used for the entire community but that the graves were scattered around the village area. The burials are all single interments placed in a shallow grave, with the body arranged in an extended position on the back, with the head toward the east. These shallow graves are usually less than 30 cm in depth, so that cultivation has disturbed many of the recorded graves.

The burials recovered are all represented by adult individuals, both male and female. All of them have some burial goods in association and these include both aboriginal items and European trade goods. The grave offerings are most common around the head or upper part of the body, but they may also occur around the hips, along the legs, or at the feet of the burial. The simplest burial reported is Burial 2, an incomplete partially damaged skeleton that had two large mussel shells placed near the feet. Because the head and upper portion of the grave were missing, additional offerings may originally have been present. In contrast to this, Burial 1, an adult male individual, had a variety of grave associations. In a small area near the knees, in what may have been a perishable container of some type, the following items were present: 1 triangular-shaped flint knife of Alibates flint, 1 diamond-beveled flint knife of Kay County flint, 2 native-made gun flints, 2 concave scrapers, 18 flakes of Edwards Plateau flint, 2 fragments of sheet brass, 13 iron fragments, including parts of a gun barrel and knife blade, and scattered red ochre. One crushed pottery vessel was found in the abdominal area, and to the left of the pelvic bone a lump of red ochre, an unfired ball of clay, 1 mussel shell, 1 lump of native asphalt, 1 small blue glass bead, and a pebble smeared with ochre were found. Other items in the plow-disturbed grave area include an elbow-pipe fragment of siltstone, 2 small brass rings, a lead ball, 2 flint flakes, and 1 additional blue glass bead.

Other items that have been found in association with burials include a rough stone chopper, sandstone arrowshaft smoothers, a tanning stone, clay and catlinite pipes, turtle shells, fragments of iron kettles, iron nails, iron arrowpoints (Benton Types A and B), hawk bells, a brass pendant, a silver alloy ornament, glass mirrors, a variety of glass beads, and cloth fragments containing a fine copper wire that acted to preserve the fabric.

Artifacts

The economy manifest at the early Wichita sites indicates great importance attached to the French trade. This is shown in the quantity and variety of French trade items found throughout the sites. It seems quite possible, however, that the abundance of these desired trade goods may bias one's view regarding the internal economics of the Wichita villages. Although trade goods such as firearms, glass beads, ornaments, or utensils were highly prized, the need for basic subsistence items remained to be fulfilled by local resources. Although hunting would be easier with horses and firearms, and gardening might be made less laborious with metal tools, both of these activities were still necessary. The desire and availability of trade goods certainly had an impact upon traditional practices, but this is difficult to assess at the present time with the data available. One has the subjective judgment that hunting assumed increased importance because of the demand for furs and animal products, but garden produce could well be of equal significance in terms of local trade. It is clear that trade, either local or with Europeans, is of greatly increased importance by this time period.

Animal-bone refuse from excavations at the Bryson–Paddock site includes bison, deer, antelope, black bear, raccoon, jack rabbit, cottontail, bobcat, opossum, grey squirrel, mouse, gopher, turtles, numerous small birds, turkey, gar, catfish, and other unidentified remains. The most common bones are those of the bison, deer, and turtle, and it seems quite likely that bison and deer provided the major meat supply. Mussel shells and fish bones indicate utilization of the river resources, but this appears as a less-important activity. Cultivated plants are represented by remains of corn, beans, and squash, as well as some additional seeds that have not been identified. Acorns, pecans, and coffee-bean seeds have also been recovered, and many other wild plant products that are not preserved must have been utilized. The presence of projectile points and hunting equipment, as well as artifacts associated with gardening, such as the bone-scapula hoe, also attests to hunting and gardening as important activities.

The Kay county flint deposits were undoubtedly an important local resource for the Wichita villages. Evidence of quarry pits, workshops, and exposed outcrops of limestone containing flint nodules provided a supply of this raw material. Flint from these sources is plentiful on the northern village sites, not only in finished artifacts, but in debitage from their manufacture. In addition, flint artifacts made of this material are commonly found on contact sites not only in Oklahoma, but in Kansas and in northern Texas. Much of this material has been heat-treated to improve the knapping process. Large flint scrapers and alternate beveled knives appear to be a popular trade item derived from this source.

Aboriginal items present at the sites include a variety of tools and implements made of stone, bone, shell, and clay (Figure 17.3). Articles made from stone by a pecking and grinding process include milling stones, various types of abraders, pendants, and pipes. Milling stones, represented by manos and milling basins, are present although most specimens found are fragmentary. The manos are bifacial, commonly with one face more flattened than the other, and frequently marked by small pits or cups apparently resulting from use as a nut-cracking stone or anvil. Most manos are rectangular or oval shaped in form and suitable for use in one hand. The milling stones have shallow oval-shaped basins suggesting grinding by a rotary motion rather than the back-and-forth motion typical of the Southwestern metate.

Sandstone abraders are also quite characteristic of the sites and were used for smoothing arrowshafts or sharpening bone tools. They are typically loaf-shaped with one or more grooves worn or ground into the surface. The arrowshaft

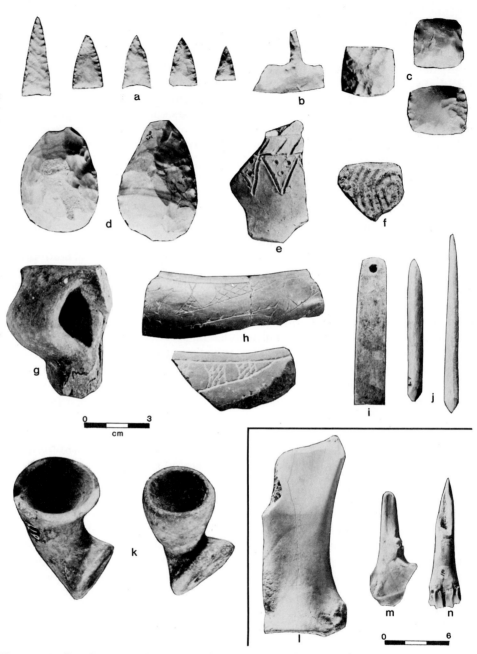

Figure 17.3 Protohistoric Wichita artifacts from the Bryson–Paddock site (J. Thoburn excavations). (a) Triangular arrowpoints; (b) flint perforator; (c) native-made gun flints; (d) flint scrapers of Kay County chert; (e) incised pottery sherd; (f) stamped pottery sherd; (g) pottery handle, shell-tempered ware; (h) sherds of Womack Engraved; (i) fragmentary bone pendant; (j) rib-edge bone awls; (k) pottery elbow-pipes; (l) bone-scapula hoe; (m) bone flaking tool; (n) cannon-bone awl.

smoothers have a typical U-shaped or rounded groove whereas the awl sharpeners have a V-shaped groove. Other specimens, some containing grooves, have flat abraded areas present, which suggests their use as a hone or file.

There is one small fragment from what appears to be a stone pendant. The perforation is present but the size and form cannot be determined from the fragment.

Stone elbow-pipes are also present. Most of the specimens are fragmentary except for examples from the Longest site. The typical pipe is elbow-shaped with the stem somewhat longer than the bowl. The pipe bowl is commonly flared and is sometimes decorated with incised designs. There are also some fragments of pipe bowls having a bulbous form, suggesting the "micmac" type pipe found in the Great Lakes region. One complete stone pipe found with a burial at the Longest site contained a metal inlay on the stem. The inlay forms a series of V designs extending from the mouthpiece toward the bowl. The design had been deeply cut into the pipe stem and was then filled with a *white metal* alloy composed of lead and zinc. The pipe is made of red catlinite from Minnesota and obviously represents a trade specimen. Although other materials were used, catlinite is commonly represented in other pipe specimens from the sites. Other stone items include pieces of hematite or limonite that exhibit abrasions and rubbed areas resulting from use as a source for pigment.

Chipped-stone artifacts manufactured from various types of flint include scrapers, projectile points, knives, drills, gun flints, preforms, cores, and utilized flakes. Of these, large scrapers and projectile points are the most abundant. The local Kay County flint represents the most common material, and the presence of debitage indicates that this was worked at the sites.

Large scrapers are abundant at the Deer Creek and Bryson–Paddock sites, and hundreds of them have been collected from the surface over the years by private collectors. They vary in form and workmanship from large flakes, in which a scraping edge has been shaped for use at one end, to those in which one or both sides are carefully trimmed, possibly to facilitate mounting. Some examples of concave scrapers also occur, but they are less frequent. Many of the scrapers show extensive wear or use polish on the scraping edge whereas others appear sharp and fresh. They are usually found scattered throughout the site deposits, but one cache of 12 specimens, neatly piled close together, has been found at the Bryson–Paddock site. The large amount of these artifacts indicates the importance of skin-working activity at the sites, which presumably was a response to the French fur trade.

Flint projectile points are the second-most-common artifact in lithic materials. The large majority of projectile points are represented by arrowpoints, although some dart points have been collected from the surface. The most typical arrowpoint is the Fresno type, a simple triangular form without notches or modification. There is considerable variation in the size, workmanship, and base form, but these minor differences appear to be of no significance. Other types of arrowpoints have been found, but they represent a small percentage of the total numbers; these include types identified as Scallorn, Reed, and Washita.

Flint knives are not plentiful although a number of fragments as well as complete specimens have been recovered. The typical specimen is represented by the alternate-beveled diamond-shaped knife (Harahay knife). Flint drills are present but are rare. Specimens recovered are made from flakes in which the flake has been trimmed to form a short drill or perforator.

Native-made gun flints are also found at all the sites. Out of 84 gun flints reported for the Deer Creek and Bryson–Paddock sites, only 12 have been identified as representing English or French gun flints; the majority are Indian-made of various materials. It should also be noted that the greatest variation in lithic materials is represented by the gun flints, which indicates widespread points of origin. Some of them, however, are locally made of Kay County material.

Other flint items include cores, preforms in various stages of manufacture, miscellaneous flakes that have been utilized for cutting or scraping, and debris from tool manufacture. Indications of heat treatment and tool making are both present.

Artifacts made from bone are also characteristic of the Wichita sites. Bison and deer bone are favorite materials but other bones are sometimes used as well. Artifacts manufactured from bone include scapula hoes, scapula knives, various kinds of awls, knife handles, pendants, hide grainers, antler flakers, bird-bone beads, and grooved rib rasps.

Tools made from the bison scapula are perhaps the most common. Hoes or digging tools are made from the shoulder blade by trimming off the spine. Although most specimens recovered are fragmentary, there is no evidence for a drilled socket or side groove to facilitate hafting. The flat portion of the scapula is commonly ground along one edge to make a bone knife or cutting tool. Many of these appear to be made from broken or damaged scapula hoes and are commonly referred to as *squash knives*. Occasionally a bone awl or perforator is made from the removed scapula spine.

The most common awl is one cut from the edge of a rib or vertebral spine that provides a thick, straight section of bone. The cross section is triangular in form and the base is typically crudely ground to a conical point. In addition to these, awls made from the deer cannon-bone have been found.

Bone handles for metal knives are also present. These are made from a rib bone that has been split by a groove or slot into which a flat metal knife blade can be inserted. The rib serves both as a handle and a mount for the knife blade. Recovered specimens do not contain the metal knife blade.

Tabular or spatulate-shaped bone pendants are also found. These are made from a flat section of bone, ranging from 1.0 to 2.0 cm in width, and have a perforation at one end. Because no whole specimens have been recovered, the length is not known, but one incomplete specimen from the Bryson–Paddock site measures 12.5 cm. Other fragments suggest that this broken example is probably from a large specimen.

What are here designated as *hide grainers* are also present. These are sections of bone ends, representing the spongy cancellous portion of the bone, that have flat surfaces and indications of usage for rubbing or smoothing soft material. The head of the bison femur was commonly used for this artifact, which was used for the preparation of hides and skins during the tanning process. Other bone items represented include cut sections of bird bones that have been used for beads, and grooved bison ribs that suggest the notched rib rasp.

Antler was sometimes utilized, chiefly for flint flakers or as tapping tools (soft hammers). One specimen has been found that is cut in half lengthwise and appears to be unfinished, or possibly it was intended as part of a composite artifact. The identification, however, remains unknown.

Shell artifacts are quite scarce. This is possibly a result of preservation because mussel shells were usually in poor condition. *Olivella* shells for beads, a small shell pendant, and a shell scraper are reported from the Deer Creek and Bryson–Paddock sites. The Longest site has produced a single shell-pendant and three large disk-shaped beads, the latter representing ear ornaments.

Artifacts made from clay include pottery, pipes, and figurines. Pottery sherds are most plentiful and over 8500 specimens have been reported from the Deer Creek and Bryson–Paddock sites. In spite of this abundance, no whole vessels have been found. The most common ware is a smooth surfaced shell-tempered pottery formed by rings or coils of clay and bonded together by the paddle-and-anvil method. The vessel form appears to be a large globular-shaped pot with a direct or slightly flaring rim and a rounded bottom, although some flattened bases do occur. Both loop and strap handles occur and were riveted to the body just below the rim on the neck area of the vessel. The sherds resemble other late prehistoric shell-tempered types, such as Woodward Plain, Cowley Plain, and Nocona Plain of surrounding regions. Two additional shell-tempered wares, however, are more distinctive. One of these is impressed with a thong-wrapped paddle and is designated *Deer Creek Simple Stamped*, and the other is a brushed surface ware designated *Deer Creek Brushed*. These sherds represent less than 10% of the total sample. The simple stamped-sherds resemble Geneseo Simple Stamped, but the brushed wares do not resemble other types found in Oklahoma. In addition, a small number of sherds having a shell tempering indicate the presence of incising and punctating, dentate stamping, and black painting as an additional surface treatment.

There are also a small percentage of sherds with different tempering materials, such as sand, grit, and/or grog that can be identified as belonging to either Womack Plain or Womack Engraved. This ware is usually covered with a red slip that is more characteristic of the Red River valley region, and it is probably an import from that area.

Elbow clay pipes are especially numerous at the Deer Creek and Bryson–Paddock sites. Although most are incomplete, a total of 649 pipe fragments have been found at these two sites. The pipes are typically made of shell-tempered clay and are shaped into small to medium elbow-pipes. The bowl usually flares to form a conical bowl and the stems are often conical in form. There is considerable variation in the shaping and workmanship represented in the pipes, and a small number of them exhibit incised or engraved designs on the bowl.

Crude clay figurines are also present. These are found chiefly as small fragments that are poorly baked so that identification is difficult. They appear to represent human figures, animals, or bird forms. Some specimens have holes in them where small sticks can be inserted to provide legs, and suggest horse or animal figurines. Occasionally a specimen is decorated with incisions or some design.

Aboriginal trade items, aside from European trade goods, reflect a widespread area of contact. Lithic materials from all surrounding states are present along with nonlocal sources within Oklahoma. Flint or chert from the following lithic sources is reported: Alibates dolomite, Shidler (Foraker), Frisco, Peoria, Boone (Keokuk), novaculite, Edwards Plateau, Bolivar (Cotter dolomite), Cresswell, Woodford, Tecovas, and Smoky Hills jasper. Other items that represent nonlocal resources include asphaltum, catlinite, obsidian, and Womack Engraved pottery.

European manufactured materials are also present at the Deer Creek and Bryson–Paddock sites. Aside from glass beads, the most frequent items are parts of guns, conical-shaped metal tinklers, copper kettle fragments, and knives. Firearms are represented by iron or brass metal parts from three types of guns: English trade guns, a good-grade French trade gun, and a good-grade French military gun. These are represented by metal pieces ranging from gun barrels to lock-plate screws; virtually all the gun mechanisms or decorative features are represented.

Household and other metal tools or implements include sheath and clasp knives, copper kettles, axe blades, hoes, wedges, scissors, punches, awls, spoon or fork handles, fine copper wire, and projectile points.

Items for adornment or personal gear include a variety of glass beads, glass mirrors, tinklers, brass rings and chain sections, a button, small bells, rivets, and some fabric fragments.

There are, of course, numerous metal scraps of iron or brass that have not been identified because of their fragmentary condition. Flat glass was sometimes treated as raw lithic material and examples of chipped knives, scrapers, and Fresno points are known.

The trade materials appear to be primarily of French origin and to date during the period from A.D. 1700 to 1760, although some later items are reported. Utilizing the data from glass beads, Sudbury (1976b) has suggested that the Bryson–Paddock site is slightly earlier than Deer Creek.

The Longest site on Red River has produced essentially similar materials except that there are some striking differences in the frequency of many items. For example, there are 4743 excavated pottery sherds from the Bryson–Paddock site and only 175 excavated sherds from the Longest site. There are 372 examples of flint arrowheads and 8 metal arrowheads from the Bryson–Paddock site, and only 8 flint arrowheads but 35 metal arrowpoints from the Longest site. This indicates that aboriginal pottery was rapidly replaced by copper kettles or trade vessels, and that hunting with the bow and arrow was replaced with firearms. Not only are the bow and arrow less utilized, but arrowpoints made of flint are replaced with those made of metal. It appears that a more bountiful supply of trade goods was available in the Red River area and that it quickly replaced many aboriginal items. In addition, some artifacts are present at the Longest site that have not been recovered at Bryson–Paddock: bone whistles, toothed or notched bone fleshers, large tabular sandstone scrapers, and metal items identified as horse trappings.

Speculations

It appears probable that the southern prairie–plains were dominated by Indian tribes that represented members of the Wichita confederacy. By A.D. 1700 to 1760 the occupations at the Deer Creek and Bryson–Paddock sites represent one division of this group—the Taovayas. These are the same people as those identified on early maps as the Paniouassa, Paniafsas, Panipiquets, or other similar names, who were living along the Arkansas River. At an earlier time these people were living farther up the Arkansas River valley in the Great Bend region of central Kansas where they were visited by the Spanish explorers in the sixteenth century. The ultimate origins of these people are to be found in the prehistoric southern plains villagers, probably the Washita river people who formerly occupied central Oklahoma.

These people established themselves in what is now Kay County, Oklahoma, because of access to French traders who were coming up the Arkansas River in search of furs and animal products. In exchange for trade goods such as firearms, household utensils, and items of personal adornment, they traded horses, slaves, furs, hides, animal products such as cured meat and bear grease, possibly honey and tobacco, and other native products. These were transported down the Arkansas River to Arkansas Post and elsewhere within the developing Louisiana territory.

Around 1760 the Arkansas River villages were abandoned as important trading centers and there was a shift to the Red River locality in southern Oklahoma. This provided an easier access to the French traders following the Red River drainage and avoided harassment from the Osage Indians who were pressing westward into the Wichita territory.

The Longest site (San Bernardo) on the Red River, along with other similar villages located across the river in Texas, provided the major concentration of this population. French trade was accelerated with increased dependence upon trade goods and "luxury" items and resulted in the replacement of many traditional customs and values.

It is not known at what time the Wichita abandoned their Red River settlements, but it is known that they were living on the North Fork of the Red River at the Devil's Canyon site in 1834. A few years later, the Wichita had abandoned the Devil's Canyon site and were to be found in the vicinity of Fort Sill and along the Washita river drainage in central Oklahoma. Today the Wichita are still to be found in this region, a locality that they have known for perhaps the past 800 years.

Reference Note

The most useful reports dealing with excavations or large surface collections are those by Bell, *et al.* (1967), Hartley (1975b), Hartley and Miller (1977), Sudbury (1976a), and Wyckoff (1964d). Other useful references include the following: Bastian (1966, 1967b), Bell (1952), Corbyn (1974), Corwin (1967), Duffield (1965), Davidson and Harris (1974), Harris and Harris (1961), Hartley (1975a), Moore (1928), Newcomb (1965), Steen (1953, 1955), Sudbury (1976b), Thoburn (1922), Witte (1938), and M. H. Wright (1946–1947a, 1946–1947b).

Bibliography

Adams, R. M.
1941   Archaeological Investigations in Jefferson County, Missouri 1939–40. *Transactions of the Academy of Science of St. Louis* 30(5):151–221.

Agogino, G. A.
1961   A New Point Type from Hell Gap Valley, Eastern Wyoming. *American Antiquity*, 26(4):558–560.

Agogino, G. A., and W. D. Frankforter
1960   A Paleo-Indian Bison-Kill in Northwestern Iowa. *American Antiquity*, 25(3):414–415.

Ahshapanek, Don C., and Robert D. Burns
1960   Mammals Associated with Prehistoric People of Oklahoma. *Oklahoma Academy of Science Proceedings*, 40:16–19.

Albert, Lois E.
1981   Ferndale Bog and Natural Lake: Five Thousand Years of Environmental Change in Southeastern Oklahoma. *Oklahoma Archaeological Survey, Studies in Oklahoma's Past*, No. 7.

Albritton, C. C., Jr.
1966   Stratigraphy of the Domebo Site. *Contributions of the Museum of the Great Plains*, 1:10–13.
1975   Stratigraphy of the Cooperton Site. *Great Plains Journal* 14(2):133–139.

Alexander, H. L., Jr.
1963   The Levi Site, A Paleo-Indian Campsite in Central Texas. *American Antiquity*, 24(4):510–528.

Amsden, Thomas W.
1958   Stratigraphy and Paleontology of the Hunton Group in the Arbuckle Mountain Region, Part VI Stratigraphy. *Oklahoma Geological Survey* Bulletin No. 84.
1961   The Frisco and Sallisaw Formations. *Oklahoma Geological Survey* Bulletin No. 90.

Anderson, Adrian D.
1975a   Archaeology of the Cooperton Site. *Great Plains Journal* 14:143–157.
1975b   The Cooperton Mammoth: An Early Man Bone Quarry. *Great Plains Journal* 14:130–173

Anderson, Adrian D., and Franklin L. Chappabitty
1968   A Bison Kill from Domebo Canyon. *Great Plains Journal* 8(1):48–52.

Anderson, Bill
      1968   Lake Eufaula Yields Partial Burial with Two Flint Knives. *Bulletin of the Oklahoma An-thropological Society* 16:155–158.
Anderson, D. C., and H. A. Semkin, Jr.
      1980   *The Cherokee Excavations, Holocene Ecology and Human Adaptations in Northwestern Iowa.* New York: Academic Press.
Anderson, D. C., and R. Shutler, Jr.
      1974   Summary and Conclusions. *Journal of the Iowa Archaeological Society* 21:155–172.
Anderson, D. C., R. Shutler, Jr., and W. M. Wendland
      1980   The Cherokee Sewer Site and the Cultures of the Atlantic Climatic Episode. In *The Cherokee Excavations, Holocene Ecology and Human Adaptations in Northwestern Iowa,* edited by D. C. Anderson and H. A. Semkin, Jr. New York: Academic Press. Pp. 257–274.
Anderson, K. L. and C. L. Fry
      1955   Vegetation-Soil Relationships in Flint Hills Bluestem Pasture. *Journal of Range Manage-ment,* 8:163–169.
Anonymous
      1929a   Coloradoans Loot Cave on Indian Relics—Discovery which Baker Hoped to Give Own State Pilfered by "Fossil Hunters". *Cimarron News,* 31(52):1 (July 19, 1929) Boise City.
      1929b   Baker Party Recovers Relics of Vanished Race in Kenton Caves. *Cimarron News,* 32(1):1. (July 26, 1929) Boise City.
      1968   Basketmaker Mummy Unearthed Near Kenton. *Boise City News Historical Edition:* 10D, Boise City.
      n.d.   Notes concerning pod corn on file with specimens at the Stovall Museum, Norman, Oklahoma.
Antevs, E.
      1955   Geologic-climatic dating in the West. *American Antiquity* 20(4):317–335.
Ayres, C. E.
      1962   *The Theory of Economic Progress, a Study of the Fundamentals of Economic Development and Cultural Change.* New York: Schocken Books, 2nd edition.
Baerreis, David A.
      1939a   A Hopewell Site in Northeastern Oklahoma. *Society for American Archaeology Notebook* 1:72–78.
      1939b   Two New Cultures in Delaware Co., Oklahoma. *The Oklahoma Prehistorian* 2(1):1–5.
      1940   The Neosho Focus. *Society for American Archaeology Notebook* 1:108–109.
      1941   Recent Developments in Oklahoma Archaeology. *Proceedings of the Oklahoma Academy of Science* 21:125–126.
      1951   The Preceramic Horizons of Northeastern Oklahoma. *Museum of Anthropology, Univer-sity of Michigan, Anthropological Papers* No. 6.
      1953   Woodland Pottery of Northeastern Oklahoma. In *Prehistoric Pottery of the Eastern United States,* Museum of Anthropology, University of Michigan.
      1954   The Huffaker Site, Delaware County, Oklahoma. *Bulletin of the Oklahoma Anthropological Society,* 2:35–48.
      1955   Further Material from the Huffaker Site, Delaware County, Oklahoma. *Bulletin of the Oklahoma Anthropological Society* 3:53–68.
      1957   The Southern Cult and the Spiro Ceremonial Complex. *Bulletin of the Oklahoma An-thropological Society,* 5:23–28.
      1959   The Archaic as Seen from the Ozark region. *American Antiquity* 24(3):270–275.
      1960   Shell Tempered Pottery in Northeastern Oklahoma. *Bulletin of the Oklahoma An-thropological Society* 8:1–2.
Baerreis, David A., and Reid A. Bryson
      1965   Historical Climatology and the Southern Plains: A Preliminary Statement. *Bulletin of the Oklahoma Anthropological Society* 13:69–75.
      1966   Dating the Panhandle Aspect Cultures. *Bulletin of the Oklahoma Anthropological Society* 14:105–116.

Baerreis, David A, and J. E. Freeman
1959   A Report on a Bluff Shelter in Northeastern Oklahoma (D1-47). *Archives of Archaeology* 1.
1961   D1-47, a Bluff Shelter in Northeastern Oklahoma. *Bulletin of the Oklahoma Anthropological Society* 9:67–75.

Baerreis, David A., Warren L. Wittry, and Robert L. Hall
1956   The Burial Complex at the Smith Site, Delaware County, Oklahoma. *Bulletin of the Oklahoma Anthropological Society* 4:1–12.

Baker, Ele, and Jewel Baker
1968a   Final Report WPA—West Texas State Archaeological Project 9249. Manuscript on file, Panhandle Plains Historical Museum, Canyon, Texas.
1968b   Final Report Archaeological Survey—O.P. 665-66-3-404 State Application 30976. Manuscript on file, Panhandle Plains Historical Museum, Canyon, Texas.

Baker, William E.
1929a   The First of the Plainsmen, Chapter I. *Southwest Wilds and Waters*, November:24–25, 61–62.
1929b   The First of the Plainsmen, Chapter II. *Southwest Wilds and Waters*, December: 16–19, 44.
n.d.   Notes on file at No Man's Land Museum, Panhandle State University, Goodwell, Oklahoma.

Baker, William E., and A. V. Kidder
1937   A Spear Thrower from Oklahoma. *American Antiquity* 3(1):51–52.

Baker, William E., T. N. Campbell, and G. L. Evans
1957   The Nall Site: Evidence of Early Man in the Oklahoma Panhandle. *Bulletin of the Oklahoma Anthropological Society* 5:1–20.

Baldwin, Jane
1969   The Lawrence site, Nw-6, a Non-Ceramic Site in Nowata County, Oklahoma. *Bulletin of the Oklahoma Anthropological Society* 18:67–118.
1970   The Lightning Creek Site, Nw-8, Nowata County, Oklahoma. *Oklahoma River Basin Survey, Archaeological Site Report* 18:1–48.

Bandy, Phillip
1976   Lithic Technology: A Reconstruction of a Northern Texas Panhandle Archaeological Assemblage. M. A. thesis, Texas Tech University, Lubbock, Texas.

Banks, Larry D.
1973   A Comparative Analysis of Lithics at the Martin–Vincent Site. Manuscript on file, Oklahoma Archaeological Survey, University of Tulsa, Norman, Oklahoma; and with author.

Banks, Larry D., and Joe Winters
1975   The Bentsen–Clark Site: A Preliminary Report. *Texas Archeological Society Special Memoir* No. 2.

Barbour, E. H., and C. B. Schultz
1932   The Scottsbluff Bison Quarry and its Artifacts. *Nebraska State Museum Bulletin* (1):283–286.

Bareis, Charles John
1955   The Brackett Site, Ck-43, of Cherokee County, Oklahoma. *Bulletin of the Oklahoma Anthropological Society* 3:1–51.

Barr, Thomas P.
1964   An Archaeological Survey of the Birch Creek Reservoir. *Oklahoma River Basin Survey, General Survey Report* (6):118–127.
1965a   Archaeological Survey of the Lake of the Arbuckles Reservoir, Murray County, Oklahoma. *Oklahoma River Basin Survey, General Survey Report* (5):40–73.
1965b   Archaeological Survey of the Arkansas River Navigational Project, Muskogee and Wagoner Counties, Oklahoma. *Oklahoma River Basin Survey, General Survey Report* 5.
1966a   Archaeological Survey of the Upper Elk Creek Watershed, Washita, Beckham, and Kiowa Counties, Oklahoma. *Oklahoma River Basin Survey, General Survey Report* (7):86–108.

1966b   Three Archaeological Sites in the Pine Creek Reservoir, McCurtain County, Oklahoma. *Oklahoma River Basin Survey, General Survey Report* No. 7.

1966c   The Pruitt Site: A Late Plains Woodland Manifestation in Murray County, Oklahoma. *Oklahoma River Basin Survey, Archaeological Site Report* No. 5.

Bartlett, C. S., Jr.

1963   The Tom's Brook Site—3Jo-1, a Preliminary Report. *Arkansas Archeology 1962:* 15–65.

Bastian, Tyler

1964   Radiocarbon Date from an Archaic Site in Southwest Oklahoma. *Oklahoma Anthropological Society Newsletter,* 12(9):1–4.

1966   Initial Report on the Longest Site. *Great Plains Newsletter* 3(1):1–3.

1967a   Recommendations for Salvage Archaeology in the Waurika reservoir: Cotton, Jefferson and Stephens Counties, Oklahoma. Manuscript on file at the Oklahoma River Basin survey, Norman, Oklahoma.

1967b   Further Excavations at an 18th Century Wichita Village. *Great Plains Newsletter* 3(7):1–6.

1969   The Hudsonpillar and Freeman Sites, North-Central Oklahoma. *Oklahoma River Basin Survey, Archaeological Site Report* 14.

Baugh, Susan D.

1982   Radiocarbon Dates from the McCutchan–McLaughlin Site, 34Lt-11. *Oklahoma Anthropological Society Newsletter* 30(2):4–8.

Baugh, Timothy G.

1968   The Edwards Site. Manuscript on file at the Oklahoma Archaeological Survey, Norman, Oklahoma.

1970   The Vandever–Haworth Site, Wg-16, Wagoner County, Oklahoma. *Oklahoma River Basin Survey, Archaeological Site Report* No. 17.

1978   The Dawson Site (My-140): an Archaic Workshop in Northeastern Oklahoma. *Oklahoma Highway Archaeological Survey, Papers in Highway Archaeology* 5.

1981   Approaches to Southern Plains Exchange: The perspective from the Duncan (34Wa-2) site. Proposal to the National Science Foundation.

1982   Edwards I (34Bk-2): Southern Plains Adaptations in the Protohistoric Period. *Oklahoma Archaeological Survey, Studies in Oklahoma's Past* No. 8.

Baugh, Timothy G., and Fern E. Swenson

1980   Comparative Trade Ceramics: Evidence for the Southern Plains Macroeconomy. *Bulletin of the Oklahoma Anthropological Society* 29:83–102.

Baugh, Timothy G., and Charles W. Terrell

1982   An Analysis of Obsidian Debitage and Protohistoric Exchange Systems in the Southern Plains as Viewed from the Edwards I Site (34Bk-2). *Plains Anthropologist* 27(95):1–17.

Bell, Robert E.

1947a   Preliminary report on archaeological activities conducted by the Department of Anthropology in the Wister reservoir area in the summer of 1947. Manuscript on file at the Department of Anthropology, University of Oklahoma, Norman, Oklahoma.

1947b   Trade Materials at Spiro Mound as Indicated by Artifacts. *American Antiquity* 12:181–184.

1948   Recent Archaeological Research in Oklahoma. *Bulletin of the Texas Archeological Society* 19:148–154.

1949   Recent Archaeological Research in Oklahoma. *The Chronicles of Oklahoma* 27(31):303–312.

1952   Fieldtrip to Kay County, Oklahoma. *Oklahoma Anthropological Society Newsletter* 1(6):1–2.

1953a   Report on the Oklahoma Anthropological Society Fieldtrip, April 12, 1953. *Oklahoma Anthropological Society Newsletter* 2(2):4–5.

1953b   The Scott Site, LeFlore County, Oklahoma. *American Antiquity* 18(4):314–331.

1953c   Basketmaker Cave of Cimarron County, Oklahoma. *Oklahoma Anthropological Society Newsletter* 2(1):3–4.

1954   Projectile Points from West Central Oklahoma: Dan Base Collection. *Bulletin of the Oklahoma Anthropological Society* 2:12–15.

1955   Projectile Points from the Oklahoma Panhandle *Oklahoma Anthropological Society Newsletter* 3(7):4–5.

1957a   Some Oklahoma Projectile Point Examples. *Oklahoma Anthropological Society Newsletter* 5(8):2.

1957b   Projectile Points from Pontotoc County, Oklahoma. *Oklahoma Anthropological Society Newsletter* 5(7):2.

1958a   Guide to the Identification of Certain American Indian Projectile Points. *Oklahoma Anthropological Society Special Bulletin* 1.

1958b   Archaeological Investigations at the Boat Dock Site, Ma-1, in the Lake Texoma Area, Marshall County, Oklahoma. *Bulletin of the Oklahoma Anthropological Society* 6:37–47.

1961   Relationships Between the Caddoan Area and the Plains. *Bulletin of the Texas Archeological Society* 31:53–60.

1967   The Cooperton Mammoth. *Great Plains Newsletter* 3(5):9.

1968   Dating the Prehistory of Oklahoma. *Great Plains Journal* 7(2):1–11.

1971   Bison Scapula Skin-Dressing Tools? *Plains Anthropologist,* 16(52):125–127.

1972   The Harlan Site, Ck-6, a Prehistoric Mound Center in Cherokee County, Eastern Oklahoma. *Oklahoma Anthropological Society Memoir* 2.

1973   The Washita River Focus of the Southern Plains. In *Variation in Anthropology,* edited by D. W. Lathrap and J. Douglas: 171–187. Urbana, Illinois: Illinois Archaeological Survey.

1977   Early Man Points from Tulsa County. *Oklahoma Anthropological Society Newsletter* 25(1):9.

1978   *Oklahoma Archaeology: An Annotated Bibliography, Second Edition.* Norman: University of Oklahoma Press.

1980a   Fourche Maline: An Archaeological Manifestation in Eastern Oklahoma. In Caddoan and Poverty Point Archaeology: Essays in Honor of C. H. Webb. *Louisiana Archaeological Society,* Bulletin 6:83–125.

1980b   Reflections on Southern and Central Plains Prehistory. Paper presented at the 38th Plains Conference, No. 7, 1980, Iowa City.

Bell, Robert E., and David A. Baerreis
1951   A Survey of Oklahoma Archaeology. *Bulletin of the Texas Archeological and Paleontological Society* 22:7–100.

Bell, Robert E., and Tyler Bastian
1967a   Preliminary Report upon Excavations at the Longest Site, Oklahoma. In *A Pilot Study of Wichita Indian Archaeology and Ethnohistory* assembled by Bell, Jelks, and Newcomb. Final report to the National Science Foundation: 54–118.

1967b   Survey of Potential Wichita Archaeological Remains in Oklahoma. In *A Pilot Study of Wichita Indian Archaeology and Ethnohistory* assembled by Bell, Jelks, and Newcomb. Final report to the National Science Foundation: 119–127.

Bell, Robert E., and Charlene Dale
1953   The Morris Site, Ck-39, Cherokee County, Oklahoma. *Bulletin of the Texas Archeological Society* 24:69–140.

Bell, Robert E., Edward B. Jelks, and W. W. Newcomb
1967   A Pilot Study of Wichita Indian Archaeology and Ethnohistory. Final report to the National Science Foundation.

Bell, Robert E., Gayle S. Lacy, Jr., Margaret T. Joscher, and Joe C. Allen
1969   The Robinson–Solesbee Site, Hs-9, a Fulton Aspect Occupation, Robert S. Kerr Reservoir, Eastern Oklahoma. *Oklahoma River Basin Survey, Archaeological Site Report* 15.

Bender, Margaret M.
1979   Letter dated December 13, 1979 detailing results of radiocarbon analyses on samples from the Spiro locality (Charles Rohrbaugh).

Bender, Margaret M., R. A. Bryson, and David A. Baerreis
1965   University of Wisconsin Radiocarbon Dates I. *Radiocarbon* 7:399–407.

1966   University of Wisconsin Radiocarbon Dates II. *Radiocarbon* 8:522–533.

1967   University of Wisconsin Radiocarbon Dates III. *Radiocarbon* 9:530–544.

1968   University of Wisconsin Radiocarbon Dates V. *Radiocarbon* 10(2):473–478.

1969   University of Wisconsin Radiocarbon Dates VI. *Radiocarbon* 11:228–235.

1971   University of Wisconsin Radiocarbon Dates IX. *Radiocarbon* 13(2):476–479.

Bender, Margaret M., David A. Baerreis, Reid A. Bryson, and R. L. Steventon

1981   University of Wisconsin Radiocarbon Dates XVIII. *Radiocarbon* 22:147–148.

Bernabo, J. C., and T. Webb III

1977   Changing Pattern in the Holocene Pollen Record of Northeastern North America: A Mapped Summary. *Quaternary Research* 8:64–96.

Blair, W. F.

1939   Faunal Relationships and Geographic Distribution of Mammals in Oklahoma. *The American Midland Naturalist* 22(1):85–133.

Blair, W. F., and T. H. Hubbell

1938   The Biotic Districts of Oklahoma. *The American Midland Naturalist* 20:425–455.

Blakeslee, Donald J.

1975   The Plains Interband Trade System: An Ethnohistoric and Archaeological Investigation. Ph.D. dissertation University of Wisconsin, Madison, Wisconsin.

Blakeslee, Donald J., and Warren W. Caldwell

1979   *The Nebraska Phase: An Appraisal.* Reprints in Anthropology, Vol. 18.

Blanchard, K. S.

1951   Quaternary Alluvium of the Washita River Valley in Western Caddo County, Oklahoma. Unpublished M.S. thesis, University of Oklahoma, Norman, Oklahoma.

Blythe, Jack G.

1959   Atoka Formation on the North Side of the McAlester Basin. *Oklahoma Geological Survey Bulletin* No. 47.

Bobalik, Sheila J.

1977a   Archaeological Investigations at Proposed Clayton Reservoir, 1976—Latimer, Pittsburg and Pushmataha Counties, Oklahoma. *Oklahoma Archaeological Survey, Archaeological Resource Survey Report* No. 5.

1977b   The Viper Marsh Site (Mc-205), McCurtain County, Oklahoma. *Bulletin of the Oklahoma Anthropological Society* 26:1–86.

1978   Archaeological Investigations at the Sallee G. Site (34-Pu-99), Pushmataha County, Oklahoma. *Oklahoma Archaeological Survey, Studies in Oklahoma's Past* No. 3. Oklahoma Archaeological Survey.

1979a   The Lee Kirkes Site (34Lt-32). *University of Oklahoma, Archaeological Research and Management Center, Research Series* 6:84–124.

1979b   The Vanderwagen Site (34Pu-73). *University of Oklahoma, Archaeological Research and Management Center, Research Series* (6):195–243.

Bohannon, Charles F.

1973   Excavations at the Mineral Springs Site, Howard County, Arkansas. *Arkansas Archeological Survey, Research Series*, No. 5.

Bolton, H. E.

1908   *Spanish Exploration in the Southwest, 1542–1706.* Barnes and Noble.

Bond, C. L.

1971   Spinach Patch site, 3FR-1, and the River Bank site, 3FR-23, west-central Arkansas. Manuscript on file, University of Oklahoma, Archaeological Research and Management Center, Norman, Oklahoma.

Bond, T. A.

1966   Palynology of Quaternary Terraces and Floodplains of the Washita and Red Rivers, Central and Southeastern Oklahoma. Ph.D. dissertation, University of Oklahoma, Norman, Oklahoma.

Bonfield, William
    1975   Deformation and Fracture Characteristics of the Cooperton Mammoth Bones. In The Cooperton Mammoth: An Early Man Bone Quarry, edited by Adrian D. Anderson : 158–164. *Great Plains Journal*:14:130–173.

Borchert, J. R.
    1950   The Climate of the Central North American Grassland. *Annals of the Association of American Geographers* 40(1):1–39.

Bousman, C. Britt
    1974a   Archaeological Assessment of Alibates National Monument. *Southern Methodist University, Archaeological Research Program.*
    1974b   Archaeological Assessment of Lake Meredith Recreational Area. *Southern Methodist University, Archaeological Research Program.*

Bowers, Roger L.
    1975   Petrography and Petrogenesis of the Alibates Dolomite and Chert (Permian), Northern Panhandle of Texas. Master's thesis, University of Texas at Arlington.

Braun, E. L.
    1950   *Deciduous Forests of Eastern North America.* New York: Hafner Press.

Bray, R. T.
    1956   The Cultural-Complexes and Sequences at the Rice Site (23SN200) Stone County, Missouri. *The Missouri Archaeologist* 18(1–2):46–134.

Breternitz, David
    1966   An Appraisal of Tree Ring Dated Pottery in the Southwest. *Anthropological Papers of the University of Arizona* No. 10.

Brighton, Harold D.
    1951   Archaeological Sites in Custer County, Oklahoma. *Bulletin of the Texas Archeological and Paleontological Society* 22:164–187.
    1952   The Archaeological survey of Keystone reservoir: A preliminary Report. Manuscript on file at the Department of Anthropology, University of Oklahoma, Norman, Oklahoma.

Briscoe, James
    1976   A Preliminary Report on the Plantation Site, Mi-63, An Early Caddoan Settlement in Northern McIntosh County. *Oklahoma Anthropological Society Newsletter* 24(8):9–12.
    1977   The Plantation Site, An Early Caddoan Settlement in Eastern Oklahoma. *Oklahoma Highway Archaeological Survey, Papers in Highway Archaeology* No. 3.

Brown, James A.
    1966a   *Spiro Studies, Vol. 1, Description of the Mound Group.* First Part of the Second Annual Report of Caddoan Archaeology—Spiro Focus Research. University of Oklahoma Research Institute, Norman, Oklahoma.
    1966b   *Spiro Studies, Vol. 2, The Graves and Their Contents.* Second Part of the Second Annual Report of Caddoan Archaeology—Spiro Focus Research. University of Oklahoma Research Institute, Norman, Oklahoma.
    1967   New Radiocarbon Dates from the Spiro Site. *Bulletin of the Oklahoma Anthropological Society* 15:77–80.
    1971a   The Dimensions of Status in the Burials at Spiro. In Approaches to the Social Dimensions of Mortuary Practice, edited by J. A. Brown. *Society for American Archaeology Memoir* 25:92–112.
    1971b   *Spiro Studies, Vol. 3, Pottery Vessels.* First Part of the Third Annual Report of Caddoan Archaeology—Spiro Focus Research. University of Oklahoma Research Institute, Norman, Oklahoma.
    1975   Spiro Art and its Mortuary Contexts. In *Death and the Afterlife in Pre-Columbian America,* edited by E. P. Benson, pp. 1–32. Washington, D.C.: Dumbarton Oaks Research Library and Collections.
    1976a   The Southern Cult Reconsidered. *Mid-Continental Journal of Archaeology* 1:115–135.

1976b   *Spiro Studies, Vol. 4, The Artifacts.* Second Part of the Third Annual Report of Caddoan Archaeology—Spiro Focus Research. University of Oklahoma Research Institute, Norman, Oklahoma.

1980   Interaction and Exchange among Mississippian Societies. In *Reviewing Mississippian development,* edited by Stephen Williams. Albuquerque: University of New Mexico Press.

1981a   The Potential of Systematic Collections for Archaeological Research. In The Research Potential of Anthropological Museum Collections. Anne-Marie E. Cantwell, James B. Griffin, and Nan A. Rothschild, eds. *Annals of the New York Academy of Science* 376:65–76.

1981b   The Search for Rank in Prehistoric Burials. In *The Archaeology of death,* Robert Chapman, I. Kinnes, and Klavs Randsborg, eds. Cambridge: Cambridge University Press.

n.d.a.   Spiro Studies, Volume 5: Burials, Chronology and Overview. MS in preparation.

n.d.b.   How Marginal were the Southern Ozarks in Prehistory? *Missouri Archaeological Society, Special Publication.*

Brown, James A., Robert E. Bell, and Don G. Wyckoff
1978   Caddoan Settlement Patterns in the Arkansas River Drainage. In *Mississippian Settlement Patterns,* edited by Bruce D. Smith: 169–200. New York: Academic Press.

Brown, Margaret K.
1975   The Zimmerman Site: Further Excavations at the Grand Village of Kaskaskia. *Illinois State Museum,* Reports of Investigations No. 32. Springfield, Illinois.

Broyles, Bettye J.
1966   Preliminary Report: The St. Albans Site (46La-27), Kanawha County, West Virginia. *The West Virginia Archeologist* 19:1–43.

1977   Second Preliminary Report: The St. Albans Site, Kanawha County, West Virginia. *West Virginia Geological and Economic Survey, Report of Archeological Investigations* No. 3.

Brues, Alice M.
1958   Skeletal Material from the Horton Site. *Bulletin of the Oklahoma Anthropological Society* 6:27–32.

1959   Skeletal Material from the Morris Site (Ck-39). *Bulletin of the Oklahoma Anthropological Society* 7:63–70.

1962   Skeletal Material from the McLemore Site. *Bulletin of the Oklahoma Anthropological Society* 10:69–78.

n.d.   The Spiro Skeletal Material. In Spiro Studies, Vol. 5: Burials, Chronology and Overview. Manuscript in preparation.

Bruner, W. E.
1931   The Vegetation of Oklahoma. *Ecological Monographs* 1:99–188.

Brush, G. S.
1967   Pollen Analysis of Late-Glacial and Postglacial Sediments in Iowa. *Quaternary Paleoecology,* edited by E. J. Cushing and H. E. Wright, Jr.: 99–116. New Haven: Yale University Press.

Bryant, V. M., Jr.
1977   A 16,000 Year Pollen Record of Vegetational Change in Central Texas. *Palynology* 1:143–156.

Bryson, Reid A., David A. Baerreis, and Wayne Wendland
1970   The Character of Late-Glacial and Post Glacial Climatic Changes. In *Pleistocene and Recent Environments of the Central Great Plains,* edited by Dart and Jones. University of Kansas Department of Geology, Publication No. 3:53–77.

Buck, Dewey A.
1958   A Preliminary appraisal of the Archaeological resources of the Short Mountain Reservoir, Eastern Oklahoma. Manuscript on file at the Department of Anthropology, University of Oklahoma, Norman, Oklahoma.

1959 The Custer Focus of the Southern Plains. *Bulletin of the Oklahoma Anthropological Society* 7:1–31.

Buck, P. and R. W. Kelting
1962 A Survey of the Tall-Grass Prairie in Northeastern Oklahoma. *The Southwestern Naturalist* 7:(3–4):163–175.

Buckner, H. F.
1878 Mounds in Indian Territory. *American Antiquarian* 1:14.

Buehler, Kent J.
1978 A Model of chronology and subsistence/settlement systems for the Salt Creek locality, North-central Oklahoma. Unpublished manuscript on file, Department of Anthropology, University of Oklahoma, Norman.

Burchardt, Bill
1958 Black Mesa. *Oklahoma Today Magazine* 9(1):2, 28–29.

Burke, J. L., III
1959 Sedimentology and Paleohydraulics of the Terraces of South Canadian River. M. S. thesis, University of Oklahoma, Norman, Oklahoma.

Burnett, E. K.
1945 The Spiro Mound Collection in the Museum. *Contributions from the Museum of American Indian, Heye Foundation* 14:9–47.

Burt, W. H., and R. P. Grossenheider
1964 *A Field Guide to the Mammals.* Second edition. New York: Houghton Mifflin Co.
1976 *A Field Guide to the Mammals.* Third edition, Series 5. New York: Houghton Mifflin Co.

Burton, Robert J.
1971 The Archaeological View from the Harvey Site, Sq-18. *Oklahoma River Basin Survey, Archaeological Site Report* No. 21.

Burton, Robert J., and Susan S. Burton
1969 An Archaeological Survey of the Lake Altus Shoreline, Greer and Kiowa Counties. *Oklahoma River Basin Survey, General Survey Report,* No. 12.

Burton, Robert J., Tyler Bastian and Terry J. Prewitt
1969 The Tyler Site, Hs-11, Haskell County, Oklahoma. *Oklahoma River Basin Survey, Archaeological Site Report* No. 13.

Burton, Robert J., and Robert J. Stahl
1969 The Harkey-Bennett Site, Sq-33, Sequoyah County, Oklahoma. *Oklahoma River Basin Survey, Archaeological Site Report* (12):111–135.

Burton, Susan Sasse
1970 The Hugo Dam Site, Ch-112, Choctaw County, Southeast Oklahoma. *Oklahoma River Basin Survey, Archaeological Site Report,* No. 16.

Burton, Susan Sasse, and William L. Neal
1970 The Dickson–Haraway Site, Sq-40, Sequoyah County, Oklahoma. *Oklahoma River Basin Survey, Archaeological Site Report,* No. 20.

Byington, E. S.
1912 Arkansas and Oklahoma Notes. *The Archaeological Bulletin* 3(3):81–82. Council Grove, Kansas.

Byrd, Clifford Leon
1971 Origin and History of the Uvalde Gravel of Central Texas. *Baylor Geological Studies,* Bulletin No. 20, Baylor University.

Caldwell, Joseph R.
1958 Trend and Tradition in the Prehistory of the Eastern United States. *American Anthropological Association, Memoir* 88.

Caldwell, W. W.
1977 Review of: Fay Tolton and the Initial Middle Missouri Variant edited by W. R. Wood. *Missouri Archaeological Society, Research Series,* No. 13.

Campbell, Richard G.
    1969   Prehistoric Panhandle Culture on the Chaquaqua Plateau, Southeast Colorado. Ph.D. dissertation, Department of Anthropology, University of Colorado, Boulder, Colorado.
    1973   An Archaeological Survey of the Dry Cimarron, Northeast New Mexico and Western Oklahoma. Abstracts of papers, Archaeological Society of New Mexico, Annual Meeting April 1973, Sante Fe, New Mexico.
    1976   The Panhandle Aspect of the Chaquaqua Plateau. *Texas Tech University Graduate Studies*, No. 11.

Cannon, P. J.
    1967   Pleistocene Geology of Salt Fork and North Fork of Red River, Southwestern Oklahoma. M. S. thesis, University of Oklahoma, Norman, Oklahoma.

Carley, Denny
    1974   Three Skeletons Exhumed from Wa-4. *Oklahoma Anthropological Society Newsletter* 22(9):2–4.

Carpenter, J. R.
    1934   Seasonal Aspection in Certain Prairie and Savannah Communities. Master's thesis, University of Oklahoma, Norman, Oklahoma.
    1937   Fluctuations in Biotic Communities, III. Aspection in a Ravine Sere in Central Oklahoma. *Ecology* 18:80–92.

Carter, Richard and Mary Ruth Carter
    1958   The Pickett ruin in Hutchinson county, Texas. Manuscript on file, Panhandle Plains Historical Society Museum, Canyon, Texas.

Carter, W. A.
    1967   Ecology of the Nesting Birds of the McCurtain Game Preserve, Oklahoma. *The Wilson Bulletin* 79(3):259–272.

Cartledge, Thomas R.
    1970   The Tyler–Rose Site and Late Prehistory in East-Central Oklahoma. *Oklahoma River Basin Survey, Archaeological Site Report*, No. 19.

Champe, John L.
    1949   White Cat Village. *American Antiquity* 14(4)1:285–292.

Chapman, Carl H.
    1980   *The Archaeology of Missouri, II*. Columbia: University of Missouri Press.

Chapman, Carl H., and others
    1960   Archaeological Investigations in the Table Rock Reservoir Area, Missouri. Report on file with the National Park Service, Lincoln, Nebraska.

Cheek, Annetta L.
    1976a   Report of the ten percent archeological reconnaissance of proposed McGee Creek reservoir. Report submitted to the Bureau of Reclamation, Tulsa, Oklahoma.
    1976b   Excavations at At-90. *Archaeological Research Associates Report* 5.

Cheek, Charles D.
    1977   A Cultural Assessment of the Archaeological Resources in the Fort Gibson Lake Area, Eastern Oklahoma. *Archaeological Research Associates Research Report*, No. 15.

Cheek, Charles D. and others
    1980   Archaeological Investigations at the Graham Site, 34At-90: 1975, 1977, and 1978. *Archaeological Research Associates Research Report*, No. 23.

Chomko, S. A. and G. W. Crawford
    1978   Plant Husbandry in Prehistoric Eastern North America: New Evidence for its Development. *American Antiquity* 43(3):405–408.

Clark, Cherie
    1980   Bone Tool Manufacture and Use by Pre-Pottery Occupants of the McCutchan-McLaughlin Site. *Bulletin of the Oklahoma Anthropological Society* 29:19–48.

Clark, M. B.
    1959   A Study of the Flowering Plants of Tulsa County, Oklahoma, Exclusive of the Grasses, Sedges, and Rushes. Master's thesis, University of Tulsa, Tulsa, Oklahoma.

Clark, Tim
   1969   Some Petroglyphs from the Black Mesa Area of Cimarron County, Oklahoma. *Proceedings of the Oklahoma Academy of Sciences* 48:138–141.
Cleland, C. E.
   1966   The Prehistoric Animal Ecology and Ethnohistory of the Upper Great Lakes Region. *Museum of Anthropology, University of Michigan, Anthropological Papers*, No. 29.
   1976   The Focal-Diffuse Model: An Evolutionary Perspective on the Prehistoric Cultural Adaptations of the Eastern United States. *Midcontinental Journal of Archaeology* 1:59–76.
Clements, Forrest
   1943   Basketmaker Culture in the Oklahoma Panhandle. In Geology and Groundwater Resources of Cimarron County, Oklahoma, edited by Stuart Schoff. *Oklahoma Geological Survey Bulletin* (64):122–124.
   1945   Historical Sketches of Spiro Mound. *Contributions from the Museum of the American Indian, Heye Foundation* 14:48–68.
Cline, L. M.
   1960   Ouachita Mountains, Oklahoma. *Oklahoma Geological Survey Bulletin* No. 85.
Coe, Joffre L.
   1964   The Formative Cultures of the Carolina Piedmont. *Transactions of the American Philosophical Society Vol. 54, No. 1.*
Cook, H. J.
   1927   New Geological and Paleontological Evidence Bearing on the Antiquity of Mankind in America. *Natural History* 7:240–247.
   1928   Further Evidence Concerning Man's Antiquity at Frederick, Oklahoma. *Science* (n. s.) 67:371–373.
   1931   The Antiquity of Man as Indicated at Frederick, Oklahoma; a Reply. *Journal of the Washington Academy of Sciences* 21(8):161–166.
Cooper, Paul, and Earl H. Bell
   1936   Archaeology of Certain Sites in Cedar County, Nebraska. In *Chapters in Nebraska Archaeology* by Earl H. Bell. Lincoln: University of Nebraska Press. Pp. 11–145.
Corbyn, Ronald C.
   1974   Progress Report on the Photogrammetric Mapping of the Deer Creek Site in Kay County. *Oklahoma Anthropological Society Newsletter* 22(4):15–16.
Corwin, Hugh D.
   1967   The Oldest Ghost Town—San Bernardo, Jefferson County. *Prairie Lore* 4(1):14–15.
Crabb, Martha
   1968   Some Puebloan Trade Pottery from Panhandle Aspect Sites. *Bulletin of the Texas Archeological Society* 38:83–89.
Crane, H. R.
   1956   University of Michigan Radiocarbon Dates I. *Science* 124:664–672.
Crane, H. R., and J. B. Griffin
   1959   University of Michigan Radiocarbon Dates IV. *Radiocarbon* 1:173–198.
   1963   University of Michigan Radiocarbon Dates VIII. *Radiocarbon* 5:228–253.
   1965   University of Michigan Radiocarbon Dates X. *Radiocarbon* 7:132.
   1968   University of Michigan Radiocarbon Dates XII. *Radiocarbon* 10:61–114.
Crawford, D. D.
   1965   The Granite Beach Site, Llano County, Texas. *Texas Archeological Society Bulletin* 36:71–97.
Crook, W. W., Jr. and R. K. Harris
   1952   Trinity Aspect of the Archaic Horizon: The Carrollton and Elam Foci. *Bulletin of the Texas Archeological and Paleontological Society* 23:7–38.
Curry, B. R.
   1974   The Climate of Oklahoma. In Officials of the National Oceanic and Atmospheric Administration, United States Department of Commerce, *Climates of the States*, Vol. II, *Western States including Alaska and Hawaii.*

Curtis, N. M., Jr., and W. E. Ham
    1957   Physiographic Map of Oklahoma. *Oklahoma Geological Survey Educational Series Map* 4.
            (Reprinted in 1972: Geology and Earth Resources of Oklahoma, *Oklahoma Geological
            Survey Educational Publication* 1).
    1972   Geomorphic Provinces of Oklahoma. In Geology and Earth Resources of Oklahoma:
            An Atlas of Maps and Cross Sections. *Oklahoma Geological Survey Educational Publication,*
            No. 1.
Cutler, Hugh C.
    1959   Plant Remains from Six Oklahoma Sites. *Oklahoma Anthropological Society Newsletter*
            8(3):4–7.
Cutler, Hugh C., and Leonard W. Blake
    1973   *Plants from Archaeological Sites East of the Rockies.* Missouri Botanical Garden, St. Louis,
            Missouri.
Dale, Vincent
    1973   A Unique Vessel from the Oklahoma Panhandle. *Bulletin of the Oklahoma Anthropological
            Society* 21:187–190.
Davidson, Claire C., and R. K. Harris
    1974   Chemical Profile of Glass Trade Beads from Archaeological Sites in Texas and
            Oklahoma. *Bulletin of the Texas Archeological Society* 45:209–217.
Davis, E. M.
    1962   Archaeology of the Lime Creek Site in Southwestern Nebraska. *University State Mu-
            seum, Special Publication,* No. 3.
    1970   Archaeological and Historical Assessment of the Red River Basin in Texas. In *Arkansas
            Archeological Survey, Research Series* No. 1, edited by H. A. Davis. Pp. 27–65.
Davis, Michael K.
    1965   A Study of Wear on Washita River Focus Buffalo Scapula Tools. *Bulletin of the Oklahoma
            Anthropological Society* 13:153–58.
Davis, William
    1962   Appraisal of the Archaeological Resources of Sanford Reservoir, Hutchinson, Moore
            and Potter Counties, Texas. Manuscript on file at Southwest Regional Office, National
            Park Service, Santa Fe, New Mexico.
Deevey, Edward S., Richard F. Flint and Irving Rouse
    1967   *Radiocarbon Measurements: Comprehensive Index,* 1950–1965. New Haven: Yale University
            Press.
DeJarnette, D. L., E. B. Kurjack, and J. W. Cambron
    1962   Stanfield–Worley Bluff Shelter Excavations. *Journal of Alabama Archaeology,* Vol. 8, Nos.
            1–2.
Delcourt, H. R.
    1979   Late Quaternary Vegetation History of the Eastern Highland Rim and Adjacent Cum-
            berland Plateau of Tennessee. *Ecological Monographs* 49(3):255–280.
Delcourt, P. A., and H. R. Delcourt
    1979   Late Pleistocene and Holocene Distributional History of the Deciduous Forest in the
            Southeastern United States. *Veroffentlichungen de Geobotanischen Institutes der ETH, Stif-
            tung Rubel (Zurich)* 68:79–107.
Dellinger, S. C., and S. D. Dickinson
    1942   Pottery from the Ozark Bluff Shelters. *American Antiquity* 7:276–289.
Dibble, D. S., and D. Lorrain
    1968   Bonfire Shelter: A Stratified Bison Kill Site, Val Verde County, Texas. *Texas Memorial
            Museum, Miscellaneous Papers* No. 1.
Dillehay, T. D.
    1974   Late Quaternary Bison Population Changes on the Southern Plains. *Plains Anthropolo-
            gist* 19(65):180–196.

Drass, Richard D.
1979   Roulston–Rogers; a Stratified Plains Woodland and Late Archaic Site in the Cross Timbers. *Bulletin of the Oklahoma Anthropological Society* 28:1–135.

Duck, L. G., and J. B. Fletcher
1943   A Game Type Map of Oklahoma. *State of Oklahoma Game and Fish Department.*
1944   A Survey of the Game and Furbearing Animals of Oklahoma. *Oklahoma Game and Fish Commission, Division of Wildlife Restoration and Research.*

Duffield, Lathel F.
1953   The Brewer Site: A Preliminary Report. *Bulletin of the Oklahoma Anthropological Society* 1:61–68.
1964a   Engraved Shells from the Craig Mound at Spiro, LeFlore County, Oklahoma. *Oklahoma Anthropological Society Memoir* No. 1.
1964b   Three Panhandle Aspect Sites at Stanford Reservoir, Hutchinson County, Texas. *Bulletin of the Texas Archeological Society* 35:19–82.
1965   The Taovayas Village of 1759: In Texas or Oklahoma? *Great Plains Journal* 4(2):39–48.
1969   The Vertebrate Faunal Remains from the School Land I and School Land II Sites, Delaware County, Oklahoma. *Bulletin of the Oklahoma Anthropological Society* 18:47–65.
1970   Some Panhandle Aspect Sites in Texas: Their Vertebrates and Paleoecology. Unpublished Ph.D. dissertation, Department of Anthropology, University of Wisconsin, Madison.

Duncan, Kelley C.
1976   Excavations at At-90. *Archaeological Research Associates Research Report*, No. 5.

Dye, D. H.
1973   An Alexander phase in the Tennessee Valley and adjacent areas. Paper presented at the Southeastern Archaeological Conference, Memphis, Tennessee.
1980   Primary Forest Efficiency in the Western Middle Tennessee Valley. Unpublished Ph.D. dissertation, Department of Anthropology, Washington University, St. Louis, Missouri.

Dyksterhuis, E. J.
1948   The Vegetation of the Western Cross Timbers. *Ecological Monographs* 18:325–376.

Eighmy, Jeffrey
1969   The Fine Site: A Caddoan Site in Eastern Oklahoma. *Oklahoma River Basin Survey, Archaeological Site Report* 13:1–50.
1970   Edwards II: Report of an Excavation in Western Oklahoma. *Plains Anthropologist* 15(20):255–281.

Ellzey, Tom
1966   A Panhandle Aspect Site (Preliminary Report). *Midland Archaeological Society Special Bulletin* 1:59–65.

England, Gary
1975   *Oklahoma Weather.* Oklahoma City: England and May.

Engle, F. E.
1934   Survey of a Wagon Road from Fort Smith to the Colorado River. *The Chronicles of Oklahoma* 12:74–96.

Etchiesin, Gerald Meeks
1979   Archaeological Testing at the South Ridge Site, Lake Meredith Recreational Area. *Archaeological Research Laboratory, Killgore Research Center,* Canyon, Texas.
1981   Archaeological Survey at Lake Meredith Recreational Area, Moore and Potter Counties, Texas. *Water and Power Resources Services, U. S. Department of the Interior.*

Evans, O. F.
1930a   The Antiquity of Man as Shown at Frederick, Oklahoma, a Criticism. *Journal of the Washington Academy of Sciences* 20(19):475–479.
1930b   Probable History of the Holloman Gravel Pit at Frederick, Oklahoma. *Proceedings of the Oklahoma Academy of Sciences* 10:77.

1951   Archaeological Evidence of Recent Filling in the Present Channel of the Washita River. *Proceedings of the Oklahoma Academy of Sciences* 32:121–122.

1952   Some Factors That Controlled the Location of the Villages of the Prehistoric People of Central Oklahoma. *Proceedings of the Oklahoma Academy of Sciences* 33:320–322.

1958   Analysis of Flint Materials from the Lee and the Lacy Sites. *Oklahoma Anthropological Society Newsletter* 6(7):2–3.

Ewers, John C.

1955   The Horse in Blackfoot Indian Culture. *Bureau of American Ethnology, Bulletin* 159.

Eyerly, T. L.

1907   The Buried City of the Panhandle. *Transactions of the Kansas Academy of Science* 21(1):219–228.

1910   The Indian Remains of the Canadian River Valley. *The Archaeological Bulletin* 1(3):77–80.

Farley, J. A. and J. D. Keyser

1979   Little Caney River Prehistory, 1977 Field Season. *University of Tulsa, Laboratory of Archaeology, Contributions in Archaeology*, No. 5.

Fay, Robert O.

1930   Dolomites of Western Oklahoma. *Oklahoma Geological Survey Bulletin* No. 49.

1965   Geology of Woods County, Oklahoma. *Oklahoma Geological Survey Bulletin* No. 106.

Fenneman, Nevin M.

1931   *Physiography of the Western United States.* New York: McGraw-Hill.

1938   *Physiography of Eastern United States.* McGraw-Hill.

Ferguson, C. W.

1969   A 7104-Year Annual Tree-Ring Chronology for Bristlecone Pine, *Pinus aristata,* from the White Mountains, California. *Tree-Ring Bulletin* 29(3–4):3–29.

1970   Dendrochronology of Bristlecone Pine, *Pinus aristata:* Establishment of a 7484-Year Chronology in the White Mountains of East-Central California, U.S.A. In *Radiocarbon Variations and Absolute Chronology,* edited by I. U. Olsson. New York: Wiley. Pp. 237–239.

Ferring, C. Reid

1978   An Archaeological Reconnaissance of Fort Sill, Oklahoma. *Contributions of the Museum of the Great Plains,* No. 6.

1982   *The Late Holocene Prehistory of Delaware Canyon Oklahoma.* Denton, Texas: Institute of Applied Sciences, North Texas State University.

Fessler, E. J.

1928   Captain Nathan Boone's journal. *The Chronicles of Oklahoma* 7:58–105.

Finkelstein, J. Joe

1940   The Norman Site Excavations near Wagoner, Oklahoma. *The Oklahoma Prehistorian* 3(3):2–15.

Fischer, F. W.

1972   Schultz Site Ceramics. In The Schultz Site at Green Point, edited by J. E. Fitting: 137–190. *Memoirs of the Museum of Anthropology* 4, University of Michigan, Ann Arbor, Michigan.

Fischer, LeRoy

1979   The Historic Preservation Movement in Oklahoma. *The Chronicles of Oklahoma* 57:3–25.

Fishman, A. G.

1936   The Relative Distribution of Herbaceous Plants in Oklahoma County, Oklahoma. *Proceedings of the Oklahoma Academy of Science* 16:40–41.

Flint, R. F.

1957   *Glacial and Pleistocene Geology.* New York: John Wiley and Sons.

Flynn, Peggy

1983   Preliminary Analysis of Materials from the Zimm's Site (34Rm-72). *Oklahoma Anthropological Society* Newsletter 31(3):6–9.

Folk, Robert L.

1965   *Petrology of Sedimentary Rocks.* Austin: Hemhill's.

Forbes, Jack D.
1960   *Apache, Navajo, and Spaniard.* Norman: University of Oklahoma Press.
Ford, J. A.
1969   A Comparison of Formative Cultures in the Americas. *Smithsonian Contributions to Anthropology,* No. 11.
Ford, J. A., and C. H. Webb
1956   Poverty Point, a Late Archaic site in Louisiana. *American Museum of Natural History, Anthropological Papers* 46:1–136.
Ford, Richard I.
1972   Gift, Barter, or Violence: An Analysis of Tewa Intertribal Exchange. In Social Exchange and Interaction, edited by E. N. Wilmsen. *University of Michigan, Anthropological Papers,* No. 42:21–45.
Ford, W. J.
1954   Subsurface Geology of Southwest Logan County. *Oklahoma City Geological Society Shale Shaker* 5(2):5–19.
Foreman, G.
1937   *Adventure on Red River: Report on the Exploration of the Headwaters of the Red River by Captain Randolph B. Marcy and Captain G. B. McClellan.* Norman: University of Oklahoma Press.
1939   *Marcy and the Gold Seekers: the Journal of Captain R. B. Marcy, with an Account of the Gold Rush over the Southern Route.* Norman: University of Oklahoma Press.
Fowells, H. A.
1965   Silvics of Forest Trees of the United States. *U. S. Department of Agriculture, Agricultural Handbook* No. 271.
Fowler, George M., Joseph P. Lyden, F. E. Gregory, and W. M. Agar
1934   Chertification in the Tri-State (Oklahoma–Kansas–Missouri) Mining District. *The American Institute of Mining and Metallurgical Engineers, Technical Publication* No. 532.
Fowler, M. L.
1959   Summary Report of Modoc Rock Shelter 1952, 1953, 1955, 1956. *Illinois State Museum, Report of Investigations* No. 8:1–72.
Frankforter, W. D., and George Agogino
1959   Archaic and Paleo-Indian Archaeological Discoveries in Western Iowa. *The Texas Journal of Science* 11(4):482–491.
Freeman, Joan E.
1959a   The Neosho Focus, A Late Prehistoric Culture in Northeastern Oklahoma. Ph.D. dissertation, Department of Anthropology, University of Wisconsin, Madison, Wisconsin.
1959b   An Archaeological Report on a Cave Deposit (D1-30) in Northeastern Oklahoma. *Archives of Archaeology,* No. 2: 1–104 (microcard).
1960   Site D1-29, a Rockshelter in Northeastern Oklahoma. *Archives in Archaeology,* No. 8:1–308 (microcard).
1962   The Neosho Focus: A Late Prehistoric Culture in Northeastern Oklahoma. *Bulletin of the Oklahoma Anthropological Society* 10:1–26.
Freeman, Joan E., and A. D. Buck
1960   Woodward Plain and Neosho Punctate, Two Shell Tempered Pottery Types of Northeastern Oklahoma. *Bulletin of the Oklahoma Anthropological Society* 8:3–16.
Frison, George C.
1978a   Animal Population Studies and Cultural Inference. *Plains Anthropologist* 23(82) Part 2, Memoir 14:44–52.
1978b   *Prehistoric Hunters of the High Plains.* New York: Academic Press.
Frye, J. C., and A. B. Leonard
1963   Pleistocene Geology of Red River Basin in Texas. *University of Texas, Bureau of Economic Geology, Report of Investigation,* No. 49.
Gallaher, Art
1951   The Goodman I Site, Custer County, Oklahoma. *Bulletin of the Texas Archeological and Paleontological Society* 22:188–216.

Galm, Jerry R.
    1978a   Archaeological Investigations at Wister Lake, LeFlore County, Oklahoma. *Archaeological Research and Management Center, Research Series* No. 1., University of Oklahoma, Norman, Oklahoma.
    1978b   The Archaeology of the Curtis Lake Site (34Lf-5A), LeFlore County, Oklahoma. *Archaeological Research and Management Center, Research Series* No. 2, University of Oklahoma, Norman, Oklahoma.
    1981   Prehistoric Cultural Adaptations in the Wister Valley, East-Central Oklahoma. Unpublished Ph.D. dissertation, Department of Anthropology, Washington State University. Pullman, Washington.

Galm, Jerry R., and P. Flynn
    1978a   New Radiocarbon Dates for Sites in the Wister Valley, Eastern Oklahoma. *Oklahoma Anthropological Society Newsletter* 26(5):2–5.
    1978b   The Cultural Sequences at the Scott (34Lf-11) and Wann (34Lf-27) Sites and Prehistory of the Wister Valley. *Archaeological Research and Management Center, Research Series* No. 3, University of Oklahoma, Norman, Oklahoma.

George, Preston
    1978   Folsom Point Section Found at Kaw Lake. *Oklahoma Anthropological Society Newsletter* 26(9):10–12.

George, Preston, and Don G. Wyckoff
    1980   Clues to Archaic Occupations in North-Central Oklahoma. *Oklahoma Anthropological Society Newsletter* 28(8):6–8.

Gettys, Marshall
    1975   Preliminary Report on Archaeological Investigations at Lukfata Reservoir, Southeastern Oklahoma. *Oklahoma River Basin Survey, General Survey Report* No. 14.
    1976   Paleo-Indian and Early Archaic Occupations of Oklahoma. *Papers in Anthropology* 17(1):51–74. Norman: University of Oklahoma.

Gettys, Marshall, Robert Layhe, and Sheila Bobalik
    1976   Birch Creek and Skiatook Reservoirs: Preliminary Report upon Archaeological Investigations in 1974. *Oklahoma River Basin Survey, Archaeological Site Report* No. 31.

Gidley, James W.
    1926   Explorations of a Pleistocene Spring Deposit in Oklahoma. *Smithsonian Institution Exploration and Fieldwork in 1925. Smithsonian Miscellaneous Collections* 78(1):27–28.

Gilmore, Melvin R.
    1931   Vegetal Remains of the Ozark Bluff-Dweller Culture. *Papers of the Michigan Academy of Science, Arts, and Letters* 14:83–102.
    1932   Methods of Indian Buffalo Hunts, with the Itinerary of the Last Tribal Hunt of the Omaha. *Papers of the Michigan Academy of Science, Arts, and Letters* 16:17–32.

Glasscock, Keith, and Alma Glasscock
    1955   A Preliminary Report on CR-1, An Indian Campsite in Moore County, Texas. *Panhandle–Plains Historical Review* 28:96–106.

Gould, C. N.
    1898   The Timbered Mounds of the Kaw Reservation. *Transactions of the Kansas Academy of Science* 15:78–79.
    1899   Additional Notes on the Timbered Mounds of the Kaw Reservation. *Transactions of the Kansas Academy of Science* 16:282.
    1903   Notes on Trees, Shrubs and Vines in the Cherokee Nation. *Transactions of the Kansas Academy of Science* 18:145–146.
    1926   Fossil Bones and Artifacts at Frederick, Oklahoma. *Proceedings of the Oklahoma Academy of Science* 9:90–92.
    1929   On the Recent Finding of Another Flint Arrowhead in the Pleistocene at Frederick, Oklahoma. *Journal of the Washington Academy of Sciences* 19:66–68.

Gray, F., and H. M. Galloway
    1959   Soils of Oklahoma. *Oklahoma State University Experimental Station, Miscellaneous Publication,* No. 56.
Gray, F., and M. H. Roozitalab
    1976   Benchmark and Key Soils of Oklahoma: A Modern Classification System. *Oklahoma State University, Agricultural Experiment Station Bulletin* MP-97.
Green, F. E.
    1963   The Clovis Blades: an Important Addition to the Llano Complex. *American Antiquity* 29:145–165.
    1967   Archaeological Salvage in the Sanford Reservoir Area. Manuscript on file at the Southwestern Regional Center, National Park Service, Santa Fe, New Mexico.
Greengo, R. E.
    1964   Issaquena: An Archaeological Phase in the Yazoo Basin of the Lower Mississippi Valley. *Memoirs of the Society for American Archaeology,* No. 18.
Gregg, J.
    1926   *Commerce of the Prairies: The 1844 edition, unabridged.* New York: Lippincott.
Griffin, David E.
    1976   A Model of Culture Change for the Middle Missouri Subarea. In Fay Tolton and the Initial Middle Missouri Variant. *Missouri Archaeological Society, Research Series* (13):33–35.
    1977   Timber Procurement and Village Location in the Middle Missouri Subarea. *Plains Anthropologist* 22(78) Part 2, Memoir No. 13:177–185.
Griffin, James B.
    1943   *The Fort Ancient Aspect.* Ann Arbor: University of Michigan Press.
    1946   Cultural Change and Continuity in Eastern United States Archaeology. In Man in Northeastern North America, edited by F. Johnson. *Papers of the Robert S. Peabody Foundation for Archaeology* 3:37–95.
    1952a   Cultural Periods in Eastern United States Archaeology. *Archaeology of Eastern United States,* edited by J. B. Griffin. Chicago: University of Chicago Press. Pp. 352–364.
    1952b   An Interpretation of the Place of Spiro in Southeastern Archaeology. In The Spiro Mound by Henry W. Hamilton. *Missouri Archaeologist* 14:89–106.
    1952c   Some Early and Middle Woodland Pottery Types in Illinois. *Illinois State Museum, Scientific Papers* 5:93–129.
    1961   Relationships Between the Caddoan Area and the Mississippi Valley. *Bulletin of the Texas Archeological Society* 31:27–37.
    1967   Eastern North American Archaeology: A Summary. *Science* 156(3773):175–191.
Griffin, John W.
    1974   Investigations in Russell Cave. *U. S. Department of the Interior, National Park Service, Publications in Archaeology,* No. 13.
Grimes, Charles W.
    1938   The Grand River Survey. *The Oklahoma Prehistorian* 1(1):7–8.
Gruger, J.
    1973   Studies on the Late Quaternary Vegetation History of Northeastern Kansas. *Geological Society of America Bulletin* 84:239–250.
Guilinger, E. L.
    1971   The Archaeological Situation at the Copeland Site, a Fourche Maline Site in LeFlore County. Unpublished M.A. thesis, Department of Anthropology, University of Oklahoma, Norman, Oklahoma.
Gunnerson, Delores A.
    1956   The Southern Athabascans: Their Arrival in the Southwest. *El Palacio* 63(11–12): 346–365.
    1974   *The Jicarilla Apache, A Study in Survival.* DeKalb, Illinois: Northern Illinois University Press.

Gunnerson, James H.
1960   An Introduction to Plains Apache Archaeology—The Dismal River Aspect. *Bureau of American Ethnology, Bulletin* 173, *Anthropological Papers* No. 58.
1968   Plains Apache Archaeology: A Review. *Plains Anthropologist* 13(41):167–189.

Haag, William G.
1942   A Description and Analysis of the Pickwick Pottery. In *An archaeological survey of Pickwick Basin in the adjacent portions of the states of Alabama, Mississippi and Tennessee,* by W. S. Webb and D. L. Dejarnette. *Bureau of American Ethnology, Bulletin* No. 129:509–526.
1971   Louisiana in North American prehistory. *Melanges* No. 1. Baton Rouge, Louisiana: Museum of Geoscience, Louisiana State University.

Hall, G. D.
1981   Allens Creek: A Study in the Cultural Prehistory of the Lower Brazos River Valley, Texas. *University of Texas at Austin, Texas Archeological Survey, Research Report* No. 61.

Hall, R. L.
1951   The Late Prehistoric Occupation of Northeastern Oklahoma as Seen from the Smith Sites, Delaware County, M.A. thesis, Department of Anthropology, University of Wisconsin, Madison, Wisconsin.

Hall, Roland Scott
1952   Location and Survey of Two New Sites in Grady County. *Oklahoma Anthropological Society Newsletter* 1(6):2.
1953   A Recent Photographic Survey Trip to Certain Sites Along the Canadian and Washita Rivers. *Oklahoma Anthropological Society Newsletter* 2:6–7.
1954   Ck-44: A Bluff Shelter from Northeastern Oklahoma. *Bulletin of the Oklahoma Anthropological Society* 2:49–67.

Hall, S. A.
1968   A Paleosol in Central Oklahoma and Its Archaeological Significance. *Bulletin of the Oklahoma Anthropological Society* 16:151–154.
1977a   Holocene Geology and Paleoenvironmental Studies. In *The Prehistory and Paleoenvironment of Hominy Creek Valley,* assembled by D. O. Henry: 12–42. Laboratory of Archaeology, University of Tulsa, Tulsa, Oklahoma.
1977b   Geological and Paleoenvironmental Studies. In *The Prehistory and Paleoenvironment of Birch Creek Valley,* assembled by D. O. Henry. Laboratory of Archaeology, University of Tulsa, Tulsa, Oklahoma. Pp. 11–31.
1977c   Geology and Palynology of Archaeological Sites and Associated Sediments. In *The Prehistory of the Little Caney River, 1976 Field Season,* by D. O. Henry. Laboratory of Archaeology, University of Tulsa, Tulsa, Oklahoma. Pp. 13–42.
1978   Snails from Archaeological Sites in Hominy Creek Valley. *University of Tulsa, Laboratory of Archaeology, Contributions in Archaeology* 4:79–85.

Hamilton, Henry W.
1952   The Spiro Mound. *Missouri Archaeologist* 14:17–88.

Hamilton, Henry W., Jean T. Hamilton, and Eleanor F. Chapman
1974   Spiro Mound Copper. *Missouri Archaeological Society Memoir* No. 11.

Hammatt, Hallett H.
1970   A Paleo-Indian Butchering Kit. *American Antiquity* 35:141–152.
1976   The Gore Pit site: An Archaic Occupation in Southwestern Oklahoma and a Review of the Archaic Stage in the Southern Plains. *Plains Anthropologist* 21(74):245–277.

Harden, Pat and David Robinson
1975   A Descriptive Report of the Vanderpool Site, Ck-32, Cherokee County, Oklahoma. *Bulletin of the Oklahoma Anthropological Society* 23:91–168.

Harden, Patrick L. and others
1981   *Sliding Slab Shelter: Hunting and Gathering in the Ouachitas.* Environmental Assessments, Inc.

Harper, Elizabeth Ann
   1953   The Taovayas Indians in Frontier Trade and Diplomacy 1719–1768. *The Chronicles of Oklahoma* 31(3):268–289.

Harrington, M. R.
   1924   The Ozark Bluff-Dwellers. *American Anthropologist* 26:1–21.
   1960   The Ozark Bluff-Dweller. *Museum of the American Indian, Indian Notes and Monographs,* No. 12.

Harris, R. K., and Inus Marie Harris
   1961   Spanish Fort, A Historic Trade Site. *The Record* 16(1):2–5. Dallas.

Harris, R. K., I. M. Harris, J. C. Blaine, and J. Blaine
   1965   A Preliminary Archaeological and Documentary Study of the Womack Site, Lamar County, Texas. *Bulletin of the Texas Archeological Society* 36:287–364.

Harris, R. W.
   1957   Ostracoda of the Simpson Group. *Oklahoma Geological Survey Bulletin* No. 75.

Hart, Orville D.
   1963   Eastern Winding Stair Range. *Oklahoma Geological Survey Bulletin* No. 103.

Hartley, John D.
   1974a   The Von Elm Site: An Early Plains–Woodland Complex in North-Central Oklahoma. *Oklahoma River Basin Survey, Archaeological Site Report* No. 28.
   1974b   A Report on Excavations in the Waurika Reservoir, Jefferson County, Oklahoma. *Oklahoma River Basin Survey, Archaeological Site Report* No. 26.
   1975a   Excavations at the Bryson–Paddock site (Ka-5) in Kay County. *Oklahoma Anthropological Society Newsletter* 23(6):2–5.
   1975b   Kaw Reservoir—The Northern Section. Report of Phase IV Research of the General Plan for Investigation of the Archaeological Resources of Kaw Reservoir, North-Central Oklahoma. *Oklahoma River Basin Survey, Archaeological Site Report* No. 30.
   1976   A Resurvey and Assessment of the Prehistoric Resources of Arcadia Lake, Oklahoma County, Oklahoma. *Oklahoma River Basin Survey, General Survey Report* No. 16.

Hartley, John D., and A. F. Miller
   1977   Archaeological Investigations at the Bryson–Paddock Site, An Early Contact Period Site on the Southern Plains. *Oklahoma River Basin Survey, Archaeological Site Report* No. 32.

Haury, Cherie E.
   1979   Characterization of the Chert Resources of El Dorado Project Area in Finding, Managing, and Studying Prehistoric Cultural Resources at El Dorado Lake, Kansas (Phase I). *University of Kansas Museum of Anthropology Research Series.*
   1982   The Prehistory and Paleoenvironment of the Black Mesa Locality Cimarron County, Oklahoma. *Laboratory of Archaeology, University of Tulsa,* Tulsa, Oklahoma.

Hay, Oliver P.
   1928   On the Antiquity of the Relics of Man at Frederick, Oklahoma. *Science* (n.s.) 67:442–444.
   1929   On the Recent Discovery of a Flint Arrowhead in Early Pleistocene Deposits at Frederick, Oklahoma. *Journal of the Washington Academy of Sciences* 19:93–98.

Haynes, C. V., Jr.
   1968   Geochronology of Late Quaternary Alluvium. *International Association for Quaternary Research, Proceedings* 8:591–631.

Haynes, C. V., and George Agogino
   1966   Prehistoric Springs and Geochronology of the Clovis Site, New Mexico. *American Antiquity* 31:812–821.

Haynes, Guy H.
   1932   A Report on the Excavations at Saddleback Ruin. M. A. thesis, Department of Anthropology, Texas Tech University, Lubbock, Texas.

Hefley, H. M.
   1937   Ecological Studies on the Canadian River Floodplain in Cleveland County, Oklahoma. *Ecological Monographs* 17:345–402.

Hemish, L. A.
    1980   Observations and Interpretations Concerning Quaternary Geomorphic History of
            Northeastern Oklahoma. *Oklahoma Geological Survey, Oklahoma Geology Notes* 40(3):
            79–94.
Hendricks, Thomas A.
    1947   Geology of the Western Part of the Ouachita Mountains of Oklahoma, Oil and Gas
            Investigations Preliminary Map 66 (Sheet 1), *U. S. Geological Survey.*
Henning, Dale R.
    1959   The Loftin Mound (23Sn-42). *Missouri Archaeological Society Newsletter* 128:9–10.
Henry, Donald O.
    1977a   The Prehistory and Paleoenvironment of Birch Creek Valley. *Laboratory of Archaeology,
            University of Tulsa,* Tulsa, Oklahoma.
    1977b   Prehistory and Paleoenvironment of Hominy Creek Valley. *Laboratory of Archaeology,
            University of Tulsa,* Tulsa, Oklahoma.
    1977c   The Prehistory of the Little Caney River: 1976 Field Season. *Laboratory of Archaeology,
            University of Tulsa,* Tulsa, Oklahoma.
Hester, J. J., E. L. Lundelius, Jr., and R. Fryxell
    1972   Blackwater Locality No. 1, a Stratified Early Man Site in Eastern New Mexico. *Southern
            Methodist University, Fort Burgwin Research Center,* Publication 8.
Hill, A. T., and George Metcalf
    1942   A Site of the Dismal River Aspect in Chase Co., Nebraska. *Nebraska History Magazine*
            22(2):158–226.
Hobbs, Hulda R.
    1941   Texas Panhandle Ruins. *El Palacio* 8(6):121–128.
Hoffman, Michael P.
    1977   An Archaeological Survey of the Ozark Reservoir in West-Central Arkansas. In *Ozark
            Reservoir Papers: Archaeology in West-Central Arkansas, 1965–1970.*
Hofman, Jack L.
    1971   A Surface Survey of the Ross Site, Cd-59, Caddo County, Oklahoma. *Bulletin of the
            Oklahoma Anthropological Society* 20:101–114.
    1973a   Bison Bone Flesher from Caddo County. *Oklahoma Anthropological Society Newsletter*
            21(2):5–7.
    1973b   Cd-177: A Small Archaic Camp in West-Central Oklahoma. *Bulletin of the Oklahoma
            Anthropological Society* 22:171–206.
    1974   The Hodge Site, Cu-40: A Late Prehistoric Site on the Southern Plains. In Reports of the
            ARKLA Salvage Project, *Oklahoma Archaeological Survey, Contract Archaeology Series*
            1:22–68.
    1975a   A Study of Custer-Washita River Foci Relationships. *Plains Anthropologist* 20(67):41–51.
    1975b   Bone Fleshers in Oklahoma. *Bulletin of the Oklahoma Anthropological Society* 23:169–176.
    1975c   Archaeology at the Easton Site (Lf-213), LeFlore County, Oklahoma. *Oklahoma Highway
            Archaeological Survey, Papers in Highway Archaeology,* No. 1.
    1976a   The Lacy Site, Gv-5, House Plan: A Washita River Phase House in Garvin County.
            Oklahoma Anthropological Society Newsletter 24(9):4–6.
    1976b   Comments on the Heerwald Site (Cu-27) of Custer County: A Problem in Archaeologi-
            cal Site Classification. *Oklahoma Antheropological Society Newsletter* 24(3):2–11.
    1977a   Gouge Production Stratigies: Toward the Study of Archaic Local Groups on the South-
            ern Plains. Paper presented at the 35th Plains Conference, November 17–19, 1977.
            Lincoln, Nebraska.
    1977b   Archaeological Salvage Investigations at the Henry Site, Cotton County. *Oklahoma
            Anthropological Society Newsletter* 25(2):5–9.
    1977c   A Caddoan Pipe from the Shawver Site on the Canadian River in Western Oklahoma.
            Oklahoma Anthropological Society Newsletter 25(7):7–11.
    1977d   Archaeological Investigations at the Estep Shelter, Atoka County, Southeast
            Oklahoma. *Oklahoma Conservation Commission, Archaeological Research Report* No. 2.

1977e   Bibliography of Spiro Archaeology. *Oklahoma Anthropological Society Newsletter* 25(4):6–11.

1977f   A Report on Preliminary Archaeological Investigations at the Estep Shelter, Atoka County, Southeast Oklahoma. *Oklahoma Conservation Commission, Archaeological Research Report* No. 2.

1978a   The Keith Site, 34 Cd-8: Evidence From a Custer Phase Component on the Canadian River, Oklahoma. Manuscript in possession of the author.

1978b   An Analysis of Surface Material from the Little Deer Site, Cu-10, of Western Oklahoma: A Further Investigation of the Wheeler Complex. *Bulletin of the Oklahoma Anthropological Society* 27:1–109.

1978c   The Development and Northern Relationships of Two Archaeological Phases in the Southern Plains Subarea. In The Central Plains Tradition: Internal Development and External Relationships, edited by D. J. Blakeslee, *Office of the State Archaeologist of Iowa, Report* No. 11:6–35.

1978d   An Alternative View of Some Southern Plains Archaic Stage Characteristics. *Plains Anthropologist* 23(82)1:311–317.

1980a   Notes on a Bison Kill in White Canyon, 34Cd-202, Caddo County. *Bulletin of the Oklahoma Anthropological Society* 29:1–8.

1980b   Notes on Ceramic Artifacts from the Lamb-Miller Site (Rm-25), Roger Mills County, Oklahoma. *Bulletin of the Oklahoma Anthropological Society* 29:59–66.

Hofman, Jack L., and Darcy F. Morey
1981   Bone Taphonomy and Archaeological Interpretation: A Bison Kill (?) from Oklahoma. *Abstracts of the 39th Annual Plains Conference*, p. 27. Bismark.

Holden, W. C.
1929   Some Recent Explorations and Excavations in North-western Texas. *Bulletin of the Texas Archeological and Paleontological Society* 1:23–35.

1930   The Canadian Valley Expedition of March, 1930. *Bulletin of the Texas Archeological and Paleontological Society* 2:21–32.

1931   The Texas Tech Archaeological Expedition, Summer 1930. *Bulletin of the Texas Archeological and Paleontological Society* 3:43–52.

1932   Recent Archaeological Discoveries in the Texas Panhandle. *Southwestern Social Science Quarterly* 13(3):289–293.

1933   Excavations at Saddleback Ruins. *Bulletin of the Texas Archeological and Paleontological Society* 5:39–52.

Holder, Preston
1970   *The Hoe and the Horse on the Plains, A Study of Cultural Development among North American Indians.* Lincoln: University of Nebraska Press.

Holliday, Vance T.
1977   Cultural Chronology of the Lubbock Lake Site. M.A. thesis, Department of Anthropology, Texas Tech University, Lubbock, Texas.

Hollis, M. S.
1979   The Case of the Missing Mummies. Two manuscripts on file at No Man's Land Museum, Panhandle State University, Goodwell, Oklahoma.

Holmes, Mary Ann
1972   The Black Mesa Survey. *Oklahoma Anthropological Society Newsletter* 20(9):2.

Holmes, William H.
1894   An Ancient Quarry in Indian Territory. *Bureau of American Ethnology Bulletin* No. 21.

1903   Flint Implements and Fossil Remains from a Sulphur Spring at Afton, Indian Territory. *Report of the U.S. National Museum for 1901*, pp. 237–252.

1919   Handbook of Aboriginal American Antiquities. *Bureau of American Ethnology Bulletin* No. 60, Part I.

Honea, Kenneth
1973   The Technology of Eastern Puebloan Pottery on the Llano Estacado. *Plains Anthropologist* 18(59):73–88.

Honess, C. W.
    1923   Geology of the Southern Ouachita Mountains of Oklahoma. *Oklahoma Geological Survey Bulletin* No. 32, Part 1.
House, John H.
    1978   Flat-Based Shell-Tempered Pottery in the Ozarks: A Preliminary Discussion. *Arkansas Archeologist* 19:44–49.
Howard, James H.
    1968   The Southeastern Ceremonial Complex and Its Interpretation. *Missouri Archaeological Society Memoir*, No. 6.
    1970   1969 Archaeological Investigations at the Weston and Hogshooter Sites, Osage and Washington Counties, Oklahoma. *Bulletin of the Oklahoma Anthropological Society* 19:61–99.
    1971   Radiocarbon Date for Weston Site Released. *Oklahoma Anthropological Society Newsletter* 19(3):29.
Howard, Lynn E.
    1940   Preliminary Report on Cherokee County, Oklahoma Archaeology. *The Oklahoma Prehistorian* 3(1):2–11.
    1941   Quarterly field report (third quarter, 1941), LeFlore County Archaeological Project. Manuscript on file, Archaeological Research and Management Center, University of Oklahoma, Norman, Oklahoma.
Hudson, Charles
    1976   *The Southeastern Indians.* Knoxville: University of Tennessee Press.
Huffman, George G.
    1958   Geology of the Flanks of the Ozark Uplift. *Oklahoma Geological Survey Bulletin* No. 77.
Hughes, David T.
    1976   The Bible Sites, Number 1 and Number 3, McCurtain County, Oklahoma. *Oklahoma Conservation Commission, Research Report 1.* Oklahoma City.
    1977a   An Index to Archaeological Survey Reports and Manuscripts Resulting from Assessments of U.S.D.A. Soil Conservation Service Watershed Projects in Oklahoma. *Oklahoma Conservation Commission.*
    1977b   Archaeological Testing in Atoka County, Oklahoma: Archaeological Sites 34At-160, 34At-163, and 34At-175. *Oklahoma Conservation Commission, Archaeological Research Report* No. 4.
    1978a   A Folsom Point from Comanche County, Oklahoma. *Oklahoma Anthropological Society Newsletter* 26(1):5–6.
    1978b   The Glasscock Site, 34 Ps-96, and Two Other Prehistoric Sites in Pittsburg County, Oklahoma. *Oklahoma Conservation Commission, Archaeological Research Report* No. 5.
    1979   34Wg-108, a small prehistoric site in northeastern Oklahoma. Unpublished manuscript on file, Oklahoma Archaeological Survey.
Hughes, Jack T.
    1949   Investigations in Western South Dakota and Northeastern Wyoming. *American Antiquity* 14(4):266–277.
    1962   Lake Creek: A Woodland Site in the Texas Panhandle. *Bulletin of the Texas Archeological and Paleontological Society* 32:65–84.
    1968   Prehistory of the Caddoan Speaking Tribes. Ph.D. dissertation, Department of Anthropology, Columbia University, New York, New York.
    1974   *Prehistory of the Caddoan Speaking Tribes.* New York: Garland Publishing Co.
    1976   A Review of Some References to Flint Sources in the Texas Panhandle. *Archaeological Research Laboratory, Kilgore Research Center, West Texas State University,* Canyon.
    1979   Archaeology of Palo Duro Canyon. In *The story of Palo Duro Canyon,* edited by Duane Guy. Canyon, Texas: Panhandle Plains Historical Society.
Irvine, Marilee
    1980   Ceramic Analysis from the Williams I Site, 34Lf-24, LeFlore County, Oklahoma. M.A. thesis, Department of Anthropology, University of Oklahoma, Norman, Oklahoma.

Irwin, H. T.
    1967   The Itama: Late Pleistocene Inhabitants of the Plains of the United States and Canada
            and the American Southwest. Ph.D. dissertation, Department of Anthropology, Har-
            vard University, Cambridge, Massachusetts.
Irwin, H. T. and H. M. Wormington
    1970   Paleo-Indian Tool Types in the Great Plains. *American Antiquity* 35:24–34.
Irwin-Williams, Cynthia, Henry Irwin, George Agogino, and C. V. Haynes
    1973   Hell Gap: Paleo-Indian Occupation on the High Plains. *Plains Anthropologist* 18:40–53.
Israel, Stephen
    1969   Reexamination of the Cookson Site and Prehistory of Tenkiller Locale in Northeastern
            Oklahoma. M. A. thesis, Department of Anthropology, University of Oklahoma, Nor-
            man, Oklahoma.
    1979   Re-Examination of the Cookson Site. *Oklahoma Archaeological Survey, Studies in
            Oklahoma's Past* 4.

Janzen, D. E.
    1977   An Examination of Late Archaic Development in the Falls of the Ohio River. In For the
            Director: Research Essays in honor of James B. Griffin, edited by C. Cleland. *Museum of
            Anthropology, University of Michigan, Anthropological Papers*, No. 61:123–143.
Jelinek, Arthur J.
    1967   A Prehistoric Sequence in the Middle Pecos Valley, New Mexico. *Anthropological Papers
            of the Museum of Anthropology, University of Michigan* 31.
Jelks, Edward B.
    1967   The Gilbert Site, A Norteno Focus Site in Northeastern Texas. *Bulletin of the Texas
            Archeological Society* 37.
Jenkins, N. J.
    1974   Subsistence and settlement patterns in the Western Middle Tennessee Valley during
            the Transitional Archaic–Woodland Period. *Journal of Alabama Archaeology* 20:183–
            193.
John, Elizabeth Ann Harper
    1975   *Storms Brewed in other Men's Worlds, the Confrontation of Indians, Spanish and French in the
            Southwest, 1540–1795.* College Station: Texas A & M University Press.
Johnson, Alfred E.
    1976   Introduction. In Hopewellian Archaeology in the Lower Missouri Valley, edited by A.
            E. Johnson. *University of Kansas Publications in Anthropology* 8:1–6.
Johnson, C.
    1974   Geologic Investigations at the Lubbock Lake Site. *The Museum Journal* 15:79–105.
Johnson, C. Stuart
    1934   Report to the Anthropology Department of the University of Oklahoma Concerning
            the Field Work Carried on in the Slab-House Site on the Stamper Ranch, South of
            Optima, Oklahoma in the Summer of 1934. Manuscript on file, Panhandle Plains
            Historical Museum.
    1939   A Report on the Antelope Creek Ruin. *Bulletin of the Texas Archeological and Paleontologi-
            cal Society* 11:190–202.
Johnson, Eileen, Vance T. Holliday, M. J. Kaczor, and R. Stuckenrath
    1977   The Garza Occupation at the Lubbock Lake Site. *Bulletin of the Texas Archeological Society*
            48:83–109.
Johnson, F. L., and P. G. Risser
    1975   A Quantitative Comparison between an Oak Forest and an Oak Savannah in Central
            Oklahoma. *The Southwestern Naturalist* 20(1):75–84.
Johnson, Jerry L., and Richard McWilliams
    1978   Physical Evidence on the Origins of the Panhandle Aspect. Paper read at the Nebraska
            Academy of Sciences, March 15, 1978.
Johnson, Leonard
    1950a   Preliminary Appraisal of the Archaeological Resources of the Optima Reservoir. Manu-

script on file, Department of Anthropology, University of Oklahoma, Norman, Oklahoma.

1950b   Preliminary Appraisal of the Archaeological Resources of the Eufaula Reservoir (Gaines Creek Reservoir). Manuscript on file, Department of Anthropology, University of Oklahoma, Norman, Oklahoma.

Johnson, L., Jr.
1962   The Yarbrough and Miller sites of Northeastern Texas, with a Preliminary Definition of the LaHarpe Aspect. *Bulletin of the Texas Archeological Society* 32:141–284.

1964   The Devil's Mouth Site, a Stratified Campsite at Amistad Reservoir, Val Verde County, Texas. *University of Texas, Department of Anthropology, Archaeology Series* 6.

Jordan, Julia Anne
1960   Prehistory of the Southern Plains. *Papers in Anthropology* 1(1):1–18.

Kansas Geological Survey
1964   The State Geologic Map of Kansas. Lawrence: Kansas Geological Survey.

Kapustka, Larry
1974   Vegetation of Oklahoma. In *Field Guide to Oklahoma*, edited by P. Risser. Norman, Oklahoma: Oklahoma Biological Survey.

Kay County Chapter
1963   The Fred Loomis Site, a Small Group Burial near Freedom, Oklahoma. *Bulletin of the Oklahoma Anthropological Society* 11:123–133.

Keith, K. D.
1973   Paleostomatology at the Moore Site (Lf-31), LeFlore County, Oklahoma. *Bulletin of the Oklahoma Anthropological Society* 22:149–158.

Keller, Gordon N.
1961   The Changing Position of the Southern Plains in the Late Prehistory of the Great Plains Area. Ph.D. dissertation, Department of Anthropology, University of Chicago, Chicago, Illinois.

Keller, John Esten
1975   Black Dog Village. *Texas Highway Publications in Archaeology, Highway Design Division, Report* No. 5.

Kelley, J. Charles
1955   Juan Sabeata and Diffusion in Aboriginal Texas. *American Anthropologist* 57(5):981–995.

Kelley, J. H.
1974   A Brief Resume of Artifacts Collected at the Lubbock Lake Site prior to 1961. *The Museum Journal* 15:43–78.

Kelting, R. W., and W. T. Penfound
1953   Literature on the Vegetation of Oklahoma. *Proceedings of the Oklahoma Academy of Science* 33:126–135.

Kerr, Henry P.
1964   Recent Activity at the Willingham Site, M1-5. *Oklahoma Anthropological Society Newsletter* 12(8):3–5.

Kerr, Henry P., and Don G. Wyckoff
1964   Two Prehistoric Sites, My-72 and My-79 in the Markham Ferry Area, Mayes County, Oklahoma. *Bulletin of the Oklahoma Anthropological Society* 12:55–86.

Kessel, John L.
1979   *Kiva, Cross and Crown: The Pecos Indians and New Mexico 1540–1840.* National Park Service.

Kidder, Alfred Vincent
1932   The Artifacts of Pecos. *Papers of the Southwestern Expedition* No. 6. Robert S. Peabody Foundation for Archaeology, Phillips Academy, Yale University Press.

1958   Pecos, New Mexico: Archaeological Notes. *Papers of the Robert S. Peabody Foundation for Archaeology*, Vol. 5.

Kidder, Alfred V., and Anna O. Shepard
    1936   The Pottery of Pecos, Vol. II: The Glaze-Paint, Culinary, and other Wares. *Papers of the Phillips Academy, Southwest Expedition,* No. 7.
King, J. E.
    1973   Late Pleistocene Palynology and Biogeography of the Western Missouri Ozarks. *Ecological Monographs* 43:539–565.
    1980   Post-Pleistocene Vegetational Changes in the Midwestern United States. *University of Kansas, Publications in Anthropology* 12:3–11.
    1981   Late Quaternary Vegetational History of Illinois. *Ecological Monographs* 51(1):43–62.
King, J. E., and W. H. Allen, Jr.
    1977   A Holocene Vegetation Record from the Mississippi River Valley, Southeastern Missouri: *Quaternary Research* 8:307–323.
King, J. E., and E. H. Lindsay
    1976   Late Quaternary Biotic Records from Spring Deposits in Western Missouri. In *Prehistoric Man and his Environments, a Case Study in the Ozark Highland,* edited by W. R. Wood and R. B. McMillan. New York: Academic Press. Pp. 63–78.
King, Mary E.
    1981   The analysis of textiles from Spiro Mound, Oklahoma. Paper presented at the symposium on Research Potential of Anthropological Museum Collections, New York Academy of Sciences.
King, Mary E., and Joan S. Gardner
    1981   The Analysis of Textiles from Spiro Mound, Oklahoma. In The Research Potential of Anthropological Museum Collections. Anne-Marie E. Cantwell, James B. Griffin and Nan A. Rothschild, eds. *Annals of the New York Academy of Sciences* 376:123–139.
Kivett, Marvin F.
    1953   The Woodruff Ossuary, A Prehistoric Burial Site in Phillips County, Kansas. *Bureau of American Ethnology, Bulletin* No. 154. *River Basin Survey Papers,* No. 3:103–141.
Klippel, W. E.
    1971   Graham Cave Revisited: a Reevaluation of Its Cultural Position during the Archaic Period. *Missouri Archaeological Society, Memoir* No. 9.
Kraenzel, Carl F.
    1955   *The Great Plains in Transition.* University of Oklahoma Press.
Krieger, Alex D.
    1945   An Inquiry into Supposed Mexican Influences on a Prehistoric "Cult" in the Southern United States. *American Anthropologist* 47:483–515.
    1946   Culture Complexes and Chronology in Northern Texas with Extension of Puebloan Datings to the Mississippi Valley. *University of Texas Publications* No. 4640.
    1947   The First Symposium on the Caddoan Archaeological Area. *American Antiquity* 13:198–207.
    1957   Early Man, Notes and News. *American Antiquity* 22(3):321–323.
Lamb, H. H., and A. Woodroffe
    1970   Atmospheric Circulation during the Last Ice Age. *Quaternary Research* 1:29–58.
Lange, Charles H.
    1953   A Reappraisal of Evidence of Plains Influences among the Rio Grande Pueblos. *Southwestern Journal of Anthropology* 9(2):212–230.
    1957   Plains–Southwestern Inter-cultural Relations During the Historic Period. *Ethnohistory* 4(2):150–173.
    1979   Relations of the Southwest with the Plains and Great Basin. In *Handbook of North American Indians: Southwest,* Vol. 9, edited by Alfonso Ortiz. Washington, D.C.: Smithsonian Institution. Pp. 201–205.
Lawson, M. P.
    1974   The Climate of the Great American Desert: Reconstruction of the Climate of the Western Interior United States, 1800–1850. *University of Nebraska Studies,* Vol. 46 (n.s.).

Lawton, Sherman P.

1958a   The Max Thomas Site, Gd-4. *Bulletin of the Oklahoma Anthropological Society* 6:83–88.

1958b   Report of Surface Survey of Archaeological Sites, Waurika Reservoir: Jefferson, Cotton and Stephens Counties, Oklahoma. Manuscript on file, Department of Anthropology, University of Oklahoma, Norman, Oklahoma.

1960   Archaeological Survey of the Hugo Reservoir. Manuscript on file, Department of Anthropology, University of Oklahoma, Norman, Oklahoma.

1962   Petroglyphs and Pictographs in Oklahoma: An Introduction. *Plains Anthropologist* 7(17):189–193.

1964   Test Excavations in Owl Cave. *Bulletin of the Oklahoma Anthropological Society* 12:87–102.

1968   The Duncan–Wilson Bluff Shelter: A Stratified Site of the Southern Plains. *Bulletin of the Oklahoma Anthropological Society* 16:1–94.

Leechman, D.

1951   Bone Grease. *American Antiquity* 16(4):335–336.

Leehan, D. Kevin

1977   Archaeological Investigations at Candy Lake, Osage County, Oklahoma. *Archaeological Research Associates, Research Report* No. 9.

Lees, William B.

1977   Investigations at Tx-33, Old Hardesty, Texas County, Oklahoma. *Archeological Research Associates, Research Report* No. 11.

Lehmer, Donald J.

1952   The Turkey Bluff Focus of the Fulton Aspect. *American Antiquity* 17(4):313–318.

Leonhardy, Frank C.

1966a   Test Excavations in the Mangum Reservoir Area of Southwestern Oklahoma. *Contributions of the Museum of the Great Plains*, No. 2.

1966b   Domebo: A Paleo-Indian Mammoth Kill in the Prairie–Plains. *Contributions of the Museum of the Great Plains*, No. 1.

Leonhardy, Frank C., and Adrian D. Anderson

1966   Archaeology of the Domebo Site. In Domebo: a Paleo-Indian Mammoth Kill in the Prairie–Plains, edited by Frank C. Leonhardy. *Contributions of the Museum of the Great Plains*, No. 1:14–26.

Lewis, Kenneth E.

1972   1971 Excavations at Fort Towson, Choctaw County, Oklahoma. *Oklahoma Archaeological Survey, Studies in Oklahoma's Past* No. 2.

1975   Fort Washita, from Past to Present: An Archaeological Report. *Oklahoma Historical Society, Series in Anthropology*, No. 1.

Lintz, Christopher R.

1973a   A Possible Chipped Axe from the Texas Panhandle. *Oklahoma Anthropological Society Newsletter* 21(7):2–5.

1973b   A Preliminary Report of the Two Sisters Site, A Panhandle Aspect Site from Oklahoma. Paper presented at 31st annual Plains Conference, Columbia. Manuscript on file, Oklahoma Archaeological Survey, Norman, Oklahoma.

1974   An Analysis of the Custer Focus and Its Relationship to the Plains Village Horizon in Oklahoma. *Papers in Anthropology* 15(2):1–72.

1976a   Test Excavations at the Kenton Kill Site (Ci-81), Cimarron County, Oklahoma. *Oklahoma Anthropological Society Newsletter* 24(7):2–7.

1976b   The McGrath Site of the Panhandle Aspect. *Bulletin of the Oklahoma Anthropological Society* 25:1–110.

1978a   The Panhandle Aspect and Its Early Relationship with Upper Republican. In The Central Plains Tradition: Internal Development and External Relationships, edited by Donald Blakeslee. *Office of the State Archaeologist, University of Iowa*, Report No. 11.

1978b   Architecture and Radiocarbon Dating of the Antelope Creek Focus: A Test of Campbell's Model. *Plains Anthropologist* 23(82):319–328.

1978c   Review of Campbell: The Panhandle Aspect of the Chaquaqua Plateau. *Plains Anthropologist* 23(8):341–344.

1978d   The Johnson–Cline Site (Tx-40): An Upland Dune Site in the Oklahoma Panhandle. *Bulletin of the Oklahoma Anthropological Society* 27:111–140.

1978e   An Archaeological Survey of the Keer–McGee Choctaw Coal Mine Facility, Haskell County, Oklahoma. *University of Oklahoma, Archaeological Research and Management Center, Project Report Series* No. 2.

1978f   Flake Blank Production Strategy of the Heerwald Site Cache. *Bulletin of the Oklahoma Anthropological Society* 27:179–206.

1979a   The Natural Lake Site (34Pu-71). *University of Oklahoma, Archaeological Research and Management Center, Research Series* 6:125–168.

1979b   The Blessingham Site (34Pu-74). *University of Oklahoma, Archaeological Research and Management Center, Research Series* 6:244–362.

1979c   Radiocarbon and Archaeomagnetic Dates from the Two Sisters Site, 34Tx-32, Texas County, Oklahoma. *Oklahoma Anthropological Society Newsletter* 27(6):1–9.

1979d   The Southwestern Periphery of the Plains Caddoan Area. *Nebraska History Magazine* 60(2):161–182.

Lintz, Christopher, C. Wallis, Jr., and Don G. Wyckoff
1981   The Clifford Moss Site Plainview Point, McCurtain County, Oklahoma. *Oklahoma Anthropological Society Newsletter* 29(1):6.

Little, Elbert L.
1939   The Vegetation of the Caddo County Canyons, Oklahoma. *Ecology* 20(1):1–10.

Little, E. L., and C. E. Olmstead
1936   Trees and Shrubs of the Southeastern Oklahoma Protective Unit. *Proceedings of the Oklahoma Academy of Science* 16:52–61.

Long, A. W.
1970   Ecological Factors Affecting the Distribution of Woody Vegetation near the Arkansas River, Tulsa County, with Special Reference to the Smoke-Tree *Cotinus obovatus*. M.A. thesis, Department of Botany, University of Tulsa, Tulsa, Oklahoma.

Long, Austin, and Bruce Rippeteau
1974   Testing Contemporaneity and Averaging Radiocarbon Dates. *American Antiquity* 39:205–215.

Lopez, David R.
1970   The McLemore Cemetery Complex: An Analysis of Prehistoric Burial Customs. *Bulletin of the Oklahoma Anthropological Society* 19:137–150.

1972   Archaeological Survey of Crutcho and Soldier Creek Development Project, Oklahoma County, Oklahoma. *Oklahoma Archaeological Survey, Archaeological Resource Survey Report*, No. 1.

1973   The Wybark Site: A Late Prehistoric Village Complex in the Three Forks Locale, Muskogee County, Oklahoma. *Bulletin of the Oklahoma Anthropological Society* 22:11–126.

Lopez, David R., and K. D. Keith
1976   An Archaeological Survey of U.S. 69: Pittsburg, Atoka, and Bryan Counties, Oklahoma. *Oklahoma Department of Highways, Oklahoma Highway Archaeological Survey, Papers in Highway Archaeology*, No. 2.

Lopez, David R., and Roger S. Saunders
1973   Current Lithic Studies in Oklahoma. *Oklahoma Anthropological Society Newsletter* 21(9):1–4.

Lopez, David R. and others
1979   Oklahoma Highway Archaeological Survey, Highway Archaeological Reconnaissance Program: 1972–1978. *Oklahoma Department of Transportation, Oklahoma Highway Archaeological Survey, Papers in Highway Archaeology*, No. 6.

Lorenzo, Jose Luis
1978   Early Man Research in the American Hemisphere. In *Early Man in America from a*

Circum-Pacific Perspective, edited by Alan L. Bryan. *University of Alberta, Department of Anthropology, Occasional Papers* No. 1:1–9.

Lowrey, E. J.
1932   The Archaeology of the Antelope Creek Ruin. M.A. thesis, Department of Anthropology, Texas Technical College, Lubbock, Texas.

Ludrick, John A.
1966   Ponca City Chapter Report. *Oklahoma Anthropological Society Newsletter* 14(4):5.

Mallouf, Robert J.
1976   Archeological Investigations at Proposed Big Pine Lake 1974–1975: Lamar and Red River Counties, Texas. *Archeological Survey Report* 18. Austin: Texas Historical Commission.

Mandeville, M. D.
1973   A Consideration of the Thermal Pretreatment of Chert. *Plains Anthropologist* 18(61): 177–202.

Mandeville, M. D., and J. J. Flenniken
1974   A Comparison of the Flaking Qualities of Nehawka Chert Before and After Thermal Pretreatment. *Plains Anthropologist* 19(64):146–148.

Mankin, Charles J.
1972   Jurassic Strata in Northeastern New Mexico. *Twenty Third field Conference Guidebook, New Mexico Geological Society.* Socorro, New Mexico. Pp. 91–97.

Marcher, Melvin V., and Roy H. Bingham
1971   Reconnaissance of the Water Resources of the Tulsa Quadrangle, *Hydrologic Atlas 2, Oklahoma Geological Survey.* Norman, Oklahoma.

Marrinan, Rochelle A.
1981   Analysis of the Faunal Remains from Sliding Slab Shelter. In *Sliding Slab Shelter,* edited by P. L. Harden and others, Appendix V, 36 pp. Pauls Valley, Oklahoma: Environmental Assessments.

Marshall, James O.
1972   The Archaeology of the Elk City Reservoir. *Kansas State Historical Society, Anthropological Series,* Number 6.

Marshall, R. A.
1963   A Descriptive System for Projectile Points. *Missouri Archaeological Society, Research Series* No. 1.

Martin, P. S.
1967   Prehistoric Overkill. *Proceedings of the VII Congress of the International Association for Quaternary Research* 6:75–120. Yale University Press.

Martin, P. S., and J. E. Guilday
1967   A Besiary for Pleistocene Biologists. *Proceedings of the VII Congress of the International Association for Quaternary Research* 6:1–62. New Haven: Yale University Press.

Mason, J. Alden
1929   The Texas Expedition. *University of Pennsylvania Museum Journal* 22:318–338.

Mason, R. J., and C. Irwin
1960   An Eden–Scottsbluff Burial in Northeast Wisconsin. *American Antiquity* 26(1):43–57.

Maxwell, J. A., and M. B. Davis
1972   Pollen Evidence of Pleistocene and Holocene Vegetation of the Allegheny Plateau, Maryland. *Quaternary Research* 2:506–530.

Mayo, M. B.
1975   A Resurvey and Assessment of the Prehistoric Resources of Wister Lake, LeFlore County, Oklahoma. *Oklahoma River Basin Survey, General Survey Report,* No. 15.

Mayo, Molly, and Guy R. Muto
1979   Radiocarbon Dates for Lee's Creek Region, Eastern Oklahoma. *Oklahoma Anthropological Society Newsletter* 27(4):10–13.

McBride, Earle F., and A. Thomson
    1970   Caballos Novaculite, Marathon Region, Texas. *Geological Society of America, Special Paper No. 122.*

McClung, T. L.
    1980a   A Preliminary Report: Archaeological Investigations at the W. W. Works Site, 34Wg-117, Northeast Oklahoma. *Oklahoma Anthropological Society Newsletter* 28(1):2–6.
    1980b   Some Notes on Basal Notched Projectile Points from Northeastern Oklahoma. *Oklahoma Anthropological Society Newsletter* 28(4):4–10.

McCoy, D. A.
    1958   Vascular Plants of Pontotoc County, Oklahoma. *The American Midland Naturalist* 59(2):371–396.

McHugh, W. P.
    1963   A Transitional Archaic and Woodland Site (D1-57) in Delaware County, Oklahoma. M.A. thesis, Department of Anthropology, University of Wisconsin, Madison, Wisconsin.

McKay, Douglas
    1953   Washita River Subbasin, Red River Basin, Oklahoma and Texas. *House Document No. 219, 83rd Congress, 1st session*, Washington, D.C.

McKern, W.
    1939   The Midwestern Taxonomic Method as an Aid to Archaeological Culture Study. *American Antiquity* 4:301–313.

McMillan, R. B., and W. E. Klippel
    1981   Post-Glacial Environmental Change and Hunting–Gathering Societies of the Southern Prairie Peninsula. *Journal of Archaeological Science* 8:215–245.

McRill, L. A.
    1963   Ferdinandina: First White Settlement in Oklahoma. *The Chronicles of Oklahoma* 41(2):126–159.

McWilliams, Richard
    1970   Physical Anthropology of Wann and Sam, two Fourche Maline Focus Archaic Sites in Eastern Oklahoma. *Bulletin of the Oklahoma Anthropological Society* 19:101–136.

Means, F. H.
    1969   Vascular Plants of Southeastern Oklahoma from the San Bois to the Kiamichi Mountains. Ph.D. dissertation, Department of Botany, Oklahoma State University, Stillwater, Oklahoma.

Mehl, M. G.
    1975   Vertebrate Paleomorphology of the Cooperton Site. In The Cooperton Mammoth: an Early Man Bone Quarry, edited by Adrian D. Anderson, pp. 165–168. *Great Plains Journal* 14:130–173.

Mehringer, P. J., Jr.
    1977   Great Basin Late Quaternary Environments and Chronology. *Desert Research Institute, Publications in the Social Sciences* 12:113–176.

Mehringer, P. J., J. E. King, and E. H. Lindsay
    1970   A Record of Wisconsin-Age Vegetation and Fauna from the Ozarks of Western Missouri. *University of Kansas, Department of Geology, Special Publication* 3:173–183.

Meighan, C. W.
    1960   A New Method for the Seriation of Archaeological Collections. *American Antiquity* 25(9):203–211.

Mercer, J. H.
    1972   The Lower Boundary of the Holocene. *Quaternary Research* 2:15–24.

Milby, T. H.
    1977   Literature on the Vegetation of Oklahoma, 1964–1975. *Proceedings of the Oklahoma Academy of Science* 57:176–184.

Milby, T. H., and W. T. Penfound
   1964   Additions to the Literature on the Vegetation of Oklahoma. *Proceedings of the Oklahoma Academy of Science* 44:23–33.

Miller A. F.
   1977   A Survey and Assessment of the Cultural Resources of the McClellan–Kerr Arkansas River Navigation System in Oklahoma, 1976. *Oklahoma Archaeological Survey, Archaeological Resources Survey Report* No. 6.

Miller, B. W.
   1955   The Geology of the Western Potato Hills, Pushmataha and Latimer counties, Oklahoma, M.A. thesis, Department of Geology, University of Oklahoma, Norman, Oklahoma, Norman, Oklahoma.

Miller, Juanita
   1963   Radiocarbon Dates from Oklahoma and Surrounding Areas. *Bulletin of the Oklahoma Anthropological Society* 11:115–121.

Miller, R. J., and H. W. Robison
   1973   *The Fishes of Oklahoma*. Stillwater, Oklahoma: Oklahoma State University Press.

Millsap, Mike, and Don R. Dickson
   1968   The Millsap Cache. *Bulletin of the Oklahoma Anthropological Society* 16:150–160.

Mires, Ann Marie
   1982   A Bioarchaeological Study of the Regional Adaptive Efficiency of the Caddo. M.A. thesis, Department of Anthropology, University of Arkansas. Fayetteville, Arkansas.

Mitchell, Jimmy
   1975   Archaeological Materials from the Palo Duro Creek Area of Hansford County, Texas. *Bulletin of the Texas Archeological Society* 46:217–231.

Monk, Susan M.
   1982   Utilization of Faunal Resources and Exploitation of Environmental Zones in the Southern Plains: The Edwards I Site. M.A. thesis, Department of Anthropology, University of Nebraska, Lincoln, Nebraska.

Moore, Bert
   1928   Indian Mounds in Oklahoma. *The American Indian* 2(14):13. Tulsa.

Moorehead, Warren King
   1921   Recent Explorations in Northwestern Texas. *American Anthropologist* 23(1):1–11.
   1931   *Archaeology of the Arkansas River Valley*, Andover: Phillips Academy.

Morse, D. G.
   1967   The Robinson Site and Shell Mound Archaic Cultures in the Middle South. Ph.D. dissertation, Department of Anthropology, University of Michigan, Ann Arbor, Michigan.

Moss, J. H.
   1951   Early Man in the Eden Valley. *University of Pennsylvania, University Museum, Museum Monographs*.

Murray, C. L.
   1974   A Vegetation Analysis of a Pimpled Prairie in Northeastern Oklahoma. M.A. thesis, Department of Botany, University of Tulsa, Tulsa, Oklahoma.

Muto, Guy R.
   1977   Parris Mound Archaeology Project: Phase One. Manuscript on file, Oklahoma Archaeological Survey, Norman, Oklahoma.
   1978   The Habiukut of Eastern Oklahoma. Parris Mound, Part I, Phase I: An Archaeological Report. *Oklahoma Historical Society, Series in Anthropology*, No. 3.

Muto, Guy R., and Roger S. Saunders
   1978   Cimarron County, Oklahoma: A summary of Historic and Prehistoric Cultural Resources. Manuscript on file, Oklahoma Historical Society, Office of Historic Preservation, Oklahoma City, Oklahoma.

Neal, Larry
   1972a   An Archaeological Survey and Assessment of the Prehistoric Resources in the Albany

and Parker Reservoirs, Oklahoma. Manuscript on file, Oklahoma River Basin Survey, Norman, Oklahoma.

1972b   Assessment of the Cultural-Historical Resources of Clayton Lake. *Oklahoma River Basin Survey, Special Report.*

1973a   An Assessment of the Prehistoric Cultural Resources of the Proposed Shidler Lake, Osage County, Oklahoma. *Oklahoma River Basin Survey, Special Report.*

1973b   Arcadia Lake: An Archaeological Survey and Assessment. Manuscript on file, Oklahoma River Basin Survey, Norman, Oklahoma.

1974a   Excavations at the Tucker's Knob Site. *Oklahoma Archaeological Survey, Contract Archaeology Series* (1):191–257.

1974b   A Resurvey of the Prehistoric Resources of Tenkiller Ferry Lake. *Oklahoma River Basin Survey, General Survey Report* 13.

1977   Test Excavations at Pw-63. In Archaeological Test Excavations, Sooner Generating Station Units, No. 1 and No. 2, by L. Neal and D. Wheaton. *Oklahoma Archaeological Survey, Contract Archaeology Series,* No. 2.

1982   A "fortification" ring at the Duncan Site, 34Wa-2. *Oklahoma Anthropological Society Newsletter* 30(4):7–10.

Neal, Larry and Michael B. Mayo

1974   A Preliminary Report on a Resurvey of Wister Lake. *Oklahoma River Basin Survey, Special Report.*

Neal, Larry and D. Wheaton

1977   Archaeological Test Excavations at the Sooner Generating Station, Noble and Pawnee Counties, Oklahoma. *Oklahoma Archaeological Survey, Contract Archaeology Series* No. 2.

Neuman, R. W.

1967   Radiocarbon-Dated Archaeological Remains on the Northern and Central Great Plains. *American Antiquity* 32(4):471–486.

Newcomb, W. W.

1965   Eyasiquiche. *The Mustang* 7(8):1–5. Texas Memorial Museum, Austin, Texas.

Newcomb, W. W., and W. T. Field

1967   An Ethnographic Investigation of the Wichita Indians in the Southern Plains. In *A Pilot Study of Wichita Indian Archaeology and Ethnohistory,* edited by Bell, Jelks, and Newcomb. SF final report. Pp. 240–395.

Newkumet, Phil J.

1940a   Preliminary Report on Excavations of the Williams Mound, LeFlore County, Oklahoma. *The Oklahoma Prehistorian* 3(2):2–6.

1940b   Excavation of "Black Mound" Reveals Ornate "hair pins." *The Oklahoma Prehistorian* 3(2):8–9.

1940c   Report on the Williams I Site, LeFlore County, Oklahoma. Manuscript on file, Western History Collection, University of Oklahoma, Norman, Oklahoma.

1940d   Report on the Sam Site, LeFlore County, Oklahoma. Manuscript on file, Western History Collections, University of Oklahoma, Norman, Oklahoma.

1940e   Report on the Mackey site, LeFlore County, Oklahoma. Quarterly field report (third quarter 1940), LeFlore County Archaeological Project. Manuscript on file, Archaeological Research and Management Center, University of Oklahoma, Norman, Oklahoma.

1940f   Quarterly Field Report (fourth quarter 1940), LeFlore County Archaeological Project. Manuscript on file, Archaeological Research and Management Center, University of Oklahoma, Norman, Oklahoma.

Nials, Fred L.

1977   Geology of Reservoir Area, Cowden Laterals Watershed Site No. 8. Unpublished report on file, Oklahoma Conservation Commission, Oklahoma City, Oklahoma.

1979   Appendix C: Report of Geological Investigations at Clayton Lake. *Archaeological Research and Management Center, Research Series* 6:522–526. University of Oklahoma, Norman, Oklahoma.

1980 Geological Setting. In A Reassessment of Certain Archaeological Sites in the Candy Lake Area, Oklahoma. *Archaeological Research Associates, Research Report* 22, Tulsa, Oklahoma.

Nichols, J. D.
1975 Soil at the Cooperton Site. *Great Plains Journal* 14(2):139–143.

Norton, G. H.
1939 Permian Red Beds of Kansas. *American Association of Petroleum Geologists Bulletin* 23:1751–1819.

Nowak, Michael and Kristine Kranzush
nd Report on Excavations Conducted in Cimarron County, Oklahoma. In the Fall of 1973 by Colorado College. Manuscript on file, Oklahoma Archaeological Survey, Norman, Oklahoma.

Oakes, John Underhill
1953 The Lacy Site, Garvin County, Oklahoma. *Bulletin of the Oklahoma Anthropological Society* 2:17–24.

Oklahoma Geological Survey and Oklahoma Water Resources Board
1980 Reconnaissance of the Water Resources in the Enid Quadrangle, Oklahoma. *Hydrologic Atlas* Sheet No. 7.

Oklahoma Water Resources Board
1968a *Appraisal of the Water and Related Land Resources of Oklahoma, Region Two.* Oklahoma City, Oklahoma: Mercury Press.

1968b *Appraisal of the Water and Related Land Resources of Oklahoma, Region Three.* Oklahoma City, Oklahoma: Mercury Press.

1969a *Appraisal of the Water and Related Land Resources of Oklahoma, Region Four.* Oklahoma City, Oklahoma: Mercury Press.

1969b *Appraisal of the Water and Related Land Resources of Oklahoma, Regions Five and Six.* Oklahoma City, Oklahoma: Mercury Press.

1970 *Appraisal of the Water and Related Land Resources of Oklahoma, Region Seven.* Norman, Oklahoma: Hooper Printing.

1971a *Appraisal of the Water and Related Land Resources of Oklahoma, Region Eight.* Oklahoma City, Oklahoma: Mercury Press.

1971b *Appraisal of the Water and Related Land Resources of Oklahoma, Region Nine.* Oklahoma City, Oklahoma: Lunn Printing.

1972 *Appraisal of the Water and Related Land Resources of Oklahoma, Region Ten.* Oklahoma City, Oklahoma: Mercury Press.

1973 *Appraisal of the Water and Related Land Resources of Oklahoma, Region Twelve.* Oklahoma City, Oklahoma: Mercury Press.

Oldfield, F.
1975 Pollen-Analytical Results, Part 2. *Southern Methodist University, Publication of the Fort Burgwin Research Center* 9:121–148.

Opler, Morris E.
1971 Pots, Apache, and the Dismal River Culture Aspect. In Apachean Culture History and Ethnology, edited by K. H. Basso and M. E. Opler. *Anthropological Papers of the University of Arizona*, No. 21: 29–33.

1975 A Review of Gunnerson's "The Jicarillo Apaches." *Plains Anthropologist* 20(68):150–157.

Orr, Kenneth G.
1941 The Eufaula Mound: Contributions to the Spiro Focus. *The Oklahoma Prehistorian* 4(1):2–15.

1942 The Eufaula Mound, Oklahoma: Contribution to the Spiro Focus. M.A. thesis, Department of Anthropology, University of Chicago, Chicago, Illinois.

1946 The Archaeological Situation at Spiro, Oklahoma: a Preliminary Report. *American Antiquity* 11(4):228–256.

1952 Survey of Caddoan Area Archaeology. In *Archaeology of Eastern United States*, edited by James B. Griffin: 239–255. Chicago: University of Chicago Press.

Palmer, E. J.
  1927   On Nuttall's Trail Through Arkansas. *Journal of the Arnold Arboretum* 8:24–55.
Parsons, Mark L.
  1967   Archaeological Investigations in Crosby and Dickens Counties, Texas During the Winter 1966–1967. *Texas State Building Commission, Archeological Program, Report* No. 7.
Patterson, David K.
  1974   An Analysis of Human Skeletal Materials from Antelope Creek Focus of Northern Texas. M.A. thesis, Department of Anthropology, Eastern New Mexico University, Portales, New Mexico.
Patterson, Deborah E.
  1974   Dental Variations Among the Panhandle Aspect Populations. M.A. thesis, Department of Anthropology, Eastern New Mexico University, Portales, New Mexico.
Pearson, F. J., E. Mott Davis, and M. A. Tamers
  1966   University of Texas Radiocarbon Dates. *Radiocarbon* 8:453–466.
Penfound, W. T.
  1947   An Analysis of an Elm–Ash Floodplain Community Near Norman, Oklahoma. *Proceedings of the Oklahoma Academy of Science* 28:59–60.
  1963   The Composition of a Post Oak Forest in South Central Oklahoma. *The Southwestern Naturalist* 8(2):114–115.
Penman, J. T.
  1974a   Two Archaic Sites in Southeastern Oklahoma. *Oklahoma Archaeological Survey, Contract Archaeology Series* (1):117–157.
  1974b   Faunal Analysis of the Hodge Site, Custer County, Oklahoma. In Reports of the ARKLA Salvage Project, *Oklahoma Archaeological Survey, Contract Archaeology* Series (1):69–72.
  1979   Faunal Remains from the Pate Site, Oklahoma. *Bulletin of the Oklahoma Anthropological Society* 28:147–150.
Perino, Gregory
  1972a   *An Historical–Cultural Assessment of the Proposed Birch Creek Reservoir, Osage County, Oklahoma.* Corps of Engineers, Tulsa, Oklahoma.
  1972b   *An Historical–Cultural Assessment of the Skiatook Reservoir, Osage County, Oklahoma.* Corps of Engineers, Tulsa, Oklahoma.
Perino, Gregory, and W. J. Bennett, Jr.
  1978   *Archaeological Investigations at the Mahaffey Site, Ch-1, Hugo Reservoir, Choctaw County, Oklahoma.* Museum of the Red River, Idabel, Oklahoma.
Perino, Gregory, and Jerry Caffey
  1980   *The Eufaula Lake Project, A Cultural Resource Survey and Assessment.* Museum of the Red River, Idabel, Oklahoma.
Phillips, Mel
  1975   Burned Human Finger Bone. *Oklahoma Anthropological Society Newsletter* 23(4):9.
Phillips, Philip
  1970   Archaeological Survey in the Lower Yazoo Basin, Mississippi, 1949–1955. *Papers of the Peabody Museum of Archaeology and Ethnology*, No. 60.
Phillips, Philip, and James A. Brown
  1975   *Pre-Columbian Shell Engravings from the Craig Mound at Spiro, Oklahoma*, Vols. 1–3. Cambridge: Peabody Museum Press.
  1979   *Pre-Columbian Shell Engravings from the Craig Mound at Spiro, Oklahoma*, Vol. 4. Cambridge: Peabody Museum Press.
Phillips, P., J. A. Ford, and J. B. Griffin
  1951   Archaeological Survey in the Lower Mississippi Alluvial Valley, 1940–1947. *Papers of the Peabody Museum of Archaeology and Ethnology*, No. 25.
Pillaert, Elizabeth
  1962   Text Excavations at the Lee Site, Gv-4, Garvin County, Oklahoma. *Bulletin of the Oklahoma Anthropological Society* 10:79–101.

1963   The McLemore Site of the Washita River Focus. *Bulletin of the Oklahoma Anthropological Society* 11:1–113.

nd   Notes on the Faunal Remains from the Moore Site. Unpublished papers. See Rohrbaugh 1982:563–571 for a summary of this information.

Porter, J. W.
1962   Notes on Four Lithic Types Found in Archaeological Sites near Mobridge, South Dakota. *Plains Anthropologist* 7(18):268.

Powell, M. L., and J. D. Rogers
1980   Bioarchaeology of the McCutchan–McLaughlin Site (34Lt-11): Biophysics and Mortuary Variability in Eastern Oklahoma. *Oklahoma Archaeological Survey, Studies in Oklahoma's Past*, No. 5.

Prewitt, E. R.
1981   Cultural Chronology in Central Texas. *Bulletin of the Texas Archeological Society* 52:65–89.

Prewitt, E. R., and D. A. Lawson
1972   An Assessment of the Archeological and Paleontological Resources of Lake Texoma, Texas–Oklahoma. *University of Texas at Austin, Texas Archeological Salvage* Project, *Survey Report* No. 10.

Prewitt, Terry J.
1968   Archaeological Survey of the Oologah Reservoir, Nowata and Rogers Counties, Oklahoma. *Oklahoma River Basin Survey, General Survey Report*, No. 10.

1974   Regional Interaction Networks and the Caddoan Area. *Papers in Anthropology* 15(2):73–101.

1980   Little Caney River Prehistory (Copan Lake): 1978 Field Season. *University of Tulsa, Laboratory of Archaeology, Contributions in Archaeology*, No. 7.

Prewitt, Terry J., and Pam Wood
1969   The Sheffield Site: A Fulton Aspect Component in the Short Mountain Reservoir Area. *Oklahoma River Basin Survey, Archaeological Site Report*, No. 12.

Proctor, Charles
1953   Report of Excavations in the Eufaula Reservoir. *Bulletin of the Oklahoma Anthropological Society* 1:43–60.

1957   The Sam Site, Lf-28, of LeFlore County, Oklahoma. *Bulletin of the Oklahoma Anthropological Society* 5:45–92.

Purrington, B. L.
1970   The Prehistory of Delaware County, Oklahoma: Cultural Continuity and Change on the Western Ozark Periphery. Ph.D. dissertation, Department of Anthropology, University of Wisconsin, Madison, Wisconsin.

Ralph, E. K., H. N. Michael, and M. C. Han
1973   Radiocarbon Dates and Reality. *Masca Newsletter* 9(1):1–20. Philadelphia.

Ray, G. D.
1960   Areal Geology of Farris Quadrangle, Pushmataha and Atoka Counties, Oklahoma. M.A. thesis, Department of Geology, University of Oklahoma, Norman, Oklahoma.

Ray, Max A.
1960a   The James Site, Br-11, an Archaeological Site in Bryan County, Oklahoma. *Bulletin of the Oklahoma Anthropological Society* 8:53–74.

1960b   A Preliminary Report on Excavations at the Pohly Site, My-54. *Oklahoma Anthropological Society Newsletter* 9(1):7–10.

1961a   A Resurvey of Oklahoma Archaeology (Part II). *Oklahoma Anthropological Society Newsletter* 9(9):6–11.

1961b   A Resurvey of Oklahoma Archaeology (Part III). *Oklahoma Anthropological Society Newsletter* 10(2–3):1–16.

1965   A Report on Excavations at the Pohly Site, My-54, in Northeastern Oklahoma. *Bulletin of the Oklahoma Anthropological Society* 13:1–68.

Ray, R. J.
    1959   A Phytosocial Analysis of the Tall-Grass Prairie in Northeastern Oklahoma. *Ecology* 40:255–261.

Reed, E. W., S. L. Schoff, and C. C. Branson
    1955   Ground Water Resources of Ottawa County. *Oklahoma Geological Survey*, Bulletin No. 72.

Reeves, B.
    1973   The Concept of an Altithermal Cultural Hiatus in Northern Plains Prehistory. *American Anthropologist* 75(5):1221–1253.

Reeves, C. C., Jr.
    1976   Quaternary Stratigraphy and Geologic History of Southern High Plains. *Quaternary Stratigraphy of North America*, edited by W. C. Mahaney:213–234. Stroudsburg, Pennsylvania: Dowden, Hutchinson and Ross.

Reher, Charles A.
    1977   Adaptive Process on the Shortgrass Plains. In *Theory Building in Archaeology*, edited by L. R. Binford. New York: Academic Press. Pp. 13–40.

Renaud, Etienne B.
    1929a   Basketmakers in Oklahoma. *El Palacio* 27:187–188.
    1929b   A Summer's Expedition to Northeast New Mexico and Western Oklahoma. *El Palacio* 27:247–248.
    1929c   Archaeological Research in Northeastern New Mexico and Western Oklahoma. *El Palacio* 27(23–24):276–279.
    1929d   Fieldnotes on file at the University of Denver Museum.
    1930a   Prehistoric Cultures of the Cimarron Valley, Northeast New Mexico and Western Oklahoma. *Colorado Scientific Society Proceedings* 12(5):113–150.
    1930b   A Summary of the Prehistoric Cultures of the Cimarron Valley. *El Palacio* 29(2):123–129.
    1930c   Colorado Museum. *El Palacio* 29(4):146–148.
    1930d   Les Plus Anciennes Cultures Prehistoriques du Sud-Ouest Americain. *L'Anthropologie* 40(3):233–258.
    1932   Archaeology du Colorado Oriental. *Revue Anthropologie* (July–Sept). Pp. 233–258.
    1937   Pictographs and Petroglyphs of Colorado—IV. *Southwestern Lore* 3(2):35–40.
    1939   The Clactonian Flake Technique in the Western United States. *Texas Archeological and Paleontological Society Bulletin* 11:129–138.
    1947   *Archaeology of the High Western Plains, 17 Years of Archaeological Research.* Denver: University of Denver.

Retallick, Harold J.
    1966   Geomorphology of the Domebo Site. In Domebo: a Paleo-Indian Mammoth Kill in the Prairie–Plains, edited by Frank. C. Leonhardy. *Contributions of the Museum of the Great Plains*, No. 1:3–10.

Rice, Elroy L.
    1965   Bottomland Forests of North-Central Oklahoma. *Ecology* 46(5):708–714.

Rice, E. L., and W. T. Penfound
    1956   Composition of a Green Ash Forest near Norman, Oklahoma. *The Southwestern Naturalist* 1(4):145–147.
    1959   The Upland Forests of Oklahoma. *Ecology* 40(4):593–608.

Richards, Michael K.
    1971   The Lee Site, a Late Prehistoric Manifestation in Garvin County, Oklahoma. *Bulletin of the Oklahoma Anthropological Society* 20:1–82.

Riley, Carroll L.
    1978   Pecos and Trade. In *Across the Chichimec Sea, Papers in Honor of J. Charles Kelley*, edited by C. L. Riley and B. C. Hedrick. Carbondale: Southern Illinois University Press. Pp. 53–64.

Risser, Paul, Jeannine H. Risser, and Vicki Goodnight
    1980   *Concept Plan for the Unique Wildlife Eco-Systems of Oklahoma*. Norman: University of Oklahoma Press.

Ritchie, W. A.
    1932   The Lamoke Lake Site. *Researches and Transactions of the New York State Archaeological Association* 7(4):79–134.

Ritchie, W. A., and R. S. MacNeish
    1949   The Pre-Iroquoian Pottery of New York State. *American Antiquity* 15:97–124.

Roberts, Frank H. H., Jr.
    1943   A New Site. *American Antiquity*, Vol. 8, No. 3, p. 300.
    1951   The Early Americans. *Scientific American* 184(2):15–19.

Robertson, Rev. W. S.
    1878   Note. *American Antiquarian* 1:14.

Rogers, C. M.
    1953   The Vegetation of the Mesa de Maya Region of Colorado, New Mexico and Oklahoma. *Lyoydia* 16(4):257–290.
    1954   Some Botanical Studies in the Black Mesa Region of Oklahoma. *Rhodora* 56:205–212.

Rogers, J. Daniel
    1979a   An Archaeological Survey of the Fourche Maline Valley South of Red Oak, Oklahoma. *Oklahoma Archaeological Survey, Archaeological Resources Survey Report*, No. 8.
    1979b   Excavations at Area 7 of the Rock Creek Site (34At-172), Atoka County, Oklahoma. *Oklahoma Conservation Commission, Archaeological Research Report* 6.
    1980   Spiro Archaeology: 1979 Excavations. *Oklahoma Archaeological Survey, Studies in Oklahoma's Past*, No. 6.
    1982a   Social Ranking and Change in the Harlan and Spiro Phases of Eastern Oklahoma. M.S. thesis, Department of Anthropology, University of Oklahoma, Norman, Oklahoma.
    1982b   Spiro Archaeology: 1980 Research. *Oklahoma Archaeological Survey, Studies in Oklahoma's Past, No. 9.*

Rohn, Arthur H., and Miriam R. Smith
    1972   Assessment of the Archaeological Resources and an Evaluation of the Impact of Construction of the Copan Dam and Lake. *Wichita State University, Archaeology Laboratory.*

Rohrbaugh, Charles L.
    1968   The W. H. Baldwin Site, Mc-84, McCurtain County, Southeast Oklahoma. *Oklahoma River Basin Survey, Miscellaneous Report*, No. 3.
    1971   Hugo Reservoir I. *Oklahoma River Basin Survey, Archaeological Site Report*, No. 22.
    1972a   Archaeological Resources in the Vicinity of Waurika Reservoir Dam, Jefferson County, Oklahoma. *Oklahoma River Basin Survey, University of Oklahoma.*
    1972b   Hugh Reservoir II: A Discussion of the Development of the Archaic Cultures in Hugo Reservoir into the Pre-Formative and Formative Tradition and Including the Descriptions of Three Archaic Sites Dug During the 1970 Field Season: Ch-89, The McKensie Site; Pu-58, The Hill Site; and Ch-113A, The Pat Boyd Place, Area A. *Oklahoma River Basin Survey, Archaeological Site Report*, No. 23.
    1973a   Kaw Reservoir—The Southern Section: Report of Phase II Research of the General Plan for Investigation of the Archaeological Resources of Kaw Reservoir, North-Central Oklahoma. *Oklahoma River Basin Survey, Archaeological Site Report*, No. 25.
    1973b   Hugo Reservoir III: A Report on the Early Formative Cultural Manifestations in Hugo Reservoir and in the Caddoan Area. *Oklahoma River Basin Survey, Archaeological Site Report*, No. 24.
    1974   Kaw Reservoir—The Central Section. Report for Investigations of the Archaeological Resources of Kaw Reservoir, North-Central Oklahoma. *Oklahoma River Basin Survey, Archaeological Site Report*, No. 27.
    1981   Other Conclusions. In *Sliding Slab Shelter*, edited by P. L. Harden and others. Environmental Assessments. Pauls Valley, Oklahoma: Pp. 147–192.

1982   Spiro and Fort Coffee Phases: Changing Cultural Complexes of the Caddoan Area. Ph.D. dissertation, Department of Anthropology, University of Wisconsin, Madison, Wisconsin.

Rohrbaugh, Charles L. and Don G. Wyckoff
1969   The Archaeological Survey of the Proposed Skiatook Reservoir, Osage County, Oklahoma. *Oklahoma River Basin Survey, General Survey Report,* No. 11.

Rohrbaugh, Charles, L., R. J. Burton, Susan S. Burton, and L. J. Rosewitz
1971   Hugo Reservoir I: The Description of the Archaeological Sites Excavated During the 1970 Field Season Including Ch-1, Ch-43, Ch-70, Ch-75, Pu-82 and Ch-90. *Oklahoma River Basin Survey, Archaeological Site Report,* No. 22.

Roper, Donna C.
1976   A Trend Surface Analysis of Central Plains Woldland Dates. *American Antiquity* 41(2):181–189.

Rucker, Alvin
1929   Cavern Holds Evidence of Early Tribes. *The Daily Oklahoman* July 25, 1929:14.

Salisbury, N. E.
1980   Soil–Geomorphic Relationships with Archeological Sites in the Keystone Reservoir Area, Oklahoma. *Archaeological Research Associates, Research Report* 23:59–78.

Sappington, Robert L.
1980   X-Ray Fluorescence Analysis of Obsidian Items from the Edwards I Site (34Bk-2). Letter report submitted to the Oklahoma Archaeological Survey.

Satterthwaite, L.
1957   Stone Artifacts at and near the Finley Site near Eden, Wyoming. *University Museum, Museum Monographs.* Philadelphia.

Saunders, Roger S.
1973   The Zimm's Site, a Late Prehistoric House Site in Western Oklahoma. *Oklahoma Anthropological Society Newsletter* 21(6):7–8.

1974a   The Clements Site (Gd-57). In reports of the ARKLA Salvage Project, *Oklahoma Archaeological Survey, Contract Archaeology Survey* 1:113–116.

1974b   The Clay and Roberts Sites, Two Lithic Workshop Sites in Western Oklahoma. In Reports of the ARKLA Salvage Project, *Oklahoma Archaeological Survey, Contract Archaeology Survey* 1:73–112.

1976   A Radiocarbon Date from the Perry Ranch Site, Jackson County, Oklahoma. *Oklahoma Anthropological Society Newsletter* 24(6):3–6.

1978   Archaeological Resources of Black Mesa State Park, Cimarron County, Oklahoma. *Oklahoma Archaeological Survey, Archaeological Resource Survey Report,* No. 7.

1982   The Kenton Caves: Examples of Cultural Resources in the Western Oklahoma Panhandle. In *Man and the Oklahoma Panhandle,* edited by B. Jackson, J. Carlisle and I. Colwell. North Newton, Kansas: Mennonite Press.

Saunders, Roger S., Jack L. Hofman, and Don G. Wyckoff
1972   *Synopsis of Survey and Recommendations Concerning Archaeological Resources along the Proposed Anadarko Pipeline Project of Arkansas Louisiana Gas Company.* Final report in Partial Fulfillment of Project 1869. University of Oklahoma Research Institute, Norman.

Saunders, Roger S., and John T. Penman
1979   Perry Ranch: A Plainview Bison Kill on the Southern Plains. *Plains Anthropologist* 24(83):51–65.

Saunders, Roger S., and Kenneth E. Saunders
1982   Distribution and Density Patterns of Lithic Materials in Cimarron County, Oklahoma. In *Pathways to Plains Prehistory: Anthropological Perspectives of Plains Natives and Their Pasts,* edited by Don G. Wyckoff and Jack L. Hofman. Oklahoma Anthropological Society Memoir 3, pp. 99–110. Duncan, Oklahoma.

Sayles, E. B.
1935   An Archaeological Survey of Texas. *Medallion Papers,* No. 17. Globe, Arizona: Gila Pueblo.

Schaffner, J. H.
   1926   *Observations on the Grasslands of the Central United States.* Columbus: Ohio State University Press.
Schambach, F. C.
   1970   Pre-Caddoan Cultures in the Trans-Mississippi South: A Beginning Sequence. Ph.D. dissertation, Department of Anthropology, Harvard University, Cambridge, Massachusetts.
Schlesier, Karl H.
   1972   Rethinking the Dismal River Aspect and the Plains Athapaskans, A.D. 1692–1768. *Plains Anthropologist* 17(56):101–133.
Schmitt, Karl
   1950   The Lee Site, Gv-3, of Garvin County, Oklahoma. *Bulletin of the Texas Archeological and Paleontological Society* 21:69–89.
Schmitt, Karl and Raymond Toldan, Jr.
   1953   The Brown Site, Gd-1, Grady County, Oklahoma. *Bulletin of the Texas Archeological Society* 24:141–176.
Schneider, Fred
   1967   Eight Archaeological Sites in the Webber's Falls Lock and Dam Area, Oklahoma. *Oklahoma River Basin Survey, Archaeological Site Report,* No. 7.
   1969   The Roy Smith Site, Bv-14, Beaver County, Oklahoma. *Bulletin of the Oklahoma Anthropological Society* 18:110–179.
Schoenwetter, J.
   1975   Pollen-Analytical Results, Part 1. *Southern Methodist University, Publications of the Fort Burgwin Research Center* 9:103–120.
Scholtz, Sandra C.
   1975   Prehistoric Plies: a Structural and Comparative Analysis of Cordage, Netting, Basketry and Fabric from Ozark Bluff Shelter. *Arkansas Archeological Survey, Research Series,* No. 9.
Schroeder, Albert
   1962   A Re-analysis of the Routes of Coronado and Oñate in the Plains in 1851 and 1601. *Plains Anthropologist* 7(15):2–22.
   1979   Pecos Pueblo. In *Handbook of North American Indians: Southwest 9,* edited by Alfonso Ortiz, pp. 430–437.
Schultz, C. B., and L. E. Eiseley
   1935   Paleontological Evidence of the Antiquity of the Scottsbluff Bison Quarry and its Associated Artifacts. *American Anthropologist* 37:306–319.
Scott, Douglas D.
   1976a   Fort Towson Powder Magazine. *The Chronicles of Oklahoma* 53(4):516–527.
   1976b   Preliminary Report on the Excavation of the Commanding Officers Quarters, Fort Towson. *Oklahoma Anthropological Society Newsletter* 24(2):5–10.
Sears, W. H., and J. B. Griffin
   1953   Fiber-Tempered Pottery of the Southeast. In *Prehistoric pottery of the Eastern United States,* Museum of Anthropology, University of Michigan, Ann Arbor, Michigan.
Sellards, E. A.
   1940   Early Man in America: Index to Localities and Selected Bibliography. *Bulletin of the Geological Society of America* 51:373–432.
   1955   Fossil Bison and Associated Artifacts from Milnesand, New Mexico. *American Antiquity* 20(4):336–344.
Sellards, E. H., G. L. Evans, and G. E. Meade
   1947   Fossil Bison and Associated Artifacts from Plainview, Texas. *Bulletin of the Geological Society of America* 58:927–954.
Shaeffer, James B.
   1957   The McCarter Site, A Late Archaic Occupation at Muskogee, Oklahoma. *Bulletin of the Texas Archeological Society* 28:240–268.

1958a   The Horton Site, A Fultanoid Village near Vian, Oklahoma. *Bulletin of the Oklahoma Anthropological Society* 6:1–26.

1958b   Salvage Project Activities. *Oklahoma Anthropological Society Newsletter* 6(7):4–5.

1961   Six Sites on the Fort Sill Military Reservation. *Plains Anthropologist* 6(12)2:13–54.

1965   Salvage Archaeology in Oklahoma, Vol. I, Papers of the Oklahoma Archaeological Salvage Project, Nos. 8–15. *Bulletin of the Oklahoma Anthropological Society* 13:77–153.

1966   Salvage Archaeology in Oklahoma, Vol. II. Papers of the Oklahoma Archaeological Salvage Project, Nos. 18–21. *Bulletin of the Oklahoma Anthropological Society* 14:1–86.

Shafer, Harry J.
1973   Lithic Technology at the George C. Davis Site, Cherokee County, Texas. Ph.D. dissertation, Department of Anthropology, University of Texas, Austin, Texas.

Sharp, Lauriston
1968   Stone-Age Australians. In *Economic Anthropology: Readings in Theory and Analysis,* edited by E. E. Leclair, Jr., and H. K. Schneider. New York: Holt Rinehart and Winston.

Sharrock, Floyd W.
1959a   Preliminary Report on the Van Schuyver Site, Pottawatomie County, Oklahoma. *Bulletin of the Oklahoma Anthropological Society* 7:33–40.

1959b   Test Excavations at the Willingham Site, M1-5, McClain County, Oklahoma. *Bulletin of the Oklahoma Anthropological Society* 7:41–50.

1960   The Wann Site, Lf-27, of the Fourche Maline Focus. *Bulletin of the Oklahoma Anthropological Society* 8:17–47.

1961   The Grant Site of the Washita River Focus. *Bulletin of the Oklahoma Anthropological Society* 9:1–66.

Shelburne, Orville B., Jr.
1960   Geology of the Boktukola Syncline, Southeastern Oklahoma. *Oklahoma Geological Survey, Bulletin* No. 58.

Shelford, V. E.
1963   *The Ecology of North America.* Urbana: University of Illinois Press.

Shirk, G. H.
1967   A Tour on the Prairies along the Washington Irving Trail in Oklahoma. *The Chronicles of Oklahoma* 65(3):1–20.

Sholes, Mark Allen
1978   Stratigraphy and Petrology of the Arkansas Novaculite of Arkansas and Oklahoma. Ph.D. dissertation, Department of Geology. University of Texas, Austin, Texas.

Skinner, Hubert C.
1957   Two Artifact Flints of Oklahoma. *Bulletin of the Oklahoma Anthropological Society* 5:39–44.

Slater, Lee
1975   Oklahoma Historical Society. *1975 Directory of Oklahoma.* Oklahoma State Election Board, pp. 202–204.

Slaughter, B. H.
1966   The Vertebrates of the Domebo Local Fauna, Pleistocene of Oklahoma. *Contributions of the Museum of the Great Plains* 1:31–35.

Slocum, R. C.
1955   Post-Boone Outliers of Northeastern Oklahoma. *Oklahoma Geological Survey, Circular* No. 35.

Slovacek, Charles
1966   Kay County Chapter News. *Oklahoma Anthropological Society Newsletter* 14(5):20.

Smiley, Terah, Stanley Stubbs, and Bryant Bannister
1953   A Foundation for the Dating of Some Late Archaeological Sites in the Rio Grande Area, New Mexico. *University of Arizona Laboratory of Tree Ring Research,* No. 6.

Smith, Bruce D.
1975   Middle Mississippi Exploitation of Animal Populations. *University of Michigan, Anthropological Papers,* No. 57.

Snider, L. C.
   1915   Geology of a Portion of Northeastern Oklahoma. *Oklahoma Geological Survey, Bulletin* No. 24.
Spaulding, G. F.
   1968   *On the Western Tour with Washington Irving: The Journal and Letters of Count de Pourtales.* Norman: University of Oklahoma Press.
Speth, John D., and William J. Parry
   1978   Late Prehistoric Bison Procurement in Southeastern New Mexico: The 1977 Season at the Garnsey Site. *University of Michigan, Museum of Anthropology, Technical Reports* No. 8.
Spier, Leslie
   1928   Concerning Man's Antiquity at Frederick, Oklahoma. *Science* (n.s.) 67:160–161.
Spradlin, Charles B.
   1959   Geology of the Beaver's Bend State Park Area, McCurtain County, Oklahoma. M.A. thesis, Department of Geology, University of Oklahoma, Norman, Oklahoma.
State of Oklahoma, Wildlife Conservation Department
   1960   Game Mammals of Oklahoma. *Oklahoma Wildlife Commission, Educational Pamphlet* No. 1.
Steen, Charlie R.
   1953   Two Early Historic Sites on the Southern Plains. *Bulletin of the Texas Archeological Society* 24:177–188.
   1955   Baked Clay Figurines From the Spanish Fort Site. *Panhandle–Plains Historical Review* 28:107–109.
Steila, D.
   1976   *The Geography of Soils: Formation, Distribution and Management.* Englewood Cliffs: Prentice-Hall.
Stevens, Dominique E., and T. R. Hays
   1977a   Archaeological Mitigation at the Waurika Lake Reservoir, Southwestern Oklahoma. *North Texas State University, Archaeology Program, Institute of Applied Sciences.*
   1977b   Recommendations Concerning National Register Eligibility of Archaeological Sites at the Waurika Lake Reservoir, Southwestern Oklahoma. *North Texas State University, Archaeology Program, Institute of Applied Sciences.*
Stipp, J. J. and others
   1962   University of Texas Radiocarbon Dates I, *Radiocarbon* 4:43–50.
Stoltman, J. B.
   1978   Temporal Models in Prehistory: An Example from Eastern North America. *Current Anthropology* 19:703–746.
Story, Dee A., and S. Valastro, Jr.
   1977   Radiocarbon Dating and the George C. Davis Site, Texas. *Journal of Field Archaeology* 4:63–89.
Stovall, J. Willis
   1938   Letter to Crompton Tate dated April 23, 1939. On file, Western History Collections, Manuscript Division, University of Oklahoma, Norman, Oklahoma.
   1940   Field Notes dated May 28, 1940. On file, Western History Collections, Manuscript Division, University of Oklahoma, Norman, Oklahoma.
   1943   Stratigraphy of the Cimarron Valley (Mesozoic Rocks). In Geology and Ground Water Resources in Cimarron County, Oklahoma, edited by Stuart Schoff. *Oklahoma Geological Survey*, Bulletin No. 64.
Strong, William D.
   1935   An Introduction to Nebraska Archaeology. *Smithsonian Miscellaneous Collections*, Vol. 93, No. 10.
Studer, Floyd V.
   1931a   Archaeological Survey of the North Panhandle of Texas. *Bulletin of the Texas Archeological and Paleontological Society* 3:70–75.

1931b   Some Field Notes and Observations Concerning the Texas Panhandle Ruins. In *Archae-ology of the Arkansas River Valley*, W. K. Moorehead. Andover, Massachusetts: Phillips Academy.

1934   Texas Panhandle Culture Ruin No. 55. *Bulletin of the Texas Archeological and Paleontologi-cal Society* 6:80–96.

1939   Report to Annual Meeting of the Panhandle Plains Historical Society at Canyon, Texas, May 12, 1939. *Panhandle-Plains Historical Review* 12:91–95.

1952   Pueblo Ruins in the Texas Panhandle. In *Handbook of Texas*. Austin: Texas State Histor-ical Association.

1955   Archaeology of the Texas Panhandle. *Panhandle–Plains Historical Review* 28:87–95.

Sudbury, Byron
1968   Ka-131, the Bowling Alley Site: A Late Prehistoric Site in Kay County, Oklahoma. *Bulletin of the Oklahoma Anthropological Society* 17:87–135.

1976a   Ka-3, The Deer Creek Site, An Eighteenth Century French Contact Site. *Bulletin of the Oklahoma Anthropological Society* 24:1–135.

1976b   Relationship of the Deer Creek (Ka-3) and Bryson (Ka-5) Sites to the Love Site (Ka-2). *Oklahoma Anthropological Society Newsletter* 24(5):3–4.

Sutherland, P. K., and W. L. Manger
1979   Mississippian–Pennsylvanian Shelf-to-Basin Transition, Ozark and Ouachita Regions, Oklahoma and Arkansas. *Oklahoma Geological Survey Guidebook* No. 19.

Sutton, George M.
1967   *Oklahoma Birds: Their Ecology and Distribution, with Comments on the Avifauna of the South-ern Great Plains*. Norman: University of Oklahoma Press.

Swanton, John R.
1942   Source Material on the History and Ethnology of the Caddo Indians. *Smithsonian In-stitution Bureau of American Ethnology, Bulletin* No. 132.

1946   The Indians of Southeastern United States. *Smithsonian Institution Bureau of American Ethnology, Bulletin* No. 137.

Swineford, Ada, and Paul C. Franks
1959   Opal in the Ogallaha Formation in Kansas. Silica in Sediments (A Symposium with Discussion), edited by H. Andrew Ireland. *Society of Economic Paleontologists and Miner-alogists, Special Publication* No. 7:111–112. Tulsa.

Taff, J. A.
1928   Preliminary Report on the Geology of the Arbuckle and Wichita Mountains in Indian Territory and Oklahoma. *Oklahoma Geological Survey, Bulletin* No. 12.

Tamers, M. A., F. H. Pearson, and E. Mott Davis
1964   University of Texas Radiocarbon Dates II. *Radiocarbon* 6:138–159.

Tate, Crompton
1938   Letter to Willis Stovall dated April 27, 1938. On file at Western History Collection, Manuscripts Division, University of Oklahoma, Norman, Oklahoma.

n.d.   Progress Report on Works Progress Administration Project 465-65-3-146 S-189 for the Period April 15, 1938 to May 15, 1938. On file at Western History Collection, Manu-scripts Division, University of Oklahoma, Norman, Oklahoma.

Taylor, J.
1965   Shortlead pine (*Pinus echinata*) in Bryan County, Oklahoma. *The Southwestern Naturalist* 10(1):42–47.

Taylor, Lyonel
1973   A Descriptive Report on Certain Material from the Lowrance Site, Murray County, Oklahoma. *Bulletin of the Oklahoma Anthropological Society* 21:157–180.

Thoburn, J. B.
1922   Kay County Village Site. *Proceedings of the Oklahoma Academy of Science* 2:112–113.

1926   Oklahoma Archaeological Explorations in 1925–26. *The Chronicles of Oklahoma* 4(2):143–148.

1930   Professor Thoburn Still Digging. *The Oklahoma Engineer* 1:6–7.

1931   The Prehistoric Cultures of Oklahoma. In *Archaeology of the Arkansas River Valley*, by W. K. Moorehead: 53–82. Andover: R. S. Peabody Foundation.

Thomas, Alfred B.

1935   *After Coronado: Spanish Exploration Northwest of New Mexico, 1696–1727.* Norman: University of Oklahoma Press.

Thwaites, Reuben G.

1905   Nuttall's Travels into the Arkansa Territory, 1819. In *Early Western Travels 1748–1846* 13. Cleveland: Clark Co.

Todd, Lawrence C., Jr.

1978   Initial Analysis of Butchering Patterns in a Cody Complex Bison Kill Site. Paper presented at the 36th Annual Plains Anthropological Conference, November 8–12, Denver, Colorado.

Toth, A.

1974   Archaeology and Ceramics at the Marksville Site. *University of Michigan, Museum of Anthropology, Anthropological Papers*, No. 56.

Troike, Rudolph C.

1955   Anthropological Theory and Plains Archaeology. *Bulletin of the Texas Archeological Society* 26:113–143.

Twenhofel, W. H.

1919   The Chert of the Wreford and Forakier Limestones along the State Line of Kansas and Oklahoma. *American Journal of Science*, Fourth Series 47(282):907–929.

United States, Environmental Data Service

1966   *Climatological Data: Oklahoma.* Vols. 75–90. National Climatic Center, Asheville, N.C.

United States, Weather Bureau

1892–   *Climatological Data: Oklahoma.* Vols. 1–74. Asheville, N.C.: U.S. Weather Bureau.
1966

Valastro, S., Jr. and E. Mott Davis

1970   University of Texas at Austin Radiocarbon Dates VII. *Radiocarbon* 12(1):249–280.

Valastro, S. Jr., E. M. Davis, and C. T. Rightmire

1968   University of Texas at Austin Radiocarbon Dates VI. *Radiocarbon* 10(2):384–401.

Valastro, S. Jr., E. M. Davis, and A. G. Varela

1972   University of Texas at Austin Radiocarbon Dates IX. *Radiocarbon* 14(2):461–485.

1975   University of Texas at Austin Radiocarbon Dates X. *Radiocarbon* 17(1):52–98.

1977   University of Texas at Austin Radiocarbon Dates XI. *Radiocarbon* 19(2):280–325.

Van Zandt, K. L.

1979   Late- and Postglacial Pollen and Plant Macrofossils from Lake West Okoboji, North-Western Iowa. *Quaternary Research* 12:358–380.

Vaughan, Sheila

1975   Archaeological Investigations for the Copan Reservoir, Northeast Oklahoma and Southeast Kansas. *Oklahoma River Basin Survey, Archaeological Site Report*, No. 29.

Vehik, Rain

1982   Synopsis of the Prehistory of Jackfork Valley, Southeast Oklahoma. Manuscript on file, Archaeological Research and Management Center, University of Oklahoma, Norman, Oklahoma.

Vehik, Rain, and Jerry R. Galm

1979   The Prehistory of the Proposed Clayton Lake Area, Southeast Oklahoma: Phase I Investigation. *Archaeological Research and Management Center, Research Series* No. 6, Norman: University of Oklahoma.

Vehik, Susan C.

1976   The Great Bend Aspect: A Multivariate Investigation of Its Origins and Southern Plains Relationships. *Plains Anthropologist* 21(73)1:199–205.

1977　　Bone Fragments and Bone Grease Manufacturing: A Review of their Archaeological Use and Potential. *Plains Anthropologist* 22(77):169–182.

1982a　A Model for Prehistoric Cultural Change in North-Central Oklahoma. In Pathways to Plains Prehistory. *Oklahoma Anthropological Society Memoir* 3 and *The Cross Timbers Heritage Association Contributions* 1. Duncan, Oklahoma. Pp. 65–75.

1982b　Acquisition and Distribution of Florence-A Chert: A Preliminary Consideration of Spatial Distribution Models. Paper presented at the University of Tulsa, Tulsa, Oklahoma.

Vehik, Susan C., and Richard A. Pailes

1979　　Excavations in the Copan Reservoir of Northeastern Oklahoma and Southeastern Kansas (1974). *Archaeological Research and Management Center, Research Series* No. 4.

Voegeli, Paul T., Jr., and Loyd A. Hershey

1965　　Geology and Ground Water Resources of Prowers County, Colorado. *Geological Survey Water-Supply Paper* No. 1772, Washington, D.C.: U.S. Geological Survey.

Wallace, Benny J.

1962　　Prehistoric House Patterns of Oklahoma. *Bulletin of the Oklahoma Anthropological Society* 10:27–68.

Wallis, C. S.

1959　　Vascular Plants of Oklahoma. Ph.D. dissertation, Department of Botany, Oklahoma State University, Stillwater, Oklahoma.

Wallis, Charles S., Jr.

1974　　Comments on Flake Analysis. *Oklahoma Archaeological Survey, Contract Archaeology Series* 1:228–236.

1976　　An Archaeological Assessment on the Effects of Construction of Impoundments 6 and 8, and a Portion of Impoundment 21, Lower Clear Boggy Creek Watershed Project, Atoka County. *Oklahoma Conservation Commission, General Survey Report.*

1977a　Archaeological and Historical Resources to be Effected by the Construction of Multi-Purpose Structure M-19, Lower Black Bear Creek Watershed, Payne and Pawnee Counties, Oklahoma. *Oklahoma Conservation Commission, General Survey Report.*

1977b　Report on the Status of Archaeological Survey Work, Quapaw Creek Watershed Project, Lincoln and Pottawatomie Counties, Oklahoma. *Oklahoma Conservation Commission, General Survey Report.*

1980　　Cultural Resource Survey. Lost-Duck Creeks Watershed, Kay County, Oklahoma. *Oklahoma Conservation Commission, General Survey Report,* 1980, No. 30.

1981　　Survey of Heart O'Hills Resource Conservation and Development Program, Critical Area Treatment Project, Cherokee County, Oklahoma. *Oklahoma Conservation Commission, General Survey Report* 1981, No. 9.

Walthall, John A.

1981　　Galena and Aboriginal Trade in Eastern North America. *Illinois State Museum, Scientific Papers* No. 17.

Waring, Antonio J., Jr.

1968　　The Southern Cult and Muskhogean Ceremonial. In The Waring Papers: The Collected Works of Antonio J. Waring, Jr., edited by S. Williams. *Papers of the Peabody Museum of Archaeology and Ehtnology* 58:30–69. Cambridge: Harvard University.

Waring, Antonio J., Jr., and Preston Holder

1945　　A Prehistoric Ceremonial Complex in the Southeastern United States. *American Anthropologist* 47:1–34.

Warren, A. H.

1979　　Historic Pottery of the Cochiti Reservoir Area. In Archaeological Investigations in Cochiti Reservoir, New Mexico 4: Adaptive change in the northern Rio Grande Valley. *Albuquerque Office of Contract Archaeology, University of New Mexico.*

Watson, Virginia

1947　　A report of archaeological Reconnaissance in the Wister Reservoir area, LeFlore

County, Oklahoma. Manuscript on file, Archaeological Research and Management Center, University of Oklahoma.

1950a   The Optima Focus of the Panhandle Aspect: Description and Analysis. *Bulletin of the Texas Archeological and Paleontological Society* 21:7–68.

1950b   *The Wulfing Plates, Products of Prehistoric Americans.* St. Louis: Washington University Press.

Weakly, Harry E.

1943   A Tree Ring Record of Precipitation in Western Nebraska. *Journal of Forestry* 41(11):816–819.

Weakly, Ward F.

1972a   Archaeological Resurvey in the Fort Gibson Reservoir, Oklahoma. Manuscript on file, Arizona Archaeological Center, National Park Service, Tucson, Arizona.

1972b   Archaeological Salvage at the Martin–Vincent Site, Wg-8, Wagoner County, Oklahoma: 1968–1969. Manuscript on file, Arizona Archaeological Center, National Park Service, Tucson, Arizona.

Weaver, J. E.

1968   *Prairie Plants and their Environments: A Fifty-Year Study in the Midwest.* Lincoln: University of Nebraska Press.

Webb, Clarence H.

1970   Settlement Patterns in the Poverty Point Cultural Complex. *Southeastern Archaeological Conference, Bulletin* 12:3–12.

1977   The Poverty Point Culture. *Geoscience and man XVII.* Louisiana State University Press, Baton Rouge.

Webb, R. G.

1970   *Reptiles of Oklahoma.* Norman: University of Oklahoma Press.

Webb, T., III, and R. A. Bryson

1972   Late- and Postglacial Climatic Change in the Northern Midwest, U.S.A.: Quantitative Estimates Derived from Fossil Pollen Spectra by Multivariate Statistical Analysis. *Quaternary Research* 2:70–115.

Webb, W. S.

1974   *Indian Knoll.* Knoxville: University of Tennessee Press.

Webb, W. S., and D. L. DeJarnette

1942   An Archaeological Survey of Pickwick Basin in the Adjacent Portions of the States of Alabama, Mississippi, and Tennessee, *Smithsonian Institution, Bureau of American Ethnology, Bulletin* 129.

Wedel, Mildred M.

1981   The Deer Creek Site, Oklahoma: A Wichita Village sometimes called Ferdinandina, an Ethnohistorian's View. *Oklahoma Historical Society, Series in Anthropology,* No. 5.

Wedel, Waldo R.

1959   An Introduction to Kansas Archaeology. *Smithsonian Institution, Bureau of American Ethnology, Bulletin* No. 174.

1961   *Prehistoric Man on the Great Plains.* Norman: University of Oklahoma Press.

1974   *Prehistoric Man on the Great Plains.* 4th printing. Norman: University of Oklahoma Press.

1975   Chalk Hollow: Culture Sequence and Chronology in the Texas Panhandle. *Actas del XLI Congreso Internacional de Americanistas I.*

Wedel, Waldo R., and Mildred M. Wedel

1976   Wichita Archaeology and Ethnohistory. In *Kansas and the West,* edited by F. R. Blackburn, J. W. Snell, and H. E. Socolofsky. Kansas State Historical Society, Topeka, Kansas. Pp. 8–20.

Weir, F. A.

1979   Greenhaw: an Archaic site in central Texas. *Bulletin of the Texas Archeological Society* 50:5–67.

Wendorf, Fred
    1975   Summary and Conclusions. *Southern Methodist University, Publications of the Fort Burgwin Research Center* 9:257–278.

Wendorf, Fred, and James J. Hester
    1962   Early Man's Utilization of the Great Plains Environment. *American Antiquity* 28:159–171.

Wenner, David J., Jr.
    1947   Preliminary Appraisal of the Archaeological Resources of Fort Gibson Reservoir. Manuscript on file, Department of Anthropology, University of Oklahoma, Norman, Oklahoma.
    1948a   Preliminary Appraisal of the Archaeological Resources of the Eufaula Reservoir (Onapa and Canadian Reservoir Areas). Manuscript on file, Department of Anthropology, University of Oklahoma, Norman, Oklahoma.
    1948b   Preliminary Appraisal of the Archaeological Resources of Tenkiller Ferry Reservoir. Manuscript on file, Department of Anthropology, University of Oklahoma, Norman, Oklahoma.

Weymouth, John W.
    1981   Magnetic Surveys of the Edwards I (34Bk-2) and the Taylor (34Gr-8) Sites in Western Oklahoma. Report submitted to the Oklahoma Archaeological Survey, Norman, Oklahoma.

Wheat, Joe Ben
    1972   The Olsen–Chubbuck Site, a Paleo-Indian Bison Kill. *Society for American Archaeology, Memoir* No. 26.
    1974   First Excavations at the Lubbock Lake Site. *The Museum Journal* 15:15–42. Lubbock, Texas.

White, Theodore E.
    1953   A Method of Calculating the Dietary Percentage of Various Food Animals Utilized by Aboriginal Peoples. *American Antiquity* 18(4):396–398.

Willey, Gordon R.
    1966   *An Introduction to American Archaeology*, Vol. I, *North and Middle America*. Englewood Cliffs: Prentice-Hall.

Willey, Gordon R., and P. Phillips
    1958   *Method and Theory in American Archaeology*. Chicago: University of Chicago Press.

Willey, Patrick S., Billy R. Harrison, and Jack T. Hughes
    1978   The Rex Rodgers Site. In Archaeology at Mackenzie Reservoir, edited by Jack T. Hughes and Patrick S. Willey. *Texas Historical Commission, Office of the State Archeologist, Archeological Survey Report* No. 24:51–114.

Williams, Bob
    1953   The Ward Site, LeFlore County, Oklahoma. *Oklahoma Anthropological Society Newsletter* 1(9):2–9.
    1955   A Preliminary Appraisal of the Archaeological Resources of the Fort Cobb, Foss and Norman Reservoirs. Manuscript on file, Department of Anthropology, University of Oklahoma, Norman, Oklahoma.

Williams, J. E.
    1974   *Atlas of the Woody Plants of Oklahoma*. Oklahoma Biological Survey and Robert Bebb Herbarium, Norman, Oklahoma.

Willoughby, Charles C.
    1952   Textile Fabrics from the Spiro Mound. In The Spiro Mound, Henry W. Hamilton. *Missouri Archaeologist* 14:107–118.

Wilson, L. R.
    1966   Palynology of the Domebo Site. *Contributions of the Museum of the Great Plains* 1:44–50.
    1972   Geomorphology of Tesesquite Creek Valley, Cimarron County, Oklahoma. *Oklahoma Geological Survey, Oklahoma Geology Notes* 32(6):195–208.

Winship, George P.
1896   The Coronado Expedition, 1540–1542. *The 14th Annual Report of the Bureau of American Ethnology*, Washington, D.C.: U.S. Government Printing Office.

Winters, H. D.
1968   Value Systems and Trade Cycles of the Late Archaic in the Midwest. In *New Perspectives in Archaeology*, edited by S. R. Binford and L. R. Binford. Chicago: Aldine. Pp. 175–221.
1969   The Riverton Cutlure. *Illinois State Museum, Reports of Investigations* No. 13.
1974   Introduction to the new edition. In *Indian Knoll*, W. S. Webb. Knoxville: University of Tennessee Press. Pp. v–xxvii.

Winters, Joseph C.
1975   Maize Remains from Two Western Oklahoma Sites. Manuscript on file, Oklahoma Archaeological Survey, Norman, Oklahoma.

Witte, Adolph Henry
1938   Spanish Fort, an Historic Wichita Site. *Bulletin of the Texas Archeological and Paleontological Society* 10:234–244.

Wittry, W. L.
1952   The Preceramic Occupation of the Smith Site, Units I and II, Delaware County, Oklahoma. M.A. thesis, Department of Anthropology, University of Wisconsin, Madison, Wisconsin.

Witty, Tom
1978   Along the Southern Edge: The Central Plains Tradition in Kansas. In Central Plains Tradition: Internal Development and External Relationships, edited by Donald J. Blakeslee. *Office of the State Archaeologist, Report* 11:56–66. Iowa City: University of Iowa.

Wood, W. Raymond
1963   Breckenridge Shelter—3Cr-2: An Archaeological Chronicle in the Beaver Reservoir Area. *Arkansas Archaeology 1962*. Fayetteville, Arkansas. Pp. 67–96.
1968   Mississippian Hunting and Butchering Patterns: Bone from the Vista Shelter, 23SR-20, Missouri. *American Antiquity* 33(2):170–179.
1971   Pottery Sites Near Limon, Colorado. *Southwestern Lore* 37(3):53–85.
1974   Northern Plains Village Cultures: Internal Stability and External Relationships. *Journal of Anthropological Research* 30(1):1–18.

Wood, W. R., and R. B. McMillan
1976   *Prehistoric Man and His Environments, a Case Study in the Ozark Highland*. New York: Academic Press.

Woolverton, Donald G.
1974   Electron Microprobe Analysis of Native Copper Artifacts. In Spiro Mound Copper, by H. W. Hamilton and others *Missouri Archaeological Society, Memoir* No. 11:207–212.

Word, James H.
1963   Floydada Country Club Site. *Bulletin of the South Plains Archeological Society* 1:37–63. Floydada, Texas.
1965   The Montgomery Site in Floyd County, Texas. *Bulletin of the South Plains Archeological Society* 2:55–102. Floydada, Texas.

Wright, H. E., Jr.
1968   The Roles of Pine and Spruce in the Forest History of Minnesota and Adjacent Areas. *Ecology* 49(5):937–955.
1972   Interglacial and Postglacial Climates: the Pollen Record. *Quaternary Research* 2:274–282.

Wright, H. E., Jr., and D. G. Frey
1965   *The Quaternary of the United States*. Princeton, New Jersey: Princeton University Press.

Wright, Muriel H.
1946–   Pioneer Historian and Archaeologist of the State of Oklahoma. *The Chronicles of
1947a   Oklahoma* 24(4):396–413.
1946–   Exhibit of Objects Discovered by the Marland Archaeological Exhibit in 1926. *The Chron-
1947b   icles of Oklahoma* 24(4):491–494.

Wright, M. H., and George H. Shirk

    1950   The Journal of Lieutenant A. W. Whipple. *The Chronicles of Oklahoma* 28:235–283.

Wyckoff, Don G.

    1961a   The Question of the Origin of the Central Plains Complex. *Papers in Anthropology* 3(1):1–16.

    1961b   Report on Archaeological Survey of Broken Bow Reservoir, McCurtain County, Oklahoma. Manuscript on file, Oklahoma River Basin Survey, Norman, Oklahoma.

    1963a   The Kerr Dam Site, a Stratified Site in the Markham Ferry Reservoir Area, Mayes County, Northeast Oklahoma. *Oklahoma River Basin Survey, Archaeological Site Report* No. 1.

    1963b   Archaeological Survey of Pine Creek Reservoir, McCurtain County, Oklahoma. *Oklahoma River Basin Survey, General Survey Report* No. 3.

    1963c   Mangum Reservoir Archaeological Survey, Greer and Harmon Counties, Oklahoma. *Oklahoma River Basin Survey Project, General Survey Report* No. 2.

    1964a   The Cultural Sequence at the Packard Site, Mayes County, Oklahoma. *Oklahoma River Basin Survey, Archaeological Site Report* No. 2.

    1964b   The Jug Hill Site, My-18, Mayes County, Oklahoma. *Bulletin of the Oklahoma Anthropological Society* 12:1–53.

    1964c   The Archaeological Report of the Buncombe Creek Site, Marshall County, Oklahoma. *Bulletin of the Oklahoma Anthropological Society* 12:103–140.

    1964d   The Archaeological Survey of the Kaw Reservoir, Kay and Osage Counties, Oklahoma. *Oklahoma River Basin Survey, General Survey Report*, No. 6.

    1964e   Two Radiocarbon Dates from the Jug Hill Site, Mayes County, Oklahoma. *Oklahoma Anthropological Society Newsletter* 12(9):5–7.

    1965   The Biggham Creek Site of McCurtain County, Oklahoma. *Oklahoma River Basin Survey, Archaeological Site Report* No. 3.

    1966a   The Hughes, Lamas Branch, and Callaham Sites, McCurtain County, Southeast Oklahoma. *Oklahoma River Basin Survey, Archaeological Site Report* No. 4.

    1966b   The Pruitt Site, Mr-12, Radiocarbon Dates. *Oklahoma Anthropological Society Newsletter* 14(8):2.

    1967a   The E. Johnson Site and Prehistory in Southeast Oklahoma. *Oklahoma River Basin Survey, Archaeological Site Report* No. 6.

    1967b   Woods Mound Group: A Prehistoric Mound Complex in McCurtain County, Oklahoma. *Bulletin of the Oklahoma Anthropological Society* 15:1–76.

    1967c   Radiocarbon Dates from Oklahoma River Basin Survey Excavations. *Oklahoma Anthropological Society Newsletter* 15(2):6–8.

    1968a   The Beaver Site and the Archaeology of the Broken Bow Reservoir Area, McCurtain County, Oklahoma. *Oklahoma River Basin Survey, Archaeological Site Report* No. 9.

    1968b   The Bell and Gregory Sites: Archaeological Chronicles of Prehistory in the Pine Creek Reservoir Area, Southeast Oklahoma. *Oklahoma River Basin Survey, Archaeological Site Report* No. 11.

    1968c   The Prehistoric Site of Spiro, LeFlore County, Oklahoma: Its Archaeological Significance and Developmental Potential. *Oklahoma Archaeological Survey.*

    1970a   1970 University of Oklahoma Field School in Archaeology: Research in Western Oklahoma (Abstract). Abstracts of Papers, 28th Plains Conference, November 26–28, 1970:17. Tulsa, Oklahoma.

    1970b   Archaeological and Historical Resources of the Red River Basin in Oklahoma. In *Archaeological and Historical Resources of the Red River Basin*, edited by Hester A. Davis. *Arkansas Archeological Survey, Publications on Archeology, Research Series* 1:69–134.

    1970c   The Horton Site Revisited, 1967 Excavations at Sq-11, Sequoyah County, Oklahoma. *Oklahoma Archaeological Survey, Studies in Oklahoma's Past* No. 1.

    1973   The Lowrance Site of Murray County 1969 Excavations by the Oklahoma Anthropological Society. *Bulletin of the Oklahoma Anthropological Society* 21:1–156.

1974   *The Caddoan Cultural Area: An Archaeological Perspective*. New York: Garland.

1976   1976 Archaeological Field Work at the McCutchan–McLaughlin Site, Latimer County, Oklahoma. *Oklahoma Anthropological Society Newsletter* 24(8):1–9.

1977   Appendix I: Soils at the Sooner Generating Station Site (Pw-63), Pawnee County, Oklahoma. *Oklahoma Archaeological Survey, Contract Archaeology Series* 2:103–122.

1979   Dating the Prehistoric Habitation of the McCutchan-McLaughlin Site, Lt-11, Latimer County, Oklahoma. *Oklahoma Anthropological Society Newsletter* 27(2):7–8.

1980   Caddoan Adaptive Strategies in the Arkansas Basin, Eastern Oklahoma. Ph.D. dissertation, Department of Anthropology, Washington State University, Pullman, Washington.

1981   Radiocarbon Dates from the Lawrence Site, 34Nw-6, Nowata County, Oklahoma. *Oklahoma Anthropological Society Newsletter* 29(8):10–11.

Wyckoff, Don G., and Thomas P. Barr

1964   1963 Archaeological Activity in the Markham Ferry Reservoir Area, Mayes County, Oklahoma. *Oklahoma River Basin Survey, General Survey Report* No. 4.

1967a   The McCully Site: A Preceramic Site in the Webber's Falls Lock and Dam Area, Muskogee County, Oklahoma. *Oklahoma River Basin Survey, Archaeological Site Report* No. 8.

1967b   The Cat Smith Site: a Late Prehistoric Village in Muskogee County, Oklahoma. *Bulletin of the Oklahoma Anthropological Society* 15:81–106.

Wyckoff, Don G., and Lyonel Taylor

1971   The Pumpkin Creek Site, an Early Archaic Site in the Southern Plains Border. *Plains Anthropologist* 16(51):20–50.

Wyckoff, Don G., and T. V. Woody

1977   1977 Field Work at Lt-11: The OAS Spring Dig and the University Field School. *Oklahoma Anthropological Society Newsletter* 25(8):1–13.

Wyckoff, Don G., Philip Robison, and Thomas P. Barr

1963   Markham Ferry Reservoir Archaeological Resources, Mayes County, Oklahoma. *Oklahoma River Basin Survey, General Survey Report* No. 1.

Yarnell, Richard A.

1977   Native Plant Husbandry North of Mexico. In *Origins of Agriculture, edited by C. A. Reed*, pp. 861–875. The Hague: Mouton.

1981   Inferred Dating of Ozark Bluff Dweller Occupation Based on Size of Sunflower and Sumpweed. *Journal of Ethnobiology* 1:55–60.

Young, Wayne

1977   Five Nonceramic Sites in Western Atoka County, Oklahoma. *Oklahoma Conservation Commission, Archaeological Research Report* No. 3.

1978   Kaw Reservoir—The Northern Section: Part II. Report of Phase Va Research of the General Plan for Investigations of the Archaeological Resources of Kaw Reservoir, North-Central Oklahoma. *Oklahoma River Basin Survey, Archaeological Site Report* No. 33.

Index